Renovating & Restyling Older Homes

the professional's guide to maximum value remodeling

by Lawrence Dworin

Craftsman Book Company
6058 Corte del Cedro/ P.O. Box 6500 / Carlsbad, CA 92018

Acknowledgments

With thanks to my assistants, Neil Gilbert and Paul Gilbert, for their valuable help with much of the work featured in this book. Also, to my wife, Mary, without whose help and encouragement none of this would have been possible.

The following companies kindly provided materials used in the preparation of this book:

Renovator's
P. O. Box 2515
Conway, NH 03818
(800) 659-2211

Vintage Wood Works
South End of Eagle Street
P. O. Box 980
Fredericksburg, TX 78624
(903) 356-2158

Wolverine Vinyl Siding
17199 Laurel Park Drive North
Livonia, MI 48152-2679
(800) 521-9020

Library of Congress Cataloging-in-Publication Data

Dworin, Lawrence, 1953-
Renovating & restyling vintage homes : the professional's guide to maximum value remodeling / by Lawrence Dworin.
p. cm.
Includes index.
ISBN 1-57218-029-3
1. Dwellings--Remodeling.   2. Historic buildings -- Conservation and restoration.   I. Title.
TH4816.D87   1996
690'.8--dc20   96-22652
                                            CIP

Contents

Chapter 1

Maximum Value Remodeling

I've looked at just about every book on the market on the subject of remodeling. I've found they fall into two types. One is the "do-it-yourself" book. These give you detailed instructions on how to spend all day repairing something you could have replaced for $2. The other type of book is for contractors and building professionals. They tell you to rip out fixtures worth thousands of dollars, and toss them in the trash. "Why should you care?" they say." It's the homeowner's money, not yours!" That's fine if the homeowner is rich and doesn't care about cost. But most of the people I deal with *do* care. They want to get the best value for their money. They can't afford to toss valuable items in the trash.

My objective in writing this book is to offer contractors with small remodeling businesses, or even homeowners who want to do some remodeling or repairing themselves, alternative approaches to remodeling or renovating older homes. By older home, I mean any home built before 1930. I feel that a home built after 1930 is essentially modern, and doesn't need the special attention to detail that earlier homes need. My work is based on common sense, and dollar-for-dollar value on what you do and what you get. I also have a

great admiration for the quality and the beauty that went into building homes 75 or 100 years ago. I don't like the idea of throwing away the past just because it's old. Restoring older homes to their original beauty gives me a great sense of satisfaction. Not only am I preserving the past, but every item I save is one less item that ends up in the dump to clutter up our future.

This book is also an ideal guide for those considering the purchase of an older home. If you're a buyer, take it along and use it to help recognize potential problems. Old homes can be very deceptive if you don't know what you're looking at. Some things that are relatively simple to repair may look like they'll cost a fortune, while other truly costly repairs can be hiding behind old wallpaper or paneling. Use this book to help you determine which is which. Knowing what to look for and where to look for it will help you come up with an accurate price when making an offer on the house. Not only will I point out situations that you want to avoid, but I'll tell you how to identify items of particular quality that add to the value of an older home.

For the most part, this book deals with recognizing the potential value in the older home and tells how to use sensible repair,

5

Figure 1-1
Fine Victorian woodwork

remodeling and renovation techniques to bring out that potential. The best way for anyone to get maximum value for their remodeling dollar is to take a balanced, reasonable approach. My recommendation: Don't waste time on items that are cheap; just replace them. Items that are valuable, on the other hand, should be repaired, not thrown away. Throughout this book, we'll discuss which items fall into which category, and the most cost-effective way to deal with them. I'll tell you about the common problems you're likely to come across while working on older homes, how to handle them, and what it's likely to cost you to correct them, both in materials and in labor.

We'll also discuss the options that the small professional remodeler can offer homeowners, especially those choices that will give owners working with a modest budget the most "bang for their buck." This is something you won't find in many other books. And, even though I'm writing for the remodeling professional, there is plenty of information here for the buyer, the homeowner, the handyman, and the tradesperson who wants to expand into the remodeling business as well.

Why Older Homes?

Remodeling an older home can be both rewarding and challenging. If you're used to working only on newer homes, you may not be familiar with many of the unique features

or special problems that you're likely to run into when working on an older house. This book will give you an idea of the types of things you'll find, and help prepare you to deal with them.

Many people have negative attitudes about working on older homes. They think these houses are a lot of trouble, and not worth their bother. That's too bad, because many older homes contain features such as oak woodwork, hand-carved detailing or elaborate decorations that you rarely find in newer homes. The beautiful woodwork and detail of the stairwell and hall that you see in Figure 1-1 is an example of the exceptional workmanship that went into many older homes. Some details that were once commonplace can now only be found as luxury items on houses built today — and then only on homes selling in the million-dollar-and-up category! You'll never see them in an average house — they're way too expensive. Yet in the old days, ordinary people enjoyed the kinds of features that only millionaires can afford now. If you can preserve these features, you're performing two very valuable services. You're giving the homeowners something they wouldn't otherwise be able to afford, and you're saving a piece of history for future generations.

✑ A Simpler Time

Older homes have a special feeling about them that few modern homes can equal. There's a quiet graciousness, even in the smaller homes, that cannot be duplicated today. Figure 1-2 shows the beautiful tile and woodwork around a bedroom fireplace that I found in one small home I worked on. This home also had hardwood floors and detailed moldings throughout. Homes like this one were built with care. They were built for a calmer time and a more relaxed, slower-paced lifestyle.

Standing on the street and looking at one of these older homes, you can get a feeling of what life must have been like for the people who first lived there. Many homes have wide, spacious covered front porches where friends and neighbors gathered to socialize on long summer evenings. Families spent more time at home. They ate big dinners together in their formal dining rooms, had guests over for tea on Sunday in their parlors, and spent cozy evenings reading or telling stories around the fireplaces. This is the kind of life these houses were built for, and it's clearly reflected in their design. Figures 1-3 and 1-4 show the characteristic charm you find in well-maintained older homes. As you can see, some homes are much more elaborate than others, but they are all distinctive in their own ways.

Of course, this kind of lifestyle doesn't appeal to everyone. If you crave action and excitement, the modern style homes are probably more to your taste, both for living and for working. However, for many of today's overworked and stressed-out people, an older home offers a quiet, peaceful retreat into a different world. Those who yearn for a simpler lifestyle love old homes. To them, these houses aren't just a place to live, they're part of a way of life. It's important to understand this if you intend to work on older homes. The work you do should always be in keeping with the spirit of the house.

Figure 1-2
*Victorian style bedroom
with small fireplace*

That doesn't mean that the homeowner won't want modern conveniences. Even though an antique house is charming, nobody really wants to duplicate life in the 1890s (or even 1920s). If you've ever tried it, you'll know that cooking dinner on a wood-

Figure 1-3
Typical Victorian home

Figure 1-4
Elaborate Victorian home

Figure 1-5
New home in Victorian style

burning stove gets old real fast. A kitchen and bath with modern equipment is a must. But not all of the old features need to be removed. Some are still useful, or at least decorative. Which should be saved and which should be torn out? And how can you add modern conveniences without destroying the beauty of the house? These are the real challenges. The most difficult aspect of remodeling the older home is adapting it to modern lifestyles.

🐦 Older Homes and the Community

The atmosphere created in a neighborhood of well-maintained older homes is so important to the communities that some have enacted zoning ordinances requiring that all building must be in keeping with the style of the existing buildings. This has forced people who wanted new homes in those areas to build replicas of older homes. The idea is that it's okay if it isn't old, as long as it *looks* old. This can be done, but it's very expensive. Old-time craftsmanship doesn't come cheap today. The home in Figure 1-5 is a new home built to blend with the style of the historic district in which it was built. Notice the narrow windows, roof accents and gingerbread porch rails. These are all typical of Victorian architecture.

Older homes are so desirable in some areas of the country that many new subdivisions are being built in older styles, such as the Victorian style of the 1890s, or the Craftsman style of the 1920s. Some subdivisions are even attempting to replicate complete towns, right down to the old-fashioned downtown with its main street. Many homes in these subdivisions are very nice, but they're not quite the same as a genuine older home.

With the costs of new homes soaring and the demand for older homes increasing, doesn't remodeling older homes make a lot of sense? In Europe, people live in houses that were built a thousand years ago. A 200-year-old house is considered "new." Our older homes were built as well as theirs. They can last for centuries too, if they're properly maintained. Houses that have been around a long time may have a lot of things that are worn out. Other items may not be worn or broken, but may be obsolete. Still others may be entirely usable, but not in keeping with modern lifestyles. That doesn't mean you should tear down the whole house and start over. All of these problems can be dealt with. Yes, it can be a lot of work; but you're not just fixing up a run-down old house, you're restoring a treasure!

Gaining Homeowner Trust

When it comes to remodeling, the homeowner will consider you the expert, and look to you for advice. You might tell him, for example, "It's going to cost $300 each to replace your windows." And he may answer, "Gee, I don't know if I should spend that much. Maybe I'd be better off doing something else with the money?"

What that customer really wants is for you to sit down and discuss the options with him. He wants advice, not just a price quote. Do his windows really need to be replaced, or can they be repaired? Is this a good place to put his money, or would he get more for his money with some other improvement? If you can discuss this intelligently with the homeowner, letting him know what options he has and what each will cost, you'll win his trust. Trust, according to a survey by *Remodeling* magazine, is absolutely the number one factor in getting jobs. It's more important than speed, service, or even price. More than anything else, homeowners want to hire someone they trust.

❧ Emphasizing Resale Value

It's worth taking a moment to consider what effect remodeling has on resale value. This is a subject that's very important to me because I make my living buying and renovating houses for resale. If I don't increase their resale value, I don't eat. (I discuss this in detail in my book *Profits in Buying & Renovating Homes*, also published by Craftsman Books.)

Resale value should also be important to the homeowners that you'll be working with, though they may not be thinking about it at the time they're considering remodeling. They may be planning to live in that house the rest of their lives. However, what they plan to do and what they will actually do is often quite different. They may get transferred to another part of the country and have to sell the house, whether they've planned on it or not. Most homeowners are aware of the possibility that they may have to move someday. It might just be a dim worry in the back of their mind, but it's there, along with all their other worries.

You can make this worry work for you by showing homeowners that remodeling can raise the value of their home. It isn't just an expense, it's an investment, like putting money in the bank. The added value will be there any time they need to draw on it. You'll find it easier to sell jobs if you discuss this with the homeowner. Most people worry about spending large amounts of money. I'm one of them. However, you can make the point that since the money is *invested*, not spent, it isn't really gone. It's just taken another form. Instead of cash, it's now in the form of increased property value, or equity. It's there, like money in the bank, and it can be recovered if necessary. This will usually make homeowners feel a lot better about the entire project.

It's possible for homeowners to "withdraw" this money without having to sell the house. Home-equity loans allow owners to borrow on the value of their property. The more it's worth, the more they can borrow. Work that increases the value of a house will increase the amount they can borrow as well. Most homeowners appreciate this advice. However, they don't really know what items will increase the value of a house and what won't. They expect you to know this. As far as they're concerned, you know everything there is to know about houses.

In order for you to retain the trust that homeowners have placed in you, concentrate on jobs that really *do* enhance value. Preserve beautiful features — don't destroy them. Avoid weird, quirky modifications that a future buyer will hate. Don't use bizarre colors and styles. Throughout this book, I'll identify work you can do that will raise property values, and point out the bad ideas that will lower them.

Of course, if the homeowner insists on making changes you know will detract from the home's value and you can't dissuade him, you'll have to go along with him. But let's face it, money spent this way is not an investment — it's money gone forever. No future buyer will pay extra for odd modifications. Such changes actually lower the value of the house, because another owner will have to spend money to tear them out. Modifications that fall into this category are pass-through bedrooms or other poorly-thought-out additions that create layout problems, strange color combinations, and odd wall paneling materials such as mirror or cork.

Other modifications that will not add to the value of the home, but that you may be hired to make, are handicap access ramps, extra wide doorways for wheelchairs or lowered countertops. The homeowners wouldn't put money into these changes unless they needed them, but unless they sell to someone with the same need, they will never recover the remodeling expense. For the most part however, homeowners in this position are more interested in improving their lifestyles than adding extra value to their home.

Offering Good Value to Your Customers

What you should try to do is give your customers good value for their remodeling dollar, without cutting your profit margins! I call this "maximum value remodeling." This is something a lot of remodelers don't understand. They think they can get more jobs by offering exactly the same services as everyone else, but for less money. This doesn't work. You need at least a 50 percent markup if you want to survive in the remodeling business. If you try to undercut the competition by cutting your profit margin, you'll eventually go broke.

Instead of trying to undercut prices on the same services, why not offer better services for the same price? If you can offer customers a better, cheaper solution to their remodeling problems, and give them better value for their money, without cutting your profits, you'll get the job every time. In fact, in many cases you'll be able to increase your profit margins and *still* save the homeowner money!

You can do this by focusing on the jobs that give the customer the best return on his dollar — the ones that make the biggest improvements for the least cost. Instead of just trying to do the *most* work, concentrate on doing the *best* work. When you're done, you'll have a satisfied customer who really feels like he got a lot for his money. Your competitors may leave their customers feeling like they got what they paid for, but your customers will feel they got *more* than they paid for. Customers like this will want you to come back and do more work for them. They'll brag to their friends about what a great deal they got, and that will generate more work for you.

How do you do this? Here's an example. According to *Remodeling* magazine, the average bath remodel costs $7,207 and recoups 85 percent of its cost. This means the job adds about $6,125 to the value of the house (85 percent of $7,207 is $6,125). What if you could do a similar job for $3,000? It would still add $6,125 to the value of the house, but your return would be 200 percent, not 85 percent. This is the secret of "maximum value remodeling." If you can figure out a way to do an equivalent or better job for much less money, there'll be a lot more profit in it for everyone involved.

In this book, we'll explore every possible way to get the maximum effect for the minimum cost. We'll carefully go through all the alternatives, looking at anything that might allow us to save money without sacrificing quality. I put a lot of emphasis on repairing things instead of replacing them. Most building publications don't cover this very much. They stress replacing things because it sells more products. For instance, they'd rather see you spend $1,000 on a new door than $10 on refinishing the one you've got. I'm not advertising or selling anything but my expertise. I'll tell you what's best for you and the homeowner, not the manufacturers.

Of course, sometimes there's just no good, cheap way to do a job. We'll look at those situations too.

❧ "Restyle" Instead of "Remodel"

Most remodeling magazines and brochures are loaded with pictures of beautiful, high-priced remodeling jobs. They cost hundreds of thousands of dollars, and it shows. That's fine if you have customers with unlimited budgets. It's easy to make a house look wonderful if you have lots of money to spend. It's a lot harder to take a house that looks like a pit and turn it into a nice home for $10,000.

For $10,000, most contractors would offer a complete remodel of only one room. I can restyle an entire house for that much! The reason I can do this so inexpensively is because I don't do a lot of extensive work. Instead, I concentrate on:

◆ items that really need replacing,

◆ items that attract the most attention, and

◆ inexpensive redecorating.

Concentrating on a few key items can totally change the look of the house. Without doing much work, the house will look and feel completely different.

Customers with small budgets are really underserved by the remodeling community. Many companies won't even quote small jobs. Those that do, often can't offer good value for the money. As a result there are millions of customers who would like to have some work done, but can't afford what's currently available. They just have to go without — and nobody makes any money. However, by using "maximum value remodeling," you can offer them substantial improvements for moderate amounts of money. This creates jobs where none existed before.

There are millions of customers that this type of remodeling can serve, and they can all be yours, because nobody else is interested. For example, if a homeowner doesn't like the way the house looks from the outside, there are a few things you can offer that won't cost a huge amount. Rather than saying they need new siding and windows (standard remodeling ideas), you can suggest adding some new trim and a new front door. These items, if coordinated with the style of the home, can provide a whole new character to the house at a very reasonable cost.

ૐ Work Smarter, Not Harder

Amazingly enough, you can often make more money on these small jobs than your competitors are making on big ones. That's because you're working smarter, not harder. By zeroing in on certain key items, you can make tremendous improvements that won't cost your customers a fortune. What they pay for is your cleverness and your creative solutions to their problems. In other words, you get paid for your brains, not your brawn. Nobody else will be bidding against you for these jobs, because nobody else will think of doing them.

This method works because frequently the problems in a house, or even in a room, are localized. The trouble spots make the whole house look bad, especially if they are the natural focus of attention, like the front door, the main windows or the facing wall as you enter a room. A house is so big that you can't look at the whole thing all at once. Therefore, the eye focuses in on certain key items. If these items are ugly, you perceive the whole house as ugly. On the other hand, if they're especially beautiful, they can divert attention from the fact that the rest of the house is plain. A little bit of work in these key areas can make a tremendous difference in the overall look of the house. You can get most of the effect of a complete remodeling job at a fraction of the cost. The average remodeler, one who concentrates on large jobs, will overlook this because it's too simple.

The same principle applies to each room, as well as to the house as a whole. Every room has its own focal point and this should be something beautiful, like a fireplace, a chandelier or an elaborate trim. This item can set the tone for the entire room, sometimes even for the whole house. People may remember the "fireplace room" or "the room with the exquisite chandelier." The rest of the room may be ordinary, but that one item will establish it in people's minds as a special place. If a room doesn't have any special features, you can add one. You can often get almost as much effect by installing one key item as you can by remodeling the entire room, but at a fraction of the cost.

This may seem confusing at first, but if you look at houses in this manner, you'll see what I mean. The main reason you'll be able to focus in on the particular needs of a house, and your competitors won't, is that *they simply don't look for them.* They don't even *think* of things like this. They'll either want to remodel the entire room, or turn down the job. It never occurs to them to try to zero in on the single most effective item, and just do that.

ૐ Use Your Design Skills

Many remodeling contractors approach jobs as though the customer has already made up his mind about what he wants. They assume that the design has been finalized; all they have to do is build it. This may be true for large, expensive remodeling jobs, where design consultants are called in to coordinate colors and styles. But what about customers with low-budget jobs? Paying a design consultant would probably use up their entire remodeling budget. And the design-build services offered by major remodeling firms may be more than they can afford as well. Therefore, they turn to you, the small contractor.

Even though a customer doesn't have a lot of money, he still deserves the best design he can afford. Can you help him? Yes, if you know something about design. You can offer him a nice-looking, style-and-color-coordinated design, for a price he can afford. You don't have to be an interior decorator to do this; you just need to know some basic facts about design. Most contractors with small businesses don't want to spend the time to do design work. You won't have to compete with them on price, you'll compete with them on quality. You'll get the job, not by offering cheaper services, but by offering better services.

It's unfortunate how many small contractors don't bother learning a little about design. That's one reason so many of them fail in just a few years. It takes more than skill with tools be successful, it takes ideas too.

My Favorite Jobs

My favorite kinds of jobs are the ones where everybody makes a profit. You make a profit, because you get paid good money for the job. The homeowner makes a profit because the work raises the value of his house more than the job cost. He makes money for you, and you make money for him! Everybody's happy. If you can make this point to a homeowner, you'll have an easier time selling your job.

There's a simple criterion to use to decide which jobs will best increase the value of any house:

> *The house should be brought up to the standards of the neighborhood.*

Any job that brings a substandard house up to neighborhood standards will increase its value. On the other hand, if you fix up a house *beyond* the standards of the neighborhood, you're throwing money away — at least as far as resale value is concerned. Homeowners may be willing to over-improve their house for their own use, but they won't be able to get the money back when they go to sell the house.

Every neighborhood attracts a certain type of buyer. If the house is in a middle-income neighborhood, it will attract middle-income buyers. They will be looking for a house that is neat, clean, in good repair and has a few special features. If you've loaded the house with luxury features, they'll be thrilled, but they won't be able to pay extra for them. If they want to get their money back for luxury features, they'll need to sell to people who can afford luxury features. If someone can afford to pay for luxury, they won't be looking to buy in a middle-income neighborhood.

A Good Example

I recently looked at a house that offers a good example of what I'm talking about. It was in a very expensive neighborhood. Most of the houses in the area were selling for $500,000. However, this one was priced at $300,000 because it wasn't up to the standards of the neighborhood. It had two major drawbacks. The first was the kitchen, which was bright and spacious, and had been recently remodeled. It was filled with lots of brand-new cabinets. Unfortunately, the cabinets were the cheapest kind you can buy, poor-quality particleboard. The drawers weren't even center-guided. Rather than being an upgraded feature, they actually lowered the value of the house. Whoever bought the house would have to tear them out and replace them. What a waste of time and money!

The other drawback was the lack of an upgraded bathroom. It was a large house with five bathrooms, but they were all cramped, dark, 1950s style baths. There wasn't a single modern, spacious, bathroom in the house — not even in the master bedroom. This wouldn't have been a problem in another area, but this was supposed to be luxury housing. All the neighbors had luxurious spa-type baths. This house should have had one as well.

Other than these problems and some rather tacky decorating, there wasn't much wrong with the house. It could have easily been brought up to the standards of the neighborhood. Even if the owner had invested as much as $100,000 in improvements (and it wouldn't have taken nearly that much), he would have gained 100 percent on that investment. Because he didn't or couldn't put the money into the house, he was selling it for $200,000 less than similar houses in that area. Why couldn't a buyer make the improvements and profit from them? They can, but it will cost them considerably more than it would cost the seller to do it. Remodeling a newly purchased house with a home-improvement loan is very expensive for a buyer. With no equity to borrow against, the buyer will be stuck with paying high interest rates.

A house can be bought with a mortgage which gives the buyer a low interest rate and payments spread over 30 years. Home-improvements loans, on the other hand, don't get such advantageous treatment. They're usually at a much higher interest rate, with the payments spread over only five years. It will cost a buyer more in payments to take out a mortgage on a $300,000 house and add to that a $100,000 home-improvement loan, than it would to take out a mortgage for a $500,000 house that is complete and ready to live in.

Let's look at the numbers: a 30-year mortgage for $300,000 at 7.5 percent gives you a monthly payment of $2,109.98, not including taxes. A home-improvement loan for $100,000 at 10 percent for five years, gives you a monthly payment of $2,124.70. The home-improvement loan payment costs more than the house payment! Compare this with the payment on a 30-year mortgage for $500,000 at 7.5 percent. It works out to be $3,516.64, not including taxes. As you can see, a buyer could pay $200,000 *more* for a house that needs no improvements, and wind up with a payment that's $718.04 per month *less,* at least for the first five years.

So who can afford to make these improvements? The seller. If the seller of this house took out a $100,000 home-improvement loan and brought his property up to the standards of the neighborhood, he'd be able to raise the asking price to $500,000. He'd get double his money back for this job, essentially making $100,000 more profit. The payments on the home-improvement loan might be steep, but he'd only have to make them for a few months, just until the house sold. The new buyer, on the other hand, would be able to buy the improved house on a mortgage, and get a favorable interest rate. Everybody's happy, including the contractor, who just got a nice $100,000 job out of the deal.

If a homeowner has a substantial amount of equity in his house, he might be able to take out a home-equity loan to pay for the remodeling, rather than a home-improvement loan. This will give him a better interest rate. Or, if he does take out a home-improvement loan, and wants to stay in the house instead of selling, he can probably refinance his house once the job is done, and pay off the home-improvement loan out of the proceeds. Since the house will be more valuable, he can refinance for a larger amount. Neither of these options will work for the new buyer. They don't have any equity in the house to work with.

This doesn't mean that buyers should never remodel the houses they buy, only that it will cost them more and take longer for them to recover the expense than it does for sellers. However, in the long run, it'll still pay off. The house in the example has a $100,000 profit in it for somebody. It may be the present owner, or the next owner. Whoever has the foresight to make the investment will reap the rewards. It could be you.

Chapter 2

Inspecting the Exterior

This book follows a logical progression. It begins with inspecting the house and deciding what work you will do, progresses through doing the work that's necessary to bring the house up to standard, and then covers making the improvements that make the home more comfortable, appealing or valuable. I'll go through all the repairs you're most likely to run into and how to handle them in the order that you'd actually be doing them. Then we'll get into updating the home, making modifications for lifestyles, and last but not least, design considerations. All of these have to be approached in a certain order, so that later jobs don't interfere with earlier ones. We'll start with the exterior and continue through the interior, until the job's done. But first let's cover the inspection process.

Making a List and Checking it Twice

The first thing to do on any remodeling job is to go over the house thoroughly and try to identify exactly what problems you're going to have to deal with. Not all jobs that need to be done in an older home are obvious. There can be a lot of hidden damage.

Always go through the entire house, inside and out, and check everything as carefully as possible. Make a list of all the repairs and improvements that are needed.

Your list should have two parts. First, list all the jobs that *have* to be done. This includes everything that's broken, decayed or obsolete. It also includes everything that you, or the homeowner you're working for, definitely want removed or remodeled. The second part of the list should include all the *possible* jobs. These are things that may need to be repaired or replaced. This list should also include things that you or the homeowners don't care for, but aren't yet sure whether you want to replace.

Why do we bother with the second part of the list? Because when you're working on older homes, you're never absolutely sure what you're going to have to do until you actually get into the job. What appears to be a little spot of decay might actually lead into a huge area of rot. What appears to be a tiny plumbing leak often requires replacing the entire plumbing system. It's very important to be aware of every possible defect before you begin. If you're a contractor, you need to discuss these possibilities with the homeowner before you write up a final estimate. If you submit a bid for a minor job that turns out to be a major job, you're either going to lose a lot of money on the job, or have one very unhappy homeowner. The time to find out about these things is *now,* before you submit the bid, not after you're legally bound by it.

🐦 Estimating Costs

I'll try to give you an idea of what each of these jobs will cost. Estimating can be difficult when working on older homes. Each one is unique. You're never sure exactly what you'll have to deal with until you start. Because of this, most of the figures I give you will be "ballpark" estimates. They'll give you a rough idea of the kind of money involved in each job.

When I need a more precise estimate, I check the *National Repair & Remodeling Estimator* and the *National Renovation & Insurance Repair Estimator*, both from Craftsman Book Company. They contain detailed costs for each part of just about any type of job. They also include a free computer estimating program, which is very valuable for those of you who own computers and want to automate the entire estimating process. Although my costs vary because I repair a lot of items that most people would replace, I like to use these books to compare my estimates to more conventional remodelers. It helps me keep up with my competition.

In my specialty, spec rehab, I don't have to submit a formal bid because I'm usually working on my own property. However, it's very important that I know exactly what I have to deal with before I submit an Offer to Purchase on a piece of property. Obviously, if a house needs major work, I can't afford to offer as much money for it as I can for a house that needs only minor repairs. I'm always very careful at this point in the deal. Mistakes in this area can, and do, cost thousands of dollars.

Sample Checklist

At the end of this book, on page 403, you'll find a sample of the checklist I use to estimate repair costs. It contains all the common defects you're likely to find in an average older house, as well as other information that you'll be glad to have later, such as whether the attic or crawl space has adequate work area. Feel free to photocopy it for your own use. Take it with you when you make inspections and check off the items as you come across them. If you don't like this checklist, modify it to suit your work or make up one of your own. You need to have some kind of prepared list because it's very easy to be distracted and leave out something important. This is especially true if the homeowners (and the kids, dogs, cats and/or neighbors) accompany you as you're making your inspection. When you have to make friendly conversation, it's difficult to make detailed notes as well. With a checklist to go by, you don't need to write as much — just check off boxes.

🐦 What You'll Need

In order to do a proper inspection, you'll need your checklist, a pencil, and a few simple tools. I always bring a measuring tape to get exact sizes, a flashlight for peeking into dark corners, a broom for sweeping away cobwebs and dirt, a level to check the lay of things, a hammer to tap on walls and supports to see if they're solid, and a screwdriver in case you need to unscrew any access panels. You'll also need a sharp object, like a small knife or even a nail, to poke into areas that may be rotted. Be sure to take a stepladder along so that you can examine interior ceilings and fixtures and be able to reach the access panel that leads into the attic. And, if you think there are problems with the roof, you'll need an extension ladder tall enough to reach the roof.

These things may seem obvious, but you'd be surprised how many people show up to do an inspection without any tools at all! There's no way to do a thorough inspection without the proper tools. And I can't stress enough how important the inspection is. Skip any part of this step and you could be setting yourself up for a lot of nasty surprises. Never say, "Oh, the roof is too high," or "The crawl space is too dirty. Everything is probably okay." It probably isn't okay. I've fallen into this trap a few times. I didn't want to get all dirty, and crawl spaces never were my favorite place. I've been very sorry afterwards.

Doing a thorough inspection can be a lot of work. It's very tempting to not bother doing the more difficult parts. I've seen professional home inspectors who avoid going up on roofs if they're too high. I know one that missed a bad roof because he didn't want to climb up and look it over. The roof looked fine from the ground, but the problem was obvious once you got up to the top. The roof later had to be replaced. It cost the homeowner thousands of dollars, and cost the inspector his reputation. Sure, it takes a little more effort, but failing to do a really thorough inspection could easily cost *you* thousands of dollars. Believe me, it's worth the extra effort!

The Lot

Before you even start looking at the house, examine the lot around it. Old houses, like the one shown in Figure 2-1, often have old landscaping which may need to be cleared away or redone. While the landscaping isn't actually part of the house, it can cause problems in and around the house. Unsightly landscaping also has a detrimental effect on the value of the property.

Are overgrown shrubs blocking the view? Are half-dead trees threatening to drop limbs through the roof? Are overhanging trees or bushes clogging the gutters with leaves and twigs? Are weed trees growing out of cracks in the foundation, threatening to break up the blocks? Are roots heaving up sections of the driveway or growing into plumbing pipes? All of these problems will need to be dealt with. In many cases, the lot may be so badly overgrown that you can't even get near some areas of the house. Obviously, this growth will have to be cleared away before you can start doing any kind of work.

Figure 2-1
Overgrown shrubs and trees can damage house

❧ Changing Grade Levels

Check the ground level around the house. It should slope gently away from the house, with the house being the highest object on the lot. Is the soil graded properly, or has it piled up too high on the side of the house? Or, conversely, has it washed away from the house, leaving a depression that water can collect in? Either of these conditions will need to be corrected.

If you look carefully around the foundations of many older homes, especially those with large trees, you'll notice that the house seems to have sunk several inches since it was built. The soil may be up to the level of the basement windows, or even higher, causing dirt to leak into the basement. Stairs and railings may be too close to the ground, or even partly buried. The dirt may be right up to the bottom of some doors, or even creeping in. What happened?

Actually, the house didn't sink. The soil around it rose. How? By the accumulation of 100 years of old leaves, grass clippings and other debris that has decomposed and been added to the soil. It's only a tiny amount each year, but over a century it adds up. The net result is that the soil may now be way too high. The soil level can easily be 6 inches higher than it was when the house was built. It may now be adjacent to materials it's not supposed to touch, and causing damage. The excess soil will have to be removed.

Look at the sidewalks and driveway. Are they broken, heaved or cracked? Does the concrete appear to be in good condition, but it's still heaved and cracked? If so, then the soil may be the problem. The soil might be too soft, too wet, or unstable. Or, maybe no sand was put under the concrete when it was poured. In any case, you can't just pour new concrete. You'll need to correct the soil problem first. If you don't, the cracking and heaving will happen all over again.

The Roof

A lot of people look at old homes and assume that they've always been the way they are now. This is rarely true. Even if they realize that the house has been remodeled, they'll think the house was built a certain way, and then remodeled all at once to look the way it does now. This is wrong, too. Most older homes have been remodeled again and again and again. It's not unusual to find five layers of remodeling work, one on top of another, or intermixed with no order at all. This is something we'll find in every area of the house, and the roof is no exception.

Most older homes started out with a different type of roofing than you see on them today. Chances are, the houses you'll be work-ing on now have asphalt shingle roofing, even though asphalt shingles have only been around for 50 years or so. The original roofing was probably wood shingle (usually cedar, but not always), or sometimes tile or slate. Cedar shingles can last up to 40 years. So a home that is 100 years old has obviously been reshingled, probably several times. Each roofing job has left its mark on the house, for better or worse. The roof in Figure 2-2 shows the layers of roofing I typically uncover. Notice that there are two layers of asphalt shingles over the original wood shingles. Under the asphalt shingles, in this particular area of the roof, was a patch of roll roofing. Other areas of this roof had as many as five layers of patches and shingles covering damaged spots, far more than the code allowed.

Asphalt shingle is the most common type of roofing currently in use. This includes the newer fiberglass shingles, which are still made with asphalt, but reinforced with fiberglass strands. Other roof coverings you may be working with are asphalt roll roofing, wood shingle, tile, slate and perhaps galvanized steel. In my area, over 95 percent of the houses currently have asphalt roofing.

Asphalt Shingle

Asphalt shingles are made of an asphalt-impregnated felt material which is covered with mineral granules. These granules are designed to protect the asphalt underlayer from the destructive effects of sunlight. Over the years, sunlight slowly burns up asphalt shingles. The more sunlight they are exposed to, the faster they burn up. Because of this, the use of asphalt shingles is more common in the North than in the South.

When an asphalt shingle is new, it lays straight and flat. As it begins to burn up, it begins to curl. Curling shingles are the classic sign of a failing asphalt-shingle roof. The first noticeable indication that this type of roof is getting old is when the shingles begin to look warped and wavy. The roof will look like it has ripples going through it. At this stage, the roof probably isn't leaking. It may have another year or two, but it's best to replace it

Figure 2-2
Layers of roofing on an older house

Figure 2-3
Shingles beginning to curl and crumble

before it begins leaking and ruins the interior plasterwork.

If it's left to continue to wear, the edges of the shingles will eventually begin to curl, sticking up in strange little points all over the roof. Shingles in this condition are very brittle. The corners will break off in the wind, leaving sections of roof exposed. A roof in this condition is either leaking or will soon begin to leak. It should be replaced as soon as possible. The roof in Figure 2-3 shows deteriorating shingles that are brittle, cracked and beginning to curl.

Another thing you'll notice on a worn asphalt roof is that there are areas where all the mineral granules have come off. It's not unusual for some of the grains to come off an asphalt-shingle roof. Even a new roof will shed some, so this in itself is nothing to be concerned about. However, when the shingles get old and brittle, they also lose the stickiness that holds the grains on. Large black areas will appear where the grains have been blown off or have been washed away by rain. This may be hard to see on a black roof, but on a light-colored roof, it's quite obvious. Whenever you see this, the roof is bad and needs to be replaced.

You can usually spot these defects from the ground. That's why many inspectors don't bother to go up on the roof. They assume that if there's anything wrong with the roof, they'll be able to see waviness, curling corners or black spots. They're right about 90 percent of the time, but not always! I've found that about one out of ten bad roofs didn't show up from the ground. You *cannot* depend on the view from the ground!

What You Can't See

Sometimes the shingles will be bad without looking bad from the ground. This is particularly true of certain types of shingles, such as interlocking shingles or hexagonal-shaped shingles. They don't have corners that curl up. Defects in these shingles may not be clear unless you're actually up on the roof.

Also, sometimes you may think a roof is worn when it isn't. Occasionally, you'll see a roof which appears to be very wavy, but is actually perfectly good. This is caused by the shingles having been put down over an uneven surface. Fiberglass shingles, which are very thin, are particularly prone to this. Any little lump or bump will show right through them. This doesn't mean they're not watertight, however. As long as they're still solid, pliable, and holding together properly, they'll be perfectly adequate protection against the weather. However, from the ground you can't tell the difference between harmless waves caused by an uneven undersurface, and dying shingles. Although wavy shingles may be perfectly serviceable, they'll never look good. The homeowner might want to replace them just because they look bad, but chances are, there's a better place to spend the money.

Never make the mistake of thinking you can judge a whole roof by looking at a small portion. Areas of a roof will wear differently due to exposure to sun, wind and moisture. If there's an upstairs window overlooking a porch roof, you may be able to stick your head out the window and look. This will give you an excellent opportunity to inspect the porch roof. But the porch roof and the rest of the roof may not be the same! Someone may have reroofed the porch without doing the rest of the house, or vice versa. You need to look at each side. From the ground you just can't get close enough to see details. Sometimes there are trees in the way, or other houses may block your view of portions of the roof. Or it may just be too high to see clearly. There's no substitute for going up on the roof for a close inspection, especially if you're about to submit a firm estimate involving any kind of roof work.

What to Look for on the Roof

Let's assume you go up on the roof to look around. What will you see? Take a look at the shingles. Now that you're up close, can you see any of the common defects, like curling, waving, or black spots? Take a corner of a shingle and bend it. It should be soft and pliable. If it's cracked or breaks off in your hand, that means the shingles have become brittle and are beginning to break up. Time for a new roof.

If possible, walk around on the roof, but be careful! Be sure you have something to hold onto in case you start sliding. Don't walk on crumbling shingles — the little crumbly pieces are very slippery.

How does the roof *feel* underfoot? Does it seem to hold your weight okay, or does it bounce excessively? If it bounces too much, there may be structural problems. These can be checked out from the attic space.

Rot Damage — How does the decking feel? Is it solid underfoot, or soft? If you find soft spots, try to determine how big they are. But be very careful. Soft spots are probably rot damage. If the rot is bad enough, the area may not hold your weight and you'll get a quick trip to the attic. When in doubt, check it from the inside instead. You'll need to double-check it from the attic space anyway. Rot damage can be extensive and should be thoroughly investigated.

Figure 2-4
Potential trouble areas on a roof

Molds and Moss — Another danger sign to check for is mold, moss, lichens or other plant organisms growing on a roof. Mold creates powdery black spots; mosses are green; and lichen are green with white edges. These organisms don't grow unless they have a steady supply of moisture and nutrients, which aren't normally found on a roof. Their presence may mean extensive rot damage, with wet, rotting decking providing the moisture and nutrients they need. You may even find small trees, plants and mushrooms sprouting from rotten shingles. Wood shingles are especially susceptible to this, but given the proper diet, plant organisms can grow on anything.

Before you assume that the roof is rotten, look around. Mosses, mold and lichen will also grow on a section of roof that is beneath a large tree. Leaves and drippings from the tree can provide the moisture and nutrients that they need. If the area is perfectly hard and solid, then they are probably just caused by the tree, and the problem is mostly cosmetic and nothing to worry about. If the homeowner dislikes the moss, you can kill it by pouring a dilute solution of chlorine bleach on it. You don't necessarily need to trim the tree back unless it can be done in a way that improves the look of the tree and the house in general. If trimming the tree would make the property less attractive, leave it. It's really more of a landscaping problem than a threat to the roof.

Flashings — Be sure to check all the flashings and valleys while you're on the roof. These are big trouble spots. Flashings are the most difficult part of a roof job. Some roofers don't know how to do them correctly. Check very carefully for leaks around the chimney, plumbing vent pipes, dormers and anything else that comes up through or attaches to the roof, including the joints between the roof and walls. Figure 2-4 shows some of these problem areas you'll want to check carefully. If the roof is leaking, any one of these may be the cause, rather than worn shingles. I've seen brand-new roofs that leaked because the flashings hadn't been installed correctly, or in some cases, hadn't been done at all! If this is the problem, you may be able to replace a flashing and avoid replacing a perfectly serviceable roof.

Figure 2-5
Patch job using roll roofing

✺ Roll Roofing

After asphalt shingles, asphalt roll roofing is the next most commonly-used roofing material. It is the correct, code-approved material to use for low-pitch roofs, those with a rise of 2 inches or less per foot of horizontal run. In any other application however, it's considered a poor-quality roofing material. If you see roll roofing on a house with a regular-pitched roof, *watch out!* That's a big danger sign! It tells you that someone's been doing low-quality, quick-and-dirty work with little regard for how the house looks or how long the work will hold up. They may have rolled it on over anything, including rot holes or fire damage. The patch job in Figure 2-5 is a good example. No attempt was made to blend it in with the rest of the roofing. You know the roof must have been in pretty bad shape if that's the improvement! Don't walk on a roof that looks like this without testing your footing ahead of time.

As a rule, you can't evaluate roll roofing from the ground. It doesn't curl or wave. It does get black spots as the grains come off, but on a low-slope roof these can be very hard to see from the ground. You'll have to go up on the roof and look at it. If the roll roofing has gone bad, you'll see a lot of black areas where all the grains of mineral material have washed away, a lot of cracking, and some bub-

bling. Like shingles, the material will be brittle, and crumble in your fingers.

Again, be careful if you have to walk around on the roof because you don't know what the roll roofing is hiding. It's often used to cover a roof that's in such bad shape that shingles won't hold on it. I've seen roll roofing thrown over big unpatched holes that went right through the decking and into the attic space. If you stepped on one of these spots, your foot would go right through. Obviously, that isn't the correct way to repair a roof. It should be rebuilt.

Figure 2-6 is a picture of a porch roof that I came across recently. It was a flat roof, so I wasn't surprised to find it covered with roll roofing. The dark, discolored section at the edge of the roof did make me think there was some rot damage, however. Figure 2-7 shows what I found when I pulled off the roofing. Almost the entire roof was rotted away!

Figure 2-6
Old roll roofing on a porch

Figure 2-7
Under the roofing was a rotted roof

One problem with very old houses is that they frequently belong to very old people who don't have the money to pay a reputable contractor for repair work. If I see one of these slapped-together patch jobs, I know it wasn't done by a contractor, because no contractor would ever do that kind of work. Usually it's done by a handyman who works cheap but gets the problem solved — at least for the moment. Of course, jobs like this are totally unsound. If you find one, be prepared to tear it down to the rafters. Consider yourself lucky if the rafters don't need replacing as well.

Let's face it, roll roofing looks bad on any nice house with a pitched roof. Even if the material is in good condition, most homeowners will probably want to replace it. The only point in evaluating its condition is to let you know whether you need to replace it now, or if it can wait a while.

The Right Place for Roll Roofing

Remember, roll roofing does have its place — it's the correct material to use for low-pitched or flat roofs. *Never shingle a low-pitched or flat roof. It will leak!* I can't tell you how many times I've seen low-pitched roofs that were incorrectly shingled when they should have been roll-roofed. I've seen whole blocks of identical houses done this way, and every one of them leaked. In some cases, the homeowners tried to stop the leaks by adding another layer of shingles. It still leaked. So they added another, and another, and another! I've seen some roofs with shingles eight layers deep — well beyond the three layers that the code allows. And they still leaked. It seemed that no one ever explained the problem to the owners. No matter how many layers of shingles they put on, the roof will leak until the shingles are removed and replaced with roll roofing.

Roll roofing is also a perfectly appropriate material for garages, sheds, and other utility buildings, especially if they're tucked away somewhere where they can't be seen. You don't need to replace good roll roofing on buildings like these.

❧ Slate and Tile

You may come across some houses with slate or tile roofs. Tile isn't common in Michigan where I live, but it's quite common elsewhere in the country, especially in the South and Southwest. Both slate and tile are luxury roofing materials that, with the proper care, can last hundreds of years.

Slates and tiles never wear out, but they break. You have to be very careful when you're examining this type of roof. It's best not to walk on them.

What usually ruins slate or tile roofs is a failure somewhere else in the system, such as a rusted-out flashing. Water gets into the roof decking or rafters underneath the slate or tiles and either rots out their supports, or rusts out the nails that hold them on. The slates or tiles then come loose and fall to the ground. This creates a bigger hole, which lets in more water, which causes more rot. In the early stages, this type of problem is best spotted from inside the attic area. You'll see water stains on the roof decking. Sometimes, if the flashing around a chimney is bad, you may find water leaking down inside the chimney after a rain.

These problems are very difficult to repair. Tile and slate are hard to work with. And, you have to work off a ladder to avoid stepping on them while you make your repairs. If the problem is in an easily-accessible area, you can probably do it yourself. If not, I suggest you get a professional to do the repair. This isn't an area of construction where "giving it a try" is going to pay off.

Working with slates is a special skill called slattery. Although slate is common in Europe, it isn't used much in the U.S. any longer. There are only a few slaters in the entire country. Having slate work done is very expensive. As a result, you'll usually only find this kind of work being done on registered historic landmarks, where you absolutely have to have authentic materials, regardless of the cost.

You can now get an artificial slate made of concrete. It's lighter, less expensive, and easier to work with than real slate, which is made of actual stone. However, even these are about five times more expensive and much harder to work with than the more common types of roofing materials. In most cases where slate roofs have failed, owners have had them torn off and replaced with asphalt shingle. Sometimes I find roll roofing glued on over damaged slates. This creates an awful mess which needs to be torn down to the rafters and completely redone.

❧ Steel

Finally, you may run across a few houses with galvanized steel roofing. These are rare in the city, but not quite as uncommon in rural areas. This type of roofing is used today for utility buildings, especially barns.

Galvanized steel roofing can last 40 years or more, but eventually it will rust out. What you find when this has happened is a roof that has been patched or partly covered with glued-on roll roofing. What a mess! This, too, will need to be torn down to the rafters and redone, including new decking.

Once in a while I'll come across galvanized steel roofs that are still in perfect condition. There's nothing really wrong with this type of roof. If your customer likes the rustic look, you can just leave it. On the other hand, if they think it makes their house look like a barn, they'll probably want to replace it no matter how much life is left in it.

The Chimney

Be sure to check out the chimney while you're on the roof. Mortar doesn't last forever. It eventually gets dissolved by rainwater, especially acid rain. The chimney is the piece of masonry that is the most exposed to rain, and therefore it's the one item most likely to need tuckpointing. Now is a good time to find out.

Be sure to check the concrete cap on the top of the chimney. Any cracks should be sealed. Otherwise, rain will seep inside the

Figure 2-8
Discolored chimney on left was from an old coal stove

chimney, between the bricks and the flue pipe. This will cause further damage.

If the chimney has never been tuckpointed, it may need to be completely disassembled and remortared, not just tuckpointed. Be careful, the bricks may be very loose. I've often had them come right off in my hand. Occasionally I've seen chimneys that have begun to fall apart and some of the bricks are laying on the roof. A chimney in this condition is dangerous. It could fall at any moment.

Sometimes you can't tell just how bad a chimney is. The chimney in Figure 2-8, the one with the discolored block, was one such case. This chimney was used with an old coal stove that had been removed 60 years ago. Chimneys that are no longer used are especially prone to deterioration. I decided to give this chimney a gentle shove to see how sturdy it was — and it fell right over! Anyone working near it could have easily knocked it over, either on themselves or someone working

Figure 2-9
Fallen chimney blocks

accumulate in the eaves. There it will cause major rot damage. Rotted eaves and fascia boards will often fall off as soon as you touch them. If the problem is really bad, the rot may extend up into the rafters as well, requiring major rafter repair or replacement.

Remember, rotted eaves are just a symptom of a bigger problem. Wood won't rot unless it's wet. You have to find how the water got into the eaves. There will be a leak somewhere in the roof, and you have to find it. A continuing leak can destroy all your subsequent work, not to mention destroying your relationship with the homeowner.

below. You can see in Figure 2-9 that the blocks fell with tremendous force. They buried themselves several inches into the ground. If someone had been standing there, they would have been killed. I'm not kidding when I say these things are dangerous!

There are a lot of old chimneys like these that are no longer being used. They may be from old coal or wood-burning stoves that were removed, or from old heating systems that have been replaced. If the chimneys are in bad condition, it's easier to remove them than repair them. They are really nothing more than a maintenance problem. If you remove them, you can patch over the hole in the roof where they used to be. That makes one less item that needs flashings, and one less place that is likely to leak. You should take care of this as soon as possible.

Be sure you know what a chimney is (or was) connected to before you remove it. Some may be connected to old fireplaces which were covered over. A fireplace in a house is usually a powerful selling tool. It would be a shame to discover a hidden one that you could have restored *after* you've pulled down its chimney.

The Eaves

The eaves are a common trouble-spot on any roof. If there's a leak anywhere in the roof area, the water is likely to drip down and

The Gutters and Downspouts

Other major roof problems can be caused by neglected gutters and downspouts. If these clog up, water can pool in them and back up under the shingles or into the eaves, causing leaks or rot damage. They can cause leaks in what is otherwise a perfectly good roof. See how the lower row of shingles was completed destroyed by a clogged gutter in Figure 2-10? This can also lead to rot damage in the eaves. But remember, clogged gutters may not be the only cause of rot damage to the eaves! You can have clogged gutters *and* a roof leak, both leading to rotted eaves. Be sure to check for roof leaks as well.

Figure 2-10
Shingles destroyed by clogged gutter

If the gutters and downspouts are the old galvanized steel type, you'll probably need to replace them. I rarely come across one of these old-style gutters that isn't all rusted out.

The Original Siding

The next area you'll want to inspect is the siding. There are several different types of siding you're likely to come across, each with its own good points and bad points. Let's go through them one at a time.

Wood Sidings

Most of the older homes I've worked on were originally built with wood siding. Many of these were later covered with some other material, like aluminum or asbestos. However, some still show their original wood siding. There are several common types of wood siding.

Clapboards

Clapboards are the type of siding I run into most often. These are tapered wood boards set in overlapping rows. They are tapered so that the bottom edge is thicker than the top edge. That way, the overlapping row can lay neatly on top of the thinner top edge of the row below it without sticking out too far. Having the bottom edge protrude slightly also helps the siding shed rainwater. The Victorian house shown in Figure 2-11 has clapboard siding.

Shiplap

Rather than having overlapping boards, shiplap siding is fitted together in a tongue-and-groove arrangement, similar to tongue-and-groove flooring. The finished wall looks like the side of a wooden ship, which is where it gets its name. See the example in Figure 2-12. The boards can be arranged either horizontally or vertically, although the horizontal installation is the more common. This style was popular in the 1930s and '40s. Most of the houses that you

Figure 2-11
Victorian clapboard house

Figure 2-12
Shiplap siding

see with this type of siding will date from that period.

There are other fitted-wood siding styles that are somewhat different from shiplap, but which require similar techniques to install or repair. They're not very common, so I'll just include them with shiplap siding repair when I discuss that.

Cedar Shingles

Cedar shingles as siding were very popular around the turn of the century. You'll find that many homes built between 1880 and

Figure 2-13
Rot damage to vertical wood siding

1920 were shingled in a style called "Shingle Victorian." This look continued to be popular through the 1920s. It dropped out of style in the 1930s, and few shingle-style homes were built after that — until just recently. The style is again popular and its renewed popularity has made older shingle-style homes even more desirable than they were before.

Checking for Damage

If the wood siding is 100 years old or more, it's likely to have problems. By far the most common is rot damage. It's very hard to keep moisture entirely away from wood siding for 100 years (unless you live in a very dry place). If moisture was allowed to come in contact with any part of the siding for any extended period of time, that area will have rotted out. Even if that area is now dry, there still may be rot damage from a leak that was fixed years ago. You need to check for this very carefully.

Damage to wood that comes into direct contact with the ground is common. Figure 2-13 shows rot damage to vertical wood siding on a house. This is a perfect example of the grading problem that we discussed earlier in the chapter. The soil piled up against this wall until it buried the foundation and came in contact with the wood. Looking at the photograph, you wouldn't think there was a foundation. It's there, just buried in the dirt.

Before I could make repairs to the siding, I had to remove the excess soil and correct the grade around the house.

I've seen a number of homes that have raised flower beds built with one border of the bed being the wooden wall of the house. People who do this have created exactly the kind of situation you want to avoid. If this type of flower bed isn't removed, it can rot out the entire wall of the house. A flower bed next to a house must have all the dirt contained in a structure made from masonry or treated lumber. It should also be at least 1 inch out from the wall of the house so that it doesn't conduct moisture to the house.

When checking for damage, first stand back and look at each wall. They should be flat, smooth, and even. Look for areas that are cracked, weathered, or have loose or missing boards. If the paint is peeling, it should be peeling evenly all over. If any area is peeling worse than the rest, investigate it carefully. Use a pocket knife, ice pick or even a long nail to probe for wood rot. When you poke a piece of wood, you should encounter resistance. If your knife or nail easily pushes into the wood, that piece of wood is no good.

Moss, mold or algae growing on the wall is a danger sign, just like on the roof. The moss is probably using rotting wood as its food supply. Check any green areas carefully!

Hidden Problems — There are certain areas that are particularly prone to rot that may not be readily noticed. These are the areas where water was likely to have been trapped. As I mentioned earlier, the eaves and fascia boards very often catch water, so check the siding directly under the eaves. Spillover from the eaves may have rotted the siding as well.

Also check siding that is near, or under, flashings. This includes the area around the chimney, sections of walls beneath roof valleys, or the points where wall sections connect to roof sections, such as at dormers, room additions, bay windows or porches. The area closest to the seam is the area most likely to be rotted.

❧ Brick or Stone Sidings

Many better-quality older homes were built of brick or stone. These are very durable materials. However, the walls still need to be inspected.

While brick and stone can last just about forever, mortar doesn't. After 60 or 80 years of exposure to the weather, it starts to crumble. Look over the walls from top to bottom. Do you see any missing mortar? Missing bricks or stones? You'll need to remortar and replace missing or broken bricks or stones. How about cracks? Extensive cracking may indicate a foundation problem.

Use your knife or nail to probe the mortar. Does it cut easily? It shouldn't. In some cases the mortar may be so fragile that you can scoop it out with your fingers. If it's failing, it will need tuckpointing.

Replacement Sidings

Many older wooden homes have been re-sided sometime during their life. You're likely to find one of several different types of siding, depending on when the house was re-sided. You may even find several, one on top of the other!

If the house was re-sided recently, it may have aluminum, steel, or vinyl sidings. These generally don't need any work. Of course, the homeowner may want the siding replaced simply because he doesn't like it. Look it over anyway. There are a few problems you might run into.

❧ Aluminum Siding

First of all, is the color on the siding even and uniform throughout? The paint on aluminum siding tends to wear off over the years, exposing the shiny metal underneath. This doesn't do any harm, but it doesn't look nice. Fortunately, aluminum siding can easily be repainted.

Painting is also an option if the homeowner doesn't like the color of the siding. In the early 1970s, many houses were sided with strange shades of pink and green that are no longer popular. Painting easily solves this problem. Be sure to point this out to the owner. Many people believe that since aluminum siding "never needs paint," that means that they never *can* paint. They think that they either have to live with the color, or replace the siding. Replacing the siding would be very expensive, but painting isn't.

Dents, Tears and Missing Pieces

Aluminum is a fairly soft metal, and can be easily dented or torn by rough handling. You're especially likely to find this kind of damage around garages and driveways, where someone may have driven a car into the siding and punctured it or ripped out a piece or even a section. Figure 2-14 shows a wall with torn aluminum siding. Luckily, you can still find aluminum siding in most sizes. If you need to replace a piece, you'll probably be able to find one that fits exactly. The problem is that it won't quite match. The old siding will be weathered but the replacement piece won't. The same thing applies to replacing missing pieces. Sometimes the aluminum pieces just aren't there, as shown in Figure 2-15. You may have to repaint the wall in order to get the new and old pieces all one color.

❧ Vinyl Siding

Vinyl siding doesn't dent, and is very hard to tear. However, it does have one serious problem: fading. You won't see this in white siding, but you will with other colors.

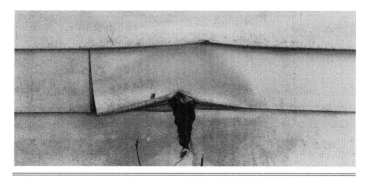

Figure 2-14
Torn aluminum siding

Figure 2-15
Missing aluminum siding

The darker colors fade worse than lighter colors, and older siding fades worse than newer.

If you're working on a house with old, dark-colored vinyl siding, it will probably have faded to several different colors. The areas with the most sun exposure will be substantially lighter than those in the shade. This is a serious problem, because you can't paint vinyl siding; paint won't adhere to it. There's really no way to correct this except by replacing the siding. And there's no reason to replace it if it's still perfectly functional. It lasts just about forever.

Another problem that I've come across with this type of siding is the color selection that has been available through the years. I've seen dozens of nicely-kept homes that look really terrible because of out-dated colors, especially the garish colors of the 1970s. Eventually, the homeowners will probably want to replace it just because the color looks so bad.

🐘 Mineral Siding

Mineral siding was popular in the 1940s and 1950s. It was manufactured to look like cedar shingles, but it really doesn't. My guess

is that you wouldn't know what it was supposed to be if someone didn't tell you. Sometimes people confuse it with asbestos siding, but it's made of a completely different material. Mineral siding shingles are made from a type of cement board and resemble cement roof shingles. The shingles come in 1 by 2 foot pieces with wavy lines cast into them to simulate wood grain. They are only about a quarter inch thick, and are very brittle. If you drop one, it will shatter like a dish. The shingles are nailed to the sides of the house in overlapping rows, just like cedar shingles.

Mineral siding holds up very well, even with exposure to weather. I've seen many houses with siding that's 40 or 50 years old, and still in fine shape. However, the shingles can't take any kind of impact. It's quite common to find a number of broken shingles on a house, like the one shown in Figure 2-16. You can replace broken shingles, but you must handle them very carefully. Also, they are very hard to find. Most of the time I have to scavenge them off old houses that are being re-sided or torn down. I keep a few on hand just in case I need them. However, if you're working on a house with more than a few shingles broken, you might as well re-side the house. It's too much trouble to find and replace a lot of shingles.

Besides, mineral siding isn't that attractive. A homeowner who wants a picture-perfect house will probably want the siding removed anyway. If they're on a tight budget, however, suggest painting the siding instead.

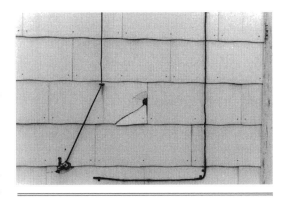

Figure 2-16
Broken mineral siding shingle

Usually, what homeowners like least about their siding is its color, and that's especially true of mineral siding. It originally came in a lot of odd colors that nobody likes anymore. Sometimes the color has faded, or the paint has largely powdered away, leaving the house looking dingy. A coat of paint can cure all these problems.

Mineral siding is very easy to paint, and it holds paint very well. Your paint job will last substantially longer on this material than it will on wood. Painting the house a dark color is a good idea — it makes the siding much less noticeable. You'd be surprised how much a simple (and inexpensive) coat of paint can improve the look of a house with this type of siding.

Figure 2-17
Asphalt siding

Asbestos Siding

Asbestos siding is in the form of shingles, like mineral siding, but the shingles are much thicker, usually almost an inch thick. They're made of a white, fibrous material (asbestos), that's fairly soft. If the shingles break, you can see these soft, white fibers at the broken edge. The shingles have a wavy bottom edge that's supposed to look like wood. They were usually installed so that they laid almost flat. This siding is even worse-looking than mineral siding. It's paintable, but even with a fresh coat of paint it looks strange.

Asbestos siding was taken off the market many years ago. Most people today are afraid of anything made from asbestos. However, as long as it remains undisturbed, asbestos siding is actually quite safe. But it isn't something you'd want to remove. It's now classified as toxic waste, and you may have to go though a whole asbestos-abatement routine if you disturb it at all. If a homeowner doesn't like it, you're better off siding over it. In most areas, removing it involves hiring a licensed contractor who specializes in asbestos removal. Even if that's not the case in your area, don't take a chance on polluting the atmosphere and yourself by throwing cancer-causing asbestos particles around. Leave that sort of thing to the professionals.

Asphalt "Fake Brick" Siding

Asphalt is the worst looking of all the old-fashioned siding materials. Fortunately, like most of these old sidings, it's no longer manufactured. It was made of exactly the same material as asphalt roof shingles. It came in sheets, usually with red bricks printed on them, though occasionally you'll see it in other colors and textures as well. The home shown in Figure 2-17 is covered in asphalt siding with a mixed-tone masonry brick look. Whether it was printed with bricks or a stone-type masonry, it doesn't fool anybody. It still looks like what it is.

Asphalt siding didn't look good when it was brand new, but it really looks bad after it has aged. It usually has some of the mineral grains washed off of it, leaving big black spots. It's quite soft and tears easily, so there are often holes in it. It isn't something that homeowners want to leave on a house. It can't be painted. All you can do is remove it or put new siding over it.

Siding Removal

Except for asbestos, all of these sidings can be removed quite easily. This is an option you might want to explore with the home-

Figure 2-18
Wall damage caused by a leaky porch roof

I've had windows fall apart in my hands when I tried to open them. You'll have to add "window replacement" to the list of jobs that need to be done.

Do the windows have usable storms and screens? If not, be sure to note that on your list. Check the glazing putty. If the windows have been exposed to the weather for any length of time, the glazing putty has probably gone bad, leaving the glass loose in the frame.

It's important to note that unless the window is very badly rotted, it may not need to be replaced. It may yet be repairable. Whether it's *worth* repairing or not is another question. We'll discuss this in detail when we get into window repair in Chapter 7.

owner. Sometimes the original wall underneath the siding is in better shape than the siding covering it. This isn't something you can depend on, though. We'll discuss what to do with siding in greater detail in Chapter 6, when we deal with siding repair.

Trim

Even though the siding on a house may be something other than wood, it might have wood trim. If that's the case, it's likely to be rotted. People with "maintenance free" siding frequently forget that the wood trim isn't. As a result, the trim is often neglected. Inspect it carefully.

Windows

Windows and the areas around them are prime candidates for rot damage. Water tends to get caught between the sashes and puddle up on the sill. It rots the sill, and then leaks down and rots the wall underneath. This is very common. Consider yourself lucky if you find windows that aren't rotted.

Check the window casing, the frame and the sashes. If any of these are rotted, it's probably not economical to repair the window.

Porches

Porches and the walls around them are also extremely common sites of rot damage. The flashings between the porch roof and the house often deteriorate, allowing water to drip down between the house and the porch. This rots both the porch and the section of the house wall adjoining it. You can see this type of rot in Figure 2-18. Another area to look for damage is in the corners of the floor. Rain will often blow onto open porches and puddle up in the corners, causing the floors to deteriorate.

Check the porch ceiling carefully for signs of water or rot damage. In many cases, people who don't have much money will allow the porch roof to leak, even if they have the main roof repaired. Since water isn't dripping on their furniture, they figured it isn't doing any harm. A leak in a porch roof can cause widespread rot damage to the porch roof structure. Even if the roof is later repaired, the unseen structural damage may not have been repaired. The entire porch roof may be unsound. If possible (if the homeowner allows), try to take down some of the porch ceiling boards and peek up into the roof structure with a flashlight. Poke the rafters and the underside of the porch decking with your knife or nail. If they're badly rotted, the entire porch roof may have to be torn off and rebuilt.

Some older porches were built directly on dirt or sand, with no proper foundation. Obviously, the part of the wall that sits on the ground will rot out, causing the porch to sag, or even collapse. Always check the bottom edge of a porch carefully. Even if it has a proper foundation, moisture can still collect at this point and cause rot damage.

❧ Second-Floor Porches

Second-floor porches were quite common on older homes, especially those built from 1880 to 1930. Some of these were covered porches. They had roofs over them, much like first-floors porches. Some were open. Often, these porches were stacked up, with the second-floor porch being built right over a first-floor porch. When that was the case, the upper porch helped protect the lower porch, with the upper porch bearing the brunt of any weather damage.

A covered upstairs porch will tend to have the same kinds of damage as a covered first-floor porch. Inspect the joint between the porch roof and the main roof or wall, and the joint between the porch floor and the section of wall it's connected to. Also inspect the corners of the floor. These are the most likely sites of rot damage.

Jump up and down on the floor. If it bounces excessively, the floor joists may be rotted. If so, the beam holding up the porch may also be rotted, which could lead to damage in the pillars or posts that support the beam. Chances are, you won't be able to tell for sure without ripping up the floor. This type of damage is something you want to discuss with the homeowner. If it seems at all likely that the beam is rotted, the upstairs porch may have to be completely torn off and rebuilt.

❧ Dust Porches

Uncovered upstairs porches are called "dust porches." They were used for shaking out rugs and dust mops when cleaning the second-floor bedrooms. They are a major problem area in an older home because they are open and continuously exposed to the weather.

Dust porches are almost always severely rotted. Let's face it, having a porch that is open to the weather is just not good design. It's asking for trouble. These porches usually need to be totally rebuilt, and that isn't an easy job. The rot often extends into the porch or room beneath the dust porch, requiring extensive repairs to that as well. We'll cover this in the section on exterior repairs.

Termites and Carpenter Ants

Porches are a frequent site of termite damage. The most important thing to remember about termites is that they need damp or wet wood to live in. Unfortunately, even a small leak can dampen a large area of wood, making it a suitable home for termites, carpenter ants, and other wood-eating bugs. Generally, termites and rot exist together, because they both need damp wood.

One source of moisture is roof leaks, as we discussed earlier. Another is moisture from the ground. Anyplace wood touches the ground, it will absorb moisture from the earth. This creates a perfect breeding ground for termites. Obviously, if the foundation of a porch has been built directly on the ground, it will very likely have termites, as well as rot problems.

Even if a porch has a proper foundation it can attract termites from the ground. Often, dirt gets heaped up against the porch. This may happen because someone has built a raised flower bed against the porch, or because the level of the soil has risen throughout the area. As a result, an area of wall that was originally well above the soil is now in contact with it, giving rise to termites and rot. Inspect areas like this carefully.

Termites pose a greater threat in coastal areas where the air is damp. There isn't any totally dry wood in these parts of the country because the moisture seeps into all exterior wood surfaces. Termites will live in fences, decks, porches, eaves and fascia boards even if the house is brick or stucco. Once they begin to burrow in, they will attack attic joists, walls, woodwork, and even kitchen cabinets.

Termites swarm in the spring, looking for new nesting areas. They look like large black or red ants with wings, though once they begin to burrow they lose their wings. If you see any bugs like this, even just a few, there's probably plenty more where you can't see them.

Termites are much less a problem in the Midwest. The air is drier and the cold winters tend to kill off termites and other bugs unless they have burrowed deep into the heated areas of the house.

Another common wood-eating bug is the carpenter ant. Carpenter ants look like perfectly ordinary big black ants, except they eat wood. Generally, if you see anything that looks at all like a big black ant in the area of wet wood, suspect an infestation of wood-eating insects.

Look at the wood. If you see a lot of little holes that look like they were made with a small drill, there are probably bugs in there. If you trace the holes (or bugs) back, you may find a large, fragile area ridden with tunnel-like holes. This is their nest.

Don't assume these insects will go away just because you've broken open their nest. They may have more than one, or they'll just make a new one. You'll never get rid of them until you remove all the wet wood, and stop the moisture, so that the rest of the wood stays dry. A house with extensive termite or other infestation should be professionally fumigated before you make your repairs. The poison kills the existing insects and their eggs.

In areas where termite infestation is common, lenders may require a pest inspection before they will grant a loan on a house. If homeowners need a second mortgage in order to have you do their remodeling, this may be something that they will have to deal with.

The Foundation

Check the foundation for any obvious signs of decay. Look for cracks, missing stones or blocks, or anything out of line or out of plumb, indicating possible settling or heaving.

Only a small amount of the foundation will be visible from the outside. We'll do a more thorough inspection when we get to the interior.

Garages

The garages on many older homes are in dire need of repair. They may have been neglected for many years. Some of them may not have been built well in the first place. They need to be checked carefully. Examine the roof and the walls using the same techniques you use on the house. The trouble spots tend to be the same, and the repairs tend to be the same, as well.

Check the garage slab and footings. These are often cracked, heaved, or settled. In some cases, the garage may have been built on sand, and a slab added later. You'll see, if you look closely, that the slab runs up to the walls, but not under them. The walls are sitting on dirt. Check the bottoms of the walls carefully. Garages that were built like this, or without any foundation at all, will probably have some rot damage. If the garage is leaning, it may have substantial damage.

If there are trees growing very close to the garage, their roots may have cracked the slab or footings. If the trunk of the tree is touching the garage, it may actually be pushing the garage over. The trees will need to be removed and repairs made.

For some reason, people seem to like to heap dirt up against garages. I've sometimes seen it 3 feet deep. Look for this, especially in areas that aren't readily seen, such as the back or side. You can expect rot and termite damage wherever dirt touches wood.

Check the garage door. Is it a modern, overhead type, or the old wooden swinging doors? Does it open and close properly? Is it rusted or rotted? New garage doors can be expensive.

Some older homes have beautiful garages. They may be former carriage houses, with elaborate brickwork and living quarters upstairs. Other garages are poorly-built shed-like structures, in bad condition. Beautiful garages are worth putting a lot of effort into. Small, poorly-built wooden ones, on the other hand, aren't worth saving. You'd get better results just tearing them down and building a new one.

That takes care of the exterior of the house. Now let's see what we'll have to deal with inside.

Chapter 3

Inspecting the Interior

s you approach the house to start your interior inspection, you can't help but notice the front door. The front door is really part of the exterior of the house, but I'll discuss it here because it's your introduction to the house — it sets the stage for what you find inside. As you walk up to any house to knock or ring the bell, where is your attention? It's focused on the front door, so you want the door to make a good impression. What kind of condition is the door in? Doors take a lot of abuse. They get slammed, kicked, rained on, snowed on, and more. They can rarely survive 100 years of this kind of abuse. Therefore, the door on the house is probably not the original door. If it is, it's probably not in very good shape.

Is the door particularly beautiful? Is it made of fine wood, carved, or set with leaded or beveled glass? If so, you may want to save it. Today a door like this can cost thousands of dollars. A nice door is worth the time and effort it takes to restore it. Doors can usually be repaired, even if they're in bad shape. We'll cover a number of techniques for saving damaged doors when we get to Chapter 7, Window and Door Repair.

If the door is not original or if it's ordinary, you're probably better off replacing it.

There's no point in putting $200 of effort into saving a $100 door.

The Living Room, Dining Room, Entry and Hall

All of the downstairs living areas will have similar problems to look for and to deal with. Except for some extra ornamental woodwork here and there, they are all basic rooms with four walls, a ceiling and a floor. To make our inspection easier, I've combined them under these features: walls, ceilings and floors. As you go through this section, you can use the same criteria to look for problems in each room. This would also apply to any bedrooms, den or family room, if the house you are inspecting has these main floor rooms.

The Walls

Your first impression of the interior of the house will probably be of the walls. What kind of shape are they in? One major problem

Figure 3-1
*Cheap paneling and drop ceiling spoil
original Victorian decor*

with older homes is that they've often been extensively remodeled. Usually they've been remodeled several times, one layer right on top of another. Peeling them off is like doing an archaeological dig. With each layer you take off, you go further back in time. You'll travel through remodeling from the 1970s, the '50s, the '30s, and so on, hitting another layer about every 20 years or so, until you get back to the original walls of the house.

You never know what you'll find under all these layers of remodeling. One older home in my area turned out to have a log cabin right in the center of it! It was an early settler's cabin that had been added onto over many, many years. The cabin was saved and moved to a historic park.

What you see when you walk through the front door of a house may or may not have anything to do with what you'll actually be working on. You'll often find yourself looking at cheap fiberboard paneling from the 1970s and a poorly-installed drop ceiling like the ones in Figure 3-1. What's under them? There might be beautiful wet plaster with fine ornamental carvings, all in perfect

condition. Or, there might be nothing more than a tangled mess of shattered furring strips. You won't know for sure until you tear the current layer off.

Finding out what's beneath the walls is one of the biggest problems you'll run into when you try to prepare an estimate. Homeowners are rarely willing to let you tear into their walls just to see what's there. And you can't just peek under a little section of paneling and guess what might be there from the little bit you see. I've tried that, and I learned the hard way not to ever do that again. The walls (and the floors, and the ceiling) are likely to be different from one area of the house, or even the room, to another. You might peek under a piece of paneling and see perfect wet plaster behind it. But when you start work and pull off *all* the paneling, you may find that the little piece of plaster you saw in your limited investigation was the *only* piece in the entire house that's still intact. If your estimate didn't include redoing the walls, you may be in big trouble.

How do you get around this problem? Consider why the paneling and drop ceiling were added in the first place. Probably, though not necessarily, to cover some kind of damage. Usually you'll find extensively-cracked plaster underneath these coverings. Sometimes you'll find big pieces of the wall missing, like the wall I uncovered in Figure 3-2. Your best bet is to always assume that the

Figure 3-2
Wall coverings often hide problems

plaster is no good, unless you can prove otherwise. If you're preparing an estimate, you need to discuss this with the homeowners. They should understand that the walls may have to be redone, and that there's a substantial amount of money involved.

ᓚ Plaster Damage

Plaster damage is extremely common in older homes. Every older house I've worked on has had some, so you should know what to look for and how to deal with it. (Even if there isn't any plaster damage when you start your work, you may cause some during the course of your remodeling.) There are three major kinds of plaster damage that you'll run into in an older home: impact damage, water damage and settling cracks. Each needs to be approached differently. Let's go through them.

Impact Damage

Impact damage occurs when a plaster wall gets hit, hard. It's not easy to break a plaster wall. Whatever hits it must have a lot of force. If the house has been vacant for a long time, you may see a lot of this kind of damage caused by vandals. Otherwise, it's usually caused by a big piece of furniture that someone was carrying roughly.

It's important to remember that when a piece of wet plaster is broken, the area surrounding it is usually loosened as well. (See Figure 3-3.) This is because the wet plaster is held up by wooden furring strips. When the wall is hit, the plaster and furring strips right at the point of impact break, leaving a hole. However, the force also causes the furring strips all around the hole to flex. Although the strips may not break, the surrounding plaster becomes separated from the furring. This plaster now has no support. If you touch it, it'll crumble under your fingers. You'll generally have to replace the plaster 6 to 12 inches around an impact hole, making it a substantially bigger job than it would at first appear.

Patching plaster holes is tedious. We'll talk about how to do this when we come to

Figure 3-3
Impact damage to plaster wall

the section on repairs. For now, we just want to decide on what work to do, and estimate the time it will take to do it. It takes about the same amount of time to patch a hole as it does to tape and finish a drywall seam. This gives you a good rule of thumb: if there's more than one hole per 4-foot by 8-foot area (the size of a sheet of drywall), you're better off replacing the whole wall.

Nail Holes — Some homeowners get very upset with the small nail holes that their walls have, over the years, accumulated from long-forgotten pictures, shelves or decorations. These are really a minor problem. Any hole smaller than your finger can easily be patched with a little spackling compound. Unless there are thousands of them (and don't laugh, because I've seen this), it takes very little time to repair them.

Here's a tip I wish someone had given me: never pry nails out of a plaster wall with a claw hammer! It will backfire on you. When you hook the claw end of your hammer around the nail and pull, if the nail is in good and solid, it won't come out. Instead, the other end of the hammer will go *in*, making a big, nasty hole that's hard to fix. A better way to remove nails from plaster is to pull them straight out with pliers. It's harder to do, but I've found it's well worth the extra effort. Sometimes, turning the nail first helps to loosen its grip in the wall. Most people don't know that nails should never be used on furring strips. Advise your customers to use screws if they need to connect anything to a lath and plaster wall.

Water Damage

The next most common cause of wall damage is a water leak. A telltale sign of water damage is bowing, where a big lump of plaster seems to be falling away from the wall. This happens when the plaster becomes softened by water, and slumps away from the wall. If it remains wet, it will eventually break free and fall to the floor.

The first thing you want to do when you spot water damage in a wall is to touch the area and see if it's still wet. If it is, you have an active leak. You can't begin to repair the plaster damage until you locate and fix the leak. The leak may be from a water pipe, a plumbing fixture, a poorly-installed window or door, a vent, a damaged roof or any one of a number of other possibilities.

Damage caused by a single leak is usually confined to one area. As the water leaks and runs, it tends to follow a particular path on its way down to the basement or ground floor. All the plaster along that path will be ruined. Everywhere else, the plaster will be fine. However, you should never assume you have only one leak. If the house has a bad roof, you could have dozens of leaks, each creating its own path down the walls. Check each wall carefully. Whenever you find old water damage in the plaster, always locate the cause. It could be caused by something that will reoccur with the first rain, snow or shower.

It's also important to keep in mind that even if the plaster is now dry and the leak repaired long ago, the plaster all along the route of the water may still be ruined and in need of repair. Once it's been softened, its bond to the furring strips is broken. If it is hit, even with your hand, it will all come crashing down. This is one way to check out the extent of the damage. If it feels solid when you pound on it, it's probably okay. Spoiled plaster will flex and crack when you pound on it, or fall right off. Of course, you don't want to start knocking the plaster off the walls before you get the job. Homeowners aren't very understanding when you destroy what looks to them like perfectly-good walls.

With leak damage, you're usually dealing with one big hole or area rather than a lot of little holes. This is often easier to repair than many small holes. However, if the hole takes up a large percentage of the wall, or if it's in a very obvious place, you may be better off replacing the whole wall. We'll discuss this in more detail in the section on wall and ceiling repair.

Cracks

Cracking occurs when plaster walls are subjected to stress, usually as the house settles. Houses can continue to settle for decades. For instance, poor soil conditions, like excessive wetness, can cause a house to settle very slowly for over 100 years. You may find that the plaster has been cracking under the wallpaper very slowly, never tearing the paper. You may not even know the cracks are there until you remove the wallpaper.

Another major cause of settling stress is foundation failure. Often, the mortar between the stone or blocks in the foundation will crumble and fall out of the joints. As the stones or blocks move closer together, the foundation can get several inches shorter. When this stress gets to be more than the plaster can bear (which doesn't take much — it's not designed to bear stress) it cracks, relieving the pressure. Like leaks, you should investigate stress cracks thoroughly before you think about making repairs. If the house is still actively settling, your repairs won't hold. You need to be sure the house is stable before getting involved in this type of plaster work.

Repair or Replace — One thing to check for when you're looking at cracks is whether the cracked sections are still laying flat, or whether they're heaved out of line. If the pieces are out of line, the problem becomes much greater. The pieces that are pushed up have probably lost their connection to the furring strips. If you try to push them down, they'll probably break off in your hand. This kind of cracking may have to be treated like a hole, rather than just a crack.

As with other kinds of damage, the extent of the cracking will determine whether you need to repair or replace the plaster. If all you have is a few cracks that are laying neatly in place, still attached solidly to the furring strips, you can just fill them with spackling compound. On the other hand, if you have more than three or four cracks per hundred square feet, or if the cracks are bigger than a quarter-inch, or if sections of the wall are heaved, the wall won't patch up well. You're better off replacing the plaster.

However, before you replace a wet plaster wall with drywall, you should consider how it will affect the value of the house. Is the house in historic, original condition? Is it in an area of historic homes? Is it in an area where wet plaster walls are highly prized? If so, replacing wet plaster with drywall may lower the value of the home. "Wet plaster throughout" is considered a very desirable sales feature for upscale housing. If you replace some of this plaster with drywall, the sellers will have to say "Mostly wet plaster," which is not as appealing. Wet plaster includes lath and plaster, plaster over wire mesh (common after the 1930s), and plasterboard, which requires a finish layer of wet plaster, used since about 1950.

If the home has been previously remodeled using drywall, or if it's in a middle-income neighborhood, then it doesn't matter as much. The average middle-income homeowner isn't as interested in maintaining a particular level of quality as in having a nice home at an affordable price. Generally, unless they're into restoration or renovating to the original standard, they won't be willing to spend a lot of extra money for plaster.

Rough Walls

In some cases, you may find walls that are very rough and uneven. This could be from many old repairs, or just poor-quality workmanship in the original construction. These walls can be difficult to repair. Often the easiest way to deal with a rough wall is to just drywall over it.

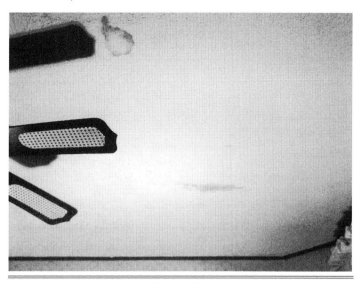

Figure 3-4
Water stains indicate leak above

The Ceiling

Since ceilings are constructed the same way as the walls, they tend to get the same type of damage. However, the frequency that you find the various types of damage is different. You rarely find impact damage here — it's hard to slam heavy objects into the ceiling. Cracking is somewhat more common, due to sagging ceiling joists. Leaks are the most common cause of ceiling repairs. If there's water loose in the house, the ceiling is usually where it will wind up.

🐦 Water Damage

Water damage from a leak can easily destroy an entire ceiling. The damage here is usually more obvious than with the walls. A section of plaster on the walls can be loose without anybody knowing it. It'll stay put for years, as long as nobody disturbs it. With the ceiling you can usually spot leaks fairly soon, especially if the ceiling is a light color. The leak will show up as a discolored stain, like the ones in Figure 3-4. If the stains are ignored and the ceiling continues to collect water, eventually the plaster will loosen and the force of gravity will pull it right down. Holes 2 or 3 feet across are common. You

Figure 3-5
Plumbing leak caused plaster to fall off ceiling below bath

Figure 3-6
Broken plaster caused by foot slip in attic

don't need a major leak to cause the kind of damage shown in Figure 3-5. Given enough time, just a few continuous drops from a leaky pipe can do it.

If there's a drop ceiling in the house, it's probably covering up this type of damage. If possible, remove a tile and peek under to see if you can get any idea of what you're dealing with. It's a remote possibility that someone might have installed a drop ceiling because they actually liked it, and the plaster underneath is still fine. But that's really a remote possibility in an older home. More likely, you'll find a mess of peeling, cracking, falling plaster.

Repairs made to a ceiling are much more obvious than repairs to a wall. You can't hang a picture over them, or wallpaper them, or put a big piece of furniture in front of them. It's also harder to patch a ceiling than a wall. It's better to replace a heavily-damaged ceiling than try to repair it. Of course, if it has beautiful ornamental plaster work, it may be worth saving, even if it's in really bad shape. Again, we'll discuss how to do that in the section on repairs.

🙚 Cracking

If there's extensive cracking to the ceiling, with no evidence of water, you're probably looking at a failure of the joists that hold up the ceiling. Check upstairs, either in the room or the attic space above. You'll probably find the floor is seriously sagging. You may have to tear out the ceiling, repair the joists, and put up a new ceiling. The condition of the room upstairs will have a lot of bearing on what you finally decide to do. We'll cover that later.

Foot Slips

One common type of ceiling damage is a cracked or broken chunk of plaster hanging down in just one area, like the one in Figure 3-6. This kind of damage usually occurs in a ceiling that has an attic space above it. If someone tries to walk around in the attic space they often learn too late that plaster and furring strips can't hold the weight of a person.

You usually only find this kind of damage in one spot. After a person's foot goes through the ceiling the first time, they usually don't try to walk around any more. This type of plaster damage only affects the immediate area. It doesn't spread much further than about 6 inches into the area around it. It can usually just be patched.

Floors

The best way to check a floor is to walk on it. How does it feel? Jump up and down on it. Is it rock solid? I'd be surprised if it was. The floors of most old houses have some give to them. A little give is normal. However if the entire floor heaves up and down like the deck of a ship in a storm, you've got some joist failures. Joist failures are a common problem in older homes, and nothing to get upset about. They aren't too hard to fix, provided you have access to the underside of the floor.

If the floor is over a basement, you're in luck. If it's over a crawl space, be sure the space is workable and accessible before you estimate the repair cost. You couldn't make repairs to joists through a crawl space like the one in Figure 3-7. You'd have to tear up the floor, make your repairs, and then replace the floor. That will certainly increase your costs. So when the homeowner tells you there's a crawl space, you'd better check it out before you make your estimate. Repairing a joist in an upstairs room creates a similar problem. You're either going to have to pull up the floor of the upper room or tear out the ceiling of the room below in order to gain access to the joists. Be sure to include that in your estimate.

❧ Floor Surface Defects

As you walk back and forth over the floors, pay attention to how they feel underfoot. You can feel many floor defects, even through carpeting. Do you feel any soft spots? This would indicate holes, possibly rot damage. Do you feel or see any ridges or seams? These usually indicate old repairs. Check them out carefully; they may or may not have been done correctly.

The house may very well have had its heating system updated at some time during its life. When this was done, the old vents or ducts would have been removed, and patches put over the holes they came through. If the house is 100 years old or more, the heating system may have been redone several times, for several different types of systems. As a result, the floor may be a crazy quilt of patches, with many as large and as awkwardly-placed as the one in Figure 3-8. If the homeowners are planning to install carpet, the patches don't matter, as long as they're solid. However, if they were hoping to have

you restore the original hardwood floor, there may be a problem. Be sure to remove all floorcoverings and inspect the entire floor before making any plans about restoring it. Don't just peel back part of the carpet and assume the rest of the floor is the same as what you're seeing. Since you do your peeling back at the edge, what you'll see is only the damage that occurred close to the wall, where not much activity goes on. There could be some nasty surprises under the middle part. Inspect all the floor.

Electrical Features

Now is a good time to check the electrical outlets and switches. The living room (and family room, if there is one) should have

Figure 3-7
This crawl space is too low to work in

Figure 3-8
Patch on floor where furnace used to be

at least three duplex outlets, the dining room and bedrooms should have a *minimum* of two, and the bathroom at least one. The *National Electrical Code* states that outlets should be placed along the floor line so that no point is more than 6 feet from an outlet. If the home has large rooms, you may want to add more than those mentioned above to bring the house up to code.

The kitchen will need outlets for the refrigerator, stove and at least one outlet for each counter space. Countertops separated by a sink, range top or refrigerator count as separate tops, so each should have its own outlet. Even if a kitchen has only one countertop, I would still recommend at least two duplex outlets to accommodate all the small appliances used commonly in a modern kitchen. The outlet in the bathroom should be protected by a ground fault circuit interrupter, and some local codes require that kitchen outlets near the sink should have them as well.

All the rooms need either a switch-operated overhead light, or a switch-operated plug that a lamp can be plugged into, so that anyone entering a dark room can immediately switch on a light.

If the rooms don't have these basic electrical features, you should add them. This is one area that building inspectors are very touchy about. Code standards for remodeling vary from city to city. You may be required to add basic electrical service to any room you're remodeling whether the homeowner wants it or not. We'll discuss the electrical system further when we look at the basement.

The Kitchen

The kitchens in most older homes usually need to be updated. We'll cover kitchen remodeling in Chapters 21 and 26. Right now, we only want to determine the overall condition of the kitchen so we'll know what we've got to work with.

❧ Kitchen Ceilings

The kitchen ceiling is the most likely ceiling in the house to need replacement. That's because most upstairs bathrooms are located directly above the kitchen to facilitate the plumbing runs. If anybody has spilled a substantial amount of water in the bathroom during the life of the house, or if there have been any plumbing leaks, chances are the kitchen ceiling has been affected. It may be that the kitchen ceiling has been replaced at least once already. Check it carefully. If it hasn't been replaced before, it probably needs to be now.

❧ Kitchen Walls

Are you planning to keep the kitchen cabinets? If not, don't bother inspecting the walls. The plaster will probably come down when you pull the cabinets out. Plan on drywalling them.

❧ Kitchen Floor Coverings

Look at the edge of the kitchen floor, where it abuts the dining room, or any other room. Is the kitchen floor at about the same level, or is it substantially higher? If it's higher, that means the kitchen has many, many layers of floor coverings, one on top of the other. I've seen floor coverings piled up 3 inches deep! Removing them can be a lot of work, so make sure you know what's there.

❧ Water Problems in the Kitchen

Sooner or later, almost all kitchen sinks leak. This is probably your first chance to look at the plumbing in the house, but for now, you just need to check and see if there's an active leak. The sink may be in fairly good repair, or it could be so rusted that it may fall apart at any moment. You need to determine if it's in need of emergency repair work. We'll look at all the plumbing in greater detail in the next chapter.

The kitchen sinks in most older homes have had plenty of opportunity over time to leak and cause considerable damage. Inspect the area around the sink carefully. Look at the bottom of the cabinet under the sink. Is there any evidence of moisture damage? See if you can peek through any seams or holes in the bottom of the cabinet. Is the floor below rotted?

Check the floor in front of the sink. Is there any evidence of moisture? Check for loose floor tiles, or soft spots under the linoleum. Check the entire kitchen floor for soft spots or dips. Look carefully! You're almost certain to find rot damage here.

If there's an active leak causing the problem, it needs repair. Otherwise, it doesn't much matter, because you'll probably be replacing the items that have been damaged anyway. Almost all older homes need new fixtures, cabinets and floor and wall coverings in the kitchen. And, unless the electrical system has been updated, you'll have to include bringing that up to today's standards as well.

Downstairs Room Additions

Many older homes were quite small when they were originally built. Over the years, living space was added on as needed. In some cases, there may have been several additions, spaced many years apart. The workmanship on these additions may have been quite different than on the original part of the house. Sometimes it was better, but unfortunately, many times it was worse. Additions were often the work of the homeowner or an amateur handyman, who didn't understand basic principles of engineering. As a result, they may not be sound. I've sometimes seen room additions in the process of shearing off from the rest of the house, almost as if they were trying to break free and go off on their own!

Additions are most likely to be found either at the rear of the house, or on the second floor, where there was room to expand. You rarely find them added to the side of the house, because urban lots were usually narrow. There wasn't room to go out on the sides very far without going over onto the neighbor's property.

🌰 Kitchen and Bathroom Additions

Kitchen and bathroom additions are the ones most commonly found in the rear of older homes. Family rooms are less common, unless they're recent additions. If the house was built before 1920, it probably didn't have a bathroom, and had very little plumbing in the kitchen. Adding plumbing to a kitchen and a separate room for a bathroom presented problems. The easiest place to put a bathroom was at the back of the house. It was too difficult to get the plumbing into existing space.

Pre-1920s kitchens were often quite large, with little plumbing and no built-in cabinets. Storage and work space were provided by freestanding pieces of furniture. They kept their dishes in china cabinets and cut up food on butcher-block tables. The only built-in was the sink. If you find an old kitchen still in original condition (which is rare), it will be completely empty, except for the sink.

Installing modern plumbing in a bare kitchen like this was quite difficult. It was often easier to build on an addition for a new kitchen. This also added extra living space to the house. In many cases, the old kitchen was turned into a dining room when the new kitchen was added on.

It's not unusual to find an older home with both the kitchen and bathroom added on at the back, usually one at a time, with the kitchen being the earlier addition. Laundry rooms, mud rooms or utility rooms were also added at the back of the house. All these rooms require running water, so they were added only when running water became commonly available, usually after 1920.

If the house is an old mansion, it may have had running water before 1920. Some expensive homes built after the 1870s had ingenious systems of attic-mounted storage tanks which were filled by servants to provide "running water" at the turn of a tap. You will probably find little trace of these original gravity-feed systems today. However, because of them, some houses may have had fully-plumbed kitchens and baths at a very early date.

❧ Identifying Additions

A well-built addition is hard to distinguish from the original building. You can sometimes see faint outlines of doors or windows on the dining-room walls where the original doors and windows were filled in. In some cases, the old windows weren't removed, they were just plastered over. If you tear into the dining room wall, you may uncover one.

One indication that rooms have been added on is an irregular shape to the house. The original design was most likely a neat, uniform rectangle, or in the case of a Victorian home, a T- or L-shape. If the house has little boxy rooms sticking out all over it, they've probably been added.

You can also check for changes in the roof line. Builders used to keep their roofs pretty simple. They may have added some dormers or towers as part of the style, but they generally didn't have roof sections jutting out in all directions (unlike some modern buildings). An abrupt change of the roof line may indicate an addition.

The Foundation

The best way to check for an addition is to look at the foundation. Builders rarely bothered to try to blend a new foundation with the old one. The basement was considered utility space. Nobody cared what it looked like.

The newer foundation may be made of a completely different type of material. The main part of the house foundation may be stone, while the addition may be cement block. Or, they may be made of different types of cement block. At the turn of the century, it was common to use cement block that had a fake stone texture cast into it. It was supposed to fool people into thinking it was cut stone. If you see this kind of block, you know you're looking at work done prior to 1925. They weren't used much after that time.

It's also quite common to find a basement only under the original part of the house, with a crawl space under the addition. In a few cases, this arrangement may be the original design. Sometimes older homes were built with only partial basements. In that case, the basement and the crawl space would all be made of the same material and workmanship.

❧ Addition Problems

You'll commonly find problems with additions. Differential settling can pull the addition away from the house. If the addition settles more than the original house structure, it can cause the foundation to crack off and tilt. Sometimes it's slight, and sometimes it's enough to spot immediately. The joint between the original roof and the addition roof is a common place to find a leak. You may also find rot damage in the wall seam between the addition and the house, especially if the roof joint leaks. If the settling is enough to cause the addition to break free of the house, you'll very likely find both problems.

An addition that is structurally weak, particularly if it's on a crawl space that's too low to work in, may be essentially unrepairable. It may be cheaper to tear it off and start over. Obviously, this would be a major expense. That's why identifying problems is so important at this time.

Heating Room Additions

Any addition may suffer from heating problems. It may not have been adequately tied into the central heating system, or may not have central heat at all. We'll talk about heating systems more in the next chapter. For now, just take a moment to check and see what kind of heat the addition has and ask the homeowners if they've had any heating problems.

The Upstairs Rooms

On the upper floor of most older homes you'll find the bedrooms, and often the only bathroom in the house. Of course, some homes have a bedroom and a bath on the main floor as well. Just about everything that we will discuss will apply equally whether these rooms are upstairs or down.

❧ The Bedrooms

Inspecting the bedrooms is almost exactly the same as inspecting the living and dining rooms. This is because all these rooms are essentially just boxes. They have no plumbing or special fixtures, no particular tendency to leak, rot, or in any other way decay more than normal. The walls and ceiling should be checked the same as the living and dining room.

❧ The Floors

Pay special attention to the floors upstairs. Do they have too much bounce or in any other way indicate signs of structural problems? These floors are much harder to fix than the floors downstairs. You'll have to lay open the structure of the floor and strengthen it from within. This means either tearing up the floor upstairs, or tearing down the ceiling on the main floor. In either case, it's a lot of work.

❧ The Bathroom

In a two-story older home, the main bathroom will probably be upstairs with the bedrooms. If the home has been modernized, it may have at least a half bath downstairs as well. Like the kitchen, the bathroom is an another room that will probably need updating. It's also an area that has a lot of special problems. Because of the constant humidity and moisture, it's much more prone to rot damage than any other room of the house. It also has a lot of plumbing which can leak.

Ask the homeowners about their plans for the bathroom. Do they want to keep it the way it is, or do they want to remodel? If they want to tear the bathroom out and start over, you don't really need to worry about minor defects. It's all going to wind up in the dumpster anyway. You just have to worry about two things right now. One, are there any active leaks? If so, these have to be stopped to prevent them from causing further damage. And two, is the room structurally solid? If not, the structural repairs will have to be made before any remodeling can begin.

Plumbing Leaks

Even tiny leaks can cause a great deal of damage over time. One of the first signs you'll notice will be loose ceramic tiles, either on the walls or the floor. Water gets under them and loosens their attachment to the substrate. Of the two, loose tiles on the floor indicate more of a problem. Wall tiles can come loose fairly easily, depending on what was used as a substrate. Floor tiles, on the other hand, usually don't come loose unless there's substantial rot damage.

It's important to check rot damage carefully, even if the bathroom is going to be torn out. Lift up the loose tiles on the floor and poke the wood under them with a sharp object. If the wood is totally rotted and crumbly, there's probably more rot damage below. You'll have to do a lot of work on the floor, and possibly on the joists as well.

Peeling paint is another sign of a problem. Check for this, especially along the baseboards. Look very carefully around the bathtub, sink, and toilet. Probe any peeling areas to see if the wood underneath is rotted.

If there have been any long-term leaks, they may have damaged the floor joists, causing the floor to lose strength. It's vital that a bathroom floor be absolutely rock solid, especially if you plan to install ceramic tile. Ceramic tile won't tolerate even the tiniest bit of give. Any motion, no matter how

Figure 3-9
Standing water in tub indicates a plumbing problem

slight, will cause the tiles to pop. So, if the floor joists have been damaged, they'll have to be repaired. Again, this means either tearing up the floor in the bathroom, or tearing down the ceiling of the room below. Usually any leak that's bad enough to rot out a floor joist will have already destroyed at least part of the floor and even more of any ceiling below it. You'll have a big repair job on your hands.

Moisture Problems — Is the bathroom damp and dank? Is there a lot of mold or mildew? If so, the bathroom has a moisture problem, either from leakage or from inadequate venting. Check for leaks first, then consider what you want to do about venting problems. Most codes will require that a bathroom have either an operable window or a fan. However, there are bathrooms that seem to trap moisture and hold onto it. If you've repaired all the leaks and still have moisture problem, adding a fan will usually do the trick.

The Plumbing Fixtures

If you're going to replace the fixtures, all you need to check for are active leaks. If they aren't going to be replaced, check each fixture carefully. Is the sink rusted or chipped? What about the tub? Make sure the faucets turn on and off, and don't leak or drip. Check the inlet lines. Do they have proper

cutoffs? Do you see any rust or leakage? Run the water. Do the fixtures drain properly? Do they leak? Check for rust or leakage on the outside of the visible drain pipes. If the tub or shower has an access panel, take it off and look inside. Do you see any rust or evidence of leakage? Flush the toilet. Does if flush vigorously? Does it leak? Does it overflow? Does it refill properly?

Figure 3-9 shows water standing in a tub. Standing water in a fixture is a sure indication of a plumbing problem. Usually it means that the drain is totally blocked. Tub, shower or sink drains frequently get partially blocked with hair, lint and soap. It may sometimes take hours for them to drain. But if the water has been sitting for days, you know it's a more serious blockage. The drain line is probably a mass of rust and crud. Most likely it will have to be torn out and replaced. That can mean tearing out walls or ceilings to get to the line, and that can be very expensive.

Installing new fixtures and plumbing repairs will be covered along with bathroom remodeling in Chapters 20 and 26.

Upstairs Additions

Bedrooms and bathrooms make up the most common upstairs additions in older homes. These additions can create particular problems. I've seen more botched upstairs additions than any other kind. Some of these are almost impossible to repair.

❧ Bathroom Additions

If the house was built before 1920, the bathroom was probably added on, and not necessarily over the kitchen. It could be anywhere. That's because the house probably didn't have any bathroom when it was built, so when one was added, it was usually by taking a chunk out of the upstairs hall. This kind of addition tends to have awkward plumbing runs with a whole slew of problems. Expect to find a lot of water damage, both obvious and hidden, in whatever room is under an upstairs bathroom addition.

Figure 3-10
Second-floor additions

🐚 Inadequate Support Problems

When extra rooms are added to the top of a house, some provision needs to be made for carrying the extra weight. If the addition is a full second story, the weight of the addition will rest on the existing exterior walls. These additions are usually fine, because the exterior walls are strong. They can generally hold an extra set of walls on top of them.

Most problem additions are done as dormers, as shown in the sketch in Figure 3-10. A dormer addition isn't built on top of the existing walls, its weight is centered on the existing ceiling joists. Room additions are heavy; they can add 10 to 20 tons of extra weight to the structure. The original structural support for the house may not be able to support this added weight. Over time, the ceiling joists will begin to bow under the load. This will put the walls in the original structure under tremendous stress. Usually there's only one load-bearing wall in a one-story house. It goes right down through the middle of the house and holds up the ceiling joists. However, this load-bearing wall is only intended to carry about 1,000 pounds, not a multi-ton dormer addition. The other walls are only built as partitions or dividers and can't hold a lot of extra weight. Eventually, the walls will crack. The load-bearing wall commonly rests on the center of the main beam of the house, which runs crossways under the floor. This is the weakest point of the beam, and it will also bow under the added stress. Amateur carpenters don't seem to understand that the walls, and especially the partition walls, cannot carry unlimited weight. And, even if by some chance they could support the addition, the floor under them couldn't. It would still begin to sag.

The clearest sign of this is a severe dip in the main floor beneath the addition. What happens is that the weight of the addition pushes the center of the house right into the ground. The diagram in Figure 3-11 shows this

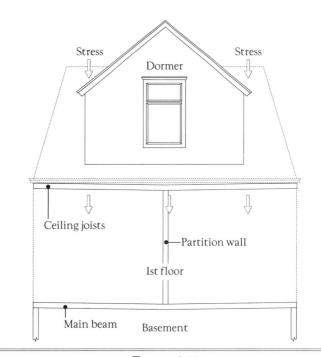

Figure 3-11
Dormer addition puts original structure under stress

process. Sometimes this isn't easy to see. You need to check the angle of the floor with your level. Most old houses are a few degrees off level, but if you find a tilt of 15 degrees or more, you've got some kind of structural problem.

As the dormer puts downward pressure on the roof, the seal between the dormer and the roof will tear free. This will allow rainwater to seep in, ruining the plaster and causing rot damage. If there's a bathroom in the dormer, the sagging structure will cause the pipes to bend. But pipes can only bend so far. After the dormer has settled 6 inches or so, the pipes will crack, causing plumbing leaks.

This is a very serious problem, and much more common than you may think. I've been in many houses like this. A poorly-constructed addition can so totally disrupt the structure of the house that there is no practical way to fix it. Often, the cost of making repairs is greater than the house is worth, and the house has to be demolished.

I don't mean to imply that you can't ever build dormer additions. Contractors build fine dormers every day, but they have to be engineered. Additional supports, in the form of beams, posts or bearing walls, need to be built to provide for the extra weight. Of course, amateur carpenters don't bother with engineering or building permits, and that's where these kind of problems originate. We'll discuss structural repairs in Chapter 12.

✌ Heating Problems

Again, check and see what kind of heat the addition has and ask the homeowners if they've had any heating problems upstairs. Right now, all you want to do it identify trouble spots. We'll discuss heating problems in detail in Chapter 14.

✌ Stairs

Another common problem with upstairs additions is an inadequate stairway. You'll often find stairways that are very steep and narrow. This may be because the builder didn't know how to build a staircase, but more often

than not, it's because the stairway was originally designed to be an attic access. An attic stairway could be narrow and steep, because it was rarely used. But when the attic space was converted into living space, the original stairway should have been remodeled as well.

I've sometimes seen some very extreme examples of attic access stairs that were inappropriate for the room additions. One house I looked at when I was house shopping not long ago was advertised as a three-bedroom home. Two of the bedrooms were downstairs and the third one was upstairs. In order to get upstairs, you had to go into the closet of one of the downstairs bedrooms, push the clothes aside, and squeeze up a dark, narrow staircase. At the top was the third bedroom. Seriously! They actually tried to sell the house that way! I don't think they got a very good price for it; certainly not what a real three-bedroom house would get anyway.

Meeting Code Requirements

In order to be up to code, a stairway must be no less than 32 inches wide. Each stair must rise no more than 8¼ inches, and be at least 9 inches deep. The stairway also needs to have at least 6 feet 8 inches of headroom throughout. If the stairway doesn't meet code, it'll have to be rebuilt. The only exception would be if your local ordinances allowed it to be "grandfathered" in as a stairway that was built before the code standards came into effect.

Keep in mind that a new staircase will take up more space than the old one. You may have to take a chunk out of one of the downstairs rooms. You'll probably have to tear out at least one wall. Be sure to include all these things into your estimate.

The Attic

Investigating the attic space carefully is very important. A lot of people don't bother to check the attic, and that can be a big mistake. You can miss serious problems, such as roof or pest damage.

If you're lucky, the house may have an old-fashioned "Grandma's Attic," designed to be used as storage space. In that case, it will have a stairway going up, a ceiling high enough to stand up in, windows, and maybe even lights. It's almost like a room. Do the homeowners need more space? Perhaps this attic could be remodeled into living space. We'll discuss attic conversions in Chapters 22 and 26.

If you're not lucky, the attic won't even have a stairway. You may have to shimmy up through a little access panel in the ceiling of a closet. That's why you need to bring a stepladder. It may be the only way you can get up into this space.

The Work Area

Check out the work area in the attic. Are you planning on doing any major electrical work? If so, the wiring will probably have to come through the attic. If you're planning to do any major heating work, you may have to bring ductwork through here as well. Take this opportunity to look around and get an idea of what you're going to have to deal with later on. Sometimes slanting roof lines completely block access to parts of the attic. Is there enough space above each of the rooms to do what needs to be done?

Attic space is typically only about 4 feet high, and it's dirty, dusty and hot. Better get used to it — you may be spending a lot of time working there. I've spent so much time in attic spaces that they don't bother me any more.

Roof Problems

It's especially important to inspect the attic if you're planning on doing any roof work. That's the only way to tell for sure how bad the roof damage really is. A roof that just looks a little over-age from the outside might turn out to have severe rot damage when you look at it from the inside.

Shine your flashlight on the underside of the roof. What condition is the decking in? Is it new or old? Solid or spaced apart, as for wood shingles? Keep in mind that if the roof has to be torn down to the decking, you won't be able to put modern shingles over spaced-apart boards. You'll either have to put in new decking, or fill in all those little spaces.

Look for discoloration that might be caused by leaking water. Pay special attention to the area around the chimney (the number one leak spot), the plumbing vent, or anything else that sticks out through the roof. Also check the eaves as well as you can (they can be hard to see from the inside). That's another common place to find rot damage.

If you find any discoloration, probe it to see if the wood is rotted. Check any discolored rafters very carefully. If the rafters are rotted, the roof could cave in under you when you try to work on it. All rotted wood will have to be replaced.

Termites

The roof is another favorite area for termites. Termites like wet wood, and even a small roof leak can dampen a large area of wood. Damp wood is also a suitable home for carpenter ants and other wood-eating bugs. Check carefully for little bore holes in the rafters and for little piles of fine sawdust. The wood droppings are left by the insects as they chew through the wood. It indicates an active insect infestation. Even if you don't see any current infestation, look for old damage that has weakened the roof structure.

Vents

All attic spaces should be carefully vented. A vented attic keeps the roof cool, which makes the shingles last a lot longer. It also vents out the summer heat and helps keep the rest of the house cool.

A vented attic also stays dry in the winter. As long as you can keep the roof dry, you won't get rot damage, and termites won't move in. Keeping the attic free of moisture also makes your insulation work better. Insulation loses almost all its R-value when it gets wet.

At one time I didn't believe that venting the attic in winter was a good idea. I thought it would make the house colder. So I tried an experiment to test this theory. I sealed up my attic vents in the fall, just before the first frost. A few weeks later I checked the attic space to see what was happening. I was astounded to find ice all over my rafters! Moisture from the house was getting into the attic space, condensing on the cold rafters, and freezing. I realized that as the ice thawed, it would sink into the rafters and wet them, leading eventually to rot damage, and possibly termite infestation. I immediately opened my attic vents. Now, I always make a point of checking to make sure that all attics are well vented.

Unfortunately, attic vents are not common in older houses. Sometimes roof vents are added when new roofs are put on, but usually not nearly enough. There should be at least 1 square inch of vent space for each square foot of attic space. My experience has been that the more vents you have, the better off the roof will be. If you don't find enough vents, plan to add them.

Attic vents may not be an easy item to sell to your homeowners. They may not appreciate their value. However, adding vents is not an expensive job. If you explain how vents will save them money, lowering both their heating and cooling bills as well as prolonging the life of the roof, most homeowners will agree to having them installed.

❧ Insulation

Older homes have a reputation for having high heating bills. Lack of insulation is one of the main reasons. They almost never have enough attic insulation. At best, you'll usually find only a couple inches of rock wool. Adding attic insulation is fairly quick and inexpensive, and it has tremendous benefits. It not only keeps the house warmer in winter, it keeps it cooler in summer. The difference it makes is really amazing. Adding attic insulation is one of the ways you can give your customers the most "bang for their buck."

The Basement

I've saved the best for last! The basement is the single most important area of the house to inspect. More of the "guts" of the house are visible to you here than anyplace else. Be extra careful in your inspection here; it really counts!

Many basements in older homes are dark and dirty. It's a good idea to carry a flashlight with you whenever you do an inspection, and bring your broom along too. Then you can sweep away the cobwebs and peek into those dark corners. Don't shy away from this part of the inspection because it's dirty and dark. The dark corners are exactly the places you need to inspect most. That's where problems are most likely to be found.

As I mentioned earlier, many older homes have a partial basement under one part of the house, and a crawl space under the rest. Try to see into the crawl space as much as possible. This may not seem a pleasant place to be poking around, but you may have to be working in there. If you don't like it now, you'll like it a lot less after spending a couple of days in it!

❧ Moisture Problems

If the basement is damp, you'll notice it as soon as you go down the stairs. "Damp" takes on a whole new meaning when you're working with older homes. When I'm out looking for property to buy, real estate agents will sometimes say, "The basement in this house is a little...a...umm...damp." What they really mean is "Bring your scuba gear!" Many older homes have no basement floor drains. If water gets in, it can't get out. It just gets deeper and deeper.

Obviously, if the water is so deep that you can't even go down into the basement, you're going to have to pump it out. Fortunately, this isn't very common. *Common* is a basement with water 2 or 3 inches deep. If someone tells you the basement is "damp," bring galoshes.

Standing water in a basement, even small puddles, will cause damage over time. The water needs to be removed. We'll discuss how to do this in the section on structural repairs in Chapter 12.

Even if there's no standing water at the moment, the basement may still be damp. The cause may be an intermittent leak that just doesn't happen to be leaking while you're there (because it isn't raining?), or the basement may just have high humidity. You can usually smell it. The basement will smell dank and musty. A sour smell usually means there's mold growing. Check for mold, slime, or mildew spots on the walls, floor and ceiling. Look for rust on the furnace, or any other metal objects. All these indicate a moisture problem.

The Basement Walls

You won't find poured-concrete basement walls in an older home. If the house was built after 1900, you'll probably find cement block, or possibly brick. If it was built before 1900, you'll probably find stones, such as uncut fieldstones, although brick is also possible. The mortar between the stones or bricks may be failing by now, especially if the house is in a damp area. Rub your finger on the mortar. Does it crumble when you touch it? If so, the basement walls may need to be tuckpointed or remortared.

The walls are the most likely place for moisture to be entering. Do you see any obvious wet spots or cracks? Look for little piles of dirt in corners and along the base of the walls. This dirt will have been carried in by flowing water. The water may have flowed away or evaporated by now, but the dirt that came with it will remain.

As water oozes through stone or block walls, it will form little droplets that cling to the inside walls. These will often dry in place, leaving behind the calcium or other minerals that were dissolved in the water. You'll see a pattern of white, powdery crystals over the surface of the wall. These crystals are quite soft, and will come off on your fingers. If you see these, you know water is oozing through at these points. The crystals will often follow the seams or borders around blocks or stones, outlining the problem areas for you.

Figure 3-12
Hand-hewn beams set in notches

The Basement Floor

What is the basement floor made of? Is it concrete, or just dirt? If it's dirt, moisture will rise up through it any time there's a substantial rain. Unless the house is in a very dry place, it's going to have moisture problems.

If the floor is concrete, what kind of shape is it in? Is the concrete solid, even, and smooth? Or is it lumpy and full of dips and holes? Many older homes originally had dirt floors in the basement, and concrete was added later. The concrete work may not have been done by a competent workman. I've seen basement floors that looked like someone just dumped a couple of wheelbarrows of concrete on the floor and made no attempt to finish it. In some cases, the concrete was in such poor condition that you could pull it up with your fingers. Concrete like this isn't of much use, and should be replaced.

Joists and Upstairs Flooring

Old houses weren't built with the kind of modern, dimensional-lumber joists you're used to seeing in new construction. You might find odd sizes of lumber or beams, which may have been cut locally to no standard size. Figure 3-12 shows floor joists made from hand-hewn beams set in notches. The joists in Figure 3-13 are made from old tree trunks that still have the bark on them! There's nothing necessarily wrong with these, even though they look strange to you. Some of these tree trunks or beams are many times stronger than the lumber we use today.

Figure 3-13
Floor joists made of tree trunks still have the bark on them

Figure 3-14
Cut-out weakens floor joist

Even if they show evidence of damage, they may not need to be repaired. In many cases, these old beams are so strong they can be half-rotted and *still* be stronger than modern joists.

Did you notice excessive give and bounce on the upstairs floors when you walked on them? If so, the basement is where you find the cause. Check all the joists carefully. Look for any evidence of rot, water marks, or insect damage. Determine if any decay you see is currently active, or if it's old, caused by some problem that was repaired years ago. Are discolored areas still wet? Do

you see any live bugs? If so, you will have to trace the problem to its source and make repairs before you can repair the joists.

Pay close attention to the area around the chimney. Water leaking through and around the chimney is very likely to cause rot damage to the floor and joists. Also examine the wood near the furnace for excessive drying and cracking caused by the heat. You're more likely to find cracked joists here than anywhere else.

Check the joists around ductwork and plumbing pipes. Plumbing leaks may cause rot damage, but improper installation of plumbing or heating lines can create problems as well. I frequently find that joists have been cut, like the one in Figure 3-14, during the installation of piping or ductwork. Sometimes several joists in a row are cut all the way through! You have to wonder why someone would do something like that. Apparently they didn't realize that cutting through the joists would cause serious problems. Cut joists are often the cause of excessive floor bounce. They have to be repaired.

Check the main center beam. You won't find a steel I-beam like the ones used on modern homes. It will most likely be a massive wooden beam made of several 2 x 12s nailed together. If the home was built before 1920, you may even find a huge, hand-hewn piece of oak. This beam is very important. What condition is it in? If it's rotted or cracked, it's very important to repair it. The whole house will sag if you don't.

The center beam is usually held up by wood or iron posts. Look these over carefully. Pay particular attention to their bases. Moisture tends to accumulate around the bases of these posts and rot the wood or rust out the iron. If dirt is piled up around them, sweep it away (You brought the broom, right?) If there's rust or rot damage here, the posts will need to be replaced.

Check the joists and the floors under the kitchen and bathroom very carefully. These areas are understandably prone to leakage. Look for discoloration that might indicate water damage. Long-term water leaks may have rotted the joists as well as the floors. Check for rot damage with a sharp object, like a pocket knife or a nail, using the same technique I mentioned when checking for exterior rot. When you poke the wood, you should meet resistance. It shouldn't just sink right in. If it does, the wood is rotted and needs to be replaced.

Turn your flashlight on the underside of the other floor areas. Are there any patches? If you weren't able to pull up the floorcovering in the living or dining room, you can check for patches in the floor now, from the underside. Past repairs may or may not be adequate. They may now need to be repaired as well.

❧ Termites

The basement is another area where you're likely to find termites, powder-post beetles, carpenter ants, and other wood-eating insects. Remember, termites like to live in wet wood. The basement and the roof are the areas most likely to be wet, so they're the areas most likely to have termites. If your basement has a moisture problem, it's a perfect place for insects. If it's completely dry, then wood-eating insects are unlikely.

If you find any rotted areas, or any areas with evidence of moisture damage, also inspect them carefully for bugs. Most of these wood-eating bugs look a lot like large ants. Are there any insects like this in the basement? If so, try to follow them and see where they go. If they're going in and out of wood, they're probably termites or carpenter ants. Again, look for little holes in the joists or beams and for piles of tiny wood grains, indicating an active infestation.

Getting rid of the moisture problem will generally get rid of the insects. However, it's not always possible to entirely eliminate all moisture in a basement, especially if the house is located in a wet area. You may have to call in an exterminator to make sure the bugs are completely eliminated. Any wood that's been extensively damaged by the bugs will have to be replaced.

Now that we've covered the structural part of the basement, we'll go on and look at all the systems that are usually found here.

Chapter 4

Inspecting the Plumbing, Electrical and Heating Systems

ith luck, you'll find the plumbing, electrical and heating systems located in the basement. If the house doesn't have a basement, the plumbing system will still be under the house, accessed through the crawl space. The electrical service panel and heating system will be located somewhere on the first floor, usually in the service porch or utility room, or sometimes crammed into the corner of the kitchen.

The Plumbing System

Inspect the plumbing system carefully, even if you don't plan to do any plumbing work. Why? Because in many cases, the plumbing systems in old houses are so fragile that just touching them can cause major leaks. Even if you don't touch them, they may fall apart all by themselves while you're working there, and you'll be blamed for it! When you inspect a system and discover a potential problem, be sure the homeowner is aware of it *before* you touch anything in the house. In fact, unless you (or a subcontractor) are planning to replace the plumbing system, you should state in your written proposal that you will not be held responsible for any problems with the plumbing. This will head off legal difficulties down the road.

You may think I'm being overly cautious about this, but I'm not. If the house was built in the 1920s or before, and has the original galvanized steel plumbing and cast iron drain lines, the entire system is about to disintegrate. Seventy years is about the most you can expect from this kind of system. By now the metal is paper thin, almost completely rusted out, and has hardly more strength than tin foil. You can easily rip pipes like these to pieces with your bare hands. And if any part of the plumbing system goes, the whole thing will go. You're looking at thousands of dollars to replumb the entire house. Be sure you — and the homeowner — are aware of this before you start.

🐚 Checking the Lines

Your inspection should begin with the inlet lines. Are they copper or galvanized steel? If they're copper, you're probably safe. Copper plumbing lasts practically forever. Unfortunately, I've found galvanized steel more often than copper.

Figure 4-1
*These cast iron drain lines are
rusty and leaky*

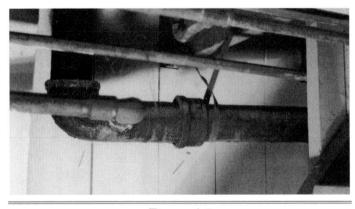

Figure 4-2
Streaks and white calcium deposits indicate leaks

Check the pipes for evidence of leakage. Gently run your hands over them. Are they wet? Are there any puddles or water marks on the floor under them? What about the joists and beams they go through or around? Is there any evidence of water damage, rot or rust on them?

Horizontal pipes are more likely to rust out than vertical pipes. Look along the pipe lengths for rust or calcium streaks, blobs or buildups. If you see water drops, or evidence of water, along any of these pipes, look closely for cracks. They can be very small, even hairline-thin. If you see one, it means that this pipe, and possibly the entire system, is ready to fall apart at any moment. Don't touch it! That might be all it takes to spring a major leak.

Look at the joints between the pipes. Do you see any blobs of white or rust-colored material oozing out of them? If so, the pipe probably had a leak that has rusted itself shut. Don't touch that either! If you disturb the rust or calcium buildup, the leak may start up again.

Drain Lines

Check drain lines carefully. If they're 70 years old or more, they may need to be replaced as well. You can see examples of warning signs around the cast iron pipe in Figure 4-1. Look at the floor joists above and basement floor below. Both these and the pipe itself indicate leakage problems. Again, look for rust streaks, drips, or cracks. You can see the calcium buildup and streaks on the pipe in Figure 4-2. Sniff around. A bad smell may indicate sewage leaking out.

The best way to check drain lines is to tap them with a hammer. However, don't do this without discussing it with the homeowner first. If the drain lines are in good condition, tapping them with a hammer won't hurt them. It normally takes a sledgehammer to break pipe. But if the drain lines are rusted out, your hammer will go right through, creating a leak where there wasn't one before. Homeowners have a tendency to get upset about things like this — even when they're warned ahead of time. You'd better give them a very clear picture of the possible outcome before you start tapping. If they're prepared for the worst, any good news will be welcome relief. A drain line should go "bong" when you tap it, making a sound almost like a gong. If it goes "thud," something's wrong. It's either rusted, or clogged. In either case, it will need attention.

Drain lines are normally hung from the joists by pieces of metal called hanger iron. Over time, some of these may have been broken or removed so that the pipes are no longer positioned correctly. The pipes should be level, or tipped a little bit downstream, so gravity causes water to flow through them and out into the sewers. If they're tipped backwards (upstream), water will pool up in them. Solids will settle out at this point, causing blockages. Pooled water will also cause excessive rusting. Use a level to check the angle of the pipes. If they're tipped backwards, you'll probably have trouble with them.

Plumbing Updates

If the plumbing has already been replaced, you still have to check for problems. Replumbing jobs aren't always done competently. Examine the new plumbing carefully. Is it a neat, professional-looking job, with quality materials assembled correctly? Or is it a crazy quilt of different plumbing materials that have been stuck together? It isn't unusual to see one area of the house plumbed with one material and another area with a different material, even in a professional job. You can't expect everything to match in an older home. However, if you see a lot of different materials stuck together in the same area, it's usually an indication of sloppy work.

Another thing to look for is irregular plumbing runs. A professional plumber keeps his plumbing runs neat and straight. If you see plumbing sticking out at odd angles, or drooping down into your headspace, you'll know that an amateur did the work. That means it's likely to have problems.

The Hot Water Heater

Hot water heaters have a life expectancy of seven to ten years, so you know the one in the house isn't the original. The oldest operating hot water tank I've ever come across was installed in the 1950s. That was very unusual. Anything older than that would probably be a collector's item (if anybody collects hot water tanks).

Check the hot water tank for leaks, or signs of possible leaks, like rust and calcium marks. Check for puddles or water damage under it. If you find any of these things, the tank will have to be replaced.

If the house was built before 1920, the hot water heater system was added later. Check to make sure it was properly installed. A gas hot water heater should be located near a chimney, with the flue pipe running directly to the chimney. The flue pipe gets quite hot so it shouldn't be located where it touches any wood, or where people are likely to touch it or bump into it. I've seen many poorly installed water heaters. One had the flue pipe running up along the basement stairs, right next to the handrail. It was difficult to go down the stairs without touching the pipe and risking a severe burn. Obviously, this was a code violation, but apparently the house had never been inspected. If the water heater is in a place it doesn't belong, it may have to be moved.

The Electrical System

Check out the electrical system while you're in the basement. Again, this is something you want to take a look at it even if you're not planning to do any electrical work. You may find that the house has been improperly wired. It could be ready to catch on fire, or someone could be electrocuted at any moment. If you're working on the house when something happens, you may be blamed for it. It's better to be aware of problems before anything unpleasant happens.

Also, some of the work you do may require electrical hookups. For instance, if you're planning to remodel the kitchen, you may want to put in a garbage disposal. The electrical code requires that garbage disposals be connected to their own separate circuit. Are any circuits available on the fuse or circuit breaker box? If not, what are you going to do about it? Better think about it now!

Figure 4-3
Old fuse box has only four circuits

ᘓ The Wiring

You can inspect the wiring at the same time you inspect the joists. It should be going in and around them. (If there isn't a basement, and you're looking in the crawl space, check whatever wiring you can see under the house.) What kind of wiring is it? Is it cable, or the old two-wire system, with two separate conductors spaced apart on insulators? There's nothing wrong with old wiring, even two-wire, as long as it's properly installed and in good condition. How can you tell if it's in good condition? It should be neat, straight, intact, unbroken and with all the insulation still on. There should be no bare or frayed wires, or loose wires dangling down where someone could touch them.

Don't assume that the wiring is okay just because it appears new. Unfortunately, home wiring is an area where you find a lot of amateur work. Some people who do their own wiring don't have any idea what they're doing. I've often found bare, live wires dangling down where people are likely to touch them, circuits wired into dead shorts, big tangled knots of wire barely tacked together, and lots of other obviously unsound and unsafe wiring. If you find any evidence of amateurs at work, check out the entire system carefully. All unsafe wiring should be removed or redone before it can start a fire or hurt someone.

ᘓ The Main Service Panel

Locate the main service panel. Does it have fuses or circuit breakers? Newer boxes have circuit breakers, but there's nothing wrong with fuses. Circuit breakers are convenient, but fuses are actually safer. Occasionally a circuit breaker fails to trip; this can't happen with a fuse.

How many amps of power are available to the system? The number of amps is usually written somewhere on the box, although with rust and dirt it may not be easy to read. If you can't tell, look at the main fuses. You can almost always read the amperage rating on them.

Older homes were originally supplied with very little power. There weren't many electric appliances, so they just needed power for electric lights, and maybe a radio or vacuum cleaner. As a result, 40 amps was considered plenty. Today, our convenience-oriented lifestyles require at least 100 amps of power. Luxury homes are now being built with 200 amps.

How many circuits does the electrical box in this house have? If the electrical system was installed or hasn't been updated since the 1920s, it probably has 40 amps on four circuits and looks like the one in Figure 4-3. It's almost impossible for a modern family to survive on 40 amps of power. If you consider that an electric stove draws 50 amps of power and an electric clothes dryer draws 30, you realize that 40 amps doesn't go very far. The house will definitely need a service upgrade.

If the electrical system was installed or upgraded in the 1940s or '50s, it probably has 60 amps of power on about eight circuits. That's a little better. If the homeowners have a gas stove and dryer, they can get by on 60 amps, especially if they are remodeling on a budget. But they'll eventually want a service upgrade.

🐛 Auxiliary Boxes

You may find what seem to be several electric service boxes. These may be of different ages, like the ones in Figure 4-4, and some may have fuses and some circuit breakers. These are auxiliary electrical boxes. These were added by someone who wanted to add extra circuits without doing a complete service upgrade. They are perfectly acceptable, as long as they're installed in a neat, safe manner.

If the house has an electric hot water heater, you may find that a separate service box was added just for that. In some cases, you may even find a separate electric meter just for the water heater. That's because some electric utility companies have special rates for electric hot water, and meter it separately. If the house has electric heat, you may find a similar arrangement. This is fine as long as all the parts are in good condition.

Auxiliary Box Problems

There are a lot of amateur electricians around who can correctly wire a simple plug or switch, but who don't really understand the principles of electricity. They all tend to make certain mistakes which I see over and over again.

The most common error is trying to add power by adding extra circuits. All that does is split the existing power into more branches. It's a useful means of preventing the individual circuit breakers or fuses from blowing all the time, since it reduces the load on each one. But it *doesn't* add any additional power. If you had 40 amps before, you still have 40 amps. You may now have eight circuits instead of four, but you still can't draw more than 40 amps total without blowing the main fuses. The number of appliances you can turn on at one time is still limited. If you want to fully utilize all these circuits, you have to do a complete service upgrade. That means replacing the main service box, electric meter, and the wiring from the house to the utility pole. That's the only way to bring more power into the house.

Very few amateurs know how to do a service upgrade, but that doesn't stop them

Figure 4-4
Electric service boxes added on in an attempt to improve service

from trying to get more power out of the system. They sometimes add 10 or 15 extra circuits to a 40 or 60 amp main box. If they're installed neatly, they're not doing any harm, but they're also not doing much good.

Dangerous Modifications

Some amateur modifications can be quite dangerous. On several occasions I've seen situations where someone decided to bypass the main fuses when they added circuits in an effort to solve the problem of constantly blown fuses. The auxiliary boxes were installed above the main fuses, not below them, so that they were connected directly to the lines coming from the meter. These new individual circuits had fuses, but there were no main fuses for them.

The main fuses are there for a reason. They protect the meter and the outside wiring from overloading. Bypassing them allows you to draw more power through the meter than is safe. If you ran all the circuits at full power, you could start a fire.

One house I worked on had several 100 and 200 amp service boxes wired to one 60 amp meter. If they had turned everything on at once, they would have drawn 400 amps through a meter and wiring designed to handle only 60! The only reason the house hadn't burned down was that the former owners were very careful never to turn on more than one high-watt appliance at a time. But what would have happened if someone had come along (a new owner, for example) who didn't know that you couldn't turn on more than one thing at a time? The house would have burned down, possibly with someone in it.

Checking Auxiliary Boxes

In order to see how auxiliary boxes are wired, you need to remove the cover of the main service box and follow the wires. You should see three heavy wires coming in from outside. Two of these, the black and red, should be screwed into terminals which are attached to the main fuse or circuit breaker holder. Below the main fuse or circuit breaker should be two metal rails. All the other circuits should be connected to these rails. *Nothing* should be connected above the main breaker. If anything is, then it's not protected by the main fuse, and you have the possibility of a dangerous overload.

If you can't take the cover off the fuse box, there's another way to test it. Pull out the main fuse, or shut off the main breaker. This should turn off all the power to the house. There should be nothing left working — no lights, no plugs, nothing. If anything still has power, it's connected improperly.

🐚 Improper Service Upgrades

Some amateurs do try to attempt a service upgrade. The common mistake here is to replace the fuse or circuit breaker box without replacing the meter and wiring. This results in a system that looks okay, but is actually dangerous. You have a nice, new 100 or 200 amp circuit breaker box hooked up to an ancient meter designed to supply 40 or 60 amps of power. How can you tell if there's a problem? The shiny new circuit breaker box should have a shiny new electric meter to match. They should be replaced at the same time. If the circuit breaker box is new, but the meter is old, the job wasn't done right.

Look at the main breaker on the new circuit breaker box. It should have a number on it: usually 100, 150, or 200. This is how many amps it's rated for. Now check the meter outside. It should say how many amps it's rated

for as well. If the numbers don't match, it's time to call an electrician.

Wrong Fuse/Breaker Sizes

Another mistake made by amateurs is to install fuses or circuit breakers that are too big for the circuit they are supposed to protect. They don't understand what fuses are for. Fuses or circuit breakers are designed to blow or shut off if too much power is drawn through the circuit. They prevent the wiring from overheating and starting a fire. If you don't have fuses or circuit breakers, you can keep plugging more and more appliances into a circuit. Eventually these appliances will draw more power than the wiring in the wall can handle, and the wiring will catch fire. The same thing can happen if you use a 30 amp fuse or circuit breaker with wiring that is rated at 15 amps. It allows too much power to be drawn through the circuit. The wiring in most older homes is rated at 15 amps, so the circuits should have 15 amp fuses or circuit breakers.

The trouble is, 15 amps isn't a lot of power by modern standards. Because of this, people often have blown fuses. The proper remedy for this is to add more circuits. But if someone doesn't know this, they may try to solve the problem by other means, such as installing a fuse or circuit breaker that's way too big for that circuit. I've often seen 30 amp fuses on 15 amp circuits. These should be replaced with the correct size fuse or circuit breaker as soon as possible.

Not all larger fuses or circuit breakers are bad, even in an old box. They may be all right, *if they're connected to heavy-gauge wiring that's designed to handle that amount of power.* Check the wiring coming out of the box. Is there heavy-gauge cable corresponding to the large fuses or breakers? If so, it probably means that a new, high-power circuit was added at some time. As long as the breaker and the cable are rated for the same amount of power, there's no problem. However, if you see old, light-gauge cable or two-wire wiring, and there are new, high-amperage fuses or circuit breakers in the box, something's wrong. Better call an electrician.

❧ Awkward Modifications

Another amateur favorite is adding a new main service panel without removing the old one. Normally, when you do a service upgrade, you disconnect all the wires from the old fuse box, hook them up to the new circuit breaker box, and throw the old box away.

For some people, this is just too much trouble. They add a new main service panel, but they don't bother to disconnect the old fuse box. Instead, they reconnect it as a sub-panel of the new box. That is, they connect the main cable that leads into the old fuse box to a large circuit breaker on the new box. The old box now draws power from the new box, instead of from the meter as it did before.

If the hookup is done correctly, it isn't dangerous, but it can be very awkward. If a circuit goes out, you have to check the circuit breakers in the new box and the fuses in the old box, since they're both still hooked up. This is really inconvenient when the new circuit breaker box is in the basement, right where you'd expect to find it, but the old fuse box is tucked away in a closet somewhere upstairs. Locating fuse boxes in closets was quite common in the old days. You may not even know there's a fuse box connected until a circuit mysteriously goes out without any of the breakers being tripped. Since fuses on old 15 amp circuits tend to blow fairly often, this can quickly become a very irritating situation. An electrician can easily connect these circuits to the circuit breaker box and solve this annoying problem.

❧ Improper Rewiring

Amateur rewiring is another problem you're likely to run into in an older home. If someone has replaced some or all of the wiring in the walls with new cable and brought it through to a new circuit breaker box, you may want to double-check the circuit layout. They may not have understood that the electrical outlets and lighting should be evenly distributed among the circuits. If there are, for example, 10 circuits, you want to have about one-tenth of the electrical needs of the house on each. If you have 10 light fixtures and 20 outlets in the house, you should have one light fixture and two plugs on each circuit, so that the power demands are evenly divided. You can usually have five or six items on each circuit if necessary. It's just poor planing to have five on one and one on another if you can divide them up.

Many amateurs just start wiring things up without any plan. They gather together as many light fixtures and outlets as they can reach, and hook them all up to the first circuit breaker. When they realize that they still have nine circuits left, they begin to spread things out a bit. The next few circuits will get maybe one light or plug each, but the last few may have nothing connected to them at all.

When the wiring is done this way, the homeowner will find that although they have a nice new circuit breaker box with lots of power and lots of circuits, they can barely turn on a light without tripping a breaker. They may be unable to use half their appliances because of poor circuit planning.

You may think that all you have to do is take the cover off the circuit breaker box and see what breakers are connected to what wires. You can also look for breakers which don't have wires connected to them. But that doesn't work. All the breakers will be connected to wires; the problem is, the wires may not be connected to anything. You may find the other ends of the wires cut and dangling in the attic or the basement. The only way to check the circuits is to turn off the breakers one at a time and see what goes off. Normally, several lights and plugs will go off every time you turn a breaker off. If many of the breakers don't seem to turn off anything, and then suddenly one or two turn off practically everything, you've found the problem.

The Heating System

The first thing you're likely to see when you go down into the basement or into the utility room is the heating system. The furnace or boiler, ducts and pipes, and all the rest of the heating system are usually right out in the open. Take a moment to look it over. Unless you're in the heating and air conditioning business, you're probably not going to be doing any repairs, so you don't need to do a detailed inspection. However, there are a few things you will need to think about. How is your remodeling going to affect the heating system? Are you going to be adding any living space that will require additional heat? If so, will you be able to tie into this system? Is your remodeling going to require moving any ductwork, radiators or baseboard heaters? If so, what effect is this going to have on the heating system? Will your remodeled room still heat properly? You need to think about this now, while you're still in the inspection/estimating phase. You don't want the unexpected expense of trying to work it out later.

It's also possible that the homeowners may be considering replacing the heating system with a different type. If they've already decided on a new system, you don't need to worry about the system that's there now. Instead, make your plans with an eye to the new system that's going to be installed. However, if the homeowners haven't decided on a new system, they may ask your advice. Replacing a heating system, after all, can be very expensive. Is it a good idea? Is it cost-effective? What kind of heating system would be best?

You don't have to be an expert to be able to work with heating systems, but you do need to know some basics about the different systems you'll come across.

Types of Heating Systems

You are likely to run into a wide variety of heating systems on older homes. Some of these will be quite different from those you may be used to seeing. If a house is over 100 years old, it probably didn't have any central heating when it was built. It would have been heated with wood-burning stoves or fireplaces, then a newer system added later. If it's less than 100 years old, it most likely had some form of central heating built into the design.

The Floor Furnace

The cheapest and simplest heating system in use during the early part of this century was the floor furnace. It consisted of a big heater, installed in the middle of the basement, with one large heat duct in the center of the house, usually in the living room/dining room area. You fed coal into it, it got hot, and hot air rose through the grating. That was the extent of it.

As you might imagine, it wasn't a very good system. The living room and dining room got too hot, the rest of the house stayed too cold. The grating over the main duct got so hot that it would burn your feet if you walked over it without shoes. Most of these heaters were torn out years ago. If you find a large patch in the floor, right in the center of the house, that's usually from an old floor furnace.

Gravity Heat

The next most common system was gravity heat. This type used the big "octopus" furnaces that you can still find in older homes. Many of these have been converted to use gas instead of coal and are still working.

The gravity furnace originally used a coal fire in the combustion chamber to warm air in a heat exchanger. The warmed air was then distributed by a ducting system to the various rooms of the house. There was no fan in this system. The air movement was based on gravity — hot air rising and cold air falling. The main difference between this and the central floor furnace was the ductwork which carried the heated air to all parts of the house.

Gravity furnaces work pretty well, even today. Some people prefer them to forced-air furnaces. They make very little noise, and the gentle flow of the warm air heats more slowly and evenly than fan-forced air. Many gravity furnaces are still in use. The main drawback for the homeowner is that they are not especially energy efficient. They tend to run up a big gas bill.

The main drawback for you, as a remodeler, is the huge ductwork you need to work around. Since there's no fan, they needed big ducts and relatively straight runs for gravity to move the air. You can see these large octopus arms on the gravity furnace in Figure 4-5. This type of system seriously interferes with your options as far as relocating ductwork during remodeling. If you interfere with the airflow to a room in any way, the room simply won't heat. You'll either have to modify the plans to avoid disturbing the existing ducts, or add auxiliary heat to the remodeled rooms. And that would create a whole slew of new problems.

Another problem with a gravity furnace system is that it's very difficult to extend heat to new areas. You need to add on relatively short, straight runs of huge ductwork. You can't run a new duct across the basement to supply heat to an addition on the back of the house. The air simply won't flow through it. About the only new area you could heat would be a previously unheated attic. Since the attic is located directly above the furnace, the warm air would flow up into it. However, even this could be a problem. You'd have to sacrifice a substantial chunk of the main floor to accommodate the new ducts. Remember, you'll need to add both hot air ducts and cold air return ducts. If you tried to extend the ducts from a bedroom, you may end up with two poorly heated rooms. The ducts may not be big enough to service more area. You'd be better off using some other heating system for the added space, like electric baseboard heat.

Steam Heat

Steam heat was considered a deluxe system in the old days. There was even a popular song written about it in the 1920s. Steam actually heats quite well, as long as the system is well maintained and in good condition. (If you need more information, you'll find steam systems in *Profits in Buying & Renovating Homes.*) They provide an even, gradual heat, with just the little bit of humidity that many people like. Like the gravity systems, many steam systems are also still in use. As a matter of fact, you can buy brand-new, high-efficiency boilers for these systems from Sears. With a

Figure 4-5
Octopus-type gas gravity furnace

new boiler, these systems are as efficient and easy to use as any modern heating system.

A steam heating system consists of a boiler, steam pipes and room radiators. Water is heated in the boiler, located in the basement, until it boils. The steam created by the boiling water rises up, by gravity, through the large steam pipes and flows into radiators located in the various rooms of the house. The radiators become hot, and radiate heat into the rooms.

Homeowners whose steam heat systems work well generally have only two complaints: One is that you can't add central air conditioning to them. The second is that they sometimes make furniture placement difficult.

You can work around a steam system, but it's awkward. You can put the radiators anywhere you want, move them from one part of the room to another, or even add radiators to additions or previously unheated spaces. However, installing new radiators and piping is tricky. The pipes leading into them must be precisely angled or the radiators will

Figure 4-6
Old gas-fired hot water furnace

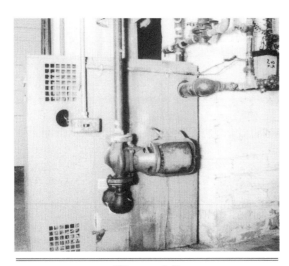

Figure 4-7
Recent model gas-fired hot water furnace

heat poorly and make a lot of noise. This isn't a job for an amateur plumber. You'll need an experienced plumber who knows steam heating systems — and they're not easy to find. Most of the guys who did this kind of work are pretty old now. You may have to pull someone out of retirement to get this kind of work done.

Hot Water Heat

Another form of heat you may find is a circulating hot water system. These are very nice systems, similar to the ones which are used in some luxury properties today.

At first glance, you may think you've come across a steam system. The old hot water systems use large radiators (unlike today's systems, which use baseboard heaters) and have a boiler in the basement to heat the water. The difference is that they circulate water, not steam. An electric motor is used to pump the water through the pipes and into the radiators in the various rooms, which get hot and radiate heat. Figure 4-6 shows an older model gas-fired hot water furnace and Figure 4-7 shows a more recent model.

This system is as good as any in use today. With a new boiler which incorporates a water chiller, a circulating water system can even be fitted with central air conditioning. If the radiators are a problem, you can replace them with baseboard heaters.

This system doesn't present a problem when it comes to remodeling work. You can put radiators anywhere you want; and since the water is pumped through the pipes under pressure, the exact angle of the pipes doesn't matter. It's no more difficult than any other plumbing job.

Forced-Air Heat

A home built before the 1940s wouldn't have included a forced-air heating system, but it might have one today. Forced-air heat could have been added any time since the '40s. So the system you come across today may be brand new or 50 years old.

All forced-air systems work roughly the same. Fuel is burned in the combustion chamber, which heats air in the heat exchanger. The fuel may be oil, natural gas, or propane. The hot air is circulated by means of an electric fan, which distributes it evenly to all the rooms. That's why these systems are so popular. Most homeowners are happy with these systems and have no reason to replace them unless the furnace is very old.

This is the easiest system to work with. Because the air is fan-forced, you can run ductwork anywhere you want, and the fan will force the air through it. Of course, if a run is extremely long or convoluted, you might need a booster fan to help the air get to where it's supposed to go, but that isn't a major problem.

Another nice thing about forced-air furnaces is that they used to be installed with a lot of excess capacity. Until recently, it was common practice to install a furnace that had 50 percent more capacity than it needed, to ensure it would keep the house toasty warm even in the coldest weather. This makes heating room additions very easy. Unless you're going to increase the heated space in a house by more than 50 percent, the existing furnace will probably be able to heat the added space easily.

Installing oversized furnaces is no longer common practice. Oversized furnaces aren't fuel-efficient. When fuel was cheap, no one worried about efficiency. If you're working on a home with a new furnace, you may have more problems than if the home had an old furnace. The new furnace may not have enough excess capacity to heat added space. Check this carefully.

🐚 Heating Fuels

Most homes more than 50 years old were originally heated with coal. This was the fuel of choice for central heating systems from around 1860 to 1940. I've never seen coal still in use, although I've occasionally come across old coal bins still full of coal! Through the years these systems have been updated to some degree or another. Most have been modified to use gas.

Coal-to-Gas Conversions

The majority of these coal-to-gas conversions were done in the 1940s and '50s, so they're now pretty old. That doesn't mean they don't work, however; they were built to last. Coal-fired furnaces were built to withstand higher temperatures than you get by burning gas. As a result, they almost never burn out. But they were built to use cheap coal, and they're not very efficient as gas-burning furnaces. In fact, they're probably the lowest-efficiency furnaces you're likely to come across.

Coal-to-gas conversions were amazingly simple. All they did was stick a burner inside the old furnace where the coal used to go. They attached it to the gas line, and then added burner controls and a thermostat to turn it on and off. That's it. The rest of the system was left the same.

This modification was done on a variety of coal-fired systems, including gravity furnaces, steam boilers and hot water boilers. You won't find gas forced-air systems converted from coal forced-air systems, because there never were any coal forced-air systems. You will find gas forced-air systems converted from oil, however. Many of these were done during the oil crisis in the early 1970s, when fuel oil became very expensive and hard to get.

Oil

Oil-fired systems are common in rural areas, where gas line connections may not be available. You may also still find them in urban property as well, but less frequently. Most oil-fired systems are the forced-air type, but I sometimes see oil-fired steam and hot water heating systems.

There's nothing really wrong with oil-fired systems, but some people just dislike them and want them replaced. They do require somewhat more maintenance than gas-fired systems. Oil-fired burners need to be cleaned annually, and the fittings, pipes and tank that the oil flows through must be kept sealed tight so they won't leak. If they don't get proper maintenance, you'll wind up with a lot of sooty smoke and puddles of smelly fuel oil. That's what gives oil heat a bad name. Some people think the smell and dirt are normal. They aren't. A properly-maintained oil system won't have any more dirt or odor than a gas-fired system. Unless you see the oil tank, you can't tell the difference.

Oil heat is actually safer than gas. If you have a leak in your oil system, you'll get a puddle of fuel oil on the basement floor. It smells bad, but doesn't really do any serious harm. It won't even burn unless you actually drop a match in it. But if you have a leak in a gas system, escaping gas can fill up a house in a matter of hours. As soon as someone strikes a spark: KABOOM! There's a big hole in the ground where your house (and you) used to be. Of the two, I'll take a puddle of fuel oil any day. Of course, city codes require that all gas furnaces be worked on by licensed contractors so that the danger of leaks is minimal if the furnace is well maintained.

There are a couple of other drawbacks to oil. One is that it has to be delivered by truck, which can be a nuisance. If you forget to put your order in, you may wake up really cold one morning. Also, the holding tanks take up a lot of room in the basement. This isn't usually a problem unless someone wants to turn their basement into a recreation room. However, most older home basements aren't really suitable as living space.

The second drawback is the possibility that heating oil may still be hard to get in some areas, or that there will be another oil shortage. Some people were so traumatized by the last oil crisis that they refuse to ever have oil heat again. And finally, a lot of people just think of oil as old-fashioned. It isn't, really. You can get brand-new high-efficiency oil furnaces that are as good as any gas furnace.

However, if you run into people who have a negative attitude about oil, chances are you won't be able to talk them into keeping their oil-burning system. They don't want it in their house, and that's that! You can point out the advantages of oil, if you think it will do any good, but it's their decision, and usually it's already made.

Propane

Propane-fired systems are common in rural areas, where gas service isn't available. Or, if it is, the cost of bringing the lines to the house is sometimes prohibitively expensive. Gas companies charge by the foot to bring the gas lines to a house. If the house is several miles from the nearest gas line, the connection cost could be more than the property is worth. In this situation, most people opt for propane. It offers all the advantages of natural gas, without the expense of having gas lines installed. Most appliances need only a minor modification to be converted from natural gas to propane.

You never see propane appliances in the city. There wouldn't be much point in having propane storage tanks and truck deliveries if a house could easily be connected to a natural gas line. Almost all houses in urban areas have gas hookups. If, by chance, you come across a house that doesn't, it shouldn't cost much to have the lines brought in. You only have to pay for the distance between the house and the nearest house that has gas. You'll probably only need to have the lines extended 10 or 20 feet.

I once bought a house that didn't have natural gas hookups. I got a very good deal on the house because most buyers weren't interested in a house that didn't already have gas. If they had taken a few minutes to call the gas company, like I did, they would have found out that it would only cost $200 to have the gas lines extended from next door. I saved thousands of dollars by making a simple phone call!

❧ Repair or Replace?

What I've told you so far about heating systems should be enough for you to help homeowners make some decisions about their systems. A lot will depend on their budgets. If money is no object, you might as well replace the system if it's not up to standard. But if they're on a tight budget, you'll probably leave the existing system in place unless it's totally inadequate. Remember, having a new heating system is nice, but it's not that much fun. For the same cost, the homeowner could have a remodeled kitchen or an extra bath. Unless improving home heating is a high priority with them, they'll probably get more pleasure putting their money into something else.

Of course this decision shouldn't be strictly about the what's more fun for the money. There are other things to consider as well. Are you going to need to tie into the existing heating system? As we discussed earlier, some systems, like forced-air, are easy to tie into. Others, like gravity heat, are almost impossible. This means that a system that's adequate before the remodel may be inadequate afterwards. But you don't need to give up on the remodeling plans just because you can't tie into the existing system. You can always add an auxiliary heater in the new room. They're never really as good as tying into the central heating system, but they're better than nothing.

If you put in a new heating system, what modifications would you have to make to accommodate it? How will these modifications fit in with the remodeling plans, or with the existing house, for that matter? For example, if you want to take out a steam system, which uses pipes, and replace it with a forced-air system, which uses ducts, you're going to have to make room for those ducts. If the house is one level, the ducts can go in the basement or crawl space. (I'll warn you, though, installing ductwork in a crawl space is not fun!)

On the other hand, if the house has two or more stories, you're probably going to have to tear out walls on the main floor in order to get the ductwork upstairs. If you were going to tear out these walls anyway, it doesn't make much difference. But if you weren't planning to, having to do it will increase the cost of the project tremendously. Maybe the owners would be better off selecting a system that uses pipes, like hot water. Or, when faced with having walls torn out, they might decide the old system isn't as bad as they thought. All these problems will have to be considered.

Finally, what's the condition of the existing furnace? The furnace is the most expensive part of the heating system. If it needs to be replaced, replacing the rest of the system won't cost that much more. But if it's a perfectly good furnace, replacing the system is far less cost effective.

When should a furnace be replaced? Furnaces are amazingly durable. They rarely need to be replaced. I've seen many furnaces

manufactured as early as 1920 that work as well as the day they were made. They survive in spite of abuse and lack of maintenance. Once in a while you might have to replace a fan motor or thermostat, but even that's fairly unusual. The furnaces in most older houses just need minor repair or adjustment to keep them working perfectly for decades.

The only time a furnace absolutely needs to be replaced is if the heat exchanger is burned through. That will cause it to leak carbon monoxide into the house. It's rare to find a situation like this in an older furnace. They were built to last. They're actually less likely to burn out than the newer ones, which are much flimsier.

Look for Danger Signs

Take the time to check the furnace and the area around it for gas leaks. Sniff around it. Do you smell gas anywhere? Check the gas pipe. This is most commonly steel "black pipe." Is it in good condition? You may find copper tubing connected to the black pipe at some points. Copper tubing is generally used to connect gas appliances, like dryers. Look it over carefully. Copper tubing is fragile. It can easily be torn or cracked, causing dangerous gas leaks. Even though copper tubing is acceptable for gas lines, *soldered* copper pipe is not. Gas can eat through solder joints, causing dangerous leaks. Any soldered gas pipe should be removed immediately.

Also, check to make sure the flue pipe is in good condition. If it's rusted through or torn, it may be leaking carbon monoxide into the house. This is dangerous, and needs immediate repair. The furnace should have its own chimney flue. It can share the flue with a water heater, but it shouldn't share it with some entirely different device, like a fireplace. There's not enough capacity in a single flue to accommodate the fumes from both a fireplace and a furnace. If they were both being used at once, fumes would back up into the house. This can be very dangerous. Let the homeowners know it should be corrected immediately.

Sharing a flue is not the same thing as sharing a chimney. One chimney can have several flues. You can tell by the number of flue pipes coming out the top. If the house has a gas furnace and a fireplace, but only one chimney, that chimney should have at least two flue pipes. If it doesn't, you may have a problem. It doesn't necessarily mean you have to replace the entire system, but the flue does need immediate attention.

Consider Efficiency

One big reason a homeowner may want to replace an old furnace is to save money on fuel bills. Many of the old furnaces, while they work just fine, are gas hogs. This is especially true of coal furnaces that have been converted to gas. A homeowner may simply want a more efficient system.

At one time I owned a house with a gas-gravity furnace that dated back to the 1920s. It worked perfectly, but during the coldest months the gas bill was over $300. That was a lot for a house that had only 1,500 square feet! It was enough to discourage prospective buyers, and make the house hard to sell. Replacing the old furnace with a new gas forced-air model brought the monthly heating bill down to around $100. That was a good investment. If the homeowners aren't sure how much they'll save with a new heat-ing system, have them call the gas company (or oil company) and find out exactly what the fuel bills have been for the house during the last few years. That could make all the difference.

However, other factors besides fuel efficiency, can affect a fuel bill. Check the insulation in the house. You'll probably want to add some, regardless of what you do with the furnace. The windows and doors may be leaky. These will also need to be repaired or replaced. These improvements may lower the heating bill substantially, without doing anything to the heating system.

Homeowners may feel that they need to replace their furnace because it doesn't heat well. Check out the system carefully. It may just need a minor repair. Poor heating is often caused by very simple things, like a rug placed over a heating vent, or rubbish blocking a duct. It would be a shame to spend thousands to replace a furnace, when all you really needed to do was move a rug!

This completes your careful and thorough inspection of the house. You've looked at every part of the house and know exactly what you're going to have to deal with. Now it's time to get to work.

Chapter 5

Urgent Repairs

*A*n older house may need a tremendous amount of work, both interior and exterior, to bring it up to date. Just getting organized can be a challenge when you're looking at a whole-house remodel. There are so many things that need attention. What should be done first? What should be done at all? Luckily, there's a logical way to approach this dilemma. All you need to do is ask yourself, "What will happen if I don't do this job right now? Will it get worse? Will it damage anything else? Will it cause tremendous problems for the homeowners?" Answering these questions will help you decide where you need to begin.

Obviously, all of the repairs you're considering on this job are causing some kind of problem, otherwise you wouldn't have been hired to take care of them. Some, however, are major and others are just minor problems. Poor decorating is a good example of a minor problem. The wallpaper may be awful, but it isn't going to get any worse in the next few weeks. Major problems, like a gas leak, will get worse.

Gas Leaks

Leaks need to be taken care of right away. Of all the types of leaks you could pos-sibly have, the most urgent are gas leaks. Fortunately, serious gas leaks aren't too com-mon. But they do exist, and you may just run across one at some time in your career. Even seconds count with a serious gas leak. If you don't do something immediately, the house could blow up. What should you do?

First of all, if you open the door to a house and there's a strong smell of gas, don't go in. You have no way of knowing how much gas has leaked out. It may have filled up the whole house. While you're poking around trying to find the problem, the house could go. It probably won't, but it might. Why take a chance? Don't go inside. Instead, call the gas company immediately. Leave the door open to help vent the gas until the gas company arrives.

While you're waiting for the gas compa-ny, look for the gas meter. If it's located outside the house, you may be able to turn the gas off yourself. That will stop any fur-ther gas from leaking into the house. The meter usually has an in-line valve on it. If it's lined up the same direction as the pipe, it's on. If it's going crossways, it's off. You generally need a wrench or a pliers to turn it off.

If the gas meter is located on the inside, let the gas company take care it off. They'll turn the gas off at the street, and let the gas

Figure 5-1
Uncapped gas line is a hazard

clear out of the house before they go inside to find the problem.

Serious gas leaks are usually caused by a careless occupant breaking a gas line when they're moving out. They may break the gas line to the stove or clothes dryer when they're disconnecting the appliance, and not even know it. Often the gas is turned off when people are moving, so no one notices. When the gas is turned back on by new the owners, the broken pipe may be overlooked for a while. The leaking gas will eventually fill up the house. If it reaches a pilot light or spark, the whole house will blow up.

One house I owned had exactly this problem. The former tenants had ripped their gas dryer out, tearing off the copper gas pipe at floor level, so it couldn't be seen. When the gas was turned on, I had no idea that the broken pipe even existed. Luckily, it was summertime, and I had all the windows wide open while I was working on the house. The open windows vented the gas out. If the windows had been closed, the house could have exploded, and me with it.

🐚 Minor Gas Leaks

You're much more likely to run into minor gas leaks than major ones. In this case, rather than an overwhelming smell of gas,

you'll notice just a little hint of gas. Sometimes you're not even sure what it is. Something just smells funny.

Gas from a tiny leak will usually escape from the house at about the same rate it leaks out of the line. It generally won't build up and explode, but don't count on it. The leak still needs to be attended to right away. Minor leaks can get bigger, and it's always possible that large amounts of gas could build up over time.

The best way to find these leaks is sniff them out. The smell will get stronger as you move towards the leak. There are usually just three areas in the home that are supplied with gas: the kitchen, the laundry area, and the furnace. The leak will most likely be in the kitchen or laundry area, since these pipes are the ones most often disturbed by occupants as they move. If it's not there, it'll be somewhere near the furnace. If there are any plumbed-in gas heaters or wall furnaces, check them as well.

If you're lucky, the problem will be a minor one, like a supply line that was never properly capped or completely turned off. Figure 5-1 shows an example. Often, just turning a valve fully to the off position will solve the problem. Code requires that unused supply lines be both turned off and capped, to make sure this type of problem doesn't occur. Professional moving companies are very careful about this, but other people are not so reliable. When tenants or former owners move themselves, check items like these carefully.

The next most likely cause is a loose fitting. These aren't always easy to find. But if you can zero in on the general area that the leak is coming from, you can turn off the gas to that area and stop further leakage. If the problem's in an area that isn't vital, like a line to a clothes dryer, it's not an emergency. You can wait until it's convenient to get a plumber in to take care of it once the leak is stopped.

If you can't find the leak, you may have to turn off the gas to the whole house until you can find and correct the problem. Of course you'd rather avoid this if possible, especially in winter. No gas means no heat. That makes the house unlivable until the heat is back on again. Call the gas company before you resort to turning off the gas. They may be able to send an emergency crew out to locate the problem.

Natural gas is not the only kind of gas leak that can be a problem. Blocked or improper flues can cause carbon monoxide to leak into the house. This won't make the house blow up, but it will make everyone sick. If people in the house are complaining of headaches and nausea, carbon monoxide poisoning may be the problem. If the house is closed up, as it might be in the winter, it could be a deadly problem! The hot water heater shown in Figure 5-2 was improperly vented and created just this type of situation. It had a piece of old downspout attached that was used as the flue pipe. The improper connection leaked fumes into the house. I shut the gas to the water heater off immediately, and left it off until I had a regular flue pipe installed.

Figure 5-2
Downspout used as flue pipe was leaking fumes into house

plumbing runs traveling through them as well. If so, these areas will also need to be heated.

Close off the rooms that you know for sure have no plumbing, such as the bedrooms, sitting rooms or family room. This may shut off as much as half the floor space in the house. A few electric heaters should be able to warm the rest. The house doesn't have to be kept toasty warm. It only needs to be above 32 degrees to keep the pipes from freezing. This isn't hard to do, unless the temperature outside is sub-zero.

Be sure to keep all combustible materials well away from the space heaters. Also, don't plug more than one heater into each electric circuit. This type of heater draws a lot of power, usually about 1,500 watts each. A 15-amp circuit can provide a maximum of 1,800 watts. You can see that this doesn't give you much to spare. More than one heater per circuit will just blow a fuse. If you're in a hurry and get careless, you can blow a fuse and not notice it. Then your heating plan will fail, and the pipes will freeze.

Heating Emergencies

In some climates, lack of heat can be an urgent problem during the winter. Not only will this make the house unlivable, but if it's cold enough, the pipes may freeze and break. This can cause major damage. And that's my definition of urgent. You need to takes steps to prevent this from happening.

❧ Using Electric Heaters

If the heat is only off for a couple of days, you may be able to use electric heat to keep the house warm enough to protect the pipes. Just plug in a bunch of electric space heaters. I always keep about a half-dozen of these around. They're useful for all sorts of little jobs, like warming up the garage before you work on your car. You don't need to heat every room, just the ones that have plumbing. Usually these are the basement, kitchen and bathrooms. However, in some older homes the living and dining rooms may have

❧ Using the Stove

The stove is another valuable source of heat in the house, especially if it's electric. If you turn the oven on at medium heat, 300 to

71

350 degrees, and leave the oven door open, enough heat will pour out to keep a 1,500 square foot house warm in 20-degree weather. It's almost like a little furnace.

Don't do this with a gas oven. It isn't safe to leave the oven on all the time in an occupied house. The oven is, after all, an unvented gas heater. When it burns, it uses up oxygen and throws out a lot of carbon dioxide. In normal cooking, this isn't a problem. However, if you use the stove as a heater, this can build up unsafe levels of carbon dioxide and make you sick. A gas stove should be used for heat only for very short periods of time, and only in a house that's vacant.

An electric stove doesn't generate fumes. You can run this for as long as you want. It's the equivalent of a big electric space heater. I've heated entire houses with electric stoves for days on end, without any problems.

The only drawback to electric heat is that it's expensive. If you're running the stove and some space heaters, you're probably drawing 5,000-10,000 watts of power continuously. While electric rates vary, most utilities charge something like 1 cent per 100 watts per hour. If you figure this out, it comes out to between 50 cents and $1 per hour. That's $12-$24 per day. You clearly don't want to let this go on very long.

🐚 Winterizing the House

If for any reason a house needs to be left without heat for several weeks or months during the winter, it should be winterized. This consists of shutting off the water and draining all water pipes in the house. If there's nothing to freeze, then you won't have freeze damage.

To do this, you first shut off the main water supply. Then open all the faucets, starting with the ones in the basement. Be sure to open all of the faucets, including the ones outside. If any are left closed, water may be trapped behind them, which will freeze and break the pipe. As you open the faucets upstairs, siphoning should cause all the water to flow out of the system through the basement faucets.

You will need to completely drain the hot water tank on the water heater. Then flush all the toilets. This empties the water out of the toilet tanks, but not out of the bowls. You will have to either pump the water out of the bowls, or add a couple of cups of antifreeze to them. All the sink traps will have to be either pumped out, or have antifreeze added to them as well. You should check your local ordinances about putting antifreeze into the sewer system before you do this. Because of water pollution standards, it may be illegal in your area. You can pump the water out with a toilet plunger. Be sure you plug up the sink and toilet bowl openings with plastic or some old rags after you do this. Once you pump the water out of the traps, you break the water seal that keeps sewer gas out of the house. Sewer gas will come up through the openings if they aren't plugged, and make the house smell like a sewer. It won't hurt you, it's just really awful.

Remember that water always flows to the lowest point. Usually that's a basement laundry tub, or some other faucet in the basement. If you don't have any faucets in the basement, you may have to disconnect a pipe to drain the water. Pick the lowest pipe you can find that will drain the most water.

Winterizing an older home is not only a lot of trouble, but it isn't always reliable. Avoid it if you can. Because of the many plumbing modifications in older homes, there may be odd loops of pipe running through out-of-the-way places that won't drain correctly. If even one small section still has water pooling in it, that water will freeze and break the pipe. When you turn the water back on, water will come gushing out of the ceiling, or wherever the pipe was. I've even had water come gushing out of a light fixture! Then you have to tear open the ceiling, find the broken pipe, repair it and repair the ceiling. That's a lot of extra work!

It's better to keep the house heated throughout the winter. Winterizing should be done only if there's no practical alternative. Of course, winterizing is better than nothing. I've seen houses that weren't winterized. Believe me, they're a lot more work to repair than the few minutes it takes to drain the water and pump out the fixtures — or even to repair a single broken pipe, for that matter. In one house I saw, the toilets were shattered as though they'd been hit with a sledgehammer. The sink traps were all broken, the water heater was ruptured, and most of the inlet lines were cracked. The house needed to be completely replumbed, at a cost of thousands of dollars. If the house had been winterized, there might still have been a little damage, but at least the entire system wouldn't have been destroyed.

Water Leaks

Water leaks are common problems that require immediate attention. They're not as urgent as gas leaks. Seconds don't matter, but days do. You can't just let a water leak go until you get around to it. A few drops of water going on continuously can be tremendously destructive. Even a small leak can do thousands of dollars worth of damage in just a few days.

There are three types of water leaks that you will have to deal with most often:

◆ Roof leaks, which let in rainwater

◆ Plumbing leaks, which let water out of the plumbing system

◆ Basement wall leaks, which let ground water into the basement

Of the three, basement wall leaks are the least urgent. There's usually very little of value in a basement that the water can harm. Most of the time the water just goes down the drain. If the homeowners do keep valuables in their basement, you should advise them to find a new storage area for the time being.

🐌 Plumbing Leaks

Plumbing leaks, even tiny ones, can be amazingly destructive. And the higher up they are in the house, the more destructive they are. A plumbing leak in the basement really won't do much more damage than a

Figure 5-3
Vacuum cleaner hose used as drain line

basement wall leak. The water usually just drips onto the cement floor and goes down the drain. A plumbing leak in an upstairs bathroom, on the other hand, can destroy the first floor plasterwork throughout the entire house. Look for wet spots on the ceiling below the bathroom. They indicate an active plumbing leak above.

Emergency Repairs

There's an emergency plumbing repair you can do that requires no tools or materials, and takes literally only a few seconds of your time. It's so simple that most people don't even think of it. *Turn off the water supply!* If the water's turned off, it can't leak. Ideally, you can turn off the water supply to the area or fixture that's leaking. If you spot really serious problems, turn off the water and disable the fixtures feeding into those lines immediately. What's a serious problem? Here are a couple. In Figure 5-3, you see a vacuum cleaner hose being used as a drain line. Figure 5-4 shows a rusted drain pipe and uncapped drain line leaking sewage and gases into the basement.

You don't even have to be on the job to make this simple "repair." You could do it when you go to deliver your estimate. Then you can say to the homeowners, "I may have saved you thousands of dollars by stopping

73

Figure 5-4
*Rusted drain line and uncapped pipe
leaking sewage and sewer gas*

Figure 5-5
Loose plaster indicates roof leak

this leak from doing any further damage." If that doesn't get you the job, I don't know what will.

Of course this only works if there's a cutoff available to that section of the house, or if a leaky fixture has a cutoff. Unfortunately, many old houses with the original plumbing don't have cutoffs for the various sections of the plumbing system. That means the only way to stop the leak is to turn the main water supply off. That makes the house unlivable. If the house is vacant, it won't matter too much. The homeowners will have to wait until the plumbing is repaired before moving in. If they're living in the house, however, it's best to go ahead and turn the water off and advise them call a plumber immediately.

You may run into one other problem when you turn off the main supply. While there's always supposed to be at least one shutoff for the system, they don't always work. In that case, the only way to shut off the water is at the curb. To do this, you need a special tool called a "curb key." This is a very useful thing to have, and only costs about $5. You won't need it very often, but when you need it, nothing else will do. You can buy one at any good hardware store.

Roof Leaks

Roof leaks can be the most damaging leaks of all. They start at the top of the house and work their way down, often destroying everything in their path. If you leave them long enough, they can completely destroy a house. Crumbling, loose plaster (Figure 5-5) or water marks on wallpaper (Figure 5-6) are good indications of an active roof leak.

Bad weather creates additional problems when you need to make roof repairs. If the whole roof needs to be torn off and replaced, you'll be temporarily exposing the house to the weather. You really don't want to start a job like this too late in the season, unless you have a big crew and can get the job done in a day or so. If you start the job and the weather turns bad, it may be weeks before you can finish it. In the meantime, the interior of the house could suffer major damage. All you can do if you have the roof off and the weather turns, is to put tarps over the house until the weather breaks. This will help a little, but some water will still get in and cause damage. Always check the weather forecast before starting a roof job!

Because of weather problems, most people wait until spring to tackle big, difficult roof jobs. The job may still be interrupted by a day or two of bad weather, but time will be on your side. The weather will be getting better every day, instead of worse, as it does in the fall.

Emergency Roof Repairs

What if the roof is already leaking, and the weather has already turned bad? What can you do? Some people think that in order to do an emergency roof repair in winter you have to risk your life and climb up on a wet, icy roof in the middle of a blizzard to try and fill the leaks with tar. There's actually a much quicker, easier, and safer method, and it works just about as well.

The worst damage from roof leaks occurs when the water gets into the plasterwork, as it did in the house shown in Figure 5-7. The plaster becomes saturated and eventually just falls off the wall. If you can catch the water as it enters the attic space, *before* it gets to the plasterwork, you've headed off almost all the damage. Once again, there's a solution that's so simple most people never think of it. Go up into the attic space and find the leak. If it's a big leak, it'll be pretty obvious. Then, *put a bucket under it!* That way the water will drip into the bucket, instead of working its way into the plasterwork below. Unless the hole is the size of your fist, you won't even need to empty the bucket very often. It usually takes more than a week to fill a good-sized bucket, one drip at a time. This gives you time to wait for the weather to clear to do a permanent repair on the roof.

As simple as this is, you'd be amazed by the number of people who just do nothing. I was in a home not long ago that had a serious roof leak. The owners planned to have it repaired in the spring, as soon as weather permitted. In the meantime, water was leaking in, causing damage to their living room ceiling. I advised them that they should go up into the attic space, which was easily accessible, and put a bucket under the leak so that they could save their ceiling. Their answer was, "It's too much trouble." Instead, they allowed their entire living room ceiling to cave in. The leak caused hundreds of dollars worth of damage, as well as inconvenience —

Figure 5-6
*Water marks on wallpaper
indicate active leak*

Figure 5-7
Falling plaster indicates major roof leak

and it could have been prevented by a simple, five-minute job!

Hidden Leaks

In some cases, you may not be able to tell exactly where or how the water is coming in. This is one of my least favorite situations — the dreaded "mystery leak." However, even in this case there's an emergency repair which usually works.

Even though you can't tell exactly where the water is coming from, you do know

Figure 5-8
*Broken light fixture with exposed wires
is a dangerous hazard*

where it's going. You can tell by the spot on the ceiling where the paint is discolored or peeling, since those are the first signs of a leak. Go up into the attic, above that spot, and lay down a big piece of heavy plastic sheeting, like Visqueen. Arrange it over the ceiling joists so that the edges are a bit raised. This will make a cup-shaped depression that will hold water.

Check the plastic after the next rain. You should find a good-sized puddle — a puddle that would otherwise have dripped down into the plasterwork below, causing more damage. If the leak is serious, you may have to mop up the puddle after each rain, since the plastic, unlike a bucket, can't hold very much water. A wet-and-dry vacuum works well for this. It will suck up the water quickly and neatly, and it's a lot easier to work with than a bucket and sponge.

This may seem like a lot of trouble, but believe me, it's a lot less trouble than replacing the ceiling. The homeowners may be willing to do some of this work. It doesn't take any particular skill to go up and empty a bucket or sponge up water. It's little enough to do for the hundreds of dollars they'll be saving by not having to replace the entire ceiling or other damaged plasterwork.

Electrical Problems

In your inspection, you should have identified any wires that were loose, frayed, hanging where people might touch them, or dangerously close to objects that might short them out. These should be removed, or at least disconnected. The broken light in Figure 5-8 is a good example. Turn off the whole circuit if necessary. Never say, "I know where those wires are. I'll be careful not to touch them." Remember, other people will be going through this house while you're working on it. They don't know where these wires are. Ignoring dangerous wiring is like leaving traps for people. Always choose safety; get rid of any bad wiring.

Security

A vacant house is always a security problem. Never leave anything valuable in a vacant house, no matter how nice the neighborhood. I've learned this the hard way. I've had valuable tools and materials stolen from vacant houses in what were supposed to be the city's best and safest neighborhoods. No matter how well sealed-up the house is, people can get in if they really want to. The only thing that really protects a house is the owner. If there's no one living there, there's no real protection.

❧ Windows

Broken windows are a security problem. Anyone can climb right in, and this is very likely to happen if the house is vacant. Even if there's nothing to steal in the house, someone might come in just to vandalize it. Broken windows are common in houses that have been vacant for a while. It's best to fix them immediately. If you can't fix them, at least board them up, or cover them with something. Otherwise insects, birds, rain or vandals can get in and damage the house.

Of course, boarded-up windows look terrible. Instead of using boards, I keep a supply of old storm windows around. I can usually find one that's roughly the same size as the broken window, and screw it in over the frame. It may not fit exactly, but it's better than nothing, and it doesn't look as tacky as a board. To keep relations friendly, you have to think about how the neighbors feel.

❧ Doors

One of the first things that should be done on any newly-purchased property is to change the locks. If it hasn't been done already, advise the owners to do it now. They have no way of knowing who might have a key to the old locks. There might be one floating around the real estate office, various service people might have them, the former owners may have given keys to friends, or friends of friends, and so on. This is especially true if the house has been vacant for a while. People tend to be very careless with keys to a vacant house. After all, if it's empty, there's nothing to steal. Of course, if someone really wants to get in, they can still break in. But don't make it easy for them. They shouldn't be able to just walk in with a key.

Bad Doors

What if the doors are broken, and can no longer be locked? Or if they're going to be replaced? The owners won't want you to put new locks on doors that are going to be thrown away.

In this case, the best way to deal with the situation is to pick one door to use for the time being, and seal all the rest. The quickest and easiest way to do this is to run a few 3-inch drywall screws right through the door and into the door jamb. This works well even on a door that's broken or in poor shape. Once you've done that, the only way get the door open from the outside is to break it

down. Another good thing about doing this is that if you should need to open the door, it only takes a few seconds to spin the drywall screws back out.

If the door is already shattered, or completely rotted, there may not be enough left of it to screw down. In that case, screw a sheet of plywood over the opening. It's ugly, but it works. You can put it on the inside if it will show less that way.

What about the one door you plan to use? See if you have another lock that's the same brand and type as the one that's currently on it. It doesn't need to be new. It'll take only a couple of minutes to switch the locks. All you have to do is release the screws that hold in the cylinder mechanism (where the key goes), and screw in another one. All the rest of the parts can be left in place. Sometimes even a cylinder of another brand will fit.

I keep a box full of old locks around for this purpose. I've got at least one of all the popular brands. You can usually get these from people who are throwing away old doors — lock, keys and all. You can also find them at garage sales for only a dollar or so.

If all else fails, you may have to install a whole new lock assembly in the door. But since you don't plan to keep the door, you don't have to do an especially nice job. It's just a temporary fix. You can just whack a hole in the door and stick the lock in. It only has to last a few weeks at most, until you install the new door. Once all this is taken care of, you'll know exactly who has a key to the house.

The house should now be safe and secure, with all the urgent repairs made, or preventive steps taken to prevent further damage. You can now get on to the regular work.

Chapter 6

Roof and Siding Repair

It's time look at the other repairs we listed in our inspection. We'll go through them in the same order as we inspected them, starting with the exterior. Whether or not you should actually start with the exterior will depend on several factors: the weather, the occupants and the urgency of the exterior work among them.

The main factor is the weather. If the weather is unsuitable for working outside (3 feet of snow, for example), you can't begin with the exterior repairs no matter how much you may want to. Your only option is to start on the interior, or do nothing at all. Since good weather is in short supply in Michigan, I usually work on the exterior whenever there's a nice day, but I always find that I finish my interior work first. The weather rarely permits me to work outside as much as I would like. Remember, you can do your interior work on sunny days, but you can't do your exterior work on rainy days. So I suggest you always save your interior work for rainy days if possible. Otherwise, a prolonged stretch of bad weather can really mess up your schedule. You'll be stuck with a half-done job, with no work to do until the weather clears.

In scheduling your work, another factor to take into consideration is whether there are people waiting on a particular part of the job. Is the house vacant, with people anxious to move in? In that case, you may need to do the interior work first. People can move in as soon as the interior is finished, even if there's a lot of work still to be done on the exterior. It's much harder to work inside an occupied house than a vacant one. You've got to move furniture, protect or remove carpeting, be careful not to track dirt into the house, and so on. The job takes a lot longer, and it's nerve-wracking having to worry about upsetting the occupants. So if you can do the interior work before anyone moves in, grab the opportunity. Working on the exterior of the house isn't such a problem for people. You don't need to invade their privacy or worry about damaging their furnishing while you're working outside. In many cases, they're at their jobs the same hours you're working. You may never even see them.

The last factor you need to look at in scheduling is whether any of the exterior damage threatens the interior. Does the house have a leaky roof, for example? There isn't much point in replacing all the ceilings, only to have them destroyed again after a big

Figure 6-1
A one-layer tearoff

rain. Any exterior damage that may cause interior problems needs to be fixed first, if at all possible. If the weather makes major work impossible, at least do emergency repairs, as we discussed in the last chapter.

Roofing an Older Home

The roof is normally where you'd want to start your repairs. A leaky roof can cause tremendous damage — nothing in the house is safe until the roof is repaired. Basic roofing is generally pretty simple, so I'm not going to give you step by step instructions on how to install a new roof. I did my first roof with nothing more to go by than the instructions on the shingle package! As long as you get the shingles on straight and neat, fastened securely, with the proper spacing, they'll be fine

One thing stands out in my memory about my first roofing job that's worth mentioning. When I read the instructions on the package of shingles, they said to start by lay-

ing out five rows of shingles, each set back from the one below. I wondered about that. Why couldn't I just do one row, all the way to the end, and then come back and do another? So I tried it. You can do it that way, but you have to move your ladder a lot more often. If you start five rows at a time, you'll be able to shingle everything that's in reach from that ladder location before having to move your ladder. It saves time and effort to follow instructions.

If you feel that you need more installation instruction than you get on the package, any "how to" book will give you adequate information. What I'll cover, instead, are the problems you might run into working on an older home. You could do a thousand roofs on newer homes without ever running into the problems you'll run into on one old one.

Just remember, I said roofing is *simple*; I didn't say *easy*. It's a hard, heavy job that nobody really likes. It's especially unpleasant to work on a roof in the middle of summer. It can easily get up to 120 degrees. I've been working on a roof when it was so hot that the shingles melted in my hand. For each shingle I put on, I ruined five. I've learned to work early in the morning or late in the evening in the summer when the weather is hot.

⚘ The Tearoff

Your roofing job may begin with tearoff, removing all the old roofing material down to the decking. This isn't something you need to do unless a house already has three layers of roofing. (Two in some areas. Check your local code). If you figure that a layer of roofing lasts 20 years, the house has to be 40 to 60 years old before tearoff becomes necessary. Some cities will allow you to do what's called a one-layer tearoff. You remove just the top layer and replace it. Figure 6-1 shows a one-layer tearoff I did last summer. Removing only the top layer of shingles saves a lot of work on a roofing job, but you can't always do it. Many cities are very touchy about tearoff. They not only insist on having all the layers removed down to the decking, but may require new decking as well. This is one area where you need to check with your building department before bidding on the job.

Tearoff is an unpleasant job. You're generally looking at 6 to 8 tons of old, crumbly roofing material that has to be removed and disposed of. There's a special tool for removing old shingles called a roofer's spade. It looks like a flat shovel with a serrated edge. The edge hooks under shingles, and rips them up, nails and all. If you're lucky, you can pry up a big section of roofing all at one time. However, it still takes a long time, and a lot of muscle. Plan on about 1½ hours for every 100 square feet of roof shingles for a moderate angle roof. You'll need to increase the time if the roof is steep.

Disposal

Getting rid of all of this decayed roofing material can be a major expense. Tearoff generates a lot of trash. You'll get a cubic yard of trash from every 2½ squares (250 square feet) of shingles. And no matter how neat you try to be, it gets all over the place. It's not safe to leave lying around because it's full of nails. If someone steps on one, they'll be sure to sue you. The yard needs to be cleaned up at the end of each day. You should figure in at least four manhours for this.

You'll need a dumpster to put all this stuff in, possibly more than one. You'll also have to pay dumping fees. These vary tremendously from one part of the country to another. Some municipalities have exclusive trash hauling contracts. You may be required to use their trash haulers, no matter what the charges. Be sure to check these out completely before you submit any firm bids.

Many disreputable remodelers try to keep their costs down by using their own pickup trucks to haul old roofing material away and dump it illegally. Not only does this break the law, it also uses up a lot of time and effort. It may take dozens of trips to haul all the old roofing away. This could only be worthwhile if you work very, very cheap.

Once I tried loading all the old roof material from a house into trash bags. Since I was working on quite a small house at the time, there was less roofing material than average. However, it still took 200 trash bags! You can imagine how long it took to fill all these. I decided my time was worth more than that!

🐚 Decking

During the inspection, you should have been careful to identify areas of rot damage. Any rotted decking will have to be removed, and damaged rafters replaced or doubled. This kind of damage can be very spotty. One area may be very bad and need complete replacement, while another area may be in perfect condition.

Houses that originally had cedar shingles have a different kind of decking than modern homes. They have boards spaced 1½ to 2 inches apart, rather than placed close together to form a solid decking. I've found this type of decking in eight out of ten older homes that I've worked on. This is correct for cedar shingles, but not appropriate if you're going to put on new asphalt shingles. Asphalt shingles need a solid surface.

It's possible to fill in the spaces between the boards by nailing 1 x 2s between them, but it's tedious. Time is important when you're doing this kind of work. You need to get the new roof on before it rains. It's quicker and easier to cover the old boards with new plywood decking.

Cedar Shingles

You won't have to redo the decking if you're planning to install cedar shingles. The original decking will be fine, assuming it's still in good condition.

Personally, I don't like cedar shingles. I think they're a fire hazard. Occasionally you may come across a house with an old cedar shingle roof that has burn holes in it. When cedar shingles get old, they get very dry and just a little spark can set them on fire.

I prefer to use cedar-look shingles made of fire-resistant materials, like asphalt. If you look at them up close, they don't really look like cedar shingles. But from a distance, like the ground, they look very close to the same.

Figure 6-2
*New cedar-look asphalt shingles used
to cover old cedar shingles*

They are the same color, and have the same type of shadow pattern, created by raised layers of asphalt glued to alternating points to make the hills and valleys that cedar shingles have. Figure 6-2 shows a partially completed roof done with cedar-look asphalt shingles. You can compare them to the original cedar shingles just above. One of the advantages of these shingles is that they are ultra-heavyweight. You can install them over an uneven surface, as I did in this particular job. They bridge the gaps and create a nice finished surface. They were designed especially for this type of use.

If the homeowners want a cedar shingle roof and the local fire code allows it, you'll have to go along with it. However, you might mention that their fire insurance may be higher with cedar shingles than with asphalt. They may want to check with their insurance company before making a final decision.

🐦 Choosing a Shingle

One problem you'll commonly find with older roofs is that they're uneven or look like they're rippling. This can be caused be settling, by the warping of some of the roof materials, or by lumpy layers of roofing underneath. This problem is particularly noticeable under fiberglass shingles, which are very thin, and show every little lump.

If you're working with a roof that appears uneven, consider using ultra-heavy-weight shingles, like the cedar-look asphalt shingles. They'll smooth out the bumps and make the roof look like new. Of course, they're a lot heavier than fiberglass shingles, so they're a little more work to handle. They weigh 320 pounds per square instead of 240. Because of this, they come in four bundles to a square, instead of three. That way, each bundle weighs about the same as a bundle of regular shingles. These shingles make a nice-looking roof. Figures 6-3 and 6-4 show before and after photographs of a roof job I completed recently. You can see that the ultra-heavyweight shingles covered the uneven and broken cedar shingles completely. These shingles also come in several other textures and colors, including a slate-look style which is quite attractive.

Figure 6-3
Original cedar shingle roof

Figure 6-4
*New roof with ultra-heavyweight
asphalt shingles*

Asphalt Shingles

I prefer high-quality asphalt shingles to other roofing materials. I consider everything else to be either too expensive, too much trouble, or a fire hazard. Asphalt shingles are now made in a wide variety of colors, styles, and textures. You can get just about any kind of look you want with them.

If your customer has an unlimited budget and wants a more exotic roofing material, such as copper, slate or the new anodized steel, you can't very well say no. However, handling exotic roofing materials is a specialized skill. Since jobs like this only come up once a decade, I subcontract them out to a specialist. Often these materials are only available through manufacturer's authorized dealers anyway.

Walls

Now, let's take a look at the kind of exterior wall repairs you might need to do on an older home. Again, I'll concentrate on the special problems you're likely to run into, with the biggest problem being the siding. We'll look at ways to deal with the existing siding in this chapter. If it isn't worth repairing, we'll discuss new siding in Chapter 18. First let's see what options you have open to you.

≈ Siding

As I mentioned in the section on inspections, it's quite likely that the house has already been re-sided. If the siding is fairly recent and in good condition, you can probably just leave it.

Sometimes I run into a house that has perfectly good siding, professionally installed with acceptable materials, but it just doesn't look very nice. It's in good condition — it simply isn't attractive. When you find a situation like this, take a second look at the house as a whole. Usually the siding doesn't look right because the original features that made the house distinctive have either been removed or covered up with the new siding. What had been a nicely decorated home now looks like a plain box. This isn't a siding problem; it's a trim problem. Replacing the siding won't help; you need to replace the style. The house is supposed to have decorative trim, and it'll never look right without it. This is a fairly common situation, and one we'll discuss in detail when we get into recreating a home's original style and character later on in the book. Right now, we're going to concern ourselves with the siding that does need attention.

Most of the time the siding doesn't look good because it's inferior siding, or an old-fashioned siding that nobody uses or likes anymore. Inferior sidings are generally to blame for 80 percent of the siding problems that I've come across. The three I dislike the most are asphalt "fake brick," asbestos, and mineral siding. Of the three, the only one I consider even halfway acceptable is mineral siding. It doesn't look too bad with a fresh coat of paint over it. But, to be honest, it doesn't look too good either. So what should you do when you're faced with ugly siding? It depends on the type.

≈ Mineral Siding

When you're considering what to do about mineral siding, your first concern should be your customer's budget. Replacing mineral siding doesn't give the best "bang for the buck." New siding costs a lot of money and provides only a minor improvement in this case. What you want to do for your customer is just the opposite: provide a major improvement for a little money.

If the house is supposed to be a picture-perfect showplace and money is no object, by all means, the siding should go. But if it's a choice between the siding and some other improvement, like an extra bathroom or a kitchen upgrade, the homeowner will get a lot more value out of the other improvement.

Painting the Siding

The best compromise is to give the siding a fresh coat of paint for now, with the idea of

Figure 6-5
Painted mineral siding

the house was done, I had almost half the paint I bought left over. I didn't skimp on paint, either. The house looked fine. In fact, it still looks fine, and I painted it 10 years ago.

You can see in Figure 6-5 how nicely the paint covers mineral siding. This house was an ugly dark brown. I painted it a light green with only one coat, and the siding looked like brand new! Since this material is so easy to paint and takes so little paint to cover, why not give it a try? If there's any question in the homeowner's minds about whether to paint or replace the siding, the cost and ease of maintenance may settle the question.

Siding Repair

One thing that can complicate the job is damaged siding. Obviously, if it's heavily damaged, you won't want to bother trying to fix it. You'll have to replace it. But, if it's only slightly damaged, with just a few broken shingles, what do you do? That sounds easy enough; you replace the broken shingles, and then go ahead and paint. Unfortunately, it isn't that easy. Mineral shingles are no longer manufactured.

You may be able to scavenge some shingles from someplace, such as a house that's being torn down or re-sided. I've had to do that. Now, to save time, I've started saving my own small supply of mineral shingles. Whenever I re-side a house that has mineral shingles, I save some in case I need them for another job in the future. It's always good to have some of these obsolete or hard-to-come-by materials on hand.

Another possibility is that you may be able to move a few shingles from someplace on the house where they don't show. Be extremely careful when you remove them. They break very easily. The first time I tried to take mineral shingles off, I broke five for every one I got off intact. Don't try to pry or pull them off. And don't try to pry the nails out with the claw end of a hammer. The pressure of the hammer head will break the shingle. The only way to remove them in one piece is to use a pair of pliers and carefully pull out each nail holding them in place.

replacing it in a few years when more money is available. This is practical because mineral siding is so easy to paint. It requires very little prepping. All you have to do is just wash it down to remove the dirt or any powdery paint. You have to do this before any paint job. If you use a power washer, you can have the whole house washed down in just a few minutes. The siding won't need any scraping, caulking, or priming, although the windows and trim might.

Mineral siding takes much less time to paint than regular wood siding. The paint can be rolled on, or even sprayed (I prefer rollers). It's almost as fast as painting interior walls. You can figure on covering about 200 square feet per hour, at least for the first story. Once you get to the second story and above, you'll have to work off a ladder, which will slow you down a bit. It's still a fast job, though. It'll probably take you longer to paint the trim and windows (assuming they're wood) than it will to do all the siding.

Another interesting thing about mineral siding is that it uses very little paint. It's a nonporous material, so the paint doesn't sink in. I've found that a gallon of ordinary latex house paint goes almost twice as far on this material than it does on wood. The first time I painted a house with this type of siding, I bought the paint based on the manufacturer's recommended coverage for wood. When

Take the shingles from hard-to-see places like the edge of a porch that's covered by evergreens, or from a wall right next to a privacy fence. The back of the garage is another area that may not be readily seen, especially if it's near the rear of the property. If necessary, you can take all the mineral shingles you need off one obscure area and re-side that area with a different type of siding. It won't match, but in a location that no one will notice, it doesn't matter.

If all else fails, you can make a few fake shingles using pieces of quarter-inch exterior grade plywood. Cut them the same size and shape as the mineral shingles. Prime them carefully, and fit them into the spots where the shattered shingles were removed. Once the wall is painted, the fake shingles should blend right in.

Removing the Siding

If the homeowners want their mineral siding removed, there may still be an alternative to replacing it. You might find that you can work with the wood that's underneath. However, you won't know for sure until you remove all of the old siding. That isn't a problem. If you're going replace the siding, you'll have to remove the mineral shingles anyway. You can't side over them. If you try to drive nails through them, they'll shatter. Re-siding is a lot easier if you just tear all the old shingles off and get them out of the way.

So, once the old siding is off, check to see what's underneath before you decide to replace it. The wall underneath may be in good condition. You might decide to restore the original wood, rather than putting up new siding. This is especially true if the original walls were an especially beautiful or unique wood. Strangely enough, it's not uncommon to find beautiful, decorative walls in good condition covered with terrible siding. Siding was often added primarily to "modernize" a house, to cover up the out-dated style or decorations — detail that today would be highly prized and cost a fortune to duplicate. If you discover this type of decorative detail beneath old siding, it would be a shame to cover it up with a new layer of siding.

Fortunately, mineral siding is quite easy to get off. You don't have to be careful how you remove the shingles if you don't want to save them. You can just grab the shingles and pull. They'll break off in your hand. Any difficult pieces can be tapped with a hammer; they'll shatter, leaving nothing behind but the nails. You may find tar paper underneath the shingles. It just tears right off. The only thing that takes any time is pulling all the nails out. You can easily clear off about 200 square feet of shingles in an hour.

&. Asphalt "Fake Brick" Siding

Your choices of what to do to improve asphalt siding are limited: you can remove it or side over it. Painting is not an option and neither is leaving it — it just looks awful.

Asphalt siding is the same material as roof shingles. It's easy to drive a nail through, so siding over it is no problem. You can install new siding just as you would over a plain wood wall, except you'll need to use longer nails.

I can never bring myself to just side over it, however, because I have to know what's under it. What if there's something really wonderful under there? If you side over it, you'll never know! Unless I know for sure that the wood underneath can't be salvaged, I just have to take the old siding down. I know of one remodeler who found a whole set of perfectly-preserved turn-of-the-century circus posters attached to the original siding. They were collectors' items, and worth a great deal of money.

You probably won't find circus posters, but you may find ornamental woodwork, or interesting sidings. It was common on Victorian homes to use several different kinds of siding on one wall to make interesting patterns, like the varied sidings shown in Figure 6-6. You rarely see this kind of detail put into houses today. If you do, it's certainly worth preserving. More often than not, however, you'll just find a plain old clapboard wall, usually in poor condition. So what if you don't discover buried treasure? You won't have lost much by taking the siding off. You

Figure 6-6
*Several types of sidings used to make
an interesting pattern*

don't necessarily have to clear all the walls. If the first wall looks unpromising, just quit there.

This kind of siding is very easy to remove. Just grab a corner, and pull. Huge chunks will tear off in your hands. The claw end of a hammer or crowbar are both good tools for getting this stuff off. It'll tear right through it, and allow you to pull off good size pieces. As with mineral siding, the shingles come off and leave the nails behind. Pulling these out is the most time-consuming part. However, you can still remove 300 to 400 square feet an hour, with no problems.

As you can see, it only takes about an hour to clear a wall. That's why you won't lose much time if you decide to clear one wall to check what's underneath. At worst, you've wasted an hour of work. At best, you may find that you can use the original siding, or better yet, you may discover something really worth preserving! These little discoveries are what makes remodeling older homes fun.

Asbestos Siding

When you find you're dealing with asbestos siding, you again have two choices. You can paint it, or side over it. Removing it isn't a good idea because of possible asbestos contamination.

Generally, I prefer to side over asbestos siding. It's easy to paint, much like mineral siding, but it never looks as good. Homeowners aren't always happy with the way it turns out. Usually they'll still want new siding as soon as their budget will allow for it. Of course, if they can't afford new siding now, painting is the next best choice.

Asbestos siding is easy to side over. It's soft and nails go through it easily. However, it has no holding power. You'll need to use a nail long enough to go clear through the siding and grip the wood underneath.

Wood Siding

If you've removed one of the sidings we just discussed, you'll probably put up wood siding. But more likely, the home was finished with wood siding in the first place. You might find some that's in good shape, or it may have been replaced with new wood at some time. But in most cases the original wood siding (or perhaps even the replacement wood siding) will need some work.

Now is the time to repair any rot or insect damage you discovered during the inspection. Damaged clapboards should be pried loose, and new ones fitted on. Clapboard design, such as that shown in Figure 6-7, hasn't changed much over the years. You can probably get some almost exactly the same as the original. If there are tiny differences, they won't be noticed.

Cedar shingles are also about the same as they were years ago. You should be able to buy new ones similar to the ones on the house. Cedar is supposed to be rot-resistant, but even cedar rots if it stays wet long enough. Any rotted shingles should be replaced.

Shiplap, or other less common types of siding, can be more of a problem. Again, you don't need a perfect match. As long as it's close, no one will notice. People don't expect older homes to be absolutely perfect. If you can't find anything close to the same, you can always take some from an out-of-the-way area on the house or garage and use it to repair visible sections. Or you can try to make some pieces of similar siding. Most likely you'll be dealing with 1 x 4s that have edges cut into them. With a router you can come up with something pretty close. However, this is practical only if you need just a few pieces. If you have extensive damage to a wall with unusual siding, you're better off replacing all the siding so you can keep the exterior look uniform.

Exterior Painting

Once you've made your repairs, you'll need to paint the wood siding. A lot of people take painting for granted. They think it's an easy job that anybody can do, with or without experience. Not true — not if you want quality work! Sure, you can just slap the paint on; but it won't look good and it won't last. That's the kind of work that a "fly-by-night" remodeler would do. They're not worried about how it's going to hold up. By the time the homeowner complains, they've either left town or gone out of business. If you intend to stay in business, you need to do quality work. A good businessperson can count on the repeat customers and referrals that quality work ensures, especially in slow times. Since painting is one of the jobs you'll be doing most often in this line of work, it's important that you do it right.

Figure 6-7
Old clapboard siding

🌿 Preparation

Painting an old house isn't an easy job. It usually takes a lot of prepping to remove peeling paint and repair weathered and cracked wood surfaces.

First of all, the wood needs to be carefully scraped and any loose paint removed. Your choice of scraper makes a difference. You can use a flat scraper, like a putty knife, or a curved one, like a Red Devil. I've found that the Red Devil seems to grip better, and pull off more flakes. I've also had good results with the Wagner Power Scraper. It has a curved blade, like a Red Devil, but it vibrates up and down at high speed, knocking the paint chips loose with less effort. The only drawback is that you need to plug it in, which can be inconvenient when you're working in a hard-to-reach area.

Usually a scraper won't remove all the paint. You'll find that in some areas, the paint adheres so tightly to the wood that you can't scrape it off. You can generally paint right over these areas. If the paint bond is that good, it'll probably be okay under a new coat of paint. But you may not want to leave it that way. Painting over patches of existing

Figure 6-8
Remove old paint with a heat gun

paint may create a rough, uneven texture. On some parts of the house, it may not show. However, in highly-visible areas, imperfection in the paint can ruin the whole look of the house.

You need as smooth and perfect a surface as possible on and around the front door, and on the front porch and entrance trim or decor pieces. This also applies to pillars, door frames, edge trim, wooden ornaments, and anything else that's highly visible as you enter the house. Remember, the front porch, entranceway, and front door are the first things visitors will see. They're right at eye level. They need to be as perfect as possible. A bumpy paint job here will create an overall bad impression.

On the other hand, there are many areas of the house that can't be seen up close. The eaves and fascia boards, for example, are too far up for really close inspection. Unless you're on a ladder, you'll probably will be at least 10 feet away from them. You can't see little flaws from that distance.

Paint Removal

For areas where you need a perfect surface, there are a number of ways to clean off those last little bits of paint. The most common are chemical paint removers, sanding, and heat.

There are two general classes of chemical paint removers. The first group are the fine, furniture-quality removers, like acetone, used for stripping furniture and interior trim. Stripping down a house with one of these paint removers would take a year. They're much too slow for exterior work. We'll discuss these when we get into the interior work.

The other type of chemical removers are harsh jellies designed to quickly remove large quantities of exterior paint. I don't like these jelly-type paint removers. First of all, they're caustic. If you get any on you, they'll burn your skin. Second, they generate nasty fumes that burn your nostrils. Third, even though they work faster than the interior removers, they're still too slow to work with. You have to paint them on, wait for them to work, and then scrape off the dissolved paint a few inches at a time. But the main reason I don't like them is that they simply don't do a good job. They always leave a little residual paint behind. You have to go over them twice, which takes twice as long, and then they often dissolve the top layer of wood. When you're finished, the wood ends up in worse condition than it was before.

There are some new types of jelly paint removers that are non-caustic, release no fumes, and clean up with water. These are an improvement, but I still don't like them. They just don't do an efficient job.

Sanding is another alternative. It works fine and leaves a nice surface, but it's far too slow unless you're only doing a very small area.

I prefer using a heat gun to remove paint. A heat gun looks like a hand-held electric hair dryer, but it's much hotter. (Don't dry your hair with it!) The heat softens the paint, allowing you to scrape it off. It only heats a few inches at a time, so it's still slow. But if you have more than one small area to clean off, it's the only practical way to get a really perfect surface. I used a heat gun to remove the alligatored old paint on the siding shown in Figure 6-8. It took me about an hour to do 10 square feet of surface. It takes longer if you're working on fancy moldings, or the detailed convoluted surfaces that you find on Victorian spindles, turnings and gingerbread. You only want to use a heat gun for very visible areas, like the front entrance to the house. It would take months to do the entire house that way.

You can also use a propane torch to soften paint, though I prefer a heat gun. A heat gun doesn't get hot enough to scorch wood, but a propane torch does. If you're not careful, a propane torch will leave burn marks. But even a heat gun can get hot enough to scorch you. Always work carefully. It's a good idea to wear gloves.

੨ Primers

If the wood is very weathered (which it probably will be), you won't get sufficient coverage from any standard house paint with just one coat. You'll get better results by first using a quality primer. The primer will seal and protect the wood, and provide a good surface for the finish paint coat.

Some people don't want to bother with a primer. They think it's too much trouble and expense. If the wood you're covering is in perfect condition, you might be able to get away with not using a primer. However, on an older house, the wood is most likely far from perfect. Weathered wood is so absorbent that paint just soaks into it, leaving it looking as though it's only half-painted. The only solution is to apply another coat of paint. If you have to put on two coats of paint, you've lost any savings in time and materials that you might have had by skipping the primer. In fact, it will cost you more. Primers not only give you better results, but they're cheaper than paint.

Some primers, like Kilz, are especially formulated to cover problem areas. They even cover knot holes, which tend to bleed through regular paints. I've had knotholes bleed through several coats of ordinary paints, but nothings bleeds through Kilz.

੨ Testing Paints and Primers

If you're not sure what you'll need, try a little experiment. Often, before I launch into a big painting job, I test the paint on a small area of the surface in an out-of-the-way spot. I try several paints and primers in different combinations to see what works best on that particular wood. I might try latex and oil or alkyd-based house paints, with and without primer, in one or two coats, on a few square feet for each combination. I leave them for a few days and then check to see how they look. The differences are often dramatic. Very often four out of five test areas look terrible, and one looks great. I'm often surprised. What would have been my first choice may look the worst. The paint or paint combinations I finally choose are sometimes the ones I didn't think would work, but just included for comparison. Sometimes none of them look good, and I have to start over with different paints.

Why don't some paints look good? Generally, it's because of poor coverage. A cheap, thin paint just doesn't have enough substance to fill in all the little cracks and pores in the wood and provide a smooth, nice surface. After three or four coats it would probably look okay, but then you've used up a lot of paint. Any price advantage you may have gotten with the cheap paint will be lost. It can easily cost you more to use cheap paint than a good brand. Remember, time is also money. Do you really want to paint the same house three or four times? Isn't it better to do it right the first time?

What do I mean by "cheap" paint? Generally, an off-brand that you've never heard of, or the discount store house brands. They are frequently priced temptingly low. I've seen them for as little as a dollar a gallon. This is because there's actually only one dollar's worth of paint in the can — the rest is water. You're not really getting a deal at all. Compare test areas of the cheap paint versus the good stuff. You'll see the difference instantly.

What do I recommend? I use a lot of Sears brand paints, and I've always had good luck with them. I've also had good results with Dutch Boy and Sherwin-Williams. Glidden is okay for interiors, but I don't like their exterior paint. It doesn't cover well with one coat. I've noticed that quality varies a little on many brands. Even at Sears, you can see quite a range of quality. There's a big difference, for example, between Sears "Good" and Sears "Best." Sears "Best" covers a lot better. I only use Sears "Good" for less-demanding jobs, like utility buildings. Try several brands to see which you like the best. I also like Sears because they give you a Paint Contractor's Discount Card. The discount brings the regular price on paint down to about the same as the sale price.

Paint tests not only help you decide which paints look best, but they also help homeowners see clearly that one paint will work better than another. Sometimes the only way to convince them is to let them see it for themselves.

My biggest reason for suggesting that you test your paints is because every house is different. After years of working with paints, I can't be sure which will work. I always use my favorite paints when I can. But what worked on the last house may not work well on the next. The wood may be different, its condition may be different, or the conditions in and around the property may be different. The only way you can really tell is to test it out.

It may seem like a lot of trouble, but if you're working on a big job, you'll be spending hundreds, maybe thousands of dollars on paint. You also may be investing hundreds of hours of work. If you use the wrong paint, it can all be wasted. It's worth the time it takes to make sure that the job comes out right.

🐟 Spray Painting

People are always suggesting that you spray-paint houses. Paint sprayers seem to be all the rage right now. I know some remodelers who just love them. They'll spray anything. Personally, I don't like paint sprayers at all. I never use them. I'll tell you why.

First of all, they don't save as much time as you might think. Most of the time you spend on painting a house is in the prepping, not the painting. Brushing the paint on doesn't really take that much time. You still have to prep a house, even if you spray the paint. In fact, spraying actually requires more prepping because you have to mask off all the areas that you don't want painted, like windows, trim, or brickwork. That's tedious work, but it has to be done. I've seen jobs where the painters didn't bother masking anything; they just painted the windows, the chimney, the shrubs — even the grass! You can imagine how it looked. It didn't look like much of an improvement to me.

Second, paint sprayers do a lousy job. Sprayers can't handle thick paints. You either have to use a light, enamel-type paint, or thin down a regular house paint. Light enamels are totally inappropriate for weathered wood. They don't have enough substance to penetrate into the pores of the wood and seal it. You'd need to apply 20 coats before you got enough paint on to provide adequate protection from the weather.

Thinning regular house paint doesn't accomplish much either. Remember, the thinner the paint, the more coats you need. There goes your time savings. Also, most modern house paints have a warning on them in big letters: DO NOT THIN! That's because these paints are a scientifically-formulated balance of pigments, binders, and thinners. The combination of ingredients has been carefully worked out for optimum performance. If you thin the paint, you change the formula and completely void any guarantees the paint might have.

I've examined a number of wooden houses that have been painted with a sprayer. The results were generally bad, reflecting poorly on the quality of painters and their workmanship. In each case, the coverage was terrible, with bare wood showing through at points, and none of the homes had been adequately masked. They certainly weren't very professional-looking paint jobs. If I had been one of those homeowners, I'd have refused to pay for the work.

One reason you see so many jobs like that is because painting can be done without a building permit. It's one of the few jobs that can. As a result, paint jobs never have to pass a city inspection or come up to a minimum standard. That's lucky for some of the painters out there, because very few spray jobs would pass.

I was involved in one case that did require an inspection. A homeowner had a house that was up for sale. He had a buyer lined up for it, but the buyer wanted to buy via FHA mortgage. In order to sell a house FHA, you need to have it inspected by a government inspector. The inspector determined that the house needed to be painted before he would okay the loan, and the loan had to be okayed prior to the close of the sale.

Since the homeowner had a buyer, he opted for the quickest, cheapest job he could find. He had it sprayed. It wasn't the worst job I'd ever seen, but it wasn't good either. Going for the cheap job really cost him! The FHA rejected the paint job. It wasn't up to their standards. The homeowner was advised that the house would have to be painted again. He refused, and lost the deal. The cheap paint job actually took away from the value of the house, rather than adding to it. I came along a short time later and was able to buy the house at quite a savings. I painted it myself, and turned it over for a nice profit.

Good Uses for Sprayers

Actually, paint sprayers work fine for almost anything except wood. Remember mineral siding? Sprayers are fine for painting them. Mineral siding is nonporous. It only takes a light coat of paint to cover it.

Sprayers are also fine for metal, brick (if you want painted brick), stucco, or cement block. None of these surfaces need protection from the weather. You just paint them for a certain look; they don't need a heavy coat for coverage. Spraying is actually the best way to go when painting aluminum siding too. You can get a nice, smooth finish with no brush marks, almost like the finish on a car, if you know how to handle a sprayer. Because aluminum is totally nonporous, you have to be very careful not to spray too much paint on one area. If you do, you'll end up with drip marks. It takes a little practice to get it right.

Sprayers are also a good choice for applying clear wood preservatives, or other light oils or stains. These coatings are normally quite thin. They'll spray well without further thinning. If you want to put a coat of clear

Figure 6-9
*Solid-colored stain used
on weathered wood*

wood preservative on a privacy fence, a sprayer can save you a lot of time. The fence probably won't need any prepping (unless it was painted before), and most fences don't have brickwork or trim to be masked off. Wood preservative penetrates well. As long as you spray plenty on, you'll get good coverage and protection.

Stains

In some cases, you may prefer to use an exterior stain on the house instead of paint. I used to think that stains were only suitable for rustic-style new construction, but that's no longer true. There's quite a large selection of solid color stains that look and cover very much like a thick paint. I've recently begun using these on heavily weathered wood, and I've had very good results. Their coverage is excellent. They cover, provide a good seal, and protect weathered wood — all in one coat.

I used a solid-colored stain on the barn in Figure 6-9. One coat gave very good coverage on this difficult surface. Solid-colored stains are the only coating I've found so far that will do this. None of the house paints I've tried have covered as well. Stains are also supposed to resist peeling. According to the manufacturer, they will eventually weather away, but they'll never peel. I haven't been using them long enough to make this promise myself. But so far, everything I've used an all-weather stain on still looks good. I intend to keep an eye on them over the next several years to see how long they hold up.

Weathered Wood Siding

A few years ago, the "weathered wood" look was popular. This look was accomplished by putting up raw wood siding, and leaving it uncoated so that it would weather to a mellow gray color. Uncoated cedar shingles were especially popular for this style. This look can be found on everything from 100-year-old shingled Victorians to brand new construction.

The problem with the weathered look is that the wood rarely weathers evenly. The more exposed areas usually end up with the desired color, but protected areas, such as under the eaves, often remain unweathered and retain their original wood tone. A house with varying weather exposure can end up with every possible variation of wood tone between brand new and weathered gray. That usually isn't the look homeowners had in mind, and they're not likely to be very happy with the result. I've seen some cases where the homeowners were so upset that they had the house completely re-sided.

While re-siding is certainly an option, it isn't the only alternative. A coat of gray stain can often create the mellow gray tone that the homeowner had in mind in the first place. This is a possibility that's worth discussing with the homeowner, especially if the wood siding is in perfect condition. It seems a shame to tear it all off just because it's the wrong color.

Some homeowners prefer the original warm wood tones and don't like the look of the wood as it weathers. Rather than staining the siding, they may want to restore it. There are several products available on the market to clean and protect unpainted exterior wood surfaces. Generally these fall into two categories: protectants and cleaners. Protectants can be used on wood that's in good shape to preserve it and maintain the wood tones. A protectant won't brighten discolored wood, it will only stabilize it. If you put it on discolored wood, the wood won't get any worse, but it won't get any better either. It should be applied every year or so, since it will be worn away by severe weather.

If the wood is damaged or discolored, it needs to be cleaned first. Cleaners can restore and brighten damaged wood, if it isn't too badly weathered. Once the color is restored, then you need to put on a protectant to keep it that way.

I use Dekswood Exterior Wood Cleaner and Brightener, from The Flood Company, to restore weathered wood. They also make deck preservatives, and other exterior clear wood coatings. You can call them for information and a free Wood Care Guide at 1-800-321-3444.

❧ Other Wood Surfaces

Many homes have unpainted exterior wood surfaces, such as decks and wood privacy fences, that also need care. These wood structures are usually made of rot-resistant cedar, redwood, or pressure-treated pine. Lumber yards are full of promotional brochures for these materials which say that you can leave them out in the weather for 40 years with no preservative coatings of any kind. Maybe you can, but that doesn't mean you should. While these woods may not actually rot away without preservatives, they'll still decay. Within a few years, the surface will get cracked, checkered, dry-looking, and dull.

Homeowners are often upset with the weathered look of their decks and fences. They may not mention it, however, because they don't realize that anything can be done about it. If you're working on a house with a weathered-looking deck, ask the homeowners if they'd like it brightened up. You're likely to see the homeowners brighten up as well! A wood cleaner will bring back most of the original wood tones, and a preservative will keep the wood looking good. Remind the owners that the wood should be recoated every year or so to keep it looking nice. It will not only please them to have a nice-looking wood again, it may provide you with steady annual work. I think these wood preservatives are well worth the effort and cost. I never leave any kind of wood, even pressure-treated pine, out in the weather without some kind of preservative coating.

When you're working on a restored older home, keep in mind that unpainted wood usually doesn't fit with the original style. Pressure-treated lumber didn't exist in the old days. Therefore, any pressure-treated decks or fences added to an older house are obviously not original and can clash with the style of the house. There's a simple solution to this problem: paint them. Just because you don't *have* to paint them, that doesn't mean you *shouldn't* paint them. Not only will paint help preserve the wood, it will make the additions blend better with the rest of the house. Pressure-treated wood should be primed before you paint to keep the chemicals from bleeding through the paint. A primer, such as Kilz, that's designed to prevent bleed-through will give you a good base for your paint.

Window and Door Repair

Window and door repair is a subject that you won't find much information on. Most contractors prefer to replace these items rather than spend time trying to make repairs. That's okay if remodeling fairly modern homes is your main business, but often won't work with older homes. Modern windows and doors don't always match the design and character of an older house, and ordering custom replacements is very expensive. This chapter provides you with information that will give you the option to repair some of these classic older windows and doors that you may find hard to replace.

Windows

The windows in older homes usually need a lot of attention. This is especially true if they've been without storm windows for any extended period. The window shown in Figure 7-1 was badly weather damaged because it wasn't protected by a storm window. The sash joints were weakened and needed to be reinforced; the glazing putty needed to be replaced; the swollen, rough wood had to be sanded smooth so that the

window would open and close without sticking; and it had to be painted. Most of this work could have been avoided if it had been covered during the winter months. Windows without storms suffer weather damage a lot faster. That's one of the reasons storm windows were invented in the first place.

Storms and Screens

During your inspection, you should have noted whether the house had storm and screen windows, and if so, their condition. If not, they probably had them at one time. Houses built after 1920 would have had them, and those built before that time most likely had them added them later. The original types were a wood-framed screen for the summer, like the ones shown in Figure 7-2, and a separate framed window unit for winter. Every spring the ritual of taking down the storm windows and putting up the screens would take place. The process was reversed in the fall, when the screens came down and storms went up. This was a lot of work, compounded by the problem of storing the out-of-season windows or screens.

I've found these types of storm windows and screens in many older homes. Sometimes

Figure 7-1
Weather-damaged window

Figure 7-2
*Porch has original storm and
screen windows*

they're in perfect condition. I think that's because they were so much trouble to put up and take down that nobody bothered. They just sat in a stack in the garage for 70 years. Unless a homeowner insists on total historical authenticity, they're not going to want to use this kind of screen and storm window today. They'll want the modern, self-storing type that just slide up and down.

Storm-and-screen assemblies are slowly being edged out of the housing market by the more modern thermopane replacement windows that have built-in screens. These don't require storm-and-screen assemblies. This type of window is being used in almost all new construction. And, as windows in older homes are replaced, eventually the storm-and-screen assemblies will disappear. However, this won't happen overnight. It will take quite a few years. There are still many homeowners who are unwilling to replace their older windows. If they intend to keep their existing windows, good storm-and-screen assemblies remain a must.

Before you decide whether to repair or replace existing storm-and-screen assemblies,

check the underlying window. Does it need replacing? If so, you may as well buy a thermopane replacement window with a built-in screen, and not worry about the storms or screens.

Old Storms and Screens

Very often I find three or four different kinds of storm and screen windows on the same house. The homeowners apparently replaced them only when it was absolutely necessary, and then only those that *had* to be replaced. They replaced one here and one there over the years, so that in many cases, not only are the original storm and screen windows in poor condition, but some of the replacements need replacing as well.

Self-storing storm-and-screen windows were first used in the 1940s. Many of these were made of galvanized steel. They probably lasted a long time, but now most of the ones still in use are badly rusted, and won't slide up and down. In the 1950s, aluminum storms and screens became popular. Over time, aluminum becomes oxidized and pitted, so most of these are no longer working well either. Another common problem you'll run across is that the rubber stripping holding the glass in the frame has rotted, and the glass has either fallen out or is just about to fall out. And, of course, broken window glass and torn screens are constant problems.

One of the houses I bought a few years ago had no storms or screens on any of the windows. In the garage, however, I found modern, self-storing storm-and-screen assemblies to fit every window of the house. They were in perfect condition, except that the glass in every single one was broken. I couldn't figure out how this could have happened, until I talked to a man I knew who had worked on the house before I owned it. He told me that the former owners had taken all the storm-and-screen assemblies down in order to paint the windows, and had stacked them neatly in the back yard. The temptation was just too much for one of the neighborhood kids, who discovered that he could break all of the windows at the same time with one big rock. The owners couldn't deal with this. They just put the broken windows in the garage and left them. You'll find situations like this are not uncommon when you're working on older homes.

Repair or Replace? — I've found that it doesn't pay to put much effort into repairing old storm-and-screen assemblies. If they need a lot of work, it's cheaper to replace them. New storm-and-screen assemblies usually cost from $30 to $50, depending on size and quality, although you can spend a lot more if you want the best.

Old storm-and-screen assemblies tend to be troublesome: They don't slide up and down smoothly; they won't stay in place when you slide them up, or lock-in positively when you slide them down; the glass tends to be loose in the windows; the screens generally have tears; the frames are pitted or rusted; and the plastic snap-in pins that hold the windows in place are frequently broken off.

However, most of these problems can be repaired. Hardware stores carry rubber stripping and a selection of plastic window pins.

You can buy screening by the roll, and glass can be cut to size. Be careful, though. By the time you add up the cost of replacing all these items, you can easily spend more than the $30 it would cost you to replace the whole assembly. You should also take into consideration the value of your time and labor. Even if you can replace all the parts for under $30, you'll still have a pitted, balky window that won't slide smoothly. If it were your own home you might polish off all the little pits, but when you're working for someone else, that would be too time-consuming to be cost effective.

If the window has only one minor problem, a torn screen, for example, and is otherwise in pretty good shape, it pays to repair it. Screening is cheap and easy to replace. The same is true of replacing a single broken window, or a few missing pins. However, if it has several things wrong with it, it's not going to be worth your time.

Remember that big storm-and-screen assemblies cost more than little ones. My $30 to $50 estimate is for an average-sized window. Storm-and-screen assemblies for oversized windows can easily cost $100 or more. I put a lot more effort into repairing large storm-and-screen assemblies than small ones.

❧ Window Repair

As I said before, most remodelers don't bother trying to repair damaged windows. They just replace anything substandard. Some replace anything, whether it's substandard or not. There's a lot of money to be made in window replacement. As far as these guys are concerned, all windows need replacing, even if they're in perfect condition.

Why bother repairing windows at all? There are a number of reasons. First of all, unlike storm-and-screen assemblies, windows can be quite expensive. You can easily pay $200 for a nice-quality replacement window. It makes a lot more sense to spend $30 to $50 repairing a $200 window than it does to spend $30 repairing a $30 storm-and-screen assembly.

Figure 7-3
Fancy Victorian windows should be saved

Secondly, many old windows are really very beautiful. They may have leaded glass or elaborate woodwork like ones shown in Figure 7-3. It isn't reasonable to compare the value of windows like these to $100 or $200

Figure 7-4
These windows are historically accurate

off-the-shelf standard-grade replacement windows. Today, you can't even buy windows like these. They have to be custom-made, and that can cost thousands, rather than hundreds, of dollars. It's certainly worth putting some time, money and effort into repairing fine-quality windows.

Finally, original windows are historically accurate. They're made of good quality wood, have genuine divided lights, and use the original hanging systems. Figure 7-4 shows some unusual historic windows. If you replaced these with modern vinyl windows, the house wouldn't look right. For a job like this, you have to get custom-made, historically-accurate reproductions which could cost thousands of dollars. It's a lot cheaper to save the original windows whenever possible.

Evaluating the Window

In order to decide whether any particular window is worth saving, you'll need to look at how difficult it will be to repair, and whether the quality of the window justifies the time and labor involved in making the repairs.

First of all, what is the overall condition of the window? Certain defects are common to almost all older windows. The glazing putty on old windows usually needs to be replaced; cracked panes need to be replaced; corners may be weakened and need repair; minor rot damage to the top and/or bottom edges of the sashes need repair; and many layers of paint may have to be sanded off the wood so that the window can open and close properly. These are relatively minor repairs, and certainly worth doing if they're the only problems.

In some cases, however, you'll find more extensive damage. The wood parts of the sashes may be completely rotted through. If you try to open the window, it might come apart in your hands. The sill or frame may be rotted, with rot possibly extending into the wall below. A window like this can't exactly be repaired, but it can be rebuilt. This is a little more difficult, and requires more evaluation.

Figure 7-5
Fine quality oak windows

Fine Quality Windows — Now you have to consider the overall value of the window. Even in the old days, there were quality windows and cheap windows. Quality windows had heavier frames made of better wood. They had more detail work, like divided lights, leaded glass, or carvings. They also used better hanging systems, such as counterweights. Figure 7-5 shows the kind of quality windows that I always try to preserve. They are counterweighted windows with heavy oak frames and divided lights that add detail and interest to the room. It would be a shame to replace windows like these with modern ones.

What kind of materials were used on the window you're evaluating? Is it made of the finest materials, with leaded glass and elaborate woodwork? How does the window fit in with the rest of the house? Will a replacement window look out of place? Is the window one of a set? You can't very well have three leaded-glass windows in a row, and then one vinyl one. If it's part of a set, they all need to match. If you can't repair the one that's damaged, you will have to replace all of them. A quality window is always worth repairing, or even rebuilding, if necessary. On the other hand, if it's a cheap window, even if it's very old, it may not be worth putting a lot of effort into.

Lesser Quality Windows — How can you tell if it's of a lesser quality? The cheaper windows had flimsy frames made of less expensive wood, like cheap pine. They usually had one or two large panes of glass, rather than many divided lights. They also used cheaper hanging systems, such as spring pins. Spring pins are little pins located on one side of the window frame. You have to pull them in to open the window. When the window is opened to the desired height, you let go of the pin and it snaps into a hole in the window frame, holding the window open. Spring pins don't work well. They slip, jam, and balk. They were never used in good-quality windows. If it's a spring-pin window, in anything less than perfect condition, you're better off replacing it.

To make your final decision on whether to replace a window, add up all the costs of repairs and compare them to the benefits. Don't forget to include the storm-and-screen assemblies, if they're needed. An average cost could be $30 to $50 for a new storm-and-screen assembly, and probably about $50 to repair the window. That's $80 to $100. Is the window worth $100? If it's a beat-up poor quality window, it's not. Replace it.

Common Repairs

I've done a lot of reading about remodeling, but none of the books I've read has covered the subject of window repair. Everyone seems to think old windows should just be replaced. I don't agree. Therefore, I'm going to devote a lot of space here to covering the subject of repairing old windows. I'm doing this partly because I like old windows, and partly because it's a subject nobody else seems to care about.

Let's assume that a particular window is worth saving, either because it's especially beautiful or high quality, or because you can't match it. What repairs are you going to need to do?

Replacing Glazing Putty

Almost certainly you'll need to replace the glazing putty. Reputtying windows is a standard, bread-and-butter job for most remodelers. However, if you work mostly

Figure 7-6
Multi-paned windows

with newer construction, you may not be familiar with how it's done.

If you look at an older window, you'll notice that the glass is held in by a lip of wood on the inside, and glazing putty on the outside. Sometimes the putty has so many coats of paint on it that it's impossible to tell what it is. Glazing putty doesn't last forever, but it can last 40 or 50 years if it's properly protected with a storm window. Without protection from severe weather, it'll only last 5 or 10 years. In any case, if you're working on an older home, the glazing putty will probably need replacing. If you look closely, you may see cracks in it, or chunks missing, or the putty may be missing altogether, leaving the glass loose in the window frame. If you don't reputty it, the glass will fall right out. If the window pane is cracked and needs to be replaced, you'll always have to reputty. The old putty has to be removed in order to get the broken glass out.

Choose a good-quality glazing putty. It makes a big difference in the application. I strongly recommend Borden's Glaze-Tuff. It's smooth, creamy, and easy to work with. Most of the others I've tried are too hard to spread.

You can apply glazing putty with a putty knife (or even a butter knife), but I suggest buying a special glazing putty tool. Red Devil makes a good one, and you can find it in most hardware stores for about $5. It will

save you enough time to pay for itself on the first job.

The hardest thing about reputtying a window is getting all the old glazing putty off. Ninety percent of it will crumble off right away, but the last little bit won't come off no matter what you do. I've only found one solution for this. When I get a little bit that absolutely refuses to come off, I just take my pocket knife and cut under it and shave off a little sliver of wood, putty and all.

It usually takes about 15 minutes to reputty one pane of glass. And for some odd reason, it takes just about as long to do a small pane as a large one. So if you're working on a house with colonial-style windows that have many small panes of glass, you can expect to spend a long time reputtying. For example, the windows in Figure 7-6 each had eight panes of glass. It took me two hours to reputty each window, and there were a lot of windows on that porch! I wouldn't have believed how much time that job took, if I hadn't timed it myself. It's one of those jobs that just refuses to get done! There isn't much to it, but it just drags on and on and on. Be sure to figure all this time in when you write up your estimate.

Replacing Glass Panes

If you need to replace any cracked or broken panes of glass, take the window out of its frame and lay it down flat on a newspaper to work on it. That way you can break the old glass out into the newspaper. When you're done, just fold up the newspaper, broken glass and all, and throw it away. This prevents broken glass from getting all over the place.

Measure for replacement glass carefully. Be sure to measure all the way to the end of the glass, under the glazing putty. If you're not thinking, you'll measure to where the glass appears to end, at the glazing putty, instead of under it. If you do that, your new glass pane will be a quarter-inch too small. This is a common mistake. It's also a good idea to double-check the measurements of your new replacement glass before you leave the hardware store. They sometimes cut it wrong. If you wait until you're back on the job, you'll have to make another trip to the hardware store. Double-checking can save you a lot of wasted time.

Some remodelers cut their own glass. This seemed like a good idea to me, since I always have a lot of extra panes of glass lying around that don't fit anything any more. Unfortunately, I just don't have good luck with cutting glass. Half the time I break the glass; and the rest of the time I wind up with a jagged cut that's hard to work with. I've been told that this is because glass gets hard and brittle and difficult to work with as it gets old. I'm convinced! One thing is for sure; trying to cut my own glass isn't worth my time. I just buy it cut to size.

Sash Repair

The sash frames (the wood part that goes around the glass) of older windows are often in need of repair. Opening and closing them all the time can work the joints loose. The joints are also common areas for rot damage.

The easiest way to strengthen loose corners is to apply glue to the corner joints, and then screw steel reinforcement angle braces over them. Figure 7-7 shows this type of repair on the weather-damaged window from Figure 7-1. Once the window was painted the braces were hardly noticeable. Also, the new storm-and-screen assembly I installed covered that part of the window sash.

Some sashes may be swollen due to years of exposure, and now stick in the window frame, preventing the window from opening.

Figure 7-7
Steel angle brace used to reinforce sash

You can sand them down to operate smoothly again. Other sashes may have shrunk, causing them to rattle around in the frame. The best way to deal with this it to glue a thin strip of wood to one side of the sash. This increases the size of the window so that it fits in the frame properly. The wood strip won't show. It should be thin enough so that it isn't visible around the stops.

Rebuilding the Sash Frame — If the window is badly rotted, you may need to rebuild the sash frame. This isn't worth doing unless the window is especially beautiful, or part of a set. In many cases, only one side of the sash frame may be rotted, commonly the bottom edge. Water often pools around the window sill and sits there. After a while, it will rot away the bottom of the sash. If you're lucky, you'll only have to replace one piece. However, if the rot extends up the sides, you may have to replace the whole frame.

People don't often think of repairing rotted windows. They're so used to just replacing damaged windows that it doesn't even occur to them that the window can be rebuilt. It's really no different from any other carpentry job. It just needs to be done carefully.

If you examine a window sash frame closely, you'll see that there's really nothing mysterious or complicated about it. It's nothing more than four pieces of wood with dovetailed corner joints, and a little lip routed out to hold the glass. If you have a wood shop, you can easily copy one. If you don't have a wood shop, you can copy it anyway. In fact, even if you're a lousy carpenter, you can still put together something that will work fine and look good. I'll tell you how.

Pick a piece of standard-sized wood that's close to the size of the frame. You may not be able to find anything that's exactly right, since old windows are sometimes odd sizes. If all else fails, start with something that's too big, like a 2 x 4, and cut it down to roughly the right size.

You'll notice that the original sash piece had a square groove on one side. This is the lip that the glass sets into. On the other side

Figure 7-8
Victorian home with stained glass windows

of that lip there's usually a scalloped edge. This is decoration. You'll need to take a router with a square bit and cut a lip into the piece of wood for the glass. It would be nice if you could create a decorative edge on the other side to copy the original scalloping. You may not be able to copy it exactly, but anything close will do. If you have a problem doing this, the decorative edge can be omitted. The window will work anyway.

If you don't have a router, there's another way to do this. Buy a piece of very small quarter-round molding. The quarter-inch size is good for this. Put a layer of carpenter's glue along one of the flat edges, and lay it on top of your piece of wood, spaced back from the edge about a quarter-inch. Nail it on with brads to hold it until the glue dries. This gives you the same effect as routing out a square groove. You have a lip where the glass can go. If you're lucky, you might even be able to find a piece of quarter-round molding with a scalloped edge on one side. Once this is in place, it'll give you a very believable copy of the original sash frame.

If you have a wood shop, you can make dovetail joints for the new sash pieces. If you don't, any strong joint will work. You can even butt them together, as long as you use both glue and screws to hold them. If in doubt, add steel reinforcement corner braces, like the one shown in Figure 7-7, to give the corners extra strength. The steel braces will also help hold the frame flat and square.

Your rebuilt sash frame doesn't need to be absolutely perfect. It needs to fit in the same frame, and hold the same size panes of glass. It can be slightly taller or thicker without anybody noticing. Even as much as a half-inch difference won't really show once it's painted to match the others. Of course, all of this detailed work is very time-consuming. It takes about two hours to make one simple sash. This includes cutting and assembling the wood, and setting in one pane of glass. If you need more than one pane, it will take longer. You can use this same technique to make custom windows. You can turn out a surprisingly nice-looking window, even if you're not very good at fine carpentry.

I'm not suggesting that you replace all the windows in a house this way. That would be far too time-consuming. This technique is best used for only one window, or just part of one window. If fabricating one piece of wood allows you to save the entire window, it's well worth the time. If the window is part of a matching set, rebuilding one window, or part of one window, can save you from having to replace the whole set.

Adding Leaded or Fancy Glass Windows

This technique is especially valuable if you're working with fancy windows that have leaded, beveled, or colored glass. Windows like these are usually one-of-a-kind. If one has to be removed, you won't be able to match it.

Fancy glass windows really add to the atmosphere of an older home. The window in Figure 7-8 is a good example of how stained glass windows were used as part of the architectural composition of some Victorian homes. The home isn't really elaborate, but the porch, molding, stained glass window and varied use of siding give it a distinctly individual look. If the house you're remodeling doesn't have any leaded glass windows, my technique offers you a fairly economical way to add some. Whether or not you want to do this is a question of style, which we'll discuss a little later.

You can often find gorgeous pieces of stained, beveled or leaded glass at antique stores. They are usually reasonably priced — much less than it would cost to buy something similar new. I've seen quite a nice selection for around $100. If you can find a pane of fancy glass that's roughly the same size as one of the windows in the house (give or take a few inches), you can make a custom sash to hold it. You just have to make the sash a little bigger or smaller, as necessary, to hold the glass in the window you choose.

For the maximum effect, use fancy glass in a window that's very visible. If possible, try to find several different-sized windows in the house that would be good locations for fancy glass. That way, if the homeowners really want to add this special touch, you're more likely to be able to find at least one pane of glass that you can use. You can even inset a glass pane into a built-in cabinet if there isn't a window that it will fit. I added a decorative pane of leaded glass to the cabinet in Figure 7-9 and turned it into an interesting centerpiece for the room.

If you find a large sheet of fancy glass, you may have the option of removing both sashes from a window to accommodate it. Of course, the window will no longer open, so be sure you select a location that's not important for ventilation. Since this antique glass is old and fragile, when I use large sheets I like to glaze in a sheet of plain glass on the outside as a backing. This protects the fancy glass from weather and dirt, and adds strength.

The Value of Antique Glass — Adding antique window glass may seem like a lot of trouble, but a new leaded glass window can easily cost $1,000. In some houses, spending $1,000 is a worthwhile investment, because these windows can add several thousand dollars to the value of a house. This is one of my favorite "maximum value" additions, because it can raise the value of a house many more times than it costs.

Figure 7-9
Cabinet with fancy glass door

Fancy windows are also good "distracters." They catch the eye and tend to distract everyone's attention from the less attractive parts of the house around them. This can be especially valuable if there's an unattractive aspect of the house that you can't easily change. People won't notice the ugly paneling or strange trim, they'll only notice the beautiful window. They'll say, "Oh wow! Look at that gorgeous window!" instead of "Look at that awful paneling."

I've had very good results with all the fancy windows I've installed. You'd be surprised how much difference a beautiful window in a good location can make to a house. It's especially nice if you can locate it so that the sun shines through it. I've even had neighbors come and ask me to do the same for their homes. It makes such an obvious improvement that the entire neighborhood will take notice.

Another nice point about this kind of a job is that, unlike conventional window replacement, you'll never have to deal with competitive bidders. Very few remodelers do work like this. The only ones that I've ever known to do window restoration are historic renovation specialists — and they don't work cheap. Most general remodelers have never even thought of doing this, and wouldn't know how to do it if they had. You can charge just about any (reasonable) amount of money for your work, and people will be happy to pay. Remember, a beautiful stained glass window can raise the value of the house by several thousand dollars. Even if you charge a lot, the homeowner will still come out ahead.

Cost — What will this type of work cost you to do? Installing the window will take four to eight hours, depending on the size and complexity of the window. The only significant material cost is the window. And they can range in price anywhere from $100 to $1,000, depending on the size and detail. The more expensive windows are truly gorgeous. They're the sort of thing you'd expect to find only in the finest homes. A thousand dollars isn't a lot to pay to end up with a million dollar effect.

Often, the hardest part is finding the right piece of glass to fit the window you've chosen. You may have to go through a lot of antique stores before you find anything that will do. This isn't a job you want to do on a tight schedule. However, once you've done it a couple of times, you'll become familiar with the antique glass sources in your area. You'll have a pretty good idea about what you can get, and where you can get it. That makes finding the right glass a lot easier.

Of course, there's always the possibility that the homeowner may not appreciate fancy windows. Some homeowners don't even want you to repair the windows they have. They may even want you to take all the old windows out and replace them with new thermopane windows. If they have nice antique glass windows, this is very foolish, and will substantially lower the value of the house. However, if you can't talk them out of it, ask if you can have the old windows. You may be able to use them on another job. If not, you can always sell them to an antique dealer. Fancy windows bring $25 to $100, even in poor condition. Whatever you do, don't throw them away. You'll be throwing out hundreds of dollars!

Jammed Windows

Old windows that don't open or close easily are one of the most common complaints of homeowners. Sometimes a house is full of windows that won't open and close at all. Homeowners often think they need to replace their windows in order to correct the problem. This is rarely necessary. Jammed windows can usually be repaired with very little cost.

By far the most common cause of jamming is paint. Over the years, windows are painted many times, one layer over another. These layers build up until the thickness becomes enough to jam the window. This is particularly true of the top sash, which usually isn't opened as often as the bottom. If the homeowner doesn't care about opening the top sash, you can just leave it painted shut, but most likely you'll need to get them both back in operation. You can test to see if the windows are jammed with paint by taking a sharp object and cutting into the paint on the window casing. Most likely, a half-circle-shaped piece will break off. Under it, you'll see layer upon layer of paint, often each one a different color.

The best way to take care of this is to remove the paint build-up with a heat gun. You need to remove the interior stop and take the sashes out, the same as if you were going to replace the glass. Use a heat gun and a scraper to remove all the paint from the casing. Remove the paint from the sashes as well. Build-up may be jamming the sashes against the stop. Be careful to keep the heat gun away from the glass. The extreme hot air from the gun can crack cold glass.

Fit the windows back into the frame and try them out. They'll probably be fine. If they're still jamming, it's usually because the sash frame has absorbed moisture and expanded. A little bit of sanding should solve the problem.

Once you have the window working properly, you can repaint the window casing and sashes. The build-up from a single coat of paint won't do any harm. This entire job usually takes about two hours per window.

🦜 Counterweighted Windows

Counterweighted windows were common in quality-built older homes. When working properly, they are still a very good window system. They were usually very well made, with good quality wood, and sturdy assembly. Unfortunately, the ones you come across today are rarely in working order. In fact, the only ones I've ever seen working properly are the ones I fixed myself.

Counterweighted windows work by means of heavy weights inside the wall that are attached to the window by ropes. Each sash, top and bottom, has two weights, one on the left and one on the right. The weights weigh exactly the same as the window, so that when you lift the window to a certain height, it stays there. Figure 7-10 shows the parts of a counterweighted window and the location of the weights, pulleys and ropes in the wall.

By the time I get to them, the ropes are almost always broken. The homeowners may not even be aware that the windows are supposed to be counterweighted. They often think that the only way to hold them up is to put a stick under the sash. If you're not sure whether they're counterweighted windows or not, look in the upper corners of the window frames. There should be a pulley wheel on each side to guide the rope that attaches to the weight. You may even see the broken ends of the rope sticking out of the wheel, or out of the top of the window sash. Sometimes all trace of the rope is gone, but the wheels will always be there.

A common problem with counterweighted windows is that a rope has broken on one side, but not the other. This pulls the sash over to one side, causing it to jam. Windows in this condition can be very difficult to open and close. Sometimes the window problems have become so aggravating for the homeowners that they just want to get rid of them and replace them with something that works. However, if this is the only reason they want to replace the windows, you can offer them a good alternative. These windows are fairly simple to repair. With a little work, you can restore them to like-new condition.

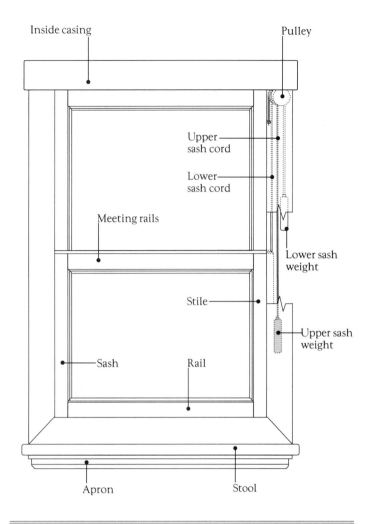

Figure 7-10
Weight assembly in counterweighted windows

Repairing Counterweighted Windows

Most of the time, all that needs to be done to repair a counterweighted window is to replace the broken ropes. This is simple, but not easy. The weights are difficult to get at. You'll need to work on this from the inside of the house.

First, you need to remove the inside stop. On a top-quality window, the stop will be held in with screws for easy removal. Since removing this piece is necessary for many other common window repairs, such as replacing broken glass, I really appreciate working with quality windows that have these thoughtful little touches. If the stop isn't screwed in, it'll be held in with small nails that you'll have to carefully pry out. Once loose, lift the sash up off the sill and swivel it out of the window frame. With luck, you'll only need to remove it on one side.

There's supposed to be a little door, held in by a screw, under the inside stop on each side. This door is designed to provide access to the counterweights. Unfortunately, the door usually isn't there. If that's the case, you'll have to pry off the outer casing boards on the sides of the window. Be careful not to break them. They're usually held on with 4-inch trim-head nails. If these have rusted, they can be very hard to get loose. Don't put too much pressure on one spot — you'll either break the trim board, or knock a hole in the wall. Work all around the board until you get it loose.

When you get the trim board off, you'll be looking at what appears to be a blank wall. Your first thought will be "Oh no, there's no weight here at all! I'm wasting my time!" Have faith. It's there. The window assembly was installed before the furring strips and plaster went on. The outer casing boards were put on top of that. The weight is under the furring strips.

You'll need to cut through the plaster and furring strips at the bottom of the window frame. Don't worry, the hole won't show once you put the trim board back on. Cut carefully so that you don't break any big chunks of plaster loose.

You may not see the weight at first. It's recessed a little below the bottom edge of the window frame. That's to give it someplace to go when the window is all the way up. If you stick your fingers into the hole, you'll feel the top of it. It's usually a rough cast-iron cylinder, with a loop on top for attaching the rope.

Now you need to replace the rope. I usually use cotton clothesline, because it looks just like the rope that was there originally. Feed an end over the pulley until it appears in the hole. Tie the end to the loop on top of the weight.

If you look at the outside edge of the sash frame on each side, you'll see keyhole-shaped cutouts where the rope is supposed to go.

Cut the rope to the proper length and tie a knot in the end. The knot goes in the round hole part of the keyhole-shaped cutout. The long thin part of the cutout acts as a guide for the rest of the rope. Once you fit the sash back in the frame, the rope will be held in place by pressure.

Before you put the window back together, check and see that the window moves properly. If you've done this repair correctly, you'll be amazed at how nicely the window slides. You can open or close it with one finger, and it stays exactly where you put it. Very few modern windows can match this. If it doesn't move easily, it may have dirt or paint caught in it, and need cleaning or sanding. Make sure the rope is the right length. The window should go all the way up to the top of the frame, and all the way back down to the bottom.

This repair only takes about an hour per window. However, it can be complicated by the fact that it's very easy to break the trim boards or knock chunks out of the plasterwork while you're doing it. If that happens, you'll have to repair the new damage, and that adds extra time to the job.

I find this job especially worthwhile when I have other work to do on the window or the wall. If you have to take the window apart to replace broken glass, for instance, why not repair the counterweights while you're at it? It won't be that much extra work, and everyone will be really happy with the results when you're finished.

Heat Efficiency and Counterweighted Windows

To be honest, not everybody likes these windows. *This Old House* on PBS recommends that you replace them because they're not heat efficient. I don't think that's a good idea. If the counterweighted windows are in good condition (not loose, leaky, or full of holes), and have good storm windows as well, they'll provide decent thermal performance. The storm windows are what make the difference. You can even get low-E, high-performance storms if the homeowners want to pay a little extra for them.

Replacing counterweighted windows with new thermopane models is an expensive job. Even if you can get a good price from a window replacement specialist, it's still going to cost roughly $200 per window, installed. Multiply this by an average of about 10 windows, and you're looking at a total bill of about $2,000. The new windows probably won't save more than about $100 a year on an average heating bill (if the old windows are in good repair and have good storms), so you're looking at a payback period of 20 years. If the homeowners are real sticklers about heat conservation, they may want to go ahead and replace the windows anyway. However, this is clearly not going to pay off right away. Certainly, if the windows are in poor condition, heat efficiency is yet another reason why you might want to replace them. However, if heat efficiency is the only reason to replace them, in my opinion it's not worth doing.

❧ Repair vs. Replace

If you've been adding up the times for each of these window repair jobs, you can see that a window that needed all of the repairs we've discussed would consume a huge amount of work. That's why most remodeling books don't recommend window repair. I certainly don't recommend putting many hours of work into a cheap window in poor condition. However, many windows can be saved by no more than one hour's work. It seems a shame to replace a window that's so easily saved.

I generally don't put more than $50 total (materials and labor) into trying to save a window. If it's going to cost more than that, you need to ask yourself what makes the window special or worth saving.

- ◆ Is it an especially high-quality window? Does it have leaded, beveled or colored glass? Does it have ornate woodwork?

- ◆ Is it part of a set?

- ◆ Is it one of a kind? Does it have historic value?

If all the answers are "no," you're better off just replacing it. If there's even one "yes," you're looking at a window that could cost $1,000 to replace. Wouldn't the homeowner prefer a $50 repair to a $1,000 replacement?

❧ Window Replacement

Simple window replacement is a fairly easy job. It doesn't require much in the way of special tools or skills. You can special-order a replacement window to be the exact size and shape of the window that you're replacing. When the new window comes in, it fits exactly into the old frame. It also comes with an installation kit and complete instructions. Figure 7-11 shows a double-casement window that was too rotted to repair. It had a nice shape and suited the location perfectly, so I replaced it with the thermopane window shown in Figure 7-12. As you can see, the new window is modern and functional but retains the look of the original.

Figure 7-11
This rotted window had to be replaced

Figure 7-12
New thermopane window retains the look of the original

Figure 7-13
Unusual historic windows are hard to replace

I don't do a lot of this kind of work. I can't compete with the window replacement specialists as far as price. They work in volume. The only time I ever do simple window replacement is when I need to replace just one or two windows. You can't get a good price from the window replacement specialists unless you're replacing at least half-a-dozen windows. They're not interested in doing just one. As a rule, window replacement specialists deal in inexpensive vinyl windows. If your customers want a better window, like a Pella or Andersen, they won't find any discount installers who can make them a better deal than you can. You can compete with any installer when dealing in high-quality products.

Simple window replacement is another one of those jobs you can find out about almost anywhere. In fact, the instructions that come with the window are usually all you need.

Custom Windows

Some windows can't be replaced with standard order replacements, they have to be custom built. If you can't repair or rebuild an unusual window, like the one in Figure 7-13, you may have to have a duplicate window made. That's what I do if I need one window to complete a set, or one that holds a pane of

fancy glass that can only fit in an exact duplicate of the old window. A good wood shop will have no problem doing this kind of work. They can even provide you with the best of both worlds — a window that looks just like the antique one, but is up to modern standards of performance. Unfortunately, you have to pay dearly for this luxury. Custom windows can be very expensive. Even a relatively ordinary window, a Colonial-style for instance, can cost $500. If you need something really expensive, such as one with duplicated leaded-glass work, it can run upwards from $1,000. That's why I rebuild as many windows as I can.

🌰 Adding a New Window

What if you want to add a window where there isn't one now? Your clients may want more light or ventilation, or maybe they want to improve the look of a room or gain a view. Or, you might suggest adding a new window if you find a really beautiful antique window that you can't use in any of the existing window frames.

This is a big job, not like a simple window replacement. You have to tear out a chunk of the wall that's substantially bigger than the window. This is a job you have to plan out carefully.

First, you'll need to cut a hole through the wall where the new window is to be installed. That includes cutting through any studs that are in the way. When you remove studs, which are load-bearing structural members, you need to make some arrangement to hold up the weight that they carry. You'll have to double the studs on either side of the opening and build a header, made of two 2 x 4s, to install across the top of the opening. The header will redistribute the load.

Next, you need to build a frame the size of the new window to set the window assembly in. Then you have to repair and trim up the wall opening with new drywall on the inside, and siding on the outside. You'll also need to install window casings, and other trim.

Figure 7-14
Original windows

Figure 7-15
*New larger windows take
advantage of view*

Figures 7-14 and 7-15 show a window replacement job that I did recently. It was similar to installing new windows, because both openings had to be enlarged considerably. The original windows were too small to take in the beautiful view offered from the back of the house. The only problem was that the new windows weren't historically accurate. We felt this was justifiable since the changes were made to the back of the structure, not the front. Keeping style consistent is less important in the back of the house; especially in this case, where the view was more valuable to the owners than historical accuracy.

An average job like this takes about 12 hours per window. The cost is whatever you pay your carpenters per hour, times 12, plus the cost of the window, and a fair mark-up for you. The benefit to the owners, in this particular home, far outweighed the cost of the improvement. If they decide to sell the house, the new window additions will easily add double or triple the cost of the windows to the selling price.

Exterior Doors

In every home, doors take a lot of abuse — even more than windows. In older homes they're often in very poor condition. Many of the doors you'll come across in this type of work won't be the originals. What are the problems you're likely to encounter with these old doors? There are several, and I usually divide them into two categories: the front door; and all the other doors to the house.

❧ The Front Door

The front door is by far the most important door in the house. In fact, it's actually one of the most important items in the house. It's the first thing most visitors will see when they approach. It's where the all-important first impression is made, and there's no way to correct a bad first impression. A rough-looking front door can certainly spoil the look of the entire house.

Homeowners are usually aware of the importance of the main entry door. If not, tell them. Having a nice looking house is as important to you as it is to them, especially if you like to use finished projects as advertisements of your work. If the house doesn't look good, it won't bring you any referrals.

Should you Keep the Existing Door?

There are a few things you need to look into before you decide what to do with the front door. First of all, is it the original door, or a replacement? It's more worthwhile to repair an original door than a replacement, because the original door will be a perfect match for the style and design of the house. Finding another door that will match as well can sometimes be very difficult and expensive. On the other hand, if the door's already been replaced once, it won't make much difference if you replace it again.

How can you tell if the door's original? Usually, replacement doors look like replacements. They don't complement the style of the house. I've seen many 1960s-style blond, modern doors on 1920s houses. They look pretty bad. When you come upon something like this, you'll want to replace it with something that's a better style for the house.

What if the replacement door matches the house perfectly? This is rare, but it can happen. My rule is: if it looks original, treat it as if it is. We'll spend more time on the front door later on in the chapter.

❧ Side and Back Doors

What about the second group of doors I mentioned? These include the side doors, back doors, and any other door that isn't immediately visible from the street.

These doors are much less important that the front door. They're not often noticed by visitors, and even homeowners pay very little attention to them. That was probably the case when the house was new as well. Most of these doors were originally rather plain and ordinary. There usually isn't anything special about them that makes them worth saving.

If the doors are in poor condition, replace them. If they're serviceable, leave them alone. If they're ugly, a fresh coat of paint will usually brighten them up enough to make them passable.

If you believe door specialists, they'll tell you that all old doors need to be replaced. They'll give you the following reasons why you should replace side and back doors:

1. They leak heat.

2. They're a security problem.

3. They're ugly.

4. New doors will raise the value of the house.

Let's consider these reasons one at a time.

Leaky Doors

First of all, old doors do leak heat, but unless they fit very badly, they probably don't leak all that much. You can usually fix minor leaks by replacing or adding weatherstripping. If that's the only problem, you can add a lot of weatherstripping for a lot less money than replacing the door. Of course, this solution may not be as heat efficient as a new, perfectly-fitted insulated door. However, the amount of money saved on heat with the new door will be very small. Like window replacement, it's something on the order of 20 years before the money saved equals the cost of a new door. Certainly, replacing doors like this will provide the homeowners with other benefits as well, but it's a poor return for their money. If budget constraints require that some jobs be omitted, this is a good one to skip.

Storm and Screen Doors — Remember that most doors will need storm and screen doors that are in good repair. Storm doors cut drafts in the winter, and the screens keep bugs out and let ventilation in during the summer. If a door without screens is used much in the summer, the house will quickly fill up with bugs.

Storm and screen doors take a lot of abuse. Unless the ones on the house are fairly new, they probably need replacing. This job does give you good cost effectiveness. Well-maintained storm and screen doors really make a difference. Homeowners will get better heat efficiency by replacing a bad storm door than by replacing the door itself — and it's a lot less expensive. A good-quality pre-hung storm door assembly costs about $100, depending on size, and takes only about an hour to install.

Unlike windows, replacement doors don't come with storms and screens. These are separate items. If the storm door is bad, it will have to be replaced regardless of whether you replace the door or not. This is one reason that door replacement is generally even less cost-effective than window replacement.

Security

Door specialists like to point out that old wooden doors can be easily forced open, and new steel doors can't. I won't argue with that. However, if somebody really wants to get into a house, they'll find a way. If they can't get in through the door, they'll come in through a window. If security is the main concern, why not put in a burglar alarm? There are quite a few now, like the Schlage Keepsafer, that are radio operated. They're cheap, too. They start at around $200 and go up, depending on the number of sensors you want to install. At that price, they're cheaper and more effective than new doors.

Radio-operated systems work by means of radio transponders attached to door and window sensors inside the home. They don't need to be hardwired in. Not only does this make them easy to install, but it also makes them easy to move. This is an especially nice feature for people who are renting and want that extra security. If they decide to move, they can take their alarm system with them. A hardwired system always stays with the house. Because burglar alarm systems don't generally raise the value of a house very much, the portability of these systems is a big advantage. Owners only have to make a one-time investment in an alarm system.

Of course a radio-operated system doesn't really offer the same protection as a hardwired system. Professional burglars can get around them. But most of us are more concerned with common burglars, who are looking for some quick cash or a stereo system that they can pawn. These burglars aren't going to be able to cope with even the simplest system. However, if you're dealing with the kind of client who keeps piles of diamonds or gold bricks in their home, they'll need a really good alarm system. A radio-operated system is designed more to scare off intruders with a lot of noise. They're fine for protecting the average house, whose owners keep their valuables in a bank safe-deposit box.

Ugly Doors

While it's true that new doors may be more attractive than the existing doors, this is, again, not a cost-effective job for the side and back doors. It's only cost-effective for the front door or doors. Any doors that can be seen from the street must look as good as possible. Side and back doors generally can't be seen from the street.

Side and back doors are forgettable. Nobody pays much attention to them. They don't look at them, and they don't remember them. Think of houses that you've visited. Unless the side or back doors were really special, or really awful, did you remember what they looked like? For that matter, did you care what they looked like? Well, neither does anybody else.

If looks are the only problem with the side and back doors, just put a fresh coat of paint on them. Use an attractive color that goes well with the house. If possible, use a darker color. It will make them show up even less. Painting costs very little — figure about a quart of paint and one hour's work per door. New paint almost always gives you good results for a fraction of the cost of a door replacement.

Resale Value

Another favorite of the door specialists is the idea that new doors raise the resale value of a house. They do a little, but the homeowner won't get back anywhere near as much as the cost of the new doors. Resale value is an area where I have a lot of first-hand knowledge, since buying and selling houses is my main occupation. Buyers don't pay any more attention to the doors than anyone else. Except for the front door, they generally don't notice doors. When I point out the lovely new doors I spent a small fortune on, they just yawn. What they really care about are the kitchen, the bathrooms and the overall appearance of the house. Believe me, an extra bath will always help sell a house; new doors won't!

ॐ Replacement Costs vs. Repair Costs

As with window repair, this is probably the only place you'll ever read about door repair. Most "how-to" books tell you to just replace exterior doors. They'll tell you that door repair "doesn't pay." But, they haven't ever actually figured it out. Let's go through some numbers and see.

Replacement Costs

The minimum you can expect to pay for a decent exterior door for any part of the house is $150-$200. All you'll get for this is a usable, functional door. If you want one that's attractive, especially for the front of the house, you'll have to pay more. You can easily spend $2,000 for something special.

Let's use $200 as a general figure. For this money, you can either get a builder's quality (cheap) prehung steel door, or a better-quality solid wood door. Figure at least an hour to hang the door.

If you want to install a new door, you can't just "go pick up a door." It has to be selected. It has to be the right size and style. This takes time. It then has to be transported and stored until you install it, and the old door has to be removed and disposed of. All of these steps require a substantial amount of handling, and also a lot of time. People forget to put all these details into their time estimates. They only count the actual installation time for the door, as if it magically appeared where and when you wanted it, and the old door magically disappeared. In reality, material handling takes a lot of time, for this and any other work you do on the job. All this time adds up. If you don't figure this into your estimates, you'll wonder why you're not making any money. You're looking at a minimum of one and a half hours for selecting and handling a new door. Then add an hour for installation, which brings it up to two and a half hours.

Now you need to put a finish on the door. New doors come from the store either plain, unfinished wood, or primed metal. You can get prefinished doors, but they're more expensive. If you decide on a prefinished door, you'll have to take the time to select the right finish; add a little more to your selection time. Doors that aren't prefinished will need to be painted or varnished. Add on at least another half-hour.

If you add this all up, you've put in at least three hours work and $200 for the replacement door. I'm not including the price of a lockset in this computation, because I'm assuming that you'd need to replace the lock in the old door anyway. For the purposes of comparison, it just cancels out. However, if you want to figure that cost in separately, you can figure about $50 for a decent quality lockset, such as Schlage. Your new total is $250, plus three hours labor.

Simple Repair Costs — Now, what about repairing the old door? What will that cost? The average old door will only need minor, cosmetic repairs, like filling old nail holes with putty. This takes a half-hour or less. It will also need refinishing or repainting. If the old finish needs to be stripped, stripping will take about two hours, assuming you plan to repaint it. If you want to varnish a previously painted door, stripping will take longer. Even if the door doesn't need stripping, it will still take a half-hour to an hour for prepping. Applying a new coat of paint or varnish takes about half an hour. The total repair/refinishing time will generally run one and a half to three hours, depending on your choice of finish.

When you decide to repair a door, there's very little handling time required. You just need to pick up the wood putty, paint, varnish or stripper when you pick up your other supplies. It doesn't require a special trip to a supplier, transporting large materials, or removing or disposing of materials. Materials cost? About $10 for paint or varnish, $20 if the door needs to be stripped. The total is $10 to $20 and one and a half to three hours labor.

Let's compare costs. Installing a new door will cost (minimum) about $200 for materials plus three hours of labor. Fixing and refinishing an old door will cost (maximum) about $30 materials plus roughly the same three hours of labor! Of course we're only talking about simple repairs here. More complex repairs will cost more, but you would only make them on valuable doors where the return on your time and investment would be greater. We'll go into this in more detail later on in the chapter.

Labor — Now, for the bottom line: how much can you charge for this? Door manufacturers would have you believe that you can charge $400, installed, for a $200 door. In that case, you'd be making $200 for your three hours of labor, or almost $70 an hour! That would be great, but it won't work. There's vicious competition for jobs like door replacement. You'll be competing against others who are willing to do the same job for something like $250. Now you're down to $50 for three hours labor. That isn't such a great deal anymore.

What about door repair? There's very little competition for this job, because most people don't know how to do it. They've been told it's better to replace doors, and that's what they do. Your door repair costs only have to compete against door replacement costs, so you'll come out way ahead.

Because materials costs for minor door repairs are so low, you can greatly undercut the price of any door replacement, and still make good money. You could easily charge $175 for this job. If the door to be repaired is especially nice, $175 is a bargain. It's well worth paying $175 to save a $2,000 door. At that price the repair is still cheaper than the cheapest replacement door, and you'll make over $50 an hour for your work.

This job is a perfect example of the "best bang for the buck" type of job. You save the customer hundreds of dollars, and make good money for yourself doing it. Your customer is happy, and you're happy. The only one who isn't happy is your competition.

Door Repair

The first step in repair work is evaluating the door. You need to balance the amount of work it needs against the cost of replacing it with a door of equal quality. Remember, repair only pays if repairing the door would cost substantially less than replacing it.

If the door needs only the work we just discussed, it's almost certainly worth repairing. Even the least expensive replacement door will cost more. This assumes that, for a front door at least, the door is an attractive design. There's no point in repairing an ugly front door. Even if it's in perfect condition, it will still be ugly. With a side or back door, however, style doesn't matter; only the condition is important.

If the door is going to need more than three hours of work, you'll have to look at it very critically. How much is the door worth? Is it especially nice? I'll totally rebuild a really great door. It's worth it, even if it takes days. I patched, repaired, stripped and varnished the door in Figure 7-16. It was a lot of work, but you don't find doors with fancy glass like this one has very often. A truly beautiful door can cost thousands to replace. You can charge the homeowners $500 or more to repair the door, and they'll still be getting a bargain. An ordinary door, on the other hand, really isn't worth more than the three hours. If it's going to take much more time than that, you'd be better off replacing it.

Figure 7-17 shows another example of doors that were worth saving. They're extra-wide French doors set with thick, beveled glass. New doors like these cost between $1,000 and $2,000. You definitely wouldn't want to throw these doors away. The doors

Figure 7-16
This door was worth saving

were very dirty and the bottoms scarred and damaged. I cleaned them with detergent and covered the damaged areas with brass kick-plates. It took me less than two hours and cost me $50 to restore them to almost new condition. They were worth putting a lot of time and effort into repairing. Luckily, in this case, I didn't have much to do. Let's consider some of the common repairs that other valuable doors are likely to need.

Refinishing

The most common problem you'll run into with any old door is simply a bad finish. Lumpy paint or alligatored varnish can make an otherwise attractive front door look really nasty. Many times the finish on the front door looks so bad that the homeowners will be inclined to simply replace the door. However, if the finish is the only problem, you need to assure them that you can refinish it nicely — and for a lot less money than they would have to spend on a new door.

Cleaning — If the door has a varnish finish that has darkened, try washing it before you strip it. It's possible that the finish may only

be dirty. This is especially likely if the door has several layers of wax on it. Wax can hold dirt and make the door (or any varnished woodwork) look really bad.

Scrub a small area with a powerful detergent such as 409 or Fantastic. If you see the color changing dramatically, dirt and wax buildup could be the problem. In that case, it's worth cleaning the entire door. It may look fine once it's been cleaned, and refinishing may not be necessary. Of course, cleaning doesn't always do the job, but it's worth a try. When it does work, you'll get a really nice effect for only a few minutes work.

Stripping — A heat gun is the best tool for stripping a door. It will soften up all the old paint or varnish, allowing you to scrape it off easily. You may want to take the door off its hinges for stripping. They're usually easier to work on when you lay them flat.

Once you remove all the old paint, you'll have the option of either painting the door, or varnishing it. If it's a beautiful door, made of a nice quality wood, you'd be better off varnishing it. It brings out the beauty of the wood, and makes the door look more like a valuable antique.

Varnishing — If you decide to varnish, first you'll need to wash the door with acetone to remove any residues that might have escaped the heat gun. These residues won't show through paint, but they will show through varnish.

Figure 7-17
Repaired French doors

When you use acetone, you need to work in a well-ventilated area (a porch is good) because of the fumes. Pour some acetone into a jar with a tight lid. Dip a piece of extra fine steel wool in it and then gently scrub the surface of the door. Work only on a few inches at a time. Don't scrub hard; let the acetone do the work. You'll see the residue dissolve, and the original wood surface appear. After a few minutes, the steel wool will get clogged with old paint or varnish. Rinse it out in the acetone, then continue scrubbing. Be sure to keep the jar of acetone capped between dips. Otherwise, it will all evaporate into fumes in just a few seconds.

Before you varnish, examine the wood tone. Do you like the color? If it's too light, you might want to stain it. If it's too dark, you might be able to bleach it. Light sanding may also lighten the tone a little. If you have to do all of these steps, stripping, acetone wash and then varnishing, the total refinishing job can take up to six hours. However, the door will look like new when you're done.

This may seem like a lot of work, but remember, installing a new door is a lot of work, too. Plus, you'd need to spend hundreds, perhaps thousands of dollars to get a door that looks really nice. It's far less time-consuming if you can salvage the door that's already there.

Painting — In some cases, it may be better to paint the door than varnish it. This is especially true of doors that are damaged. Paint will hide repairs that varnish or stain won't. You can varnish over tiny repairs, such as nail holes filled with wood putty. Tiny imperfections won't interfere with the look of the door. However, any big repairs, like a filled-in hole from an old lock, will show. Wood putty takes stain differently than wood. If you varnish or stain it, the repair will take on a different color than the rest of the door. If you desperately want to stain the door, it's possibly to buy colored wood putty that matches a particular stain and try to blend it that way. But it's very difficult to get a precise match. It's only worth

the time and effort if you're working on an extremely nice door. With most doors, your best bet is to just paint it.

Antiquing — Another alternative is antiquing. Antiquing is actually a paint finish, but it looks like old wood. Essentially, a phony wood grain is painted on. This may not sound too good, but the results look surprisingly believable. You really have to stick your face in it to tell it's not actual wood grain.

Most paint stores carry antiquing kits. They come with complete instructions and all the materials you need, including a special tool for making the fake wood grain.

Antiquing is time consuming. The door, or any antiqued surface, requires three coats: a base coat, the antique wood-grain coat, and a coat of varnish on top. Each of these needs to dry overnight before the next coat can be applied. Figure about three hours for the whole job, not including any other repairs the door might need.

One drawback to an antique finish, besides the time involved, is that it's rather fragile. It can't be used in exposed areas, or areas of high wear. Because of this, you probably won't find yourself applying an antique finish very often. It's really only good for situations where you desperately want wood grain, and damage to the surface makes using the original wood grain impossible. In special situations, though, it can be a real lifesaver.

Repairing Holes

Holes are a big problem in older doors. They range from small nail holes, where a decoration was hung, to large poorly cut or unused lock holes as big as your fist that go completely through the door.

Filling with wood putty works fine for small holes. Even fairly large nail holes will fill nicely. The repair may be visible up close if you're looking for it, but back a few feet, it will disappear into the overall texture of the door. Wood putty is designed for use with relatively small holes. It doesn't work well on large holes. These require a different technique.

Filling Large Holes — Most people don't try to repair large holes. They consider the door ruined, and throw it out. That's too bad, because many large holes are fairly easy to fix if you know how.

The most common large hole you'll find in an older door is an unused lock hole. These are usually the result of poorly installed lock sets that never quite fit. You may also come across doors that have been forced open, causing the lock mechanism to be smashed right out of the door. That makes an awful hole. In some cases, the door may have a ragged hole the size of a softball. Hardly anyone, except me, would even try to repair a hole like that. However, it is repairable.

My favorite material for repairs like this is an auto body filler, like Bondo. I use it for all kinds of miscellaneous repairs. It's strong, weatherproof, workable, paintable, and fairly cheap. You can get it on sale at K-Mart for as little as $10 a gallon — and a gallon goes a long way.

If you've ever done auto body work, you're probably familiar with how this material handles. Auto body filler is a gooey, clay-like material that you mix with a hardener (which comes in a separate tube) when you're ready to apply it. I usually use a putty knife to mix it together. You need a flat surface for mixing it up on, like a piece of scrap wood or heavy cardboard. Use something disposable, because it's almost impossible to get this stuff off when you're done. Be careful not to get it on your skin; it burns.

The more hardener you add to the mix, the faster it hardens. If you add too much, it'll harden before you have a chance to use it. I've had it turn into a solid block with my putty knife right in the middle of it, and had to throw the whole thing away, putty knife and all.

Because body filler is semi-liquid, it tends to ooze and run when you use it on a vertical surface. It's easier to work with if you take the door off its hinges and lay it flat. If the hole you're repairing goes completely through the door, you'll need to block the back side. Otherwise, the body filler will ooze right on through and out the other side. Use a piece of cardboard to block up the hole. Remember, whatever you use will be glued securely onto the door. Cardboard is a lot easier to take off than a piece of wood. If you use wood, you'll have to chisel it off. That's a lot of work, and may damage the door.

You may have to apply the body filler in more than one layer. That's because it's impossible to get the body filler to make a smooth surface on the first application. It always has hills and valleys in it when it hardens. It seems to be unavoidable. If you try to smooth out the ripples while it's still wet, they just get worse. You have to let the filler harden. Then cut down the hills and fill in the valleys. In auto body work, three applications are considered the minimum. For carpentry, you probably won't need more than two. You may even be able to get away with only one, once you get used to working with the material.

I've found that the best tool for cutting away excess body filler is a Surform plane. It has hundreds of little cutting surfaces, each of which trims out a little bit of material. The resulting cuts look almost like someone clawed the material with their fingernails. It's an easy tool to work with because you can hold it at any angle, and you don't have to worry about taking off too much material at one time. The Surform will cut away the hills and blobs in seconds, leaving you with a flat, although rough, surface. A power sander with coarse sandpaper will even out the marks left by the plane. The result is a smooth, solid, strong surface.

You'll have to paint over this type of repair. It won't take a stain. However, once the door is painted, the repair will be completely invisible. When I think about the condition of some of the doors I've worked on, and the size of the holes I've filled, many of the repairs I've made using auto body filler are really quite amazing.

Installing a New Lock — Once the hole is repaired and you have a smooth, featureless door, you'll have to install a new lock. The door will look almost new, like a door that's never been cut for a lock. Where will the new lock go?

This is important: *Do not* cut through the body filler to install the new lock. It's likely to break loose. If not now, then later, after the lock has been used for a few months. Install the new lock either higher or lower than the old lock, but not in exactly the same place.

If you must install the lock at the same height, flip the door around, so that the hinge side is now the lock side, and vice versa. The hinge side has never been cut for a lock, so you'll have nice, clean wood to work with. The problem, of course, is that the hinge side has been cut for hinges. You'll have to fill in the mortise cuts with body filler and make mortise cuts for the hinges on the other edge. This may sound like a lot of work, but it actually only adds about half an hour to the job.

You can also use this method if you want to install a modern, round lockset in a door that was cut for an old-fashioned mortise lock. You can buy conversion kits for this, but I don't recommend them. The kits include an escutcheon plate which fastens over and covers the old hole. The new lock is mounted in the plate. Unfortunately, the plates aren't very strong and don't hold up well. The result is a flimsy lock conversion that doesn't provide good security. My technique may be more work, but it's stronger and far more attractive. The finished door will look like new.

Figure 7-18 shows a door that had the full treatment. This door had been kicked in and the old mortise lock burst out, leaving a huge, ragged hole. The photograph shows the door after I filled the hole with Bondo, flipped the door around and filled in the old mortise cuts. The next step was to cut new holes for the lock and hinges. Figure 7-19 shows the same door, painted and installed. The complete job, including repair, painting, and installation, took about four hours, and cost about $20, not including the lock.

Figure 7-18
Door has been patched with Bondo

Figure 7-19
Repaired door, painted and installed

Repairing Loose Seams

Loose seams are another common problem you'll have with older doors. Depending on the degree of deterioration, repairing these may or may not be a problem.

Most older doors (and newer ones too, for that matter) are a panel-type construction. They actually consist of a number of

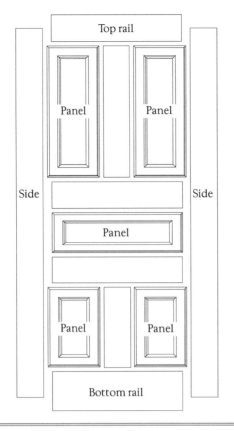

Figure 7-20
Diagram of a panel door

Figure 7-21
Moisture destroyed this garage service door

separate pieces, usually 10 or 12, depending on the style of the door. Figure 7-20 is a diagram which shows an exploded view of a standard panel door. As you can see, the top and bottom rails are each one piece, the sides are each one piece, the panels are each single pieces, and the dividers between the panels are each single pieces. The more panels a door has, the more pieces there are. All these pieces are held together with glue. Unfortunately, glue doesn't last forever. If the glue decays, the door will come apart.

Partial Repairs — Is it an important or highly-visible door, like the front door? Or is it a relatively unimportant door, like a garage service door? Is it totally disintegrated or just weak? If the door is totally falling apart like the one in Figure 7-21, you should just discard it. You don't want to put a lot of effort into painstakingly reassembling a garage service door. It isn't worth it.

However, I don't often find this to be the case. It's much more common to come across doors that are merely weak. That is, the seams are loosening, but they haven't completely come apart yet. Sometimes, you can save the door so quickly and easily that it's a shame not to do it. With a door like this, there's a simple repair I use. It doesn't result in a very attractive door, so I only use it on unimportant doors, like service doors.

I get four large, flat corner irons. They have to be the flat kind that won't interfere with opening and closing the door. When I say large, I mean as big as will fit on the rails. The bigger the better. Put these at the four corners of the door. Install them on whichever side of the door is less noticeable. In the case of garage service doors or basement doors, it's usually the inside. Make sure the steel pieces cross the seams between the rails, so that some of the screws will be on each side of the seam. Coat the corner irons liberally with glue before installing them. That way, they'll be both screwed and glued to add strength to the repair. It's also a good idea to dip the screws in glue before installing them. That will keep them from working loose.

If the center rails seem loose, you can get T-shaped steel pieces to strengthen them as well. Install these the same as the corner pieces. You now have a door that has steel reinforcements at all the seams. It may not look too great, but it will definitely be strong. And once the door is painted, no one will really notice the reinforcements. They'll be obvious enough; but as I said before, people just don't pay attention to the way most doors look as long as they're neat and serviceable.

This repair will take about half an hour, and will cost between $5 and $20 for materials, depending on how much you pay for the corner irons. It may seem like a makeshift repair, but some of the doors that I fixed like this are still in use after 10 years. They'll have to be replaced someday, but an extra decade of use isn't bad for a $10 to $20 investment.

The alternative is replacing the door. A decent exterior-grade door will cost you about $100. I have bought a few cheap, particleboard exterior doors for as little as $50. However, I haven't had good results with them. They're ugly, heavy, hard to work with, and they don't hold up well. A repaired door will look better and last longer than a cheap replacement.

One thing I should point out about corner irons is that their price varies tremendously, depending on how you buy them. If you buy them in bulk, unwrapped, you'll pay about a quarter of the price that you'll pay if you buy brand-name irons, shrink-wrapped onto a little card with matching screws and a pretty logo. If you use a lot of corner irons, buying them like that will really add up. I always buy them in bulk. I don't get the matching screws, but that's okay. I just buy a box of screws that are the right size for my purpose. Much of the time the matching screws won't work for what I want to do anyway. All these little savings add up. You'll be surprised how much money you can save at the end of the year by simply watching prices on items like these. And, that's also less expense to be passed on to your customers.

Rebuilding Doors

Of course, you can't just screw corner irons onto a highly visible door, like a front door. You'll need a repair that's not only strong, but doesn't show or detract from the beauty of a nice door.

When you have an entry door that's worthy of repair, it's best to completely disassemble the door and rebuild it. As you might imagine, this takes time, but it's not as hard as you might think. It usually takes me about six hours. I wouldn't put that kind of work in on a cheap door, but for an expensive door, the time spent is a bargain. You can charge $50 an hour for your time, and the labor cost will still only come to $300. That isn't much to save a $1,000 door.

You can make the repair on-site, but it's easier to do it in a wood shop if you have one. Either way, the door will have to be off the hinges for a day or two, so you'll need to board up the opening.

Taking the Door Apart — Rebuilding a door with bad joints is a lot like repairing an old piece of furniture that has come unglued. First of all, you need to take it completely apart. Pry the joints apart carefully, working from the edges so you don't leave tool marks where they'll show. The joints usually come apart easily. After all, the reason you're repairing the door is because the joints are loose!

There are several different kinds of joints used in old doors. They all have small, interlocking pieces that are glued together. Try not to break any of them. Don't worry if some of them are broken already; I'll tell you how to deal with that in a minute. If some of the joints seem to be hung up and refuse to come apart, look for small nails that may have been driven in at right angles. Remove these very carefully, or you may damage the joint when you pull it apart. Remember, everything you break is just one more thing you'll have to fix.

The outside rails are the hardest to get apart. That's where the strength of the door is — or rather, was. Once you get these apart, the center panels and rails will usually just fall right out.

What you're likely to find inside the joints is old, powdery glue. Glue failure is usually the reason that old doors fall apart. You have to remove all the old glue before you can repair the door. If you don't remove all the glue, you may have problems with your repair.

Often the old glue is so powdery that you can just wipe it off. A little hand sanding will take off the remainder. If the glue won't wipe off, use a sanding disc to remove it. The disc will take off most of the glue in seconds. You'll just need to do a little hand sanding to get out the bits the disc can't reach.

Reassembling the Door — Once you've removed the old glue, you need to reglue and reassemble the door. Use a good carpenter's glue, and clamp the joints together with bar clamps. Be careful to wipe up any glue drips; it's really hard to get them off once they're dry. Make sure the door is lying flat and straight, and all the corners are true. If it's crooked or out of line, you need to straighten it before the glue sets or it will be crooked forever. Once clamped, leave the door undisturbed overnight to ensure that the glue is properly set.

If any of the joints have been damaged, you can strengthen them by adding screws through the joint. Use long, thin wood screws, usually about 8 or 10 inches long, and a drill bit to match. Drill a hole on the edge of the door going right through the joint. The screw should be long enough to go through one rail and into the next. Dip the screw in glue and screw it in tightly. Since you're installing it from the edge of the door, the only place the screw head will show is on the edge, so it won't detract from the look of the door. Adding screws substantially strengthens the door. If there's any doubt in your mind about the door's strength, add screws. It can never be too strong.

If you think about it, this isn't really a complicated job. All you're doing is taking the door apart and putting it back together the way it was, except with fresh glue. Of course, it has to be done carefully. If you try to rush through it, you won't get good results. But it doesn't require any special skills. You could even have a semi-skilled helper do it as long as he's a careful worker.

Replacing Parts — What if you find that some parts of the door are totally unsalvageable? This is bound to be the case every once in a while. The part that's most likely to be badly damaged is the bottom rail section. It's usually weakened from being kicked too many times, or from sitting in a puddle of water winter after winter. Sometimes, the door will be perfect except for the bottom section, and that may be totally destroyed.

You'll need to remove the bottom section and make a duplicate of it. If you're lucky, it'll be a standard size and thickness. Sometimes you can take a bottom section off a similar door and use it for a replacement. But that's pretty rare. Most old doors are odd sizes. You may not even be able to find a piece of wood the right size and type for the repair. Many times I've had to laminate two pieces together to get the right thickness, or plane down a thicker piece.

If you can't find the right type of wood, you may have to use a totally different kind. This isn't too great a problem. I've used a piece of 2 x 10 pine to rebuild the bottom door section. It made a perfectly sturdy repair, but the new piece didn't match, so I had to paint the door.

The best way to attach the new piece is with dowels, the way furniture is put together. If you've made or repaired furniture, you're probably familiar with how to do this. You can buy precut furniture dowels that are grooved to improve their grip.

Drill a hole in the replacement piece half the length of the dowel and set the dowel in place. Then drill another hole the same size in the old door, lining it up with the dowel. When you put the new piece on, the dowels should extend half way into the new piece and half into the old door, holding the two parts together. Use three or four dowels, if possible, to provide sufficient strength. Take care to precisely line the new piece up with the door. This is hardest part of this job. The pieces never seem to want to go together quite right.

Apply glue liberally to all the parts. Anything that can be glued, should be. Clamp the whole assembly together with bar clamps, and leave it overnight. When it's dry, you may find that the new piece is not quite lined up exactly with the door. Well, that's what power sanders are for! A power sander can clean up slight imperfections and make the whole door assembly look almost as good as new.

Salvaging Parts — You may find a beautiful door that's unsalvageable. Sometimes there's just not enough left of it to work with. Before you throw it out, however, look it over. What is it that makes the door beautiful? Does it have leaded glass windows, brass fittings, carved ornaments? Many of these things are removable. Take them off and save them. You may be able to use these special features on another door. You may even be able to transfer fittings or other features onto the replacement door. If you can, it will make the replacement door look more like the original. This is especially true if the ornamentation on the door matches the rest of the house.

Sometimes, you can find a new panel door that has a center panel roughly the same size as the leaded glass window from the old door. You can remove the panel and set in the leaded glass window, creating a door that's almost an exact replica of the original door. The more similar the new door is to the old door, the better the door will look. If you can't find a door that's suitable for the fittings and ornaments you take off the old door, keep them anyway. Sooner or later you'll find just the right place to use them.

Chapter 8

Porch Repair

The porches on older houses frequently need a great deal of repair. Porches take the brunt of the weather, and their maintenance is frequently neglected because they're not part of the regular living space. As a result, they often suffer serious damage. In Chapter 2 we discussed some of the problems you're likely to run into with old porches. Now let's see how you should deal with them.

Porch repair is one of those areas where you can get a step up on your competitors. Why? Once again it's because most contractors would rather tear off the old porch and replace it than try to deal with minor repairs. They'll charge their customer a lot of money for the demolition and dumping of the old porch, a lot of money for new porch materials, and a lot of money for the labor to build it. When they're done, they'll usually have a porch that's ugly and inappropriate because it doesn't match the house. A new porch rarely looks as good as the original porch would look if it were properly repaired.

Look at the porch in Figure 8-1. It looks like a simple covered front porch. But imagine the house without that porch; it would be totally different. The angled roof, varied siding, and intricate woodwork give the house its warmth and charm. It really isn't as simple

as it looks. It's an integral part of the overall architectural style of the house. Whether you're working on a simple porch, or an elaborate wraparound porch like the one in Figure 8-2, you should preserve as many of the original features as possible. That requires an attention to detail that few remodelers want to put into a project.

A careful investigation will usually reveal problems that you can repair with a little time, effort and resourcefulness. You can save the original porch and all the features that made it beautiful and a perfect match for the house. Plus, you'll be able to save a great deal of money on labor, materials and disposal fees. You'll be able to offer this service to the homeowner for a fraction of what your competitors would have charged, while still making a lot more profit than they would have made.

Of course, there are some cases in which your competitors may be right. Some porches *do* have to be torn off. What did you find on your inspection? If the roof was rotted, but the floor, understructure and foundation were okay, you can just replace the roof. If the understructure or foundation were damaged (this is very common), but the roof and supports were okay, you can just repair the

Figure 8-1
Simple covered porch on Victorian home

Figure 8-2
Elaborate wraparound porch

understructure and/or foundation. However, if they're *all* rotted, then your competitors are right — the porch will have to be torn off.

Let's go through the repairs in the same order as we did during the inspection, start-

ing with first-floor porches. Since wood porches are a lot easier to repair than masonry porches, we'll start by looking at wooden porch structures.

Wooden Porches

The point at which you and your competitors will most often differ is in repairing the understructure. This is a touchy job which requires careful thought and planning. Moreover, it requires crawling under the porch and working in a cramped, dirty space for sometimes days on end. Most of your competitors aren't willing to do this. If you are, you'll have a big advantage.

🐌 Evaluating the Problem

If the understructure of the porch is damaged, you'll have a porch that's sagging, uneven, or unsteady. This is a common problem with wooden porches.

The first stage of a damaged understructure becomes evident when the porch seems unsteady under a load. If several people walk on it at once, or one person jumps up and down, the porch shakes violently. Some people think this is normal; it's not. A porch, even a wooden one, should be fairly steady. You can expect a little vibration if somebody is jumping up and down, but if there's so much bounce that people's drinks fall over, you have a problem.

If nothing is done about this problem, it will progress to stage two — unevenness. The floor will noticeably tilt to one side or the other. It's supposed to tilt slightly towards the front for rain run-off. However, if it's tilted to the left or right, that means the supports on the low side have failed, and the porch is beginning to sag.

The final phase is definite sagging. The porch drops noticeably on one or both sides, and begins to pull away from the house. If the porch is not repaired at this point, it will break free of the house and fall right off.

It's best if you can catch a porch repair when it's still at stage one. It's a lot easier to fix then. The further along the deterioration progresses, the harder it is to fix. If the porch is shaky but not sagging or uneven, all it needs is strengthening. This is done much the same way as strengthening a weak floor in the interior of the house. However, in order to evaluate the extent of the problem and find out exactly what's causing it, you need to get under the porch. That can be a job in itself. In fact, many remodelers never even get that far, which is why these repairs are so rarely done.

Porch Access

Your first question will be: "How do I get under the porch?" In some cases, there may be an access panel on one or another side that can be removed, as in Figures 8-3 and 8-4. If there isn't a panel, and the base of the porch is partially or totally enclosed with wood lattice, you can sometimes remove one section of lattice to gain access. Often the area behind the stairs isn't sided, leaving a hole behind the stairs that you can slip into. In some cases, the stairs can be temporarily removed. The hole behind them is often as wide as a doorway, although somewhat shorter.

Sometimes there's no way under the porch at all. This is especially true with porches that are very close to the ground. Obviously, you're not going to be able to go under a porch that's only 6 inches off the ground. However, it's still important to get a good look at what's under the porch. You won't be able to tell how much work needs to be done under there until you do. In this case, you're going to have to take part of the floor up to get at the problem. If the problem is only in one small area, it may not be necessary to tear up too large an area. Try to locate the source before tearing into the floor. You may be able to save yourself a lot of work.

Creating Adequate Access — If you're going to be doing a lot of work under the porch, you'll need good access. You can't be squeezing through a small opening under the stairs twenty times a day. If you're only going to have to go under the porch once or twice,

Figure 8-3
Porch access panel

Figure 8-4
Access panel for small back porch

the existing opening might be good enough. That's why a little opening under the stairs or an access panel, even if it's tiny, is the place to start.

If the porch is only weak, not uneven or sagging, repairing it may be surprisingly easy. You may only need to make two trips under the porch: one to inspect and measure, and one to bring in your materials and do the work. However, if the porch *is* uneven or sagging, you'll have to spend some time under it.

In that case, you'll need good access. So if there's not an access panel big enough to get through easily, you'll have to make one.

Cut out an access panel on whichever side of the porch is less obvious. If there are shrubs on one side, use that. You can put ropes around the shrubs and tie them out of the way while you're working. When you're done, you can release the ropes, and the access panel will be hidden behind the shrubbery.

Having an access panel for the porch is a valuable asset. It not only makes this job easier, it makes it easier to do future work that might be needed. Be sure to point this out to the homeowners so that they will view the new access panel as a useful improvement, not just an ugly hole you cut in their porch for your own convenience.

Making an access panel is a little like making a window. You cut a hole through the siding, frame it up, and then screw a plywood cover over it. Whenever anyone needs to get in or out, they can just unscrew the cover.

If you can see into the porch from another point, *make sure the area where you want to locate your access hole is clear.* If you can't see under the porch, drill a couple of test holes before you start cutting. Use a stick or a piece of wire to probe into them to make sure there's nothing blocking the space where your access panel is going to be. You don't want to cut out a panel and then find your access blocked by a masonry pier or some other obstacle. You can probably guess how I came up with this tip: I learned it the hard way!

You want to cut through as few studs or other support members as possible. Avoid the corners, since that's where the main support posts are most likely to be. If you cut through the supports, you'll weaken the porch. Make your hole big enough so that you can get yourself and your tools in and out easily, but no bigger than absolutely necessary. Access panels are ugly enough. The smaller they are, they less noticeable they are. Be sure to header off any studs you cut through, as you would with a window. Otherwise, you'll weaken the porch. When you're done, paint the plywood access panel cover to match the rest of the porch.

Inspecting the Porch Understructure

First of all, you'll need a good light to make your inspection. It's dark under the porch. Use either a powerful flashlight, or a trouble light. I prefer a 100-watt trouble light. Although the cord is a bit of a nuisance, it throws a lot more light than a flashlight. And since it plugs in, I never have to worry about the batteries running down.

Under the porch you'll find dirt, cobwebs and bugs, to name a few. Take a broom and sweep it out. Take the time to do a good job; the cleaner it is, the less unpleasant it'll be to work in. It usually only takes me about five minutes.

After you clean out the area, take your light, a tape measure, a hammer, a sharp object for probing, and a pencil and paper. Then crawl under the porch for a good look. It's best to get everything you're going to need together before you go in, because getting in and out is a nuisance. The fewer times you have to do it, the better. You'll be annoyed with yourself if you have to come all the way out just to get a tape measure; and really annoyed if you have to do it again for a pencil.

Inspect all the supporting members of the porch carefully. Start with the floor joists. Do you see any cracks, rot, discoloration or water marks? Probe any discolored areas. Are they solid, or soft with rot? Any rotted areas will need to be repaired.

I'm never sure what I'm going to find when I go under a porch. Even two houses which appear to be identical will often have different structures under the porch. In many cases, you'll find that the porch has been worked on in the past, so that there are sometimes two or more sets of supports, with each entirely different.

The Foundation — What's holding the porch up? Is it sitting on piers, beams, or stud walls? Are the walls sitting on a proper foundation, or are they just sitting on the dirt? Are the supporting members rotted, cracked, crumbling or discolored? Any weakness in the supporting members will cause the porch to become shaky.

I've often found wooden porches built without a proper foundation, or with no foundation at all. They're often held up by wooden stud walls sitting on sand or dirt, with corner posts made out of three or four 2 x 4s nailed together. They weren't very solid when they were new, and after 60 or 80 years, they're a lot worse.

Sometimes you'll find the porch held up by masonry piers. They may be original, or they may have been added later. Original piers are usually made of brick or stone like those in Figure 8-5, while later additions tend to be made of cement block. Often there are just two piers, each one holding up an outside corner. However, I've come across porches with six or eight piers. You're more likely to find these under Victorian porches, which were often built in complicated shapes. There's usually a pier at each corner, which is good. The more piers there are, the more solid the porch will be.

Check each pier to be sure they are all solid and plumb. If they didn't have good footings, they may have settled or been heaved out of alignment. That's a common problem with old piers. If they're only slightly out of line, they may still be providing adequate support. However, if they're substantially heaved or settled, some other support may be needed.

Porches may also be supported by posts. These could be made of anything, from modern treated 4 x 4s to old tree trunks. Check these for rot damage. Old tree trunks standing on wet ground are very likely to be rotted through.

If the porch is shaky, but not sagging, you're likely to find that one or two floor joists, or a beam or pier, has failed. Had more than one beam or pier failed, the porch would probably have progressed to the sagging stage. However, you may find that some of the other supports, while not yet failing, have begun to decay. You should repair those as well. If you fix them now, it'll save you or someone else a trip under the porch at a later date.

Figure 8-5
Porch with stone piers

❧ Repairing Weak or Damaged Floor Joists

If one or two floor joists are clearly damaged, you can repair them by simply doubling the joist. Use a piece of treated lumber the same size as the existing joist. If you nail the new piece securely to the old, the load will be transferred to the new joist.

If you do this correctly, you should be able jump up and down on the porch without getting any significant movement. Try it. If the porch still bounces, it either needs more strengthening, or you haven't identified the entire problem.

It's not always easy to tell which floor joist is causing the problem. Rather than having just one completely-failed joist, you may find that all the joists are a little weak. If I find this to be the case, I build a beam to support the joists in the middle. I use two 2 x 12s nailed together. If the weakness is in only one area, it may not be necessary to run the beam all the way across the porch. You only need the beam on the weak side. However, if you're in doubt, run it across the whole porch. It can't hurt to make it too strong.

Figure 8-6
Old porch with poor support structure

It's often difficult, or even impossible, to work with long pieces of lumber under a porch. Piers, posts, or other obstructions can interfere with your ability to attach the beam where it should be attached. If this happens, you can use two smaller beams instead of one big one. The two beams don't have to line up in an exact line. They can be offset to clear an obstruction. The important thing is that you support the center of the floor joists with something strong. The exact type or location of the support doesn't matter very much. You could even use three of four small beams, if necessary, as long as each beam has its own supports. Of course, the more beams you use, the more work it will be.

Supporting the Beams

If there are solid, well-supported posts or piers under the porch, you can attach your new beams to them for support. Unfortunately, the supports under an old porch, like the one shown in Figure 8-6, are rarely good enough for this. There usually aren't enough supports in the first place, and those that are there aren't often in the best condition. Usually, I end up having to add some new posts or piers.

I've tried adding both wooden posts and masonry piers as support beneath porches. They work equally well, but the masonry piers are a lot harder to build. Now, I primarily use treated 4 x 4s which I set on concrete pads. I place them under the header, and attach them with post caps. That transfers the load directly to the post. It also prevents the post from breaking free, as it might if it were attached to the side of the header.

Using Floor Jacks — You'll need to use floor jacks to get the new support members to fit tightly. For this job, you should have short jacks, the kind designed to fit in a limited space. They adjust from 2 feet to 4 feet in height. You'll need at least two, but it's a good idea to get three or four. Once you have them, you'll find you use them a lot. They're good for all kinds of things.

When you have the beam constructed, you need to set it in place under the floor joists. This is often easier said than done. The beam has to be supported under the underside of the floor joists. There isn't a lot of room to work under the porch, so you can't always approach the job from the best angle. It would be helpful if you could have someone hold it for you, but you'll be lucky if there's room enough for just you under the porch, much less a helper.

What I usually do is hold up one end of the beam and tack it into place. Then I move to the other end and tack that into place. Now the beam is suspended from the bottom edge of the floor joists in more-or-less the correct position. Position the jacks near where the posts will be, but *not* in exactly the same place. In order to get a tight fit, the posts will have to be installed before the jacks are removed. You won't be able to do that if the jacks are blocking the spot. This may seem obvious, but if you're not thinking ahead, it's very easy to place the jacks in such a way as to block the place you need to work in. I've done this many times, even though I know better.

The bottom end of the floor jack needs to sit on something solid so that it doesn't sink into the ground when you tighten it (see Figure 8-7). A cement block works well for this. Place one of the steel plates that come with the jack between the top of the jack and the beam, so that the jack doesn't dig a hole in the beam. Tighten the floor jacks until they are pressing the beam securely up into the floor joists, but no further.

Now you need to check the porch floor from the top side to make sure it's stable. It's a lot easier if you have a helper that can do this for you. That will save you from having to come out from under the porch over and over again. Even with good access, getting in and out from under a porch is difficult. You don't want to do it any more often than necessary.

If the jacks are adjusted correctly, the porch will now be rock solid. If it still shakes, try tightening the jacks a little more. Be careful! If you over-tighten the jacks, you'll make a bulge in the porch floor.

Installing Support Posts — The posts should be installed near the ends of the beam for best support. The exact location will depend on how much clearance and room you have to work in under the porch. Anywhere within 8 inches of the ends should be fine. Don't try to get away with just putting one post right in the middle. The ends of the beam won't have adequate support. If the beam is longer than 10 feet, or the porch is especially heavy, you might want to add an extra post in the middle of the beam. This usually isn't necessary, but it's not a bad idea. It gives you an extra margin of safety in case anything goes wrong. I don't think it ever hurts to make things extra strong. If you make it strong enough to last a lifetime, you'll never have to go under the porch again! I'm in favor of that.

Once the jacks are adjusted correctly, it's time to cut the posts. They should fit snugly between their concrete pads and the beam. If they're the same height as the jacks, they'll give you the same support you have with the jacks. They'll be high enough to make the floor rock solid, but not so high as to cause a bulge. This is one of the main reasons I use floor jacks for this job, as opposed to just levering the posts into place. You get a much more precise fit with floor jacks.

Figure 8-7
Floor jack supporting porch

When you remove the floor jacks, the load will be transferred to the posts. The porch will be stronger than it's ever been. In fact, if you've used a full-width beam and two or more posts, you'll have built a structure strong enough to be the entire support for the porch. Even if all the other support structures under the porch fail, the porch will still stay up.

Does this sound like a lot of work? It isn't. I've often done a job like this, including cutting an access panel and installing a beam and two posts, in about six hours. The materials run about $50, depending on the length of the beam and the number of posts you need. Since the posts will usually be fairly short, you can cut two or three out of one 8-foot 4 x 4. In fact, I can often make them out of 4 x 4 scraps left over from another job. (I never throw anything useful away.) Then the cost for the posts is zero!

You could charge quite a bit for a job like this, and still have the homeowner jump at the deal. After all, the alternatives are to either allow the porch to continue decaying until it's unsalvageable, or to tear it off and replace the whole thing. In both cases, it'll cost a lot more than what you're going to charge for repairs. Since few contractors bother with this type of repair work, you'll probably be the only one offering this service.

Figure 8-8
New stairs, railings and siding

Figure 8-9
A coat of paint to finish the job

You can charge any reasonable amount of money, and still get the job. Figures 8-8 and 8-9 show the same porch as the one in Figures 8-6 and 8-7. This job required new stairs and rails, and I enclosed the base of the porch with new siding. You can see the finished porch in Figure 8-10. Once the house and porch were painted, it looked like a brand new porch had been added!

Figure 8-10
Completed porch project

❧ Repairing Sagging Porches

What about porches that have gone on to the next stage, serious sagging? What's the best way to deal with these?

When I say sagging, I mean a porch that has dropped roughly 4 to 10 inches below its original level. Keep in mind that most wooden porches were not built level from front to back. They were built tilted away from the house to allow the rain to run off. This tilt isn't what I mean by sagging. A porch should be level from left-to-right. If one side is now much lower than the other, it's sagging.

Sometimes both corners sag. When that happens, it's only a matter of time before the porch starts pulling away from the house. You'll see a substantial gap between the porch rim joist and the wall of the house. Corners rarely sag the same amount, so there may also be a lot of unevenness on the porch. It can be so extreme that it's difficult to walk on the porch.

Here's what you may be looking at: A porch that's shaky, pulled away from the house, uneven, and sitting at a weird angle, sometimes as much as 8 inches out of plumb. Ninety-nine out of a hundred contractors will tell the homeowner the porch should be demolished and replaced, at a cost of perhaps several thousand dollars. If you're going to be the one that says it's salvageable, we'd better consider just what has to be done.

Can This Porch Be Saved?

If the porch has completely broken free of the house and hit the ground, it's not sagging, it's collapsed. In this case, the other contractors are right — it needs to be replaced.

How far out of line can a porch be before it's unsalvageable? I use 8 inches as a rule of thumb. More than 8 inches and it's likely to be so twisted out of shape that it will fall apart if you try to put it back into line.

An important factor in your decision to save the porch is the condition of the floor and joist structure. Even thought the porch may be sagging, the floor and joist structure may actually be fine. What happens is that one or more support posts or piers fail, and with nothing to hold it up, the porch sags. Simply replacing the post or pier can make the porch perfectly serviceable again.

Sometimes this easy fix won't work because extensive rot damage has set in. This is especially true of porches that have been sagging for a long time. The porch floor gets twisted and eventually cracks open up in it, allowing rainwater to enter, causing rot. When this happens, the joist and floor structure of the porch will begin to fall apart. A porch like this cannot be saved.

You must inspect the porch carefully before you make the decision to try to save it. The ideal candidate for repair has solid flooring, solid joists, good siding, good stairs, but is sagging substantially due to post failure. Essentially, there's nothing wrong with the porch except the support posts. Repair those, and the porch will be almost as good as new.

Another point to take into consideration is the workmanship of the porch. How elaborate is it? A simple, unenclosed, deck-like porch is not worth a great deal of time and effort. It would be easier to just replace it. An elaborate two-story Victorian porch, covered with ornamentation, is a different story. A porch with a lot of detail would be very difficult and expensive to replace. The more elaborate the porch is, the more it's worth saving.

Saving a Doomed Porch

Figure 8-11 shows a porch I worked on not long ago that was sagging extensively. One corner had dropped a full 6 inches. As you can see, the porch was roofed and enclosed, had operable windows, and was styled distinctly to match the house. The porch had pulled several inches away from the house and the window frames (shown in Figure 8-12) were all out of alignment, causing the windows to jam. Cracks had opened up between the window framing and the siding as well. Several contractors had looked at the porch before me. They all agreed that the porch should be demolished and replaced.

Replacing the porch was a very costly option. Just demolishing a porch this size is an expensive job. It would have produced about two dumpsters of trash, which would cost

Figure 8-11
Enclosed porch with sagging foundation

Figure 8-12
*Inside view of porch shows misaligned
windows and cracks in siding*

Figure 8-13
Damaged porch has easy access for repairs

about $500 each to have picked up and dumped. That's $1,000 just for trash removal. Next is the cost of the new porch. Labor and materials to build a comparable porch in the same style would run approximately $9,000. That's an estimated cost of about $10,000 for the new porch. Although the porch looked pretty bad, I decided it was an ideal candidate for repair. It even had a usable access panel! You can see the small opening in Figure 8-13.

Straightening the Porch — Repairing a sagging porch is a lot like strengthening a shaky one. It's the same kind of work — there's just more of it. The biggest difference is that the sagging porch needs to be pushed back into its original position before it can be stabilized.

You start this job by establishing a good access, clean out the cobwebs, and take a look around. Good access is especially important in this case, because you'll have to go into and out from under the porch many times.

When you get under the porch, you'll probably find that one or more posts or piers

have failed. This is the place to start. Set floor jacks on either side of the bad post (or pier) and tighten them. Check all the posts. Put jacks around any posts that are bad, and at intermediate points between them. Now you can remove the bad posts without causing the porch to sag any further. Plan on using at least four jacks to support the porch. It's not a bad idea to use six or eight. A porch is a heavy structure. You can't lift it with only one jack. If you tried, you'd put too much stress on one point, and rip the porch to pieces. Using several jacks distributes the upward pressure evenly.

Once the jacks are in place, you can start moving the porch back into the proper position. This has to be done very slowly and carefully. That's why you'll need to make a number of trips under the porch. If you try to jack it back into place all at one time, it will probably tear apart. Remember, it took the porch a number of years to sag into its current position, maybe 20 years or more. You can't expect to put it back into place in 20 minutes.

Tighten each jack one or two turns, until you feel a lot of resistance. Start at one end and work towards the other, tightening each jack in turn. When you're done tightening each jack once, go back and do it again, in the same order. You'll be surprised to find that the first jacks, which you had tightened just about as tight as you could, are now loose. That's because each jack down the line takes some of the load off the one before it as it is tightened.

You may hear a lot of creaking and groaning from the porch as you jack it back into line. Pay attention to this. Too much creaking may mean that something is ripping loose. If the porch is making a lot of noise, stop tightening, and check it out.

After you've tightened each jack a couple of times, check up on top to see how the work is progressing. Is the porch moving back into line the way you wanted it to? Make sure the porch isn't twisting and becoming more distorted, or moving in the wrong direction. If it is, you've either tightened one or more jacks too much, or you've placed them wrong. In either case, you'll need to back them off a bit and try again.

If the porch is uneven to start with, you may not want to tighten each jack the same amount. For instance, if the right corner of the porch has dropped 6 inches and the left corner has dropped only 3, you'll need to tighten the jacks on the right side twice as often as the ones on the left side.

You shouldn't try to move the porch up more than an inch or so a day. You can often feel the point at which you should stop. You'll begin to encounter a lot of resistance, almost as if the porch was fighting you. When this happens, stop and let the porch "rest" overnight. This allows it to settle into its new position gradually. The next day you'll find that the jacks that were too tight to budge the night before have become almost loose. That's because the porch is no longer fighting; it settled into its new position. Now you can move it up another inch or so. This process will take three to five days, depending on how many inches the porch has sagged.

Figure 8-14
Interior view of repaired porch

Once you have the porch back in line, you can strengthen it using the techniques we covered earlier in the chapter. Replace any bad posts or piers, double any weak joists, and add beams and posts any place it looks like they're needed. When in doubt, add more. It's a lot of trouble to jack up a porch; you don't want to have to come back and do it again — ever.

The porch in Figure 8-11 needed surprisingly little work other than jacking it up. Once it was straightened, everything shifted back into place. All the jammed windows came unstuck, the parts that were pulling away from the house went snugly back into position, and the gaps in the walls closed up. The roof didn't even need repair, it just needed to be caulked, as did the walls and windows where the gaps had been. To be honest, I was extremely lucky on this job. I was amazed how everything fell into place on its own. You really can't count on every job running this smoothly.

When it was done, it seemed like nothing short of a miracle had taken place. The completed porch is shown in Figures 8-14 and 8-15. This is just a sample of what you can do. Some of my colleagues looked at it before I went to work and said, "Larry, you've gone too far this time. You'll never be able to save this porch!" When I finished the job, they

Figure 8-15
Completed porch repair

couldn't believe their eyes. It looked like a new porch. Not only that, but it was rock-solid. There wasn't a sign anywhere that it had ever sagged.

Cost — Total material cost for this porch repair ran about $220: $100 for the treated lumber and a couple of bags of concrete for the understructure, $7.50 for five tubes of caulk, $40 for paint, and $70 for rebuilding the porch railings. I'm not including the cost of the floor jacks because they're tools which you should have on hand. You'll use them over and over on many jobs. (They're fairly inexpensive, usually about $25 each.) It took about 22 hours of labor to complete this porch job.

On average, jacking up and repairing a porch understructure takes 8 to 12 hours, depending on the severity of the problem. Of course, that's spread out over a few days. The porch in Figures 8-11 through 8-15 took me 10 hours to complete. Stretching the time out over several days wasn't a problem on this job because, as you can see from the photographs, I had a lot of other work to do on the house. I had to be there anyway. If the porch were the only job I had to take care of at that particu-

lar location, I'd have figured travel time into my estimate for the three to five trips I made to jack up the porch. The labor and material costs I mentioned did include painting, caulking, building the porch railing and minor trim repair. Even if the job had taken twice the time and material cost (even three or four times!), it was still a lot cheaper than tearing off the porch and rebuilding it.

One of the best things about this type of job is that you won't be competing with other contractors for the repair job. You'll be submitting a bid for repair, while they're submitting bids for replacement. Even if you charge $2,500, you'll most likely be $7,500 cheaper than your nearest competitor, and still make over $100 an hour for your labor!

One thing you may notice as I go through these repair jobs is that my material costs are usually very low compared to my hours of labor. That's because of the way I approach remodeling jobs. I try to save and reuse as many materials as possible, and that keeps my material costs to a minimum. Sometimes it takes longer to save materials than to just go out and buy new ones, but I don't mind spending a few extra hours if it saves me thousands in the long run. Most contractors throw everything out without a second thought. It may be easier to work this way, but it will make your material costs sky-rocket. I don't think you should try to save every little thing, but I encourage you to take the time to evaluate items and decide what is worth saving and what isn't.

&. Repairs to Porch Pillars and Walls

It's been my experience that the understructure of the porch is the area most likely to need work, so that's where I've placed the emphasis in this chapter. However, there are other repairs that you'll need to make on wood porches.

One important way in which a porch differs from the rest of the house is that it generally doesn't have walls. If the porch does have walls, they don't usually have a structural function, such as providing support for the roof. The walls are often full of windows, which have no weight-bearing capacity. Porch roofs are generally supported by beams which rest on pillars. The reason is so the sides can remain open (or filled with windows) to allow light in and provide a view out. As a result of this construction, any repairs you have to make to the walls are usually cosmetic, such as patching, caulking and painting, rather than structural.

Figure 8-16 shows a fairly typical house with a large downstairs porch as well as an upstairs dust porch. The porches are supported by the house at the back, and by a large beam set on two massive pillars at the front corners of the downstairs porch. The beam and pillars provide enough support so that the sides and front of the lower porch can remain totally open, giving the porch a spacious, airy feel.

I don't usually have a lot of trouble with porch pillars. Again, the most common cause of damage in porches is rot. This generally occurs either from the bottom up, from wet ground coming in contact with the porch, or from the top down, when the porch roof leaks. Since the pillars are in the middle, they're the last to be affected by rot. I've often seen houses where both the porch roof and floor have been replaced, but the original pillars are still in use. As a matter of fact, I've come across 150-year-old pillars that appear to be in like-new condition.

If the pillars are damaged, the damage is usually pretty easy to spot, since the pillars are right at eye level. In order to make repairs or replace a pillar you have to provide a temporary support for the roof. If you have to replace the pillars, be sure you make the new ones as similar as possible to the original.

Sometimes damage may be hidden under vinyl or aluminum siding. If the pillars are sided over, it may be a good idea to check and see what's underneath. The house in Figure 8-16, for example, provided a surprise. It appears to have square pillars. Underneath, they're not. When I tore into this job, I discovered that the original supports were actually round columns! Whoever sided this house couldn't cope with the round columns,

Figure 8-16
Two-story house with upstairs dust porch

so they just boxed them in and made them square — which totally changed the style of the house! The original columns were still in pretty good shape, so I just left everything alone. However, you never can tell. You might find rotted pillars or columns hiding under the siding.

The Porch Roof

The porch roof is an area that's likely to cause trouble. The main culprit here is neglect. I've often seen houses where the owners had re-roofed the main part of the house but not the porch because they didn't think it was important.

As a porch roof begins to wear out, rainwater seeps in and starts to cause rot damage. The decking goes first, then the joists, then the beams. Figure 8-17 shows an example of this kind of deterioration. This is the porch roof of the house in Figure 8-16. The decking on the upper dust porch had rotted away, and several of the joists were badly damaged. Luckily, the beam is still okay. As long as the beam is okay, a porch roof is repairable. If the beam has rotted, you'll have to tear the whole roof off and build a new one.

Figure 8-17
Rotted decking on porch roof

Dust Porches

Structurally, dust porches are just flat deck/roof areas above the lower porch that were built to walk on. They were designed to make upstairs cleaning easier by providing an exterior place to shake out rugs and dust mops.

Dust porches are a particular source of trouble because most roofing materials aren't meant to be walked on. Originally, dust porches were decked with tin, galvanized steel, or, in the case of one porch I saw, welded steel plates! The welded steel worked quite well for about 30 years, but then it rusted through, and no one knew how to fix it. Most of these porches developed leaks many years

ago, and many were never adequately repaired. Often the repairs were made using typical roofing products, such as asphalt shingles, which don't hold up under foot traffic. As a result, many are likely to have serious rot damage.

Porch roofs and dust porches are repaired roughly the same way. Any difference in the work depends on whether the dust porch is going to be walked on or not. The deteriorated dust porch in Figures 8-16 and 8-17 was no longer used as a porch. The homeowner considered it just a decoration. That made my job a lot easier. I was able to repair it as though it were a low-pitched roof, using standard roofing techniques and materials.

Figures 8-18 and 8-19 show this repair job in progress. I doubled all the damaged joists, replaced the posts, and then installed new decking. Because this porch was very low-pitched, I couldn't roof it with shingles. I had to use roll roofing, which was the correct material for this application. The main difference between reroofing a dust porch and most other porch roofs is that the other roofs are steeper. Other than that, the job is exactly the same.

Figure 8-20 shows the finished job. It's quite attractive, and the homeowners can even step out onto it now and then, if they're careful. However, roll roofing is not designed to hold up under heavy foot traffic (or even

Figure 8-18
New joists, posts and decking being installed

Figure 8-19
New roof decking in place

light traffic from a woman in high heels — she'd punch a hole in it with every step).

What if the homeowners had wanted to use the dust porch as an outdoor sitting area? The only roofing material available that's both waterproof and walkable is rubber roofing. It's a tough rubber material that comes in a big seamless sheet that's laid over the whole porch. According the manufacturer, it's sturdy enough to survive heavy foot traffic, as well as loads from patio furniture. With this material, the dust porch can be used just like any other porch. Unfortunately, you can't just go out and buy it, it's only available through specialty subcontractors. If a homeowner wants to use the dust porch, you'll have to subcontract the job out.

On rare occasions, you may find a tin roof that's still serviceable. If the homeowner doesn't want to walk on it, you can preserve the roof by giving it a coat of mobile-home roof coat. This is a quick and easy job. It only takes about half an hour to brush a covering of roof coat on an average-size dust porch. A 5-gallon bucket of roof coat costs about $25, and would cover two roofs about the size of the dust porch in Figures 8-16 through 8-20. A coat of roof coat will extend the life of a tin roof by about 10 years, which isn't bad for $12.50 and a half an hour of your time.

Other Porch Roof Repairs

The porch roof in Figure 8-21 involved a different kind of repair. It already had brand new shingles, yet it was sagging and out of line. It really had me puzzled. In fact, that's me on the ladder trying to figure out what's wrong. It turned out to be another amateur fix-it job. The roof was re-shingled but not all the necessary structural repairs had been made. This house had been neglected for decades before the new porch roofing was installed. During that time, serious rot damage had occurred and several rafters were rotted out. Whoever put the new roof on had replaced the shingles and decking, but hadn't bothered with the rafters. That was the cause of the sagging.

Luckily, this was a fairly easy repair. After studying the situation for a while, I

Figure 8-20
Completed dust porch roof

realized that all the damage was within 4 feet of the end of the roof. I could reach the area through the hole I had opened up at the end. I cut 2 x 4s to fit, put them in through the hole, and forced them into place by levering and hammering them in between the wall of the house and the porch beam. The pressure I exerted on the roof as I forced the new rafters into place pushed the roof back into its proper shape. I screwed the new rafters securely into place, and the problem was solved!

The best part of this job was that I didn't have to tear out the existing roof, or the porch ceiling in order to make the repair. Of course, I was lucky. Only four rafters were

Figure 8-21
Sagging porch roof was a mystery

Figure 8-22
Rotted porch stairs need to be replaced

rotted, and the beam on the outside edge supporting the posts was fine. If the rot had extended much further, I would have had to replace the whole porch roof. As it turned out, the repair took about four hours, and cost $20 for materials. The most time-consuming part of the job was trying to figure out how to do it!

❧ Porch Stairs

Another part that often fails on wooden porches is the stairs. That's because they're generally positioned in front of the porch, and not under the roof, so they aren't protected from the weather. Between the sun, rain, and foot traffic, porch stairs take a lot of abuse. A coat of paint will protect them for a year or two, but few people are conscientious enough to repaint them that frequently. Once the paint is worn away, rainwater will begin to soak the wood, and then the rot begins.

Figure 8-22 shows a fairly typical set of rot-damaged stairs. The treads were badly deteriorated. When I tore into these stairs,

the wood was sopping wet even though it hadn't rained for quite a while. The wood was so soft it crumbled under my touch.

The type of repair needed for rotted stairs depends on how far the rot has progressed. If only the treads are rotted, you can just pull them off and replace them. Be sure to use treated wood for the new treads — that way they'll never rot out again. You can use two pieces of 2 x 6 for most treads. If that's all the damage there is, you have a quick and easy repair job that will cost about $50 in materials, and take about two hours to complete.

If the stairs are badly rotted, it's very likely that the rot will extend into the risers as well. When the risers are rotted, the stairs are ruined. You'll have to tear them off and build a new set of stairs.

If rotted stairs aren't replaced, they'll eventually collapse all by themselves. That's what happened to the stairs for the porch in Figure 8-23. (This is the same porch repair job that we discussed earlier in the chapter.) When these steps collapsed, someone replaced them with a stack of loose cement blocks. This was a very dangerous arrange-

Figure 8-23
Collapsed stairs were replaced by a stack of loose concrete blocks

ment, and an obvious building code violation. I refused to let anybody, even my helpers, come or go by the back door until I built a new set of stairs. It didn't take long; a simple set of porch stairs is easy to build.

The most important part of any staircase is the risers. These provide all the strength for the stairs, as well as support for the treads. Cutting risers can be tricky. If you don't get the cuts exactly right, the stairs will come out crooked. Fortunately, you can buy precut risers made from treated lumber for most common porch heights. They only cost about $25 apiece. For that price, it isn't worth the time and effort for me to cut them myself.

Be sure to inspect precut risers carefully before you buy them. I've found a few risers that were cracked, or had big knot holes in critical locations. If you buy defective risers, the staircase won't hold up. Remember, its strength is in the risers.

The staircase I built for the porch in Figure 8-23 needed three risers. I used joist hangers to attach the risers to the porch. Then, all I had to do was cut two pieces of 2 x 6 for each tread and screw them into place with deck screws. And that's all it took! The new stairs were up and usable. You can see the finished stairway in Figure 8-24. You can make them more formal-looking by enclosing the backs, but it isn't necessary, especially for a rear or side porch.

If the porch is painted, paint the stairs to match. Treated wood doesn't necessarily need to be painted. It won't rot, but green-colored treated wood just won't look nice on a painted porch. Remember that treated wood needs to dry out good before it's painted. It's often still oozing chemicals when you get it from the lumberyard. You can't paint it until it's completely dry. That can take a couple of weeks of sitting in the sun. Also, be sure to undercoat it with a good primer/sealer as well.

Sometimes the original wood stairs on a porch rotted away long ago and they were replaced by concrete steps. The concrete steps may now be in bad shape. I'll discuss how to repair these later on in the chapter.

Figure 8-24
New stairs and railings on repaired porch

🦜 Railings

In many cases, you may be able to save the existing railings when you rebuild steps. However, in a case like the porch in Figure 8-23, where no trace remains of them, new railings need to be built. Railings can be either very easy, or very difficult, depending on how fancy you want them to be.

I usually try to construct a railing that matches the style of the house — something similar to what would have been there originally. The house in Figure 8-23 is a Craftsman, so I built a Craftsman style railing using simple, straight geometric shapes. I try to avoid buying prefabricated railing parts, unless I really need them. They're too expensive. In this case, the top and bottom rails are ordinary treated 2 x 4s, and the balusters are treated 2 x 2s. You can buy plain balusters like the ones I made for $3 each, but why? They're no different from a piece of treated 2 x 2 as far as I can tell. If I cut them myself it only takes a few seconds, and saves me $2 each. If I were going to build a Victorian railing, with turned balusters, I would buy them. That's a different story. It's not worth my time to try to make turned balusters on a lathe.

If you make your own balusters, be sure to select really nice pieces of 2 x 2. Discard any that are cracked, warped, or have big knot holes. People will be looking at the railing for a long time and any defects will really show up.

Constructing the Railing

Railings like the one in Figure 8-24 are really quite easy to make, and they look nice in a lot of different applications. I've made dozens of them. They are also very sturdy, much stronger than a lot of the prefabricated railings you can buy. I tried buying pre-made railing sections once. The flimsy construction made me uneasy. They're held together with staples, rather than the deck screws that I use. One section actually fell apart in my hands while I was trying to install it! I took all the pieces back to the store and demanded my money back. That was the last time I tried to save a little time on a railing. It's important that railings be sturdy. The higher up the porch is, the more important this becomes. People lean on railings and even sit on them. What if several people lean on your railing at once, will it support the weight? It had better!

For residential applications, the building code specifies that railings be at least 36 inches high. Personally, I don't think this is always high enough. I often build railings up to 42 inches, especially if the porch is very high off the ground. My thinking here is that people like to have parties on their porches. Some of their guests might have a little too much to drink and could easily flip right over a 36-inch railing. If you build a 40-inch railing, they'll just bounce off of it and land back on the porch, instead of over the side.

Now, you might say "How likely is this to actually happen?" I don't know. However, my attitude is "better safe than sorry." I don't want to be sued because someone fell through or over an unsafe railing.

Spacing

According to the building code, railings must be constructed in such a manner that a 4-inch diameter sphere can't pass through them or under them. The triangular opening between the step and the railing can't be more than 6 inches on any side. Be sure your railings match the code regulations or they won't pass inspection, and all your work will have to be done over.

The first thing I do when constructing a railing is cut all the 2 x 2 balusters. Then, I cut the top and bottom rails to length. I mark a line every 5 inches on the rails. If you space the balusters 5 inches apart on center, when you subtract the width of the wood, you get openings that are $3\frac{1}{2}$ inches wide. That's well within code. Not even a baby could squeeze through these. When measuring, don't start at one end and work across. Unless your rail is an exact multiple of 5 inches (unlikely), your last baluster will wind up crammed against a post. Instead, start in the middle and work in both directions. That way, the balusters will be centered.

Once I've marked every 5 inches, I make another mark at the center of each line. I drive a deck screw just barely through at each of these spots on the bottom rail, until the point starts to show on the other side.

Then, I hold a baluster section onto the point, and drive the screw into it. I do the entire bottom rail this way, attaching all the balusters on the bottom side. Then I take the top rail, drive screws into it, and attach it to the top. If I wasn't going to paint the railing, I'd use 16d galvanized finish nails on the top instead of screws, because the screw heads don't look nice. However, I'd still use screws on the bottom where they wouldn't show. It only takes about an hour to construct an 8-foot railing section this way. It costs about $40 in materials.

Posts

If the original porch posts or pillars are still in good condition, you can attach the new railings to them. Otherwise, you'll have to add more. When in doubt, add more. Again, the stronger the railing is, the better.

I usually use treated 4 x 4s for posts. My favorite method of attaching them to a porch is with ½ inch chromed bolts. Unlike nails, these bolts will never work loose. I attach the rails to the posts with 6-inch long lag bolts. I drill through the post, parallel to the rail, and into the rail, lengthwise. Then, I screw in a chromed lag bolt, and that railing is there to stay! Remember, when you attach the railings, the opening between the floor of the porch and the bottom of the railing must be less than 4 inches.

Repairing Masonry Porches

Masonry porches are much more difficult to repair than wooden ones. There's not a lot you can do with crumbled masonry. Most of the time a deteriorated masonry porch *does* have to be demolished and rebuilt. However, you don't have to demolish a porch at the first sign of cracking. There are a few things you can do to save them. Let's consider the possibilities.

❧ Causes of Cracking

Most masonry porches, like the one shown in Figure 8-25, have walls built of cement block, brick, or stone. The interior is filled with sand, and the top is a slab of concrete which is cast in place and rests on the sand base.

Cracking can be caused by a number of things, but most of the time it's caused by some degree of settling or heaving in the footings. Usually this is because the footings were constructed on ground that was too soft or too wet. If the settling is severe, a crack will run up from the ground, through the bricks or blocks, and right through the slab on top. Sometimes the bricks or blocks will crumble and fall out along the crack. This allows the sand inside the porch to pour out. It's very common to see a big pile of sand beside a damaged masonry porch. It looks like someone piled it up there, but they didn't. It seeped out from the inside.

Once the sand seeps out from the inside of the porch, there's no longer anything to

Figure 8-25
Brick masonry porch

Figure 8-26
Small masonry porch needs work

hold the top slab up. The top slab is usually 4 to 6 inches thick. It's pretty strong, but it's also pretty heavy, and it wasn't designed to be left unsupported. It was designed to lie on the bed of sand inside the porch. If the sand seeps out, the slab is likely to crack and settle to the level of the remaining sand.

Figure 8-26 shows a small, deteriorated masonry entry porch on a house I recently considered renovating. Taking a closer look, (Figure 8-27) you can see that the top slab which used to be the floor of the porch is completely gone. At one time, someone had attempted to stop the deterioration by trowling on a new layer of concrete. However, the new cement didn't bond with the original and eventually broke up and peeled off. You

Figure 8-27
Badly deteriorated porch will have to be demolished

Figure 8-28
Damaged brickwork needs repair

can see what is left of the resurfacing job crumbling off the remaining steps. This porch will have to be demolished and completely rebuilt.

The Time Factor

If a porch is actively crumbling, it will have to be demolished. In many cases, however, porches may crack a little bit, and then stop. This is because a footing has settled an inch or two, and then stopped. The porch may get one or two cracks in this manner, and that's it. The footing will have settled as far as it's going to go, and there may be no further problems for decades.

How can you tell? If the homeowner has had the house a long time, you can ask him. Otherwise, the best way is to ask the former owner, or a neighbor. What you want to know is: How long has this porch been like that, with that degree of cracking? If they say "Gee, I don't know. It must be new. I'm sure it wasn't there last year!" That's the signal to give up. The porch is actively deteriorating. You might as well just tear it off now, before it crumbles completely. However, if they say "Oh, the porch has been like that for as long as I've lived in the neighborhood — must be 20 years now" then you're in luck. The porch may be cracked, but it's stable. Maybe even repairable.

🐾 Replacing Damaged Bricks, Blocks and Mortar

You need to start your repairs from the bottom up. Examine the bricks or blocks in the porch walls. What condition are they in? If they're all in terrible condition, cracked or crumbling, you won't be able to save the porch. If they're all fine, except for a few, as in Figure 8-28, you may be able to chip out the bad ones and replace them. Keep in mind that if you take a brick or block out, the sand behind it will want to pour out through the hole. You'll need to plug the hole immediately to prevent this from happening. The sand performs an important function in holding up the top slab. You want to keep as much of it inside the porch as possible.

Frequently, the bricks or blocks will all be fine. The cracks only run through the mortar, or in some places, the mortar has come loose and is missing. In that case, tuckpointing may be all that's needed.

Parging

What if some of the bricks or blocks are cracked, crumbled a little, pitted or weathered? Will you have to demolish the porch? Maybe, or maybe not. It depends on how far the deterioration has progressed. If substantial chunks have broken off, leaving the top slab unsupported and broken, you probably won't be able to save the porch. However, if the deterioration is mostly on the surface, with no (or hardly any) blocks broken completely through or missing, you may be able to save the porch by parging.

Parging is the process of coating masonry with a layer of concrete. You can't just use ordinary concrete for this. It won't stick. However, there are special concrete mixes designed for this type of repair work. One is *sand mix,* made up of portland cement and sand, without any of the aggregate (small stones) found in regular concrete. It also contains a higher proportion of portland cement, giving it greater strength.

Another material designed for concrete repairs is latex concrete strengthener. It's available in many forms, but I usually buy the liquid form. Latex is a sort of rubber-like material, which, when added to the concrete mix, greatly increases the stickiness and flexibility of the concrete. A mix with a latex additive is much less likely to crack than plain concrete, and it will stick to another layer of concrete or masonry. It's quite expensive — about $20 a gallon. However it's worth it, because it allows you to do jobs that would otherwise be impossible.

Sand mix with a latex strengthener gives you the strongest, stickiest mix available. It has the consistency of mortar, only it's finer and stickier. When you apply it, dampen the surface of the bricks or blocks, and trowel the sand mix evenly over the entire surface. Work it in carefully, making sure to fill all the cracks, pits, and holes. Put it on about a half-inch thick over the entire wall. It's a very time-consuming job; you'll only be able to do about 20 square feet an hour. But don't rush it; take the time to do it right.

When you're done, you'll have a wall that looks like poured concrete. It will be smooth and featureless, with all the pits, holes and cracks filled. Any loose blocks or pieces will be glued together. The new layer of concrete will protect the wall from further weathering. With all the cracks and holes filled, water won't get into the wall and cause further cracking through freezing and thawing. Plus,

the half-inch layer of strengthened concrete will add a substantial amount of strength to the porch wall. It will help make up for the strength the wall may have lost through past deterioration.

Of course, the big question here is: Will this repair last? The answer is yes, as long as the deterioration did not extend all the way through the wall. This technique works best on surface damage, pitting, chipping, weathering, mortar loss, and surface crumbling. It will control some small cracking as well, even if the cracking goes clear through the wall. It can't repair a wall that's completely broken up, however, and it won't do anything about heaving or settling. As a rule, I see more surface damage than any other kind, especially damage caused by weathering. Parging can make a severely-weathered surface look like new. More importantly, it stops the weathering, and extends the life of the masonry by decades.

Parging is a useful technique. I've used it to repair chimneys, for interior basement waterproofing, and many other kinds of masonry repair.

❧ Damage to the Porch Surface

Even if the damage to the support walls of the porch is minor, there can still be serious cracking of the cement top slab. Repairing cement isn't an easy thing to do. In fact, most people won't even try. Here's another area where you're not likely to have much competition.

Concrete looks tough, but it can be surprisingly fragile. Its biggest weakness is that it requires good support. It must be held up by a solid undersurface. If there are any problems with the support, the concrete will crack, heave, or settle. That's what usually happens to porch slabs. If the sand supporting the slab leaks out or the foundation supports settle, the top slab will crack and settle too. The slab will continue to settle until it sits on something that will support it. If the support doesn't settle more, it may stay cracked, but stable, for decades.

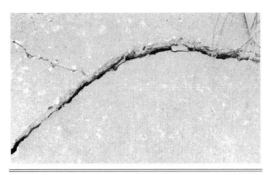

Figure 8-29
Cracked sunken porch slab

What you commonly find is a cracked, sunken spot on a porch, like the one shown in Figure 8-29. The edges around the crack may have crumbled somewhat as well, and the rest of the surface may be pitted and weathered, giving it a very rough look. It may still be quite strong, and easily support the weight of people plus patio furniture or anything else that's likely to be on a porch, but it's uneven and doesn't look very nice.

The simplest way to deal with this is just tear the top off the porch and cast a new slab. That's what most contractors would do. That's not the only solution, and may not be the best solution — it certainly isn't the cheapest.

In order to repair the damaged concrete top slab, you'll need to know about concrete repair in general. The techniques you'll use for this kind of job can be used on all kinds of concrete flatwork. Knowing how to make these repairs can be a very valuable asset for you. I have frequently been able to save thousands of dollars worth of concrete that others would have torn out and replaced.

Concrete Repair

If the porch is stable, it may be possible to pour a new layer of concrete over the old one. This will fill the cracks and level out the sunken area. It sounds easy, but there's a very particular way this repair has to be done. You can't just add a layer of ready-mix concrete over an existing slab. Ordinary pre-mixed concrete doesn't work well for repairs. It isn't designed to be used in thicknesses of less than 2 inches, and won't bond well to previously-laid concrete. It's supposed to be used for new work, not repairs. If you try to use it to layer over old surfaces, or to fill holes, it will crumble and fall off after a few months. Most contractors believe this is inevitable and so they don't even consider repairing concrete. They just demolish damaged concrete and replace it.

My favorite material for concrete repairs is a latex-strengthened sand mix, like the one I use for parging. It's the strongest, stickiest concrete mix you can get. If this doesn't fix the problem, nothing will.

Applying a New Surface — First of all, clean the area you're going to repair. Remove loose stones and bits of concrete. Then mix up a batch of sand mix, adding latex strengthener according to the directions on the bottle. Wet the porch surface and then spread the sand mix evenly over the damaged area. Trowel it out so that it fills any holes, cracks, pits or sunken areas. It's best not to feather out the edges of the repair. Concrete doesn't work well when it's applied thinly. Instead, cut down the edges of the area to be repaired as shown in Figure 8-30. That way, you'll be able to keep your repair thick and still have it come out even with the rest of

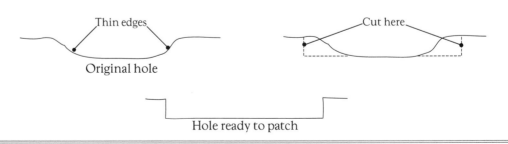

Figure 8-30
Chisel away edges so the hole does not taper

the porch. Use a level to make sure that everything is coming out straight. Be sure to keep the surface damp as it cures, as you would any concrete work.

It's not necessary to coat the whole porch if only one part is bad. However, if you do coat the entire porch, you'll have the effect of resurfacing the concrete, as well as filling the holes. If you do it correctly, the porch will look almost like new.

This material, like all concrete mixes, tends to work best when applied in thick layers. It isn't a good idea to put it on thin. Try to keep it at least ½-inch thick at all points. This is one reason you might not want to coat the entire porch. You may not want to add ½ inch to the sections of the porch that are already the correct height.

Durability — Once the surface repair is complete, the big question is: Will it last? Yes, it will, as long as the porch is stable. I've done a few repairs like this that are still in perfect condition after ten years. However, if a porch is still settling or shifting, the repair will eventually crack. It may last a few years, but you're simply delaying the inevitable replacement of the porch surface. You cannot provide a permanent repair on an unstable surface.

What this boils down to is that I wouldn't offer an unconditional guarantee with this type of repair. You can offer a repair job to the homeowner as a less expensive option, that may or may not provide a permanent fix. It'll probably work, and it's certainly cheaper than replacing the slab, *but there's always an element of risk.* Make sure the homeowner is aware of this — and *get it in writing.* People often "forget" that you warned them the repair might not work.

Cost — How much will the repair cost? That will depend on the size of the porch, and the degree of cracking. Figure 8-31 shows a large porch I repaired. The top slab was 15 feet by 18 feet, and 4 inches thick. It had a cracked, sunken area roughly 8 feet long and 2 feet wide. At its lowest point, the slab had dropped 3 inches. The porch had settled years ago, and though it was damaged, it was quite

Figure 8-31
Large porch with severely damaged slab

Figure 8-32
Quarry tile conceals concrete repair

stable. I made the repairs in four hours using two bags of sand mix and about a quart of latex strengthener. The materials cost about $20. It was a lot cheaper and easier than demolishing the slab and replacing it! Once the slab was level, I laid quarry tile over it to conceal the repair and all the old cracks. Figure 8-32 shows the completed repair and the new tile. This additional work added $400 and 10 hours to the job.

⁊⬤ Repairing Stairs

You can use this same technique to repair concrete stairs. It's especially worthwhile with cast-in-place stairs, as opposed to

Figure 8-33
Cast-in-place stairs need repair

Figure 8-34
Repaired stairs are not very attractive

the hollow, moveable kind. Cast-in-place stairs, like the ones in Figure 8-33, are solid concrete. Demolishing them is a big job. Then you'd still have to build and install another set of stairs. For about the same amount of work it takes to demolish them, you can repair them instead.

New or not, cast-in-place stairs are not particularly beautiful. You can repair the cracks using my concrete repair technique, as I did with the stairs in Figure 8-34, but that does nothing to improve their overall appearance. Because the stairs shown here belonged to a particularly nice house, I decided to do

something special with them. Like the cement porch we just discussed, I covered them with exterior-grade quarry tile.

Adding Tile

As you can see in Figure 8-35, the tiles gave the stairs an expensive, custom look. They are covered with the same type of tile I used on the porch. Tiles are a great way to improve the appearance of any concrete repair.

Installing quarry tiles on exterior concrete surfaces is much the same as installing them on interior surfaces. The main difference is that you need an adhesive that's approved for outdoor use. You can often find quarry tiles very reasonably priced. One reason I decided to use quarry tiles to cover these stairs is because I had just found a great deal on tile. A builders' warehouse store was selling boxes of 1-square-foot tiles for $12.39. With 21 tiles to a box, it worked out to 59 cents a square foot. That's just about the cheapest floor covering you can buy. However, rather than looking cheap, it looks quite expensive.

The problem with installing tiles on stairs is that they're all corners and very little flat area. If you've ever installed tiles, you know that the easy part is covering the large

Figure 8-35
Quarry tile and new railings complete the repair

flat areas. The hard part is fitting the corners. You have to do a lot of cutting to get them to fit properly. It takes longer than you might think to do a stair job. The stairs in Figure 8-35 took me about 10 hours of labor, but the material cost was quite reasonable — only about $75.

Besides stairs and porches, this kind of tile can be used on walkways, patios, walls, and anything else that might look nice tiled. Not only is tile beautiful and weatherproof, but it covers up a wide variety of surface defects. You can also use it to cover a less attractive material, such as cement block. Keep it in mind whenever you have a surface that's solid but weathered, pitted, or just plain ugly.

I'll cover general decorating projects, style, and design in later sections of the book. However, installing quarry tile is one of those overlapping areas where a design element is also part of the repair, so it fit very nicely here.

Chapter 9

Repairing Concrete Work, Foundations and Drainage Problems

*I*f you've ever had concrete flatwork done, you know that it's very expensive. Most of this is the cost of the concrete itself. The cost of the labor involved is minimal. That's why I usually contract it out. Doing the work myself doesn't save much.

Concrete work requires a great deal of back-breaking, unskilled, minimum-wage work. I try to avoid work like this and concentrate on jobs that require the special skills and expertise that I can charge a lot of money for. Hauling wheelbarrows full of concrete for $5 an hour isn't exactly my idea of a good time.

The only concrete jobs I do myself are very small ones. Subcontracting small jobs is impractical because contractors need to charge a minimum amount just to make it worth their time. You might as well do it yourself as pay the minimum charge for a tiny job.

The quality of concrete work varies tremendously. I've seen some that's so poor you can crush it with your bare hands. Obviously, concrete like this isn't worth repairing. Age is not necessarily a factor in determining if concrete needs replacing. In many cases, I've found that concrete poured in the old days is better than the work done today. I've seen concrete flatwork, especially sidewalks, stamped 1901 that was in perfect condition, while other concrete, dated 1987, was falling apart. Today, a lot of contractors pour concrete too late in the season, use too many additives, and don't cure the concrete well enough. This tends to shorten the life of concrete. If concrete is properly mixed, installed, and cured, it can last for centuries.

Concrete Mixes

There are a few different types of concrete mixes that you will be dealing with in repair work: ready mix, mortar mix, sand mix and, on occasion, transit mix. While all these products are similar, each is a designed for a different purpose.

The basic ingredient of all concrete is portland cement. It's the sticky stuff that holds it all together. Portland cement, sand, gravel and water are mixed together to make standard concrete. If you buy ready mix, the sand and gravel are already added in the correct proportions. That's why it's called ready mix; all you have to add is water and it's ready to use. Ready mix is ideal for small concrete jobs, like cementing in a fence post, or putting in a small patio or sidewalk.

Mortar mix is used to mortar masonry materials together. It has more portland cement than ready mix, and only very small pieces of gravel. As a result, it's stickier than ready mix, so it's better for holding block or brick together. You would get a very poor result using ready mix for masonry work — the units wouldn't hold together well.

Sand mix is made of portland cement and sand, without any gravel. That's why it's called sand mix. It has a lot more portland cement in it than ready mix, so it's very sticky, but also very expensive. It costs about twice as much as ready mix and is designed specifically for concrete repairs. Sand mix should be used in any application in which concrete will be poured in a layer 2 inches thick or less. A 2-inch layer of ready mix would crumble if you used it in a repair, but sand mix won't. Sand mix is substantially stronger than ready mix. However, you only want to use it for small repairs because of the cost.

Most lumber yards sell bags of pure portland cement that you can buy to make your own mixes with. You add the sand, gravel and water in the proportions that you want for your concrete. You should know what you're doing if you mix your own. The wrong proportions can make your concrete weak.

For large jobs, concrete is ordered by the cubic yard in what's called transit mix. This is what you get when the big cement-mixer trucks deliver it to the job site. You would use transit mix for driveways, foundations and large patio and sidewalk jobs. It's usually delivered in 5 cubic yard minimums. Even if you only need 1 or 2 cubic yards, you would have to pay for 5 cubic yards of transit mix. That's why I subcontract out large concrete jobs. I rarely have a need for that much concrete, and if I do, it's too much for me to work without experienced help. I stick to jobs that I can do with ready-mix concrete.

Repairing Concrete Flatwork

The technique we described for repairing porch slabs in the last chapter will work on all kinds of concrete flatwork. It also works well on pits, holes or surfaces where the damage is limited to a fairly small area. The repair mix is somewhat expensive; so it wouldn't be cost-effective to try to use it over too large an area. Big slabs of concrete that are heaved or settled should just be replaced.

Sometimes I come across concrete that's in reasonably good condition, except for one or two bad spots. This is especially true in the case of sidewalks. For some reason, the edges of sidewalk sections that abut each other often crumble, even though the rest of the walk may be fine. This is a code violation; and you may be required to rip up the sidewalk and replace it, especially if the house is being fixed up to sell. However, if you can do a solid, nice-looking repair job, building inspectors often let it go. That can easily save your customers a thousand dollars or more. Then they can use the money towards paying you to do something more interesting, like a new bathroom. If you can save a sidewalk and use the money for a bathroom instead, from the homeowner's point of view, it'll be almost like getting the bathroom for free. As a rule, building inspectors will only be looking at the remodeling work that you are hired to do. If the homeowners aren't interested in concrete repair, you won't be required by an inspector to do concrete work that isn't part of the job. However, if you are doing a whole house rehab, concrete work is often part of the repairs.

Begin the repair by clearing away dirt or weeds from the damaged area. It's impossible to tell just how much damage there is until the area is clean. It might be much more than it appears, or much less. You should also remove loose stones or crumbling concrete. When the damaged area is clean, fill it with strengthened sand mix. Be sure to add or replace the crack control lines between the slabs. That will help prevent the spread of damage in the future.

Repaired slabs look repaired, but that doesn't usually matter. Most people don't worry too much about having beautiful sidewalks, unless it's the one leading to the front door. But they *do* want their walkways to be safe to walk on. Most building inspectors will accept a good repair job. If you're in doubt and don't want to spend time on something that you're not sure will pass inspection, ask the inspector ahead of time.

I've found this type of repair to be quite durable. I recently checked on one that I did 12 years ago, and it was still in fine condition. That isn't bad, especially when you consider that some new sidewalks don't last that long.

❧ Other Concrete Repairs

As I said before, concrete flatwork that has suffered extensive damage should be torn out and replaced. However, you only need to tear out what absolutely has to be removed. Sometimes, that's only one or two bad blocks of concrete. A driveway or sidewalk that appeared at first to be unsalvageable might be just fine after one or two bad areas are replaced.

This kind of repair works best if it involves a section of concrete that has crack-control lines or expansion joints. The cracking, heaving, or settling will often stop when it reaches the line or joint. That's why they're cut into sidewalks and other big concrete pours. Unfortunately, not everyone understands the purpose of these lines. I've seen huge slabs of concrete poured with no crack-control lines at all. Once a crack develops, there's nothing to stop it. It will go from one end of the slab to the other.

If there's a damaged area that's circumscribed by crack-control lines, you can just break out the bad piece and replace it. But if there aren't any crack-control lines, the job isn't so clear cut. Does that mean you have to tear out the whole slab, even if it's the size of an entire patio? Not necessarily. There's another alternative. You can cut out or cut off the bad area with a cement saw.

A cement saw is a big machine with a saw blade that can cut through concrete. You have to hook it up to running water while it's cutting so that the blade remains cool. They're available to rent for about $100 at most any store that rents tools. Cut a neat rectangle around the damaged area, and break it out. The resulting hole can be filled with ordinary concrete. You don't need to use the sand mix that I recommended for small repairs because the new piece of slab will be 4 inches thick or the full thickness of the rest of the slab. It won't need to bond to an underlayer. It's just like pouring any other small slab of concrete. There will be a seam where the new slab was added, but when it cures, it won't be particularly noticeable. Repairing a 3- or 4-foot damaged area, using a cement saw and ready-mix concrete, will run about $200 including labor and materials. Making a repair like this is only worthwhile if the damaged area is relatively small. The bigger the damaged area is, the more the repair costs, and the less worthwhile it is to try and save the slab.

❧ Patio Repair

There's another way to save a patio that's in bad shape. You can level it out with sand and then cover it with patio blocks. This even works on a patio that's broken up and heaved. Essentially, what you're doing is burying the old patio under a new layer of patio material. Since that's the case, it doesn't matter what shape the old patio is in. Of course, you could tear out the old patio and put the cement patio blocks in the space instead, but why bother? Tearing out concrete is a lot of work, and it creates a disposal problem. If you leave it, it will act as a nice solid underlayment for your patio blocks — and save you a great deal of work.

You may be wondering why I go to all this trouble to save concrete flatwork. The reason is because concrete flatwork is very expensive to put in, and it doesn't add much to the overall value of the house once it's there. So you don't want to go to a lot of expense to put in new flatwork if you can avoid it. Also, unless you're in the concrete business, you're probably going to have to subcontract the work. That means thousands

Figure 9-1
Mortar between stones has worn away

of homeowner dollars going into someone else's pocket, not yours. If you can save homeowners that money, they'll be able to spend it on something *you* can do for them. That makes everyone happy.

Foundation Repairs

While we're on the subject of concrete and masonry repairs, let's talk about the foundation of the house itself. You'll find that most serious foundation problems are below grade. That means they either have to be fixed from beneath the house (usually from under the crawl space or inside the basement), or the foundation has to be dug out from the outside. Many of these problems involve the same types of repair that we discussed when we were dealing with porch foundations, only on a larger scale.

Damaged foundations can be a serious problem. If the entire foundation of the house is crumbling and unstable, it may have to be completely replaced. This would be the case if, for example, the footings had deteriorated and the basement walls were collapsing. Replacing an entire foundation is a job best left to contractors who specialize in this kind of work. It's possible to replace the foundation of a house while the house is still in place, but it's a touchy job.

❧ Minor Foundation Damage

Luckily, I rarely come across foundation problems that are this severe. Most of the problems I see are either fairly easy to repair, or the damage is localized. Problems like these can often be repaired by just one or two men, with floor jacks and ordinary tools.

How can you tell whether the damage to the foundation is minor or major? First of all, inspect the house itself. Is there any evidence of sagging? Do the walls seem to be dipping down at any point? Is the interior plaster cracked? If so, do the cracks appear to be coming from one point?

If the answer to any of these questions is *yes,* then the house may have lost support from the foundation — although that's not the only cause of these kinds of problems. However, if none of the above is true, then the damage is probably minor, just on the surface.

Stone Foundations

The foundations on most older homes are built of brick, cement block, or stone. Poured concrete foundations are not often found on houses built before 1950.

A very common problem with stone foundations is that the mortar holding the stones in place has gone bad, and many of the stones are just held together by the pressure of one stone against the other. Figure 9-1 shows a foundation in just that condition. Bricks and stones last practically forever, but mortar doesn't. Mortar is highly alkaline and rainwater is slightly acid. Over the course of a hundred years or so, rainwater will dissolve the mortar between the stones. If a house is about 100 years old, chances are it's time to replace the mortar. Older homes with brick or block exterior walls and foundations are usually tuckpointed periodically. If the foundation isn't too badly damaged, tuckpointing these foundations may solve the problem. However, if the foundation is made of stone, the problem is a little more difficult. Stones are irregular shapes, and that makes them harder to handle.

Fortunately, a lot of old stone foundations were massively overbuilt. It isn't unusual to find a stone foundation that's 2 feet thick! They can sustain a lot of damage, and still be strong enough to hold up a house. In many cases, the deterioration may be almost entirely on the surface. Damage like this is caused by exposure to weather. Since only the surface is exposed, that's the only part that deteriorates. Often, the damage may consist of nothing more than a few stones that have come loose and fallen out. Loose stones are fairly simple to fix. You just have to clean out any old and crumbling mortar, and remortar the stones back into place. If any of the stones appear to be cracked or crumbling around the edges, replace them with stones of a similar size and shape.

Old-time masons knew that mortar would cause problems, not stones. The best-built stone foundations were those where the stones fit together tightly, and required very little mortar. If you find a foundation like this, try to preserve the fit. If you can't make the stones fit tightly back into their original positions and you try to make up for it by using more mortar, you'll wind up with an inferior foundation.

It's often difficult to work with these kinds of foundations because the stones are such irregular sizes and shapes. A stone, like the one in Figure 9-2, that falls out of a particular spot, will only fit well in that one spot. When you're making repairs and you have to remove a few stones, it's important to keep track of exactly where each loose stone came from. If there are several, you might want to either number them, or lay them out on the ground in the same order that you removed them and make a little diagram of how they fit together.

If you don't keep track of the stones, you'll be sorry. A pile of loose stones is like a jigsaw puzzle. It can take you hours to figure out how they were put together. When the foundation wall was originally built, a century ago or so, life moved at a slower pace. The mason who built it wasn't in a hurry. He probably spent weeks fitting all the stones together just perfectly. You can't afford to

Figure 9-2
Each stone fits into its own space

spend weeks reconstructing it. So, whatever you do, don't get the stones mixed up!

You may occasionally come across a foundation made of rectangular cut stones, like the one shown in Figure 9-3, rather than irregular fieldstones. This type of foundation was more commonly used to build luxury homes. They're a lot easier to work with. They're about the same size and shape as cement blocks, and handle about the same, except they're a lot heavier. (The early cement block foundations, those cast with a stone texture in their surface, were supposed to look like these cut stone blocks.) You won't have the problems fitting cut stones together like you will with fieldstones.

Figure 9-3
Foundation made with cut stones

Figure 9-4
Cracked cement-block foundation wall

What if the foundation is made of stones that are poorly fitted together, with a lot of mortar to make up the difference? By "a lot," I mean a band of mortar 2 to 4 inches thick. In some cases there's almost as much mortar as stone. If the mortar in a foundation made like this is crumbling, the foundation has serious problems.

You'll have to determine how deep the damage goes. Take out a few surface stones and probe the inner layers of mortar. Is it crumbling all the way through? If it is, you'll be able to work your probe completely through the wall. There'll be nothing really solid to stop it. A foundation like this will need to be replaced.

Brick Foundations

Besides the need for tuckpointing, the other common problem I've found with brick foundations is crumbling bricks. If only a few are bad, you can just chisel them out and replace them. Brick foundations, like stone foundations, are usually quite thick. You can remove a few bricks from the surface layer without disturbing the house. The nice thing about bricks is that they're all the same size. Unlike stones, you don't have to remember where each one went, or find one just the right size to replace a bad one.

Block Walls

I don't see as much damage to cement block foundations as I do other materials. In fact, they're often in better condition than poured concrete foundations, even though the poured foundations are newer. The most common defect I see in block walls is cracked mortar, like that shown in Figure 9-4. You can repair this with tuckpointing. Tuckpointing will take care of lot of minor damage, including cracked blocks, as long as the wall is still stable. You can see that the blocks in Figure 9-4 were also slightly out of line, probably the result of settling. The wall was still stable, so tuckpointing was all that was needed to take care of the problem.

If the blocks themselves are crumbling, the problem is more serious. Block walls are only one block thick. Because of this, you can't just take out a few blocks. There'll be nothing in their place to hold up the house. You'll have to support the house at that point before you can make the repairs.

Serious Foundation Problems

Many of the repairs that require supporting the house are serious and may be beyond your capacity. We're going to discuss repairs here that are suitable for a foundation that has failed at a single point. For example, a foundation that is mostly solid, but has one bad spot, like a few cracked blocks in one location. If the overall foundation isn't generally solid, or if it has many bad spots, it needs to be replaced.

Constructing Supports

If the house has begun to sag in one area, or you need to make foundation repairs that will temporarily weaken its structure, you'll have to support the house before you can proceed any further. You'll have to build a support in the basement or crawl space to hold up the section of the house where you'll be working. To simplify our discussion, let's assume that you're working on a house with a basement. The technique you use to make these repairs is very similar to the one we used when repairing the porch foundation, especially if you're working in a crawl space. In a basement, you usually have the advantage of being able to stand upright to work.

First, you'll need to construct a beam. Two 2 x 12s nailed together usually work well for this purpose. The beam should be long enough to support all of the floor joists that are over the bad section of foundation.

Position the beam in the basement parallel to the bad wall, about 1 or 2 feet away from it. You want it to be close enough to the foundation wall to adequately hold up the ends of the joists, yet far enough away to give you room to work. When the beam is in the correct location, nail it to the joists so that it hangs there, suspended by the nails. This will prevent it from falling on your head later, when you take the jacks out from under it.

Support the beam by placing at least two floor jacks under it — three or four jacks aren't a bad idea. The more jacks you use, the less stress there is on each one. Be sure that they're perfectly vertical before you start tightening them. Remember, they'll be under a lot of pressure. If they're crooked, the pressure could cause them to shoot out sideways at high speed.

Place a steel plate on the basement floor under each jack post. The plates help distribute the stress over a wider area of floorspace. Otherwise, there's a chance that the pressure created when you jack up the beam may push the jack post right through the basement floor, creating a big hole. This won't happen with good quality concrete, but that's not usually what you'll find in an old basement. Basement floors in older homes are often very poor quality. If you should accidentally punch a hole in the floor, you can patch it. But the fewer things you have to fix, the easier your work will be.

You need to increase the pressure on the jacks slowly and carefully, as we did with the porch. If part of the house has sagged, you'll want to level it back out, but again, this kind of work must be done with patience. You need to be even more careful than you'd be if you were working on a porch. The main part of the house is much more fragile. You now have the upstairs plasterwork, the subfloor and the floorboards to worry about. Remember, the sagging occurred over many years. You can't just jack it back into place in

a few minutes. Don't plan on more upward movement than $1/8$ to $1/4$ inch per day. If you try to do more, the house will fight you. It will be very difficult to tighten the jacks. If you let it adjust to its new position overnight, the next day you'll find that the jacks you couldn't budge the night before have become easier to tighten. Some of them may almost be loose!

If you find the jacks very difficult to tighten, don't force them. Don't pound on them, or use an extra-long wrench for leverage. If you do, you're likely to knock them out of position. Instead, use more jacks. When the weight is distributed over more jacks, each one will be easier to tighten.

If you're in doubt as to whether it's necessary to add support to make your repairs, do it anyway. Even if the part of the wall you're working on appears to be adequately supported and you're not tearing out the entire wall, it's still a good idea to support the house with a beam and jack posts. A beam should be used if anything more than surface repairs is to be done. After all, if you tear out half the thickness of the wall, can you be sure that the other half will still support the house? If it doesn't, the house may sag further, causing massive cracking upstairs. By supporting the load with a beam, you can do anything you want to a wall and you won't have to worry about what might happen.

Rebuilding the Foundation

Once the weight of the house has been transferred to the new beam, you can begin work on the foundation. You don't need to wait until the house has been jacked back into the correct position to begin repairs. Bringing a sagging house back into a level position can take weeks. As long as the weight of the house is being held up by the beam and jacks, and not by the foundation wall, you can begin working on the foundation. If necessary, you can tear out the entire foundation wall, including the footings, and replace everything.

If you decide to tear out the entire wall, you'll have dig the dirt away on the outside of the basement first. Otherwise, the dirt that's supported by the basement wall will pour into the basement once you break through the wall. If the wall is stone or brick, cutting completely through the wall may not be necessary. You only need to replace the part that's deteriorated. Working from the inside, that's often only a few inches into a thick wall. However, if the wall is cement block, one block thick, replacing any part will involve going completely through the wall, and you *will* have to dig it out from the outside as well.

Sills and Joists — While working on the wall, check the sills and the ends of the joists for damage. They may be rotted, or damaged by termites. It's always a good idea to replace the old sill with treated wood when you rebuild a foundation wall, and bolt the new sill to the new wall. Set the anchors for these bolts when you rebuild the wall. Rot-damaged joists should be doubled to ensure proper support.

If the sills or joists are rotted, the house may be sagging, even though the foundation may be perfect. In that case, replacing the sills and doubling the joists may be all that you need to do. You still need to jack up the house and support it in order to replace the sill. Otherwise, the whole weight of the house will be pressing down on the rotted sill, making it impossible to get it out and put another one in.

I've heard a lot recently about how bad it is for untreated wood to rest on masonry. Supposedly, untreated wood which touches masonry will quickly rot. Some contractors are now tearing out large amounts of wood just because it comes in contact with masonry.

I've never found this to be a problem in Michigan. I've worked on many buildings where untreated pine has been sitting directly on masonry for 100 years or more, and it's still fine. Perhaps this rot problem exists in moist regions, such as along the coasts, but it's never been a serious problem in the Midwest, as far as I know. Of course, I always check carefully for rot damage anyway. Many basements and crawl spaces have had long-term leakage or moisture problems which can cause serious rot problems to any wood, not just that sitting on masonry.

Rebuilding the Wall — How you rebuild the wall depends on whether it's important to the owners to retain historical accuracy. If it is, you'll need to rebuild it exactly as it was. If not, you might want to consider some easier construction method. This is especially true of stone foundations.

As I mentioned earlier, stone is very difficult to work with. In many cases, the original masons used very large stones for the lower parts of the wall to provide extra strength. This can make the lower part of the foundation extremely hard to work with. Some stones I've seen were up to 3 feet across. It must have been a heck of a job getting them positioned there in the first place, especially when you consider that most of the work was done by hand, with the hauling being done by horses. You know that it will be a heck of a job working with them now! Stone foundations may be very pretty from the outside, but if your repair is in a dark corner of an unfinished basement, how much do looks matter?

My experience has been that, unless you're working with historic properties, it's a lot easier to rebuild the foundation with cement block. Putting stones back together, or replacing stones with ones that fit just right, is far too time-consuming. Blocks are all the same size; all you have to do is put them in. You'll save a tremendous amount of time using blocks. If a stone wall is very thick, you may need to use two layers of cement block to match the thickness. But putting in two layers of cement block is still a lot easier than building up a 2-foot-thick stone wall. Figure 9-5 shows a stone foundation repair using cement blocks.

If you're working on a house where the look of the foundation *does* matter to the owners, and you have to rebuild the foundation all the way through to the exterior surface, you may be able to finish the outside with a stone facade. Use cement block for the interior of the wall and then cement a layer of stones to the outside. It will look like a stone foundation, but you'll only have to use a single layer of stones. That'll save you a lot of work.

It's also possible to use poured concrete to replace a section of foundation. The problem with doing this is that it's often difficult to build the forms in the small space you have to work in. For small repairs, 4 feet wide or so, I've found cement block to be the easiest way to solve the problem. However, if a larger section needs to be replaced, poured concrete might save time. I prefer to subcontract this out to a contractor who specializes in these kinds of repairs. Figure 9-6 shows a foundation repaired in this manner. A large triangular section of the foundation was torn out and replaced with poured concrete. The stones on each side of the newly-poured section were still strong, so they were left in place. The contractor blended the new concrete in with the stones on each side of the repair.

Permanent Beams and Posts

Once the wall is repaired, you need to decide what to do with the beam you made. I prefer to leave the new beam in place and install permanent posts to add extra support to the house. As far as I'm concerned, you can never have too much support. The more support the house has, the less likely it is to sag in the future.

The main drawback to doing this is that the new posts and beams are usually fairly ugly and they take up room in the basement. That may not be a problem if the basement is just used for storage and laundry facilities. Most older homes don't have basements with enough headroom to be used for living space anyway. It rarely matters to the owners whether the basement is pretty. Given a choice, they would rather have the extra support.

If you intend to leave the beam installed permanently, it should be supported by treated 4 x 4 posts. The new posts should be standing on post anchors and footings poured just for them. This is especially important if the concrete on the basement floor is poured thin or is a poor-quality concrete, as is often the case in older homes. I've worked in

Figure 9-5
*Foundation wall repaired
with cement blocks*

some basements where the concrete was so poor that you could dig right through it with the point of a spade! If the posts don't have their own footings, they'll eventually push through the basement floor.

Cost

Foundation repairs usually don't cost very much in terms of materials, but they are very time-consuming. For example, if you have to take down a stone wall, clean out the bad mortar and then remortar the stones back in place, it'll take about ½ hour per cubic

Figure 9-6
Poured concrete used to repair damaged foundation

157

foot of stonework. If the stone wall is 2 feet thick by 8 feet tall, and you need to rebuild a section that's 4 feet wide, you'll be working with 64 cubic feet of stonework. That's about 32 hours of work, almost a week, to rebuild just one little section of wall! It's very labor-intensive work. It's no wonder people don't build with stone much any more.

Stone walls also use large amounts of mortar, depending, of course, on how closely the stones are set. I've found that I average one bag of mortar for every 2 cubic feet of stone. So the repair to that same 4-foot section would take 32 bags of mortar. Luckily, mortar is cheap. The stones, of course, cost nothing, since you can reuse the original stones. It's your time that costs! As a point of contrast, if you were to make the same repair using cement block, it would take you about an hour, 40 cement blocks and less than one bag of mortar to do a one-layer repair. If the repair required you to replace the whole 2-foot thick wall section, you'd need approximately 120 cement blocks for a three-layer thickness and three bags of mortar. Your material costs would be under $100 either way; the only change would be in your labor. However, even if it took you five or six hours, that's still a huge time savings when you consider the labor involved in working with stone. You can see why I prefer to use cement block.

Keep in mind, however, that none of these techniques will repair a massively-deteriorated foundation. These are localized techniques to deal with localized problems. These kinds of repair are only adequate for fairly small areas. If major areas of the foundation are heaved or settled, or if the footings are bad, the entire foundation will probably have to be replaced. This means that the house will have to be jacked up, and the foundation removed and replaced by someone with the specialized skills and equipment to handle that kind of work.

Directing Water Flow

Another area you may want to look at, especially if the house has foundation damage that appears to be caused by excessive weathering or erosion, is the exterior drainage system. This is something that you may have to deal with anyway. Many basement problems originate with poor drainage outside the house. The first place to check is the ground around the exterior foundation of the house. If there is standing water or very wet soil around the foundation, you'll need to determine the cause. What does the grade around the house look like? When the house was originally constructed, it should have been graded so that the house was a little bit higher than the surrounding land. The lot should slope away from the house so that rainwater and other runoff flow away from the house, not towards it.

As I pointed out during the inspection process in Chapter 2, all sorts of things can happen to the soil over the years. It could be that the house is now the lowest point on the lot, instead of the highest. In this case, water would tend to run toward the house and pool up around it. This water can erode the foundation or soak through it and find its way into the basement.

You might think that the simplest way to deal with this problem is to get a few loads of topsoil and pile it up around the house. But this isn't always the best idea. Check the level of the soil around the house. It may already be higher than it should be, due to a buildup of leaves and sod over the last 100-odd years. Remember, you must keep the soil well away from the wood parts of the house, or you'll cause serious rot problems. It's best to have at least 6 inches from the soil to the sill. If adding more topsoil would fill in this space, don't do it. It would be better to change the grade around the house by removing soil from the lot instead.

Removing soil is easier said than done. You may have to take away a couple of dumptrucks-full in order to level out the lot. That will probably totally destroy the lawn and other landscaping. This isn't a job you'll want to do yourself; leave this one to landscapers with heavy equipment.

❧ Gutters and Downspouts

Without resorting to landscapers and heavy equipment, there are a few other measures you can take to redirect water runoff. People tend not to take gutters and downspouts seriously. However, they're extremely important in keeping water away from the foundation and preventing basement leaks. They're the first line of defense against rainwater. If you look at the roof of a house during a rainstorm, you'll notice that there's a tremendous amount of water pouring off of it. If that water is allowed to pour onto the ground around the house and sit there, the soil will become totally soaked. If there's no drainage around the foundation, the water will remain there until it can find someplace to go, and that's usually into the basement. Properly-installed gutters and downspouts catch the water that's coming off the roof and direct it away from the house. This may be all you need to do to keep the ground around the house reasonably dry.

A key point here is that you need to run extensions on the downspouts as far away from the house as possible. You can't just let the downspouts empty out on the ground next to the house if the grade around the house is wrong. That won't accomplish anything. You need to make sure that the water runs off in a direction away from the house.

A good place to send the water is out onto a concrete driveway. If the driveway has been poured correctly, it should then direct the water away from the house and into the street. If a driveway isn't available, any other nonporous surface, like a patio, will do. Failing that, try to direct the water toward a part of the lawn that slopes away from the house. If none of these is available, just run the extension out as far as you can. This will allow the water time to soak into the soil before it gets to the house.

This seems very simple, but it's amazing how often it will solve a drainage problem completely. Since it's simple and cheap, it should be one of the first things you should try.

Gutter Problems

Some older homes have no roof gutters. If the house is over 100 years old, the roof may not be designed to accommodate them. Houses this age often have fascia boards that slope backwards at a 45-degree angle, instead of straight up and down, like more modern homes. You can't use spikes to attach a gutter to a fascia board like this. However, there are roof-mounted brackets that can hold the gutter. Of course, roof gutters aren't historically accurate on a house this old. They won't look quite right. You'll have to decide which is more important: a perfect-looking roof, or proper drainage.

I worked on one 100-year-old home that had never had gutters. Interestingly enough, I found a complete set of very old-fashioned, round steel gutters in the garage. They dated back to around 1940. Apparently, someone had bought them over a half century ago, but had never gotten around to putting them on. *That's* what I call procrastinating!

Be sure that the house has enough downspouts. I've often seen gutter runs of 40 feet or more with only one downspout. This may work okay in a drizzle, but in a downpour the single downspout won't be able to handle the flow. Also, if there's only one downspout and it becomes clogged, the gutters won't work at all. They'll simply fill up and spill over. This won't do any good in terms of keeping the water away from the house. It's also possible that the spillover in the gutter may go back towards the house and flow in behind the fascia boards or under the shingles, causing interior leaks. Avoid problems like this by adding downspouts. I always try to have one downspout for every 20 feet of gutter.

Extension Problems

The biggest problem with long downspout extensions is that they are sometimes in the way, and no one really understands why they are there. People often just think they're a nuisance; they have to mow around them and avoid them when they're walking around the house. If you don't carefully explain the importance of the extensions, they can cause a few difficulties.

159

For example, I own and rent out a couple of houses that had basement leaks. I eliminated the leaks by installing gutters and downspouts with extra-long extensions. However, every time a new tenant moves into one of these houses, I get a call a few months later telling me that the basement is leaking. When I check it out, I find that either the downspout extension has been stepped on and crushed so that water can't get through it any more, or it's been removed (or both). The tenants usually tell me they took it off because it was in the way. They didn't think it would make any difference. I have to put on a new extension, and explain to them why they shouldn't take it off. This solves the problem until I have a new tenant. Even if I explain the problem to them very carefully when they first move in, eventually they forget, and I have to go through this all over again. They just can't seem to make the connection between the downspout extension and the basement until the basement begins filling with water!

The point I'm trying to make here is that if you use long downspout extensions, be sure the homeowner understands their purpose and how important they are. They won't do any good if they're taken off.

🐌 Exterior Barriers

Another way to keep water away from the house is to put something over the soil that water can't get through. If you can keep the rainwater out of the soil for 3 or 4 feet around the house, the odds are that the soil next to the house will stay dry and so will the foundation and the basement. A little bit of water won't cause problems; you don't need to keep the soil dry as dust. It's only important that the area around the house not be soaked.

If the house has a driveway on one side, that side is taken care of. The rain should run down into the street. A concrete patio also makes a good barrier. If the house doesn't have one, consider adding one. Not only will it help solve the drainage problem, but it's a nice feature in itself. It does double duty, making it even more worthwhile.

If a concrete patio would be too expensive, making one out of cement patio blocks will work almost as well. If you put a layer of heavy plastic underneath the blocks, any water that seeps through the seams between the blocks will be caught by the plastic and directed away. Patio blocks are cheap, and easy to install.

Porches also act as barriers against general deterioration and water runoff. If there are problems under the porch, they're probably caused by water pouring under the porch and puddling up there. Check the grading around and under the porch and fill in any low spots.

With a porch, driveway, and patio, you conceivably have three sides of the house protected. What about the last side? What you do here depends on how a barrier will fit in with the landscaping, and how visible it is. If it doesn't show much, you might be able to add a layer of patio blocks over plastic to make a walkway, or even pour a concrete sidewalk along the side of the house. This can be attractive if it's carefully designed.

If concrete is not in keeping with the homeowner's landscaping plans, you can lay down a layer of heavy plastic covered with small stones or wood chips. It will look like a flower bed, but still protect the house around the foundation. Be sure the soil underneath the plastic is graded away from the house. You want the rain to be caught by the plastic and directed *out* into the grass, not the other way. This approach isn't as good as concrete, but it's better than nothing. Its biggest advantages are that it's cheap, and you can use it anywhere. If the house doesn't have a patio, driveway, or porch on the side, and the homeowner doesn't want to add one, you could use the plastic on any or all sides of the house, where necessary. With a few decorations, it won't look bad at all.

The biggest problem with plastic is that it can be easily torn, especially if people walk on it. Once it's torn, it won't work anymore. Another problem is that, while the area may look like a flower bed, you can't actually plant flowers in it. Be sure the homeowners understand this. If they cut holes in the plastic for flowers, water will get under the barrier, defeating its whole purpose. It's possible to have flowers in this area, but they need to be in aboveground planters.

You can buy enough plastic to surround an average size house for about $20. The greater cost will be for the stones or chips to cover it. They need to be laid 3 inches thick in order to look good. If you're doing an extensive area, you could wind up using several cubic yards of material. You'll need to check the price of the materials at a local dealer. However, it will probably cost $100 to $200, depending on what you use, and how much. It takes about four hours to do one side of a house in this manner.

Figure 9-7
New driveway will direct water runoff into street

Driveway and Patio Problems

On rare occasions, you may come across a house that has foundation problems or a basement leaking badly on the driveway or patio side. Instead of solving the drainage problem, the driveway seems to be making it worse! In a case like this, check the grade on the driveway or patio. Most likely it's angled wrong, and tilting towards the house instead of away from it.

The driveway in Figure 9-7 was just such a problem. The driveway was level, but it was built higher than the house it belonged to, and lower than the house next to it. As a result, the runoff from the neighboring house, as well as from the driveway, ran down the slope and settled around the foundation of the house. The porch foundation at the front of the house was rotted and decayed and there was water in the basement. I had the old driveway removed, the excess dirt hauled away, and contracted out the installation of a new concrete driveway. You can see that the new driveway slants away from the house and is several inches lower than both houses. By laying the driveway in two sections, each angled towards the middle, the driveway provides a natural channel for water runoff. I had the driveway brought right up to the house, covering an old cracked and broken walkway that ran from the garage to the side door. Having a new driveway built with the correct grade solved the drainage problem, eliminated the water in

the basement, and prevented future problems with the repairs I made to the porch.

Although laying a new driveway is the ideal way to repair a problem like this, it's expensive. This job took three days and cost $3,000, including the demolition and removal of the old driveway and regrading the slope. It was a big project, and one I had to subcontract out to a concrete contractor. Homeowners may not want to spend that kind of money to tear out an existing driveway or patio and pour a new one, even if it's graded incorrectly. In this particular case, the problem was severe and warranted the expense.

A less expensive solution may be to add a concrete seal between the house and the driveway or patio. This seal is essentially a triangular-shaped piece of concrete fitted into the point at which the main concrete slab touches the foundation of the house. It should fill in the low spot at the foundation, and direct water back out onto the main slab and away from the house.

You can make the seal with a batch of my favorite concrete patching mix — latex-strengthened sand mix. Remember, ordinary concrete can't be applied in a thin layer like this. It would crumble. Don't add too much water to the sand mix. You want it fairly stiff, so that it stays where you put it. Pour the mix over the joint between the foundation and the slab. Trowel it out so that it goes up the foundation a little way, and out onto the slab until it reaches the point at which the slab levels out.

Ideally, you should extend this additional piece of concrete out onto the slab until you hit a point that's level. This would make sure the water runs away from the house, and down the driveway or patio. If you don't extend the repair to a level point on the main slab, water will puddle up between the high points of your repair on one side, and the high edge of the main slab on the other. This may or may not be a problem, depending on how the driveway or patio lies. At worst, moisture trapped in this area might tend to freeze over in the winter, creating a dangerous slick spot.

In some cases, it might be necessary to extend the repair completely across the slab before it comes to a spot that's level enough to direct water away from the house without puddling. This is a different technique, called an overlay. It works, but uses a lot of concrete. It's almost like putting another driveway over the old one. The best candidate for an overlay is a driveway that's solid and in good condition, but angled incorrectly. If the slab is massively heaved, badly broken up, or more than a few inches out of line, this type of repair won't work. Slabs in that bad a condition should be replaced.

The cost for materials to add a concrete seal between the house and the driveway is about $20, and it only takes about two hours to do. An overlay on a driveway is a big job, one that should be subcontracted out to a concrete contractor. For a driveway like the one in Figure 9-7, an overlay would take a crew of six one day and cost approximately $1,000. You may have to shop around for a contractor that will do this type of job. Overlays are tricky. If they aren't done right, they'll break up. Because of this, many concrete contractors don't want to do them.

Laying Asphalt — If the driveway is solid, but out of line, you have one other option. You can have it covered with asphalt and have the asphalt laid to correct the angle.

Asphalt is a lot cheaper than concrete; and laying it over the old driveway saves the trouble of tearing the driveway out. Asphalt can be poured right over concrete, as long as the concrete is solid. Don't have asphalt poured over a driveway that's badly broken up. The cracks will eventually come through.

The disadvantage of an asphalt driveway is that not everyone likes asphalt. It's hot in the summertime, and it smells when it's new. Asphalt driveways never look as nice as concrete drives. However, they're not at all as expensive, either. Tearing out an existing drive and replacing it with concrete will cost roughly five times as much as simply covering the old one with asphalt. This option is not suitable for patios. Nobody would want an asphalt patio! They might be willing to park their car on asphalt, but no one wants to have a party on it.

Handling asphalt requires special equipment. Resurfacing a driveway with asphalt is another job you'll have to sub out to a specialty contractor.

Chapter 10

Garage Repair

I find old garages in varying conditions. Some were built of oak, and well-maintained throughout the years. These may still be rock-solid, even after 75 or 80 years. Others may have been cheaply built when new, not taken care of, and not worth trying to salvage. Garages built on sand, with no proper foundation, are often severely rotted. In fact, it's surprising that they've lasted at all!

A garage is generally considered a necessity for a home today, but not all older homes have them. If they do have a garage, it's often too small or in poor repair. Figure 10-1 is an original garage that was built in the early part of the century to go with a Craftsman-style home. What I found unique about this garage was that it was in reasonably good repair *and* it was designed for two cars.

Don't try to save an old garage that's in poor condition, especially one built without a proper foundation. New garages aren't that expensive to build. By the time you've put in everything the old garage needs, you'll have spent more than it would cost to build a new one. Besides, unlike the garage in Figure 10-1, most older homes have only a one-car garage, about the size of a modern shed. That's too small to meet today's needs. You may be able to fit one compact car in it, but nothing else,

not even a lawnmower. A garage like that, even in perfect condition, isn't very useful.

The only time I try to save a deteriorated garage is if it's a particularly attractive structure. Chances are, if it's an exceptional building, it wasn't built to be a garage at all. Originally it may have been a carriage house or a workshop, and then later converted to a garage. These are sometimes beautiful buildings, with elaborate ornamentation that matches the house. You don't want to tear down one of these beautiful buildings if you can avoid it.

The Grandfather Clause

Be sure to check the zoning ordinances before you tear down a garage, or anything, for that matter. The zoning regulations have undoubtedly changed since the house was built. If you tear the garage down, you might not be allowed to build a new one, which isn't going to endear you any to the homeowner! This is especially true if the house is on a small lot or the garage is very close to the property line. New regulations may restrict you from building any new structure on the

Figure 10-1
Original two-car garage

Garage Doors

The garage door, of course, is a feature that is different from the rest of the house. It's also the most obvious and important feature on the garage, and the one item most often used. The garage door is what makes the garage functional. If it doesn't work, the whole building is useless.

Figure 10-2 shows an old garage in its original condition. Typical of old garages, this building has wooden doors which swing out to open. In good condition, like those in Figure 10-3, these doors have a certain charm. But for the most part, they're a pain to use. They're heavy, they usually don't open and close easily, and you can't use an automatic garage-door opener with them. If the garage is in otherwise-good condition, you should probably replace doors like these. You can

lot. However, the existing garage is "grandfathered" in. That is, since it was there before the law changed, it's allowed to remain.

The "grandfather clause" allows you to make repairs on an existing structure, but any new structure must conform to the new rules. Sometimes the new regulations may require you to build something smaller in order to fit the lot size, or build it in a different location, or they may prevent you from building anything at all. Never tear down a structure that you intend to replace until you've checked zoning to see if you'll be allowed to replace it! Sometimes a building will qualify as a remodel even if there's just one original wall standing.

Figure 10-2
Old garage with swing-out doors

Repairs

Most garages are repairable. Even those that look pretty bad can usually be saved. Garages have the same kind of problems as the house. They need roof repairs, paint, new siding, and window and door repair. All of these should be handled in the same manner as the house — that is, using the same materials so that they match the work done on the house. You don't want the garage to look like an add-on, even if it is. It should be as closely coordinated with the house as possible.

Figure 10-3
Renovated garage with original doors

find old-fashioned-styled modern doors that retain the antique charm of the originals, but are a lot easier to use.

A good garage door is an expensive item. The smallest, cheapest doors will run you about $300, and you can spend three times that amount for a nice one. Be sure the garage is in good condition before you consider putting a lot of money into replacing the doors. There's not much point in putting an expensive new door on a garage that's about to fall over.

Starting in the 1940s, the most common garage doors were the overhead doors, like the one shown in Figure 10-4. They are generally made of steel, but you can also find wooden doors in areas where the climate is mild. I often find this type of door in poor, but usable, condition. If the homeowner's budget is tight, and the door isn't too rusted, you can keep these old garage doors. They don't look too bad if you bang out the dents and put on a fresh coat of paint. They may not be as nice as the new roll-up doors, but most of the time they still have many years of service left in them.

Door Springs

In many cases, a few minor repairs are all that's necessary to get an old garage door into perfect working order. There isn't much information available on garage door repair, at least not in any remodeling books I've read. Maybe I'm the only person who ever repairs garage doors. Like so many other things, most remodelers just replace them. That's fine, if you're working with an unlimited budget. However, if homeowners are short of money, they'll probably appreciate a $50 repair a lot more than a new $600 door.

If you have a door that doesn't open and close properly, it may just need a new set of springs. Springs don't last forever. Overhead doors have two springs, one on each side. If one spring is broken or weakened and the other isn't, the door will pull to one side and jam.

Detach the springs and take them to a garage door specialist. They can get you new springs to match the size you need. I've been

Figure 10-4
Garage with overhead door

able to get replacement springs for doors up to 50 years old. You may have to special-order them, and wait a couple of weeks, but you can get them. With new springs, most old garage doors will open and close like new. Replacement springs cost about $20 each.

Installing the springs is pretty easy. They just hook onto an adjustable loop on the door. It takes about 10 minutes to install and adjust them. The loop should be adjusted so that the tension on both sides is the same. If the springs are the only problem, $40 and a few minutes work will save the homeowner the cost of a new garage door.

Door Locks

Garage door locks are another problem area. Most of them work with a very simple mechanism. The spring-load latch type have latches on both sides of the garage door that fit into cutouts on the metal garage door framework. They're attached by cables to the garage door handle. When you turn the handle, it pulls the cable, and unlatches the door so it can be opened. If the cable breaks, the door remains permanently in the locked position. Replacing the cable will solve this problem.

Another common problem with garage door locks is missing keys. If you don't have a key, you can't lock or unlock the door. This is solved by replacing the lock mechanism. Replacements are easy to come by. Most

Figure 10-5
Roll-up garage door fits this door opening

Figure 10-6
Garage door frame is slightly out of square

hardware stores carry them for about $10. They're very simple to bolt into place.

Door Frames

Sometimes the steel framework of the door will come loose from the wood door frame and cause the door to jam. Years of opening and closing can cause the nails to work loose from the wood on the door frame, making the door shift in its frame. Refastening the metal door framework to the wooden door frame solves this problem.

A more serious problem can occur if the garage has started to lean. An overhead garage door is a rectangle and has to fit into a rectangular door opening. If the garage is out of alignment, the door opening will look more like a parallelogram than a rectangle. The door will no longer fit into the opening; the corners will jam.

There are two solutions to this problem. The first one is to replace the overhead door with a sectional roll-up door. Roll-up doors ride up on their own frames, independent of the garage door framing. They can cover any opening, regardless of shape, as long as the opening is reasonably straight. A deviation of as little as an inch can often prevent a slab-type overhead door from opening and closing. Small deviations like that are not a problem with a sectional roll-up door. Figure 10-5 shows a roll-up door that was installed to solve this problem. If you look at the top edge

of door frame on this garage, you can see that the door frame is out of square. Figure 10-6 shows the roll-up door in a partially raised position. Its framework sits inside the garage and, as you can see in Figure 10-7, it is separate from the framing around the garage

Figure 10-7
Roll-up tracks are installed independent of the frame opening

door opening. When you look at these pictures, you can also see why the garage is starting to lean — it has no foundation. It is slowly sinking on one side, so the roll-up door is only a temporary fix for a continually worsening situation. This particular garage needs the second repair option as well!

The second way you can repair the garage door alignment is to straighten the garage and restore the door frame to its original shape. This will allow the door to fit into the opening again. We'll cover this option in detail in a little later in this chapter.

Other Door Problems

You may come across a few garages with roll-up doors that need repair. The rollers used on these doors are little nylon wheels. They are mounted on the sides of the door and fit in the roller track. If one or more of the wheels break, the door will stick. These roller assemblies can easily be unbolted and replaced. Replacement rollers are available at most hardware stores or can be ordered through a door specialist. You may also need to replace some of the little hinges that fasten the sections together. If these are broken or loose, the door will jam when you try to open it. Again these can be found in hardware stores or ordered from a specialist.

I've seen a few sectional roll-up doors with some of the sections bent out of shape. Apparently, when some of the hinges came loose causing the door to jam, the owners became frustrated and kicked the doors. Of course kicking a door rarely works as a method of repair, though it may relieve some stress. A door that's been kicked out of alignment may seem unsalvageable, but it isn't always. If you go over it carefully and replace all the bad hinges and straighten out the bent sections, you can often get the doors working as good as new again for about $100. But this kind of work takes a great deal of patience, and maybe more time than it's worth. I would only go to a lot of work to save an especially nice or especially big door. A 2½ or 3-car door can easily cost $1000 to replace. That's the only type of door you can rationalize spending a day's work on. If it's an ordinary small door, just replace it. If you're not sure whether it's repairable or not, call in a door specialist. They can sometimes solve problems in a very short time, or tell you right away that the door isn't repairable. Don't spend hours trying to repair a door without checking it out first.

The only thing I've found that can make a garage door totally unsalvageable is rust. If the frame of the door rusts through, it will destroy the integrity of the door. You can patch this back together by bolting some scrap metal over the rusted-out spots, but it won't last and it looks terrible. A rusted door has to be replaced.

🐚 Leaning Garages

As a garage deteriorates, it will begin to lean. If you don't correct this, it will continue to get worse until the garage falls right over. I've found two predominant causes for this type of deterioration: wood damage at the foundation due to rot or insects, and foundation damage due to settling or heaving by tree roots. People often neglect the area around the garage. They let trash and weeds build up and frequently allow large trees to grow right next to the foundation. Trees and their roots can put tremendous pressure on a structure. If this pressure continues, over time it will undermine the foundation and cause the garage to lean. If you plan to repair a garage, any trees that touch it should be removed.

Straightening Walls

As long as the garage is in pretty good condition, it can usually be straightened by using come-alongs. I start by attaching a 2 x 4 horizontally to the inside of the garage, going along all the studs. Then I drill a hole in the garage wall and attach one end of the chain to the 2 x 4. The other end of the chain can be attached to any solid object, such as a big tree, even if it's a distance away. The come-along operates by applying pressure by means of a handle you pull that ratchets the chain along. It's kind of like an automobile bumper jack, except it pulls instead of pushes. Like a jack, it allows you to exert a tremendous amount of pressure without too much effort. By attaching the chain to the 2 x 4, the pressure is distributed all along the garage wall as the come-along is tightened, rather than in just one spot. As always when doing any kind of straightening, apply just a small amount of pressure, then check to see what's happening. *Never* apply a lot of pressure to *anything* without periodic checks. You can use this method only if the garage is slightly out of line, no more than 6 to 8 inches.

Done correctly, this technique won't do any further damage to the garage, provided that the garage is in fairly decent condition to begin with. You can't use this method on a garage that's totally rotted and crumbling, it will just tear it to pieces. A garage like that should be torn down and rebuilt.

If you're lucky, the garage will go back into place easily. I've worked on some that you could almost push back in place by hand. Others required a little creativity, such as pushing a wall back in line with the bumper of my pickup truck. (I don't recommend this method, especially if you have a nice new truck!)

Once the garage has been pulled up straight, it needs to be braced to hold it in place. You can use 1 x 4 bracing for this, but I prefer to use sheets of $^5/_8$-inch plywood. I run these along the entire back of the inside garage wall, butting them up tightly next to each other, and screwing them securely to every stud at 1-foot intervals. Most freestanding garages (as opposed to attached garages) have no interior finish, so the studs are exposed and the plywood goes up very quickly. Usually, the plywood is best attached to the rear garage wall. Garages lean from side to side, not from front to back. The plywood locks the wall together into one big, immovable mass. Since it is butted tightly into the corners of the garage, and each piece is butted tightly to the next one, the garage can't lean without splintering all the plywood. It would take a bulldozer to do that. Using plywood also insures that the garage is absolutely straight. The plywood sheets have straight edges and 90-degree corners. They won't set into the corners properly unless the garage is absolutely straight. This acts as a

double-check mechanism, to ensure the garage has been straightened perfectly.

If the garage is basically sound but has been pushed over by a tree, the plywood bracing may be the only repair it really needs, except for some caulking and paint. Often there's nothing wrong with the garage; it's simply not as strong as the tree.

As far as rot repair around the foundation, you need to consider how severe the damage is, and what other repairs are needed, before you decide to straighten the garage. Start adding up the costs for all the repairs. You want to make sure that your repairs don't add up to more than the cost of a new garage.

I've made that mistake myself. I looked at a garage in parts, and just began fixing each part without keeping in mind the total expense of the overall project. The garage rafters were rotted, so I doubled them; the studs were rotted, so I doubled them too; it needed a new roof and new siding, so I re-roofed and re-sided it; the door was rusted, so I installed a new door. About that time I realized "Hey! I just built a new garage! I replaced every part." If I had thought the job through a little better, I would have just demolished the old garage and built a new one. It would have been a lot easier. My mistake was not looking at the project as a whole. Each job was worth doing, but overall, they added up to a project that wasn't worthwhile.

If the only damage is around the foundation, you may be able to straighten the garage, repair the foundation and have a sturdy garage at very little expense.

There is one other thing that can make a fairly solid garage lean, but this is not as common. You may come across a garage with four or five layers of asphalt shingles built up on the roof. This is more than code allows, but occasionally garages are re-roofed without much thought of the consequences. The average two-car garage uses five squares of shingles, at 240 pounds per square. That's 1200 pounds for each layer of shingles, or as much as 6000 pounds if there are five layers. That's like parking two medium-size cars on the roof! Even if a garage is well built, it will

Figure 10-8
Garage in very bad shape

Figure 10-9
Crumbling foundations

eventually begin to lean with this much weight on it. Besides straightening up the garage, you'll have to strip off the old roofing material, at least down to one layer, and get rid of it. Then you can re-roof the garage. That should eliminate any future problems.

🐟 Dealing with a Broken Foundation

Garage foundations may be broken, settled, heaved, or in some cases, missing altogether. Because of this, you may find a wall that's broken or rotted free from its base or bottom plate. I've seen walls that flap in the breeze. Obviously, there's not a whole lot left to a garage like this. Ideally, you'd want to tear it down and build a new one. But sometimes, as I pointed out earlier, building

regulations won't allow you to do that. Most contractors would just say "Sorry, I can't help you," and walk away. However, there are still possibilities in this situation.

Figure 10-8 shows a garage I found in teardown condition. The foundation, shown in Figures 10-9 and 10-10, was just a mass of uneven rubble. The deteriorated back wall wasn't even attached to any base. There was no way I could build anything on a foundation

Figure 10-10
Garage wall is no longer attached to foundations

Figure 10-11
Jack and new 4 x 4s used to build new wall

like that. I decided to ignore the foundation, and support the structure with 4 x 4s set directly into the ground.

I demolished the flapping wall, and used jacks to support the structure while I worked on it. In Figure 10-11 you can see one jack set on a log. I had to use the log to bring it up the proper height. I placed treated 4 x 4 x 12s in the corners, and at 4-foot intervals across the back of the garage. They were set directly into the ground, like fence posts. In order to get them to fit tightly, I set them in their holes loosely, and then screwed them securely to the top plate. Then, I filled the holes with concrete. Once the concrete hardened, the 4 x 4s were locked into the correct position, at both the bottom and the top.

With the 4 x 4s in place, the garage structure was strong and stable. I then covered the back wall with rough-sawn wood siding. This entire repair can be completed in about 12 hours, and costs about $200 for materials. It's not a perfect repair; it may not even be code-approved in some areas. However, it's solid and safe, and it allows you to get another 10 or 20 years out of a garage that would otherwise have to be torn down. On this particular job, I re-sided the rest of the garage to match the new wall. In some cases, if the wall is not easily seen, you can just paint it, and no one will notice if it matches exactly. If the homeowner is on a tight budget, or the garage is grandfathered in, a repair like this may be the only alternative to no garage at all.

Recycling What You Can't Use

If you find it necessary to demolish a garage, porch, or any other large structure, you should give some thought to how you're going to dispose of the trash. The cost of trash removal is skyrocketing. In some areas of the country it's become a major remodeling expense. Having a dumpster brought in is the easiest method of disposal, but once you find out how much it's going to cost, it may not be the best.

Recycling Valuable Building Materials

Consider the following: Are there any materials in the structure that can be recycled? Some old buildings that have to be demolished are made of woods that are no longer available, or that have become very valuable. This is particularly true in the East, where there are large numbers of very old houses. Many of these houses have heartwood pine floors, or heavy oak beams that are not only valuable, but salvageable. They can be remilled into new lumber and flooring. Throwing wood like this away is like

throwing away money. If you work in the eastern states, you're probably already aware of this. Some remodelers think of the demolition of an older structure as a treasure hunt. It's an opportunity to discover all kinds of valuable items and materials.

Remodelers in the Midwest and West tend not to think this way, but they should. As time goes by, there are going to be more and more opportunities to work on older homes. Most of the homes in the Midwest and West aren't old enough to have been built with the really unique types of wood, like heartwood pine. However, there are other types of valuable lumber to be found. Don't overlook the possibilities in outbuildings, either. Old sheds, barns and chicken coops were often built out of heavy oak planks. Building like that would be extravagant today. However, at one time, oak was standard construction lumber. It was used in the same way we use pine today. I've come across oak planks 12 feet long, 18 inches wide, and a full 4 inches thick in old outbuildings! You don't even find new lumber like this anymore. I never throw this kind of lumber away unless it's so badly rotted that it's totally unusable.

Just keep this in mind when you have to tear down old structures. Even if the surface of an old board is worn or weathered, the interior may still be perfect. Remember, these boards can be remilled. You can trim the bad parts off a 2-inch-thick plank and still have enough good wood left for two ¾-inch boards.

🐚 Firewood

Unfortunately, most of the structures you'll be tearing down will be made of plain old pine. However, even old pine is useful for something. How about firewood? Old furring strips make particularly good kindling; so do cedar shingles. Pieces of old cedar make nice firewood, and they smell nice when they burn. Oak scraps also burn well. Pine 2 x 4s aren't the best firewood, but when they're free, they become quite appealing. The only wood you don't want to burn is treated or painted wood. So, if you know anyone who heats with wood, or has a wood-burning fireplace, ask them if they would like to take it off your hands.

My point here is not that this wood is so valuable as firewood, but that it has a *negative* value as trash. It's going to cost you money if you have to have it hauled away in a dumpster. If you can use it, or you can get somebody to take it, even for free, you're that much ahead on your dump fees.

I use a lot of wood to heat my house each year; 15 cords of firewood plus all the scrap I can salvage. Some people claim that burning pine will soot up your chimney, but I haven't found that to be a problem. If you clean your chimney once a year, as recommended, you're not going to have any significant buildup. If you normally have a lot of scrap wood, consider putting a fireplace or wood-burning stove in your home. It will lower your home heating bills, raise the value of your house, and give you something useful to do with bulky trash that will otherwise cost you money to dispose of.

Recyclers, Antique Dealers and Junk Collectors

Interest in recycling is growing every day. Some Home Depot outlets are now opening recycling centers at their store locations. Soon you'll be able to sell them your glass and scrap metal, then go inside and buy new supplies. That's really one-stop shopping!

The value of scrap metal is increasing every day. Don't throw out old aluminum doors and windows, copper pipes and wire, or old electric motors. They're all worth money to recyclers. Even scrap steel is becoming valuable. Junk yards will pay a penny a pound for it. You won't get rich this way, but it beats paying to have it hauled away. Before you throw it in the dumpster, call a scrap dealer or recycler.

🐚 If You Don't Want It . . .

Old cabinets are always useful. Ugly kitchen cabinets make useful work benches, or great storage in the garage. If you don't want them, maybe one of your crew does. They take up a lot of space in a dumpster. Anything you can give away will leave space for other things.

Old windows, doors, fixtures, and fittings can all be recycled. Antique dealers sometimes pay a lot of money for them, depending on their age, style and condition. Of course, if they're just ordinary windows and doors, or are in poor condition, you probably won't be able to sell them. However, you might be able to get someone to take them for free. Try putting them, or any other items you need to dispose of, by the curb with a sign that says: *Free*. I'll bet they'll be gone the next day.

If you have to tear out flatwork, many concrete manufacturers will accept broken concrete pieces. They grind it up and recycle it into new concrete. They may charge a small fee to take it, but that's usually less than you'd have to pay to have it hauled away by a waste disposal company. In my area the concrete manufacturers charge about $5 per pickup-load.

🐚 Garage Sales and Flea Markets

Do you, or any of your friends, like garage sales? A lot of reusable building materials can be sold at garage sales or flea markets. They're only worth a dollar or two, but if you multiply that by thousands of items, it all adds up. If you don't want to bother with it yourself, see if you can get in touch with a flea market dealer who will. You may be able to get them to take the whole lot off your hands, and give you a few dollars for it as well.

There's also the possibility that you can donate usable building materials to schools or charities. Not only does this get rid of them, it also builds good will. Don't give them garbage, though. That'll do the opposite.

🐚 Advertise

Another valuable means of disposing of odds and ends is an ad in the paper. It doesn't need to be long. It can just say something like "Free wood" or "Free bathroom fixtures" and either a phone number or an address. Junk dealers check these ads for anything they can use or resell. There are people who make quite a bit of money this way. After all, they're getting the stuff free, so anything they sell it for is almost 100 percent profit. You can almost give it away and still come out ahead. The space you save in the dumpster will more than make up for the few dollars you spend on the ad. If I have to order a dumpster to haul off things that could have been recycled or reused by someone, it only costs me money. At $500 apiece, dumpster costs add up real fast!

So far, the only item I've been able to find absolutely no use for at all is old asphalt shingles. They're heavy, crumbly, and full of sharp nails. The dumpster is the perfect place for these. By recycling useful items, I save dumpster space for things like shingles that are a serious disposal problem.

As the cost of trash disposal continues to increase, strategies like this are going to become more and more important. By recycling, you'll be conserving valuable resources, helping the community, and saving a heck of a lot of money.

Structural Repairs, From the Basement Up

We've gone through just about all the necessary repairs to the exterior. We'll discuss the exterior again when we get into making improvements to the home. Now it's time to start on the interior repairs. We'll look at these repairs in the order in which you would actually do them, starting in the basement with basic structural repairs, and working upwards and outwards to wall repairs and trim.

I intend to generally limit the discussion to repairs at this point, and consider modifications later. However, if we want to go through the work in the order in which it's actually done, we'll have to consider certain kinds of modifications at the same time we're doing the repairs. After all, it doesn't make much sense to repair a wall, and then decide to tear it out later. This kind of thing happens, but I'm certainly not going to recommend it!

Also, as a matter of good business practice, you may have to alter the order of some of these jobs to suit the needs of the homeowner. Unless you're doing a whole-house remodel on a vacant house, you'll probably be working around the people living there. Certain repairs may need to be done first in order to make the house livable. For example,

you'll have to make sure there's always at least one functional toilet available (your crew will appreciate that as well). Since we can't anticipate the needs of every homeowner, I'm going to assume that the house is empty or that any urgent repairs have been dealt with.

The most serious problems you're likely to encounter are those involving the basic structure of the house: the floors, walls, ceilings and anything that operates within them, such as plumbing, electrical and heating systems. After the urgent repairs we discussed in Chapter 5, and any repairs needed to reinforce the foundation (Chapter 9), these structural and mechanical problems need to be dealt with before you do anything else to the inside of the house. You can't build anything unless you have a solid structure to build it on. Structural problems need to be addressed from the bottom up, and since the lowest part of the house is the basement, let's start there.

The Basement

We've already covered the foundation repairs that you have to make from inside the basement. These involved repairing and reinforcing damaged basement walls and adding additional support to the foundation in the form of new sills, posts and beams. As we discussed, joists and beams can become rotted or damaged by dampness and insects over the course of the years. Basement moisture problems are very common in older homes. In order to prevent further damage to the structure of the house, you'll need to eliminate the leaks in the basement. There may be instances where this will be among the urgent repairs that you have to do first. I've been to more than one house that had "moisture problems in the basement," and found not moisture, but several inches of standing water! In situations like this, the leaky basement has to be drained and stabilized before you can make repairs to the foundation or other structural members.

There are many different ways that water can gain entry into the basement. Groundwater can get in through cracks or holes in the basement walls. Or it can seep in through porous materials such as cement blocks, even if they're entirely intact.

Houses built today have a number of systems in place to prevent water from seeping through basement and foundation walls. First, the outside of the foundation wall is covered with waterproofing material. Secondly, drain tiles are installed at the base of the foundation to drain away groundwater, and to stop it from pooling around the basement. And finally, the area around the foundation is backfilled with gravel and sand, so that water drains through to the drain tiles, and doesn't puddle up around the exterior of the house.

When you're dealing with older homes, chances are that any exterior waterproofing that used to be on the house has dissolved away over the years. If the house is over 100 years old, it was probably built without foundation drainage. Even if it's newer than that, the drainage may not work any more because of broken or clogged lines. The only way to replace these systems is by digging out the area around the exterior of the basement. This is very difficult and expensive, not to mention hard on the landscaping. I prefer to leave jobs like these to contractors with back-

hoes. I'd rather approach the problem from a different direction.

🐛 Dealing with Leaks

I always double-check the exterior grading and drainage around the basement before I do anything else. If none of the exterior measures we discussed in Chapter 9 solves the basement leakage problem, then I go to work on the problem from the inside. Remember, do try all the exterior measures available to you first. They are, for the most part, cheap and easy, and they solve the problem an amazing number of times.

If the exterior measures *don't* work, it may be because the water table is very high. That means that the ground around the basement is constantly saturated with water. This is common in houses built in very low-lying areas, such as reclaimed swamp land or along canyon or valley floors. If a basement in such an area has no drainage, it will eventually fill with water to the level of the water table.

A high water table is a very difficult problem to deal with. It's as though the house was built in the middle of an underground lake. The basement is constantly surrounded with water and sooner or later that water will find a way in. Ideally, houses in areas like this should be built on piers and without basements. However, when you come across a home like this, and it does have a basement, you have a problem. It isn't going away, so you'll have to deal with it.

Waterproofing

First of all, check to see if there are any visible cracks or holes in the walls. Figure 12-1 shows one type of hole you may run into. It was drilled through this basement wall to accommodate a pipe which was no longer being used. The hole was larger than necessary for the pipe, allowing a lot of water to leak into the basement. I removed the pipe and filled in the hole. I've found latex-strengthened sand mix usually fills holes like this pretty well. In some cases, that may be enough to solve the problem. Patch any holes and cracks you find in the walls. I've seen

Figure 12-1
*Hole in wall allows water to
leak into basement*

Figure 12-2
Parging helps to seal leaky basement walls

some basements that were essentially intact, except for one small crack that was leaking. When the crack was filled, the problem was solved.

It's nice when moisture problems can be solved that easily. Unfortunately, most of the time that isn't the case. Usually, if you patch one crack, the water just comes in some other place. It may be coming in through micro-cracks that you can't even see. If the basement is made with cement block, the block itself is porous, and will continue to seep water even if you seal up every crack and hole you can find.

Many stores sell waterproofing paint which is supposed to solve this problem. My experience has been that, while waterproofing paint helps, it can't deal with the severity of a groundwater problem. In time, the paint just peels off.

Parging

I find that parging the basement walls is a much better solution to the problem. We discussed parging techniques earlier, in Chapter 8. It's useful for all kinds of repairs. In this case, it will seal all the little micro-cracks that you can't see, as well as seal the pores of cement block. As you can see in

Figure 12-2, it provides a smooth, unbroken surface of fine, close-grained concrete.

Another advantage to parging is that it cements together any loose or damaged masonry materials in the basement walls. This can add substantial strength to the walls. It's often worth parging the basement for this purpose alone. If the walls leak, and they're in poor condition as well, parging will kill two birds with one stone.

However, even a parged surface has tiny pores that water can squeeze through over time. After parging, the surface should be sealed with a coat of waterproofing paint. This is really the best use for waterproofing paint. It can't hold back a flood, but it can keep out an occasional drop of water. A combination of parging and waterproofing paint will stop most basement leakage.

Constant moisture will eventually wear out waterproofing paint. Over time, all the little drops seeping through the tiny pores in the wall will break down the waterproofing paint's ability to adhere to the wall. After two or three years, the paint will start to peel, and the wall will begin to leak again. Often, the peeling will indicate the level of the water table outside the wall.

One time I owned a house with a basement that would peel every three years from the floor to a point 2 feet up the wall, and then stop. The paint above that point always remained in perfect condition. That's because there was no water above that point. The water pooled underground at a level of 2 feet above my basement floor. If the basement had been built 2 feet higher, I would never have had a problem. As it was, I decided that painting this 2-foot strip every three years wasn't too much of a problem. So I just continued to do that for as long as I owned the house and the basement always remained dry.

Severe Problems

There are some cases of basement leakage so severe that even parging won't keep the water out. This occurs where there is tremendous water pressure outside of the basement wall. I've seen water spouting through a wall with such force that it looked like a faucet was wide open and shooting water out through the wall. Parging will slow down a leak like this, but it won't stop it completely. Some water will still seep in.

In a situation like this, you need to install a basement dewatering system. These systems are designed to catch the water as it comes in and direct it into a drain or sump before it can cause any damage. They don't try to stop the water, just control it.

One common way to do this is to make a trench all around the perimeter of the basement floor. If it's concrete, you'll need to use a cement saw to get a nice cut. Cement saws are kind of a pain to use, because they're big and heavy and have to be connected to running water while they're in use. The constant flow of water keeps the blade from overheating, but it also makes a big mess. Unfortunately, they are the only tool that will make a neat cut through thick concrete. You can rent them at any rental store that has a good selection of tools.

Cut out an 8-inch-wide strip of concrete as close to the wall as possible. Then dig out the dirt to a depth of 8 inches. You'll want a trench that is 8 inches wide and 8 inches deep all along the entire base of each exterior facing wall. If there are any walls that don't leak, you won't need to make a trench there.

Usually, if the water table is high, all the exterior walls will leak. Somewhere in the basement there should be either a sump or a floor drain. Run the trench to this point. If there isn't a drain or sump, you'll have to install one.

Put 4-inch drain pipe into the trench to direct the water flow. I use corrugated plastic pipe. It's cheap and it works well. Connect the pipe all around the basement, and bring it to the sump or drain. Be sure the pipe is either level, or angled toward the drain or sump. If it isn't, add some gravel to the low points in the trench until the pipe is raised to an angle that is correct. If the pipe isn't angled correctly, it won't drain well.

Now, check the end that's connected to the drain or sump. You should see water start to pour out of it almost immediately. In some cases, the water flow will be the equivalent of a faucet turned on full, and may continue 24 hours a day, seven days a week, for months! That's an indication of just how serious the water problem was.

The rest of the trench can now be filled with gravel up to the level of the floor. The floor will have a strip of gravel around its perimeter that is solid enough to walk on without damaging the system. When any water seeps in through the walls, it will drip down onto the gravel where it will filter through and be caught by the drain pipe. The pipe will then direct it into the drain or sump. This will keep the center floor area dry, since there's no way that water can get past the gravel-filled drain trench. The basement will probably always be humid, since water is constantly flowing through it, but it won't be waterlogged.

Installing a Sump

Unfortunately, many older homes were built without any kind of basement drainage. Since any drain system you install will depend on a working floor drain or sump, you may have to put some kind of drainage in.

Floor drains are generally installed when a house is built. It's very difficult to put one into an existing house. You'd have to tear up the basement floor, and do major excavation on the outside to hook it up to a sewer line. Installing a sump is usually more practical.

A sump is basically a hole in the floor with a crock for collecting water. You'll have cut a hole through the cement at the place where you want to locate the sump, usually in some unused corner where it will be out of the way. Then, dig the hole deep enough to accommodate the sump crock. These are generally made of plastic. They look like big plastic buckets with cutouts for connecting drain lines.

When the crock is installed and the drain lines connected, the sump will fill up with water. You'll need a sump pump to pump the water out. This is the key to the entire installation. Sump pumps have a switch that's activated by the water level. When the sump starts to fill, the switch turns on, pumps the water out, and then turns off when the water level has dropped below the activating switch. If there's a lot of water, it will cycle on and off every few minutes. The sump pump has an outlet that connects to standard size (usually 1 inch) pipe. You need to pump the water into a plumbing drain line, or at least, into a line that will carry it out of the basement.

The nice thing about moving water with a pump, as opposed to using gravity, is that you can send the water up, sideways or in any other direction you need to, in order to get rid of it. If there are no accessible drain lines, you'll have to pump the water outside. Try to direct the it onto a driveway, or some other surface that will carry it away from the house. If you just have it pour onto the ground outside, it's likely to seep into the ground and end up leaking back into the basement. Be sure to angle the outside part of the pipe downwards, so that the water always drains out of it completely. Otherwise, any water trapped in the pipe may freeze in the winter, blocking the pipe.

I've had good results with this kind of dewatering system. I once worked on a house that had 2 inches of standing water in the basement all throughout the spring. The problem was so severe that there were actually frogs living in the basement! The frogs

Figure 12-3
Drain pipes will be connected to sump which will pump water away

kept the homeowners awake all night with their constant "ribbit, ribbit, ribbit!" As soon as I installed a drain system (and the sump, shown in Figure 12-3), the water disappeared, and so did the frogs. The basement never had a problem with standing water again. The frogs had to find another home.

There are other ways to control water flow in a wet basement. Some, like the B-Dry Basement De-Watering System, use a baseboard water collector. This is installed around the perimeter of the basement. This baseboard performs the same function as the trench. It catches any water leaking in, and directs it to a drain before it can do any damage. The advantage of this system is that it doesn't require any concrete cutting or digging. The disadvantages are that it takes up space, and it's easily damaged. If someone kicks a hole in it, it won't work anymore. The trench, on the other hand, is almost impossible to damage.

Cost

Digging a trench and installing drains and gravel around the perimeter of a basement will only cost about $200 for materials.

However, it's a hard, heavy job. It can take 12 to 20 manhours of labor to do an entire basement. Most contractors charge $2,000 to $3,000 for this job. B-Dry Systems, for instance, charges about $3,000 to do all the walls of an average-sized basement. Even though it's hard work, you can see that this job has a lot of profit potential.

If you have to install a sump as well, there will be additional costs. An ordinary residential-type sump pump costs about $100. You'll also need an electrical connection for the sump pump, and it should be on its own circuit. The other materials you'll need are fairly cheap. About $300 should cover everything, including the pump. Cutting through the concrete and digging out the hole for the sump crock is difficult and time consuming. Figure another 12 hours for this part of the job.

Strengthening the Floors

Now that the basement walls are solid and waterproofed, we need to turn our attention to the structural problems of the first floor and above. The basement is the perfect place to get a good view of the underside of the floor joists. This is where you're most likely to find the cause of any first floor problems.

Weak floor joists are usually to blame for excessive bounce, or even serious sagging, in the main floor. And by far the most common cause of this weakness is some poorly-done installation in which a big chunk of one or more of the joists was cut away! It never ceases to amaze me that people think they can whack chunks out of the floor joists without anything bad happening. What do they think the floor joists are for? Decoration? I've seen this kind of joist damage in probably 90 percent of the older homes I've looked at. Cutting a little notch out of one or two joists may not cause a problem. But cutting joists clean through, or having half-a-dozen joists in a row deeply notched, *will* cause problems. It undermines the strength of the entire floor system, and causes major weaknesses upstairs.

A second cause of joist failure is cracking, due to excessive drying or defective lumber. Less common is failure caused by undersized or overspanned joists, generally due to improper construction. Interestingly enough, I rarely see this in houses 100 years old or more. Many of these houses were built with the old fully-sized dimensional lumber. That is, with 2 x 4s that were actually 2 full inches by 4 full inches, not 1½ x 3½, like they are today. The old lumber was, and in most cases still is, substantially stronger than the stuff we use today. Also, many old houses were built with oak framing, instead of the pine we now use. These houses were built like rocks. I've rarely seen any kind of joist failure in these. This old framing could survive a tremendous amount of mistreatment. I've seen houses where the framing was exposed to the weather for decades, and still remained solid.

Hand-hewn Beams and Logs

In some older homes, you may find the floors supported by massive beams, or even logs (with the bark still on) sawn in half. This kind of construction was common in rural areas, where trees were plentiful. The trees were cut down to clear the land for farming, and because there were so many of them, they were used very liberally in building the farmhouses. A floor supported by logs is strong enough to park a truck on. I know. I've done it!

A house may be in the middle of a city now, but that doesn't mean it wasn't in a rural area when it was built. Most cities have grown tremendously in the last 100 years, gobbling up the farms and outlying communities in the process. It's not uncommon to find an occasional 1880s farmhouse, surrounded by 1920s bungalows, sitting in the middle of a city.

These massive beams and logs can take a lot of abuse, but even they can fail sometimes. Usually their failure is caused by a moisture problem that was left unrepaired for decades, resulting in massive rot or termite damage. In many cases the damage may only be in one small section of the beam, but that's enough to weaken the floor above.

You don't necessarily have to replace the rotted beams with beams of the same size. Some of these massive beams weigh over 500 pounds and they are very difficult to work with. It's almost impossible to fit a new 500-pound beam into the same slots that you took the old one out of when you're working in a cramped basement. I tried it once; it was way too much trouble. A couple of 2 x 10s will give you roughly the same strength, and they're a whole lot easier to handle.

The experience of trying to handle beams of that size was valuable. Not only did it give me a greater appreciation for the old builders, but I realized that whoever came up with the idea of building houses out of 2 x 4s was a genius; 2 x 4s are incredibly easier to work with.

ॐ Joist Repair

Before you begin to repair the understructure of the floor, you need to check and see if the floor is level. Is it sagging or out of line? If it's out of line, you'll have to jack it back into proper alignment before you do any other work. If it's level, but weak, you can go ahead and make repairs. Since that's the easiest of the two alternatives at this point, let's start there.

Bridging

Lack of bridging between floor joists is one common cause of weak floors. Bridging consists of two small pieces of wood or metal strips nailed diagonally, crisscross, between the joists. Or, it can be a single piece of lumber, the same size as the joists, nailed cross-wise between the joists. This last type is called solid bridging. Solid bridging gives the floor a lot more strength than the regular bridging members. It's usually used under areas that carry a heavy load, such as the bathroom. You won't often find it under the main spans of the floor, because it's more difficult to install, and the extra strength isn't necessary.

Figure 12-4
Underside of floor shows leak from bathroom above, and no bridging between joists

All floor joists should have some type of bridging installed between them to keep them absolutely vertical, and to distribute the load evenly. If the joists aren't braced with bridging they may twist or turn, and then they can't support the floor properly. Missing bridging is very common in older homes. It may have been removed for some kind of installation, or it may never have been installed. A few pieces of missing bridging generally won't matter, but if there isn't *any*, you can have problems. Figure 12-4 shows the underside of a weak floor. There was no bridging of any kind used to support the flooring in this house.

When I have to install bridging to repair a problem floor, I generally use solid bridging. While solid bridging isn't usually needed in an ordinary floor, an ordinary floor doesn't bounce. The fact that the floor has a problem indicates the need for extra care to be taken in its repair.

Installing solid bridging may be all that's needed to stabilize the floor, especially if the problem isn't too severe and there are no other obvious defects, such as cracked or broken joists. Bridging pieces should be placed every 8 feet, and offset from each other so that each one is nailed directly to the joist, not toenailed. Once the pieces are installed, release the floor jacks, then test the floor. Go upstairs and jump up and down on it. You may find all the floor problems solved.

Figure 12-5
*Jack holds small beam in place while
repairs are made to joists*

Bringing the Floor into Alignment

If the floor is sagging or out of line, it will need to be jacked into place before it can be worked on further. The technique I use for this is the same as I use for porch and foundation repairs: Construct a beam, and support it with post jacks; then tighten the jacks slowly, over a period of several days if necessary, until the floor is level once again.

Watch out for plumbing and heating lines when you're setting the beam. They're often right in the way of where you want to work. In fact, they're often the cause of the damage you have to repair. Most of my repairs are on joists that were cut for the installation of plumbing or heating lines. Unless you're planning to replace the run of pipe or ductwork that's in your way, you'll have to work around it. Be especially careful of cast iron drain lines. If they're old, they'll often crumble at the slightest touch — and what a smelly and disgusting mess they make! Working around existing pipe runs often means using two small beams instead of one big one. That way you can position one on either side of the plumbing or heating line.

Also watch for plumbing lines that are almost level with the joists, but not quite. They may be hanging down an inch or so below the joist, so that you'd hardly notice them. If you push the beam right up against them, you'll force them up level with the joists. That may be all it takes to break the lines loose from their attachments, and send water pouring all over the basement. You'd be

better off to notch your beam to accommodate the lines, and leave the plumbing undisturbed. You can add a post under the notch to make up for the loss of strength. An alternative to this is to use a small 4 x 4 as a little beam, as shown in Figure 12-5. This particular area of floor had so many low hanging pipe runs that there was no place to put a full beam. This small beam was just what I needed to hold up the joist while I reinforced it. Notice how much of the joist has been cut away. It was no wonder that this floor sagged!

Reinforcing the Joists

A sagging floor has obviously sustained more severe damage than a floor that just bounces or shakes. In addition to bridging, you'll most likely need to repair some of the joists. The problem joists are not usually hard to find. One or more will probably be cracked or cut. The easiest way to repair these is to double them, that is, just add another piece of wood the same size right over them. Nail the new joist securely to the old one, and then add solid bridging on both sides of the doubled joist. Do this to all the joists that are noticeably damaged.

Once you've doubled all the damaged joists, carefully loosen the floor jacks and see if the floor stays put. Go upstairs and jump up and down. The floor should be solid. If it isn't, add more floor joists, and more bridging. Keep adding them until the floor is rock solid.

A Permanent Beam

Another option is to install a permanent beam using the same technique we covered in foundation repair. The advantages and disadvantages of doing this are the same. A permanent beam takes up basement room and isn't a very attractive addition; but it's a lot less work than doubling all the joists, and usually works just as well.

A permanent beam should be installed right in the middle of the span of joists, since the middle is usually where the greatest weakness is found. Once installed, the joists will have half the unsupported span as before. Even if they've lost a large percentage of their strength, the joists should still be able to maintain their strength for this greatly reduced distance. This extra support is usually all that's needed to make the floor above quite solid.

Figure 12-6 shows a permanent beam in place. Before I put this beam in, the floor above bounced so badly that items on the dining room table would bounce over the edge and fall off when someone walked by. Now the floor is totally sound. Posts and beams should be positioned very carefully to do the maximum good. If you can't put them exactly in the middle of the weak section, install them as close to that area as possible. In the case of the beam in Figure 12-6, I had to position it about 6 inches away from the optimum location because of all the ductwork. That was still close enough to give the floor the support it needed.

🐾 The Main Support Beam

Floor joists are generally held up by the foundation wall on one side, and the main support beam on the other. This is the beam that runs right through the middle of the basement. On newer homes, those built since about 1950, this beam is made of steel. On homes built between 1910 and 1950, it's usually made of many pieces of 2 x 12 nailed together. On homes built before 1910, it's often a single heavy oak beam.

This beam is absolutely crucial to the support of the house. It supports all the floor joists for the first floor. If it fails, the first floor will sag. It also supports the main load-bearing wall that holds up the second floor. This wall is built right over the main beam. The load-bearing wall serves the same function for the second floor that the main beam serves for the first. That is, all the floor joists for the second floor rest on the load-bearing wall, which in turn rests on the main beam. In other words, the main beam is holding up the entire house. If this beam fails, the whole house could collapse into the basement.

There is supposed to be a continuous, unbroken line of support at this point, running from the main beam all the way up into

Figure 12-6
Permanent beam stabilizes floor above

the attic. If this line of support is weak, problems with the main beam often show up on the second floor. It may seem strange, but if the floor on the second floor of the house is shaky, the first place you should check for the problem is the basement!

Repairing the Beam

The main beam is usually held up by steel or cast iron posts. These were used instead of wood because they don't rot. However, they do rust. I've found rusted-out support posts to be the most common cause of main beam failure. Figure 12-7 shows a cast iron post with the bottom 3 inches totally rusted away. The post is hanging from the main beam, instead of holding the beam up.

In some cases, the fact that the posts are rusted out may not be immediately obvious. This is especially true if the posts are sitting on a dirt floor, or if dirt has accumulated around the base of the posts. If there is a lot of dirt at the base, you don't actually see the bottom of the post. So, as the post rusts, the

Figure 12-7
*Bottom of this cast-iron post
has rusted away*

Figure 12-8
Steel post supports the main beam

beam sags, and forces the post down into the basement floor. You won't see a jagged rusty edge, like you would on a rusty car, because that edge had been forced into the floor by the tremendous pressure of the main beam. The post may look just fine. You may not even be able tell that it's now a lot shorter than it used to be; a lot shorter than it needs to be. A level will help you detect this problem. The beam will dip towards the post or posts that are bad.

Once you find the bad post or posts, you'll need to jack the beam back into place. Be careful; there's a tremendous amount of weight resting on this beam. If it's a two-story house, you'll probably need to use at least four jacks to move the weight. If you try to lift the beam with fewer than that, you'll soon get to a point where the jacks just won't turn. Don't force them; use more jacks.

As with jacking up other parts of the house, take it slowly and carefully. Don't try to raise the beam more than $1/8$ of an inch per day. Otherwise, you'll cause extensive cracking upstairs. If the beam has sagged substantially, it may take a couple of weeks to safely get it back into place.

Once the beam is back in place, you'll need to replace the post. Use a new steel post like the one shown in Figure 12-8, or a treated 6 x 6 wood post. It's also a good idea to add several more posts, one on either side of the new post, and one or two more at any other point along the beam that looks less than perfect. You need to do this because both the years of sagging, and the pressure of moving it back into a level position, may have weakened the beam. This is especially true of beams that are made of many pieces of lumber that have been nailed together. You can't be sure that all this movement hasn't caused their attachments to loosen. Adding a few more posts will make up for any loss of strength.

Finally, you may run into situations where the main beam itself has decayed, due to rot or termite damage. Adding more posts to a substantially-damaged beam won't help, because it's no longer solid enough to remain in one piece for long, even if it's supported. Your best bet in this situation is to replace the beam with steel. The new beam should set on new posts, with their own footings.

Costs

In most cases, these types of structural repairs don't cost much in materials. All you'll need are a few 2 x 12s and 4 x 4s, some miscellaneous hardware (joist hangers, post caps and bases, etc.), and a few bags of cement. About $300 should more than cover it.

Jobs that don't require jacking the floor back into position are fairly quick. For example, strengthening a shaky (but not sagging) floor by doubling a few joists and adding a dozen pieces of solid bridging should take three to five hours, depending how easy the basement is to work in. A clear, open space with a high ceiling is a lot easier to work in than a cramped, cluttered space. (The work goes faster when you have room.) Installing a permanent beam takes about eight hours, including pouring new footings.

If you have a job that does require jacking the floor back into proper position, it's quite a bit more labor-intensive. Installing a temporary beam, jacking up the floor, doubling all the joists, adding solid bridging, and removing the temporary beam will take about 16 hours. In terms of labor, the most tedious part of this job is coming back every day to jack the floor up another 1/8 inch. If you're doing other work on the house, the few minutes that it will take you to tighten the floor jacks won't be a problem. However, if you have to drive across town from another job just to tighten the jacks, you can easily spend two hours a day commuting to do a five minute job. Figure this time into your estimate.

Second-Floor Structural Problems

Now that we've dealt with the structural problems in the basement, we need to go on to examine the second floor. Shaky, sagging floors occur on the second floor as well. The causes are similar, but they're much harder to repair. The bottom side of the second floor is covered by the first-floor ceiling. In order to see the floor joists and to determine what the problem is, you'll have to take the ceiling down. This is a big job in itself. Also, you can't just stick a bunch of posts and beams wherever you feel that the ceiling needs strengthening. They would probably end up right in the middle of the living room. All your repairs need to be integrated into the existing walls and ceiling, so they don't show.

As I mentioned earlier, many second-floor problems are caused by structural failures that begin in the basement. This is especially likely if both the upstairs floor and the main floor are sagging or bouncy. In that case, the part that has failed is a part that supports both floors. You may find that after you've stabilized the first floor, the problem upstairs will go away. If not, go back to the basement and take a second look.

Look carefully for any part of the structure that still may not be adequately supported. If you think you've found a weak spot, or even if you're not sure, try this experiment. Place a few jack posts at the places that may be weak, or at any areas that take considerable stress. This includes major joints, corners, or the middle of long spans. Tighten the jack posts until you encounter substantial resistance. Now, check the upstairs. Many times you'll find the upstairs has stabilized.

If that's the case, you've just saved yourself a great deal of work, and avoided tearing out a perfectly good ceiling. More importantly, you could have torn out the ceiling, added any amount of strengthening to the underside of the upstairs floor, and then found that it didn't correct the problem. If the problem is in the basement, you want to find that out *before* you start tearing up the rest of the house, not after! On the other hand, if everything in the basement is fine, and the first floor is rock solid, but the upstairs still sags or bounces, the problem must be in the upstairs structure.

❧ Amateur Carpenters

In Chapter 3, during the inspection process, we discussed some of the serious structural problems you may find on the second floor. One of the examples I used was an improperly-installed second-floor dormer addition. Amateur carpentry, especially when it comes to room additions like these, is the biggest cause of major second-floor structural problems that I've come across.

I rarely find these kinds of problems on a professionally-built home. Most contractors know enough basic engineering to avoid creating structural problems. However, in my experience, the older a house is, the more likely it is that one or more amateur carpenters have passed through its doors. That's why you're going to run into quite a few problems like these if you work on older homes.

In addition to poor carpentry, weak second-story floors can be caused by some of these problems:

◆ Floor joists that have cracked due to excessive or improper drying

◆ Joists that have been weakened by rot or moisture damage, usually from a long-term plumbing or roof leak

◆ Joists that have been cut through in the course of an improper installation of plumbing or heating ducts

These types of damage are more likely on the main floor than the second floor. That's because the plumbing and heating systems are usually in the basement and so have a greater effect on the first floor. The second-floor joists are usually fairly well protected by the main floor ceiling.

Taking Down the Ceiling

Before you can make any direct repairs to the floor structure, you to have to take the ceiling down. Probably the ceiling is a mess anyway. Weak or sagging upstairs floors almost always cause extensive cracking to the main floor ceiling, so taking it down isn't usually a big loss.

Salvaging the Special Features — Don't start tearing down the ceiling without salvaging any nice wood moldings or decorations that you may find. Are there any plaster medallions, rosettes, borders or other special features? If so, remove them carefully. They can probably be reinstalled when you're done. Keeping these features intact will make the new ceiling blend in better with the rest of the house. Many old-fashioned moldings are unique. You'll never be able to match them, unless you want to have them custom-made. It's a lot easier, and less expensive, to save them.

Of course, it's only worth saving these features if they're original, or are especially nice. Don't bother trying to salvage plain pine moldings that you can buy anywhere. It's a lot easier to just replace them with new ones.

Removing plaster decorations requires special care. Most original decorations were not carved into the ceiling, but were cast separately, then added on. This means you may be able to get them off in one piece, or, at least, in a few pieces.

Start by cutting away the ceiling around the decoration. This will allow you to look at the decoration from the edge. You may then be able to see how it was attached. If not, carefully take down the entire piece of ceiling, decoration and all. Once it's on the ground, you might be able to just peel the ceiling pieces away from the plaster. That will allow you to reinstall the decoration in one piece once you're done with the repairs. If the plaster will not separate from the decoration, you can trim around the edges of the decoration leaving a layer of plaster attached to the back. Instead of laying the decoration on top of the new drywall, you'll have to cut a hole in the drywall and set the decoration into it. It may stand out a quarter of an inch or so farther than the drywall, but it's supposed to stand out. It'll just stand out a little more. Smooth the edges with drywall compound.

You never know what's going to happen when you work with decorations on old plaster. Sometimes the plaster turns to dust when you touch it; other times you can detach 4 x 8 sheets of it without breaking it. You won't know until you start to take it down. You just have to tell the homeowner, "I'll do my best to save the plaster decorations, but I can't guarantee it." If the decoration breaks, don't despair. Plaster is fairly easy to work with. You can just glue it back together. A little drywall compound will fill in any cracks or chips. Once it's back up on the ceiling and painted, it will look fine.

This may seem like a lot of trouble, but if you check the price of these kinds of decorations, you'll see that your efforts will be worthwhile. Really nice plaster decorations can cost hundreds of dollars. And besides, you'll never be able to find matching decorations if there's more of these in the house. Salvaging the originals is the only way to get a perfect match.

If all else fails, you can buy reproductions. Many of the new ones are made of plastic, which is a lot easier to work with than cast plaster. Write or call for free catalogs from the manufacturers. A few sources are:

FYPON Molded Millwork
22 West Pennsylvania Ave.
Stewartstown, PA 17363
Phone: (717) 993-2593
and
Renovator's
P.O. Box 2515
Conway, NH 03818-2515
Phone: 1-800-659-2211

They have a good selection and fairly moderate prices. If you're lucky, you might be able to find something close to the one you need to replace. If you can't find a really close match, get the closest one you can find. People are less likely to notice that the ceiling decorations don't match exactly than they are to notice that the decoration is missing completely.

Demolition — Remove the ceiling carefully. I've often seen workers gleefully slamming huge chunks of ceiling down onto the floor below. Before *you* do that, stop and think about the result. Are you going to want to refinish the floor? It's going to be a lot harder to do if it has big dents caused by falling plaster. If you think that you, or anyone else, may want to preserve the floor, then take care of it. Keep it covered at all times, and don't let your workers drop junk on it.

Figure 12-9
Remove main floor ceiling to reveal second-story floor structure

Once the ceiling is down (see Figure 12-9), you'll be able to check out the source of the second-floor problem and get some idea about what you'll need to do. The basic repairs will be much the same as those we considered when we discussed repairing wooden porches. Once again, you'll be dealing with a wooden understructure that needs to be strengthened. Of course, you'll be working in a living area, so the repairs will be a little more difficult.

🐚 Shaky Floors

A shaky floor, one with excessive bounce, is the easiest of the second-floor structural problems to fix. How much bounce would I call "excessive?" Most wooden floors will move a little bit if people jump up and down on them. However, you should be able to walk across a floor and not have it bouncing up and down like a ship in a storm. If simply walking on it causes the furniture to sway and glasses to tip over, the floor has excessive bounce. Generally, the homeowners will tell you if there's more bounce than they feel comfortable with. For some people, even a little bounce is too much.

The most common cause of excessive bounce is improper framing. The floor may have started out as an attic floor, and was never framed in heavily enough to support the live load of a bedroom or bathroom. In some cases, it may have been framed simply as a ceiling. There may not even have been an attic room above the main floor when the house was built. Whoever added the second floor may have just floored over the existing ceiling joists, without building them up to handle the extra load. This will definitely result in shaky floor.

Reinforcing the Joists

Floor joists should be 2 x 6s or 2 x 8s, depending on the distance they're going to span. If the floor joists are smaller than this recommended size, you'll need to add more joists of the correct size. The simplest way to do this is to just add another set of joists in between the old ones. There's no need to take the old ones out. Make sure that the new joists fit snugly up against the bottom of the floor, and are properly attached at the ends.

What if the existing joists are the correct size? If they are, they're clearly not doing their job. They must have lost strength for some reason. Doubling them will usually solve the problem.

It's a good idea to go upstairs and check the floor periodically as you work on this problem. I like to check the upstairs floor after each joist is added. If you're doing it right, you should notice substantially less bounce with each added joist. I find this work very satisfying. I enjoy feeling the floor grow more and more solid with every joist I install.

If it isn't getting more and more solid, then you're doing something wrong. Most likely, there's a gap between the new joists and the upstairs floor. This happens frequently because the flooring nails from the upstairs floor are protruding through the bottom side of the subfloor. If you're not careful, the new joists may hang up on these nails. The joists will butt against the points of the nails, instead of against the subfloor. As long as this separation remains, the floor will continue to bounce.

To avoid this, you'll need to hammer the bottoms of the new joists upward until you drive the joists onto the points on the flooring nails. Sometimes the points of these nails will be enough to hold the joist up, even

though it hasn't been securely nailed yet. But don't count on it staying there for long. I've sometimes made the mistake of letting go of the joist and stepping back to see if it was positioned correctly, only to have it come crashing down on my head. It's never a good idea to let go of a new joist until it's well attached.

Ideally, new joists should be supported in the same way as the existing joists. Each end should be supported by a wall or beam. Sometimes this isn't possible. The existing joists may be set into notches in a solid oak beam, for instance. In this case, joist hangers would be the best way to support the new joists. If, for some reason, you aren't able to securely attach the ends of the new joists, you may be able to get good results by just attaching them to the existing joists, thereby doubling the joists. In most cases, the weak spot in the existing joist is in the middle, not on the ends. If you securely attach the new joist to the old, this should solve the problem. If you have any doubts about whether this will solve the problem, attach the new joist with screws rather than nails. That way, you can easily remove the screws and try positioning the joist elsewhere.

Once you have the new joists in place, the upstairs floor should be rock-solid. If not, you may have to add more joists. This is another one of those jobs that you don't ever want to have to come back and do again. I like to make floors strong enough to park my truck on (though I only actually did that once). A floor like that will never be a problem to anyone again.

Normally, you won't need to add solid bridging to the new joists unless the room above is a bathroom with a ceramic tile floor. In that case, there is a lot of weight on the joists, and ceramic tile won't tolerate even the tiniest bit of bounce. Solid bridging under a ceramic tile bathroom floor is never a bad idea.

Structurally, what solid bridging does is tie all the joists together into one big, solid unit. Without bridging, each joist is independent. If you put a lot of weight in one small area, the joist right under it might bow. With solid bridging, all the joists are attached and one can't bow unless there is enough weight to make them all give. A bathtub full of water can weigh over a thousand pounds. That's enough to make one joist bow, but not enough to bend all the joists if they are bound together with bridging. (Remember, of course, bridging does no good at all unless you're adding them to joists that are good and solid.)

Jacking Up the Floor

If the upstairs floor is sagging or bowed, simply adding more joists isn't enough. All that will do is stabilize the floor in its present shape. In order to get it back into the right position, you'll need to jack it up.

The technique here is pretty much the same as the one we used to make structural repairs in the basement. However, jacking up a second floor is trickier. The space you're working in is higher, making the underside of the upstairs flooring harder to reach. Also, the floor under you isn't as solid.

Once again, you'll need to construct a beam. I mentioned earlier that it's a good idea to save your temporary beams from other jobs. By now you can see why; you can use them over and over again. The beam should be as long as the floor you're jacking up. Place it under the joists in the middle of the floor — that's usually where the sagging or bowing is worse.

If the ceiling is high, as it often is on older homes, your post-type floor jacks may not be long enough to reach the beam. If they're only a little short, you can rest the bottoms of the jacks on one or two cement blocks to make them taller. Some people attach 4 x 4s to the jacks to give them more reach, but I don't recommend it. The whole assembly becomes unstable, and it's likely to break loose and fall. Also, if it takes more than two cement blocks to make a jack tall enough, don't keep piling up cement blocks. The pile will also become unstable. Remember, the jack is going to be under a lot of pressure once you tighten it. If it's not absolutely plumb, and on a solid surface, the pressure could cause it to shoot out sideways at high speed. This can be very dangerous. Always treat floor jacks with great respect.

There's another technique you can use when screw-type floor jacks won't fit. You can use a couple of automobile-type hydraulic bottle jacks and 4 x 4s. Bottle jacks are quite strong. They are, after all, designed to lift cars. They're also quite small, and easy to handle. Their biggest drawback is that they only have a few inches of extension. That's where the 4 x 4s come in. You'll need to get 4 x 4s long enough to reach from the bottle jack to the beam. Attach the 4 x 4 securely to the beam so that it will hang from the beam if the jack is removed. That will ensure that it won't slip out of line and come crashing down on your head. Securing all these parts may seem like a lot of trouble, but if you've ever had one of these temporary assemblies fall on you (like I have), you'll realize that the extra trouble is worthwhile.

Be sure to protect the floor before you set your jacks on it. A piece of ¾-inch plywood under the jacks provides a good base and protects the floor from being dented by the pressure of the jack. The number of jacks you'll need for this operation will depend on how long the beam is, and how badly the floor is bowed. When in doubt, use more. You're much better off with too many than too few.

One thing that makes this operation complicated is the fact that the floor on which the jacks are resting is only made of wood. It isn't tremendously strong. Before you can start jacking, you'll need to reinforce the points your jacks are setting on. Otherwise, when you start jacking, instead of the floor upstairs moving up, the main floor might move down! This would do more harm than good.

To prevent this from happening, you need to temporarily reinforce the main floor from beneath, down in the basement. Place floor jacks or 4 x 4s directly under the part of the floor that the upstairs floor jacks are resting on. Each jack must have its own support to stop the floor from sinking when you start jacking. When you're done, you'll have a two-part support column reaching from the

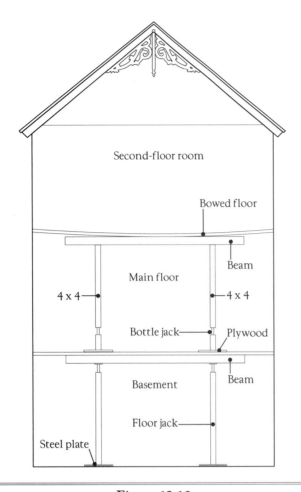

Second-floor room

Bowed floor

Beam

Main floor

4 x 4 — — 4 x 4

Bottle jack — Plywood

Basement

Beam

Floor jack

Steel plate

Figure 12-10

Support structure should run in straight lines from the basement to the second floor

basement floor to the second floor, as shown in Figure 12-10. If you look at it starting from the top, you have the second floor joists, the beam, the 4 x 4, the bottle jack, the ¾-inch plywood, the main floor, another beam, a 4 x 4 or a floor jack under that, and the basement floor at the base of it all. The entire support structure is essentially resting on the basement floor. As we discussed in the section on first-floor structural repairs, be sure to place a steel plate under the jacks in the basement, so that they don't punch a hole in the floor.

Now you're ready to start jacking, and again, you must tighten the jacks slowly and carefully. Pay attention to creaking and groaning. The floor probably sagged over many years. If you try to jack it back into

place too fast, you may rip it to pieces. Don't try to move it more than ¼ inch per day. It may take several days to get it back into position without damage.

Once the floor is back in the proper position, you can strengthen it by adding more joists. Loosen the jacks, but before you remove them completely, check to make sure the floor is rock-solid. If it isn't, add more joists until it is. Also, check the floor for floorboards that may have worked loose during the repair process. You can usually hammer them back down without any problem.

❧ Cost

Strengthening a floor that isn't sagging is a fairly easy job. It should take no more than about eight hours, not counting putting up a new ceiling. Your only material cost will be the lumber for new joists. This is usually under $200.

Straightening a sagging floor is more difficult. That will take you about 20 hours. And remember, you'll need to strengthen the main floor from the basement, too. That means you'll need two beams and two sets of posts, not just one. In terms of materials, you'll need the same joists, plus 4 x 4s and lumber for two beams and four posts. This should still come to under $300. Keep in mind that you'll be able to save the 4 x 4s and beam and use them another time. (Or you may already have some from another job.) They always come in handy.

If you want to add in the cost of taking down and replacing the ceiling at this point, I'll include that here. These are usually considered two separate jobs; one is drywalling and the other structural repairs. You'll need separate permits for each.

For estimating purposes, I'll assume that you are working on an average size room, no more than 12 by 20 feet, with no fancy moldings or ceiling decorations to deal with. Tearing down the ceiling is quite easy — often they're already falling before you start. The hardest part is removing the old furring strips. They leave nails behind, and every single nail has to be removed or driven in.

Otherwise, you'll have nails poking holes through your new drywall from the back side. Figure about two hours labor for the tear down, plus trash removal. An average ceiling will generate about 400 pounds of trash. That's a little less than half a pickup truck full. In my area, that will cost about $15 in dump fees, plus time and gas for the trip to the dump.

The ceiling will take about nine sheets of 8-foot drywall at $4 each, and drywall compound, which will run about $10. The most costly part of the job is labor. It will take two to three men 10 hours to hang drywall on the ceiling of an average size room. Most of the time is taken up with taping and finishing, which is tedious and time-consuming work. You can use 12-foot sheets of drywall if it will save time, but I never do. You need a lot of space and at least four men to work with 12-foot sheets. I've found that dealing with 8-foot sheets in most old houses is hard enough. Large materials are best left for large jobs and large crews.

Sagging Second-Floor Additions

The most serious second-floor structural problem is a sagging room addition. These are caused by someone adding another floor to a one-story house without adequately strengthening the basic structure of the house. Poorly-constructed addition problems can be very difficult to fix. Sometimes they can't be fixed at all, and the house has to be demolished.

A second-floor addition is tremendously heavy. Supporting it is considerably harder than just supporting the live load on an existing upstairs floor. Even if there's a grand piano in an original upstairs room, a dozen new 2 x 10s will hold it up, with strength to spare. But an addition weighs many tons. In some cases, that extra weight can be enough to crush the entire house into the ground.

❧ Partition Walls

One reason an addition sags is because an amateur carpenter used first-floor partitions as load-bearing walls. Partition walls are designed to divide the main floor up into various rooms. They aren't intended to carry a lot of weight. Many amateur carpenters don't seem to understand this basic fact of building. They set additions right on top of partition walls and assume the walls will hold everything up.

To add to the problem, first-floor partition walls are not well supported themselves. A load-bearing wall would have a post or a beam under it in the basement, to help carry the weight. In that case, the upstairs would rest on the wall, the wall would rest on the basement beam or post, and that would rest on good, solid concrete. Everything would be well-supported, and you wouldn't have any problems.

Unfortunately, if you check the basement, you'll probably find that the partition wall that is supposed to hold up the second-floor addition is only held up by the first-floor joists. The joists can't handle the tremendous weight of the addition, so the first floor sags, causing the upstairs floor to sag in turn. If you don't do something about this situation, the floor will eventually break, and the house will collapse inward into the basement.

If you find a problem like this, you may be able to repair it from the basement. You'll need to make a permanent beam and install it under the partition wall. Then you'll need to jack the beam up, slowly and carefully, until all the floors are level again. You can expect this to take from several days to possibly a few weeks.

This same repair can be done from a crawl space, but it takes a lot longer, and it's a lot more unpleasant. Working in a crawl space is like working under the porch. It's dirty, cramped, and often wet. Your only consolation is that you can charge just about anything you want for this job, because probably nobody else will even bid on it.

No Wall at All

In some cases, an amateur carpenter may have added the upstairs room without giving any thought at all to its support. We discussed additions like these in Chapter 3, when we were inspecting the house. There may be no walls under it, load-bearing or otherwise. It may be just sitting in the middle of the living room ceiling, causing serious sagging.

You approach this problem the same way you would if you were straightening a sagging floor. You'll need a beam, and a number of jacks. However, you may need a bigger beam, and more jacks, depending on the weight of the addition.

More than likely, because of the tremendous weight involved, adding joists alone won't provide enough support. You'll need to install a permanent beam, creating a post-and-lintel arrangement, with your beam as the lintel. Be sure you position it carefully, because the homeowners are going to have to live with it. However, if you do a nice, neat job it will look fine, once it's drywalled and painted.

Jacking up the beam can be tricky. You'll have to lift a lot of weight, so it may take a lot of jacks. Be sure each jack is adequately supported by posts in the basement, or the pressure can break the living room floor joists.

If you try to lift too much weight with one jack, you'll notice the piece of wood it's attached to (the beam or 4 x 4) will begin to be crushed. In that case, stop, and distribute the weight better by lifting with some of the other jacks instead. As with the porch, you want to lift a little bit with each jack, so that none becomes overstressed.

Attaching the Beam

You'll need to give some thought to how you're going to support the new beam. You can't just have a bunch of 4 x 4s standing in the middle of the living room. You'll need to connect the beam to something inside the walls.

The best way to do this is to cut away some of the plaster and build posts into the first floor walls. You may be able to use 4 x 4 posts, but if you're not sure they'll be strong enough for the weight involved, use 6 x 6s or steel columns. The posts need to be set into the walls with their bottom ends resting on something solid — either the top of the foundation wall or a special support built in the basement. This is an absolutely crucial support point.

Beams and Walls

You may also find a combination of inadequate support situations. That is, there may be a load-bearing wall under part of the addition, but not the rest. In that case, you may be able to strengthen the wall, and then attach a new beam to that. Or, you may be able to transfer all the load to the beam, and not have to bother about the wall at all. You will want the repair to be as unobtrusive as possible, but a lot depends on how much weight there is to support. If the addition is really heavy, you may have to use all of these techniques.

If there's a lot of weight to support, a wooden beam may not be your best choice. Rather than using a beam that is so thick that it interferes with headroom or that it looks unsightly, you might want to use a steel I-beam. I try to avoid using steel beams. They're heavy and hard to work with; but they're amazingly strong. Sometimes that's what you need to get the job done.

Cost

Supporting an addition is a touchy job that needs to be approached with great care. If it's a fairly simple and straightforward problem, you may be able to engineer it yourself. Check with the building inspector to make sure you will be able to get approval for your project. You may want to consult a structural engineer before you begin, just to make sure that your plans are going to work. Having your plans approved by an engineer will also makes it easier to get approval from the city building department. Often, when the problem is really severe — and I've seen several houses like this — the building department will just want to condemn the house before it collapses and someone is hurt. Having an engineer approve your plans may be what it takes to convince the building department that the house can be saved. Check with a couple of engineering firms to get bids; engineers don't work cheap. In general you can expect to pay $500 to $1,000 for engineering work.

The material costs are fairly low on this job. All you're using is some lumber to build a beam and some posts. The exact cost will depend on how big a beam you need and how many posts, but generally about $400 will cover it easily. The main cost factor in this job, besides engineering fees, is the labor. It takes me between 20 and 40 hours, working alone, to do a job like this. It's hard to pin the labor down any more than that, because each job is different, and involves varying degrees of difficulty. Sometimes everything drops right into place, and sometimes it fights you every inch of the way.

The alternative to making these repairs is demolishing the house. That, and the fact that many contractors have no idea how to do a job like this, cuts down the competition and makes this work very profitable indeed.

You can figure repairs to the walls and ceilings separately using the costs we discussed for drywalling the ceiling earlier in this chapter. I always estimate the finish work separately because usually I'm doing plaster repair work and painting throughout the house.

Stairways

A nice stairway is often a central feature in the downstairs living area. If there is a problem with the stairway, you need to deal with it before you do any further work on the main floor living area.

There are many different types of stairways found in older homes. Some are beautifully constructed, with gracious fea-

tures that look like the ones you might see a movie star using for a grand entrance. Others are cramped, dark, narrow little steps which appear to ascend up into a closet. And of course, there are other styles in between these extremes.

Obviously, if a house has a grand staircase, you'll want to do everything you can to preserve it. Features like this add to the beauty and value of an older home. Cramped, dark little steps, on the other hand, should be torn out and replaced with a new staircase.

Stairway Problems

Stairways are a major source of structural problems. This is particularly true of open stairways — those with railings on both sides instead of a wall on one side. Open stairways can be very attractive, but they frequently have support problems. If the house you're working on has an open stairway, take a look at the floor above it. What's supporting the floor? In many cases there's nothing at all. You're likely to find a sagging floor and a cracked first-floor ceiling above this kind of stairway.

Another common structural problem is found with stacked stairways. That is, the basement stairs are right under the stairs to the second floor. This minimizes the space that stairways take away from the living area, but then the stairs are essentially supporting each other. If there's a lack of support in the basement, it can cause problems all the way up to the second floor.

Strengthening the Structure

Usually, the first place to go to check out an unstable or sagging stairway is the basement. Look at what's under the stairway. A properly-constructed house will have at least some kind of beam, even if it's only a doubled floor joist, supporting the stairs. This support was probably adequate when the house was new. However, the beam may not be as strong as it used to be, and the entire stairway structure may now be inadequately supported. In many cases an extra post or two placed at this point may solve the support problem.

193

If adding support in the basement doesn't solve the problem, you'll need to add support on the main floor. This is more difficult. You can't just stick a 4 x 4 post in the living room. The repair needs to be unobtrusive. This is especially true if you're working on a beautiful staircase. You don't want to spoil the effect with awkward, ugly repairs.

One good place to add strength to an open stairway is at the newel post. In most open designs, these posts extend about 4 feet off the floor. However, there are some designs in which they extend all the way to the ceiling. How about redesigning the style of the stairway and constructing a post that goes to the ceiling? Try to make the new newel post as similar as possible to the rest of the stairway. Use the same kind of wood, and stain it to match. When you're done, it should look like a decorative element rather than the support column it really is. Be sure there's a post beneath it in the basement as well. The upstairs corner, which was probably cracking and sagging, will now be held up by this column, which is in turn held up by the post in the basement. This gives the same required line of support that you need for a room addition or any other weight that pulls on the structure of the house.

The overall effect may not be quite as attractive as the original open stairway. However, if you do a very careful job, matching the new pieces to the old as closely as possible, the difference should be minimal. The only other way to deal with this problem would be to tear down the ceiling and add a beam, as we discussed in the last section. That would be a shame if the ceiling was in otherwise good condition. It would also be lot more work, and when it was done the beam might look more awkward than the new newel post.

❧ Unsuitable Stairways

Another problem with stairways in older homes is that a stairway built to a second-floor addition may not have been built to code. As I mentioned during the inspection, many of these stairways were designed solely as an attic access. They were never intended for regular use, and were not rebuilt to suit the need when the attic was converted into additional living space. In other cases, the stairs were added by amateur carpenters who simply didn't know how to do the job right. In either situation, the stairway should be rebuilt to meet the existing need of the homeowners.

The major concern now will be space. The new stairway will most likely need to be bigger than the old one. An inadequate stairway is usually too narrow, too steep, the treads aren't deep enough, or any or all of the above. The new stairway may have to be wider, and longer, to accommodate a larger number of stairs, each of which is deeper. Where is the extra space going to come from?

The exact placement of the stairway is going to depend on several things, such as available space, traffic flow and livability. No matter where you place it, a relocated stairway will more than likely end up taking a chunk out of the living room or dining room. And it will have an impact on the structural plan of the house.

Figure 12-11 shows a dark, narrow, steep stairway that I had to rebuild. I was fairly lucky with this one. The plaster was damaged and when I tore into the walls to see how bad the damage was, I found that the stairway was enclosed with partition walls. Figure 12-12 shows the interior of one of the walls. The studs had been set sideways, creating a weak, thin wall. Modern construction techniques wouldn't allow this. I had expected to find load-bearing walls, especially since it appeared that the upstairs floor joists were resting on the top of the staircase walls. Unfortunately, these walls served no structural function at all — they weren't even fully framed!

I removed the old staircase and constructed a new one that was wider and less steep. The new walls were framed correctly and offered more support than the useless walls I took out. I had to take some space from a downstairs room in order to widen the stairway, but it wasn't really noticeable. The finished staircase, shown in Figure 12-13,

Figure 12-11
*Dark, narrow stairway leads
to second-floor addition*

Figure 12-12
Partition wall has studs set sideways

Figure 12-13
The new stairway

looks a lot like the original. Once I've installed the handrail, it will function as a safe and easy access to the upstairs bedrooms, no longer dangerously steep or uncomfortably narrow.

This job was about as simple as stair building ever gets. However, it was still a big job. The plaster was already ruined, so I didn't have to tear out any good walls. Even if the stairway had been in good condition, I would still have had to install new drywall on the walls. I used plain pine risers and treads for the stairs, because the stairway was going to be carpeted. There was no fancy woodwork necessary, except for a little bit of trim molding. It was a pretty simple, straightforward job. It took me 60 hours and cost about $500, including the drywall.

New Stairways

Style and design considerations are very important when planning new stairways. A stairway is a highly visible design element and should coordinate with the overall design of the house. It doesn't necessarily need to have the same layout as the old stairway. It doesn't even need to begin and end at the same place. In many cases, you wouldn't want it to. The original stairway, especially if it was an attic access, may start in a closet. This is obviously an inappropriate place for a stairway that's used for everyday living. Ignore the old stairway and start fresh.

What spaces would you like to have the stairway connect? A downstairs hall would be a good place for the new stairway to start, if there's a downstairs hall. Otherwise, someplace near the front door is usually a good

Figure 12-14
2 x 4 blocks added for strength

Figure 12-15
New tread fastened into place

location. Of course, the other end of the stairway needs to come out in a reasonable position upstairs as well. It should come out in a hallway too, if possible, not in the middle of a room. What if there isn't an upstairs hallway? You may need to make one. We'll deal with this in depth when we talk about improvements that enhance livability.

One advantage to building new stairways is that there are designs to fit many different shapes and sizes. The stairway doesn't have to be a straight shot from the first floor to the second. It can curve, or have a landing, or even more than one landing if necessary. This flexibility makes it easier to use the stairway to tie the desired areas on both floors together.

Stairway design is a very complex subject, one that could easily fill its own book. If you're thinking of designing and building a stairway, you might want to consult *Rough Framing Carpentry*, or *Wood-Frame House Construction*, also published by Craftsman Book Company (see the order form in the back of this book). These contain far more on the subject than I could possibly cover here.

✌ Stairway Repair

Stairways take a lot of abuse. They're often one of the most heavily-traveled areas in the house, especially if all the bedrooms are upstairs. In an older home, the stairs are

likely to need some minor repairs to the treads, posts or railings even if their basic structure is sound. The most common problem is broken treads. After 60 or 80 years of being stomped on, it's no surprise that some treads break. In fact, it's surprising that any of them are still intact!

Broken Treads

Start your repairs by carefully prying out the old tread. This sounds easy, but it's not. The treads are usually nailed in place with the nails entering at a 45 degree angle. This allows the nails to grip into the stringer as well as into the riser of the next stair. You may be able to cut through the nails with a hacksaw blade, or a Sawzall. Pry the tread up slowly and carefully, so that you don't break any of the pieces. You might need to reuse the wood.

If the stairway isn't especially attractive, or if it's going to be carpeted, you can replace the broken tread with a piece of plain pine. Figure 12-14 a staircase that had a broken tread. To make the repair, I pulled back the carpet and removed the tread. There was no way that I could make a new tread that would sit into the stringer exactly like the original tread, so I screwed pieces of 2 x 4 to the sides of the stringers to add extra support. You can see one in Figure 12-14. Then I replaced the tread with two pieces of 2 x 6, which I screwed into the 2 x 4 supports. Figure 12-15 shows the new tread in place.

The finished stair, shown in Figure 12-16, looks perfect.

This method generally works very well, but you must be sure that the replacement tread is as sturdy as the original. Remember, pine isn't as strong as oak. If you're replacing an oak tread with pine, the pine needs to be much thicker. However, using a thicker piece of wood may cause the one stair to be higher than the others, and this won't do. The irregular height might make someone trip. The simplest way to deal with this problem is to just get another piece of oak.

Matching the Tread — If the staircase is constructed of beautiful wood, you can't just use any old piece of wood as a replacement. It needs to match. This can be a problem, especially if the staircase is made of unusual wood, or assembled in an unusual pattern, like parquet.

The best way to deal with this situation is by trying to salvage the old tread. Of course, if the old tread is broken; it won't hold weight, but it still may be useful cosmetically. It still matches. You can construct a new underlayer to support the broken tread.

The easiest way to do this is from under the stairway, working upwards. However, you can also work from the top down, if necessary. I take a piece of 2 x 12 and cut it to fit into the open space just below where the tread used to be. It should sit level with the top of the riser, so that the old tread can sit on top of the 2 x 12, and be the same height it was originally. Screw the 2 x 12 securely into the risers. When I can, I like to put a couple of support blocks under it as well. This will make it the strongest stair in the stairway. Glue the original tread onto the pine underlayer and you'll have a strong, rebuilt tread that exactly matches the rest of the staircase.

It will no longer matter that the tread lacks strength. The weight will be supported by the 2 x 12 pine underlayer. The old tread is just there for looks. If you do this carefully, the repair should be practically invisible. The stair will match perfectly, and be stronger than ever.

Figure 12-16
Completed tread repair

Surprisingly, I've found construction like this on original stairways in old homes. What appeared to be a tread made of solid mahogany was actually a thin strip of mahogany glued over a pine underlayer. I guess starting about in the 1920s, fine woods were beginning to be too expensive to use for ordinary stairways.

Loose Newel Posts

Newel posts and hand rails tend to become wobbly over the years. It's often because the glue has lost its strength and the nails have worked loose after years of being pulled back and forth. If that's the case, adding some carpenter's glue and hammering the nails back in is all that's needed.

Occasionally the problem is more severe. The base of the newel post, or the wood it's attached to, may be cracked or splintered. The best way to fix it is to try to get around to the underside of the staircase. You may be able to reach it from a closet, from the basement, or by removing a tread. Once you can get to the base, you can add screws and glue from the inside, where the repair won't show.

If you can't get to the inside of the staircase, you may have to add screws and glue to the newel post from the outside. It won't look as nice, but it's better than having the newel post come off in your hands. If you countersink the screws and cover them with matching wood putty, the repair should be fairly unobtrusive.

Chapter 13

Plumbing Repair

The next subject we need to take a look at is plumbing. The basement is the heart of the plumbing system, so you may have run into some of these problems there already.

Major plumbing modifications require tearing out walls, so you'd better do them before you begin the wall repairs. Also, plumbing leaks can ruin any kind of plasterwork. Never do any plaster repairs until you're absolutely sure that all leaks of any kind have been permanently repaired. Otherwise, you risk having all your nice new work ruined.

Galvanized Steel Inlet Lines

Most older homes have inlet lines of galvanized steel. These lines have a limited life span, usually about 70 years. That means, if a house was built in 1920, the pipes are due to expire any day. Don't even touch them until you're ready to start working on them. Just moving them slightly may be enough to cause leaks. Old pipes are sometimes as thin as tinfoil.

Plumbing problems on newer pipes tend to be at the joints — the points where two or more pipes are fastened together. Old pipes have problems at these points, but they also have problems with cracking. You rarely see this in newer pipes. Look for cracks whenever you have an old pipe that's leaking and the reason isn't apparent. A crack will first show up as a very faint line, only about a hair's width, and will appear to be drawn on the pipe. You would never notice it if you weren't looking for it.

Pipes crack because they have rusted through almost completely. If you put a wrench to a cracked pipe and turn, the pipe will break apart. Not only that pipe, but the pipe next to it will break apart, and the one next to that! You'll end up having to replace the entire horizontal run of pipe.

Usually, vertical pipes rust much more slowly than horizontal ones. So you may not need to replace the entire plumbing system — just the horizontal runs. That's actually pretty lucky, because the vertical pipes are the ones that run through the walls. They're much harder to get at. If you have to replace the vertical piping as well, you'll probably have to tear up walls to get them out.

Figure 13-1
*This mass of leaky plumbing connections
should be replaced*

❧ The Plumbing Runs

In a modern house, the plumbing runs are carefully planned to be as compact as possible. Pipes will run from the basement to the kitchen. The bathroom will be located directly over the kitchen. An additional bathroom or lavatory will be on the opposite side of a common wall with the other bathroom or kitchen. If there are bathrooms in another part of the house, they'll be grouped together as well. All the plumbing is grouped together in one or two areas. You won't find pipes running all over the house.

In older homes, this isn't necessarily the case. Since the plumbing may have been added after the house was built, it may run anywhere. An upstairs bathroom may have been located in an unused bedroom, and that may not be above the kitchen. If the rooms don't line up, you know that the kitchen plumbing hasn't been extended vertically up into the bathroom. Check the basement. Is there a vertical run feeding the bathroom? If not, it must be supplied by a horizontal run

coming out of the kitchen. This horizontal run is likely to be a trouble spot. Any mysterious water damage in the living room, dining room or other downstairs area is probably caused by that pipe.

If you discover any horizontal runs of pipes after removing the ceiling in any of the main floor rooms, don't just blissfully drywall over them. Examine them carefully. Even if they aren't leaking now, they may be soon. Any work that you're doing will disturb them. The vibrations from hammering and cutting may be all it takes for them to crack and spring a leak. Replace any old galvanized steel pipe that you suspect may be 70 years old or so. Otherwise, the leaks may start showing just as soon as your new drywall is finished, ruining all your work, and your good will with the homeowner.

❧ Patched-Together Plumbing

It's not unusual to find three different kinds of plumbing within a few feet of each other in an older home. I've often found galvanized steel, leading to copper, leading to plastic, all in the same area. Each of these materials is a different age, and is the result of several layers of modifications.

There isn't necessarily anything wrong with this work. It may have been competently done, and it may not leak. However, looking at it doesn't tend to give you confidence. All of the joints are potential trouble spots. Of course, all plumbing systems have joints, and I'm not suggesting that you should worry about every single one of them. A joint that has been properly done by a competent plumber is not likely to leak. However, a competent plumber will use only as many joints as necessary. If you see a plumbing system that has lots of extra joints added for no good reason, you know it was done by an amateur. Amateurs do all kinds of crazy, unsound things. Figure 13-1 is an example of a plumbing nightmare. It would be hard to imagine fitting more joints into this convoluted jumble of leaky pipe connections. Any time you find something like this, you know it has to be replaced immediately.

The reason that joints between different piping materials can be a problem is that different materials expand at different rates. Since pipe materials are constantly expanding and contracting, the joints between them are more likely to work loose than joints between the same materials. The more of these joints there are, the more trouble you're likely to run into. In a properly laid out system, you might find the main part of the system of galvanized steel with an add-on section of CPVC plastic pipe. You will only have one point where different materials are joined, and that is where the new section comes off the old section. This joint will probably be okay.

If the system was done incorrectly, you're likely to find galvanized steel pipe connected to copper, which is connected to CPVC, which is connected to more galvanized steel, and so on. It will be a crazy quilt of all kinds of materials and each connection will be a potential trouble spot. All of these materials are fine in themselves, but they're *not* fine all hooked together! If a system like this isn't leaking now, it will be soon. It's best to tear out the least used types of pipe and replace them with whatever has been used the most. Rebuild the system with one or at least not more than two types of material — not a half-dozen.

Most of the time when I find a run of old and new pipe joined together that appears solid and the pipes are in the exposed area of the basement, I leave them alone. They'll be easy to get at if the joints should begin leaking in the future. They can't do a lot of harm in the basement, anyway. On the other hand, old and new runs of piping joined inside a ceiling or wall should be replaced. A leak there can cause too much damage. Interior leaks have the potential to destroy the plasterwork in several rooms. Never leave any substandard plumbing inside ceilings or walls. The risk is just too great.

Water Hammer

If you've always worked on properly-constructed houses, you may never have come across *water hammer*. It's an odd effect caused by sudden pressure changes in the inlet lines. If you turn a faucet on and off quickly, the pipes will go WHAM! It's very loud, and the whole system shakes!

This happens a lot in older homes, especially those with patched-together plumbing systems. Whoever put the system together didn't understand the need for air chambers. An air chamber, in its simplest form, is just a piece of pipe coming up off the inlet lines that contains air. When the pressure in the pipe changes suddenly, the air absorbs the shock. This simple addition to the pipe line will eliminate water hammer problems.

I've occasionally found an air chamber installed upside down! The installer clearly didn't know what it was supposed to do. If it's upside down, it'll fill up with water, not air, and it won't work. You may also find air chambers that are properly installed, but don't appear to be working. They may be filled with water. In that case, shut off the water supply, and drain the line. This should clear all the water out. When you turn the water supply back on, air will automatically be trapped in the air chamber.

Drain Lines

Drain lines commonly rust out, especially the parts where water can pool. The longer the water sits in the pipe, the more the pipe rusts. That's why the traps under sinks rust out so often.

When the house was built, the drain lines were installed so that water couldn't pool in them. Water can't pool in vertical lines, and the horizontal lines should have been hung so that they were either level, or angled down towards their outlets. That would keep pooling to a minimum, and allow the drains to empty quickly and easily.

Over the years the drains may have become partially clogged, or they may have shifted or settled, so that the angles are no longer correct. This could allow water to pool up in some parts of the system, and these parts will be the first to rust out.

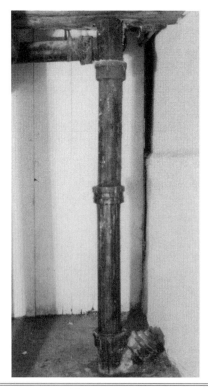

Figure 13-2
Rusted section of cast iron pipe

Check the angles on all the drain lines in the basement. If there are any that are angled wrong, look for rust damage. Even if there isn't any damage now, correct the angles to prevent future rust damage. Proper angles will also improve drainage, which is especially important on drain lines coming from toilets. If these lines don't drain quickly and easily, solid matter from the toilets won't clear completely. It can build up in the pipes and cause constant clogging problems.

Cast Iron Drain Lines

The main drain lines in most older homes are 4-inch cast iron pipe. Examine them carefully. Look for hairline cracks, or for mysterious puddles on the floor nearby. Be sure to check them carefully before you spend a lot of time and money waterproofing the basement walls. You don't want to put a lot of work into the walls, only to discover that the leak was in the plumbing. This may

seem pretty basic advice, but sometimes it's hard to tell where water is coming from. The leakage from pipes may not be obvious. If pipes run near a wall, it may look for all the world like the wall is leaking. The only way you can tell the difference is by checking the pipes very carefully.

When you're ready to deal with the pipe lines, start by tapping them with a metal tool. We discussed earlier why you shouldn't do this during your inspection. Just tapping on them may be enough to make them spring a leak.

Once you begin working on the plumbing system, you can be fairly aggressive about checking out cast iron piping. Cast iron is a very tough material. When it's in good condition, it takes a sledgehammer to break it. Jabbing it with a screwdriver or tapping it with a small hammer shouldn't hurt it. If it does, the pipe is badly rusted and needs replacing.

If you find one bad spot in a pipe, the entire pipe will have to go. You can't just cut out the bad spot. The rest of the pipe will be so crumbly that you won't be able to work with it. This is especially true of horizontal runs; if one spot is bad, the entire run is probably bad. It's often easier to replace the whole thing than to try to save a few existing pieces of pipe here and there anyway. Putting in all brand-new pipe makes sense. This is a hard, messy job. You won't want to do it over; and you know that the homeowners will call you back if the same pipes begin leaking again.

Cast iron pipe can be difficult to work with. The rusted parts may be so fragile that they just fall apart in your hands, while other parts are as solid as the day they were cast. You'll have to break those out with a sledgehammer. I usually use a 4-pound mini-sledgehammer for this, although if the pipe is especially tough you might need a larger hammer. I find that most pipe tends to comes off fairly easily, but there's always some last little bit I have to slam the heck out of before I can get it out.

Figure 13-2 shows a vertical pipe line that I had to replace. You can see the discoloration in the top section of the pipe. That's a pretty

Figure 13-3
Rusted section crumbled and fell apart

Figure 13-4
All the bad pipe has been removed

good indication of a problem, even without the corroded joints and water stains. When I tapped the top of the pipe with my mini-sledge, a great big chunk shattered and fell out (Figure 13-3). I removed the bad section of pipe, leaving the top and bottom joints (Figure 13-4). Always be very careful when you're breaking out cast iron pipe. The good

pieces are heavy and you don't want to be under any when it falls. Figure 13-5 shows the newly-installed vertical pipe. I used one long piece of PVC pipe to replace the two old sections. The bottom fit snugly into the old joint and I used a rubber pressure-seal to join the old and new pipes at the top (Figure 13-6).

This job can be very messy, especially if you're removing a horizontal pipe that has been angled wrong, and there's a substantial buildup of solids inside. It'll smell really bad. This isn't a job for someone with a weak stomach. The sludge tends to get all over the place when you're working. Pounding on the pipes splatters it around the basement. Be sure the area you're working in has been

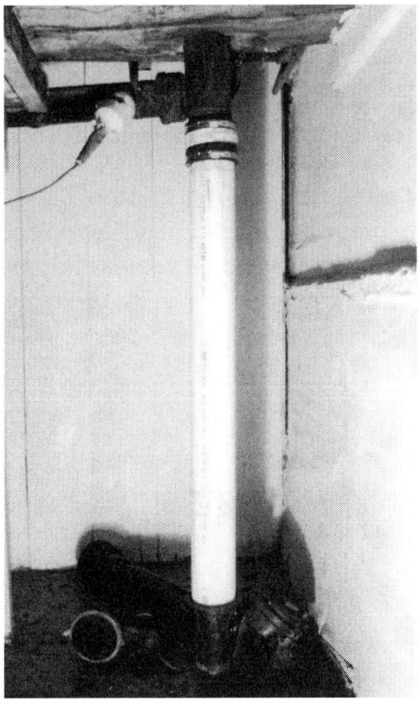

Figure 13-5
New PVC pipe

Figure 13-6
Rubber connector joins old and new pipe

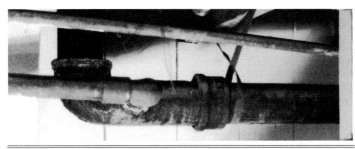

Figure 13-7
Horizontal pipe shows signs of rust damage

Figure 13-8
New PVC pipe line

totally cleared of any of the homeowner's belongings before you begin. That way, you can hose the area down and wash all the sludge away when you're done.

It's also a good idea to turn off the water supply and flush all toilets to drain the tanks before you start. You don't absolutely need to turn off the water, but if you don't, you can be sure that someone will flush the toilet while you're standing right under the open drain. Warning (or even threatening) people ahead of time is useless. Someone always forgets! You can take my word for it, or you can learn the same way I did.

This is especially true if you have to leave the job unfinished, even for a few minutes. You'll come back, and the basement floor will be covered with water and crud. If the toilets *can't* be flushed until the water is turned back on and the toilet tank is refilled, this won't happen.

🐘 Working with PVC Pipe

I generally replace cast iron lines with PVC pipe. It's strong stuff, yet it's lightweight, cheap, and easy to work with. You can cut it with a hacksaw, although I usually find it's more convenient to cut the large sizes with a saber saw. You can get connector pieces of PVC pipe in all sizes and angles. You just glue the pieces together with plastic cement. It's almost like making model airplanes.

Be sure you have a good selection of fittings and connectors on hand before you start work. I've wasted endless hours making unnecessary trips to the hardware store to get the pieces I should have had before I started. And since not all hardware stores stock a complete selection of 4-inch PVC, I sometimes had to go to several different stores to get the right fittings. Four-inch PVC isn't used as commonly as the smaller sizes. You can save yourself a lot of aggravation if you make sure you have every possible part before you start.

When you're working with PVC pipe, you need to remember that once it's glued into place, you can't change it. If a piece is angled wrong, you'll have to cut it out and throw it away. Even though it's cheap, that's still a nuisance. To avoid extra work, fit all the pieces together first without glue. Make sure the angles are correct and the pieces fit snugly together. And here's a tip that'll save you the price of this book: Once you've assembled the pieces correctly, mark them. I draw arrows on each piece in pencil, and then all I have to do is line up the arrows when I put the pieces back together with glue. If you do that, you'll be sure that all the angles will line up exactly the same way.

Plastic cement sets up very quickly. You only have about 30 seconds to get the pieces positioned together correctly before it sets. Because you have to hurry, it's easy to make a mistake and get the angle connectors turned around. Marking all the pieces clearly will save you a lot of trouble, especially if you're working on a complicated connection. Figure 13-7 shows a rusted out horizontal pipe run that I had to replace. It took several pieces of PVC pipe in varying sizes, fitted together at different angles, to complete the run of new pipe shown in Figure 13-8. The vertical pipe running up off the horizontal section goes all the way up to join the plumbing in the main floor bathroom. You can bet I marked these carefully!

Figure 13-9
Rusted pipe patched with duct tape

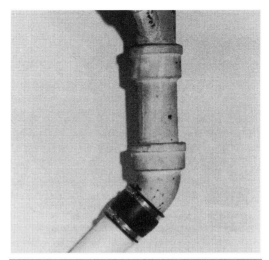

Figure 13-10
New PVC pipe with rubber connector

🦜 Connecting Old and New Pipe

If parts of the old pipe are still usable (many times, the vertical runs are okay), you can join the new pipe to the old with rubber pressure-seal connectors. These are rubber sleeves that fit over both pipes, and seal tightly with clamps that look like radiator-hose clamps. They're used to connect different types of pipe to one another. I replaced the rusted section of cast iron pipe shown in Figure 13-9 with PVC. The new section is now joined to the old with a rubber connector (see Figure 13-10), making a nice neat repair.

Rubber connectors can also be used as size adapters. You can get them with one end larger than the other to join two different sizes of pipe. Since they're rubber, they're flexible, allowing you to join two pieces of pipe, like the ones shown in Figure 13-11, that aren't the same size and don't line up exactly. A situation like this would be a real headache without flexible connectors. They are code-approved, even for use in exterior underground piping.

Figure 13-11
Rubber connector joins pipes of different sizes that don't quite line up

advantage of doing this kind of job is that homeowners expect it to cost a lot of money, so you can charge a high price and no one will complain. No one will do a job like this cheap, so you don't have to worry about anyone substantially underbidding you, especially plumbers. Most of them really dislike this job (for good reason), and would just as soon let someone else do it.

Bathroom Leaks

It's important to correct any problem leaks in bathrooms before proceeding with the wall and ceiling work. Of all the possible

Cost

Replacing the main 4-inch drain line is a difficult, messy job. Doing all the lines in a typical basement will take six to eight hours. It will only cost about $100 for materials. The plumbing leaks in the house, those from the bathroom are the most damaging. Basement plumbing leaks will just drip on the basement floor. Kitchen leaks will drip on the joists below, but it takes years before any serious damage occurs. A leak in an upstairs bathroom, however, can cause thousands of dollars in damage to the plasterwork in the rooms below in just a few days. Always make absolutely sure the bathroom plumbing is solid. Examine all the pipes carefully and replace anything that looks substandard.

The bathroom is a prime site for a "mystery leak," one that is very hard to find. A mystery leak may only occur under very specific circumstances. To find it, you need to try every imaginable thing that could be done with the plumbing in the bathroom, and see if it leaks when you do it. Turn on the water in the sink and bathtub, and let it run for a long time. See if any leaks develop. Turn on the shower as well as the tub. Sometimes the shower plumbing leaks, when the tub doesn't. Fill the tub up with water. The added weight of the water will sometimes cause pipes to shift and leak. Flush the toilet several times. Sometimes it will leak only after the second or third flush. You need to locate these leaks now, before the plasterwork is put in any more jeopardy.

ᓚ Floor Leaks

One type of mystery leak that I find quite often in older homes is an unsealed bathroom floor. This is a problem that's unique to the bathroom. Normally, a bathroom floor will be covered by a waterproof material, like ceramic tile, or a single, unbroken sheet of resilient floor covering. The flooring material should be sealed to a cove base or tile molding. If it's fully sealed, any water spilled on the floor will just puddle up and stay there until it's either mopped up or dries up by itself. It won't be able to penetrate the floor.

In older homes, the bathroom floor seal is often broken. It may be because the tiles have broken loose, moldings have rotted or come loose, or holes have been cut for pipes or other installations. Once this seal is bro-

ken, any water spilled on the floor will seep through the gap, and ruin the plasterwork in the room below.

This kind of leak is almost impossible to find when you're working on the bathroom. You can check all the plumbing, and it will be in perfect order. You can run water for an hour without any sign of a leak. And yet, in a day or two, you'll get a call from the homeowner about water damage appearing on the ceiling below the bathroom.

What makes this leak particularly maddening is that it will only leak when there's a lot of water spilled on the floor. It's most common when there are small children living in the house. Children love to play in the tub; diving like mermaids or having water fights that send gallons of water over the edge and onto the floor. However, splashing isn't limited to children. I've known older people who like to exercise in the bathtub, and I guarantee that an adult doing legs lifts can splash as much water as a junior mermaid any day! Another problem you'll run into with older couples is that they may purposely dump a bucket of water on the floor to wash it. I guess this is how they used to do it in the old days. You can't very well tell someone how to clean their own bathroom floor. They won't listen even if you do!

Another thing to consider is that the leak may be new. Your work, even in other rooms, may have jarred some of the tiles or moldings loose, breaking the seal along the bathroom floor. If the problem has existed for some time, there would be water damage to the downstairs ceiling. Check out each leak carefully. You can't automatically assume all water damage is from a plumbing leak, even if there is a plumbing problem. Believe me, there's no rule that says you can't have leaks from more than one cause.

You can check out the floor seal by simply dumping a bucket of water on it. If the floor is intact, the water will just sit there. If it disappears, it's probably seeping through a break in the floor. If the ceiling in the room below has been removed, you'll be able to see a wet spot developing on the joists. If the ceiling is still up, a wet spot will eventually develop on the plaster. You may have to be patient, however. It sometimes takes hours, or even overnight, before a wet spot will become visible on plaster. The water has to seep through several layers before you'll be able to see it. Check the entire area carefully; there may be more than one leak. Once you've identified the leaks, seal them thoroughly.

Kitchen Plumbing

Kitchens are a lot easier to work on than bathrooms because they're generally located on the first floor, and have a basement or crawl space below. You can usually get at the plumbing from underneath, and there's room available to run piping. In an upstairs bathroom, all the pipe runs have to fit into the ceiling, and either the ceiling must come down or the floor come up in order to work on the pipes.

There are a couple of plumbing problems that are unique to the kitchen. One of my least favorites is a drain pipe that's clogged with grease. People are supposed to know better than to pour grease down the kitchen sink. Grease hardens in the drain lines producing a clog that can be *very* hard to get out. And it doesn't just clog the trap. I've seen 4-foot runs of 2-inch pipe completely blocked by hardened grease. The only way to open the pipe back up is with a power auger, and even then it's a difficult job. Often I don't even try to clear the line. If I have other plumbing work to do, I just cut out the clogged section and replace the pipe!

The other common kitchen problem is loose fitting connections around the kitchen sink trap. This is the only trap where you'll find this happening as a rule. It's caused by vibrations from the garbage disposal. A disposal creates a lot of vibration when it runs, and in most kitchens, it runs several times a day. Eventually the vibrations cause the trap fittings to work loose, especially PVC fittings, which are only finger-tight in the first place. All you need to do to fix the problem is to tighten the fittings. If you're working with PVC pipe, you don't even need any tools — you can tighten them with your hands.

This problem may reoccur every couple of years. Be sure and advise the homeowners. If you show them what to watch for and how to fix it, usually they can take care of it themselves.

Heating and Electrical Modifications

After the plumbing system is repaired, it's time to tackle the heating and electrical systems. Again, if you're going to make any changes or adjustments to these systems, you need to do them before you make repairs to the walls.

Installing a New Heating System

Major remodeling or alterations to the house will inevitably affect the heating system and any changes to the heating system may require alterations to the house. Working on the heating system is always a big job. You'll probably need to install new runs of ductwork or pipes through the walls of the downstairs living areas. This means tearing out the plasterwork on several, or maybe all, of the walls. If the walls need repair anyway, you can kill two birds with one stone. But even if the walls are perfect, they may still need to be torn out to accommodate new ductwork. Needless to say, I prefer doing major heating alterations on houses that need wall work anyway. Having

to tear out perfectly good walls adds considerably to the cost of doing the work.

We talked a lot about the various types of heating systems in Chapter 4. We don't need to go into heating design in depth here, but there are a couple of things to consider about repairs that affect the main floor living area.

🐚 Heating Design

If you'll be doing any major modifications to the heating system, it will involve the first-floor rooms. First, you have to run the new pipes or ductwork up to the main floor. This actually isn't too difficult because most of the runs will be in the basement or crawl space. The only alterations may be registers for the ducts or holes for the pipes. If you only plan to bring heat to the main floor (in a one-story house, for example), you shouldn't have too many difficulties with the heat distribution.

The real problems occur when you want to extend heat to the second floor. In order to do this, you'll have to tear out large sections of plasterwork in the main floor living area. That's the only way to allow the runs of ductwork or pipes to reach the second floor in as short and direct a route as possible. Unlike electrical wiring, you can't just run it anywhere you want. The longer and more convoluted the runs of ductwork are, the harder it is for the heat to get to its destination. A room at the end of a long run of ducting will not heat well.

When working with heating systems you must always remember that warm air rises, and cold air sinks. You want to work with this principle when laying out heating runs. This is pretty basic, but you'd be surprised how many people forget it. Try always to locate the cold air return registers near the floor, so that the cold air, which naturally sinks, will fall towards them. The cold air will then naturally flow towards the furnace, aided by suction from the furnace fan.

Place the hot air registers near the floor as well, so the warm air will rise up and disperse throughout the room. It's best to locate them on an outside wall, preferably under a window, so that the warm air from the register can counteract any cold air that might come off of the window.

No doubt you've been in houses in which these suggestions weren't followed. It's very common, for example, for a single story house without a basement to have some of the ductwork running through the attic space. I've lived in houses like this. Believe me, I can tell you from experience that it isn't a very efficient way to heat a home. If you put the hot air registers near the ceiling, the warm air will tend to just collect in a layer next to the ceiling. This means that people, who are closer to the floor than the ceiling, will be cold. The higher the ceilings are, the worse the problem will be.

If the cold air return registers are located near the ceiling as well, the problem will be even worse. The cold air registers won't suck up cold air, they'll suck up warm air — because that's what's there. Warm air will come out of the hot air registers and accumulate near the ceiling, where it will get sucked into the cold air registers. The warm air will never make it to the lower parts of the room. There will always be an undisturbed layer of cold air down by the floor. A

room like this is uncomfortable. The temperature will never be "just right" anywhere.

Ideally, you'll place hot air registers on exterior walls underneath windows, with the cold air returns on the opposite interior walls. This will give you optimal heating and air circulation. It will also take advantage of the basic principals of physics to help the furnace move air properly: Warm air will rise up through the ducts and diffuse through the rooms, and cold air will fall back towards the furnace to be reheated.

Each room should have both a hot air register and a cold air return. The only exceptions to this are the kitchen and bathroom. These rooms should not have cold air returns because they would draw in odors and too much humidity. By using these principles, it's possible to heat a house without using fan-forced air at all. This is how a well-designed gravity furnace system works.

Missing Cold Air Returns

I can't tell you how many times I've seen rooms with hot air registers, but no cold air returns. Why is that a problem? The warm air can't get into the room unless the cold air has a way to get out. Otherwise, pressure will build up in the room to the point where the fan can no longer overcome it, blocking entry of the warm air.

This may not be a serious problem in a room that is normally open, such as a dining room that's not separated from the living area by doors. As warm air enters the room, the cold air will just flow out to the adjoining room or rooms, and go down the first available cold air return. If there are plenty of cold air returns in nearby rooms, you may not notice a problem.

This can be a major problem in a bedroom, however. A bedroom without a cold air return will only warm up if the door is open so cold air can flow out into the hallway. When the door is closed, the cold air becomes trapped. With no way for the cold air to get out, the hot air can't get in, and the temperature will plunge. I've slept in bedrooms like this. They're uncomfortably cold all winter long.

If homeowners never close their bedroom door, they may never be aware that they have this problem. A couple with no children and who rarely have overnight company, for example, may not have much occasion to close their bedroom door. Bedroom doors are only for privacy. However, if they ever decide to close their bedroom door at night, they'll notice the problem as soon as the weather gets cold!

You want to avoid creating this type of problem. If you're installing new ductwork, put in enough to create optimal heating and cooling — and don't leave out the cold air returns!

❧ Locating New Ductwork

Since hot air rises, a furnace directly under the main part of the house will provide the most effective heating. Locate it as near the center of the house as possible. That way, the air will be able to rise up almost vertically into most of the rooms in the house. Try to always keep the air travel as vertical as possible. The longer the horizontal distance the air has to travel, the less heat will get to its destination.

Keep this in mind if you're installing ductwork runs. For effective heat circulation, you need runs in almost all of the main-floor walls. If you plan to drywall all the first floor walls anyway, it doesn't matter. It'll be easy to install the ductwork in the proper locations. However, if the old walls are in perfect condition, you have a problem. Either you'll have to install the ductwork in a substandard location and get poor heating, or tear out perfectly good walls. Neither option is very attractive.

Minimizing Wall Damage

In some cases, you may be able to minimize the damage without compromising the heating. This requires thoughtful planning. Look over the layout of the house carefully. Is there any one wall that's centrally located, right under all, or most all, the upstairs bedrooms? If so, it might be possible to group all

the cold air returns here. That way, you'd only have to tear out one wall, instead of several.

I managed to group ducts like this in a house I recently renovated. The original owners had never bothered to install heat in the upstairs bedrooms. They didn't use the upstairs, so they weren't worried about it. There were two bedrooms and a bathroom upstairs that needed heat. That meant I needed three heat ducts, plus cold air returns for both bedrooms. I was able to manage this with just three runs of ductwork. One duct brought heat up for the larger bedroom; the second brought heat up for both the smaller bedroom and the bathroom; and finally, one large cold-air return served both the bedrooms.

I couldn't run new ducting through a central wall because the ideal wall was sitting on the main beam, and I didn't want to cut through the beam. Instead, I ran the ducting through the floor in out-of-the-way locations, using my "nooks and crannies" approach. I didn't have to worry about preserving any nice plaster walls in this house, because there weren't any. A roof leak had caused extensive damage to the plaster, and I had to install new drywall throughout the house anyway.

Figure 14-1 shows the first duct I ran from the basement through the main floor and up through the ceiling to the upstairs bedroom. It came out in a new closet I built for the smaller bedroom (shown in Figure 14-2) and then turned the corner to carry heat into the larger room next to it. I boxed in the duct inside the closet, and once it was painted, it was hidden from view. Figure 14-3 shows the finished bedroom with its new closet — and no sign of the ductwork. Downstairs, I also boxed in the duct with drywall. You can see the finished work in Figure 14-4. Because this duct is located behind the living room door, no one ever notices it. It just blends into the corner.

Another duct was routed through a corner in the kitchen, shown in Figure 14-5, and ended up in a small storage area under a corner of the roof. This area was accessed through a door in the smaller bedroom (Figure 14-6). The storage area was perfect for

Figure 14-1
*New duct running from basement
below to bedroom above*

Figure 14-2
*Ducting will be concealed
inside new closet*

running the upstairs ductwork. I ran hot air ducts to the adjoining bedroom and the bathroom, as well as the cold air returns for both bedrooms through this open space. Because the area was unheated, I insulated the ducts carefully. When the work was done, I removed the door to the storage area and drywalled over the opening. Since the area was all taken up with ductwork, there was no longer any need to have access to it.

Figure 14-3
Finished bedroom with new closet

Figure 14-4
Boxed-in duct isn't noticed in corner

Downstairs, in the kitchen, I boxed in the ductwork and concealed the box with new cabinets.

Running duct up an outside wall where it will show and boxing it in isn't really a good idea. Unless it's done very carefully, it looks terrible. However, if the alternative is no heat at all, boxing it like that may be the best you can do. Boxes should always be located in out-of-the-way places, like behind a door. Now and then you can find a spot to tuck one of these in without it showing at all. Older homes often have these odd little nooks, crannies, or protrusions where you can add a duct without making it look any stranger than it already does.

Figure 14-5
New duct will run through corner of kitchen and be hidden by new cabinets

Utilizing Available Spaces

Are there any spaces where you could run a duct downstairs without it showing? Closets are often ideal for this, especially if they're located on or next to an exterior wall. If you can run a hot air duct up through a closet, you may be able to have it come out in an almost ideal location upstairs. Once you drywall over the duct in the closet, like I did in my renovation, it won't even show. The only loss will be a portion of the closet. Figure 14-7 shows the ductwork for a cold air return that I ran under a set of stairs. Little spaces like these are also ideal locations for hiding ductwork. It pays to search out areas where you can install ductwork without making a mess.

Figure 14-6
Upstairs duct runs are hidden in attic space behind this wall

Old homes often have other odd little spaces that you might be able to use for ductwork. Laundry chutes are a good example. If the homeowners won't miss it, a laundry chute is just the right size for a duct. They go from the basement to the second floor, which is exactly what you need.

Finally, there may boxed-in areas, dead spaces, or even old ductwork left over from some other modification that isn't being used any more. I often find these in older homes. They are sometimes quite large, offering plenty of space for a duct, or even two. Of course, they may not be in a usable spot, but it's worth checking for them anyway. If you use all of these available spaces, you may be

Figure 14-7
Dead space under stairs is a good place to conceal ducting

able to minimize the damage to the main floor walls. You might only have to tear out one or two, instead of all of them.

Planning ductwork runs carefully is worth the effort, even if you're not doing the installation yourself. If a heating contractor plans and installs a new furnace and the ductwork, he's going to plan the layout for optimal heating. He won't care about the damage to the walls or plasterwork, that's not his job. You'll be the one doing the wall repair!

If you can minimize the amount of wall work that needs to be done, you can save your customers a lot of money. This money can then go into something special that they'll enjoy more. After all, if you have to tear out perfectly good walls and then replace them, your customers have spent a lot of money on something that doesn't even show. They had walls before, and they have walls now. They'll realize that the work had to be done, but they won't be really happy about it. On the other hand, if you can save the walls and use the money for something else, you can give the customers a lot more value for their money, without any cost to you. You'll make your customers a lot happier, and happy customers are always good for business.

Solving Heating System Problems

While we're on the subject of heating systems, let's discuss how you can solve some of the more common heating problems that you'll run into. Drafty uncomfortable rooms are, unfortunately, fairly common in older homes. That's one of the reasons why some people dislike older homes. They think cold, unpleasant rooms are an inevitable part of owning an older home. But they're not. There's always something you can do about them.

First of all, you need to consider the type of heating system. Different heating systems require different solutions. I devoted a lot of space to heating systems and their problems

in *Profits in Buying & Renovating Homes*. I'm not going to repeat it all here. We'll just go over the problems that come up most often, and what you can do about them.

Forced-Air Problems

Forced-air heating systems, whether fired by natural gas, oil, or propane, are identical in terms of air circulation. They all rely on a powerful fan to blow warm air through the house. Unfortunately, there is a limit to this fan's ability. If anything interferes with the airflow, a room doesn't get heated.

Bad Thermostat Location

One problem I run into frequently is an incorrectly-placed thermostat. The thermostat should be centrally located so the temperature around it is typical of the temperature in most of the house. If it's tucked into some out-of the way corner, warm air may not reach it. The furnace will run longer than it's needed and the house will become uncomfortably warm. On the other hand, if it's located too close to a hot air register, or hot air blows directly on it, it will cause the furnace to shut off before the rest of the house has warmed up. Much of the house will always be cold.

Moving thermostats is fairly easy. Find a good location for it in a central area, like the living room. It should be on an interior wall, away from doors, windows, and hot or cold air registers. Thermostats are usually connected to the furnace by three small wires. Disconnect these wires (make a note of which one went where), screw the thermostat to the wall in its new location, and reconnect the three wires. It's as simple as that.

Missing Ducts

If a room is missing a hot air register or a cold air return, that may be the cause of the heating problem. If you're planning to tear out walls or install ducts, then you need to include this room. But what if you weren't? Is there a cheaper, easier way to deal with the problem?

If the room is missing a cold air return, you might be able to get by with a passive duct. This is essentially a hole in a wall with a register plate over it. The hole needs to lead to a hallway or some other space that has a cold air return. Line the hole with sheet metal to prevent cold air from infiltrating the space between the walls. If the only reason the room remains cold is because the warm air can't displace the cold air, this will do the trick. When you give the cold air a way out, even if it's just through a hole, the room will heat better.

What if a room has no hot air duct-work? This is actually quite common in older houses, especially those that have forced-air systems that were converted from gravity systems. The gravity systems used only a few very large, centrally-located ducts. The air from these had to spread out and fill the house. There wasn't usually a duct in every room.

In many cases, the existing ducts were retained when the system was converted to forced air. This isn't an ideal installation. Gravity ducts just don't work properly with a forced-air furnace. However, the alternative would probably have required ripping up perfectly good walls to install new ducts. To avoid this, many people just used the existing ducts.

Check the adjoining rooms for ducts. Do any of them have heating ducts on walls that are common with the problem room? If so, you can cut through the wall and tap into that duct. There's probably enough warm air there to heat both rooms. This is especially true if it's an old gravity-furnace duct. These ducts are much larger than they need to be for a forced-air furnace. There should be more than enough air there to heat two rooms.

But what if you do tap into a common duct, and you don't get enough air to heat both rooms? You may be able to get some more by raising the pressure elsewhere in the system. You can do this by partially blocking the registers in the other rooms, especially the warmest ones. In some cases, just closing the dampers part way will do it. Or, you can permanently block off part of the register by attaching a little piece of sheet metal on the inside, where it doesn't show. If all the warm air can't get out of these partially-blocked registers, it'll go where there's less resistance. Since the cold rooms have wide-open registers, the warm air will flow out there. This is one way to distribute the warmth more evenly through the house. Try this technique with any room that isn't heating adequately. It doesn't always work, but it's easy, and it costs practically nothing.

Inadequate Air Pressure

If there's a long, convoluted run of duct-work leading to a room, the room probably won't heat well. That's because air under pressure seeks the path of least resistance. A long, complicated run of ductwork has a lot more resistance than a short, simple one. Most of the warm air in the system will follow the short, straight route out the ducts near the furnace. Some air will make it all the way to the end room, but not enough to keep it from being chilly. The rooms near the furnace will be too warm, and room at the end of the convoluted duct will be too cold. Partially blocking the registers in the warmer rooms might help, but in some cases the resistance in the ductwork leading to the cold room is just too great.

You can solve this problem with a device known as a booster fan. I use booster fans quite often. They're good little problem-solvers. You can install a booster fan inside the ductwork to help move the warm air through to the desired destination. They come in a variety of sizes to fit most duct-work. You can even get them already built into a piece of ductwork, so that it will fit your ductwork exactly. All you have to do is cut a piece out of the existing ductwork, and replace it with the new piece containing the fan. It's quite easy.

Figure 14-8 shows a small length of duct containing a booster fan next to the longer run of duct that I'm going to fit it into. Figure 14-9 shows a close-up of the ducting with the booster fan installed. I placed the duct section with the fan close to the room that the duct was going to serve. With the help of this short run of duct, I was able to heat a large 12- by 20-foot upstairs room that

Figure 14-8

Smaller section of duct contains booster fan

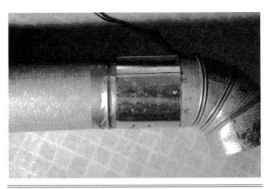

Figure 14-9

Booster fan installed in duct section

had previously been served by its own gas heater (which was very noisy and unsightly) at a considerably higher cost. It's always best to place the fan in the ductwork as close to the chilly room as possible. You get the best heating result that way.

If you can't put the fan close to the room you want to heat without tearing up walls, put it anywhere you can, as long as it's in the duct leading to that room. Even installing a fan near the furnace will greatly increase the airflow to the room. Once the booster fan assembly is installed, you can wire it in parallel with the furnace fan. Then, when the relay turns the furnace fan on, the booster fan will go on as well. The booster fan will provide a tremendous increase in air flow to the room, and will almost always solve this type of heating problem.

I've had very good results using the Evenair Air Boosters that are sold at Builder's Square. They can add up to 250 CFM per duct branch, yet they only draw 40 watts of power. And they're inexpensive to install. The 6-inch model shown in Figure 14-8 only cost $21.

Just a note: In some cases, this solution may work too well, causing the room to become overly warm. This isn't too serious a problem. You can solve it a couple of ways. The easiest is to just partially close the hot air register damper. This blocks out part of the airflow, so that the room gets less heat. A more elegant solution is to wire a motor speed control into the booster fan circuit.

Changing the speed setting will make the room warmer or colder, allowing you to adjust it to whatever setting works best.

Other Advantages Offered by Booster Fans — There are some other advantages to using booster fans. You can also use them to help overcome heating problems created by missing cold air returns. At first, this may not seem logical. How can more air get in when the cold air can't get out? The problem here is pressure. When the warm air tries to enter an unvented room, the pressure in the room rises until it equals the pressure in the duct. The air in the duct can't overcome this resistance, so it flows out someplace else, leaving the room cold.

When you add a booster fan to the duct, you tremendously increase the pressure in that duct. The warm air pressure becomes great enough to force its way into the room, making the cold air seep through the crack under the door, or any other tiny openings that may exist. You can help this process by creating a means for the air to get out, like a passive duct. If nothing else, you can trim a little bit off the bottom of the door so there's a larger slot for the air to flow through. This may sound too easy, but it works.

Booster fans also work well in homes with long runs of horizontal ducting. Some single-story houses have ductwork runs that are almost entirely horizontal. This is unavoidable with a forced-air furnace system in a house without a basement, but it doesn't always provide good, uniform heating. Often the rooms nearest the furnace are warm but the rooms farthest from the furnace remain cold. The extra pressure provided by a booster fan can force the air through the long, horizontal duct runs, overcoming the fact that warm air prefers to go up rather than sideways.

A booster fan will also help in situations where the hot air registers have been located incorrectly, such as at the top of a wall instead of the bottom. With the added air pressure, air deflectors attached to these registers cause the warm air to shoot down, instead of up where it forms a warm air layer near the ceiling. As the deflected warm air rises back up, it mixes with the existing air, providing good, even heating throughout the room.

Booster Fans with Air Conditioning — You can also use booster fans to solve problems caused by duct placement in forced air heating and air conditioning systems. Duct locations that are good for heating tend to be poor for air conditioning, and vice versa.

Remember, hot air rises and cold air falls. Ceiling-mounted hot air registers that heat poorly will cool very well, because the cold air that flows out will fall towards the floor. As the air falls, it will mix with the rest of the room air, and provide nice, even cooling. Unfortunately, hot air registers near the floor, which are best for heating, don't work well for cooling. The cold air that comes from those registers doesn't rise, it just sits in a layer on the floor. The only thing that will be cooled are people's feet!

Newer furnaces, which were designed with air conditioning in mind, have multi-speed fans to solve this problem. The fan runs faster with the air conditioning on to compensate for the fact that cold air doesn't rise. The extra fan pressure forces the cold air throughout the room, rather than allowing it to settle on the floor. Older furnaces, not designed to work with an air conditioning system, don't have this feature. So, when someone adds central air to an older furnace, they are likely to have this layering problem.

Luckily, booster fans can solve the problem. If you install air deflectors pointing up, the booster fans will force the cold air upwards out of the registers at high speed. As the cold air settles back down, it will mix with the rest of the room air, and provide even cooling.

If the booster fans only need to be used during one season, you can wire a switch into the circuit so they can be turned on and off. Then the homeowner can switch them on during the heating season and off during the cooling season, or vice versa.

Uninsulated Ducts

I can't tell you how many times I've found uninsulated ductwork running though an unheated space. This is clearly not very smart. Metal conducts heat extremely well, so a lot of the heat in the warm air that's passing through the duct will be lost to the cold air outside the ductwork. The furnace will have to run a lot longer to transmit enough heat through these ducts, running up the heat bill. If the heat loss is severe enough, the room at the end of the duct run can be unheatable.

The solution is simple: Insulate any ductwork that runs through unheated space. I also insulate ductwork that runs through partially-heated spaces, like the basement. This may make the basement a little colder, since it was being warmed in part by the escaping heat. However, I've found that most basements stay warm enough just from waste heat off the furnace itself. If the homeowners want to use the basement for living space, then insulating the ductwork there would be counterproductive. Generally, the basements in older homes don't make very good living space and are used mostly for storage. In that case, it won't hurt if it's a bit chilly, and insulating the ductwork will lower the homeowner's heating bill.

Adding Auxiliary Heating

What do you do if a room has no heat duct, and no way to bring one in, short of ripping up half the house? If the house is constructed with beautiful, ornate plasterwork that's in good condition you don't want to tear it up to install a duct for one cold room. Refinishing the walls with plasterwork of the same quality would be tremendously expensive. On the other hand, the room needs to be heated to be usable in the winter. Probably your best bet in this situation is to add an auxiliary heating unit.

Some people use gas-fired space heaters in rooms like this. They're economical to operate, and it's possible to plumb in the gas line without causing damage to other rooms. However, I don't like these heaters for a number of reasons. They don't heat evenly, they're noisy, they're not really easy to install, and they're ugly. They need to be mounted in the wall, with their own vents, and plenty of clearance on all sides. This may require tearing up a wall, which is exactly what you wanted to avoid. They also interfere with furniture placement, since they get very hot. My experience has been that anybody who's lived with these heaters for any length of time has grown to hate them. They may be okay for a cabin or a trailer, but they don't really fit in a nice home.

I prefer easy-to-install electric baseboard heaters. They're wired in like any other electric appliance. You'll need to fish a 220-volt line through the walls for the heater, and put it on its own 220-volt, 30-amp circuit, but that's not too difficult. The nice thing about electric lines is that, unlike ductwork, you can run them anywhere that's convenient. If you can't get the line up from the basement, you can run it around through the attic.

Another advantage of electric baseboard heaters is that they're unobtrusive. They fit along the baseboard, out of sight, and don't interfere with furniture placement. They heat by convection — that is, they heat the air around them, which then rises, drawing in more air to be heated. This is a gentle, quiet process, although it's a little slower than other types of heaters. You can't turn them on and expect the room to be warmed up instantly. They take about an hour to warm an average room. Because of this, many people leave them on all the time during the winter. They come with matching thermostats, which install right into the baseboard unit. Once the correct setting is established, they can be left on to keep the room an even temperature all the time.

Electric baseboard heaters are also inexpensive to purchase. A 4-foot unit, which can cost under $20, is adequate to supply all the heat for a small room or supplemental heat for a larger room. The size you need will depend on the cubic footage (not square footage) of the room. A tall room has more cubic feet and will take more heat than a room with a low ceiling, even if the floor space is the same.

The biggest drawback to electric heat is the operating expense. Using electric baseboard heat for an average-sized bedroom will cost about $100 a year. On the other hand, if you tear out several walls, run ductwork to the room, and replace the walls, it will cost the homeowner around $2,000. That's 20 years worth of electric heating. Most Americans don't stay in the same house for 20 years, so the homeowner will really come out ahead by using the electric heaters. Of course, anything else you can do to make the room warmer, such as adding insulation or sealing air leaks, will also help lower the electric bill.

I'm only recommending the use of electric heat as supplemental heat, not as the primary heat source. That is, I'm assuming that the room in question is already partially heated by the furnace, even if it has no ductwork. It should pick up a substantial amount of heat from the rest of the house unless it's totally isolated, like a garage conversion. If the room is chilly, I'm assuming it's something like 55 degrees when it's 30 degrees outside. The job of the electric heater is to add 12 or 13 degrees, to bring the room up to a comfortable 67 or 68.

On the other hand, an isolated room with no other heat reaching it might be 30 degrees, the same as the outside. The heater would need to add 37 or 38 degrees to it to bring it up to a comfortable living temperature. That's about three times the amount of heat that you would need for a room that started out at 55 degrees, and predictably, it'll triple the cost of the electricity. That's why electric heating is practical only as supplemental heat. It's too expensive to use as a primary source of heating (except in mild climates, where you don't need as much heat).

Electric heat is especially useful in rooms that get almost enough heat, but stay just a bit chilly when the temperature drops really low. These rooms probably only need additional heat for a few of the coldest days in winter. It won't run the electric bill up that much if electric heat is used occasionally, but not every day. In a situation like this, the savings over adding ductwork is tremendous.

You can buy 8-foot baseboard heaters, with thermostats, for about $50. Most rooms will need only one. You'll probably wind up paying more for the 30-amp cable you'll need to wire them than you will for the heaters themselves. The cable usually costs me an additional $50. The time-consuming part of the job is fishing the wire through the walls. This can either be very easy or very difficult, depending on the layout of the house. The average wiring installation takes one person about four hours.

Steam Heating Problems

Steam systems are actually very nice heating systems. They heat well, and they're very reliable. Many people have poor attitudes toward steam systems because they've heard that steam heat has a lot of problems. In my experience, most of the problems are caused by lack of maintenance.

Like any system, steam heat requires a little adjustment now and then. Often these systems are neglected for decades, usually because people don't know what to look for when there are problems. When examining a steam system, you need to make sure that the radiators are level, the connections are all tight, and the little chrome cold-air release valve is properly seated, with the pointed end up. You'd be surprised how many problems can be remedied by just these three simple steps.

It's possible to extend steam heat to an additional room, but steam systems use very large pipes. That means you may have to tear up some walls to install additional pipe lines. You'll have to weigh the cost of the installation against the cost of adding auxiliary heat to the room before you encourage a homeowner to go ahead with this kind of expense.

Hot-Water Systems

From a remodeler's point of view, hot-water heat is practically ideal. It has the big advantage of using small-gauge pipe to carry the hot water. Modern systems use ½-inch copper piping; older systems often used ¾-inch galvanized steel pipe. Since the pipe is small, you can sometimes run it through the insides of walls without doing any damage to them. This is tremendously helpful when you need to bring additional heat to new or remodeled rooms. You don't have to make a tradeoff between installing proper heating and having to do a lot of expensive wall work. New hot-water systems use unobtrusive baseboard heaters. If you add heat to a room, you should locate the heaters on an exterior wall. Since they're flat and low, they won't interfere with furniture placement in the room.

If you're working on a house with an existing hot-water system, you may find a baseboard heater or an old radiator that isn't functioning properly. Here's a helpful procedure to know about. Sometimes air becomes trapped in the system and prevents hot water from entering the baseboard or radiator. They have bleeder valves just for this purpose. Open the bleeder valve and release any air. Keep the valve open until water starts coming out. The system is also equipped with an auto-fill valve. It will automatically add more water to fill up the space that was occupied by the air. Following this simple procedure should solve the problem.

I've come across a lot of old hot-water systems in my work. Hot-water heat has been around for a long time. Figure 14-10 shows a hot-water radiator from about 1925. (Steam radiators look almost exactly the same except they have little chrome cold-air release valves and hot-water radiators don't.) The original

Figure 14-10
Hot water radiator circa 1925

system in this house still worked perfectly, even though it was about 70 years old. The only change that had been made to the system in all those years was to convert it from coal to gas, probably some time during the 1950s.

Unfortunately, hot-water heat is an expensive system to install new. If the house already has a hot-water system and you can extend it into remodeled areas, great. But if it has another system that's adequate for the existing house but doesn't suit your remodeling needs, it probably wouldn't be cost effective to tear out the old system and install hot water.

Other Heating Problems

An insufficient heating system isn't the only cause of cold rooms in older homes. Sometimes there's more cold air leaking in from the outside than the heater can counteract. You have to look at leaky windows, poor weatherstripping around doors, and poor insulation as contributing causes of heat problems.

Leaky Windows

Some remodelers use high-tech devices to check for leaky windows. My feeling is that if you need to use a high-tech device, it's not leaking enough to bother with. The only device I use is a cigarette, or a smoldering piece of paper. These are much cheaper than a smoke gun, and they serve the same function. You can watch the smoke to see where the air is going.

If the window's leaking badly, you won't need any devices to detect it. You'll be able to feel cold air on your face as you approach the window, even if it's entirely closed. Windows like these usually have visible gaps all around the sashes. The window can't be closed tightly, because the sashes no longer fit properly.

You'll have to either repair or replace any leaky windows. We discussed both these options in Chapter 7. Be sure to check over the exterior storm windows before you make a final decision. If they're missing or damaged, replacing them might solve the problem at the lowest cost to the homeowner.

Interior Storm Windows

If the window's not too far gone, another inexpensive choice would be to add an interior storm window. This provides another layer of window material, either plastic or glass, to the interior surface of the window. It's much like an exterior storm, except it's on the inside.

In its simplest form, an interior storm can just be a layer of plastic. This *isn't* the most attractive option, but it *is* the cheapest. There are a number of heat-shrink plastic window kits especially made for this purpose. The plastic is attached to the window frame with adhesive, and then heat-shrunk with a hair dryer. Once they're shrunk into place, they're fairly unobtrusive. The frames are permanent, but the plastic has to be replaced every season. This is an inexpensive temporary fix that you can offer if the homeowners aren't ready to replace the windows.

It's possible to get custom-made, permanent interior storms, but it's rarely worthwhile. If you add this expense to the cost of exterior storms and repairs to the window, it will cost more than simply replacing the window. These are only worth using on windows that are so special that you wouldn't want to replace them. If that's the case, one source for interior storm windows is:

Magnetite Corporation
8356 Tom Drive
Baton Rouge, LA 70815

You can also call them at 1-800-MAG-TITE for a free brochure.

Weatherstripping

In many cases, weatherstripping can solve the problem of leaks around doors and windows. The original weatherstripping may have gone bad, or there may not have been any.

There are a number of weatherstripping products available that you can install. For windows, the old standby is spring brass. It's especially helpful for sealing windows that don't seat properly in their frames anymore. Spring brass will create a tighter fit.

The bottom edge of the window can also be sealed effectively by using one of the newer rubber seals. They are available at most hardware stores. You attach them to the bottom edge of the sash using staples or small nails. When the window is closed, the rubber is compressed, creating a good seal. Be careful not to use too much of this, however, or it will be impossible to completely close and latch the window.

While weatherstripping can help stop air leakage, you'll still need good storm windows and doors for decent thermal performance in cold climates. They help insulate the house from the cold. Without storm windows, homes can get very cold in mid-winter. I've seen ice form on the inside of the windows when the temperature drops — and when that happens, you know you have a heat problem!

Inadequate Insulation

When you go into a cold room, put your hand on the walls and the ceiling. If they feel cold, more than likely it's because of poor insulation. Unfortunately, adding insulation to finished walls can be quite difficult. Unless you're planning to take the walls down, you'll have to settle for trying to blow insulation into the walls from the attic or basement. This isn't always practical, but add insulation in any areas where you can do it easily. Additional insulation is always worthwhile.

If you're planning to drywall some of the walls, be sure to add insulation while the interior walls are down. It's also a good idea to add a layer of plastic as an air-infiltration barrier. In older homes, you should add insulation and air-infiltration barriers anyplace you can. This isn't always a good idea in a new house. A house that's too tightly sealed can become stuffy and humid, but that's never a problem with older homes. They always have far more air going through them than you want. Over the years, they have accumulated literally thousands of little cracks and holes where air leaks in. You'll never be able to seal up all these little openings, but if you seal up some, it will help keep the house warm in the winter.

Insulating the Attic

If a cold room has attic space above it, adding attic insulation may solve the problem. There's never enough insulation in an old house, so adding it can only help. Insulation doesn't cost much and it will save the homeowner money in heating and cooling bills, as well as making the house more comfortable.

Putting insulation in the attic space is a simple job, but it can be rather unpleasant. Attic spaces are often cramped and hard to work in. They can also be very hot in the summertime. Insulating an attic is one job you don't want to do on a hot, sunny day. The attic space can easily get up to 140 degrees. If you must do this job during the summer, try to work very early in the morning, before it gets hot, or on a cloudy day.

I've found that most old houses have an inch or two of rock wool in the attic, or nothing at all. The old rock wool can be left in place, but it probably won't do much good there. If you install new fiberglass insulation on top of it, the vapor barrier on the new insulation (either Kraft paper or foil) will probably block moisture at this point, causing the rock wool to become damp and useless. What I usually do is pull up the rock wool and use it to fill in any little gaps that the fiberglass won't settle into. This will provide more complete coverage without having to spend any extra money.

If the attic doesn't have any old rock wool that you can use, buy some loose insulation for filling in gaps. New rock wool will be fine for this. You want insulation that's pourable, so you can pour it into any little gaps and spaces. Make sure you don't leave any heat leaks.

Don't handle any of these materials without some kind of dust protection. Fiberglass throws millions of tiny particles into the air. Breathing these can be extremely irritating to your nose, throat and lungs. Attic spaces are also very dusty. If you disturb the old rock wool, for example, 50 years' worth of dust will fly into the air in a dense, choking cloud.

Most fiberglass installers recommend wearing a dust mask, but I've found these aren't really adequate. Dust masks don't seal well enough around your face, allowing dust and fiberglass particles to get in. I prefer to use a paint respirator. They have a soft rubber mask, which seals up well around your nose and mouth, and two big, replaceable filters. They're a bit heavy and awkward (which is why some people prefer paper dust masks), but that doesn't bother me. I've found that wearing a paint respirator actually makes the job a lot less unpleasant. The respirator filters out just about everything, so you don't smell any dust or particles. Having clean air to breathe helps a lot.

I usually install a full 12 inches of insulation in an attic. That's the recommended maximum, but it only costs a little more than installing 6 inches. If you're going to all the trouble of climbing up into the attic and dealing with insulation at all, you might as well get the maximum benefit for it.

Of course, if you live in a warm area of the country, where winter heating costs are insignificant, adding 12 inches won't really be worthwhile. I would still install 6 inches to keep the summer cooling bills down. A house with no insulation in the attic space can get very hot in the summer. The sun beats down on the roof, heating the attic space, and some of this heat will be conducted into the house through the ceiling. Insulating the ceiling blocks the heat, and keeps the house cooler.

While you're in the attic, check to make sure that there are enough vents, and that they're all fully functional. The vents are very important. They help keep the house cool in the summertime and vent out moisture in the winter. Birds sometimes build nests in them, or they can become clogged by leaves and debris.

If the house needs more venting, the gables are a good place to install them. All you need to do is cut a hole, and nail in a vent. If the hole is in a visible location, be sure to use an attractive vent. They're available in a number of decorative designs to match various trim styles.

You may not even have to cut a hole in order to mount the vent. Many older homes have ornamental windows near the peak of the gable in the attic. These windows serve no function. Some of them, like the one shown in Figure 14-11, aren't even attractive. You should remove these windows and replace them with decorative vents. The vents will be more useful and more attractive than the old windows.

Electrical Modifications

Now's a good time for you to do electrical modifications. Unlike ductwork, it's possible to run wiring within existing walls. However, it's a lot easier to do it when the

Figure 14-11
Small attic window should be replaced with vent

walls are down. If you're going to be working on the walls, any electrical work you do will be fairly easy.

❧ Service Upgrades and Rewiring

Most older homes that I work on have an electrical system that's in good working order, but way too small. They have too little power, too few circuits and far too few outlets. As we discussed in Chapter 4, a home that's over 50 years old was probably wired with something like four 15-amp circuits, or 40 amps total power. Unless it's been upgraded recently, now is the time to do it. Even if the upgrade was done 20 years ago, the home may still need additional electrical service.

Most of the time the existing wiring can be left in place. There's probably nothing wrong with it, there's just not enough of it. It doesn't need to be torn out, just more added. The existing circuits can usually be left the way they are, and when the service upgrade is done, they can be transferred over to the new circuit-breaker box. Then, additional circuits and outlets can be added to bring the house up to standard.

Cities vary tremendously as far as the type of electrical work they'll allow you to do if you're not an electrician. If you own the house, they may let you do a service upgrade, but most of the time they won't. Generally, cities will allow you do minor work, like

adding outlets or switches, but will require that you hire a licensed electrical contractor to do major work, such as service upgrades. Even if you have an electrician doing the service upgrade, it's a good idea to know what's involved.

The exterior portion of a service upgrade consists of replacing the meter, service lines, equipment and conduit that carry electrical service from the meter to connect to the power lines at the service drop. The service drop is the overhead conductor through which the electrical service is supplied by the power company. These lines belong to the power company, and any work required on the service drop or power lines has to be done by the utility company.

If the home has a basement, the main part of the service upgrade will be done there. All the old circuits leading to the original fuse box need to be disconnected and the old fuse box removed and replaced by a new circuit-breaker box. The old circuits can then be connected to the new box, each attached to the correct-size circuit breaker. The new circuit-breaker box will provide 100-, 150- or 200-amp service to the house and allow new circuits to be added. You can have the wiring for the new circuits ready before you have the service upgrade done. Just bring the wires through to where the box is going to be so the electrician can hook them up when he's installing the new box. That way, you can have everything done at one time.

Because the electrician's part of the work is done in the basement and outside, it can be done most anytime, even after the new walls or wall repairs have been done. Any in-wall wiring, however, should be done before the walls are repaired. Fishing electrical cable through existing walls can be very difficult. Rewiring while the walls are down saves a lot of time and trouble.

The existing outlets in old houses are usually wired with old two-wire wiring. If you're not tearing into the walls, and you're working on a tight budget, you can probably just leave most of this wiring as it is. A system that was properly installed, but is old, is usually still safe and usable. However, two-wire electrical wire can only supply a 15-amp ungrounded line. If you're going to be tearing into the walls, you should go ahead and replace old two-wire wiring with a 20-amp grounded line. Also, once you disturb the old two-wire, you can no longer count on it being entirely reliable. The insulation often becomes brittle and may crumble when you touch it, leaving dangerous bare wires. If there's two-wire remaining in any area that you're working in, if you've disturbed it, replace it.

❧ Adding Additional Outlets and Switches

The point of adding new circuits is to be able to add new outlets and switches. Few older homes have adequate outlets to supply today's needs. Many rooms have only one electrical outlet, and all the outlets may be on the same circuit. Often the house has only 15 amps to supply the total electrical needs of four or five rooms. This will do for a few lamps, but that's it. You can't maintain a modern lifestyle on this little power. I try to make sure each bedroom has at least two outlets, and four each for the living and dining rooms. You don't have to bring the house up to new construction code requirements, but the inspector will want to make sure the house has enough outlets for modern living. Talk to your inspector about requirements in your area. Any arrangement of outlets that makes sense will usually be okay. You don't need to put each outlet on its own circuit. You can attach one to another, and put them on the same circuit. Generally, the most you have is six outlets on one 20-amp circuit.

The kitchen needs a lot more power than it did in the old days. Be sure to add a lot of countertop plugs. Certain items, especially in the kitchen, do need to be on their own circuit. I always put the dishwasher, garbage disposal and furnace on separate circuits. It's also convenient to install separate circuits for high-watt appliances, like the refrigerator and microwave ovens. Microwaves draw a lot of power. They tend to trip circuit breakers a lot when they're on the same circuit as other appliances. I avoid this irritation by putting them on their own circuit, even though it isn't required.

GFCI Outlets

Another thing you may need to add is a ground-fault circuit interrupter outlet. These are required for all high-risk locations, which include areas next to the kitchen and bathroom sinks, the garage and any outdoor receptacles. They are easy to put in. You just remove the old outlet (if there is one) and replace it with a GFCI outlet. You may not have to buy GFCI outlets for every outlet that you need protected. It's possible to attach up to two more regular outlets to a single GFCI outlet. The circuitry in the GFCI outlet will protect all of them. The only problem you may run into is ungrounded wiring. GFCI outlets *must* have a good ground in order to work. If the old wiring is ungrounded two-wire, you may have to put in new grounded cable to the GFCI outlets.

Lights

Each room also needs to have a switch-operated overhead light, or a switch-operated outlet. This allows someone to enter a dark room and be able to immediately switch on a light. This is a code requirement that most cities strictly enforce.

I don't usually have to add many lights to old houses. While they tend to be short of outlets, they usually have enough lights. In some houses I've worked on, there were rooms that were only wired for lights and had no outlets at all! You'll often have to replace old light fixtures. They may be worn or broken, or simply unattractive. It's fairly easy to replace an existing fixture. Usually the wiring running to the fixture is okay even if the fixture isn't. That's important, because it's a lot easier to replace a fixture than to replace the wiring to it.

Make sure the homeowners have all the electrical switches and outlets they need for every room. It's inconvenient not to have enough outlets available to run electrical fixtures and appliances. People like to have radios and televisions, even computers, in their bedrooms. Discuss this with the home-owners, and make sure you add more than enough outlets to satisfy their requirements. There are more electric devices coming out every day. Even if the house seems to have enough outlets now, in a few years the home-owners will probably want more.

Adding Circuits and Cable for Specialty Items

Occasionally I deal with homeowners who have special electrical needs, usually (but not always) when I'm working with high-end properties. People who spend money on expensive electronics will want to make sure they work just right. Do the homeowners have any high-power appliances, such as a big-screen TV or a high-powered stereo? If so, consider putting in a separate circuit for each of these. Audio and video systems work bet-ter when they have plenty of power, and don't have to share with other appliances. Have you ever seen the picture dim on a big-screen TV when another appliance goes on? It would be terribly frustrating for someone to spend a lot of money on a television only to have the quality fluctuate every time the refrigerator comes on!

Audio experts generally recommend having a separate circuit for a stereo system. I put one in for mine, and it does seem to have a better sound now. Real audio fanatics go beyond this and have a separate service (meter, service box, etc.) installed for their stereo systems. They claim it makes a big dif-ference in the sound quality, and that a few hundred dollars for a separate service is a small price to pay to improve the sound of an expensive (with the best equipment and components, they can run over $100,000) stereo system. If the stereo has 100 amps available to it, you can be pretty sure it won't blow any fuses, no matter how loud it's turned up!

Homeowners appreciate having a sepa-rate 20-amp circuit added in the living room, even if they don't own a big-screen TV or a high-power stereo. They might buy one someday, and the idea that a special place has

already been set aside for it seems like a rather luxurious asset to have.

Adding Other Types of Cable

Now is a good time to consider installing any other types of cable that the homeowner might want either now or in the future. How about a hardwired alarm system or intercom? Cable for these would be a lot easier to install while you're in the midst of repairs.

There are radio-connected intercoms available now that don't require wiring. They can be plugged into any electrical outlet, and they communicate with each other by radio. These systems have a range of 500 feet. They are good systems for people who live out in the country, but not so good for populated areas. If anyone within 500 feet (a block or so in any direction) has an intercom operating on the same frequency, each will hear the others messages. That doesn't offer much pri-vacy for an intercom. As more people buy them, they'll become even less private. If a homeowner values privacy, a hardwired sys-tem is a better investment.

Video cable is another type of cable that's used more and more today. If someone has an outside antenna, satellite dish, multiple VCRs, or multiple TVs with their own video feed, they're probably tripping over a rat's nest of video cables. It's a lot more conve-nient to run these cables through the walls. They can terminate in video cable wall con-nector plates. These plates (available from Radio Shack) are the same standard size and shape as electrical outlet plates, except they have a little RF cable screw-connector, instead of a power outlet. If the homeowners know what video devices they want connect-ed, you can run the cable directly between them. Otherwise, you can run cable from each room down to a central location in the basement. The rooms can then be connected to each other by jumpers. This will allow any video device in any room to be connected to any other room. Some people may want mul-tiple lines going to some rooms. This will allow them to run more than one video device at a time. For example, they can watch one program on TV and tape another at the same time.

🐌 Installing Built-in Audio Systems

Built-in audio systems are becoming more and more popular, especially in homes where space is at a premium, or where a free-standing stereo would interfere with a decorating scheme. This may come up when you are dealing with older home renovations. Modern audio equipment doesn't always fit into a Victorian decor. There are quite a few options that you can offer the homeowner.

Generally, I would only recommend permanently installing audio speakers and cable in the walls. It's not a good idea to install electronic audio or video components, such as CD players, receivers, TVs or VCRs in walls. This type of equipment needs good ventilation, which is hard to get inside a wall. They also need to be where they can be easily removed for servicing. A built-in unit may be hard to replace — new components might not fit into the old holes. It's better to install them in a freestanding unit or build them into a closet or cabinet where they can sit on a shelf and be easily removed or replaced. Speakers and cables rarely need to be replaced or require any service. They're better off in the wall and out of the way.

Speaker Cables

Like video cable, there are special wall-mounted connector plates for speaker cable. You can put one set where the components will be located, and another where the speakers will go. That way, each can be connected to a wall plate by a short piece of cable, with the intervening cable going through the walls, instead of snaking all over the floor.

Speaker cables come in a wide range of quality. Top-of-the-line cable can easily cost $100 per foot, or more! I wouldn't use that for in-wall installations, however. Use a moderate quality, like Monster Cable. If the homeowner wants something better, try Audio Advisor, at 1-800-942-0220. They stock premium-quality cables in all price ranges, including some specifically designed for in-wall use. They're also willing to spend time on the phone with you, and advise you on the best way to handle your project. And, it's hard to beat their prices on quality equipment.

Speakers

Electronic equipment can be placed inside a piece of furniture, but the speakers have to be out in the open where they show, or their sound will be muffled. Fortunately, there's a wide selection of speakers designed for in-wall installation. The speaker grills can even be painted to match the wall color, making the speakers practically invisible. Homeowners can have a high-quality sound system without speakers interfering with their decorating scheme.

Built-in speakers come in two types: in-wall and wall mounted. The wall-mounted type usually stand a little bit away from the wall on brackets, while the in-wall type are set into the walls themselves. The wall-mounted type are unobtrusive, but if looks are really important, the in-wall types may be the better choice.

In-Wall Speakers — You can mount any kind of speaker in a wall, but you'll get better results using speakers specifically designed for that purpose. There are high-quality speakers available for in-wall mounting. The Dynaco FL-650 is highly regarded by the experts. It's available from Audio Advisor for about $200 a pair.

The biggest problem you'll have with an in-wall installation is stray vibrations. If the sound is turned up too high, the speaker will vibrate quite heavily. A speaker assembly that's not securely fastened down will buzz as well. The vibrations can be transmitted to the wall, and from there to any loose fittings, causing odd buzzing and whistling sounds. A homeowner who's paying a lot of money for high-quality sound equipment won't be happy with all these odd noises ruining the effect.

Make sure the speaker assembly is securely fastened down. It should be connected directly to the studs whenever possible. Or you can attach it to a ¾-inch piece of plywood, wide enough to bridge across the studs. When the plywood is securely screwed to the studs, it will become a stable mounting plate for the speaker.

You should also fill the space between the studs with fiberglass insulation. This will help control vibration and improve bass response. If you can, fill the entire wall cavity that the speaker is mounted in, floor to ceiling, with fiberglass insulation and pack the cavities on either side of the speaker as well. This will help control stray vibrations.

Make sure there are no other loose items, such as electrical boxes, that aren't securely fastened down. Anything loose may buzz. Finally, hook up the speakers to an audio source and try them out before you close up the wall. It's be a lot easier to remedy any problems before you hang the drywall than after.

Some speaker manufacturer's instructions may include directions that are different from these. For instance, not all speakers should be packed in fiberglass. If the manufacturer's instructions are different from mine, follow theirs. They built the speaker; they ought to know how it functions best. However, if no instructions are included, my installation procedure should work.

The big advantage of in-wall speakers is that, once they're installed, no one will even notice them. The music will just be there. The disadvantage is that they're permanently installed in one fixed location. Once they're in, you can't move them without tearing up the wall. Make sure the homeowner is happy with the placement.

Bracket-Mounted Speakers — There are a few advantages to speakers mounted on wall brackets. First, since the speaker is held away from the wall by the bracket, stray vibrations are much less a problem. Second, the speaker can be angled to point directly at the area of the room where people will be sitting. Sound is better if it's pointed toward the listener rather than off in some neutral direction. If the furnishings are changed, the speakers can be redirected to suit the new arrangement.

This is an advantage over in-wall speakers, which can never be moved.

Another big advantage is that you don't need to rip up the walls to install bracket-mounted speakers. They're surface-mounted. You just need to make a couple of little holes to fish the speaker wire through. The wall brackets should be attached to a stud or they can vibrate loose. The speakers are mounted on the brackets and connected to the amplifier by speaker wire. It's best to run the speaker wire inside the wall, terminating it in a wall-mounted speaker connector plate. The plate should be located near the place where the homeowner plans to put the amplifier. For a professional-looking installation, you want to keep all the wiring confined, and not have it dangling around the room or hanging down the walls.

The choice of speakers should be left to the homeowners. If they have no preference and ask your advice, do a little research. Call Audio Advisor, or ask any good audio shop to advise you or the homeowners.

Audio on a Budget

Fine-quality audio equipment isn't cheap. However, a homeowner can still have a good-sounding built-in music system without spending too much. You can use automobile speakers to provide an excellent in-wall installation. Automobile speakers are designed to the same specifications as home speakers. They work fine with a home receiver or an amplifier.

I've found car speakers with surprisingly good sound that only cost about $75 a pair. Auto sound shops have a wide variety of speakers that you can listen to before you buy. The larger speakers usually have a better sound. They're a good choice. Don't bother with the little dashboard speakers.

Car speakers are supposed to fit into small spaces, which makes them ideal to fit into wall cavities. You'll have room to spare. You can wire the speakers with heavy-duty speaker cable, and trim out the installation with wall-mount speaker connector plates, both from Radio Shack. Install them as I described for the other speakers, using a mounting plate with insulation around them. If the grilles that came with the speakers are paintable, you can paint them to match the wall. When you're done, you'll have a good-sounding, elegant-looking installation for about $100 (material cost).

Some homeowners may want an expensive installation in the living room, and one of these budget techniques to bring music to the kitchen or rec room. You can use these methods to extend the music all over the house. Putting top-quality equipment in every room is very expensive.

Professional Installations

A homeowner who's really into audio/video equipment may want professional technicians to do the installation. They use specialized techniques and equipment to make sure every aspect of the installation is absolutely perfect. However, these people are specialists in the selection and setup of equipment. They're not remodelers. They'll usually be happy to let you do the in-wall installation. Remember, however, that when you work with professionals like these, you must follow their instructions to the letter! Tiny details can make a big difference in the installation. If they ask you to do seemingly senseless and illogical things, do them. For reasons unknown to me, these details seem to make a difference. A top-quality audio system can run $100,000 or more, and you don't want anything to interfere with it. If the installation isn't perfect, you most certainly don't want it to be your fault!

Many remodelers don't understand the need for precision in this kind of work. As a result, audio/video technicians have a hard time finding remodelers they can work with. If you can do the kind of work they require, you may find a lot of their business coming your way. Since they're usually working with very well-to-do people, that can only be good for your business. Homeowners will remember if you do good work, and they will call again.

Adding Electricity to the Garage

Today everyone wants electricity in their garage and most old garages don't have it. Running electricity to the garage is a very useful and popular addition.

The garage should have its own 20-amp circuit — one circuit is usually enough. This circuit needs to have a GFCI circuit breaker installed in the main circuit-breaker box so that the entire circuit is protected. Use underground feeder cable (Type UF) between the house and the garage. It should be buried 18 inches below the surface and it should be protected by conduit. I like to put a layer of rocks in the trench as well. This helps prevent anyone from accidentally digging through it.

A garage should have an overhead light and at least one outlet. It isn't a bad idea to add a light or two on the outside of the garage as well. I often put up carriage lamps on either side of the garage door; they are attractive as well as useful. Mounting floodlights on the garage may also be an option that the homeowner will like. I usually put these on the side or back, not on the front, and position them so that they'll light up the back yard. It's really handy to be able to flip a switch and have the whole yard lighted.

Most older garages aren't big enough for a work area, but if there is space, the homeowner may want some additional outlets for power tools, and a work bench light. Sometimes even a small corner is enough space. Be sure there is an outlet for a radio as well. There are a lot of men who like to retreat to the garage to work on a hobby or make repairs to household items, and listen to a ball game.

Electrical work is a complicated subject. It would take an entire book to cover it completely. If you need more information, I suggest *Illustrated Guide to the National Electrical Code* by John E. Traister. It is available from Craftsman Book Company.

Chapter 15

Wall and Ceiling Repair

Up to now, we've been dealing with the structural and mechanical systems, the parts of the home that don't really show. These repairs are absolutely vital, but they're also less satisfying than the more visible improvements. The homeowners can't proudly point your work out to their friends, because most of it doesn't show. They would prefer to pay for improvements that they can admire and show off.

Now that we've covered everything that goes inside the walls and ceilings and added in anything that was needed, we can get to the more visible jobs. We're ready to repair the walls and ceilings themselves.

Repairing Wet Plaster

If you examine the walls in an older home, you'll notice that the plasterwork involves three layers. The first layer is made up of furring strips. These are little strips of wood, spaced ½ inch apart. The first layer of plaster is applied over these and it oozes around and through the spaces in the furring strips, where it hardens. This process locks the plaster onto the strips, creating a base for the next coat of plaster and a very strong wall. Figure 15-1 shows the back side of a lath and plaster wall. You can see how the plaster drips through the spaces, giving it a solid grip on the lath.

The first coat of plaster is a coarse gray plaster and often has fibers (usually animal hair) mixed into it for extra resilience. The finish coat of fine white plaster is applied on top of that. This is the surface that will be painted, and the only surface people see. Many people never know what's under the white plaster finish, or how much work went into creating their nice smooth walls.

Applying wet plaster is very tedious work. I tried it once, and it took me what seemed like forever to do one wall. I thought I was doing something wrong, until I watched a professional plasterer at work. It took him practically forever, too! He was working on one 8- by 24-foot wall, and it took him three days! I could have drywalled the same wall in three hours, and had time for a coffee break too. That gives you some idea why wet plaster work isn't done much anymore.

Figure 15-1
Back of lath and plaster wall shows how plaster fills in and grips the lath

It also shows why patching wet plaster walls *is* worthwhile. Wet plaster walls are becoming a rarity, and people who appreciate quality workmanship are willing to pay more for homes that have this kind of plasterwork. They may not entirely understand what goes into it, but they know it's desirable and they want it. Many real estate listings will mention "wet plaster" as a sales feature which adds value to the house. If you replace wet plaster with drywall, you may lower the value of the house!

I recommend repairing any wet plaster walls that are reasonably repairable. I'm not suggesting that you try to glue a million shattered pieces of plaster back together. However, if the damage isn't too great, you'll add more value to the house by repairing the walls than by replacing them.

Patching Small Holes

If you need to repair holes in plaster walls, there are a couple of different ways you can do it. I like to repair small holes with a little bit of drywall compound and drywall tape.

I find this a convenient way to deal with the problem, since I almost always have drywall tape and compound on hand. I buy ready-mixed drywall compound. It comes in a resealable plastic tub and you can use what you need and store the rest. Patching plaster comes in a powder form and has to be mixed just before you use it, and then you must use it all immediately. It's not very convenient when you only need to do a few small holes. Also, it's something of a storage problem. It has to be kept absolutely dry, or it will harden up.

The technique for repairing holes with drywall compound is the same as taping a drywall seam. You lay down a bed of drywall compound, imbed the tape in it, and cover it with more drywall compound. The problem with using drywall compound is that the repair stands up above the surface of the wall, unlike patching plaster, which will be flush. You need to feather the edges out very gradually to blend the compound into the surface. I usually have to extend the edges out about 12 inches. If you do this carefully, the repair will become almost invisible. It takes longer to repair cracks and holes with drywall compound than it does to simply tape a drywall seam because of the care you must take to blend it. Figure about 50 percent longer than taping a drywall seam. It's a tedious method of repair, but assuming a wall has only a crack here and there, it's a lot less work than tearing the wall out and drywalling the whole thing. Figure 15-2 shows several small cracks that I repaired using this technique. When the compound dries and the wall is painted, you won't be able to see the repairs.

Drywall compound isn't suitable for repairing large holes. It isn't intended to be applied more than about $1/2$ inch thick. If you try to apply it any thicker, it won't stay put. It'll ooze down the wall after a few hours. When you come back the next day, you'll find it has hardened into a strange-looking blob. You'll have to break it off, and do the repair over.

Another problem with using drywall compound for large repairs is that thick applications take a long time to dry — and when they finally do, they crack. You have to put on another layer to cover the cracks. It will eventually come out looking okay, but it's a lot more trouble than it's worth.

With all these problems, why do I even bother with drywall compound? Because the typical older home has a lot of little cracks and holes that can be repaired this way. You can easily find a hundred little holes scattered around the house. Most of them are no bigger than your little finger. A lot of them are a smaller — nail-size holes from hanging pictures or small objects on the walls. You can fill small holes with just a dab of drywall compound, and then sand them smooth when they're dry. You don't need to tape and blend little repairs like these. Many times fine cracks and holes aren't immediately visible and you won't see them until you're working on something else. If you had to stop and mix up a batch of patching plaster every time you came across one of these, you'd go nuts. It saves a lot of time and trouble to just run a little drywall compound over them.

Figure 15-2
Cracks repaired with drywall compound and joint tape

🐚 Patching Large Holes

For larger holes, patching plaster is best. If you're used to drywall, plaster may surprise you. Patching plaster handles very differently from drywall compound. It takes a little while to get used to the differences.

Patching plaster sets up fast. You have to be ready to apply it when you mix it. Within a half hour it will be completely hardened. You want to make sure it hardens on the wall, not on your tools. I use a big plastic mixing bowl to mix up batches of plaster. I find that if I mix up any more than this, it will harden before I use it all. I like to use a plastic bowl because it's easier to clean. If the plaster hardens up in it, I can flex the bowl and the plaster will break free.

Getting the consistency of patching plaster right takes a little practice. When you first mix it up, it'll seem to be too thin. However, in a few minutes it'll thicken up to the right consistency. But don't let it sit too long or it will harden completely. You have to keep an eye on this stuff until the job is done.

One thing I like about patching plaster is that it stays where you put it. I was especially pleased by this the first time I used it to patch a big hole in a ceiling. I was used to working with drywall compound, so I just assumed it would drip out all over me. I was amazed when it didn't! I troweled it into the hole in the ceiling, and it stayed there. Within an hour, it was completely hard, and ready to sand. Drywall compound would have oozed back out of the hole after a few minutes. And, even if I could have made the compound stay put, it would have taken days to dry, then shriveled and cracked when it did. This experience taught me to appreciate patching plaster. It may be a nuisance to mix up, but in situations like this, it's worth it.

🐚 Repair or Replace?

There comes a point when repairing wet plaster walls is no longer practical. If the walls or ceiling are badly damaged, with extensive cracking or many holes, it's better to replace them. It takes about the same amount of time to patch a hole as it does to tape and finish a drywall seam. That gives you a good rule of thumb to work by: if there's more than one softball-size hole per 4-foot by 8-foot area (the size of a sheet of drywall), it will be less work to replace the whole wall than to repair it.

Of course, the cheapest way to deal with a problem isn't always the best. You should discuss this with the homeowner. If the homeowner is on a tight budget, the subtle differences between wet plaster and drywall may seem unimportant in the face of the cost of repairs. If the choice comes down to having wet plaster repaired or a second bathroom, most people on a budget will choose the bathroom. Replacement is also the logical selection if the house has had a lot of modifications, and already has several drywalled walls. In that case, one more won't do any harm.

On the other hand, if you're working on an expensive or historic house, in an area where people care about authenticity or special details, it's a good idea to save the walls if you can. Drywalling destroys the historical accuracy of the house, and removes an asset that some people are willing to pay extra to have. You could seriously lower the home's value.

Repairing with Drywall

I would recommend only replacing the walls that absolutely need it, and saving those you can. Many contractors prefer to replace everything. If any wall in a room is damaged, they'll rip all the walls in the room out and replace them. I consider this wasteful and unnecessary. Remember, demolition costs money, as does waste disposal. Don't forget to add these costs in when comparing the cost of repairing a wall to the cost of replacing it.

Replacing walls that don't really need it is a waste of the homeowner's money. Sure, you can say it's necessary, or cheaper in the long run. Some other contractors would. But the homeowner will be a lot happier if you can save the walls, and use the money for something more enjoyable. Replacing walls with other walls isn't exciting. Saving walls

and updating the kitchen is. That's what makes a homeowner happy, and happy people recommend you to their friends. That will make you happy, too.

❧ Removing the Wall

If I have to replace wet plaster with drywall, I usually remove one complete wall, from corner to corner. That's because it's difficult to seam drywall to plaster in the middle of a wall without the seam showing. Corners are easier. It's really not any harder to tape a drywall wall to a wet plaster wall at the corner than to tape drywall to drywall at the corner.

Contractors routinely tear out the furring strips when demolishing a plaster wall. I don't, unless it's necessary. If I need to install insulation or ducting, for example, the furring strips will have to come out. Otherwise, I prefer to leave them. Pulling out the furring strips may make the plaster come off easier, but if the walls are in bad shape, the plaster will probably come off easily anyway. After all, if it wasn't coming off, I wouldn't be replacing the wall.

Furring strips add a lot of strength to a wall. Drywall backed by furring strips is considerably more solid than just plain drywall. You can't punch a hole in it with your fist, like you can drywall alone. I think it makes the wall feel more substantial, like the original wet plaster. That's why I try to preserve the furring strips, if possible.

❧ Creating Plaster Effects with Drywall

One of the most attractive things about wet plaster is its ability to curve. Many older homes have arched doorways and coved ceilings. For many people, these features make a house interesting. An all-drywall house has only straight lines and 90-degree angles.

If it becomes necessary to replace plaster walls that have special features with drywall, most contractors will simply break out the curves and replace them with straight lines. This saves money, but it can really spoil the look of the house. Redoing the wet plaster, on the other hand, may be prohibitively expensive. Fortunately, there are other alternatives.

You can find products like prefabricated fiberglass archways to take the place of the wet plaster features. Special order them in the exact size you need. They're squared-off on the outside, to fit a square door opening, but rounded on the inside, to create the look of a plaster archway. Just nail them into place, then tape and finish, just like drywall. One source for these products is:

Insta Arch Corporation
17 Hamden Park Drive
Hamden, CT 06517
Phone (203) 281-3270

🐌 Bending Drywall

You can also take advantage of the fact that drywall can be bent into curves. This is especially useful for replacing coved ceilings, or other areas with large curved surfaces. You may have accidentally discovered how easily drywall bends if you've ever left a drywall panel leaning against a wall too long. Once it has bent itself into a curve, it stays that way.

Normally, drywall that's kept dry will take weeks to bend itself into a curve. You can speed up the process by moistening it with a fine spray from a garden hose. Don't overdo it, however. If you get it too wet, it will just fall apart. Once the drywall has softened, you can slowly work it into a curve. Brace it in the position you want and let it dry overnight. The next day, you'll have a piece of curved drywall that will fit into the curved spot in the coved ceiling.

Unfortunately, it's not always as easy as it sounds, especially the first time you do it. You'll probably ruin a few pieces of drywall before you get it right. Luckily, they're cheap. The greatest difficulty is trying to apply the precise amount of moisture without ruining the panel. It's also hard to get the angle of the curve to come out right. You might want to make several curved pieces, then you can pick the best one to use.

Figure 15-3
A doorway being patched with drywall

Trying to curve drywall panels may sound like a lot of trouble, but the alternatives are worse. Destroying the curves and replacing them with flat, straight lines will ruin the authentic look of the house, and probably lower its value. The other alternative would be to reapply wet plaster, and that's even more trouble. You can ruin a lot of drywall pieces, and still get the job done faster and cheaper than replastering with real wet plaster.

🐌 Patching Plaster with Drywall

You may find that you can save a wet plaster wall by using drywall to patch a large hole. It can be a touchy job, and it isn't worth doing on a severely damaged wall. But it works well if you're dealing with one fairly good-size hole. I do it when I find that a door or window has been removed and the hole hasn't been filled over with plaster. That leaves a large hole in an otherwise perfect wall. It's less trouble to patch the hole than to tear out the whole wall and replace it with drywall. Figure 15-3 shows a doorway repair. The hole was left after the door was sided over from the outside. I filled in the opening

Figure 15-4
*Plumbing repair being
patched with drywall*

with drywall, and once the edges were taped and sanded, no trace of the opening remained.

Hanging drywall in situations like this is fairly simple. You just need to add a 2 x 4 or two to the doorway or window opening to provide extra support for the drywall panel. If you're lucky, there may even be a nice little lip remaining where the moldings were. The drywall panel can be set in flush against the lip.

The difficult part is taping the edges. Plaster walls aren't indented for the tape, like the edges of drywall. That means you'll have to extend the edges out about 12 inches, and feather them very gradually. In the case of a doorway, the drywall compound from the seam on one side of the door may meet the compound from the other side in the middle of the drywall panel. You can blend the two seams together, making the doorway look like one very wide seam. But remember, you're spreading the compound wide, not

thick. It will hold well, and dry without cracking. If you do it carefully, once it's sanded and painted, the old doorway will just disappear.

I use this same technique on any large holes in good walls. Often, this involves holes made for plumbing repairs. Figure 15-4 shows an area of wall where someone had cut away the plaster to get at the pipes. I carefully patched the wall with drywall. Again, when the edges were feathered, it created one large band of compound. After sanding and painting, the repair became invisible.

Sanding the Compound

Many drywall finishers tend to use a lot of drywall compound, and then sand the heck out of it. That's a lot of extra work, and it makes a big mess. I prefer to use slightly less compound, and then touch it up by adding more to the low spots after the first layer has dried. I find this to be less work, and a lot less mess.

Drywall dust gets all over the place when you're sanding. If you're in an occupied house, it can be a real problem. The dust will settle in a thick layer over everything, and the house will look like it hasn't been dusted in a thousand years. Be sure to close off your work area with plastic sheeting to keep the dust out of the rest of the house. Also, if weather permits, open a window and stick a fan in it, blowing towards the outside. This will blow most of the dust outside and keep the house cleaner. It will also make it easier for you to breathe in your work area.

If you don't think sanding drywall raises a lot of dust, stand outside while someone is sanding and the fan is going. There will be clouds of dust coming out of the house. It almost looks like the house is on fire!

❧ Ceilings

Repairing ceilings is almost exactly the same as repairing walls. This is especially true when using drywall. The main difference is that since you're working overhead, it's a lot harder to keep your materials in place. One man, working alone, can easily hang drywall on walls, but hanging drywall on a ceiling is pretty much a two-person job. It's very hard for one person to hold up both ends of an 8-foot sheet of drywall.

If you must drywall a ceiling by yourself, you can use a brace to hold up one end of the sheet while you hold the other. There are drywall braces that you can buy, or you can make one out of a few pieces of 2 x 4 fastened together in a T-shape. I just use an 8-foot step ladder; it's the perfect height for an 8-foot ceiling. If I need to add a little height, I'll fasten one or two pieces of 2 x 4 to the top to bring the height up. I slide one end of the drywall panel onto the top of the ladder and move it into place while I fasten the other end with a few screws. Once one end is secured, I can let go and fasten the end that's on the ladder. I even have a ladder in place to work off of! It's slower working this way, but it can be done. By the way, I always use screws rather than nails on ceilings. I find it very difficult to nail upwards.

Even with all the right equipment, hanging drywall on ceilings by yourself is hard work. You don't want to do it unless it's an emergency — a job that just can't wait until you can get a helper. If I have a choice, I always have someone help me with ceiling work.

Odd Angles

Another problem you're likely to encounter when working with the ceilings in an older home is odd angles. These are especially common on the second floor where the roofline often intersects the walls creating two 135 degree angles rather than one 90 degree angle. You can see this type of ceiling situation in Figure 15-5. You can also see it if you look back at Figure 15-2. Every upstairs room in this particular house had a roofline intersecting a wall at this same angle. Angles aren't a problem for wet plaster work, but they are for drywall. Drywall was designed to use in square rooms, with 90 degree angles. Odd angles make drywall work far more difficult and time consuming.

Figure 15-5
Roof lines at odd angles present special problems

In this house, the 135 degree angle in the first room I drywalled was 4 feet up from the floor. My first thought was to lay the drywall panels sideways along the base of the wall. The 4 x 8 panels fit neatly into the space between the floor and the angle in the wall with no cutting, so it made sense to place them like that. However, this turned out to be the wrong way to do the installation. That's because the seam at the 135 degree angle was almost impossible to tape properly. The compound had to go on so thick that it cracked when it dried. I had to put it on over and over again, and it kept coming out wavy, lumpy and bumpy. It took about a dozen tries to finally get it right. Taping this one seam took as long as drywalling all of a normal room. I decided there must be a better way.

The next room I did a little different, and it turned out to be the right way. I cut a 2-foot-wide piece of drywall and laid it from the floor to a point 2 feet up the wall. This may seem like a foolish way to install drywall, since I was creating an extra seam, but as you'll see, there was a logical reason for doing it. Next, I scored a full sheet of drywall lengthwise down the middle *on the back side.* Then I cracked it carefully, leaving the two pieces connected by the paper on the front. In this way, the drywall was hinged down the middle, and I knew that the hinge could bend to any angle. I installed the hinged piece so that the bottom edge lay on the 2-foot piece that was already installed, and the hinge lay exactly on the 135 degree angle. Since the hinge was never cut all the way through, it didn't have to be taped. That solved the taping problem. Of course I still had a seam to tape, but it was an ordinary flat seam, and no particular trouble to tape.

You have to handle hinged drywall pieces very carefully. Otherwise, you'll tear them before you can get them installed. If they get torn, you'll have to start all over with a new piece. It takes at least two people to work with hinged drywall; you can't handle these sheets by yourself without tearing them.

In working with older homes, you're going to come across a lot of situations where you'll need to install drywall at odd angles. I've found that using hinged drywall panels saves time and trouble, and produces a nicer finish than trying to tape odd angles using conventional methods.

❧ Replacing the Trim

Don't forget to replace any plaster trim, medallions or moldings you took down when you began. If they don't fit exactly, don't worry. You can fill in the gaps with plaster or drywall compound. Once it's painted, the repair won't show.

Replacing the trim also helps to blend the old and new areas together. If you're concerned that a repair may be visible, look at it again once the trim is in place. Most of the time, the trim will cover up minor imperfections, or lead the eye away from problem areas. I'm often surprised to find that areas that didn't look quite right suddenly look perfect when the trim is replaced. It's all the little details that bring the job together.

Floor Repair

The next area we need to turn our attention to is the floor. We've already dealt with the structural problems that affect the floor, but not the condition of the floor itself. How does it look, and what kind of repairs are needed? How deep do the problems go? Is the floor still the original wood, or covered in linoleum or carpet? Does it need a new subfloor, a new surface, refinishing, replacing or new carpet? Let's take a look at these questions.

Carpeting vs. Hardwood Floors

The simplest way to deal with floor problems is to carpet over them. Carpet can be installed over just about any surface, so long as it's solid and level. This isn't always the most appealing solution however, especially in a home that has beautiful old wood floors. Carpeting will hide this special, and potentially valuable, feature. But many times homeowners aren't aware of the value of the wood floors.

The homeowners may have already decided that they want carpeting installed.

Some people have very strong feelings about carpeting. If they have hardwood floors that need repair, and aren't sure what they want to do with the floors, you may be asked for your advice. You should be aware of the advantages and disadvantages of finishing hardwood floors or putting in carpet or other types of flooring.

It's always advisable to preserve hardwood floors, even if the homeowners don't care about them. Wood floors can add thousands of dollars to the value of the house. I try never to do any kind of work that will harm them. Carpeting over wood won't hurt it, but gluing tile to it will. You may want to advise your clients that any kind of work that damages the hardwood floors may lower the resale value of the property should they decide to sell in the future. They may not choose to follow your advice, but you should make them aware of the potential loss so they can make an informed decision.

Carpeting

Is there already carpeting down in the house? Is it going to be replaced? If so, leave it there until all the other work is done. Some people tear out old carpeting first thing, without even thinking about it. That isn't a good idea. Even the worst carpeting can serve a great purpose: it's an excellent drop cloth! It's exactly the right size for the room and it's fastened down so it won't slip around while you work. It's even padded to protect the floor from tools or materials that may be dropped. It also makes cleanup a lot easier at the end of the job. You just roll the whole thing up, paint drips, plaster pieces, bent nails and all, and put it out for the trash. The floor underneath will be clean and undamaged. Old carpeting should always be removed last, not first.

❧ Cleaning

Before you decide to use the old carpeting for a drop cloth, however, take time to check it over carefully and see if it's salvageable. Even if it doesn't look too good at the moment, it's surprising what professional steam cleaning can do. I've seen it restore carpeting that appeared to be completely worn out. Sometimes the nap of the carpet is just pushed down, rather than worn down, and the carpet isn't really in bad shape. Steam cleaning can raise the nap again, making the carpet look fine. Professional carpet cleaners also have a wide range of chemicals available for removing stains and odors. I've seen them get out marks that I was certain were there to stay.

You can always have a professional carpet cleaner take a look at the carpet if you're not sure it will clean up. They can usually tell you whether it's worth the effort or not. One of the worst substances to get out of a carpet is Kool-Aid, especially grape. If there are kids in the house who drink Kool-Aid, the carpet may not be salvageable!

If the homeowners have decided that they're ready for new carpeting, they won't want to be bothered with cleaning. But if they're undecided, you can suggest trying a professional carpet cleaner first. New carpeting is very expensive. If they can save the existing carpet, they may be able to use the money for another remodeling project. Don't forget to point this out. Don't just say "Do you want to keep this old, worn carpeting, or do you want new carpeting?" Of course they'll opt for new carpet. But what if you say this: "Would you like to clean up the existing carpeting, and add another half-bath, or shall we skip the bath and get new carpeting?" There's a good chance they'll at least try the cleaning before they give up on the bath. If they choose the carpeting, most of the money will go to the carpet manufacturer. If they choose a half-bath, most of the money will go to you!

❧ Salvaging Carpet

Even worn-out carpet may have some salvage value. Most carpeting doesn't wear out evenly. There's usually a path through the middle of the room that's fairly worn, but the areas where the furniture was placed usually remains in good condition.

If it's a good-quality carpeting in an attractive color, those areas, usually around the edge of the room, may be worth saving. They're perfect for carpeting hallways and stairs. All you need is a 3-foot wide strip of carpeting. If you're doing stairs, it doesn't even matter if the strip has seams. They won't show. If you're pulling the carpet out of a large living/dining area, the edges may be enough to recarpet all the stairs and hallways.

In a house that has the same carpeting throughout, you can use the salvageable carpet for the hallways and stairs, and only replace the carpet in the living/dining areas. Carpeting wears out first in the living/dining areas, hallways, and stairs. The bedrooms take much longer to wear out because they have a lot less traffic through them. If you use the carpeting from the living/dining area to redo the stairs and hallways, they'll all be done in matching carpeting that's in good condition. The only cost is the labor to cut and install the pieces. This works out particularly well if the owners decide to use some other treatment for the living/dining area, such as refinishing the wood floors.

For safety and convenience, it's more important to carpet the stairs and hallway than the living/dining area. People are less likely to slip on carpeted stairs than uncar-

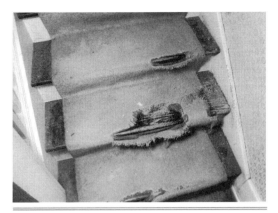

Figure 16-1
Worn carpet on stairways is dangerous

Figure 16-2
Carpeted stairways are safe and quiet

peted stairs, and less likely to get hurt if they do. Also, carpeted stairs and hallways are quieter. It's nice to keep the areas outside the bedrooms quiet, so sleeping people aren't disturbed by those walking around. Carpet like that shown in Figure 16-1 is a safety hazard, but it's not uncommon to find in older homes. The stairs almost always have the most worn carpet in a house. Figure 16-2 shows the same staircase with new carpet and refinished woodwork.

There are a lot of carpets that you don't want to salvage, even if they're in reasonably good condition. These include carpets in ugly colors or outdated types, like the shag carpets popular in the 1970s. These carpets looked terrible within a very short time, but never seemed to get really worn out. It's surprising how many homes you find that still have shag carpeting in them. Shag carpets seem almost indestructible.

Just to prove the point, let me tell you about a roll of carpet I found one time. I bought a house with a large lot. Towards the back of the lot was a mound of dirt that I tried to level out. The mound turned out not to be dirt, but a roll of old shag carpeting that had been buried, probably for 20 years. Someone had gone to great lengths to get rid of that carpet. They had tried to burn it, but it wouldn't burn, so they buried it instead. It was a brilliant, multicolored electric green. After all those years in the ground, it was still in perfect condition — and just as ugly as the day it was made!

Buying New Carpet

If the homeowners want you to install new carpeting, look into ways you can save on the purchase price. Good carpet is expensive. If you're doing a whole house, especially a big house, you're looking at several thousand dollars. I try to save as much money on carpeting as possible.

One way to save money without sacrificing quality is to buy direct from the factory. I buy most of my carpeting from the mills in Georgia. Dalton, Georgia is the carpet capital of the world. Call or write, and they'll send you a nice selection of samples. The mill I order from most often is:

S & S Mills
2650 Lakeland Rd. SE
Dalton, GA 30721
1-800-241-4013

I've found the quality of carpet from this company to be excellent, and the prices very reasonable. Their samples are attractively packaged, so you can use them for presentations to customers. I can get top-quality carpet from them for a price that would only buy junk locally. Craftsman's *National Construction Estimator*, the estimating book I use when I need a price for something I'm not familiar with, estimates the cost of good quality carpeting, installed, at $36 per yard. I can do the job for half that, with carpet that's every bit as good, if I buy it directly from the factory. A 1,500 square foot house, for example, has 166 square yards in it. At $36 a yard, that's $5,976. As you can see, carpeting really adds up. If you can do the job for half the price, you save almost $3,000. That's definitely worth looking into.

By the way, I don't own stock in S & S Mills, nor are they giving me anything for recommending them. I just happen to have found them to be a way to improve my profits without hurting my reputation by installing cheap junk. Like anyone that I have successfully done business with, I'm happy to recommend them. That's just one of the benefits you get for buying my book.

One nice thing about ordering carpet from the factory is that you can take your time to look over the samples at home, without having a salesman pressure you. I feel like I do a better job of picking out carpet under these conditions.

If you decide to order carpeting from Georgia, there are a few things you'll need to know. First, it takes about 10 days for shipping, so you'll have to plan that time into your schedule. Second, there's a 50-yard minimum. Don't plan on ordering carpet for just one room unless it's a really big room.

The carpet will arrive by truck, and you can have it delivered right to the house where you'll be installing it. It usually comes late in the day. Because it's big, the shipping company will load it first, so it will be the last thing in the truck when it comes to unloading. Someone will have to be at the house to accept the shipment. You can make arrangements to have the shipping company call you the day before the carpet is to be delivered, so you know when it's coming.

There are two big problems you have to deal with when the carpet arrives. First, you have to unload it. The truck driver isn't allowed to unload it for you. Unloading carpet isn't easy; it's really heavy! That's why it's the last item at the back of the truck. A big roll of carpeting can weigh 500 pounds, and it's awkward as well as heavy. The roll may be 20 feet long. You'll need at least two, and preferably three, men to get it off the truck and into the house. One person couldn't do it alone.

The second problem is storage. Where will you keep it until it's time to install it? Finding a place to put a 20-foot roll of anything in a house is surprisingly hard. Remember, the carpet needs to be protected. You can't leave it in the middle of a work area where it might be damaged. I often find the only place to put a roll of carpet is on the stairs, pushed to one side. That means it will be partially blocking the stairs for as long as you have to store it. Everyone will have to squeeze by it whenever they go up or down the stairs. Because of the storage problem, I try to time the delivery of the carpet so that it arrives as close to the installation time as possible.

Health Considerations

There's been a lot of news coverage recently about health hazards linked to the gases that are given off by new carpeting. The government has just issued guidelines regarding these gas emissions. Before buying any carpet, make sure that the manufacturer is complying with these new regulations. S & S Mills advertises that they meet all of the new government standards.

I haven't ever had any problems with these gases myself, but I do know that new carpeting does have a pretty strong chemical smell. In an enclosed area, the smell can be rather overpowering. Even if the manufacturers are complying with the new standards, it's easy to understand that some people might still be sensitive to the odors. I believe that it's always better to be safe than sorry, so I try not to put myself in situations where I might be sued. Since new carpeting gives off most of its gases in the first few days after it's unrolled, I try to only install new carpeting in houses that are vacant. Usually it's a few weeks before anyone moves in, and by that time, most of the smell has gone away.

If you have to install new carpeting in an occupied house, it's a good idea to try to control the gases and smell. Unroll the carpeting in an unoccupied area, like the garage, and leave it there for a few days until the smell diminishes. Of course, this may be easier said than done. Finding an area, even in the garage, big enough to unroll carpeting isn't easy.

If you can't air out the roll in advance, bring as much ventilation into the house as you can while you're laying the carpet. Open the windows as much as the weather permits. If it's cold out, open the windows a crack and advise the owners to leave them that way for a few days. It will run up the heating bill a little, but not that much. Most of the health problems associated with new carpeting were reported in sealed buildings. Keep some fresh air circulating through the house for the first few days, and buy from reputable carpet manufacturers. That should greatly decrease any health risk.

Installation

I usually contract out carpet installation. Professional installers always do a better job than I can. There are a couple of installers that I work with. They work for carpet companies during regular business hours, but are always willing to pick up some extra money on the side doing jobs for me evenings or on weekends. You can find professional carpet installers who will work like this advertised in the papers, usually under "Services Available."

Their rates are generally pretty reasonable. For instance, I just had 80 yards of carpeting installed for $220. It was a lot of work, more than I would have taken on for that kind of pay, but they set the price. Of course, some installers charge more than others. You'll just have to see what the going rate is in your area.

Hardwood Floors

The condition of hardwood floors in older homes varies tremendously. I've found some in absolutely perfect condition and others that were hopelessly chewed up. Usually they're somewhere in between these two extremes.

Floors that are in perfect condition have usually been carpeted for much of their life. In many cases, carpeting, or at least large area rugs, were put down over the floor when it was still new. As a result, the wood may not have ever been walked on. These floors are a pleasure to discover.

On the other hand, there are a lot of people who never cared about their hardwood floors. They assumed that since they preferred carpeting, everyone else would prefer carpeting too. They never stopped to think that someone might want to uncover the wood someday and restore it. As a result, they treated their floors poorly. They sloped paint, glue, and crud all over them before putting carpet down. After all, what difference did it make? The floors would always be carpeted, or so they thought. Now you have to deal with the results of their negligence.

If the floor has been treated badly, the present homeowners may be in for a shock when the carpet is taken up. This is especially true if they wanted to restore the hardwood floor instead of installing new carpet. When they bought the house they may have been told that the house had hardwood flooring. But no one told them what condition it was in.

I've seen homeowners get really depressed when they see their hardwood flooring uncovered for the first time. They often take one look and give up. "What's the use!" they think. Of course it's easier to carpet over the flooring than to deal with repairs and refinishing, especially if they don't know where to begin. This is when they're likely to turn to you for advice.

🐚 Refinish or Recarpet?

If the floor is damaged, it will probably need refinishing. This is a big job, and it'll cost the homeowner a lot of money. In some cases, it may be cheaper to put down carpet than refinish the floor. You can't really argue with the homeowner's decision to carpet under those circumstances. However, a hardwood floor is still a valuable asset, even if it needs refinishing. Encourage the homeowners to consider the value of the floor and not to give up on it forever. Even if they decide to lay carpet now, it's just like putting their asset aside for the time being. They can invest in the floor at a later date. They should think of it as putting their hardwood floor in storage.

If this is the case, don't make the same mistake that others before you made. Take good care of the floor. Just because it's going to be carpeted doesn't mean it's disposable. Don't slop paint on it or gouge holes in it. Even in bad condition, it's still valuable. It may be a mess now, but you don't need to make it worse. They may want to refinish it someday.

Floor Repairs

It's common to find patched floors in older homes. Usually the patches are the result of heating modifications, but you'll also see places where walls have been moved as well. There will be a long, thin patch, just the width of a wall, running along the floor.

Once in a while you'll find there has been some attempt at matching the patches to the flooring, but usually not. Floors are most often patched with pine or plywood. The patch needed to be strong, not beautiful. Once a floor was patched, it was assumed that it would be carpeted. If you're going to recarpet the floor, the patches aren't a problem. However, if you were going to refinish the floor, the patches will complicate your plans.

Finding a large patch in an otherwise-beautiful floor is always a big disappointment. I'll often peek under the corner of an existing rug, and find what appears to be a perfect hardwood floor. I always hope that the rest of the floor will be as good, but it rarely is. It's really frustrating when 90 percent of the floor is flawless, but that last 10 percent is a big, ugly patch.

If you find a floor with just one bad patch, and the homeowner is short of money, you might just be able to leave it there and still uncover the floor. A lot depends on where the patch is located. If it's in an area where it will be covered by a sofa or an area rug, the owner may be satisfied with just hiding the patch. No one else will ever know the patch is there. It can always be repaired later. This changes the patch from an urgent repair into something that can be dealt with when it's financially convenient.

❧ Patches

If the owner wants a really beautiful, complete hardwood floor, however, the patch will have to go. That's a lot easier said than done. The old patch will have to be pried out as neatly as possible, and new flooring strips put in. The patch will probably be nothing more than a single layer of 3/4-inch plywood. Once you remove it, you'll have a big open hole that goes all the way to the basement. Now what?

A hardwood floor consists of two layers, a subfloor and a layer of hardwood strips. The subfloor is for strength and the hardwood strips are for looks. Both are usually 3/4 of an inch thick. Before you can do anything else, you'll need to replace the subfloor under the patched area. You can use 3/4-inch plywood for this, recessing it below floor level enough so that the new oak strips you put on top will set flush with the rest of the floor.

Once the subfloor is repaired, you can determine how to repair the flooring. An amateur would repair the hole by just filling it in with oak strips, not taking the flooring pattern into consideration. I've seen this dozens of times, and it never looks good. The hole is probably a neat square or rectangle, like the one in Figure 16-3. The original strips were laid in a pattern with the stripes offset from one another. They were probably laid similar to brick, with seams that purposely didn't line up. If you just fill in the hole, the pattern won't match the rest of the floor. All the seams will line up in a straight line, and it will look very obviously like a patched square in the floor.

Figure 16-3
Floor furnace hole needs repair

Figure 16-4
*New flooring strips blend with old to
make a nice repair*

In order to make the repair not look like a repair, you'll need to recreate the original pattern. If you look at the edges of the patch, you'll see that some of the original strips have been cut through, leaving short pieces that come up to the edge of the missing section. If you remove the short pieces on each side, the original zigzag pattern will reappear. You need to fit the replacement strips into these places in order to recreate the correct pattern. The new strips will then be woven into the rest of the floor, like the repair in Figure 16-4. You can't even see where the new flooring strips were added in now that the floor is polished.

Unfortunately, most floor repairs aren't that easy to blend. The new pieces probably won't be the same color as the rest of the floor. If you're very careful, you might be able to stain them to match, but this is very hard to do. With a job like this, you always have to assume that you'll need to refinish the floor in order to blend in the new pieces.

Alternatives to Refinishing

Before you jump into a refinishing job however, examine the floor carefully. How close does the repair match, and what other areas need refinishing? If the defects in the rest of the floor are minor, just a lot of little scratches, a good coat of polish might cover them and blend the repair in. A "scratch-remover" furniture polish will sometimes do the trick. Remember that once the furniture

and area rugs are in place, you won't be able to see every little nick and scratch and variation in the floor. People don't crawl around on their hands and knees looking for defects in the floor. They look at the room as a whole. They won't notice a defect in the floor unless it's fairly major.

Old spilled or spattered paint spots are a very common problem when you uncover hardwood floors that have been carpeted. When people paint the walls, knowing that they are going to lay carpet, they very rarely worry about protecting the floors. Now, many years later, you get to clean up their mess.

Paint spots will sometimes come off easily, especially if it's latex interior wall paint. This kind of paint won't adhere well over varnish. You may already know that if you've ever tried to paint over varnished woodwork. A strong detergent and a mop may be all you need to take the paint off. If that doesn't work, try a scrub brush or very fine steel wool. Be careful with the steel wool, however. It's an abrasive. That means it will remove anything, but it may also scratch the floor. A few light scratches won't do much harm to the floor. They can usually be covered by polish.

Refinishing the Floor

If the floor is heavily damaged, it will need refinishing. The most common damage, other than nicks and scratches, is a worn path in the finish caused by years of continuous use. Even wood succumbs to heavy foot traffic eventually. You won't be able to cover up a 2-foot-wide path with just floor polish.

Even if there's not a lot of wear damage, the floors may need refinishing because the existing varnish has become cracked, alligatored or discolored by age. Nothing lasts forever. Even varnish goes bad after about 100 years.

Refinishing will tremendously improve the looks of a wood floor. I'm often amazed at how good a refinished floor looks, especially considering how some of them looked before. Many of the floors I've worked on were in such bad condition that I didn't think anything could help them. Yet, once they were refinished, they looked like new!

🌢 Color

Refinishing the floor will change its color. It was common at one time to stain all the woodwork in a home with a dark stain, including the floors. What appears to be a dark wood floor may actually be a light oak, with a heavy coat of stain. The floor in Figure 16-5 is typical of this. I often sand a small area of the floor to see how it compares to the rest of the wood in the room. It helps me to determine how large the job is going to be. Remember, once you remove the old finish, the original color will return. If it's light oak, and you like light oak, that's great. However, it won't match the rest of the woodwork any more. If there isn't much woodwork in a room, that may not be a problem. In some rooms the woodwork may have been painted over to match the walls. You can either leave it painted over or you may want to strip the paint or old finish off that as well. Chances are, the underlying wood will most likely be the same color as the floor.

If a room has a lot of dark stained woodwork and the color of the floor no longer matches it, it will spoil the look of the room. To make it right, you can either stain the floor to match the woodwork, or strip the woodwork to match the floor. When you're dealing with a lot of woodwork, staining the

floor to match the other wood is a lot less work. However, getting a stain to match exactly is pretty tricky. I usually buy a small can of every color of stain that even closely resembles the color of the woodwork, and then experiment with them. I mix the colors until I get just the right match.

This is fairly tedious work. I sometimes have to try a dozen different combinations before one comes out right. Once you get the right color combination, you can make up a big enough batch to do the entire floor. Be absolutely sure the color is right before you mix it all up. You don't want to have a great big batch of the wrong color. You also don't want to stain the floor, and then discover the color is wrong. (Don't laugh — I've done it!)

Be sure you test the stain on the wood in the room where it will be used, and look at it in varying light. Colors change during the day, and they're also different under artificial light and natural light. I usually find an area in the room, in an out-of-the-way place (but with good light), where I can play with the colors. I sand the floor down and apply various stains until I find one that matches the woodwork (Figure 16-6). You don't have to worry about the bad matches. They'll all be sanded off before you do the whole floor.

Because this job is so touchy, a lot of contractors don't want to be bothered with it. As a result, floor refinishing is a new subcontractor specialty. At the moment, there aren't very many of them. But if you don't want to do this job yourself, and you can find one of these subcontractors, you'll have the perfect person to solve your difficult refinishing problems. The cost varies, but subcontractors in my area are charging about $3.00 a square foot for refinishing.

🌢 Finish Removal

The hardest part of refinishing a floor is getting the old finish off. I've tried a lot of different ways to do this, and I'm not entirely happy with any of them. I originally tried using chemical paint removers to strip off the old varnish. That works, but it's way too

Figure 16-5
*Sand a small area to find the color
of the unfinished wood*

Figure 16-6
*Test the color of various stains to
match existing woodwork*

slow. I've found that the only practical way to strip a floor is with a power sander.

Most people recommend using floor sanders. They're like a big belt sander with a long handle so you can operate them standing up. They're very powerful, but I don't like them. I think they're too hard to control. Floor sanders take off material so fast that you can easily damage the floor. I never really get a nice smooth finish when I use one. Supposedly, in the hands of an expert, they do a good job. But I don't think there are too many experts around, because I've seen a lot of floors chewed up by floor sanders. Perhaps the operator wasn't "expert" enough. If I had more practice with floor sanders, maybe I'd be better with them. I'm afraid I'd have to ruin half a dozen floors before I got the hang of it, and I just don't have that many floors to spare.

I prefer to use a regular belt sander on floors. Belt sanders are designed for use on furniture, so they remove material slowly. I think that's an advantage, rather than a problem. You're not likely to do any damage to a floor with a belt sander. It may take longer to do the job, but you get a nice effect.

Another advantage of belt sanders is that they're small, inexpensive (about $200 for a good one), and you can use them for many different jobs. A floor sander, on the other hand, is big, expensive, and only does one thing. Even if I were going to use a floor sander, I wouldn't want to invest money into buying one. I'd just rent one, even though that's very expensive. Rental stores charge about $100 to rent one for four hours!

It takes about two hours to do an 8- by 10-foot floor with a floor sander, versus about six hours with a belt sander. However, if you figure in your time to pick up the floor sander at the rental store and return it when you're done, plus your rental costs, you might come out just about even using the belt sander, and you'll get a better-looking floor.

Of course, the bigger the floor, the less appealing the belt sander becomes. If you have to strip down a floor that's 20 by 40 feet, rather than 8 by 10 feet, you're looking at 10 times the square footage — 800 versus 80. It will take you ten times as long to sand it down with a belt sander, or 60 hours instead of six. This isn't a practical use of your time. When I run into a situation like this, I subcontract the job out to a specialist. It's a lot safer than using a floor sander myself. You can get a subcontractor to sand and refinish the floor, as we discussed above, or you can just subcontract out the sanding. They'll do that for about $1.50 a square foot. In most instances, the sanding is the hardest part of

Figure 16-7
Floor sanded and ready to be refinished

Figure 16-8
Refinished floor looks like new

the job. Once the sanding is done, I can do the refinishing myself.

I actually do very little subcontracting for floors. Most of the homes I work on simply aren't that big. I'll take on a refinishing job of 300 to 400 square feet myself, but I probably only get a job with 1000 square feet of hardwood floors once in a decade. Oak floors that are that big, but aren't ruined, are not all that common.

Once the old finish is removed, most of the work is done. The floor will look something like the one in Figure 16-7. (I hadn't finished around the edges of this one yet.) Unless you're going to stain it, the floor may need nothing more than a couple of coats of floor varnish. Be sure to keep the floor absolutely clean between the time you sand it and the time you varnish it. That means keeping people off of it. Since the floor has no finish, its pores are unsealed. If someone walks on it, the dirt from their shoes will lodge in the pores of the wood. When you varnish over the dirt, the footprints will be preserved in the floor forever.

After you varnish the floor, it shouldn't be walked on for at least 24 hours. That may be a problem if the house is occupied. Be sure to plan your refinishing work to correspond with the homeowners' absence, or at least at a time when they can avoid the rooms where you're working for a day or more. The finished job should turn out like the floor in Figure 16-8. This floor was sanded with a belt sander, then stained and varnished. The completed floor looked like new.

Softwood Floors

Not all wood floors are made from hardwoods. Some older homes were built with soft pine flooring. Softwoods can be very attractive, but they're a problem to work with and maintain. They dent very easily. The very worst thing for a softwood floor (and some resilient floor coverings as well) is a high-heeled shoe, especially a spike heel. A spike heel on a softwood floor leaves the floor looking like someone beat on it with a tack hammer. There are little round dents all over it.

If you're dealing with a floor like this, you'll need to discuss its pros and cons with the homeowners. Refinishing the floor will make it more attractive, but you can't make it any more durable. If the owners go to the expense of refinishing, in order to keep it looking nice, they will have to be very careful with it. They will need to put floor protectors under the legs of heavy furniture, avoid rolling anything with metal casters over the floor, and, of course, make sure high heels stay off of it. If this is too restrictive, they'll probably be better off with another kind of flooring.

Unsalvageable Floors

There are some wood floors that are beyond repair. Usually it's because the floors have been patched too many times. This happens when several different kinds of heating systems have been installed. If the house had a floor furnace, then a gravity furnace, and then forced air, the floor will be a jumble of patches. There may be more square footage of patches than there is of flooring!

Extensive water damage can also ruin a wood floor. It can be the result of a long term roof leak or a neglected plumbing leak. Continuous moisture will cause cupping, warping, and even rot damage. The floor will be uneven and hard to walk on. You can't even carpet over a floor with this kind of damage. The warping will be felt, even through heavy carpeting and padding.

You'll need to put down a layer of underlayment to even the floor out. I always use at least ½-inch plywood. Some people recommend ¼ inch, but I don't think it feels solid enough. The ½-inch plywood does a better job of bridging little gaps caused by cupping and warping. Nail the underlayment down every 6 inches with ring-shank underlayment nails. That will give you a nice, solid floor, suitable for any kind of floor covering.

New Wood Flooring

If the homeowners really like wood floors but the existing floors can't be saved, you can install new wood flooring. If the old flooring is solid and flat, new flooring can be installed directly on top of it. Otherwise, the new flooring should be installed on top of a layer of underlayment.

There are a lot of new wood flooring products on the market. The old standby, oak tongue-and-groove strip flooring, is still available. But compared to the newer products, it's pretty expensive. Oak tongue-and-groove is also very time-consuming to install. Each piece has to be carefully fitted to the one before it, and securely nailed. That takes a lot of time, and a lot of nails. A pneumatic power nailer can speed up the job, but it will still take quite a while.

The new wood flooring products are installed differently. They're glued down, like floor tiles. Essentially, that's what they are, wooden tiles. Even if you aren't familiar with all the new products, you've probably seen wood tiles in the parquet design. They've been on the market for about 20 years. Now this type of wood tile is available in several styles, including one that looks just like oak tongue-and-groove strips.

The new flooring products are about half the thickness of oak tongue-and-groove flooring, so the manufacturers can make twice as many of them out of the same amount of raw wood. That brings the price down. There are also some that have a veneer layer, usually about ⅛ inch thick, over an inexpensive substrate, which are less expensive still.

When I first saw these tiles, I worried about their performance. After all, they're only half as thick as the old flooring. I was sure that would affect their durability. So far, however, the tiles I've put down are holding up fine. I've even seen them used in commercial applications, where they get very heavy traffic. They seem to work well, even in demanding settings.

The tiles aren't as strong as the old oak strips. However, in most modern floors, the strength comes from the subfloor, not the floor covering. If a floor needs extra strength, it's more practical to lay down another layer of plywood subfloor than to try to use the floor covering for strength.

Besides lower cost and easier installation, there's another advantage to using wood floor tiles. They're easier to replace if a tile is damaged. The bad ones can be pried out and a new one installed, just like any other type of floor tile.

❧ Installation of Wood Floor Tiles

It's important that these flooring products be installed correctly. They must be glued neatly onto a solid, level subfloor. Use the same care you would when installing any kind of floor tile.

Like many floor tiles, these products aren't supposed to be installed directly on concrete. And I know from personal experience that it's an important prohibition. I was doing some work in a conference center that had wood parquet floor tiles laid incorrectly. They were installed directly on the concrete subfloor. I noticed a few of them seemed to be a bit loose, but I didn't think much of it. I had to run an extension cord through an occupied area, so in keeping with proper safety procedures, I neatly taped the cord down to the floor with duct tape. Imagine my surprise when I pulled the tape up, and half the floor came with it! Moisture had come up through the concrete, and partially dissolved the glue holding the floor tiles down. That's a fairly common occurrence, and the reason why you're not supposed to glue tiles directly to concrete. I was really embarrassed, even though it wasn't my fault! There was so little glue left on the tiles that all it took was a tug on a piece of tape to pull them up. (No, I didn't have to replace the floor tiles.)

These chapters have covered all the basic repairs that you're likely to encounter in an older home. Assuming that the house you're working on needs only these repairs and some paint, you could be finished. That happens sometimes. More often, however, older homes need updating and improvements to make them more convenient to live in. In addition, there's always a lot of cosmetic work that you can do to transform an ordinary old house into a very special classic home. That's what we'll cover in the next chapters.

Discovering Victorian Architecture

When making changes to any house, you always need to consider its architectural style. In the previous chapters, the style of the house wasn't especially important. Our goal was simply repairing the basic mechanical and structural items, while saving any valuable assets. However, now we're looking at making physical alterations to the house that will increase convenience, or what I call *livability*. When you make these changes, you need to make sure that they will also work well from the standpoint of the style of the house.

In other words, adding a small square room off the side of a quaint old house will surely add convenience, but it might look awkward — and that doesn't provide a net improvement to the value of the home. If you add livability, but take away from the charm of the home, you really haven't gained anything. A room addition that's obviously an add-on creates a jarring effect, like a blue car with one red door. That clashing door does make the car safer, but it doesn't make it look right.

Any alterations you make should be in keeping with the original style of the house. An ideal alteration doesn't look like an alteration at all, it blends in. An architectural expert might be able to tell that it isn't original, but that isn't what's important to your work. If the owners wanted it absolutely original, you wouldn't be making any changes. You want to make changes that create a more comfortable or convenient home without spoiling the style.

Architectural Styles

Just what do we mean when we talk about style? During various periods of our history, certain architectural designs dominated particular time periods. These were modified by individual taste, finances and location, but for the most part they followed a standard pattern. When you look at an older home, you can pretty much determine when it was built by its style. We'll look at the most common styles of older homes and help you match any modifications or additions to the original.

Victorian homes were built from around 1850 to 1910. In most parts of the country, this is the oldest style you're likely to come across. If you live along the eastern seaboard, you may occasionally come across some styles that are even older, such as Federal or Greek

Figure 17-2
Smaller Queen Anne Victorian

Figure 17-1
Large Queen Anne Victorian

Revival. However, many of the concepts (although not the designs) we're going to discuss now will apply to these styles as well. Later styles, originating in homes built from 1910 to 1930, include the Craftsman home and Frank Lloyd Wright's Prairie-style home. We'll discuss modifications to those styles toward the end of the book. Anything after 1940, I consider too modern to be included among "older" homes.

The Victorian Style

Right now, let's look at the Victorian. There are actually many Victorian styles. The most common style, the one that most people think of when they hear the term *Victorian*, is the Queen Anne style. That's the style we'll be discussing in depth. Figure 17-1 is an example of a large Queen Anne Victorian home. This is a "lumber baron" mansion, built around 1880. There are several elaborate homes like this in my area of the country, most of them built by men who made their fortunes in the lumber business. They have a lot of beautiful detail work on the inside that would cost millions of dollars to duplicate today. Of course, not all Queen Anne homes were mansions. Figures 17-2 and 17-3 are more common versions of the same style. There are many more homes like these across the country than the huge mansions.

Other Victorian styles you may see are:

◆ Stick Victorian, similar to the Queen Anne style but much less elaborate (Figure 17-4)

◆ Shingle Victorian, notable for its cedar shingle siding (Figure 17-5)

◆ Richardsonian Romanesque, which features heavy masonry resembling a medieval castle (Figure 17-6 shows a side view of one of these homes)

Figure 17-3
Well-maintained Victorian home

Figure 17-4
Stick Victorian

Figure 17-5
Shingle Victorian

◆ Second Empire style, which looks like the Addams Family home from the movie

Many smaller Victorian era homes fall under the category of "folk" Victorian. These were the more moderate priced homes. Folk Victorian homes were designed by local builders, rather than architects. They used Victorian design principles, but kept the price down by making the homes less elaborate. These were the homes of the middle-class, so there are far more of them than any of the other Victorian styles.

❧ The Exterior Design of a Victorian Home

Figure 17-7 is a photograph of a small folk Victorian home. This one is nicely restored. It looks a lot like it would have looked 100 years ago. Notice the elaborate decoration. The house may be small, but it isn't plain. This home is typical of Victorian design. The Victorians loved decoration. They decorated

Figure 17-6
The side entrance, with second story sleeping porch, on a Richardsonian Romanesque style Victorian home

Figure 17-7
Small "folk Victorian" home

Figure 17-8
*Victorian home with a 1920s
porch enclosure*

everything. To them, a plain wall was an embarrassment; somebody wasn't doing their job.

Design features commonly found on Victorian homes are high, peaked roofs, towers and turrets, bay windows, wraparound porches, many exterior doors, and of course, fancy gingerbread decorations and ornamental millwork. You've probably seen homes like this, even if you live in a city where most of the building is new. That's because the Victorian style is coming back. Many builders are building brand-new Victorian-style homes. Obviously, it costs a lot more money to build a Victorian house than the less adorned designs of the modern home. All the decorations cost money. Yet, many builders consider it worthwhile.

That's an important point to remember because it proves that the Victorian style is still valuable. You might not care for it personally, but there are lots of people who do, and they're willing to pay thousands of dollars extra to get it. If you're working on a Victorian house, you want to do everything you can to preserve and enhance the original design, not destroy it.

Sometimes it's difficult to recognize a Victorian house because of all the changes that have been made to it over the years. It could have been remodeled or added onto several times. It's important to realize that just because work is old, that doesn't mean

it was part of the original design. The Victorian look was out of fashion by 1920. The oldest Victorian houses were 70 years old by then, and many were in need of major repairs. If an owner in 1920 decided it was time to update and modernize his home, then you'll find 1920s alterations on, let's say, an 1870s house.

From the outside, you're most likely to see these alterations in the porches. Porches require maintenance. If the original Victorian porch wasn't maintained, it probably needed to be replaced by 1920. A Victorian porch is distinctive and is one of the features that clearly marks a house as Victorian. It has fancy posts and railing and often very detailed trimwork. By 1920, this style was considered old-fashioned and was no longer desirable. Homeowners tried to get rid of their old-fashioned porches. They replaced them with newer designs which they thought gave their homes a more modern look. It's quite common to see a home like the one in Figure 17-8, with a 1920s porch enclosure covering up the original Victorian design.

Of course this reasoning wasn't confined to the homeowner's of the 1920s. People were constantly modernizing and updating these old homes. As a result, you'll often find layer upon layer of remodeling, each layer representing a different age. Sometimes a house is completely changed by this process, and you can only guess what the original style was.

Figures 17-9 and 17-10 are photographs of a Victorian house, though there isn't much of the original Victorian styling left. Most of the distinctive features have been removed, including all of the gingerbread. What defines the style now is the L-shape design, the ornate siding in the gable area, and the two separate entrances at the front of the house. All these are typical of Victorian styling.

Figure 17-11 would be even harder to identify, except it still has a little piece of remaining decoration in the gable. The porch on this house is gone completely. Only a well-informed observer could identify the original style of houses like these. Luckily, by

Figure 17-9
High gable with ornate siding indicates Victorian style

Figure 17-10
Double front entrances are another feature of Victorian design

the time you finish reading this book, you'll be well informed, too.

The Victorian Gold Mine

You may be tempted to say "Who cares? What difference does it make what the style used to be if it's gone now?" Well, *you* should care. It's important to determine the original style, because with a little effort you could bring that style back. The homeowners may not even be aware that they own a Victorian home. They may just think of it as an old, ugly house with no personality. If you can show them how a few changes can transform their home into a unique, beautiful and valuable property, you may turn a simple remodeling job into a project that's lucrative for both you and the owners.

Most small contractors don't recognize the possibilities in old houses. Even if they do, they don't know what work is required to restore the style to a Victorian home, or how to do the work. Their ignorance gives you a big advantage. You won't have a lot of people bidding against you. The only ones who really understand the possibilities involved in these homes are the big design/build firms. Their architects know design and style and how to recreate it. They do fine restoration work, but they charge tremendous amounts of money for it. Their overhead is huge — architects do not work cheap. It might actually be to your advantage to have your

Figure 17-11
Missing porch makes Victorian design harder to identify

customers get estimates from a couple of these companies. After they get a quote of $100,000 for a job you're quoting at $10,000, you'll hear fewer complaints about your price.

The reason it's important to understand Victorian style is because these homes are often located in prime real estate areas. If they can be restored to their original beauty, they're often worth huge amounts of money. If they're left alone and unrestored, looking like "just any old house," they may sell for a only fraction of what they could otherwise bring.

253

If the homeowners don't believe that restoring the original style of their house will dramatically raise its value, have them check with a real estate agent. Show them a similar house that has been restored, and let the real estate agent give them a price comparison. In a nice neighborhood, a restored house will sell for at least $100,000 more than a house that hasn't been restored. Most remodeling prospects look at your $10,000 remodeling proposal differently when they learn it'll add $100,000 to the house's value.

If you understand Victorian design, you'll be in a position to make the homeowners a lot of money. For a relatively modest investment in exterior trim and design items, you can tremendously increase the value of a house. This is a perfect example of "maximum value remodeling." You can charge the homeowners a lot of money to do the work, and they'll still come out way ahead on the deal.

⁊ Style Elements

In order to understand any older home, you need to try to put yourself in the place of the original designer. It's hard to work on a Victorian home if you don't understand what its design was meant to accomplish. Some of the features on an older home may look like a lot of nonsense to you, but they're not. They were all put there for a reason that was practical for that time. Lifestyles have changed tremendously since Victorian times, and some features that were useful then are hard to understand now.

The key to understanding Victorian design is remembering that many conveniences that we take for granted today, didn't exist then. Victorian people tried to accomplish the same things we do, but they often had to do them in very roundabout ways. Many of their designs are actually very clever ways of dealing with problems that were difficult to solve at the time. Once you understand how these designs work, you'll admire the cleverness of the designers who came up with them.

Recreating the original look of an older house often requires some detective work. You have to look for the little clues that indicate what the house looked like, and these clues aren't always easy to find. They may be buried beneath several layers of remodeling. It helps if you familiarize yourself with the elements of Victorian design. The best way to do this is to look at Victorian houses, if not in person, at least in pictures. I've tried to include a lot of pictures in this book. If you look at them closely, you can begin to get a feel for the Victorian style.

You can also find many excellent books on Victorian homes in bookstores and at the library which will help you. A couple of my favorites are *Painted Ladies* and *Daughters of Painted Ladies,* by Elizabeth Pomada and Michael Larsen, published by E. P. Dutton. They're full of pictures of beautiful Victorian mansions, restored to their original designs and colors.

Some of the colors may look pretty wild, but historians have proven that these were the original colors. Victorian houses weren't designed to be painted all white, like so many of them are today. The Victorians loved decorations, and white features on a white background don't show up. Why would you want to carefully sculpt decorative features, and then have them fade into a neutral background? If someone went to the trouble to create intricate decorations, you can bet they wanted them to be noticed! Painting them contrasting colors was the best way to make them stand out.

Another book I use as a reference is *Field Guide to the American Home,* by Virginia and Lee McAlester, published by Knopf. This one contains extensive black and white photos of all the different styles of American architecture and explains how to identify each type, and their important features. It doesn't give you the colors, but it's a great help in identifying architectural designs.

There's really no substitute for seeing these homes in person. If you can, spend some time driving around Victorian neighborhoods in your own area. Better still, get out of your car and walk around. The closer

Figure 17-12
Original Victorian gingerbread

Figure 17-13
Gingerbread trim makes this little house stand out

you are to these houses, the more you'll be able to see how the design elements fit together. You will get a feeling for what the overall effect is supposed to be. That's the best way I know to prepare yourself for remodeling/restoration work.

Exterior Decoration

When most people think of Victorian style, they think of "gingerbread" decorations. These are the elaborate little millwork pieces that are usually found all over Victorian homes. These pieces may be small, but they're very important. They're what identifies the house as Victorian. The house in Figure 17-12 has a lot of beautiful gingerbread and trim work around the porch, windows and gables. It isn't a big elaborate home, but as you can see, even a moderate house can be artistically and gracefully transformed by its gingerbread decorations. The house in Figure 17-13 would be very plain and totally lacking in personality without all of its elaborate trim.

Gingerbread is such a powerful design element that you can make almost anything look Victorian by adding decorative pieces to it. This is actually quite a common practice today. I've seen countless modern buildings with Victorian gingerbread added to provide an "old-fashioned" look. This isn't the best use of gingerbread millwork, but it does give you an idea of what a powerful design statement it can make.

The impact that these decorations have on the style of the house is the very reason that many Victorian homes are without gingerbread today. When Victorian architecture went out of style, many people removed the gingerbread, hoping to give their houses a more modern look. At the time, this was considered a big improvement. The home in Figure 17-14 was once a Victorian mansion. It looks very strange without any decorative trim. The elaborate style, with its distinctive tower, is out of place without the ornamental accessories which define its architectural type.

The Layout

In some cases, the owners of older homes have been so successful at updating their homes that it's very hard to identify the original style. However, the shape of the house will usually identify it as a Victorian, if it is

Figure 17-14
*Victorian mansion stripped
of its former beauty*

one. While the former owners may have changed a lot of the trim, they couldn't change the basic shape of the house.

Victorian homes are generally laid out in a cross shape, or a 90-degree L-shape, with an overall look of a house that's tall and thin. This design layout went out of style around 1915. Figure 17-15 is an example of a house that has been stripped of its decoration but still retains its distinctive Victorian shape. It's tall and thin with a pointed gable roof that clearly identifies its original style. Houses shaped like this are always Victorians, no matter how plain they appear to be. You won't find this shape on any other type of house, with the exception of a new Victorian reproduction.

The Porch

Victorians generally had one of two types of front porch. The first is a big, wraparound porch that covered part of the front and all of one side of the house. The second is a smaller stoop-type porch, often so small that it may only have served as a covered

entrance at the front door. Original Victorians didn't have broad front porches that cover the entire front of the house, unless they extended around to the side as well. Broad front porches are typical of the later Craftsman and Prairie styles. As we mentioned earlier, however, many people replaced their Victorian wraparound porch or stoop with a broad Craftsman style front porch in keeping with the styles of the 1920s.

You will sometime find both a wraparound and a stoop porch on the same house. The wraparound porch will always be in the front of the house, extending down one side. In that case the stoop porches will be at the back and side doors. A proper Victorian house had some type of porch at every door to protect the interior from the outside elements.

Another type of highly distinctive porch that you'll find on a Victorian home is an upstairs dust porch or an upstairs sleeping porch. These may have been integrated into the design of the downstairs porch, being placed directly above the front or rear entry porch, or they can simply project out from the second story, as in Figure 17-16.

It's very common to find the porches on Victorian homes missing, especially the side and back porches. If porches aren't maintained, they deteriorate. They've had plenty

Figure 17-15
*Victorian home has lost its
distinctive identity*

of time to rot off in the last 100 years, and since porch styles have changed there was no urgency to replace them.

Figure 17-17 shows a house in which this kind of porch deterioration is taking place. The front porch can no longer be used; the steps have either fallen off or have been removed. The porch itself is rot damaged and beginning to sag. If someone doesn't repair it, it will collapse in a few years. The rear porch has been enclosed and is now used as the main entrance to the house. This is the kind of evolution of use that changes the style of a house. When the front porch is gone, it will be a lot harder to tell that this house is a Victorian.

If you look closely at a remodeled Victorian house, you may be able to figure out where the original porches used to be. The porches were designed to fit nicely into the angles of the house. A small area with only one door probably had a simple stoop porch. If the area is on the rear or side of the house, then you can be sure it was a stoop porch. Victorians often connected two or more doors with one porch. A wide area, especially one with a door on each end, probably had a porch that connected the doors. A door at the side of the house may have been connected to the front of the house with a wraparound porch. Keep in mind though, that a wraparound porch is found only in the front and along one side, never at the rear of a house. Any door leading to the exterior upstairs logically opened to a porch. The door may have been sealed off if the porch is missing, or the porch may have become a room addition.

The Doors

Victorian houses have lots of doors. In some cases, the doors are very close together, so that two adjoining rooms may each have separate entrances from the outside. This may not seem very sensible today, but at one time, these separate doors were quite useful. One of their functions was to keep formal and informal areas separate.

Victorian houses all had formal front parlors with their own entrance from the

Figure 17-16
Elaborately decorated dust porch projects out from the front of this home

Figure 17-17
Front steps have been removed from deteriorating entry porch

outside. The room was used for entertaining guests and was furnished with the family's very best pieces. The guests entered directly into the parlor, which was kept closed off from the other rooms in the house. The family used a separate entry and a second parlor for everyday activities. That way, the formal parlor was always in nice order, even if the rest of the house had that "lived-in" look. Figure 17-18 shows a Victorian home, in

Figure 17-18
*Well-maintained Victorian home
still has two front entries*

Figure 17-19
*Trapdoor leads to basement of this 1888
Victorian home*

almost original condition, that still has its two front doors. Many homes like this have had one of the doors blocked off.

Victorians had a hard time keeping their houses clean. They didn't have any of our modern cleaning devices, such as vacuum cleaners. Rugs had to be beaten to get the dirt out of them. Everything else had to be swept, mopped or laboriously scrubbed by hand. Upstairs dust porches allowed them to sweep dirt out, and shake out rugs and dust mops without carrying them downstairs. They also kept the dirt down by limiting the number of people tracking through the house. There were separate doors for downstairs service areas so that the dirt could be swept out. Anything dirty that had to come in didn't have to go through the main living areas of the house. Vegetables from the garden, wood or coal for the fire, even the laundry, came and went through side and back service doors.

The basement had a separate entrance, too. That's because most basements had dirt floors, and so were probably the dirtiest part of the house. In very early Victorian houses, the basement was only used as a root cellar, to store potatoes, onions, apples and other foods which would keep without refrigeration in a dark, cool place. It was a natural refrigerator.

Later, when these houses acquired central heating, coal was stored in the basement as well. Tons of coal came and went through the basement, getting soot and coal dust over everything it came near. I still find coal dust hiding in little nooks and crannies in these old houses, even when there hasn't been any coal in the house for 50 years. Of course, the last thing a Victorian homemaker wanted was to have coal dust tracked through the house, so the basements usually had an outside entrance.

Figure 17-19 shows a typical trapdoor basement entrance. The door lifts up from the floor, allowing access to the stairs going down into the basement. Figure 17-20 is another view of the trapdoor showing the multiple access routes to this basement. The trapdoor is located just inside the house, with an outside service door directly at the front of the stairway. There's a second door approaching from the kitchen. The kitchen has its own separate outside entrance as well. All these doors ensured that foot traffic was routed by specific needs, helping to keep the home clean.

Once you're able to visualize how the Victorians lived, you'll get a feel for the way Victorian houses were laid out. Then you'll be able to look at a heavily-remodeled Victorian and say "There should be a door here" or "There should be a porch in this area." And when you begin working on the house, you'll run into the remains of that torn-out porch or missing door just where you thought it should be.

Figure 17-20

Trapdoor leading to basement can be accessed from inside and outside entances

Renovations in Historic Neighborhoods

You can sometimes date a house by the size and position of the lot it was built on. If a Victorian house was built in a city, it was probably on a very small lot. In many older cities, the houses actually touched, creating row houses. Even if they didn't touch, there might be only a narrow walkway between them. In the country, the lots were considerably larger, since there were fewer people and less demand. Of course, there were many factors over time which influenced lot sizes.

🐚 Urban Growth

The growth rate of a community affected the way neighborhoods developed. In some old communities, a house that appears to have been built in the city may have actually been built out in the country. Most cities have grown tremendously since 1880, with much of the growth taking place around the turn of the century. So a house that was built outside the city in the 1880s may have become part of the city by 1900, with newer homes built up all around it. Since Victorian architecture was still in style in 1900, it may appear that all the houses are the same age. However, 20 years may have made a big difference in the space available for building. A house built in 1880 may have been on a generous, country-sized lot, while the newer houses around it may be on tiny city lots.

To further complicate the situation, the generous country lot may have been cut up and sold to others when land prices skyrocketed in 1900. If a house was sitting way back off the main road, even the land in front the house may have been divided up and sold off. The house may now face the wrong way, with an access road fronting the side of the house. This can really create design problems.

The evolution of the lot becomes very important if you're working in an urban area that's part of a downtown historic district. These districts try to preserve their original look. But what time factor do you use to determine what was "original?" Is it the way the house was originally built in 1880, or the way it looked in 1900?

An excellent example of this dilemma is the Cultural Center area of Detroit. In 1880, it was an area of gracious mansions located two miles outside of the city. The lumber barons who built these homes commuted downtown each day by horse and buggy. The area was very country-like, with a lot of open space. The poor and middle class, who couldn't afford to keep horses, had to live closer to the city. There was no public transportation, and the automobile hadn't been invented yet. Most jobs were downtown, and two miles was too far for most people to commute on foot, especially in a Detroit winter.

By 1900, this had all changed. Detroit had experienced a population explosion, and public transportation, via streetcar, was available out to the Cultural Center area and beyond. This meant that workers could live miles away from their jobs, and commute to the city, just like the rich folks. There was a tremendous building boom, and the Cultural Center area rapidly filled up with apartment buildings and small, single-family homes.

The rich abandoned their homes to the incoming middle class and moved further out into the country. They didn't want to live in the same neighborhood as ordinary people. They built new mansions, which were also gobbled up by the city over the next 20 years. This pattern repeated itself over and over, until there were five neighborhoods of country mansions incorporated into the Detroit Metropolitan area. A new area of executive mansions, even farther out in the country, is being built at this very moment.

Urban decay is not a new phenomenon. The Cultural Center area was experiencing urban decay as early as 1900! This process makes renovating historic urban properties very difficult. In order to restore an 1880s mansion to its original grace, you might have to tear down several smaller 1900 era homes that are in the way. However, the smaller homes have historic value, too. This can be a real headache for everyone involved.

This scenario isn't limited to Detroit. Almost all major industrial cities have downtown historic districts, with similar problems of evolution. If you understand how the changes took place over time, you'll be a lot better prepared to deal with them.

Small Towns

Urban decay hasn't been as big a problem in small towns. Many towns never experienced the kind of population explosion that leads to urban decay. The land was never in such great demand that it became necessary to divide up large parcels and build smaller houses on the lots belonging to larger, older homes. The lots usually remained a generous size, as large or larger than modern lots.

However, urban expansion may have caused some of these small towns to become suburbs of today's cities. The Victorian neighborhoods in these suburbs often consist of the most valuable real estate in the entire metropolitan area.

I like to look for homes to renovate in suburban areas where there hasn't been a lot of change over the years. This is where I find the most perfectly-preserved Victorian homes. Areas that were wealthy in 1880, but haven't had much money since, haven't undergone as much updating as areas that have experienced periods of prosperity and growth. You can often find fabulous Victorian mansions in need of repair. Many are being bought and renovated by people who don't have a lot of money, but appreciate the beauty and value of older homes. These homes are perfect targets for your brand of remodeling.

Chapter 18

Restoring Victorian Exteriors

*A*s we discussed in the last chapter, you should consider the overall design of a house before making any changes that affect its exterior. Since we're going through these jobs in the order in which you'd actually do them, now's the time to plan the entire project. You don't have to select all the final colors and trim at this time, but you need to have a clear idea of how the finished project will look. You can't start tearing into things without understanding how all the pieces are all going to fit together.

This may seem obvious, but I've seen projects that were done piecemeal, without a clear plan. Each modification was made without any thought to the changes that would follow. When all the little jobs were completed, the home was a patchwork of alterations that didn't go together and didn't suit the overall design of the home.

Designing Alterations

Essentially, what we're talking about here is designing alterations, not just making them. Many remodeling companies offer *design/build* services. Some have registered architects who do the actual designing. That's

nice, but as you might imagine, it runs up the cost substantially. The average middle-class customer can't afford expensive design services, and there are very few companies that can offer these services on a moderate-priced job. Most companies are looking for the big jobs, where they can make big profits. They certainly aren't going to include any design consultations on a job where the profit margin is already limited.

You don't have to be an architect to offer customers basic advice about design. Of course, you're not a professional designer, and you might prefer to have the customers make all the design decisions for themselves; it's certainly a lot simpler that way. However, remodeling is a very competitive business. If you *can* offer ideas and advice about design, you'll distinguish yourself from your competitors. As you probably know, most small contractors don't do design work.

Let's say a homeowner is asking for estimates on a particular job. Rather than simply submit the lowest bid for that job, you may be able to suggest an improved design, one that's better suited to the home than the homeowner's idea. Now you have a whole new ball game. You're no longer competing on price alone; the issue becomes one of design as well.

Figure 18-1
Victorian fixer-upper in need of restoration

look. If you corrected these three problems, you would have a restored Victorian beauty, at least from the outside.

Of course, these are big jobs, and not the kind of work you can do cheap. But there is so much to gain! Right now the house is an eyesore. But the same house restored to its original Victorian look will be a prime piece of property. It could be worth more than two or three times its present value. There's a lot of profit here for somebody — maybe you. Houses like this one present a tremendous remodeling opportunity. Someday, someone will want to restore it, and there will be a lot of money in it for the contractor who knows how to do the work. All you have to do is see the potential, and *show* it to the owners.

Of course, there's always the chance that the homeowner will steal your idea and have someone else build it. That can happen, especially if you quote a very high price for the job. However, if your price is close to everybody else's, it makes more sense for the homeowner to have you do the job. After all, you thought of it, you bid it, and you have the knowledge to carry it through. If the homeowner has someone else do it, they may or may not get it right. It's a lot easier to have you do it, and most people will be willing to pay a little more for someone who has really good ideas.

❧ Recognizing the Potential in a House

If you look at a Victorian house like the one in Figure 18-1, your first reaction might be "What in the world am I going to do with this thing? It's a mess!" It's true, it is a mess. However, a lot of what it needs are just simple repairs, the kind you'd do to any house. From the standpoint of style, however, there are really only three things wrong with it. It needs new siding, the porches need to be replaced and restyled, and it needs some Victorian gingerbread to give it a finished

Improvements: Style vs. Livability

Unless an older home has been updated recently, it's going to need some livability improvements. By livability, I mean the everyday conveniences and little luxuries that make a house pleasant to live in. A good example of a livability improvement is the addition of a second bathroom to a house that has only one. This would be an essential improvement to a large house. Having only one bathroom in a home otherwise designed for several people is very inconvenient.

The main reason most owners decide to do some remodeling is because there's a problem with their home. They either need some serious repair or they're anxious to improve the living conditions in their house. If they can afford it, they'd usually like to fix up the exterior, too. Here is where the dilemma of style vs. livability crops up, and there are a lot of factors that will determine how you should proceed. Will restoring the original design of a Victorian house improve the home's livability? Very often, the answer is no. So what do you do? This a more frequently a problem with the interior, but it can affect what you do to the exterior as well.

Figure 18-2
*Many of the special features of
this Victorian home are hidden under
the aluminum siding*

Figure 18-3
*This house has especially nice decorations
above and below the gable-end windows*

❧ Siding Designs

When you stand back and look at a house, the first thing you'll notice is the condition of the siding. Like the home in Figure 18-2, the original siding, with all its decorative features, has probably been covered over sometime during the life of the house. If the present siding needs to be replaced, the homeowners will have to decide whether to have you try to restore the original wood siding, or simply put on new vinyl siding. To be absolutely authentic, you'd restore the original wood, but that may not be what the homeowners want to do. Keeping up a wood exterior involves a lot of maintenance.

Before they make their final decision, check and see what condition the original siding is in, and if it has any kind of ornamentation. Victorian houses often had beautifully ornate wood designs worked into the siding. The best place to look for these decorations is on the most visible areas of the house. You're not likely, for example, to find much in the way of decoration in the rear of the house, or in other areas that aren't clearly visible. Look for decorations on the front of the house, especially at the top of the gable.

This is where you'll often find contrasting siding, like fish-scale shingles. As you continue down the gable area, you may find other decorations, such as those above and below the windows on the little house in Figure 18-3. Look also at the area around the porch, or where you think the porch used to be. This is another favorite spot for fancy millwork and other decorations.

If you find decorations like these, the homeowners have a more difficult decision to make. On one hand, they can restore the siding and paint it in contrasting colors, like the original Victorian houses. This will create a gorgeous effect, but it's very expensive to do. Elaborate paint jobs aren't cheap. Painting a home like the ones you see in *Painted Ladies* can easily cost $20,000, and it's very hard to find a painter who knows how to do it. Also, painting is a continuing expense, because it will need to be redone every few years. This adds up to a huge amount of money.

The alternative is to cover everything over with vinyl siding. Vinyl siding requires no maintenance, and costs a lot less to install than a fancy paint job. It would also provide the opportunity to add some Styrofoam insulation to the house, under the siding. This might be very worthwhile if the house is cold and drafty. The downside is that you'd be covering up desirable features and losing the opportunity to increase the beauty and value of the house.

You'll find that many people will have strong feelings about this, one way or the other. Some love Victorian decorations and will want to go with restoring the original look. Others couldn't care less about the decor, but love the idea of easy-care vinyl siding. If the homeowners don't have definite ideas about what they want to do, they may turn to you for advice on this question. What should you say?

Weighing the Costs and Benefits

If you approach this question from a logical point of view, your advice will depend on the homeowners financial circumstances and the rest of the neighborhood. Restoring the original siding will be a costly initial investment, as well as a continuing expense, but it will create a beautiful, authentically Victorian look. However, if the homeowner is short of money, vinyl may be what they can afford right now.

If their financial situation is okay, the neighborhood may be the determining factor. The value of any improvement in a house depends on the importance that the people who live in the area put on it. Neighborhoods tend to be made up of people with similar values. So if the house is in a middle-class neighborhood, the people who live there probably share middle-class values. If it's a wealthy area, they may have a different set of values. Wealthy people don't usually live in middle-class neighborhoods, and vice versa. So if the house you're working on is in a middle-class area, don't try to sell the owners on ideas that don't fit the area. They'll never get their money out of the improvements. No matter how nice a house is, it will never be worth much more than the other homes in the area.

When it comes to remodeling, you have to give people what they want, and no more. Middle-class people have different priorities than the wealthy. If you're working in a middle-class neighborhood, people may appreciate a fancy paint job and think it's very nice, but they may not think it's worth the expense. They have more urgent needs for that much money, and would probably rather have vinyl siding.

Wealthy people, on the other hand, love this kind of work. Drive through any neighborhood of upscale older homes, and you'll see what I mean. All the houses are elaborately decorated, painted in eye-catching colors, and very well maintained. These people pay a lot of money to keep up this kind of decor, and they expect their neighbors to do the same. Clearly, if you're working on a house in an upscale neighborhood, it would be best to restore the wood siding. If you don't, you're throwing away money. Original Victorian features will tremendously increase the value of a house in a very nice area, but vinyl siding will lower its value. Wealthy people prefer natural materials, like wood. To them, vinyl siding appears cheap.

Finding a Compromise

There are many neighborhoods that can go either way. They're the upper-middle class areas or the neighborhoods that are in the process of being restored. Each new restoration in an area like this increases the value of all the homes around it. If the homeowner is in this situation, and would like to restore the home but just can't afford to do a complete or authentic renovation right now, you may be able to suggest a compromise. There are vinyl sidings that reproduce some of the styles that were used by the Victorians. They come in a variety of colors and textures. One source for these is:

Wolverine Vinyl Siding
17199 Laurel Park Drive North
Livonia, MI 48152-2679

You can call them for a free brochure at 1-800-521-9020. Figure 18-4 is an example of the look that you can achieve with these new vinyl siding products. Figure 18-5 is a close up view of Wolverine's rounded clapboard vinyl siding, and Figure 18-6 shows their reproduction of the fish-scale shingles that Victorians loved to use. These examples are from the Wolverine Vinyl Siding Restoration Collection and are intended to be faithful reproductions of turn-of-the-century styles.

Not only can you recreate the look of Victorian siding using vinyl, you can also reproduce the multicolored painting style that the Victorians liked as well. These siding products come in a variety of authentic colors. In this way, you can provide your customers with some of the beauty of the Victorian styling while giving them the easy maintenance and lower cost advantages of vinyl.

You can also recreate an authentic style by adding a little decorative trimwork to a house whose trimwork is completely gone or that never had any decorations to begin with. Remember, not every Victorian house was elaborately decorated. Fancy trimwork was expensive, even then. There's no rule that says you can't make the house better than original! Now is your chance to make up for any shortcomings in the original design. You can add the kind of decoration that the original house might have had if the owners had been able to afford them. Adding a small section of varied siding in the gable area dresses up the exterior. Top this with a little gingerbread, and you've produced a whole new look to a plain Victorian. (We'll discuss adding gingerbread towards the end of this chapter.)

Courtesy of Wolverine Vinyl Siding

Figure 18-4
Vinyl siding products reproduce Victorian look

Another compromise is to restore small areas on the house that have decorative siding, and side over the plain parts of the walls. You have to carefully trim around the decorative features so they remain exposed. This isn't always an easy thing to accomplish. It works best with features that stand out from

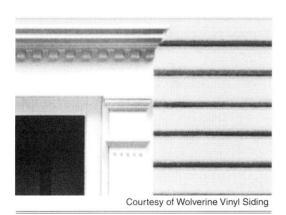
Courtesy of Wolverine Vinyl Siding

Figure 18-5
Vinyl clapboard siding and trim accessories

Courtesy of Wolverine Vinyl Siding

Figure 18-6
Vinyl "fish-scale" siding decorates gable area

Figure 18-7
*Decorative wood trim on this bay
can be restored*

Figure 18-8
*Re-siding around this bay window
would not be difficult*

the surface, like the bay windows shown in Figures 18-7 and 18-8. The wall behind these windows is just plain clapboard siding. If you put new siding on the wall, and restored the wood around the bay window, the owners would have the advantages of new siding without losing the unique features of this window. Of course, the bay window would still have to be painted every couple of years, but it's a lot less trouble to paint one window area than it is to paint a whole house.

Finally, if the present homeowners decide to put siding over the existing decorations, they shouldn't feel bad about it. It's the same as putting carpet down over oak flooring. The fancy wood features aren't gone, they're just in storage. They'll always be there, in case anyone wants to uncover them and restore them in the future. Having them is an asset that adds value to the house, even if the asset isn't currently being used.

❧ The Porch

The next major area you may have to deal with in a renovation is the porch. If the porch is a mess, like the one in Figure 18-1 at the beginning of this chapter, you don't have

to worry too much about what you do. Just about anything will be an improvement.

However, if you're working on a house like the one in Figure 18-9, the porch becomes more of a problem. This house originally had an elaborate Victorian wraparound porch covered with gingerbread, perhaps similar to the one shown in Figure 18-10. The original porch in Figure 18-9 was replaced with a cement porch around 1940, and it was enclosed with aluminum windows in the 1960s. This porch is in perfect repair. Even though the style doesn't match the rest of the house, it provides useful living space for the homeowners. Should you suggest that it be torn off and replaced with an Victorian porch?

If you want to reproduce an authentic look, I guess you could do that. But tearing off this porch will actually reduce the livability of this house. A glassed-in porch is much more useful than an original, open Victorian porch. It can be used later in the season, and it helps keep the house insulated from the cold in winter. Unfortunately, it's not very attractive.

Once again, the key to determining the right way to deal with this situation is the neighborhood. In a wealthy neighborhood, this porch would look tacky. It would substantially lower the value of the house. For the rich, a porch is primarily a design element. They're not going to sit out on the porch to do their chores or knit or paint or play with their children. They aren't interested in a porch for its livability value. They want a porch that's a beautiful addition to their home. This porch isn't beautiful.

In an upscale neighborhood, it would be better to demolish this porch and replace it with an elaborate Victorian porch. No matter how much it cost, it would increase the value of the house even more.

In a middle-class neighborhood, it's probably better to leave the porch the way it is. Middle-class people actually use and enjoy their porches. The increased space and convenience of an enclosed porch will appeal to them. An elaborate Victorian porch may also appeal to them, but not if they have to pay to demolish one good porch to build another. And in an average neighborhood, buyers won't pay extra for an elaborate Victorian porch, so it wouldn't increase the value of the house in proportion to the cost.

Discovering the Original Design

If you decide to restore the original porch design, you'll need to discover just what the design was. This is a lot like being an archaeologist and trying to recreate a lost city from a few remains. Uncovering the clues to old architectural designs will make you feel like the "Indiana Jones of urban archaeology."

Using the historical information you have about the house (sometimes you can find old photographs), or the information I have given you, try to locate where the original porch went. The existing porch may or may not be original. If it conforms to Victorian styles and fits in well with the design, then it's

Figure 18-9
Original wraparound porch has been enclosed

probably original. If it doesn't, it's probably a replacement. Check for marks on the walls or other indications that will show you where the original porch may have been.

Figure 18-11 shows the interior wall of an enclosed porch. This is a good example of the kind of detective work you can do. In the corner of the porch is a fancy Victorian turned post. It doesn't make sense for someone to pay

Figure 18-10
Victorian wraparound porch

267

Figure 18-11
Decorative turned post indicates porch was originally open

for a turned post and then build a wall over it, so you know that the post was probably there before the walls. The siding for the walls on both sides of the post is the narrow tongue-and-groove design that was popular during the 1920s. These clues tell the story of

Figure 18-12
One side of this wraparound porch has been enclosed

the porch. It was originally an open Victorian stoop porch which was enclosed during the 1920s. If you removed the walls and replaced the missing gingerbread, you'd have the original porch back.

If there's no hint of the original porch, use the logic of the home's design to figure it out. You know the following rules about Victorian porch design:

◆ A Victorian house should have either a wraparound porch or a stoop porch.

◆ The porch should fit into an angle created by the wings of the house.

◆ Two or more doors, fairly close to each other, are often connected by a porch.

◆ All doors should have some type of porch.

Using these rules, you can figure out where porches should be, even if there are no signs of porches there now.

What if you're wrong? What if there never was a porch in the location you choose? It doesn't matter! The object is to create a nice-looking house in the Victorian style. If it didn't have a porch there before, it probably should have. Therefore, you're improving the design in addition to restoring it.

Porch Decorations

Victorian porches were always elaborately decorated. Victorians used the porch as a showplace. Knowing this also helps you figure out where the front porches should be located. They should be placed in such a way that their decorations are highly visible.

The pillars on the Victorian porch were always elaborately milled. They were never plain 4 x 4s. If you see 4 x 4 pillars, you know they're replacements. The railings were always elaborate as well. The balusters would have been ornate spindles, or possibly even fretwork, but never just plain 2 x 2s. The porch in Figure 18-12 was originally a wraparound porch. The side porch on the right has been enclosed to make a room. The porch has its original turned pillars, but the railings and balusters have obviously been replaced.

Figure 18-13
*Beautiful wraparound porch with
ornate pillars and balusters*

Figure 18-14
*Lattice is not appropriate for
Victorian porch*

Figure 18-13 shows a beautifully maintained Victorian porch. Notice the pillars and ornate spindles for balusters. I'm sure that the original porch for the home in Figure 18-12 was very similar to this one.

Some people use preassembled lattice, as in Figure 18-14, to fill in the space between the handrails and the porch deck. This is *not* a Victorian style. It looks tacky on any porch, but especially bad on a Victorian. I think a lot of people believe that if a material like lattice was used at all in Victorian design, it can be used anywhere and it will look right. They haven't done their homework. Victorians only used lattice on the underskirts of the porch, below the porch deck, to fill in between the piers of posts. It's perfectly appropriate when it's used there. Lattice is a handy material, but it's often overused. It should *never* take the place of balusters. When I find it used that way, I always remove it.

A Porch Renovation

Figure 18-15 shows a Victorian house that I worked on recently. All of the outstanding features that should have been part of this simple stoop porch were missing. And, as you can see in Figure 18-16, someone had used lattice to fill in for the balusters. You know that

I had my work cut out for me! The porch had undergone some repairs and replacements over the years, and was not in very good shape. I had to do some repairs as well as restyling, and keep all the work within a reasonable, middle-class budget.

Figure 18-17 shows the roof overhang with the corner post missing. I braced the end and added a fancy turned post for support (Figure 18-18), trying to match one remaining original post at the other end of the porch. I left the two plain 4 x 4 posts in place. I replaced the lattice with turned balusters and added some gingerbread. You can see in Figure 18-19 how much these modifications improved the design of the porch. I only used lattice for the underskirts. Figure 18-20 shows another view of the completed porch. It's a big improvement, isn't it?

The Cost — I bought the post and the turned balusters at Builder's Square, but you can probably find them at Home Depot, Dixieline Lumber, Home Base or any other building supply store. They're both stock items. The post cost $25 and the balusters ran about $4 each. Making the railings was the most time-consuming part of the job. I had to make five of them (some for the back porch

Figure 18-15
Victorian house needs to be "restyled"

Figure 18-16
Porch railings need to be replaced

as well), for a total of 36 feet. It took ten 2 x 4s (at $2 each) routered into nice-looking handrails and 90 balusters to complete the job. Assembly took about 12 hours. Fortunately, I was able to do 90 percent of the work in my workshop, and then take the finished pieces to the house for the final installation. That was very helpful since I did this work in the winter, during a break in the weather. The total material cost for the railings and balusters was $405.

All of the gingerbread on the porch was gone. The only thing left were little marks where the decorations had once been. I guessed that it needed spandrels and brackets, and estimated the size. I used easily-available, inexpensive styles, again from Builder's Square. It took about 30 feet of spandrel, costing $300, and eight brackets, costing $120, for a total of $420 for decorative materials. Putting up the spandrels and brackets took about eight hours, including simple painting. A fancy, multicolored paint job would have taken longer. When I was installing the decorations, I was surprised to discover that they lined up exactly with the old marks. The original decorations may not have been exactly the same as mine, but they must have been pretty close! As you can see from this project,

Figure 18-17
Porch overhang needs repair and new corner post added for support

Figure 18-18
Rebuilt overhang with fancy turned post and new gingerbread decorations

recreating Victorian porch design isn't as hard or as expensive as you might think.

Repairs to the porch roof and supports cost $50 and took about four hours to complete. If you add all the material costs together for the whole job, it comes out to $875. My total labor for this porch amounted to about 24 hours.

In order to make good money on a job like this, you should charge at least $2,000. That would come out to about $50 an hour for your labor. Is the porch worth it? Definitely! It makes the house far more attractive and adds tremendously to its value. You could charge twice that amount and it would still be a good deal for the homeowners. In an upscale neighborhood, this job could easily raise the value of the house $20,000, or ten times the cost, often even more. For work like this, the homeowner will come out ahead in almost any area. If you point this fact out, the work will be a lot easier to sell.

The homeowners on this particular job were on a tight budget, so I kept the costs down by using standard trim items that are available at any home store. The problem with using these is that everyone has access to them. If there are a lot of homes in the area undergoing renovation, you can end up with a house that looks a lot like everybody else's. If you want to guarantee an individual look, you need to use less common types of trim. You can order unique trim pieces from specialty woodworking shops. Of course it will cost you two or three times what I paid for the trim on this porch, but the result will be striking.

When I first started doing porch restorations, very few people were into renovating homes in my area. It wasn't important to look for any really unique materials. Now, restored Victorian porches are becoming more and more common, so I try to use better-quality trim whenever I can so that my work stands out from the others. We'll discuss Victorian gingerbread and where to buy it a little later in this chapter.

Upstairs Porches

If the house has an upstairs porch, it should be trimmed out exactly the same as the downstairs porch. You should make it a mirror image of the downstairs porch.

Figure 18-19
Railings and decorative spandrels and brackets give porch a new style

Figure 18-20
Restyled "Victorian" porch

Figure 18-21
Older home has no obvious Victorian features

Victorians like the "mirror image" effect. You'll often see Victorian designs repeated over and over, sometimes the same, and sometimes upside down, as though the downstairs is a reflections of the upstairs.

The important idea in decorating porches is to stick with one theme. If you use small spandrels and fan brackets on one porch, you must use them all over. You can't switch to a different pattern on another porch. If you

Figure 18-22
Parlor door sealed off from outside

do, the porch will look like an add-on, instead of an original. Always pick a design that you can continue and repeat throughout the entire house.

🙠 Doors

One of the more unique Victorian features, the multiple entrance doors, has disappeared from many older homes. By the middle of this century, people no longer had any use for all the doors that the Victorians were so fond of. Having too many doors creates drafts and interferes with furniture placement, so the extra doors were simply closed off and sided over. You may be able to find marks on the walls, either interior or exterior, to indicate where these doors were. If not, you can guess. There should be an entrance door for the front parlor, and another entrance door for the rest of the house, as well as doors for the kitchen, the basement and perhaps another side or back door.

If these extra doors have just been blocked off, should you restore them? This is another area where livability and style may disagree. Let's face it, the people who closed off the doors were right. All these doors are a nuisance. They have no function in terms of modern lifestyles.

However, these drawbacks are also what makes having multiple doors unique. Since most people have had their extra doors blocked off, a house that still has all its doors becomes special. It might be the only one in the area to have them. The doors make a strong style statement, and have a lot of visual impact. Everybody notices them. Distinctive features like these help make an ordinary house exceptional.

So now you have yet another confusing problem to deal with. Should you restore the doors or not? You can decide this one the same way you decided on the other issues. What kind of neighborhood is the house in? Is it an upscale, historic neighborhood, where authentic features are highly prized? If so, restore the doors. The added property value will more than make up for any inconve-

Figure 18-23
Front porch before

Figure 18-24
Parlor door entrance restored

nience. In a middle-class neighborhood, however, people generally prefer livability to unusual style, so don't bother restoring the doors. The owners will dislike the cost and inconvenience more than they will appreciate the style.

Figure 18-21 shows a fairly typical older home. It appears to be a simple design, with no outstanding characteristics. The front porch was restyled around 1920, and new siding was added some time later. Aside from the shape of the house, there aren't any obvious Victorian features. When I went inside the house however, I found an unused parlor door (shown in Figure 18-22), that had been sided over and closed off from the outside. Figure 18-23 shows a view of the front entry door and the area where the parlor door used to exit. What was interesting about this particular house was that the door was still there inside, in perfect condition, but it just didn't go anywhere. I carefully trimmed back the siding and — voila! As you can see in Figure 18-24, the original parlor door entrance was restored, just as it was in 1890. In keeping with the style of the newly discovered original door, I replaced the storm/screen door on the opposite entry with a similar door.

In this case, the cost to restore the parlor entrance was very little. It was only the time it took to trim away the outside siding. As far as convenience goes, the door was always there on the inside, so the interior of the house was not changed at all. This was not a difficult decision to make. A house with virtually no personality at all suddenly regained a part of its heritage and appeal.

Screen Doors

Victorian houses had wooden screen doors, not aluminum storms. You can buy a custom Victorian screen door, or you can easily make one yourself and save a lot of money. It's quite simple. Start with a plain wooden screen door, the kind you can buy at almost any home-improvement store. A modern wooden door is very similar to a Victorian door, except it has no decoration. That's no problem; just add some. If you put a spandrel in the middle and brackets on the corners, you'll get a very credible imitation of a Victorian screen door. All the parts are available at Builder's Square or any other home supply store. Assembling them only takes about half an hour. You just have to screw the decorations on. The total cost for a project like this is only $50 to $75, depending on the amount of decoration you add.

Figure 18-25 is an old 1930s-vintage wood replacement storm door, which was missing its screen. I decided to make it into a Victorian-style screen door to add some character to the entrance of this house. The basic screen section of the door was just a rectangle made of plain pine 1 x 2s. I made it "Victorian" by doing just as I suggested in the last paragraph: I added a spandrel in the

273

Figure 18-25
Wood storm door, circa 1930

Figure 18-26
Making the screen section "Victorian"

middle and a couple of brackets in the corners. You can see the new screen section waiting for some paint in Figure 18-26. It cost me about $40 in materials (remember, I already had the door), and took an hour to make. Figure 18-27 shows an authentic Victorian screen door — or is it? It looks real, doesn't it?

The advantage to this screen is that it dresses up the entire doorway. The door behind it is quite plain. I could have replaced the door with an expensive Victorian antique or a replica of a fine entrance door, but there wasn't the money on this job to cover that extra expense. By decorating the screen, I got much the same effect at a fraction of the cost. An antique door, or even a replica of one, could cost thousands of dollars. This one may not be as elegant, but at $40, you can't beat my screen in terms of the most "bang for the buck."

You can use this same technique to make a lot of things "Victorian." All you have to do is take something plain and add gingerbread

to it. Of course, there's a limit. You can't very well make a Victorian big-screen TV! However, anything that resembles the Victorian style can be modified this way, and it will become Victorian.

Windows

Don't forget the windows as points of decoration. The Victorians liked decorative headers over the tops of windows, and running trim under them. These decorations may be missing now, but you can replace them with something similar.

You'll often find that the original Victorian windows have been replaced. If you're lucky, they will have been replaced with modern windows the same size and shape as the originals. If that's the case, it won't matter that they're modern, from an exterior design point of view. Most people won't notice the difference. If you decorate them with Victorian trim, they'll look just like the originals.

Unfortunately, the old windows are sometimes replaced with modern-styles that are completely inappropriate, like the 1950s "picture" window in Figure 18-28. If you look at the design of the house, you can see how the original window probably looked. The decorations under the eaves of the bay indicate that there were two narrow windows where the picture window is now.

The Victorians liked to group small windows. A bay like this would have two or three small windows facing out and one on each side, all matching. The picture window ruins the effect. The only way to restore this design is to replace the picture window with a couple of windows the same size and shape as the side windows. It'll be hard to recreate the original look on this window, though, because a big chunk of the wall was removed when the picture window was installed. Patching the wall and rebuilding the window openings won't be easy.

Adding Bay Windows

If a picture window is located in a fairly isolated position, you might be able to replace it with something else that will enhance the Victorian design. Often you can add a bay window (unless the picture window is in a bay, like the one just mentioned). In many cases a bay window may have been removed to put the picture window in, but not always. By putting in a bay window, you may be restoring the house to its original look, or improving the original look.

Bay windows are expensive to put in, but they're an attractive feature to have. Installing bay windows is the kind of improvement that increases both style and livability. They're not only beautiful, they're also useful. They let in more light and ventilation, and they add extra space. Everybody likes them.

The bay windows in Victorian houses were often elaborately decorated. They were a focal point of the decor, and removing them may have seriously harmed the design of the house. You can't buy Victorian bay windows today, but you can build something similar. Figure 18-29 shows a rather unique, authentic Victorian bay window. What makes it stand out, aside from the second-story location, is the decoration. Without the elaborate brackets, which appear to brace the bottom of the window, it's just a box. You can imitate this or any other style of decoration. Install a plain, square, modern bay window. Then, buy some Victorian trim, in a style that matches the rest of the house. Put brackets underneath the window, and fretwork over and under each

Figure 18-27
"New" wood Victorian screen door

Figure 18-28
Picture window is not Victorian style

Figure 18-29
Unique second-story Victorian bay window

window in the grouping. You can also add rosettes and moldings to match the house. Your completed bay window will look very Victorian. Only an expert will be able to tell that it isn't an original (the thermopane glass is what always gives it away).

The cost for adding a bay is two-part. First is the installation of a modern bay window. A large, nice-quality bay window, like an Andersen or Pella, will cost about $1,000. The labor will run another $250. The second part is the cost of the Victorian gingerbread, and the labor to install it. I would estimate that the gingerbread and the labor would be about $250 each, bringing the total cost for a Victorian bay to somewhere between $1,750 and $2,000. Of course, each job will vary depending on the size of the window, the location and how elaborate the trim work is. In terms of pricing out a job like this, you could easily charge $4,000 to $5,000 just for the one window. A nice bay window is a striking feature on any house. A Victorian bay will easily add far more value to the house than it will cost, making it a good deal for both you and the homeowners. As always,

the neighborhood will determine whether or not this is a worthwhile investment. Adding the Victorian trim almost doubles the cost of the job.

In every job I look at, I always make added value the main criterion. "How much value will this add to the house?" When you're dealing with restorations, all these Victorian trim jobs are big winners for everyone. They always add far more value than they cost. They turn ordinary plain boxes into unique Victorian homes. People don't drive by these homes and forget about them, the look sticks in their minds. For owners looking to spruce up their homes for resale, nothing pays off more than trimwork. Even though it's expensive, it really adds "curb appeal."

Leaded Glass

Leaded, beveled, and stained glass are among the favorite features of Victorian homes. If a home has these, be sure to preserve them. If it doesn't, you might want to add some. You can often find some nice authentic pieces in antique stores. If you have a place you can store them, buy fancy glass windows when you see them, and save them to use when you come across the right house. They may not fit exactly into the windows where you want to use them, but they're often close enough that you can make them fit. We discussed how to do this in Chapter 7.

Victorians typically put fancy glass in the top sash of a window, and plain glass in the bottom. If you put fancy glass in both sashes, you won't be able to see out. However, this can create a nice effect in windows you don't really want to see through, such as in a bathroom. Victorians also liked to use leaded or stained glass for certain visual focal points, like in a window on the landing of a formal staircase.

If there are several windows that are visible at the same time, either side by side, or one above the other, they should all have the same pattern of fancy glass. Remember, Victorians liked everything to match. It wouldn't look right to put fancy glass in just

Figure 18-30
Old window needs to be replaced

Figure 18-31
Antique leaded-glass window

Figure 18-32
Window opening at stairwell

one window of a group. If you only have one piece of fancy glass, put it somewhere where it will be the only window in the room, like the entry, a stairwell, or a bathroom.

It's also possible to buy new fancy glass in the Victorian style, though I've found it to be very expensive. Expect to pay at least $200 per window, just for the glass. If you decide to do this, you should probably replace the entire window assembly, and put in a new window with the fancy glass built into it. A set of matching windows could run up quite a bill, easily in the thousands of dollars.

Is it worth it, in terms of property values? For middle-class property, it probably isn't. Again, middle-class owners would like the windows, but the extra money you'd have to charge for the job may not ever be recovered in added value to the house. For upscale property, however, it would be well worthwhile. Wealthy people want a house that's distinctive and unique, and they're willing to pay for it. Fancy glass is one of those features that's highly visible, capturing the attention and imagination of everyone who sees it. The addition of features like these makes a house special and greatly increases its appeal, and therefore, its value.

Changing Out Windows — I am working on a house right now that is about 150 years old. It has been remodeled a number of times over the years, and as happens, ended up with a few oddities that I'm trying to repair. I just finished dealing with the windows. There were twelve windows in the house, all exactly the same — badly deteriorated, as you can see in Figure 18-30. I replaced most of the windows with modern Thermopane windows that look very similar to the originals. However, in a few locations, I used fancy glass windows as replacements.

Figure 18-31 shows an antique leaded-glass window that I bought at an antique store. I installed this window at the landing on the main staircase. Figure 18-32 shows the

Figure 18-33
Newly installed antique window

window opening with the original window removed. It's a highly visible location from the inside, but the view out leaves a lot to be desired. This is the perfect location for a fancy glass window. As you can probably see, the window opening was considerably larger than the antique window. I constructed a

new, smaller window opening and filled in the extra space with drywall on the inside (Figure 18-33) and OSB on the outside (Figure 18-34). Since this house needed to be completely drywalled on the inside and re-sided on the outside, these repairs were soon concealed.

Figure 18-35 shows another problem window in the same house. An old remodeling job had cut across the top of this window, leaving the window opening up into the ceiling. It looked pretty bad from the inside, and even worse from the outside. I couldn't just put in a smaller plain window because there are three windows in a row on the side of the house. I needed something different here. My solution was to add a decorative octagon window. It fit the space neatly and looks like it was designed as part of the original decorations rather than a repair.

Figure 18-36 shows the new window from the outside framed in with OSB. Another reason that this window works so well here is that it's directly below my other

Figure 18-34
Exterior view of window replacement

Figure 18-35
New ceiling blocks top of window

decorative window. You can see them both in Figure 18-37. Although the new windows aren't the same, they are very close in size and line up directly one over the other. Victorians often had unusual window treatments repeated like this to add interest to both the exterior and interior. Once the new siding was up on the outside, the new windows looked as though they had always been there. Figure 18-38 shows the side of the house with all the new windows and siding installed.

One reason replacing these windows with fancy glass was practical was that the house had to be re-sided anyway. If that hadn't been the case, patching the siding around the windows would have been a very big job. The windows still would have needed to be replaced, but I might have had to be considerably less creative, and put in windows that were closer in size to the originals. When you find you have the opportunity to make improvements like these without the extra work that they often present, you should try to make the most of it.

Figure 18-36
Decorative window in place

Other Window Treatments

Don't forget about adding simple items, like shutters, to very plain windows. Shutters are a very inexpensive and easy addition that can make a big difference to an otherwise ordinary house. You can buy simple shutters at any home improvement store. Sometimes

Figure 18-37
Exterior view of replacement windows

Figure 18-38
Unusual window treatment adds interest to house

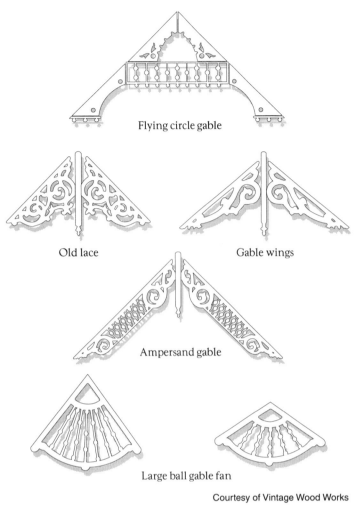

Flying circle gable

Old lace

Gable wings

Ampersand gable

Large ball gable fan

Courtesy of Vintage Wood Works

Figure 18-39
Victorian gable decorations

followed. A complete Victorian house would have spandrels or arches across any openings, such as the space between the pillars of the porch. The pillars would be columns or ornately turned posts with fancy brackets on the left and right sides, and sometimes on the front and back as well.

The gables of the house would also be decorated. They usually had wings, fans, or cross-pieces mounted on them. Figure 18-39 shows a variety of gable decorations that you can order from Vintage Wood Works and install. Other decorations used in the gable area include running trims, sunbursts and medallions. Sometimes the eaves were decorated with corbels like those shown on the house in Figure 18-40. The windows and doors had ornamental headers as well, often repeating the theme from the porch or roof trims. Notice in Figure 18-40 that the corbels and window trim both have drop trim pieces. While the decorations might lead directly from one to the other, they never cut into each other, or blocked each other out. Each decorative item had its own space.

The designs themselves were made up of simple elements, lines, circles, squares and angles, often with these elements layered on top of each other to create intricate patterns. They didn't use any free-form or organic shapes.

you can't completely restyle a house and make it into a Victorian showcase, but you can almost always make little improvements that will add to its appeal. Shutters are one of those improvements that can dress up almost any old style home. You can't just think: "Victorian or nothing." Rather you should think, "If I can't do a complete Victorian make-over, I'll do what I can."

Victorian Decorations

There were many variations in the way a Victorian home was decorated. Some houses were considerably more ornate than others, but there were certain basic rules of design that everyone who could afford decorations

🐦 Creating the Right Look

You can create just about any Victorian effect using precut millwork. That's the way the Victorians did it. They didn't hand-cut all the little pieces. Usually they bought them from Sears. Since the Victorian style is popular once again, this type of millwork is easily available, and at reasonable prices. You can even buy the more common styles at chain stores, like Builder's Square or Home Depot.

The ideas to keep in mind when using Victorian decorations are:

◆ Use as much decoration as possible; there's no such thing as too much.

◆ If a decoration will block or overlay another one, leave it out.

◆ All decorations should be symmetrical, using common shapes.

If you look closely at the porch or siding on a Victorian house, you can often find marks (like the ones I found on the porch in the work we just discussed), where the old decorations used to be. That will show you where the decorations were, but not what they looked like. For that, you have to guess.

Look for any surviving decorations on the house. The missing decorations would have matched them. If the surviving decorations have graceful curves, you want to use more graceful curves. If they have stars or balls, add more stars or balls. If you can't find anything that matches exactly, you can probably find something that's fairly close.

The two decorative elements that you can safely add to any Victorian home are spandrels and brackets. The Victorians used them almost all the time. Spandrels look like miniature railings, and were used to span the open spaces between posts. At the posts, ornate brackets would be mounted under the spandrels, so that it looked like the brackets were holding the spandrels up. The drawing in Figure 18-41, taken from the Vintage Wood Works catalogue, shows how the various trim pieces, brackets and spandrels fit together on a typical Victorian porch. The brackets can be the same style as the spandrels, with little balls or turnings which match the balls or turnings on the spandrels, or they can be a different, but complementary style, such as fretwork brackets under ball spandrels. However, all the spandrels should be the same, and all brackets should be the same, even if spandrels and brackets are different from each other.

If you're having trouble locating what you need, Vintage Wood Works is an excellent source for ordering Victorian decorations. You can call, fax or write for a free catalog:

Vintage Wood Works
Hwy 34 South
P.O. Box R
Quinlan, TX 75474
Phone (903) 356-2158, Fax (903) 356-3023

Figure 18-40
Elaborate corbels and ornamental window headers decorate this Victorian home

When you look through the Vintage Wood Works catalog, you can see how easy it would be to spend a lot of money on decorations. They have so many great pieces you can choose from. It can be very tempting to order several thousand dollars worth of elaborate decorations for a house. Before you do that, however, you have to decide whether

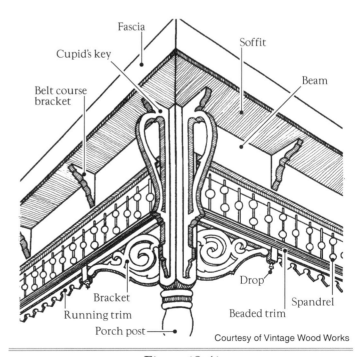

Figure 18-41
Victorian trim, posts, brackets and spandrels

the investment would be justified. In an upscale neighborhood, Victorian decorations, auth-entically applied, can raise the value of a house by $100,000. In that case, a few thousand dollars in decorations is money well spent.

If a homeowner is working with a tight budget, you can get quite a nice effect using the stock decorations available from most building supply chains. They have almost everything you need to completely outfit a house in Victorian designs. The only problem is that their selection of styles is limited. That may not be a problem if you're working on the only Victorian house on the block. But if the house next door is already decorated with the same stock decorations, it might be best to spend a little more and order decorations from a specialty supplier.

Another option is to make some of the decorations yourself. I have found a book that's very helpful if you want to try this. It's *Victorian Fretwork*, by John T. Jenson, published by Garden Way Publishing. It's a unique book, full of actual patterns that you can trace onto wood and cut out with a jigsaw. It's tedious work, but not that hard to do if you select a fairly simple design. Remember that you may need quite a few, and it takes a lot less time to cut out a simple design than a complex one. If you have the time and patience, making your own decorations can save a lot of money. (Be sure you always consider the value of your own time before you take on a project like this!)

Painting Decorations

These little decorations can be difficult to paint. It's hard to get a brush around all the little parts, and it's easy to miss a spot. I avoid this problem by dipping the decorations, rather than painting them with a brush. Just pour some paint into a tray, and lay the decoration down in it. Let it sit for a few seconds, until the paint has thoroughly penetrated. Then hang it up on a piece of wire to dry. The paint may get chipped slightly when you install the pieces, but that's easy enough to touch up.

If you want to paint the decorations in two or more different colors, in the Victorian style, you can still dip them in the base color. After they've thoroughly dried, you can add the contrasting colors using a small brush. This is a lot less trouble than painting the whole decoration with a small brush. You can do the final paint coats after the decorations are installed, or before, depending on convenience. If a decoration is going to be installed in a hard-to-reach place, like the peak of a gable, always paint it before you install it. There's no reason to paint something standing at the top of a ladder when you could do it in your workshop.

Cost

The cost of Victorian decorations varies depending on how elaborate they are. You can get nice spandrels for around $10 per foot, and nice brackets for about $15 each from Builder's Square. Vintage Wood Works charges about the same for their simple styles, but the more intricate the pattern, the more expensive they become. If you're working with a big budget, you can get some really fabulous decorations for about $40 per lineal foot. For the most part, however, the pieces are not that expensive. They run about $10 to $15 each. The problem is that you will want to use dozens of pieces to complete a whole house. Trimming out an average size Victorian house will cost between $500 and $1,000.

Installing decorative pieces is very time-consuming, fussy work. Everything has to be lined up exactly right. The decorations will be the focus of a lot of attention and any little defect will be noticed. I usually figure $50 per hour for my labor when I'm doing this type of work.

Inventing the Style

What if you're working on a house that has nothing left of the original Victorian style, not a clue as to what it might have originally been? What should you do?

Figure 18-42
Before: Plain house lacks style

Figure 18-43
*After: Victorian decorations
add charm and style*

Many Victorian houses weren't designed by architects, they were designed by builders. They were guys just like you. And, like many people in the business today, some were more creative than others. The creative ones built homes that looked very much like the ones that the architects designed. If they could do it, why can't you? If you follow the same rules, you'll get the same effect.

Victorian builders liked to make their houses interesting — you'll never find two that are exactly alike. They often let their imaginations run wild, adding all kinds of fanciful creations into their designs. You can do the same thing. While your ideas may not create exactly the same result as the original, the spirit will be the same.

If you start with a plain house, you can decorate it any way you and your clients like. Work out whatever plan you think looks good, then show it to your clients and let them make their suggestions. As long as it uses Victorian design elements, and its all symmetrical and matching, it'll be pretty close to what the Victorians would have done.

Even if the house has always been plain, you can still add Victorian decorations. There were thousands of plain, gable-roofed

houses built all over the country between 1880 and 1940. While most of these weren't designed to be Victorian, they don't clash with the Victorian style. They're just plain houses, with no particular style at all, so why not make them Victorian?

Figures 18-42 and 18-43 are before and after pictures of a house I decorated in the Victorian style. The effect was quite nice, considering I spent very little time and money on it. Besides painting the house and adding a new front door, most of the work involved restyling the front porch.

The original porch railing was a code violation. Since it had to be replaced anyway, I made a new one using spindles for balusters, in the Victorian style. The spindles were a stock item that cost about $4 each. Making the railings was the most time-consuming part of the job. I was surprised to find that it took me a full 20 hours to put them together. However, I did everything in my workshop except the final installation, so that made it a little easier.

The fretwork brackets came from the Vintage Wood Works. I put them up between the porch posts and the roof, and they really set the style. The brackets only cost $8 each, but what a nice statement they make! You can see that a $32 investment in the right place made all the difference in the look of this house. The final step was enclosing the area under the porch with lattice.

From an historian's point of view, this isn't an authentic job. It's a "Victorian look," but not a restoration. The house wasn't originally a Victorian style, but doing an historic restoration on a house like this would be rather pointless. It was never a very attractive style to begin with. My non-authentic "Victorian look" restoration gave the house a style and charm that it didn't have when it was new. Everyone in the neighborhood loved it, and the new style substantially increased the value of the house. With a little updating in the interior, as well as fresh paint and carpet throughout, I was able to sell this house for well over twice what I had paid for it.

Even though you may not be working with the aim of selling a house for profit as I do, you can keep that in mind for your clients. They'll always be pleased with your work if you can increase the value of their home while you're making a nice profit for yourself. It's a win-win situation.

Chapter 19

Victorian Interiors

*T*he interiors of Victorian homes are as unique as their exteriors. We've talked about some of these features already: formal parlors, separate entrances for formal and informal rooms and service areas, many small, specialized rooms, and so on. It's an interesting fact that house designs tend to reflect the lives of the people that live in them. That's why certain designs become popular at certain times. People feel that these designs have something to say about their lives.

Victorian Lives

The Victorian lifestyle revolved around all the little details that it took to make life as orderly, efficient and pleasant as possible. How things were accomplished was almost as important as the accomplishment itself. This attitude was reflected in everything they did. They took pride in the mastery and artistry of detail. This is also reflected in the interior design of their houses. The houses are full of intricate and interesting detail, all in perfect order, with each item having a place and job, just like the people who lived there.

It's important to remember that there were a lot of people living together in a Victorian household. Besides the mother, father and children, there were probably aunts, uncles and grandparents. That's why these houses had to have a lot of small bedrooms. Each person, or at least each adult, needed to have their own room.

During the day, there might be several activities going on in the house at the same time. This required Victorian houses to have many small rooms downstairs, too. They needed a place where mother could entertain visitors, while Aunt Matilda knitted and Grandma shelled peas for dinner. The result was a formal parlor, a family parlor and an open wraparound porch where Grandma could sit in her rocking chair and work or watch the kids at play. Each area was separate from the other, allowing each person a little privacy in their activities.

For most of us, this style of living has changed. Few people want to live with relatives today. When people can have a home of their own, that's what they want. The evolution of the single family home reflected this change in the American family. The designs which replaced the Victorian-style home early in this century, like the Craftsman and

Prairie homes, were laid out like modern houses. They had a single large living room instead of two parlors, and three or four large bedrooms, instead of six or eight tiny ones. They were designed for a single family who did things together, not a bunch of relatives who wanted to do different things and needed separate space.

Adapting the Victorian Floor Plan

The biggest problem with Victorian houses is their use of space. Many of the rooms that the Victorian lifestyle required aren't really needed today. Homeowners have to decide how to incorporate these rooms into a livable, workable plan for their lives. Changing a floor plan is expensive, and not something they should do without careful consideration.

The homeowners may be able to use some of the Victorian rooms as they are. A formal parlor, for example, makes an excellent home office, especially if it still has a separate entrance. Business associates or clients can come and go without using the family areas. Small bedrooms make good libraries, studies or nurseries for infants and small children. These possibilities are worth considering. However, for the average family, some alterations will probably be necessary.

Your first impulse might be to gut the interior and rebuild it in a more modern style. While this certainly is an option, it isn't always cost-effective. There are other factors to consider. What's the condition of the house? If the interior is a mess, you won't lose much by gutting it. On the other hand, if it's full of beautiful, perfectly preserved Victorian decorations, you could be throwing away a lot of money by tearing it out. Again, it depends on the neighborhood. In an upscale area, decoration like these can add many thousands of dollars to the value of a property. Does the homeowner really want to throw that money in a dumpster? In terms of property value, you can add more to the house by preserving the original decorations and carefully remodeling around them.

Chances are, the house won't be in perfect condition. Most of the houses I work on have been remodeled somewhat through the years, often poorly, and many times the original features that made the house special have been destroyed. However, it may be possible to save some of the remaining unique features. They can be integrated into a new design, using some modern elements and some antique elements. If you're lucky, you might be able to add the improvements needed for a modern home, while maintaining the style elements that identify the house as Victorian. This blend can be very effective, creating an "eclectic" style that is extremely attractive. Many jobs like this have won prizes for design.

Changes to the Floor Plan

Before you settle on a plan, you need to look for spaces where you can add some of the nondecorative features that Victorian houses tend to be short of, such as bathrooms and closets. The house may not have been built with any bathrooms or closets at all. Even if they've been added over the years, there probably won't be enough of either one to suit the modern household. If you're going to be altering the floor plan, be sure to set some space aside for another bathroom or two, and several closets. We'll discuss adding these features a little later.

Another feature of the floor plan that you have to consider right now is how the traffic flows from room to room. Does the flow make sense, or have past remodeling decisions made it a confusing maze? When a house is laid out poorly, it's unpleasant to live in. Many times I've had to reorganize the floor plan of a house just to make it functional.

Fixing the Floor Plan

This is particularly true of the house I'm working on now. It's a 2,400 square foot Gothic Victorian (shown in Figure 19-1) that has been massively remodeled. The original house was a small one-story structure built in the 1840s. Most of what you see now was added on in the 1860s. At one time it was one of the great houses of the area. When I bought it, it was a run-down duplex and the neighborhood eyesore. The zoning variance allowing it to be rented out as a duplex had expired, and the city insisted that the house be made back into a single-family home. Because of this, I was able to purchase it cheap, but the remodeling is a major undertaking. Figure 19-2 shows the downstairs floor plan for the duplex as it was when I bought it.

My wife did some research and discovered a small drawing of the house, dated 1880, at the local Historical Society. She also located the granddaughter of one of the former owners. The woman's grandfather had purchased the house in 1890 and she had lived there as a young child in the 1920s. She was able to tell us what the house used to look like and provide us with a sketch of the floor plan as she remembered it. Figure 19-3 shows her layout of the downstairs rooms. There were no bathrooms (it still has an outhouse in

Figure 19-1
Historic Victorian fixer-upper

the back), no central heat, and only one staircase going upstairs to the bedrooms.

The house had been converted into a duplex in the 1940s, and of course that involved major interior and exterior changes.

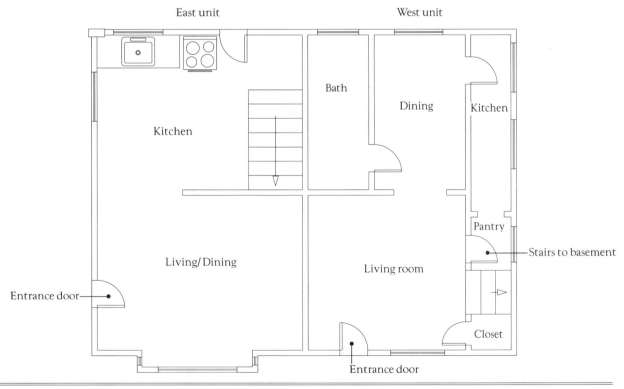

Figure 19-2
Floorplan of house 1940-1994

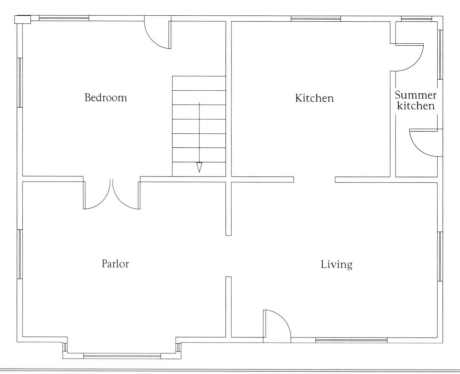

Figure 19-3
Floorplan of house 1860-1940

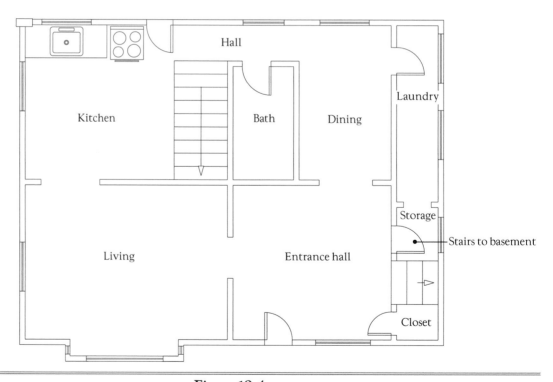

Figure 19-4
Floorplan of house 1995

Figure 19-5
Door cut through bathroom to connect dining room and kitchen

Figure 19-6
New door from dining room to hallway cut through, old door into bath still in place

It took a lot of creativity for us to design a workable floor plan suitable for modern single-family living that wouldn't cost a fortune to construct. Figure 19-4 shows the arrangement we eventually came up with. It's as close to the original as we can make it, and still be functional.

We retained the kitchen from the east unit because it was a large, pleasant room that we could work with. The cabinets, fixtures, floor covering and wall treatments all had to be replaced. I cut a hallway through the back of the house to connect the kitchen with the dining room in the west unit. This dining room was quite large and cheerful, with a big, bright window looking out to the back.

The new hallway had to go through the bathroom, and as you can see in Figure 19-5, it created quite a big mess. Tearing it up was no big loss, however, because all the plaster was bad and the bathroom was a disaster already. Even if I hadn't put the hallway through the bathroom, I would have had to make considerable changes in its layout. The only door into this bathroom was in the dining room, which is really an undesirable arrangement. Figure 19-6 shows the new door I cut from the dining room into what was to become the hall. I closed up the old door, and made a new door into the bathroom from my new hallway. This was a huge improvement. The only loss in all of these changes was the tub in the bathroom. The room was no longer large enough for a tub/shower combination, though there was still room for a nice shower stall. This is perfectly fine for a downstairs bath. The main bathrooms are upstairs with the bedrooms.

We turned the small kitchen for the west unit, which had originally been the summer kitchen, into a really nice laundry/sewing room combination. It has lots of windows which makes it light and bright and provides nice ventilation for the summer. We kept the cabinets for storage and put in a new countertop to use as a work area. It's great for

Figure 19-7
Stained glass window in living room

Figure 19-8
Exterior view of remodeled historic Victorian home

folding clothes or laying out patterns or working on hobbies and crafts. There's plenty of room to work and it's convenient to the living area of the house. This turned out to be an ideal use for a rather oddly placed room.

The former living room for the west unit is now the main entrance hall for the house, and the east living/dining room combination is now a nice large living room. We closed off the former exterior entrance to

this room and replaced it with the small stained-glass window shown in Figure 19-7. We retained both staircases leading to the upstairs. It's really quite a nice feature to have an access to the upstairs near both the front and back entrances.

All in all, I think this job will be a huge success. I've completely reoriented the first floor, and created a well-organized and pleasant layout. All the rooms had to be gutted and new drywall put up. It was difficult, time-consuming and expensive, but well worth the cost. I am still working on the interior and plan to do elaborate Victorian trim in all the rooms. Our goal is to make this a luxury home, completely restored in Victorian style. Figure 19-8 shows the exterior as it looks today. We still have exterior landscaping work to do, but that will have to wait until spring. This home is in a historic neighborhood surrounded by many beautifully renovated homes. Whatever it costs to bring the house up to the standards of the neighborhood we'll recover in appreciated value when it's ready to sell.

The Parlors

Most of the homes you'll work on will have an easier layout to deal with. This old duplex was a pretty extreme case. However, even if the basic floor plan in a house works, you may still have a problem with some of the rooms, especially the small bedrooms and the parlors. Let's start with the parlors. As we mentioned before, most Victorian homes had one formal parlor, and one informal family parlor. This is similar to the living room/family room concept in more modern houses.

If a Victorian home is large and luxurious, with a good-sized informal parlor, the owners might want to keep the formal parlor. It's a gracious feature, and helps preserve the antique atmosphere of the home. My wife and I retained the formal parlor in our 3,000-square-foot Victorian farmhouse. We use it much the same way the Victorians did, as a formal room to entertain guests. This isn't a problem for us, because the informal parlor is quite large and we're not short of space.

However, in most Victorian homes, both parlors were rather small. Modern families need at least one room large enough to accommodate the entertainment features that they enjoy together. If they can, they would like a room separate from the formal living room. When space is at a premium, however, people would rather do without a formal area, and have a comfortable family area. For them, a formal parlor is a waste of precious living space.

Fortunately, it was common for the formal parlor to be right next to the family parlor. If the wall between the two is a partition wall and not load-bearing, you can just remove it and have one large room. This will greatly increase the livability of the house. If the wall between the two rooms is load-bearing, you'll need to replace it with a beam, as we discussed in Chapter 12.

⨎ Blending the Rooms

In many cases, the trim and decorations in both parlors will be the same, so the two rooms will blend together neatly and your alteration won't show. You can make the two rooms look like they were always one big room.

The only hitch to this plan is that when you remove the wall, there will be a wall-width section missing from the floor, walls, and ceiling, where the wall used to be. You can patch the floor using one of the techniques we discussed in Chapter 16. If the walls and ceiling are plain, or need to be drywalled anyway, they won't be a problem either. However, if the walls or ceiling are decorated, patching the missing section between the two rooms can be a problem. How can you connect the decorations together? This is especially difficult if the rooms have some unique feature, like wainscoting.

Often you can salvage trim and wainscoting from the wall section that you remove. This will give you an exact match, but it's still very hard to patch it in without the patch showing. You have to cut the pieces down so that they fit perfectly, and line up perfectly with the existing pieces. You may have to shim them out with tiny shims. This is very tedious work. Allow at least ½ hour for each trim piece or molding that needs to be patched in. If there's a lot to patch, the time can really add up.

Another solution, especially if you can't salvage any trim, is to fill the space with "pilasters," or fake columns. This works best on a load-bearing wall when you need to put in an overhead beam. The columns appear to be holding up the beam. In fact, depending on your design, they may actually *be* the support for the beam. Add decorations to the columns and beam to match the style of the room. If the ceiling is decorated with rosettes, buy some small rosettes and attach them to the columns. If you do this correctly, the columns and beam will look like design elements, not structural elements. Ornate pilasters were an authentic Victorian treatment.

When one of the parlors has been modernized and one hasn't, blending them becomes a little more difficult. You may be able to coordinate the two rooms reasonably well if you can find decorations, molding and trim similar to the original room. If you can't, you may have to completely redo both rooms in order to blend them together. When you do this, be sure to preserve the antique spirit of the rooms by adding new matching Victorian decorations.

Don't forget about using some of the same decorations that you used on the exterior, like spandrels and brackets. Victorians carried these design elements into the interiors as well. If you put a spandrel and some brackets across the opening between the two rooms, as shown in Figure 19-9, the opening will appear to be part of the original design. This will help the blend finished room with the rest of the house.

⨎ Victorian Wallpapers

Some elegant Victorian rooms have what appears to be ornamental plasterwork. It looks like the walls are covered with hundreds

Figure 19-9
Use Victorian gingerbread to blend rooms

decorations embossed into its surface. It's normally painted, which makes it look like painted plaster. Lincrusta wallpaper can last a very long time. There are some houses in England that have had it in place for more than 200 years.

Lincrusta wallpaper is still available, though it's quite expensive. In spite of the cost, it may be just the design element you need to tie two remodeled parlors together, or to add an elegant touch to any other formal rooms. If you use Lincrusta, as well as other plaster decorations, you will have a room that's just as beautiful and elaborate as any Victorian original.

of raised plaster decorations. It's actually a very elaborate wallpaper, called Lincrusta. It was invented in England in the late 1700s. Lincrusta gives the effect of an incredibly detailed plaster job, at a fraction of the price. It's a very thick, heavy wallpaper, with the

🐌 Vinyl Decorations

You can also find vinyl copies of many very elaborate Victorian decorations. Some of these vinyl decorations are molded to look just like plasterwork. The ceiling medallion in Figure 19-10 is an example of this type of decoration. It's actually vinyl, but once it's painted, you can't tell the difference between this and the real thing. There are a number of sources for these decorations. One source for both the Lincrusta wallpaper and the vinyl interior decorations is:

Classic Architectural Specialties
3223 Canton Street
Dallas, TX 75226
1-800-662-1221

You can call them, or these two alternate sources for vinyl decorations, for a free catalog:

Russell Enterprises
Like-Wood Millwork
2600 Boyce Plaza Road
Pittsburgh, PA 15241
1-800-367-1076

Style-Mark Molded Millwork
960 W. Barre Road,
Archbold, Ohio 43502
1-800-446-3040

Figure 19-10
*Vinyl medallion looks like
ornate plasterwork*

Many of these vinyl decorations can be used as exterior gingerbread as well The selection of Victorian styles in vinyl isn't as varied as those in wood, but they are low-maintenance and many are attractively priced.

🐦 Ceiling Treatments

Victorian houses originally had rather high ceilings, often 10 or 12 feet high. The high ceilings gave the houses an open, airy feel, and helped keep them cool during the summer. However, they also caused high heating bills during the winter. Because of this, many people have installed drop ceilings in their houses to keep heat from rising.

The most common material for drop ceilings is some form of ceiling tile. If a house has an 8-foot-high tiled ceiling, there may be a considerable space between it and the original ceiling. The space can be as much as 4 feet. That's almost like having another room up there! I'm always in favor ripping out these ceilings to restore the original room height. If you do, it opens up the room and improves the whole look of the interior. What seemed like a cramped, uncomfortable little room will suddenly become airy and cheerful. That's because the house was designed to have high ceilings. Lowering the ceiling spoils the proportions of a room, making it seem close and unpleasant. As soon as you restore the original height, the design comes back into focus, and the beauty of the room returns.

You never know what you're going to find when you take down a drop ceiling. Usually there's just a bunch of broken plaster and furring strips. However, every once in a while, you'll find a beautiful Victorian ceiling in good or repairable condition. Then, taking down the drop ceiling pays for itself. But even if you have to put up a whole new ceiling, the improvement to the room will make the job well worthwhile.

Tin Ceilings

One attractive feature you may come across in a Victorian building is a tin ceiling.

I've often seen them in Victorian stores and saloons, and occasionally I find them in a house, although not as often. If you find a tin ceiling, try to preserve it; it's a valuable feature.

You can buy reproductions of ceiling tin. It's actually quite popular today because it provides a very distinctive, decorative look. You can order it from a number of sources. Here's one you can call for a free catalog:

Classic Architectural Specialties
3223 Canton Street
Dallas, TX 75226
1-800-662-1221

In Victorian times, ceiling tin was considered an informal treatment, suitable for kitchens or family parlors, but not for formal rooms. If your clients aren't particular about being historically accurate, you can use it wherever you think it will look nice. A patterned ceiling can dress up a house that's otherwise quite plain. Keep in mind, though, that ceiling tin has a design of its own. You don't want to use it in a room that already has other decorations, especially if they don't match. It looks best in a plain room where it becomes the focus of attention. That way you get the maximum value out of the beautiful ceiling.

Cost — Genuine ceiling tin can be rather expensive. It starts at $3 per square foot. If you want a fancier metal, like brass or copper, the price goes up to $9 per square foot. However, original brass or copper ceilings were quite rare. They were used only in very expensive buildings, like elaborate mansions, or official buildings, like courthouses. They create a very opulent look.

Installing ceiling tin or other ceiling metals is quite easy. Depending on the type you buy, it can be either nailed in place, or laid into a drop ceiling framework. It takes about the same amount of time as installing any other kind of ceiling tile. The main expense is in the materials, not the labor.

The Bedrooms

The bedrooms in a Victorian house, like the parlors, tend to be too many and too small. Once again, the solution here is to remove walls and open up space. The house will be a lot more livable with three good-sized bedrooms than six tiny ones. You'll probably also need to add closets to the bedrooms, because most of the time there weren't any in the original home.

The Victorians didn't worry about closet space. They kept their clothes in wardrobes, which were very large, often ornate pieces of furniture. You can find them in antique stores now and then, usually selling for quite a bit of money. If the homeowners want to keep the home authentic, they can buy a few wardrobes and use them instead of closets. This may work for guest rooms, but wardrobes aren't really big enough for today's needs. Most people don't want to take authenticity so far that it interferes with their own convenience. They would rather have a nice modern closet for their own use.

𝒆𝓪 Adding Closets

If you remove walls to expand the bedrooms, you have an ideal opportunity to add closet space. It's a lot easier to give up space for a closet in a large bedroom, than in one of the tiny original rooms. Taking space out of a small room can make it unusable.

When you're working on the walls, check and see if there are any unused or under-utilized spaces that you might be able to improve on. This is especially important when you're deciding where to put closets. Are there any less-useful spaces in the rooms, like areas where the ceiling slopes down, or in an awkward, out-of-the-way corner? These are ideal for closets. A space that's inconvenient for living can be fine for storing clothes. Figure 19-11 shows a walk-in closet I made from an awkward little space I found adjacent to the bedroom.

Sometimes closets have been installed in the bedrooms at some point, but they're often totally inadequate by today's standards. The strange little box in the corner in of the room shown in Figure 19-12 was supposed to

Figure 19-11
*New walk-in closet made
from unused space*

Figure 19-12
Tiny closet added in 1920s

Figure 19-14
Finished room with new closet

Figure 19-13
New closet being built

Figure 19-15
*New closet built under stairs
for first bedroom*

be the closet for the master bedroom. It was probably added in the 1920s. It was so narrow you couldn't even hang a coat hanger in it! It was quaint, in a rustic sort of way, but totally useless as a closet. Since I already had to do major work in this room because of plaster damage, I decided to put in a nice modern closet.

The end of the room, where the ceiling slanted down, seemed like the perfect location. Figure 19-13 shows the work in progress, and Figure 19-14 shows the finished room with the new closet. I used two 36-inch wide bi-fold doors for the closet doors. The raised panels gave them an old-fashioned look. They weren't a perfect match for the existing antique entry door, but they were pretty close. After the doors were painted, the new closet blended into the room very nicely.

Sometimes you can solve two bedroom problems by adding only one closet. This was the case in a small house I worked on a few years ago. The house had two adjoining bedrooms, but only one had a closet. The bedrooms were already quite small, and neither one could afford to lose more space.

Looking around, I found an unused space under the stairs that could be converted to a closet. However, it was adjacent to the bedroom that already had a closet. Having two closets in one bedroom and none in the other was not a solution. However, this arrangement offered an opportunity for some creative remodeling.

First, I constructed the new closet in the space under the stairs, shown in Figure 19-15.

Figure 19-16
Old closet closed up in first bedroom

Figure 19-17
*Opening cut from second bedroom
into old closet*

Then, I blocked off the door to the old closet in that bedroom and refinished the wall. When the drywall was painted, the old doorway disappeared, leaving a neat, boxed-out area which didn't look bad at all. You can see it in Figure 19-16.

Next, I cut a hole in the wall of the second bedroom, making a new doorway into the other side of the old closet. What I did was simply flip the closet around, so that it faced the second bedroom instead of the first. Figure 19-17 shows the new doorway being cut into the bedroom wall, and Figure 19-18 shows the completed closet for the second bedroom. When I was finished, each bedroom had its own closet. The second bedroom had the closet that used to belong to the first, and the first bedroom had the new closet I created under the stairs. This wasn't a quick or easy job, but it did solve a serious problem in a very efficient way.

One thing that you have to watch for when putting doors on closets is to make sure that they doesn't interfere with anything when they open. Before you choose the type of door, measure the room. Will there be enough space for a full-size bed, a chest of drawers, and other usual furniture without the closet door hitting them? It's easy to wind up with the only practical placement for the

bed being in the way of the closet door. That would make the new closet practically useless.

Planning out the room and the best furniture placement may seem obvious, but I've seen many bedrooms that were put together without this kind of planning. In some bedrooms, no matter how you place the bed, it's

Figure 19-18
*Finished closet now opens
into second bedroom*

always blocking something. It's in the way of the closet door, the entrance door, or a window. It's hard to envision all of this when the room is empty, but believe me, the homeowners won't fail to notice it when they try to arrange their furniture. Suddenly, your great remodeling job won't seem so great anymore!

When you see that you're going to have a space problem, you can either change the position of the door, or change the type of door you put on. Perhaps you can use two small closet doors, or a folding door, instead of a regular, full-size door. Two small doors will open in half the space.

❧ Bedroom Doors

If you take out a partition between two bedrooms and make one big room, you'll have two entrance doors to the new room. You can leave the room like that, but it's a sure sign of a poor remodeling job. One of the doors should be filled in, keeping the door that's most convenient to use.

Another option is to close off both existing doors, and add a new door in a different, more convenient location. Ideally, a bedroom door should open onto a central hall, near the stairs, and close to a bathroom. You may not always be able to get them located perfectly, unless you want to gut the entire house, but you can usually work out a pretty good arrangement.

Moving doors is a lot of trouble. I'm not suggesting that you shuffle them around like cards. However, the position of the doors is important. The layout should make sense. People should be able to come up the stairs and find bedrooms and bathrooms where they expect them. Everything should be obvious. Don't leave doors in dark corners, or create a maze of twisted hallways to get to rooms. I've seen remodeling jobs like that. The result is a house that's awkward and hard to get around in. Whatever changes you make should always be with the idea of *improving* the livability of the house.

Matching Doors

All the bedroom doors that are visible from the same hallway should match each other. If they're all closed, they're all visible at the same time. You don't want to look down the hallway and see several different kinds of doors. The doors also need to match the interior of the bedroom, and other hallway woodwork or trim.

If a door needs to be replaced or added, matching it to the others can be a problem. Some of the old panel door styles are still made, but most of the older styles have a different layout of panels than the new doors. You may have to replace all of the bedroom doors in order to have matching doors. If they're in poor condition, it isn't a great loss.

However, if the doors are all perfect, but one is missing, it's more of a problem. This is especially true if they're particularly nice doors — varnished hardwoods, for example. Before you sacrifice all the doors, look around the house for a door that you can scavenge from someplace else. Are any doorways going to be closed off? Even if the door isn't exactly the same size, it might be worth altering if it matches the other doors. Don't forget closets in your search. While it would be best if all the closet doors matched the bedroom doors, it isn't as important as having all the bedroom doors match. You might be able to steal a matching door from a closet, and use it on the bedroom hallway door. When you replace the closet door, find as close a match as possible. No one will notice the difference.

❧ Woodwork, Trim and Decorations

Victorian bedrooms tend to be much plainer than the parlors and entrance halls. That's because parlors and entrance halls were considered formal, public rooms. The Victorians liked to impress their guests, so the formal areas had the most elaborate decorations and furnishings in the house.

Bedrooms were private rooms. Since few people would see them, it wasn't as important to decorate them. In a mansion, where cost was no object, the bedrooms would be fancy. But in the average, middle-class home, the bedrooms were usually quite plain. For this reason, I never feel too bad about tearing them up. I'm not destroying irreplaceable examples of historical architecture and decorative art.

The woodwork and trim are usually the only distinctively Victorian items in the bedroom. You may have some decisions to make about preserving these in a remodeled bedroom. The trim needs to match throughout the room. Are you going to try to save the existing trim, or replace all the trim?

How do you decide? First, is the woodwork especially nice? You don't want to throw a roomful of beautiful, carved oak in the trash. In that case, you'd want to try to patch in any missing pieces. But, where in the world can you get pieces that match? From some other room in the house, that's where! If you're tearing out walls, there will be fewer total walls than before. Save the trim from the walls you tear out. You can use it to patch in missing pieces in other rooms.

The trim only needs to match within each room. The rooms don't all need to be exactly the same, because no one will be seeing them all at once. If they're similar, the minor differences won't be noticed. This gives you a lot of leeway. You can get away with a lot more in the bedrooms than you can in the parlors, where everything is visible at the same time.

If necessary, you can pick one of the least important bedrooms and use it for "parts." That is, you can take matching pieces of trim or doors and use them for matching and patching in the other rooms. That way, all the rooms will have their original, beautiful trim, except one. The remaining room can have all new trim made in an old-fashioned style. It may not be as authentic or beautiful as the rest, but it will still look nice. The only alternative to this would be to have matching trim custom made — an expense that few homeowners want to bear.

Moldings

Most Victorian bedrooms had fairly simple woodwork. It's not usually worth putting a lot of effort into restoring. If you've ever tried to patch in little pieces of molding, trying to get the pieces to match, you know that it's difficult to do. It's usually easier to replace the whole business. However, there are a few cases where patching in the moldings is worthwhile.

If most of the moldings are in good shape and you're planning on keeping the old walls, saving the moldings and patching in missing pieces is especially worthwhile. That's because the old moldings are very hard to remove. It's almost impossible to get them off without doing some damage to the walls; and if you disturb the furring strips, you'll loosen and crack the plaster. So pulling off the moldings can easily ruin the whole wall. Unless you're planning to drywall the walls, you're better off leaving the moldings in place.

Another problem is that the nails in the moldings may have rusted into place. When that's happened, the nails won't release when you pull on them. Instead, you'll end up cracking the molding into a mass of splinters, and then you'll have to rip out each splinter, one at a time. This takes a long time, and makes a big mess.

If you have to replace the moldings, you can sometimes make new moldings that are very similar to the old moldings. Similar moldings work well when all of a single room is being remodeled, because they're not side by side with the originals. Just try to preserve the spirit of the originals.

So as long as the different moldings are in different rooms, the difference will never be noticed. You can even point them out to people, and they still won't notice. I've tried it. I pointed to the moldings and said "See how these moldings are different from the ones in the other rooms?" The answer I got was "Really? They look the same to me!" I guess that means I was successful.

Paint

It's a lot easier to work with moldings that are painted than those that are varnished, especially if you need to match or patch them. If the moldings are painted, you can even use an entirely different kind of wood to make your patches. No one can see the wood beneath a coat of paint.

I almost always find that the woodwork has been painted in older homes. Varnish will turn black and alligator after a few decades. If the homeowner didn't want to strip the woodwork and varnish it again, it got painted. In some cases, this is really too bad. A lot of the woodwork I've found painted over was beautiful oak, or another fine hardwood.

Unfortunately, old paint is very difficult to get off moldings. We discussed the problem of paint removal in the chapter on repairing and refinishing doors. In the case of moldings, the problem is even worse. You can take doors off their hinges, and have them dipped in a tank of chemical paint stripper. You can't always remove moldings. They may break up if you try to take them off. The only safe way to strip them is to leave them right where they are, and take the paint off with a heat gun. Then, follow up the heat gun with an acetone wash. It's very tedious and time-consuming work.

A roomful of moldings can easily take 40 hours to clean and refinish. You'd have to charge at least $800 for this kind of job, more if you have higher labor costs. For beautiful woodwork in a central part of the house, like the living or dining room, the cost might be worthwhile. In a bedroom, it usually isn't. The Victorians were right: the bedrooms aren't worth spending a lot of money decorating, because not that many people ever see them.

Testing for Lead — You may run across lead-based paints in very old houses. If you're concerned about that, you can use a test kit to see if paint contains lead. I use one called Lead Zone, made by Enzone Incorporated. It only costs about $4. It contains a packet of test strips that change color if they come into contact with lead.

I rarely come across lead-based paint. I think that's because it has been off the market for about 30 years. Most of the woodwork I deal with was originally varnished, and was painted over fairly recently. By the time it was painted, lead-based paints were no longer used.

Maximizing Space

When you're working on a small house, every inch is precious. If it was remodeled in the past, there may be some dead spaces created when new partitions were put in. Rather than having an awkward wall around a little corner, remodelers often just run a straight wall over it, leaving an enclosed space with nothing in it. The older the house is, the more likely you are to find spaces like this. Look for odd shaped walls, walls that seem unreasonably thick, or walls that don't line up. These dead spaces can be useful for closets or storage. If you're going to be making major changes to the floor plan, you can get rid of these dead spaces, and get a few more feet of floor space.

Victorian homes also have open areas of unusable space created by the exterior design of the house or from the addition of heating ducts or plumbing pipes. Narrow or awkward corners or boxed-in areas that are useless for living space or furniture can be closed in to make additional storage areas. You can make linen closets, built-in shelving, or small cupboards. If you look carefully, there are probably a lot of these little spaces that would be good for storage: over and under stairways, behind knee walls in upstairs bedrooms, and around boxed-in flues.

If you put in a prefabricated fireplace, you'll be boxing in a large area above it. Built-in shelves would be nice there, or a built-in cabinet. These little odds and ends of space may not seem worthwhile, but they add up.

Of course, this kind of work can be expensive. Built-in shelving and cupboards require fine carpentry. You can't leave this type of work to unskilled helpers. Is the added space worth the expense? The answer to this question is determined by the size of the house. Adding a few more square feet to a large house doesn't increase its value very much. Adding the same amount of space to a small house is far more worthwhile. The smaller the house, the more valuable the added space will be. You can often find several square yards of extra storage space in varying locations throughout a house. That's

Figure 19-19
*Chest of drawers built into
dead space in wall*

almost as much space as you'd get by adding a small room. While these scavenged spaces may be expensive on a per-square-foot basis, they're a lot cheaper than building on an addition. The extra space becomes even more valuable if the house is in an area where code or zoning restrictions won't allow an addition to be built. In situations like that, the little scavenged spaces may be the only way to add any space at all.

Built-in cupboards and closets can hold items that would otherwise take up space someplace else. Figure 19-19 shows a chest of drawers that has been built into a dead space behind a bedroom wall. In a small room, built-ins like these free up valuable floor space by eliminating the need for free-standing floor units. While you aren't actually adding floor space, it makes more floor space available. This is also true if you put a closet in a dead space. That frees up the space on the floor where the closet would otherwise have been. The effect is the same as enlarging the room.

🐦 Making Built-in Closets and Cabinets

Many older homes were originally constructed with little built-in cupboards, closets, and shelves. Adding new ones won't

seem odd or look out of place, even if the house didn't have built-ins before. These features are in keeping with the spirit of an older home.

I usually concentrate on building cupboards and closets, rather than adding open shelving. Open shelving is more difficult to construct because it's in plain view all the time; it has to be absolutely perfect. When there's other woodwork in the room, new shelving has to be stained to match. This kind of shelving requires a skilled carpenter, and takes time. When you have to subcontract out the work, it's no longer a cost-effective means of adding space. I don't find it's worth doing unless the homeowner specifically wants open shelves.

Built-in cupboards and closets avoid a lot of problems. The spaces are covered by doors, and you can't normally see the inside clearly. You can use drywall for the interiors, and plain pine for the shelving. That's easier to build and finish than open shelves.

By cupboards and cabinets, I mean a built-in storage space that's covered by a small door. These spaces are generally on the order of about 2 feet by 3 feet. If a space is substantially smaller than that, it isn't worth bothering with. If it's larger, I call it a closet. A cabinet or cupboard can have built-in shelving, a closet rod for hanging clothes, a closet-organizer arrangement, or a combination of these. The choice depends on how big the space is and how the homeowner wants to use it.

Closets and cabinets are really quite easy to make. First, find a suitable unused space. If the space is walled in, open it up as far as you can. If it's deep and there's a lot of space, you can make it into a closet. If not, you can make a built-in cabinet. Essentially, a cabinet is the same as a closet, only smaller.

Figure 19-20 shows an open area over a stairway that I thought of as potential closet space. I boxed in the space and added a little cabinet door that I had salvaged from another job. The result is the mini-closet shown in Figure 19-21. While it isn't a full-height closet, it is full depth. There's room to hang shirts, coats or other short clothing items. Had the

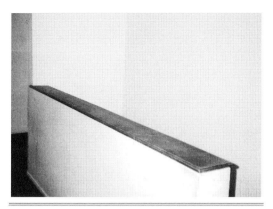

Figure 19-20
*Open area over stairway
is potential closet space*

Figure 19-21
Small closet completed in open space

owners preferred, I could have put in shelves and made it a nice, deep linen closet.

Framing in closets or cabinets can be awkward. You have to work in small spaces, without disturbing the existing walls. Aside from the problem of limited space, however, it's a lot like building any closet. In the case of a cabinet, it's like building a miniature closet. You can drywall the closet or cabinet walls, but use plywood for the bottom to provide enough strength.

Storage Closet and Cabinet Doors

There are two problems in finding doors for the closets and cabinets: First is finding a door that fits the nonstandard space. And second, finding a door that matches the style in the rest of the house. After all, the door and the trim around it are the only parts of the addition that will show. They need to look nice, and they need to be the same style and color as the other woodwork in the room.

If the space is large enough to accept a full-size closet door, you're in luck. It's a lot easier to find full-size doors than small doors. You can usually find closet doors in styles to match most any decor. But where do you find small, odd-size doors?

Actually, I've found that there are several possibilities. First of all, I always save any small doors that I remove from old homes. A lot of these come from old linen closets or

medicine cabinets. Also, you can often find inexpensive odd-size doors in antique stores or at flea markets. They're cheap because most people have no use for them, but they don't really want to just throw them away.

The advantage to using recycled doors is that they're genuinely old. Old doors will blend well with the other old features of the house. When you use old doors, no one suspects that the cabinet or cupboard is a new addition. What's the disadvantage? There's no reliable source for them. If you need several to match, you'll never find them. Also, you can't just go out and find the size you need. You just have to select from what's available at the time. Of course, since you're building the cabinet from scratch, you can make the door opening a little bigger or smaller to fit the door. All you have to do is find a door that's within a few inches of the right size.

Another source I use for doors are wooden shutters. They make good cabinet doors. They look a lot like louvered closet doors, only they're smaller. A nice thing about shutters is that they're available in a wide range of sizes. You can usually find one to fit any size

Figure 19-22
*Window shutters make good
folding doors for small closets*

Figure 19-23
Shutters used as cabinet doors in bathroom

cabinet. And they are fairly inexpensive. Figures 19-22 and 19-23 show two different cabinets I built with wood shutters for doors, one in a bedroom and the other in a bathroom.

Kitchen cabinet fronts can sometimes be used for doors on built-in cabinets. Only certain styles will do, however. You don't want the cabinet to look like a kitchen cabinet that's been set into a wall. I only use the ones that are styled in an "antique look." They have a dark finish with leaded-glass fronts. Anyplace that carries a large selection of kitchen cabinets will have this style. They're designed to look like Victorian built-in cabinetry. And, that's just exactly what you want them to be. What luck! Using these fronts on your new built-in cabinet will give it a very authentic look.

Making Cabinet Doors — If you can't find any used or new doors or shutters that will fit the cabinet, you can make the doors yourself using the same technique that you use for making windows.

First, make a frame out of 1 x 4s. I usually use steel corners to hold the 1 x 4s together. The steel corners keep the pieces straight and flat. Of course, they go on the inside where they won't show. I glue all the joints, as well as fastening them together with screws.

Next, I run a router along the back side of the frame and cut a groove ¼ inch deep. Then I cut a piece of ¼-inch plywood the

same size as the inside of the frame, and set it into the groove. It should be glued in place as well as nailed. The result is a nice little panel door. Once it's painted, it'll look just like any other antique door. It isn't really hard, but I don't suggest doing this, except as a last resort. It's very time-consuming. It's a lot easier to buy a door.

Skylights

Some rooms in Victorian homes can feel cramped and be quite dark. If these rooms have a roof overhead (as opposed to another room), you can brighten them up by installing a skylight.

You might think that a skylight wouldn't be a very Victorian addition, but it is. The Victorians had skylights, but they didn't use them in the same way we use them today. Victorian skylights were heavy, clunky assemblies made of glass set in a cast-iron frame. They were expensive, hard to work with, and almost always leaky. That's why they were rarely in homes. They were more common in large buildings where they could provide light for several floors at once, such as above stairways in apartment houses or in commercial buildings. This function was especially important in the days before electric lights became available. Gaslights weren't very bright. They weren't much better than candles at providing light. That made natural light very important, especially in factories and other work places. Highly elaborate skylights, made with opaque and light-colored stained glass and ornamental frames, were also installed in fancy hotel lobbies, multistory department stores, court houses and other official buildings to provide light.

When electric lighting became widely available, after the turn of the century, skylights fell out of favor. They were no longer necessary for lighting, and their maintenance and safety problems had given them a bad name. They didn't regain widespread popularity again until the 1970s, when plastic skylights became available.

Skylights are a good example of a modification that can follow the spirit of the Victorian style, even though their use may not be absolutely historically accurate. Of course Victorian builders didn't have modern skylights available. If they had, Victorians would certainly have used them. Their only criticism would have been "Hmm, it looks a bit plain to me. Let's dress it up with some decorations!" They would have embellished them with the same kind of fretwork that they put on everything else.

You can duplicate this look by decorating a modern skylight with Victorian fretwork. A fretwork grille, like those the Victorians used on warm-air openings, would give you a very Victorian look. You'll probably have to construct a grille like this yourself, or have it custom made. Depending on the size and shape of the skylight, you might be able to get the effect you want by assembling some pieces of standard millwork. You could also decorate around the opening with some corner braces or spandrels to achieve a very Victorian look. Or use decorative moldings around the skylight, either of wood or molded plastic, and paint them to look like plasterwork. The final result will be very Victorian.

Try to match the shape of the skylight to the shape of the room. Use a square skylight in a square room, a rectangular skylight in a rectangular room, and so on. Many modern skylight installations use multiple skylights.

This isn't something the Victorians would have done. You don't want to create an effect that would be too modern. It would be better to just use one and decorate it.

The most authentic location for a skylight in a Victorian house is at the top of the staircase, to provide light for the stairway. That's the only place Victorians actually used skylights in their homes. However, you can use skylights to brighten up a dark bedroom, the kitchen, or any room the Victorians considered an informal area. Don't use them in a formal parlor or the dining room. These were formal rooms and the Victorians wouldn't have used skylights there — the effect would have been too casual.

Victorians also used skylights to light up ceiling-mounted stained glass windows. This creates a very striking effect, which you can see in some restored Victorian public buildings. The roof is actually two layers of glass. On the inside is the fancy glass that you can see, and above is the outer layer made of wrought iron framework and plain glass, which allows light to shine through. The fancy glass on the inside is very delicate and needs to be protected. It isn't strong enough to take rough weather, or extreme changes in temperature that you find on a roof top.

If you have a nice stained-glass window to work with, you can create the same effect without actually installing a skylight. Instead, you can mount a bank of fluorescent lights behind the stained glass. These can be mounted in the joist space in the ceiling, or even in a wall cavity. Fluorescent lights don't take up much room or generate a lot of heat, so you can put them most anywhere. Since you can't see through most stained glass, you won't be able to see the lights behind it. It will appear that the glass is illuminated by daylight.

If the fluorescent bulbs do show through, you can mount a diffuser between the lights and the window. A diffuser is a piece of plastic with a lot of little star shapes cast into it. They are most often used as covers for fluorescent light fixtures. You can buy plastic diffuser by the sheet, and cut it to any size. The light that comes through the plastic is

Figure 19-24
Framing for light well between ceiling and skylight

diffused white light, like natural light on a slightly cloudy day. I've seen this technique used in homes and also in a lot of restaurants. People who put money into stained glass windows often want them to show up, day or night. Of course, if someone wants it to look like there's a real skylight behind the stained glass, they'll have to keep the lights off at night. Again, as ceiling decorations, they belong in the entry or the less formal areas of the house.

Skylight Installation

Installing skylights isn't terribly hard, but you do need to do it carefully. Sloppy installations will leak. Skylights are more exposed than windows. Most of the time, rain doesn't fall directly on a window because windows are vertical and protected by the eaves. A skylight, however, is right where it will bear the brunt of the weather. Since it's usually installed part way down the roof, it has to handle not only the rain that falls on it, but also the rain that falls on the section of roof above it and pours down over it. This can be a great deal of water, so the skylight must be sealed very carefully.

It's most cost-effective to install a skylight in a ceiling that already needs repair. Whenever you cut a hole for a skylight, you're going to damage the ceiling. In the case of wet plaster ceilings, the damage may be extensive enough that you may have to replace the entire ceiling. Unlike drywall, it's almost impossible to cut a large hole in a plaster ceiling without causing extensive cracking. If the ceiling needs to be replaced anyway, you can kill two birds with one stone. However, if the ceiling is in perfect condition, you'll have to add the cost of a new ceiling into your estimate.

Make it a habit to check the attic space carefully before cutting a hole in the ceiling. You want to be sure that there isn't any wiring going through the area you plan to cut. Cutting live wires can be dangerous, and common sense won't tell you where wires are likely to be in an older house. Remember, the house has probably been remodeled several times, so there's no guarantee that everything is in a logical position. You have to go up into the attic and check. While you're there, remove the insulation from the area you plan to cut out to prevent it from falling through the ceiling and making a mess.

It's also a good idea to peel away the shingles from the area of the roof you plan to cut out. I've tried just cutting through them, and discovered that the granules on the shingles take the edge off a saw blade almost instantly. You'll have to peel off some shingles in order to install the skylight anyway, so you might as well do it before you ruin your saw blade, rather than after.

Building a Light Well

One thing that confuses many people when installing skylights is what to do with the space between the ceiling and the roof. After all, unless the house has open beam ceilings, you won't come immediately upon the roof when you cut through the ceiling. Instead, you'll find yourself in the attic space. There may be 5 or 6 feet of space between the ceiling and the roof. What you need to do is build a light well to enclose that space. A light well is really just a box that extends between the ceiling and the roof. Frame it in with 2 x 4s and finish it with drywall. Be sure to insulate the attic side of the well to prevent the drywall from conducting heat and cold from the attic space into the house. Figure 19-24 shows the framing being constructed for a light well.

In most cases, you'll want to build just a plain box and paint it white to reflect the light coming in through the skylight. However, you may need to change the design of the box to improve the focus of the light. For example, if the roof is several feet above the ceiling, you will have a long, thin light well if you just make a straight box. The longer the light well, the narrower the focus of light coming into the room below. You can widen that focus by making the light well wider at the bottom than at the top. This will cause the light to spread out and cover a larger area, like the reflector on a flashlight. Just keep in mind that the final design needs to harmonize with the rest of the house. Victorian houses need to be formal, and any additions you make to the design of the house should be in a regular, symmetrical pattern.

Cleaning

If you're using a plastic or Plexiglas skylight, try to avoid getting it dirty. They're hard to clean without scratching. If you've ever seen a Plexiglas window that's been cleaned a lot, you'll know what I mean. They quickly turn into frosted Plexiglas. You don't want that to happen to your new skylight. If the skylight has a removable layer of plastic film on it, leave the film in place until you complete the installation, including any painting that you need to do. Then, when you remove the film layer, the plastic will still be sparkling clean, no matter what may have been spilled, splashed or dropped on the skylight during installation.

Plastic skylights rarely need cleaning. The outside will normally be cleaned by rain, and the inside tends not to get dirty. Dirt falls down, not up. If you do need to clean the skylight, wash it very carefully with a soft sponge and warm, soapy water. Never clean it dry — you'll scratch the heck out of it.

Cost

The cost of installing a skylight can be quite moderate. You can get a good-quality, non-operable skylight for as little as $100. Be sure to get one that's double glass, or double plastic, for better insulation. Otherwise it'll get very cold in winter, and cause condensation problems. Moisture will condense on it, drip down, and ruin the drywall. It may not seem like enough moisture would condense on a skylight to cause a problem, but it will. Any single-glass window or skylight can accumulate an amazing amount of condensation on a cold day, especially if the house is humid. I've seen major plaster damage caused this way.

If the room where you're installing the skylight needs more ventilation, consider installing an operable skylight, or "roof window." They're especially helpful in converted attics, which are often very hot and stuffy. A roof window can solve both light and ventilation problems. They are a little more expensive, running between $300 and $400, depending on the size and features.

The Victorian Cooling System

Heating and cooling has been a problem in home design for centuries, and the Victorians were no exception. Since there were no air conditioners and older Victorian homes had no central heat, the houses were laid out to make heating and cooling as efficient as possible with the technology they had to work with.

Passive Cooling

One hallmark of Victorian style is the high ceiling. High ceilings gave the houses an open, airy feel that is still greatly prized in homes. This design feature wasn't just for looks. It was to help keep the house cool in the summer. Hot air rises up to the ceiling, allowing cooler air to settle down near the floor, where the people are. Of course, this wastes heat in the winter, but that was less of a concern for the Victorians. They had plenty of heat. They could always put another log on the fire. Cooling was the real problem, and a passive cooling system was the only way they could deal with summer heat.

Figure 19-25
Ventilated thimble for Victorian stovepipe

Another passive cooling device is ventilation. Victorian houses have a lot of windows designed with ventilation in mind. Some of these are unique, like transom windows. A transom is an operable window over a door. Transoms over an interior door may seem strange to people today, but they were really quite clever. They allowed people to close the door for privacy, but still have ventilation flowing through the room.

The Summer Kitchen

Cooking created another cooling problem. The cast-iron, wood-burning stoves used for cooking gave off a lot of heat. That was great in the winter, but in the summer it made the house unbearably hot. Victorian women had to do a lot of cooking and baking, even in the summer. All their food and baked goods were cooked fresh, from scratch, every day. And they cooked and canned fruits or vegetables in the summer and early fall — the hottest time of the year.

The solution was a "summer kitchen," a small kitchen with its own stove built on an outside porch or away from the house in a separate building. The heat from the summer kitchen was vented outside. The regular kitchen wasn't used during the summer, to allow the house to stay as cool as possible. Most summer kitchens were removed or converted into rooms years ago, but once in a while I come across one still intact.

Victorian Heating Systems

Early Victorian homes were heated by cast-iron, wood-burning stoves or by several fireplaces. Each of these would generally serve two or three rooms. The fireplaces would sometimes be built into a common wall between two rooms and be open to each one. That way, two rooms could be heated with one fireplace. Sometimes, a central fireplace served several rooms.

Wood-burning stoves, either kitchen cooking stoves or smaller parlor stoves like Franklin stoves, were often used to heat a room downstairs and the room above it as well. They ran the flue pipe from the stove straight up through a corner of the room above, and then on up into the attic to vent it out through the roof. This wasn't just to save pipe. The flue pipe would get hot, and that heat would radiate through the upstairs room. You can still find remnants of these heating systems in old houses.

I found one in a house I worked on earlier this year. An upstairs bedroom had old linoleum covering the floor, and every time I walked across it, I felt a lump. I pulled up the linoleum and found the ventilated thimble shown in Figure 19-25. It was left in the floor after the wood-burning stove and flue pipe had been removed. You can see how the flue pipe used to come up through the hole from the room below. The pipe had continued upward into the attic, where it connected into a brick chimney. The brick chimney was still there, although in bad condition.

In the picture you can see the old newspapers that had been used as padding under the linoleum. They were all dated April, 1934! No one had done anything to this room for over 60 years! The newspapers were still in good condition, and easily readable. They were full of news about Roosevelt and the depression, the way it was viewed back then, not the way I'd learned about it in history class. Reading them in that old room made me feel like I'd stepped back in time. I didn't get a lot of work done that afternoon, but I did enjoy it. That was one of the odd surprises that make this kind of work so interesting.

Another common means of getting heat from the downstairs stove to the room above was through cast-iron grilles set into the ceiling of the downstairs room and the floor of the upstairs room. This allowed the warm air from the stove to rise up into the upstairs room and heat it. Figure 19-26 shows an original ceiling grille. The grilles always had some kind of design cast into them, and many are quite decorative. It's very common to find them still in place.

You may also find marks in the floor that indicate where the old wood-burning stove used to be, and patched-over holes in upstairs rooms where the old flue pipes or grilles were. It's not likely that you'll find any of the original wood-burning stoves still there, however. Cast-iron stoves don't last forever. After a few decades, they burn through, and have to be replaced. Not too many people keep this kind of heating in place today. The stoves take up too much space and interfere with furniture placement. Most of them were removed decades ago.

It's important to be aware of all these features so you'll recognize them when you come across them. Some homeowners may want them restored. If they want to be absolutely authentic, they may even want you to install a wood-burning stove in the original location. Modern wood-burning stoves can be quite attractive. They offer the opportunity to have a wood-burning heat source without the expense of installing a fireplace. You could offer this as a possibility. It would be a unique addition, and increase the authenticity of the home. As a rule however, I've found that this isn't a very popular option unless I'm working on a historic home.

❧ Salvaging an Existing Fireplace

While cast-iron stoves aren't tremendously popular today, fireplaces are. Some of the original fireplaces may still be in place in the house. Often the fireplaces were covered over when the house was converted to a central heating system. They were considered drafty and old-fashioned. Today a fireplace is considered one of the more desirable features

Figure 19-26
Ornamental grille in ceiling allows heat to rise into room above

of a home. It might be a good idea to restore the old fireplaces when you find them — if you can find them. Sometimes they have been walled over, leaving little or no trace of their existence.

Once again you have to look for clues to the past to uncover fireplace locations. Look in the areas where you think a fireplace should be. Are there any structures jutting out of a wall that could be brickwork that's been plastered over? Are there any chimneys outside that don't seem to be connected to anything? Nobody builds chimneys for no reason. Look for fireplaces below them. Also, count the number of flue pipes coming out of each chimney. Each flue pipe serviced a separate fireplace. If there are more flue pipes than there are fireplaces, look for the hidden fireplaces.

Some fireplaces are easy to restore. They may have just been sealed up and covered over with plasterwork, Underneath, they may be in almost perfect condition. Then the biggest problem you'll have is a missing fireplace mantel. Since the mantel stuck out, it had to be removed to make a nice smooth wall. Antique stores often have mantels, and sometimes you can find just what you need.

If you can't find an antique mantel that matches the fireplace, you can buy a reproduction. I usually order from Morgan Products Ltd., Oshkosh, WI 54903. You can call them at 1-800-435-7464 for more information.

Coal-Burning Fireplaces

Many old fireplaces were designed to burn coal, not wood. This is most likely to be the case if the house was originally located in an urban area. A coal-burning fireplace had a very small firebox and flue. If the original grille is still there, you'll see that it's quite small as well. These fireplaces were made for small hot coal fires, rather than large cool wood fires. A coal-burning fireplace isn't suitable for burning wood. An average wood fire would produce more smoke than it could handle, and smoke up the house. Rather than risk smoke damage, it would be better to either install a gas log unit, or not use the fireplace at all.

If you decide to install gas logs, be sure the flue is clear, and in good repair. After 50 years of disuse, it may be full of rubbish. Also, be sure the flue is big enough to handle the amount of flue gases that the gas logs put out. If the flue doesn't meet the manufacturer's requirements, you might need to buy a smaller set of gas logs.

Cleaning Ash Dumps

Regardless of the type of fuel the fireplace burns, you'll need to check the ash dump. The ash dump is a small space inside the base of the fireplace. It has a little trap door in the floor of the fireplace where the ashes can be swept through. The ashes go into the dump and then they can be removed through another door, either in the basement or outside of the house. This allows the ashes to be cleaned out of the fireplace without carrying them through the living room.

No one ever cleans out these ash dumps! I usually find a 50-year accumulation of ashes, trash, and garbage in them. You're not supposed to throw garbage down the ash dump, but people do it anyway. I've found old cigarette packs and beer bottles from the 1950s among the ashes. You know when you find things that haven't been manufactured in 40 years that it's been a long time since the ash dump was cleaned out!

When you finish cleaning the dump, be sure you secure the cleanout door. Otherwise, you can cause some major problems. I forget to check this once. I carefully cleaned out all the ashes in the dump, but neglected to repair the loose door in the basement. It seemed okay at the time. However, the first time a fire was made in the fireplace, some hot coals fell down the ash dump, out the loose door in the basement, and started a fire! Luckily, the smoke alarms went off, and the fire was quickly put out, but it could have been a tragedy. I've learned to always be very careful when dealing with fireplaces.

There are cases where you may not be able to find the cleanout door for the ash dump. It may have been blocked or covered over by previous remodeling, especially if the house was re-sided. Remodelers have been known to install the new siding right over a cleanout door. If you can't find the cleanout, don't worry. You don't absolutely need a cleanout or an ash dump for a fireplace. It's just a convenience. Many modern fireplaces don't have them. If there's an ash dump full of ashes and no cleanout, you'll just have to clean it out the hard way. Scoop all the ashes and trash into a bucket and carry them out.

🐟 Installing a New Fireplace

If the home has no fireplace, the homeowners may want to consider installing one — or several. Nothing adds to the charm of a house like a fireplace. Installing a fireplace can also add up to $10,000 to the resale value of the house. It's not a cheap job, but it is a job that can more than pay for itself.

Putting in a fireplace is a lot easier than it used to be, since you can use prefabricated zero-clearance fireplaces. Figure 19-27 shows a prefabricated fireplace being installed. Even though these aren't as difficult and time consuming as building a full masonry fireplace, they're still a lot of work.

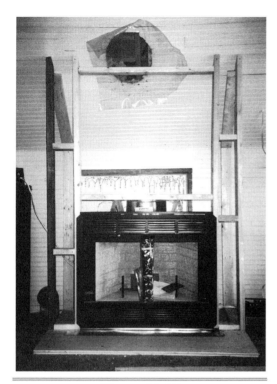

Figure 19-27
Prefabricated fireplace installation

Figure 19-28
Completed fireplace

A nice advantage to working with prefabricated fireplaces is that they only weigh about 100 pounds. That means they don't require the special supports that masonry fireplaces need. But you still have to frame, drywall and trim them, and protect the area around the fireplace from radiant heat. I use cement board for this. Figure 19-28 shows the completed prefab fireplace ready to be used.

The biggest problem with prefabricated fireplaces is installing the chimney. It's not that it's difficult, it's that the chimney takes up space. If you're installing the fireplace on the second floor, or in a one-story house, the chimney won't be a major problem. It will go up through the framed-in, drywalled enclosure, continue through the attic space, and out through the roof. It doesn't matter that it takes up space in these areas. However, if you're installing the fireplace on the first floor of a two-story house, the chimney has to go through the upstairs some place. That can be awkward. Even if it's neatly boxed-in, it might look out of place.

You need to consider what you're going to do with the chimney before deciding on the placement of the fireplace. If you can run the chimney through an upstairs closet, or in a corner, it will be much less noticeable than if it's right in the middle of a wall.

Prefabricated fireplaces can be very inexpensive. For instance, the one shown in Figures 19-27 and 19-28 only cost $175. The chimney kit was an additional $150, and the optional fireplace doors were $80. With drywall, cement board, 2 x 4s, and miscellaneous small parts, the materials for the entire project (less the cost of the tile) only ran about $450. I installed this fireplace all by myself. It took me two days to put it in and another eight hours to do the finish trim and tile work. I recommend that you have at least two men for the installation — it's a big job. I wasted a lot of time trying to line up the chimney. It would have been a lot easier if there was one person on the inside and one on the outside. I had to go back and forth, making adjustments, until I got it right. Once the initial installation is done, one person can do the finish and trim.

If there isn't a place to run a chimney, you can avoid the problem entirely by installing one of the new direct-vent gas fireplaces. These use forced-draft venting, like the new high-efficiency furnaces. They don't need a chimney at all. The gases vent through a little opening like a clothes dryer vent which you can mount in the wall directly behind the fireplace. One source for direct-vent gas fireplaces is Majestic Fireplaces. You can contact them at 1-800-525-1898 to get more information.

There are a couple of problems with these gas fireplaces. First, they're fairly expensive — $1,000 as opposed to $450 for a basic prefabricated wood-burning model. Depending on your budget, this may or may not be important. The second problem is that these fireplaces can only be used with gas logs. You can never burn wood in them. You may not think that this is a problem, but it is.

Most of your customers won't really want to burn wood in their fireplace, but they don't know that! They imagine themselves sitting around a crackling wood fire, with the pleasant smell of smoke filling the room. They'll look at the gas fireplace and say, "I want a real fireplace, not a gas fireplace." You can spend as much time as you want trying to explain to them that a gas fireplace is real. It won't do any good. In their minds, if it doesn't burn wood, it's phony.

This is not an attitude that's easily changed. When it comes to increasing the value of a house, a "phony" gas fireplace will add much less value than a wood-burning one. It will still add value, but only about half as much, even though the gas fireplace may cost more. If there's just no reasonable way to install a wood-burning fireplace, a gas fireplace is better than nothing, but it's definitely second best in the minds of the consumer.

Wood-Burning vs. Gas Fireplaces

These romantic ideas about fireplaces usually come from people who have never had a wood-burning fireplace before. People who have had experience with wood fires are well aware of their problems. Let's face it, building a wood fire can be a lot of work! As a result, most people hardly ever use their fireplaces. They only make fires when they have company or for special occasions. They hardly ever bother to make a fire just for the family.

Another problem with wood fires is the mess. You can't help getting ashes and wood chips in the house. This is especially true of prefabricated fireplaces and wood stoves, because they don't have ash dumps. Masonry fireplaces with ash dumps are a little cleaner. At least you don't have to haul the ashes out through the living area. But just scooping up the ashes can raise clouds of sooty dust. If homeowners have light-colored carpeting, and like to keep their house really spotless, they won't use their fireplace. They'll make one fire, once. When they discover how messy it is, they may never make another.

Firewood is also a problem. Unless you buy it by the cord, and have someplace to store it, it can be very expensive. If you buy the little bundles of firewood sold in supermarkets during the holidays, it's most certainly expensive. Those little bundles cost about $4 and burn up in about half an hour. Imagine trying to heat a house with them; it would cost about $35,000 a year!

You can buy a cord of firewood for about $100, but then you have to store it someplace, and it can weigh up to 5,000 pounds. Most homeowners aren't prepared to haul, store or use 5,000 pounds of wood. I know lots people who bought cords of wood thinking that they would burn it up quickly, and most of that wood is still stacked outside their homes, unburned, years later. The wood sits in the same pile as when they had it delivered. Eventually it will just rot away.

It's possible that a homeowner may have some idea about heating with wood, and may want to pay extra for a heat-circulating fireplace, or put in a wood stove for greater heat efficiency. As long as they know what's involved, that's fine. A large home can take 15 cords of firewood a year for good heating. At $100 a cord, that's $1,500 a year. That much wood can weigh 75,000 pounds. Hauling firewood may be fun in September, but by April, the romance has gone out of it!

For most people, it isn't worthwhile to spend a lot of extra money on a heat-circulating fireplace. Of course, even an inexpensive fireplace has some heat circulating features in it. It just doesn't have the blowers and ductwork the more expensive models have. Usually, the average models are plenty good for the average homeowner.

There are probably a few oddballs, like me, who are willing to put up with the mess and other problems involved with using wood for heating. I use 15 cords a year to heat my large Victorian farmhouse. Of course, I get the wood free, from dead trees on wooded land I own. I figure it saves me about $1,500 a year in heating bills, and even though I'm pretty tired of it by April, hauling firewood keeps me from getting too flabby over the winter.

Even when I lived in the city, I found there were a lot of ways to get firewood free. You have to be fairly industrious about it, and it helps if you have a truck to haul it in. Some cities give free wood to residents, from trees that the city has had to cut down. Check with the Department of Public Works in your city. You can also ask people who are cutting down their trees if they're going to use them for firewood. Most people will say "You're welcome to it if you want to haul it away." Otherwise they'll have to pay someone to haul it off. I've hauled away dozens of cords of wood like this every year. I've used several cords of wood a year for decades, and never had to buy any of it.

If homeowners have never owned a fireplace before and they think they'll use their fireplace for heating, you should warn them of these problems. However, be forewarned: they won't believe you! They've seen too many movies with people sitting in front of beautiful, crackling wood fires to see the negative side of the situation. Don't argue with them. Instead, check back in about a year. Chances are they'll say "Oh yeah, we love our fireplace. It's really nice, but we don't have time to use it much."

The Gas Log Alternative

There's a simple solution to this problem: you can install gas logs in wood-burning fireplaces. There's no mess, no fuss, no wood chips, no ashes. You just turn the logs on, and you've got a nice, cheery fire. That's really the only kind of fire that most homeowners will ever use.

The nice thing about having a wood-burning fireplace is that you have a choice. You can keep is as it is or install gas logs when you get tired of dealing with the problems of wood fires. A wood-burning fireplace can be converted to gas logs, but a gas fireplace can't be converted to wood.

A wood-burning fireplace has the advantages of being a "real" fireplace that will increase property values, but with gas logs, there's no trouble. When the homeowners decide to sell their house, they can tell prospective buyers, "This is a wood-burning fireplace, which just happens to have gas logs for our convenience. If you don't like them, we can have them taken out and you can burn wood." If the buyers are romantics, they'll want the gas logs taken out. But if someone were to check back with them in a year, they would probably be willing to pay to put the gas logs back in.

Chapter 20

The Bathroom

You'll probably have to do a lot of work in the bathrooms and kitchen to bring the house up to modern standards. Unless they've been remodeled already, these rooms generally involve enough work that they each deserve a chapter all their own. Let's start with bathrooms, since there's almost always a shortage of them in older homes.

Bathrooms and Property Values

Extensive remodeling, especially upstairs, can offer a good opportunity to put in another bathroom. Adding a much-needed bathroom can greatly increase the resale value of a house. It's another project that homeowners can make a substantial profit on, if or when they sell the house.

According to *Remodeling* magazine, the average bath addition costs $10,552, and increases the resale value of the house by 95 percent of that amount. That doesn't indicate a profit — in fact it's a slight loss. However, when I add an additional bath, it generally returns 200 to 300 percent of its cost, and that's quite a nice profit for some-

one! Why are my remodeling jobs more profitable than the average?

The *Remodeling* figures are compiled using an average of *all* bathroom additions. Some were much-needed and cost-effective additions, while others were frivolous and extravagant. You can't expect to get the same return on a fancy bathroom-spa addition that you can on a simple second bath when you're dealing with a $100,000 house. A simple bath addition is the most cost-effective type for a house in that price range. If you're working on a high-priced house that already has four bathrooms, adding a fifth bath won't increase its value very much, unless it's a fancy spa. Very few people need that many bathrooms, but the rich enjoy these little extra luxuries.

On the other hand, a large house with four or five bedrooms and only one bathroom desperately needs another bathroom. Without it, the house is below standard. People expect larger homes to have two or three baths. If they don't, it lowers the value of the house significantly. Adding another bath (or two) to a house like this repairs a defect. And that correction will greatly increase the value of the property.

After a house has two bathrooms, each additional bathroom will raise the value of the property less. If you add a second bath to a large home that has only one, you'll raise the property value a lot. Adding a third bath will raise it somewhat, but not as much. That's because a large home with only one bathroom is hard to live in. Families avoid buying houses with only one bath — unless, of course, the house is *really* cheap. With the money they save on the house they can add a second bathroom.

With the addition of a second bath, the house becomes more usable, and its value goes up. A third bath isn't absolutely necessary, but it can be nice. A half-bath is usually the most cost-effective way to go when adding a third bath to a large house. It will still return more in property value than it costs to put in. If you add a full third bath, the cost versus value benefit drops off. It probably won't return as much as it costs. Adding any more bathrooms beyond that is just extravagant.

In general, a house with three bedrooms should have at least one and a half baths. A house with four or five bedrooms should have two or two and a half baths. That's what buyers have come to expect. Any less will result in a lower value for the house. Having only one bathroom is no longer acceptable in anything larger than a small two-bedroom cottage.

Keep in mind that the increased resale value is a percentage of the original value of the house, and not an absolute dollar figure. It works out to more, in terms of dollars, on an expensive house than on a cheap house. The percentage of increase also varies, depending on the price of the house. If someone is trying to buy a house very cheaply, they have to take what they can get. They can't quibble about the number of bathrooms. On the other hand, if a house is offered at top dollar, a buyer shouldn't have to accept anything second-rate. A shortage of bathrooms will obviously hurt a house like this more than it will the cheap one.

All of these factors have a bearing on just exactly how much any remodeling job is going to be worth in the long run. The most profitable jobs, in terms of added value, are those that repair serious defects in high-priced homes. The amount of value you can add to homes in situations like this is quite remarkable. You can easily raise the value of the property by ten times what the job costs to do.

Building a Bathroom

Building a bathroom is a huge subject. There are many books devoted solely to the subject of bathroom additions. It would be pointless for me to attempt to duplicate all that information here. Instead, I'd rather discuss some of the particular aspects of bathroom additions that relate to maximum value remodeling in older homes.

❧ Converting Extra Space into a Bathroom

If you're planning to build a full bath, with a tub, you'll need a space that's at least 5 feet by 7 feet. That may not sound like much, but it can be very hard to find. Sometimes every space you find has some kind of drawback. If there's no practical alternative, you can squeeze a bathroom into a space that's only 4 feet by 5 feet, but it will be very cramped. A large bath is considered luxurious, so you should always try to build a bath in the biggest space that's available.

A half-bath, without a tub or shower, can fit in a space that's 4 feet by 4 feet or in an odd-shaped space, like 5 feet by 2½ feet. Thirty inches is the width of a standard door, and the minimum width acceptable for a half-bath in my area. Before you choose a space that small for a half-bath, check with your city building department. Their requirements may be different. A lot of closets are just about the right size for a half-bath. Because of this, turning a closet into a half-bath is a classic remodeling job. You may think it's too small, but I've found that most people would rather use a small bathroom than wait in line for a large one.

Figure 20-1
New half-bath conversion

Figure 20-2
Beginning work from the kitchen side

Figure 20-1 shows a bathroom I built using a pantry and an entry closet. The pantry shared a common wall with a coat closet that opened onto the hallway off the living room. Neither area was very large. I tore out the wall between the pantry and the coat closet to expand the space. The two closet-sized spaces combined were enough for one small 7 foot by 3 foot room. Figures 20-2 and 20-3 show the pantry side of the project, with

Don't forget about ventilation in these small areas. If the new bathroom doesn't have a window, it will need a fan that's ducted to the outside. Installing ductwork can be a problem in some locations. You may not be able to get it through to the outside without going through other rooms.

Many older homes have good-sized pantries that you can turn into a downstairs bathroom, if it's needed. One advantage to this location is that the plumbing is nearby. Locating a bathroom near the kitchen helps avoid awkward plumbing runs and the resulting damage to other rooms from installing piping.

If you use the pantry space, always try to open up another doorway so the new bathroom doesn't face the kitchen. It would be best if the bathroom opened onto a hallway. If that isn't possible, opening onto a living room, parlor or entry is better than opening onto the kitchen. However, a bathroom off the kitchen is better than no bathroom at all.

Figure 20-3
*Tearing out the wall between
the pantry and closet*

Figure 20-4
The coat closet

Figure 20-5
*The common wall from closet
side during the tear out*

the wall being removed from inside the panty. Figures 20-4 and 20-5 show the entry closet before and during the tear out process. Once the two areas were opened up, I sealed off the door from the pantry to the kitchen so that the room opened only onto the hallway.

Figure 20-6
Subflooring in very poor condition

The next step was to remove and replace the existing floor covering. The floor underneath was in poor condition, as you can see in Figure 20-6. I installed new underlayment (Figure 20-7), laid cement board over that, and then installed ceramic tile. You can see the bathroom taking shape in Figure 20-8. You can also see that there was a drain line in the floor under the old floor covering. The area that was the pantry had once had a toilet in it. Because that was all there was room for, and it was in the kitchen, the toilet had been removed and the space converted into a pantry. Now I was converting it again! However, by adding in the additional space from the entry closet, I was able to solve the space and entry problems.

I tapped into the kitchen plumbing to add the water lines for the toilet and sink. Once the walls were drywalled and wallpapered and the accessories were in, I had a cute little half-bath which opened onto the hallway. I kept the original closet door and woodwork, which matched the other woodwork in the hallway. The new bathroom blended perfectly with the rest of the house. All that was lost to add this half-bath was some underutilized storage space.

Materials for the job came to about $500, and it took about 80 hours. That was longer than I had originally estimated. It was more difficult than I thought it would be to work in such a small space. Still, the job was well worthwhile, and easily added about $10,000 to the value of the house.

🐛 Upstairs Bathroom Additions

When you're planning bathroom additions upstairs, try to avoid having to install awkward plumbing runs all through the house. Ideally, you'd like to install the second bathroom over the kitchen, to keep the plumbing runs as short as possible. However, the existing bathroom may already be there. If so, you'll have to go on to the next-best space. That is generally back-to-back with the existing bathroom, so the two bathrooms share a common wall. With luck, it will be a wall that's close to the drain stack, so that you can tap into it.

One feature you will find in many Victorian houses is an open area at the top of the stairs on the second floor. This open area is often quite large, sometimes it's as big as a bedroom. I had wondered about this design

for quite a while, and only recently found out the purpose behind this space. It was used as the upstairs heating area. A wood-burning stove would be located there, and the area left unrestricted so that the heat could spread throughout the upstairs rooms. I've found these open areas in houses built as late as 1925. A house with a furnace and ductwork didn't need this space, so if you find one of these, it tells you that the house was built without a central heating system.

The most important thing about this area today, is that it's a perfect space to use for a new bathroom. It's a room-sized space, with nothing in it. In many cases, there may already be a bathroom there. If there isn't, there should be. For a house short on bathrooms, it's like finding a bonus room. You can do anything with it, but a new bathroom would be your best improvement.

Make the New Bath Convenient

Sometimes there's just no good way to locate a new bathroom near the existing plumbing. If that's the case, it's not worth sacrificing the entire layout of the house to do it. Having awkward plumbing runs is okay if it's necessary to achieve a good room layout. It's better than a simple plumbing run in a layout that doesn't make sense. A new bathroom needs to be convenient to the bedrooms. After all, that's why you're building it.

Figure 20-7
New underlayment installed

Figure 20-8
Tile laid over cement board base

You can often make the new bathroom convenient to specific rooms by the placement of the entrance door. If the door faces one way, it will serve one bedroom or group of bedrooms; if it faces another way, it will serve another. There are times however, when you can't make this work out. No matter where you put the door, it's still inconvenient to the bedrooms. Before you decide to find a new place for the bathroom, consider altering the bedrooms instead. It may be easier to change the bedrooms than the bathroom. If you're going to be moving walls and consolidating bedrooms, consider access to the bathroom when you decide which walls to move.

In some cases, you may be able to solve the problem by having two doors in the bathroom, although this can complicate fixture placement. I've often seen doors that hang up on a sink or a toilet, and can't be fully opened. With two doors, the problem can be twice as bad. If one of the doors opens into a bedroom, you may be able to have it open outward from the bathroom and inward into the bedroom. That saves space in the bathroom. But you can't have it open outward into a hallway — people will walk right into it. I've seen doors like this, and they're dangerous. If someone suddenly opens the bathroom door, a person walking down the hall could easily get a broken nose.

One solution to the opening problem is a sliding door. It can't hit anyone in the nose, or hang up on any fixtures. Sliding doors involve a more complicated installation and they won't fit an existing doorway, but they might solve the space problem for a new doorway. Most people don't think of sliding doors in older houses. However, they have been around since Victorian times. I've seen sliding doors in original Victorian houses. If you use a sliding door in an old-fashioned style, you should be able to get a nice effect.

Other Bathroom Problems

The biggest problem with locating a bathroom upstairs is that you need room for a 4-inch drain line and a vent stack. The drain line is a difficult item to place. If you bring it straight down, it may wind up going through a bad spot in a downstairs room. You don't want a boxed-in drain line sticking out in the middle of a dining room wall. It needs to be tucked into a corner, at least. If necessary, you can run it across a room, under the ceiling. However, that means a ceiling will have to come out in order to install the drain line. Were you planning to remove the ceiling? If not, that's an added expense.

In some cases, it may be necessary to remove the ceiling under the new bathroom anyway, especially if you plan to add a bathtub. A tub full of water can weigh 1,000 pounds. Most floors weren't built to hold that much weight in one spot. You'll need to double the floor joists under the tub, and add solid bridging.

Double floor joists aren't needed if you're just planning to add a shower, or just a toilet and sink. Adding solid bridging is still a good idea, though. You need to have a rock-solid surface if you want to install ceramic tile. The floor doesn't need to hold tremendous weight, but it can't have any flex. I like to test the floor by jumping up and down on it, looking for any bouncing or squeaking. If there's any motion at all, add more bridging before you put down tile.

Remodeling an Existing Bathroom

You'll find a variety of bathrooms in older homes. Some are beautiful and elaborate, while others are simple and plain. Some are original and in perfect condition, and others are a mess. Bathrooms can be a particular problem in houses that are 100 years old or more. That's because there was no running water at all when these houses were built. They had a hand pump, and an outhouse. By the time you get to work on these houses, they undoubtedly will have had running water and a bathroom added, but the installation may leave something to be desired.

Figure 20-9
*Makeshift bathroom
in an upstairs hallway*

Figure 20-10
The bathroom sink

❧ The Worst Case Scenario

Figure 20-9 is an example of the kind of nightmare bathroom you might find in an old house. This was the upstairs bathroom in a house I bought recently. It was just an alcove with a toilet in it. There wasn't even a door — just a curtain to close off the alcove from the hallway. The "sink" was a faucet with a bucket under it! You can see it in Figure 20-10. If the bucket wasn't there, the water would just pour right onto the floor.

This rustic excuse for a bathroom may have seemed like a big improvement to people who were used to an outhouse and a hand pump, but no one will stand for facilities like this today. It makes you wonder why it remained like that for so long. Not only was the arrangement primitive, but the toilet didn't even work. When I bought the house, there were no functional toilets at all! As you might well imagine, I got it for quite a good price. Most people won't even look at a house that has no usable toilets.

Figure 20-11
Framing the new bathroom

I tore down the old alcove, and built a full bath in its place. Figure 20-11 shows the framing going in for the new bathroom. In Figure 20-12 you can see the other end of the bathroom, with the tub being framed in. In order to plumb the new fixtures, I had to tear

Figure 20-12
Framing in tub enclosure

Figure 20-13
Bathroom drain pipe and rotted ceiling in downstairs bedroom

down the ceiling in the room below. Fortunately, it was already in need of repair, so I really wasn't creating any new work for myself. You can see the downstairs room in Figure 20-13. Notice the drain pipe running up through the corner? This is a fairly common sight in many older homes. There was some pretty tacky plumbing work done during the first part of the century!

Figure 20-14 shows the downstairs ceiling completely torn out. Looking at the underside of the floor you can see the water marks left by old leaks — probably from somebody turning on the faucet upstairs without a bucket under it! The finished bathroom is shown in Figure 20-15. I took this photograph from the same angle as the one in Figure 20-9. There's quite a difference, isn't there? The biggest problem I had with this job was working in such a small space. I managed to fit in a standard-size tub, but I had to use a mini-size sink without a vanity.

Figure 20-14
Water marks indicate location of leak

ᔕ Repairs and Improvements

Most of the existing bathrooms you'll find will be in better condition than the one we just discussed. But they may still need work to bring them up to modern standards. You'll need to take the condition of the bathroom into account when deciding what remodeling will provide the best return on

Figure 20-15
New upstairs bathroom completed

the homeowners' investment. Let's consider some of the jobs you might want to do in the bathroom.

Total Replacement

From a profitability standpoint, the homeowner has the most to gain by replacing bathrooms that are in poor condition. A ruined bathroom is of no value to anybody. You might as well just tear it all out and start over.

The most common damage to bathrooms is rot, caused by long-term plumbing leaks. We talked about this type of damage in Chapter 13. These leaks may have undermined the walls and floor so badly that everything has to be replaced, right down to the rotted floor joists.

One advantage to tearing everything out is that it allows you to make a fresh start. You don't have to worry about working around features that need to be saved. You can design a completely new bathroom. This may even give you the opportunity to put in a lavish spa bath, if the homeowner's budget allows it.

Making Use of Extra Space — One nice thing about older bathrooms is that they're often quite large. Those built in the 1920s and earlier are often twice as big as those built in the 1940s and '50s. If you find one in original condition, you'll see that there's a lot

of empty space in it. That's because people used to keep furniture items in the bathroom — cabinets, vanities, wardrobes, chairs and whatever. The extra space can come in handy if you want to install some luxurious modern fixtures.

By the 1950s, bathrooms had been downsized considerably. It's actually harder to remodel a bathroom built in 1950 than one built in 1920. This is especially true if you want to install large, luxurious fixtures. However, a very old house may have a 1950s bathroom even if it was built before 1900. You'll find remodeling jobs of all different ages in older homes, often varying in quality and condition.

If you find yourself working with a small bathroom, you might want to consider taking some space from an adjoining room to make it larger. If there's a small bedroom next to the bathroom, you could combine the two rooms into one big bathroom. This is expensive, but if you're working with upscale property, it's worth it.

The rule to keep in mind is: Does this job meet the standards of the neighborhood? Do the neighbors have big, luxurious bathrooms? If they do, then this house should too. Otherwise, the house won't be up to the standards of the neighborhood. To have fewer amenities than the other homes in the area would lower its value. On the other hand, if the house is in an area where the neighbors have ordinary baths, putting in a fancy bath won't be profitable. It won't raise the value of the property as much as the job costs. Of course, the homeowners may want a fancy bath for their own use and enjoyment, rather than as an investment. If that's the case, give them what they want.

❧ Remodeling a Usable Bathroom

If the existing bathroom is usable, you may be able to keep costs down by working with what's there, rather than tearing everything out. You can often achieve a very nice effect, at minimal cost, by replacing only those items that absolutely have to be

Figure 20-16
Old sinks with separate hot and cold water spouts are inconvenient to use

Even if this is all the homeowners can afford right now, it will still be a tremendous improvement over what was there. The bathroom will instantly go from awkward and old-fashioned to modern and fully usable. That will give them the greatest "bang for the buck." If they're all out of bucks, you can stop here. They will still have a nicely improved bathroom.

Removing an Old-Fashioned Tub — Most old bathrooms will still have free-standing, rolled-edge, cast-iron tubs, without showers. These tubs can be beautiful, especially if they're part of an updated and luxurious antique bathroom. We'll discuss this situation shortly. For the moment, let's assume you want to replace the tub with something a little more modern.

If the old rolled-edge tub is in good condition, you may be able to sell it, rather than throw it away. Antique dealers sometimes buy them. They sell them to people to use for all sorts of things, like planters in the garden. You may not get a lot of money for the old tub, but at least it'll save you the trouble of trying to get rid of it.

Old cast-iron tubs are quite heavy and hard to handle. You'll need at least two men to move one. Handle it carefully. If it slips out of your hands while you're taking it down the stairs, it could demolish half the living room before it comes to a stop.

If the tub is in poor condition, it's easier to break it up and take it out in pieces. Cast iron will shatter if you hit it with a sledgehammer. It's a lot easier to dispose of a lot of little pieces of iron than one big tub.

Once the old tub is out, you'll have an open space where it used to be. This space is larger than the standard 5-foot tub pocket, which can be very helpful if you're thinking of installing an oversize tub. This is one of those situations where remodeling an older bathroom can be easier than remodeling a newer one.

If you want to install a standard-size tub/shower assembly however, you'll need to build a tub pocket. Normally, you could do this by just building a small wall at the shower end, but because of the old plumbing,

replaced. If you design a remodel that uses the existing features, you can probably quote it for a fraction of the competitive bids. The homeowners will still get a nicely improved and modernized bathroom.

Most of your competitors will submit bids based on gutting the bathroom and rebuilding it from the studs up. Homeowners on a tight budget might just give up on remodeling the bathroom if all the quotes are unaffordable. Sometimes they become so discouraged by high bids that they won't even mention the bathroom by the time they talk to you. So share any good ideas you have for the bathroom, even if the homeowners don't bring it up. They might be pleasantly surprised to discover that there are options that they *can* afford. Telling them your ideas may get you a job that wouldn't otherwise be done at all.

Replacing Old Fixtures

Old bathroom fixtures can be difficult to use. These include sinks with separate hot and cold water spouts like the one in Figure 20-16, and tubs with no showers. Fixtures like these aren't well suited to modern lifestyles. Replacing them greatly improves the livability of a bathroom.

doing this will make a pocket that's not quite the right size. To line up with the plumbing, the new tub pocket will have to be 5½ or 6 feet long, instead of the standard 5 feet. If you want to reposition the plumbing instead, you'd either have to tear up the floor or take down the ceiling in the room below. As you can see, what appeared to be a small problem can easily turn into a very big headache.

Filling Leftover Spaces — My solution is to fill in the extra space at the foot of the tub with a small shelf. Then, tile the shelf to match the rest of the tub enclosure. The shelf will be a convenient place to keep soap, shampoo, rubber duckies, or whatever else people need in the bath. I like having a shelf myself; I think they're a real improvement. People will think you've added the shelf as a convenient feature. They'll never imagine that you did it to solve an awkward space problem.

Depending on the layout of the bathroom, there may be enough space left over in the tub area to build a linen closet, either at the head end or foot end of the tub. This is a really good use for an awkward, leftover space. Linen closets are very useful in a bathroom. If you've ever been all soaped up in the shower when you realize you've forgotten your towel, you'll appreciate how nice it is to have towels stored in a handy place in the bathroom.

Bathrooms are small, but very important. The space in them is precious. You don't want to waste an inch of it. Always turn leftover spaces into linen closets, built-in cabinets or shelving.

The Window

In many older homes, you'll find a window right over the tub. This can be inconvenient if you're planning on installing a tub/shower assembly in that location. Water from the shower will puddle up on the window sill, causing rot damage. Besides that, most people don't want to have the neighbors watch them take showers. You can put a plastic curtain over the window, but that doesn't look very nice. What's the best way to deal with this?

One option is to just block off the window. This works fine as long as you block it off on the outside as well. I've seen some jobs where the window was blocked off on the inside, but not the outside. From the outside, you see a dark window, with nothing on the inside but a wall. That's not good workmanship.

To do a proper job, you'll have to match the siding, and blend it in so it doesn't show. If the house has a common type of siding, that won't be a problem. However, if it's sided with some odd material, matching it can be difficult.

If all else fails, you may be able to camouflage the repair with some kind of decoration. I had this problem with a house I worked on. It had a window which had been neatly filled in, but the siding didn't exactly match. On this particular house, all the windows were trimmed with shutters. In the old days, shutters were more than decoration, they could be opened and closed. At any particular time, you'd see houses with some of the shutters open, and some closed. I decided to take advantage of this fact by installing a set of shutters in the "closed" position over the blocked-off window. The finished effect was quite attractive. It looked like a decoration, rather than an awkward patch job.

Another way to deal with the window is to replace it with glass block. Glass block is waterproof and it lets light in, but no one can see through it. It's also attractive and quite popular today. The effect can be very nice if it's done well. Be sure to install a ceiling fan for ventilation if you're closing off the only window in the bathroom.

Accessories

Replacing a few simple accessory items can often make a tremendous improvement in a bathroom. Some of them, like toilet seats and towel bars, are inexpensive to buy but make a major difference in how a bathroom looks.

I almost always replace toilet seats in old bathrooms. They're generally worn and often downright disgusting if they haven't been replaced in a while. A new toilet seat is cheap and usually simple to put on, and it can make the whole bathroom look newer and cleaner.

You may sometimes run into problems replacing very old toilet seats. The older models may have steel nuts and bolts holding them in place, instead of the plastic bolts that are used on new toilet seats. These steel bolts can be rusted solidly in place. Getting them off is tricky. Remember, the toilet bowl is made of china. You can't put too much pressure on these bolts or you'll break the bowl.

I've tried many different ways to get these bolts off, but the only thing that seems to work for me is sawing them off. You can use a close-quarters hacksaw, but it takes too long. Instead, I use my Sawzall with a metal-cutting blade. The Sawzall will cut through them in a minute or two.

Medicine Cabinets — The medicine cabinet is another simple item that can make a big difference in a bathroom. Medicine cabinets are highly visible. If they're ugly or in poor condition, they ruin the looks of a bathroom. Unlike toilet seats, medicine cabinets can cost a lot of money. Really nice ones can run into the hundreds of dollars. If you keep it simple though, you can find one for about $50. That will be $50 well spent!

Medicine cabinets come in flush-mount or surface-mount styles. It's usually easier to use a surface-mount cabinet to replace the old cabinet. That's because a new medicine cabinet will rarely fit into the hole left by the old one. If you buy a surface-mount cabinet that's larger than the old cabinet, you can just put it right over the hole left by the old-flush-mount cabinet. It'll cover it completely. The only time I use flush-mount cabinets is when I'm going to be drywalling the entire wall. In that case, I can create a mounting hole in the new wall for any size cabinet that looks nice.

Working With Ceramic Tile

After you've got all the fixtures and built-ins done in your new or remodeled bath, you can start finishing the walls and floor. But finish them with what? Any discussion of bathrooms has to include ceramic tile. There are a lot of substitutes for ceramic tile on the market today. Some of these work well and some don't. But none of them are equal to a real ceramic tile bathroom for authenticity.

Hardboard with a ceramic tile design works well enough for the bathroom walls, but it doesn't make a good tub surround. It isn't waterproof enough. After a few years, water from the shower will get into it, and it will deteriorate.

Fiberglass tub surrounds are entirely waterproof. However, they need to be cleaned very carefully. Abrasive cleansers will scratch the heck out of them. Interestingly enough, if a fiberglass tub or surround get badly scratched, the scratches can be buffed out of it with an auto polishing wheel. This is best done by someone who's an expert at polishing cars, however. If it's done wrong, it can make the problem worse, not better.

My problem with these materials is that they just don't project a quality image. Most people expect ceramic tile or better in a bathroom. I've found it's a good idea to give people what they expect. I always install ceramic tile. Anything less looks cheap; anything more, such as Corian, is too expensive. Almost everyone is happy with ceramic tile.

❧ Installing Tile

If you haven't worked with ceramic tile, you may be surprised to find that it isn't as hard as you might have thought. My very first ceramic tile job came out pretty decent. It wasn't absolutely perfect, but the defects were so small that you couldn't see them unless you were crawling on your hands and knees. After that, I became sensitive to tile work. Whenever I go into a bathroom now, I always check out the tile work. There are almost always small defects. In fact, most work is close to the same quality as my first job. I rarely find a job that's truly perfect. When I do, I'm impressed. It's nice when somebody has the know-how and takes the time to make a job absolutely perfect.

Figure 20-17
*Water leaking through tile
destroyed drywall behind*

Figure 20-18
Damage behind tile

The single most important thing to remember when installing ceramic tile is that it has to go over a rock-solid surface. Most tile failures are caused by people skimping on the support layers. If there's any give to the surface, you'll get *tile pop;* that's when the base flexes but the tiles don't, so some of the tiles break loose. If that happens in a wet area, water will get under the tile. Unless the tile is installed over cement board, the water will damage the underlayer and then *all* the tiles will come off.

Cement Board Backing

I always install cement board as a base under any ceramic tile work I do (unless I'm tiling over cement). Cement board provides a nice, solid surface for the tiles to lay on, and it's totally waterproof.

You can install tile over any solid surface, and most of the time it will be okay. But there's always a chance that a piece of tile or some grout might come loose, and allow water to seep behind the tile. The wetter the area is, the more of a problem that can turn out to be. Bathrooms are generally fairly wet areas, with the tub/shower area being the wettest. If you install tile over wood or drywall in a shower area, and even a tiny piece of grout falls out, water will seep in and over time rot out the wood, or dissolve the drywall. A tiny grout defect can wind up destroying an entire bathroom.

Figure 20-17 shows just the kind of damage a crack in the grout can cause. When I first looked at this tub/shower enclosure, the loose tiles appeared to be a minor problem. But when I touched the wall, the whole thing fell apart! The ceramic tile had been installed over drywall. When a tiny crack opened up in the grout, water got in, and ruined the entire area. You can see part of the damage in Figure 20-18. But that's not the whole story. The water traveled through the inside of the wall, and ruined the walls several feet away as well.

Figure 20-19 shows the damage to the bottom edge of the drywall panels. The drywall on both walls in the corner melted and began to fall apart. The destruction was very apparent when I removed the baseboards. I

Figure 20-19
Leak ruined walls several feet away

Figure 20-20
Cement board on floor of new bathroom

Figure 20-21
Starting tile layout

had to gut the entire shower area and rebuild it in order to make the repair. I also had to replace the damaged drywall on the walls. This damage wouldn't have happened if cement board had been installed behind the tile in the shower. A crack in the grout wouldn't have caused any harm at all.

Installing Cement Board — Installing cement board is about like installing drywall. It even has its own waterproof tape and joint compound. Don't use ordinary joint compound with cement board; it isn't waterproof.

Cement board can be hung on walls like drywall. On floors, however, it needs a solid underlayment. You can't just lay it over joists and expect it to hold a lot of weight. It needs at least a ¾-inch layer of plywood under it for support. Figure 20-20 shows cement board being installed on the floor of a bathroom.

Tile Layout

Most tile instructions tell you to lay out tile from the center of the room, and work outward. The point of laying out the tiles from the center is to avoid having any odd pieces of tile where they'll show. If you start from the center, all the fractional tiles should wind up at the edges of the room. This is fine if you're working on a large room, but for small areas, like bathrooms, I don't like to do it this way. The space in a bathroom is too cut up. With toilet, tub, odd corners and angles, you could wind up with fractional tiles all over the place, giving the job a very patchy look.

Instead, I start from the most visible edge. That's usually the main doorway coming in. People look down as they enter the bathroom, and then look straight ahead along the floor. Therefore, you want this center stretch of floor to be as perfect as possible. So, I start at the door, and lay out my rows of tile going straight back. Figure 20-21 shows a layout in progress. This is the view from the bathroom door. With this layout, most of the cut pieces of tile wind up either under the moldings, or under the tub.

The hardest part about tile setting is cutting the tiles. The fewer you have to cut, the easier the job is. It's a lot easier to do an open, rectangular space, like an entrance hall or a kitchen. The only cutting you have to do is at the edges. Unfortunately, a bathroom isn't that easy. You have to work around the sink, toilet, tub and often a cabinet as well. Plus, the room is often an odd shape, with more corners than usual to be dealt with.

I always remove the toilet and sink before starting a tile job. That way, there are fewer things to tile around. After the floor is done, I just set the sink and toilet on top of it and grout around their bases to seal them. The other advantage to this is that if anyone decides to change the sink or toilet, there won't be a gap in the tile where the old fixtures used to be.

It's much easier to install small tiles than the larger sizes. That's because you don't need to do as much cutting with the smaller tiles, especially mosaic tiles. They're small enough to fit into most spaces without cutting. You'd probably only have to cut a handful of them on an entire job.

The bigger the tiles are, the more problems you'll have. I find the hardest ones to install are the 1-foot squares. They are very attractive, but they're not really suited for bathrooms. They work best in large, open spaces, like large kitchens, foyers, entrance halls or patio areas. They're very hard to use in a small space, like a bathroom. You have to cut them for too many complex shapes. They need to fit around drain openings, corners and small spaces. Cutting complex shapes in tile is very difficult. Working with large tiles, I often wind up with a big pile of broken pieces, usually from trying to cut one complicated shape.

Another problem with large tiles is that they're damaged more easily. For example, if you drop them, they'll shatter. The smaller the tiles, the less damage they'll suffer by being dropped. Large tiles also need better support than small tiles. Small tiles can sometimes tolerate tiny amounts of movement that will crack large tiles. If small tiles pop, they can be glued back down and regrouted — after the support problem is solved. Large tiles, on the other hand, will be ruined. They'll have to be chiseled out and replaced.

I suggest using smaller tiles for your first couple of jobs, especially in bathrooms. Otherwise you'll get frustrated, and probably end up hating tile work. The smaller tiles will save you a lot of aggravation and help you get a good start in tilesetting. Of course, you can go too far with small tiles. I've seen a lot of motel rooms where the entire bathroom,

floor and walls included, was done in plain white 1-inch mosaic tiles. That's the cheapest and easiest installation of ceramic tile in a bathroom. However, if you do something like that in a house, it'll look like a motel, and your customers won't much like that.

I also like to install a tile molding or base around the walls and seal it with grout as well. I've seen a lot of jobs without base molding, but I don't think they're very practical. Some people use wood moldings, but wood won't stop water from seeping into the walls at the seam between the wall and floor. Using sealed wood and caulking helps, but isn't as effective at waterproofing as using coved base tile around the base of the bathroom. Water can do a lot of damage, so I always try to prevent water problems before they happen when I can.

Cutting the Tiles

I find it's best to have several different kinds of tile cutting tools available for laying tile. I have a small, hand-held cutter, which is adequate for mosaic tile. It scores them and breaks them, rather than cutting through them. I also have a large, professional-type tile cutter, which can handle larger, tougher tiles. Another useful tool is a grit saw blade that attaches to a hacksaw frame. You can use it to cut curves and complex shapes in large tiles. I also have a tile and masonry blade for my circular saw. It's good for cutting up a lot of large tiles. However, the tiles need to be clamped down before you cut them with a circular saw or they'll shoot across the room. You can also rent "wet saws" from tile dealers. They're like a table saw with a water spray attachment that keeps the blade from overheating. I don't use them because they're kind of messy. I've had just as much luck using the tile cutters that I have.

There's a lot of variation in the consistency of tiles. Some are very hard, while others are relatively soft. This has a lot to do with the type of clay they're made from. Generally, the smaller tiles tend to be harder and the larger ones softer. That's a good thing, because softer tiles are much easier to cut, and the larger tiles tend to need more cutting. You'll really notice the difference if you try to cut them with a grit saw. Some of the smaller tiles are so tough that the grit saw won't even scratch them. Some larger tiles, on the other hand, are so soft they can be cut easily with a plain hacksaw.

If you need to do a lot of cutting, you should buy a few samples of the tile ahead of time, and experiment with them. If they're really hard to cut, you may be able to suggest using a different, easier to cut, tile. I've found it's a good idea to buy some sample tiles before starting a job anyway. It makes it a lot easier for the homeowners to visualize. Lay a few tiles out in the room where they're going to be installed and show them to the home-owners. This will minimize complaints like "It doesn't look like I thought it would." Tiles often don't look the same in the house as they do in the store.

Cementing the Tile

Setting ceramic tiles involves several steps, and each step has to set a day or so before the next step can be done. For instance, after the tiles are cemented down, they must be left, undisturbed, for at least 48 hours. I've had a lot of problems with this part of the job, especially when I'm working in the bathroom of an occupied house. It's hard to keep people from walking on the freshly-set tiles and knocking them all out of line. This can be very annoying. I've had to tear out big sections of tile and reset them, and then wait another 48 hour for those tiles to set. By the way, there are a number of different types of ceramic tile adhesives that you can use for this part of the job. They include wet cements, epoxies, mastics and so on. They each come with their own detailed instructions on how to apply them. Follow their directions carefully; they all work about the same if they are applied correctly.

Try to protect your fresh tile jobs. If possible, lock the door to the bathroom to keep people from using it. Bathroom privacy lock-sets always have a release mechanism for emergencies. It's usually a little hole in the center of the handle. If you stick a nail, an ice pick or any other long, thin object into this hole, it will unlock the door. Even though most people know about this, just having the door locked may reinforce the idea that they aren't supposed to enter. That helps to keep people from carelessly walking on the floor.

Grouting the Tile

After the cement sets, it's time to grout. Grouting needs to be done very carefully. Poorly applied grout looks bad, and may crumble. Be sure to mix the grout well to ensure there are no lumps. It should have a creamy consistency, like cake batter. In fact, when I mix it in my big rubber mixing bowl, it really looks like cake batter — good enough to eat! I prefer using rubber bowls because they're easy to clean. If grout gets left in the bowl and hardens, I can just flex it and the grout will break loose.

When you begin mixing grout, it always seems too thin at first. However, it thickens up after a few minutes. If you add more grout powder because you think it's thin, it will soon be too thick. Then you'll have to add more water, then more powder, and so on until you've mixed up ten times the amount of grout that you need. Remember, when all else fails, follow the directions.

I always add latex grout strengthener when I mix up grout. I find it improves the grout's consistency. It makes it easier to work with, and gives a better result. The only problem is that it makes the grout scum harder to clean off when you're done. You can buy grout that already has latex strengthener pre-mixed into it, but I don't like it. I think they put too much strengthener in it, and that makes cleaning up the grout scum *really difficult*.

You can apply grout with a sponge, but it's best to use a grout float. It's a lot faster. When grouting, you want to completely fill the spaces between the tiles. Squeeze the grout in carefully and force out all the air. If you don't eliminate all the air, bubbles will rise to the top overnight, and the grout will be full of holes the next day. Also, try not to leave a lot of grout on the tile surfaces. You will have to scrub it all off when the grout is set. The more you leave on the surface, the harder the cleanup job will be. You have to leave a little bit of it, however. If you try too hard to clean the tile before the grout sets, you'll end up scooping the grout out of the joints.

The floor needs to set another day after grouting. Then you can clean up the grout haze. This is a film remaining on the tile from the small amount of grout that was left behind on the surface. It can be surprisingly hard to get off. It's supposed to scrub off with water, but often won't, especially if you've used grout strengthener. The difficulty in removing the haze shows that the grout strengthener works. It makes the grout so strong that you can't get it off, even when you want to. Luckily, there are grout haze removers that can help. They're usually mild acid solutions that dissolve the grout haze without damaging the grout. It still takes quite a lot of scrubbing, though. I find a pot scrubber to be useful for this. Don't use anything coarse, like sandpaper. It could damage the tile. A pot scrubber won't scratch even the softest tile.

In spite of the difficulty I may have cleaning the tiles, I still think that grout strengthener is worth adding to your grout. It makes the grout very tough. It also makes it slightly elastic and allows it to survive a tiny bit of flexing without cracking. Ordinary grout will crack with even a minuscule amount of movement. Keep in mind that grout strengthener isn't a substitute for proper underlayment preparation. The amount of flex it can handle is still very tiny. However, anything you can do to make a tile job strong and long-lasting is worth doing.

ૐ Fancy Tile Jobs

It's almost as easy to do a fancy tile job as a plain one, if you plan it carefully. By "fancy," I mean a job with designs or contrasting trim, instead of just one plain, solid color. Most of the better tile jobs, like you see magazines or model homes, will have some kind of decoration, such as a contrasting stripe running around the bathroom, or a pattern in the floor.

You can buy tiles with a lot of interesting patterns already laid out in them. There are

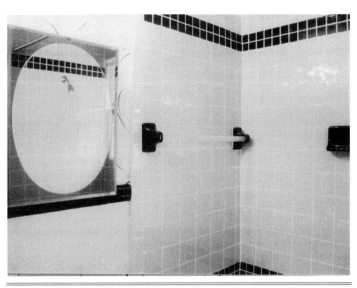

Figure 20-22
Create your own tile patterns using contrasting tiles

also tile systems that have matching trim pieces that go with solid-color tiles. Most tile stores have displays that offer a variety of combinations and interesting ideas. They will show you how to put tiles together to make simple patterns. This is an easy way to get a fancy effect without going to a lot of extra trouble. The only problem is that buying color-coordinated tile sets, especially some of their "designer" patterns, at tile stores can be rather expensive.

A cheaper way to get the same effect is to design a pattern yourself. It's easy to do if you use tiles that are all the same size. Standard 4¼-inch square wall tiles, for example, come in a wide selection of colors. That makes it easy to substitute tiles of a different color, without making any changes in your tile layout.

Figure 20-22 is an example of how I make my own decorative patterns. For this bathroom, I used gray tiles, with a contrasting black stripe. The black tiles were a quarter of the size of the gray tiles, so I just had to use four small black tiles for every one gray one. I got the idea from a nearby restaurant. They used different colors, but the effect was the same. Restaurants, by the way, are another good place to get ideas. They always have the latest and most popular decorating schemes.

The advantage to designing the pattern yourself is that you can save a lot of money by buying cheaper tiles, rather than paying a high price for a color-coordinated tile system. I bought the gray tiles in Figure 20-22 on a special closeout sale at Builder's Square for $9 a box. That's about as cheap as tiles ever get. I bought the black tiles at Color Tile. I paid almost three times as much for the black tiles, but I only needed one box, so it wasn't that expensive overall. The money I saved buying discount tiles helped pay for accent pieces, such as the matching towel bars, new medicine cabinet and mirror. Shop around for good deals on tile, and then plan your design so that the main part of the room is done in less expensive tiles, with only a few expensive tiles for the trim. That way you end up with a job that looks expensive, but really isn't.

It may seem silly to quibble about a couple of dollars on the price of tile, but the difference can really add up. The price of tile varies tremendously. You can pay anything from 90 cents a square foot, to $90! If you're doing a large bathroom, the price difference can be major.

You can often find very nice tiles at tile stores marked way down for closeout sales or specials. Many are plain, solid colors, and perfectly good quality. Sometimes you'll find another tile on the full-price rack that looks exactly the same. The only difference may be that one comes from one distributor and the other from someplace else. The closeouts are marked way down because the store doesn't have a large quantity of them and they're changing distributors. By "large quantity," I mean that they don't have enough to do a shopping center. There's often more than enough for a single bathroom.

Of course, once the tile is sold out, they won't be getting any more so it's always a good idea to buy an extra box. I always like to do that anyway. Even if a store always carries the same style, tiles bought at a later date might be from a different dye lot and may not match exactly. Give the extra box to the homeowners so they'll have matching tile in case they ever need to make any alterations to the bathroom. I find that people appreci-ate things like that. It shows concern on your part.

Of course, you have to be careful when picking out closeout tiles. Sometimes they're being closed out because the designs are out-dated. Avoid these. Nobody wants them, and that's why they're discontinued. I've often found boxes of outdated tiles left in houses I've worked on. Someone's "bargain" didn't work out, so they just left them behind when they moved. Some of these tiles are very strange. Sometimes I keep them because I think they're interesting or creative, with odd shapes and colors. I have a whole collection of unusual tiles, but I don't think I'd want to actually install them anywhere.

Finding inexpensive tiles can be important, because your ability to offer a tile job at a lower price may make the difference between getting a job and missing out. That's especially true if there's a lot of square feet to be covered in tile. If you can come up with a nice tile for $10 a box, and the competition is paying $30, you'll be able to do the same job for a lot less without cutting your profit. Let the tile stores lose money, not you! What if your customer doesn't like your limited tile selection? Just say "I can do the bathroom with any of these tiles for this price, or I can do it with these other tiles for three times the amount." That may make your tile selection look a lot better!

Tile Accents

If you can't find contrasting tiles that are exactly the same size as the ones you're using for the main part of the job, you can use any tile that's an even multiple of the main tile, like I did in Figure 20-22. The tile can be exactly half the size, or a quarter of the size or even twice the size, as long as it's an even amount. If you have a tile that's exactly half the size of the others, you can just use twice as many, and all your spacing will come out even. Watch out for tiles that are slightly off size. Your designs won't come out even. You'll wind up having to squeeze a fraction of a tile in someplace to fill an uneven space. That won't look professional — your tiles are sup-posed to all come out even.

Avoid this problem by laying out all the tiles ahead of time. This helps especially when you're doing a complicated job. It allows you to spot any problems before you cement the tiles in place.

Sometimes, no matter how carefully you plan, you'll find yourself having to fit in a fractional tile to fill a space. If that happens, try to arrange the tiles so that the fractional tile will fall in the least visible spot, such as behind the toilet. Nobody will look behind the toilet to see if the tiles came out exactly right.

American Olean Tile and Dal-Tile both have a beautiful color catalogs with lots of good ideas for tile designs. Write or call them at:

American Olean Tile
1000 Cannon Ave.
Lansdale, PA 19446
(215) 855-1111

Dal-Tile
7834 Hawn Freeway
Dallas, TX 75217
1-800-933-TILE

❧ Cost

Installing ceramic tile is expensive because it's so time consuming. You have to wait a day after setting the tile, and another day after grouting. If that's the only thing you have to do at that job, you'll have to make separate trips back to the job site to do this work. That will use up a lot of travel time. If possible, try to plan your schedule so that you can do other work on the same job when you have to be there to finish the tile. That will make the best use of your travel time.

Generally, setting tile takes about 15 hours per hundred square feet. If you're doing a 5-foot by 7-foot bathroom floor, it will amount to approximately one day's work, including grouting and cleanup (5½ hours to set the tile and 2½ for grouting and cleanup). The tile to do a floor that size usually costs me about $100, although it can cost a lot more, if you buy expensive tile.

As you can see, the cost of installing ceramic tile can be surprisingly modest. You'll have to charge a few hundred dollars for the job, but that's not much compared to the overall cost of the bathroom remodel. When you think of the benefits, it's well worth the cost. Imagine the same floor done in sheet vinyl, and you will clearly see how much tile really benefits a room. There's really no comparison. Any bathroom looks better with ceramic tile than sheet vinyl. The measly few hundred that the ceramic tile costs will increase the value of the bathroom remodeling by thousands.

Decorating the Bathroom

You may now have some modern fixtures and maybe new tile but you still have an old bathroom. Most likely the new items don't match the rest of the bathroom. That's why most remodelers believe that the whole bathroom has to be gutted and the room completely redone. But in my opinion, that's not the case. What you have is essentially a decorating problem. You need to redecorate the bathroom, creating a whole new look with paint, wallpaper, trim and accessories that incorporate the old and new features. The first step in this decorating process is deciding on a style. If you're keeping some of the old fixtures, you might want to recreate the original antique style, or a new improved version of that style (depending on budget constraints).

❧ Antique Bathrooms

Some older homes have very luxurious bathrooms. This is especially true of homes that were the "mansions" of their time. Keep in mind that a house didn't have to be huge to qualify as a mansion to the Victorians. To people in a city, where land was expensive and many were living in small apartments or cottages, a 2,000 square foot house was a luxury home. Houses were constructed accordingly and often had beautiful, luxurious bathrooms.

If a home has a beautiful antique bathroom, it's a shame to tear it out. Besides, antique bathrooms are back in style now. If you look at *Better Homes and Gardens,* or even *Remodeling,* you'll see a lot of brand-new antique-styled bathrooms being featured. People are paying a lot of money to have antique styling added. A home with an original antique bathroom is even better. The original features add substantial value to the house. If you replace anything, the owners will be spending a lot of money to lower the value of their home.

Unfortunately, a truly authentic antique bathroom is probably in need of repair, and may be awkward to use. Your job is to make the bathroom as functional and convenient as possible, without destroying its special features.

The Tub

The bathtub tends to be the biggest problem in an antique bathroom. Some old, rolled-edge tubs were beautifully made and had a lot of ornamentation. The more expensive ones also tended to be extra wide and deep, like today's luxury tubs. They're great for people who like to take nice deep bubble baths. Unfortunately, most people prefer showers for everyday use now, and these tubs weren't fitted for showers. If the homeowners are real antique buffs, they may be willing to change their lifestyle, and take baths instead of showers. That's the best solution, from the historical preservation point of view. Keep everything just exactly the way it was and encourage the homeowners to adopt a Victorian lifestyle. Not likely! For most people, that's just a bit too much to ask, even for history's sake. They may like Victorian decor, but they want to look at it, not to live it. Almost everyone wants modern convenience along with their decor.

There are a couple of ways to solve this problem. The best way is to keep the tub and add a separate, free-standing shower. If the bathroom is large, there may be plenty of room for a shower addition. This arrangement is quite popular in bathroom design today. A separate bath and shower is considered very elegant.

Some old-fashioned bathrooms have large built-in linen cupboards. These can be removed, if necessary, to make room for a shower. It's nice to have a cupboard, but a shower is more important. Of course, a shower isn't a Victorian feature and there's no way to make it look authentic. The best you can do is add tile work and trim to match the bathroom as closely as possible. What you want to do is have the kind of free-standing shower that the Victorians would have had, if they'd had showers. That's about as close to authentic as you can do.

There is a shower arrangement that was actually used in Victorian times. It's the same arrangement that's used now to add a shower to an old, rolled-edge tub. You have to install a diverter to the tub spout and attach a pipe that can carry water up to a shower head at the appropriate height. Then you need to construct a lightweight, rectangular framework, suspend it from the ceiling, and hang a shower curtain on it. This arrangement is still quite common in New York City, where a lot of these old tubs are still being used. You can also see showers like these in old movies.

The main objection to this kind of shower is that it can spoil the look of a beautiful antique tub. It also blocks a portion of the bathroom from view, making the room look smaller. Another disadvantage is that this arrangement isn't as pleasant to use as a regular shower. The space inside the shower curtain is smaller than ideal. Plus, the curtain always seems to blow up against you and get in the way while you're trying to shower. Adding a free-standing shower is a better solution, but this type of shower is better than no shower at all.

The biggest advantage to one of these added-on shower arrangements is that they can be very inexpensive to install. I've made the framework out of ordinary PVC pipe, hung from the ceiling by chains. When it's painted to match the tub, it looks fine. I used four ordinary shower curtains, one on each side, as the curtain enclosure. The only expensive part is the new tub spout with the diverter. You can find them at any good plumbing supply store for about $100. The rest of the pieces run about $40 total, depending on how much you spend for shower curtains. If everything goes smoothly, you can do the entire job in about three hours. It's a useful means of providing a shower in a bathroom remodel that's being done on an extremely tight budget. It's certainly the cheapest way I know of to add a shower to an old bathroom.

With a larger budget, you can make the framework fancier and more authentic. The original antique hardware was all finely-crafted brass. Authentic reproductions of this hardware are available. Figure 20-23 shows a more elegant arrangement. This one has the solid brass fittings and fixtures with a vinyl-lined white lace shower curtain. It's from Renovator's catalogue and costs about $500 for the fittings and fixtures and another $43 for the curtain. Using brass hardware will make the installation look as nice as the original, and that's the best you can do. Call or write Renovator's for a free catalogue:

Renovator's
P.O. Box 2515
Conway, NH 03818-2515
1-800-659-2211

They also carry other antique reproductions including kitchen and bathroom sinks, faucets and accessories, toilets, light fixtures, moldings and hardware.

The Sink

An old style sink is another problem fixture. Separate hot and cold water faucets are inconvenient to use, although some "old-fashioned" sinks are still being made with them. If the homeowners can live with separate faucets, that's fine. If the sink is especially nice, you can still get separate hot and cold water faucets to replace the old ones. If the sink isn't in good shape or isn't especially nice, or the homeowners don't like the separate faucets, you'll need to replace the sink. If the sink's okay, you may think, "Why can't I just put a new faucet assembly on one of these old sinks?" It's because the holes don't line up.

Modern faucet assemblies have hot and cold controls on either side, and a single, cen-

Courtesy of Renovator's

Figure 20-23
Brass fittings and lace provide an elegant and authentic look

tral faucet. Each of these parts mount on the sink through its own hole. You have three holes, and the size and distance is standardized. Practically every faucet made since 1950 can be interchanged with any other. The old sinks, however, have only two holes, one on each side for each faucet. There's no hole in the center. So, there's no way to mount a new faucet assembly on this sink. You could try to cut a hole in the center, but you'd probably destroy the sink in the process. And, even if you did manage to make a hole, you'll find that the distance between the holes isn't the same as the modern standard. The faucet assembly still wouldn't fit. It's easier to just get another sink.

Some models of old-style sinks have become popular again, and are easy to find in newer, more modern forms. The ceramic pedestal sink is a good example. Many new designs are available that look just like the originals, except they accept a modern, single spout faucet assembly. You may be able to find a sink that's almost exactly like the origi-

Courtesy of Renovator's

Figure 20-24
Matching "antique style" sink and toilet

nal sink you're replacing. Anyplace that carries a large selection of plumbing fixtures should have a few that you can choose from.

Some original styles aren't worth replacing with a similar design. For instance, plain, wall-hung cast-iron sinks (like the one shown earlier in the chapter in Figure 20-16) were installed by the millions between 1900 and 1920. These sinks are awkward to use, and were never especially attractive. There's no reason to replace something like that with an exact replica. Instead, buy a more attractive old-fashioned style sink. Just because you're keeping the old-fashioned look doesn't mean you can't upgrade the fixtures. Figure 20-24 shows a matching antique pedestal sink and toilet combination from the Renovator's catalogue that would be attractive in any bathroom.

The Toilet

I've never run into an original antique toilet, the kind with the high tank and pull chain. I guess those were replaced decades ago. Most of the toilets I see are fairly similar to the modern types. The design hasn't changed that much over the years. The china part of a toilet lasts forever, unless you hit it

with a hammer or put some other type of stress on it. In that case, it will shatter like a dish. The inside workings will rust out over time, but they're easily replaceable. Modern toilet parts will fit any toilet made since about 1910 — and I've never worked on one older than that. So, you may have to replace interior parts, and buy a new seat, but other than that, replacing the toilet isn't usually necessary.

Of course, there are toilets that are so dirty and rusty that it's easier to put in a new one than try to clean the old one up. You find these in homes that haven't been taken care of, not those occupied by homeowners. Generally, replacing fixtures is a homeowner option aimed at changing the style, rather than need.

Repairs

Even if you're not planning to make any major alterations to an antique bathroom, you may still need to make some repairs. The items most often in need of repair are the sink and tub faucets. After 100 years of use, they are usually pretty worn. You can sometimes find repair parts for old fixtures. Even ordinary plumbing supply stores often have parts to fit these old fixtures. With a few minor repairs, like grinding the valve seats, and some new washers, you can often have them working as good as new.

In some cases, the old fixtures may be too far gone. They might fall apart in your hands. If you can't repair old fixtures, you can often replace them with new reproductions. If you can't find one that's exactly the same, you can probably get one that's very similar. Since Victorian styles are so popular nowadays, it's often possible to find fixtures like these at plumbing supply stores. However, elaborate antique fixtures or specialty items will probably have to be ordered.

A more difficult repair problem is damaged tile work. Old tiles are quite different from the ones made today. They're different sizes and have different kinds of glazes. Even plain white tiles made 100 years ago look different from plain white tiles made today. If some of the old tiles are broken, you'll probably never find replacements that match.

Before you throw up your hands in despair, try looking in odd corners of the basement and attic for old tiles that have been stored away. Once in a while I find some original, unused building materials that were left from work done many, many years ago. People have always understood the value of keeping spare items to use for repairs. And tile is one of the few materials that doesn't deteriorate, even if it's been underwater, or buried in the yard. Tile can last for thousands of years. Archeologists have found tiles from ancient Babylon that were still in good shape. If you find any tile, it'll be as good as new.

Even if you don't find any matching tile, there are still ways to deal with the problem.

My favorite technique is to steal a few tiles from somewhere in the bathroom that's hard to see — behind the toilet tank, for example. Plan on taking more tile than you need to make your repairs, because some might get broken during removal. Replace these tiles with tiles that are as similar as you can find. It won't be an exact match, but no one will notice if they're behind the toilet tank.

Also, if you're going to be making any alterations, such as adding a shower or changing the sink, you may be removing tiles to make room for the new fixture. Save these tiles so that you can use them for repairs elsewhere in the room. If you don't need these tiles for repairs, save them anyway. It's always a good idea to have a few spares.

Chapter 21

Victorian Kitchens

If you should ever come across an original Victorian kitchen in a vacant house, what you'll find is a big, almost empty room. The only permanent fixture will be the sink. The Victorians didn't use built-in cabinets. Instead, they used free-standing furniture. If all the furniture is removed, there's literally nothing left but the kitchen sink.

You can look at this space as an opportunity. You don't have to work around any existing installations. You can put in anything your customer wants, and you've got plenty of room to work in.

However, it's pretty rare to find an original Victorian kitchen today. In the last 80 years or so, someone will have had some remodeling done. It's more likely that you'll find a mixture of remodeling jobs, all different styles and designs combined together over the years, with little of the original look of the kitchen remaining. The resulting kitchen may or may not have anything of use to you in your present remodeling project. Because there have been so many improvements in kitchen appliances and accessories in the last few decades, you may want to start from scratch and redesign the kitchen.

The Expanded Kitchen

You've got to consider the modern lifestyle when you begin your kitchen design. Kitchens have gone through a lot of evolutionary changes. The Victorians had large open kitchens, but they were closed off from the rest of the house. Over the years, kitchens, like bathrooms, were downsized. Today, the trend is to have living areas open to the kitchen: breakfast nooks, family rooms, even a kitchen office space, with a phone, desk, and maybe a computer. An open kitchen allows the cook to be included in activities, even during meal preparation. It's especially nice for a family with small children or for people who entertain informally. No one wants to be shut away in the kitchen. The other living areas should open onto, but be apart from, the kitchen work area since these activities aren't a part of cooking.

A breakfast area or eating bar is ideal for quick meals on the run. Most people don't want to use the formal dining room for every meal. The kitchen should also have space for a telephone and maybe a small TV to watch while cooking. If there isn't room for these things in the kitchen, a small nook off the kitchen with a desk would be handy. That way the homeowner can make phone calls, schedule the day, pay bills or sit down and watch the evening news while the food's cooking.

Basic Kitchen Design Considerations

The most important element in the design of the kitchen work area is the triangular path between the stove, refrigerator, and sink. This is the "work triangle," the area where most of the food preparation is done. It's very important that the work triangle be set up for maximum efficiency. Otherwise, you'll have a kitchen that's inconvenient and unpleasant to use.

A good kitchen design will keep the total perimeter of the work triangle between 14 and 22 feet. If there's too much distance between any of the three corners of the triangle, people working in the kitchen will waste a lot of time and energy walking back and forth to get things. There should also be workspaces handy to both the sink and the stove. When you think about the work that's done in a kitchen, this design is just common sense. People need to get food out of the refrigerator, wash it in the sink, cut it up on a countertop workspace, and put it on the stove. An inconvenient kitchen quickly becomes irritating. In fact, many remodeling jobs are done specifically to correct this problem.

You should also design the work triangle so that no traffic goes through it. It's hard to cook if people keep walking in front of you; it can be dangerous as well. In a U- or L-shaped kitchen, this is fairly easy to arrange. With a corridor kitchen, it can be a little harder. You may be able to close off one end of the corridor with a bar or some added countertop space and eliminate the through traffic.

There are a number of references available that provide full details on how to design a functional kitchen. I recommend *Professional Kitchen Design,* also published by Craftsman Book Company. It tells you exactly what you should and shouldn't do in remodeling any type of kitchen.

❧ Cabinetry

Probably you'll find some kind of built-in cabinetry has been added to the kitchen. Whether or not this cabinetry is usable will depend on the design you've selected for the kitchen as a whole.

You can easily spend a great deal of money on cabinetry. According to the National Kitchen & Bath Association, the average kitchen remodeling job in 1995 cost $23,243. Of this cost, 52 percent was for cabinetry. In other words, the average set of cabinets costs about $12,000. That's a lot of money. For that amount of money, you want to pick cabinets very carefully. I like to consider alternatives before I commit that kind of cash to a project, even if I'm not the one who's paying.

In terms of added value, the kitchen should be brought up to the standards of the neighborhood. If the neighbors have brand-new luxurious kitchens, this house should have one too. In that case, $12,000 for cabinets isn't a bad investment. The kitchen is one of the most important areas of the house. You can't afford to skimp on it in an expensive house.

However, standards aren't as high in an average-income neighborhood. The kitchen still needs to be attractive and functional, but it doesn't have to have all the latest features. People don't expect the very best of everything in a moderately-priced house, and cost control can be more important to people than fancy features. Everyone would like to have a kitchen with all the new accessories, but not everyone has the disposable income to pay for one. If you're careful in your choices, you can achieve 90 percent of the look of an expensive kitchen, for about 30 percent of the price. That will generate a lot of happy customers!

The Existing Cabinetry

In general, a kitchen requires a minimum of 10 feet of base cabinets, 10 feet of wall cabinets, and 8 feet of countertop space. You won't always find this in an older home. If you plan to gut the kitchen, it's easy

Figure 21-1
*Double-swinging kitchen door closes
kitchen off from dining room*

Figure 21-2
*Beautiful wood cabinetry in restored
Victorian pantry*

enough to bring the house up to standard. However, if you want to work with the existing cabinets, you'll have to add more storage space without spoiling the style of the kitchen. This can be very challenging.

An old kitchen that hasn't been remodeled in 20 or 30 years probably doesn't have a garbage disposal or dishwasher. These are basic conveniences that people expect now, so you'll want to add them. The garbage disposal isn't a problem. However, a dishwasher has to be installed under the counter near the sink. You may have to take out some of the existing cabinets to make room for it. If that's the case, you might need to add a cabinet someplace else to make up for what you've taken away. Be sure to consider this in your design.

Examine the existing cabinets carefully before you decide whether or not to tear them out. The existing cabinetry could be any age, from the 1920s to the 1970s. Some cabinet styles are more useful than others when it comes to remodeling, and many of the old-fashioned designs have come back in

style. You don't want to tear out all the old cabinetry, only to replace it with something that looks practically the same.

An important point to keep in mind is that up until the 1950s, the kitchen was considered a service area, not a formal area. It didn't receive a lot of decorating attention. The people who could afford serving help never went into the kitchen. They didn't need fancy kitchens. Their kitchens were designed to be plain and functional, much like a restaurant kitchen.

In fact, many kitchens had restaurant-type double-swinging doors, like the one shown in Figure 21-1. These were designed for the help to use when serving meals. That way, the door could be kept closed at all times and guests couldn't see into the kitchen. Most kitchens were simple, with plain pine cabinets, painted white. Only mansions had deluxe cabinetry. Figure 21-2 shows the kitchen pantry cabinetry in a beautifully-restored Victorian mansion. Cabinetry like this is always worth preserving.

The condition of the cabinets is often the deciding factor when comes to refinishing existing cabinetry. Many old cabinets are in very poor condition. They've been beaten to pieces over the decades. That isn't surprising, considering the amount of use a kitchen normally gets. Don't bother trying to repair plain pine cabinetry that's all beat up. It isn't worth the effort. You may as well just tear it out and start fresh.

Surprisingly, I often find a lot of old cabinetry in perfect condition. Sometimes it seems hardly to have been used at all during the last 50 years. Cabinets like these may be worth working with, if you can integrate them into the overall design.

If you're planning a very formal kitchen, or a modern kitchen, perfectly-preserved plain pine cabinets won't do, even if they're in good condition. However, if you have a different style in mind, the cabinets might be useful, especially in an old-fashioned style.

Discuss the cost factors related to different kitchen designs with the homeowners. If they haven't decided on a style for the kitchen, you might be able to use many of the existing features to design an attractive old-fashioned kitchen. If the homeowners are set on a modern kitchen, by all means, build one for them. But if they're not sure what they want, or they're on a tight budget, the old-fashioned style would give them an attractive design for a fraction of the cost of a modern kitchen.

Countertops

Kitchen countertops also take a lot of abuse. They're likely to be chipped, cracked, worn or damaged. Don't feel that you have to replace the kitchen cabinetry just because the countertops are worn out. Countertops often look so awful that they make the cabinetry look bad too. Try to imagine new countertops with the existing cabinets. How would the kitchen look? In many cases, it would be just fine.

It's important to match the countertop to the cabinetry. Don't put in an ultramodern granite countertop with antique cabinets. It will look out of place. But finding a countertop that looks antique may be difficult. There are fewer countertop designs to choose from than cabinet designs. It's an odd situation. There are hundreds of different kinds of cabinets, but only a dozen or so different countertops to put with them.

One problem with installing a new countertop is that modern prefabricated countertops won't fit over old base cabinets. New countertops are about 4 inches deeper than old cabinets. That means there will be an awkward 4-inch overhang in front of the cabinets. This overhang will also make sink installation difficult. When you cut the hole for the sink, if you're not careful you could cut right through the front of the base cabinets! This problem can be solved by disconnecting the old cabinets and moving them forward 4 inches from the wall. You can fill in the 4-inch gap with a 1 x 4. The patch won't show because it's in the back and at the bottom of the cabinet.

You can then install ceramic tile on the new countertop. Ceramic tile is an authentic old-fashioned approach, and there are a tremendous number of ceramic tile designs to choose from. You can find something to match any decor.

The big drawback with ceramic countertops for me is that countertop tile work is hard to do. Remember, large flat surfaces are easier, and small surfaces with lots of corners are harder. A countertop has a small surface with a lot of corners. You can figure about twice as much time to do a countertop as for the same number of square feet on a floor.

The problem will get even worse if you use large tiles, instead of the smaller sizes. You sometimes see 6-inch tiles, and even larger, used on countertops, but I prefer using 3-inch to 4½-inch tiles. I rarely use anything bigger on a countertop. If you do, you'll spend all day cutting, trying to get them to fit around corners and cutouts.

Of course, there are some beautiful tiles in larger sizes. And if larger tiles would be the perfect thing for your decorating scheme, installing them will be worth the work. There's no sense trying to save a few dollars and ending up with something that isn't quite right. Just be sure to allow enough time in your estimate to cover the job.

If you decide to tile a countertop, don't try to lay the tiles over a preformed countertop base with a curved backsplash. It won't give the tile the proper support it needs. Use a countertop with a straight backsplash. I also think it's a good idea to install cement board on top of the countertop base as an underlayment for your tile. This is especially important if you've moved the base cabinets out from the wall. The cement board will provide a surface that's rock-solid, and totally waterproof. In the long run, the tile countertop will give better performance with a good underlayment than if it's just installed over a particleboard base.

Finally, if the kitchen is one of the few that had beautiful fine-quality cabinetry that's still in good condition, you can use a fine-quality countertop, like Corian, with it. A luxury material like this is appropriate if the cabinets are all a fine wood, like the oak cabinetry in Figure 21-2. Corian looks like marble and will fit right in with the antique look. It will give the kitchen a very elegant look. However, it's impractical and a waste of money to install an expensive countertop material like Corian with plain, pine cabinets.

"Old-Fashioned" Looks in Kitchen Design

There are quite a few different looks that are considered "old-fashioned" that are in style today. "Old-fashioned" isn't limited to Victorian designs, but also includes an awakened interest in 1940s and 1950s styles. Antique collectors aren't the only ones nostalgic about these styles. They're being featured in design magazines like *Better Homes & Gardens* too. I use *Better Homes & Gardens* as a reference quite often, because their styles reflect the taste of middle-class America. They never feature anything too strange, progressive or avant-garde. Since most of my customers are middle-class, I know I can't go too wrong if I try to create

the same kind of look that this magazine projects.

If you're interested in recreating an authentic old-style decor, you can get some very good ideas from old magazines. It's easy to find old *LIFE* or *Saturday Evening Post* magazines from the 1940s and 1950s at used bookstores. They usually cost about $5. If you're lucky, you might even find an old copy of *Better Homes & Gardens*. All of these magazines had ads for kitchen products, with pictures of kitchens that were the height of style at the time. They'll show the authentic kitchen layouts, including cabinets, furniture, floorcoverings, and appliances. Color ads are harder to find but especially valuable. They show the color schemes that were popular as well.

Of course, a kitchen doesn't have to be absolutely accurate. You're not building a museum exhibit. Most people won't want to cook on a stove that they have to light with a match, for example. We're pretty conditioned to automatic pilot lights. But you can reproduce the look by simply copying the styles used for the most visible items: the cabinets, wall treatments, and floorcoverings. These account for about 90 percent of the overall design. If you get them right, you'll have the "look" of the period, without the inconveniences.

Remember, you'll be finding a variety of styles in the existing kitchens of older homes. They can be anything from the original Victorian to 1990s modern. Let's discuss some of these styles and how you can work with them.

The Antique-Style Kitchen

If the house has an original Victorian kitchen, you have the option of restoring it to something very close to its original look. For example, you could furnish it with antique kitchen furniture in the Victorian style. That would include china cabinets, butcher-block cutting tables, and small cabinets placed where they would be useful. You can actually outfit a kitchen in this way and have it just as convenient to work in as a

Figure 21-3
1930s kitchen

modern one. After all, there's no real reason why dishes have to be kept in a cabinet that's attached to the wall. They can be stored just as easily in one that's free-standing. The only real problem with free-standing furniture is that it takes up a lot of room. However, if you have a large kitchen to work with, that isn't necessarily a problem. Victorian kitchens were built a lot bigger than the kitchens in later periods, such as the 1950s and '60s.

If the homeowners don't like the idea of free-standing furniture, you can still achieve an original look by using built-in cabinets in an old-fashioned-style. There are plenty of these to choose from. You can even find built-in cabinetry that's designed to look like free-standing furniture. The pieces don't quite match, just like real antiques. They even have "distressed" surfaces so they look like used antiques. Unfortunately, they are

also quite expensive. It seems silly to me to pay more for cabinets that look like free-standing antique cabinets than you would for real free-standing furniture. It's actually cheaper to use the real thing. You can always fasten it to the walls.

1930s Kitchens

The 1930s glass-front cabinets are back in style, and they're very popular. If the house has a nice set of these, it would be better to keep them and add to them if necessary, rather than replace them. If they're dingy, a coat of paint will brighten them up. Because they are so similar to the modern version of the design, you'll be able to add new cabinetry where needed, and coordinate everything so that it all looks like the same style.

One thing that identifies a 1930s kitchen is the style of the trim. Trim from that era has a lot of decorative curves and scallops. You can remove the trim to give the cabinets an updated look. Or replace the trim with something a little more current. Figure 21-3 shows a 1930s kitchen in almost original condition. Notice the high thin cabinet style, and the curved pattern and rounded corners on the bottom of the cabinet above the sink.

The biggest problem with older cabinetry is the paint buildup. The cabinets may have been painted so many times that the doors will no longer close. Removing old paint is always a problem, but when you're dealing with cabinets, there's a shortcut. You can remove the doors and send them out to be dipped in solvent. The rest of the cabinet can be cleaned up with a heat gun and acetone. It isn't as hard as it may seem, because there really isn't much to a cabinet other than the doors. There's just a framework and a couple of sides. And those pieces are easy to strip because they're fairly straight and simple. When you compare stripping the cabinets to the cost of buying all new cabinetry, the expense is minimal.

I find it amusing that distressed antique-look cabinets are very stylish right now. The cabinets are designed to look old, beat-up,

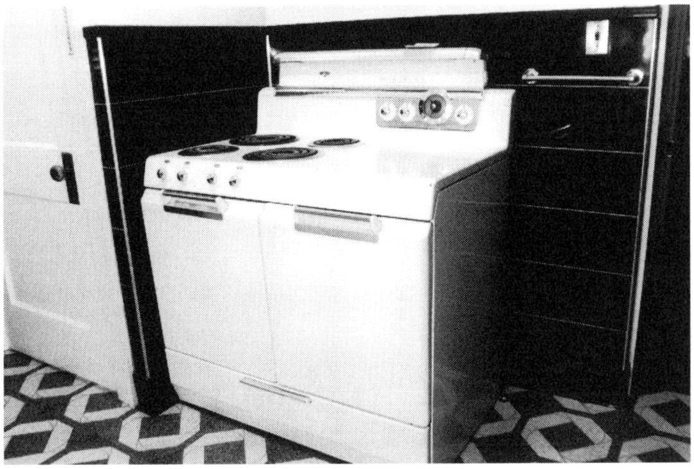

Figure 21-4
Old appliances match period styles

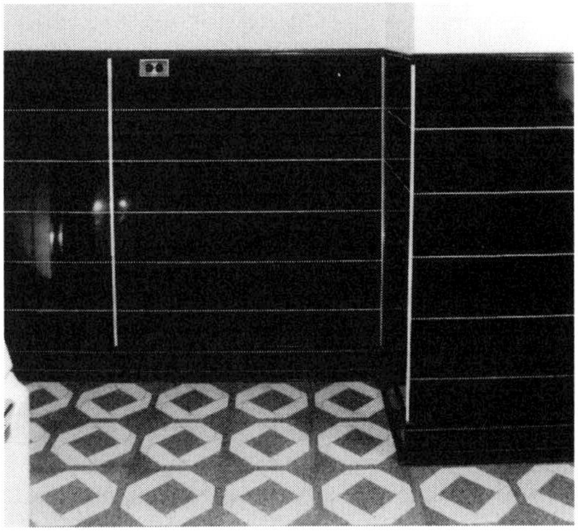

Figure 21-5
1940s style black wallboard wainscoting

and, in some cases, to look like they were painted at one time, and then incompletely stripped. They have little bits of different colors in the wood, like bits of paint that got left behind. I've spent years trying to avoid having my cabinets look like that, and now people are making them look that way on purpose!

The '40s Look

The '40s look is also back in style. The May 1993 issue of *Better Homes & Gardens* featured an entire section on '40s decorating, including a 1940s kitchen. It was featured again in the August 1995 issue in an article called "Quest for Color." The '40s kitchens were very similar to the 1930s kitchens. They had a lot of space in them, but only a few cabinets, which were tall and plain. There was still room in many of these kitchens to include a few pieces of free-standing furniture. The transition from free-standing furniture to built-in cabinets was under way, but not complete at this time. By the 1950s, built-in cabinets had taken over. There was no longer space for free-standing furniture in the '50s kitchen.

Designers are going to a lot of trouble today to find appliances to match period styles. I often find old appliances, like the stove in Figure 21-4, that are still in excellent working condition. They usually come with the houses I buy. Everything in this 1940s kitchen was in the original condition, including the shiny black wallboard wainscoting shown in Figure 21-5. This was all part of the "streamlined" look that was popular in the '30s and '40s. Figure 21-6 shows the 1940s sink unit, still in perfect condition. You can buy new sinks made in exactly the same style if you want to recreate an authentic '40s look. If you find items like these in homes you're working in, be sure to preserve them. They're valuable. If the homeowners don't want to keep them, there are people looking for these pieces who will happily pay a good price for them.

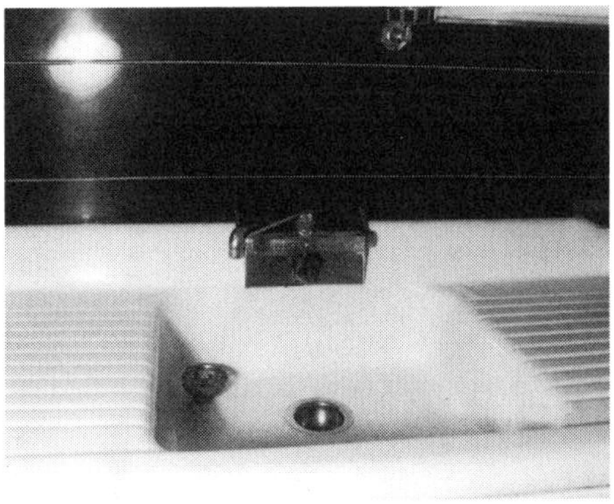

Figure 21-6
1940s sink unit

Since I knew this look was valuable, I decided to preserve the existing style in this kitchen. All it needed was a little freshening up. I repainted the kitchen in 1940s colors, and added '40s-style light fixtures and floorcoverings. The result was an attractive, stylish kitchen. By keeping the existing appliances, I was able to carry out a period theme and redecorate for very little money.

Another popular 1940s look included bright color accents against a white or pastel background. Simple designs or small pictures of animals, flowers or fruit were stenciled, painted or applied as decals to painted cabinets and trim pieces. The theme was carried throughout the kitchen, even in matching accent pieces, such as bread cabinets or canister sets.

My wife decorated a kitchen in this style a short time ago. She discovered that 1940s-style decals are still being made, and are available in many hardware stores. Using the decals, along with flowered wallpaper and pastel paints, she created an attractive 1940s look for only a few dollars.

This style doesn't appeal to everybody. But if the homeowners like it, you may be able to create an inexpensive, but fully-coordinated, *Better Homes & Gardens* '40s look kitchen for them.

❧ The Fabulous '50s

Most people have seen the new "Fabulous '50s" look. It's very *in* right now and many restaurants have spent a great deal of money redecorating their businesses in that style. As I mentioned earlier, restaurants always keep up with the latest styles. If you see it in a new restaurant, you know it's fashionable.

It's not unusual to find a 1950s kitchen in a Victorian home, or in any older home, for that matter. If the home has a 1950s style kitchen in good condition, you might want to leave it pretty much as it is. You'll probably need to make some repairs, and replace items that have worn out, like the floorcoverings. However, since the '50s look is fashionable now, you won't have any problem finding

floorcoverings, trim and other decor items to match the style. One very popular design during the '50s was black-and-white checkerboard tile. That's easy to recreate. Just buy a few boxes of plain white tiles, and a few boxes of plain black, and alternate them. It's a good design to suggest if your clients can't find floorcoverings that they like in their price range. You can always find plain black and white tiles.

The cabinets and walls in the kitchen probably won't be painted the original colors any more. That may make it hard to tell what the original decorating scheme was. Redecorating in the original colors will bring the design back together. Often, all it takes is a new coat of paint and some wallpaper to make a kitchen look like new. Repaint any painted surfaces in '50s color combinations, like salmon and sky blue or pink and green. Fabulous '50s wallpaper is available again, as well. The homeowners can complete the '50s look with a chrome dinette set. The result will be a stylish and "fun" kitchen. Once again, this look isn't for everybody. However, if the homeowners like it, you can recreate a great style for a very small amount of money.

❧ 1960s Style

A period that's just beginning to return to popularity is the 1960s. The 1960s were characterized by clear, bright colors, like reds with blue accents or black with turquoise, hot pink or bright green. You can find reproductions of 1960s styles in all the department stores. In fact, if you missed having a lava lamp in the '60s, now's your chance to pick one up! Because this style is really catching on, preserving '60s styles in homes is worthwhile. You just need to freshen it up a bit with a new coat of paint and some accent pieces, and you'll have the latest style!

1960s kitchens still look fairly modern. In many cases, they're just as functional as a new kitchen. One thing that you won't find in them however, is an island work center. Kitchen islands hadn't become popular yet. You can sometimes find a kitchen with a big empty area in the middle of the floor that would be perfect for an island. Adding an island would be one way to update a '60s kitchen. If you're going to paint the existing cabinetry, you may be able to install an island, or additional cabinets, without too much difficulty. Just find a cabinet that's roughly the same shape and style as the existing cabinets, and paint it to match. The 1960s cabinets were usually quite plain, so once they're all painted the same color, nobody will notice if one is slightly different from the others.

1970s Kitchens

Nobody likes a 1970s kitchen today. The style hasn't come back, and shows no sign of coming back in the next few years (although it probably will someday). The 1970s were characterized by the "Mediterranean look," dark heavy wood cabinets and earthtone color schemes, with olive green and harvest gold appliances. These kitchens look really dark and dreary compared to the light, bright kitchen styles today.

In terms of being functional, however, a 1970s kitchen will have almost everything a 1990s kitchen has, only in ugly colors. The cabinets are very nearly identical to new ones, except for the wood tone. Before you tear everything out, consider some lower-cost alternatives. First of all, how about painting those dark cabinets white? It's amazing what that can do. If you also replace the drawer pulls and cabinet handles with something stylish, and install a new, brighter light fixture, it's amazing how much more cheerful the kitchen will be.

Another problem with many 1970s kitchens is that they tend to have very few windows. That was part of the 1970s "dark and dreary" look. It was also a side effect of the fuel crisis. Older windows leaked heat, so some people decided to eliminate them when they remodeled. Unfortunately, there's no cheap way to remedy this now. Installing new windows is a big job. And, in order to install them, you'll have to take down some of the cabinets that were put up where windows used to be. If you do that, you'll probably find that the old cabinets will no longer fit in the new spaces you're creating. So, you may wind up having to buy all new cabinetry as well as new windows. If that's the case, you may as well just gut the whole kitchen and start over.

If there isn't a room above the kitchen, a skylight might be a better way to solve the light problem. You don't have to move any cabinets to install a skylight, and it's amazing how much light they bring in. One skylight will bring in almost as much light as a whole wall of windows. Of course, there are other drawbacks to not having windows. There's not much of a view out of a skylight. However, if your main concern is adding light to a dark kitchen, a skylight will definitely solve the problem.

Newer Kitchens

If the house has a kitchen that was remodeled in the 1980s or later, it's essentially new. You can change the color scheme and freshen the look, but you can't "update" it very much. That means that remodeling the kitchen won't add much value to the house. If the homeowners hate the kitchen and want to replace everything, of course you'll do it. But they can't expect the job to raise the value of their house.

Kitchen Flooring

Kitchen flooring takes a lot of wear and tear. As a result, the floorcovering in most kitchens is usually pretty worn unless it's been replaced within the last 10 years. There's a wide variety of floor treatments and styles to choose from today. The homeowners need to give some thought to the type of flooring they want installed so that it will coordinate with the style of the kitchen.

Wood

The original Victorian kitchen had a wood floor — either oak or plain pine. Remember, the kitchen was considered a service area. Unless it was in an elaborate home, Victorian builders wouldn't have put much effort into trying to make the floor especially nice. A worn, pitted, pine floor in the kitchen wouldn't have been considered a problem.

There are some very nice oak flooring products being used in kitchens today. They're supposed to be more water-resistant than the old wood floors were. I haven't used any of these new products in a kitchen yet, so I can't say how good they are. In the old days, however, wood flooring was a problem in the kitchen. The constant change of temperature and dampness from spills caused the wood floors in the kitchen to warp and become discolored. That's why linoleum was immediately popular when it became available and all those troublesome oak floors were quickly covered up.

There may be an oak floor in near-perfect condition under the kitchen linoleum. If the homeowners are considering wood flooring for the kitchen, it's worth peeking under the linoleum to see what's there. If the wood is in good shape, you might want to work with it, rather than cover it up again. A few coats of a good heavy-duty varnish might be enough to adequately protect it from the dampness now. It depends on the family. If they're very careful people, who rarely spill water or drop things, a varnished wood floor can last them many years. On the other hand, if they have children or pets, a more durable floorcovering may be needed.

The advantage to keeping or installing wood flooring is that it recreates the original look of the kitchen. That's something the homeowners will want to consider if you're designing an antique-style kitchen.

ꙮ Tile

Quarry tile or ceramic tile can also be used to achieve the antique look. It was a common floorcovering at the turn of the century. If the homeowners are concerned that a wooden floor won't hold up well, you can install quarry tile instead and still have an authentic floorcovering.

You have a substantial amount of open space to work with on the kitchen floor, so laying large tiles isn't a problem. There aren't as many corners or fixtures to cut around as in a bathroom, and there's certainly more room to work in. This gives you the opportunity to use some of the beautiful larger-size tiles that are available. Pick the tile that looks best in your design. Avoid using small tiles on the kitchen floor. They make it look too much like a bathroom.

For safety, I think it's good idea to use unglazed quarry tiles or glazed tiles with a rough texture in a kitchen. Large, high-gloss tiles can be very slippery if liquids or grease are spilled on them. Fortunately, all tiles always have grout lines. The extra texture helps you keep a grip on the floor, even if it's slippery.

Tile is highly wear-resistant. It will last a long time, no matter how many kids and pets the homeowners have. A properly-installed ceramic or quarry tile floor can last literally hundreds of years. Another advantage to tile is that it provides a quality look. There's a strong emphasis on "the look of quality" in remodeling products today. Tile achieves this look very nicely. It's clearly a premium product. The fact that tile can last practically forever gives the entire job a feeling of permanence that many people have come to appreciate. In this age of throwaways, disposables and planned obsolescence, it's nice to know that you have something that will never have to be replaced.

There are a few drawbacks to tile flooring that you should consider. First, it's a very hard surface. Some people complain that it makes their legs or feet hurt, especially if they're older or have arthritis. Also, when a dish or glass is dropped on a tile floor, it's almost guaranteed to break. Another thing to keep in mind is that tile is very difficult to remove. Once it's in, it's there to stay. If a single tile is damaged, it's possible to chisel it out and replace it. (You should always leave some spare tiles with the homeowners for this purpose.) But, I wouldn't want to chisel out a whole floor. If homeowners like to redecorate frequently and keep up with the latest styles, they might be better off with a resilient floorcovering, like vinyl. It's fairly easy and inexpensive to change.

Preparing the Floor

Remember, the underlayment needs to be rock solid before you install any kind of ceramic tile. Check the floor carefully for any bounce, and strengthen it where it's needed. If the surface is damaged, install new plywood underlayment. Never install ceramic tile over damaged or rotted wood.

Also check for a build-up of old floorcoverings. Often, new floorcoverings were installed on top of old ones, accumulating several layers over the years. It's okay to install resilient floorcoverings over old coverings, but there's a limit. After 100 years, that limit has probably been reached.

You can easily find 20 layers on older floors. They may have piled up to the point where the kitchen floor is now 2 inches higher than the dining room floor, even though they were once even. When this happens, there's an odd little step up where people don't expect one to be. It's very easy to trip over, and doesn't look good. If you find a floor like this, it's time to start tearing it down a few layers. Not only can it be dangerous, but a buildup like this isn't suitable as a base for tile. All those layers of linoleum are too soft. They compress when you walk on them, creating an unstable surface that won't hold the tile.

You can install resilient floorcoverings over surfaces like this, but it isn't a good idea. You'd just be adding one more layer, and making the pile deeper. It's better to tear the whole mess out and get rid of it. This can be a big, difficult job. The layers turn into a sticky mess when you begin to pull them up. They fall apart in your hands, so you can't pull up very large pieces. And they're all full of sharp little nails and splinters that catch on everything. It can easily turn into a pile of trash 6 feet high. Be sure to allow plenty of time for this job. It can take all day to pull up and dispose of 2 inches of old floorcoverings from a large kitchen. Don't forget this when you're figuring out your price!

Installing Tile

As in the bathroom, I like to lay tile with an eye towards the areas that are going to be the most visible. This can sometimes be a little difficult to visualize in a large kitchen, especially if it's completely empty, with all the cabinets removed. That's why most manufacturers recommend that you lay your tiles out starting from the middle and work out in all directions.

However, this doesn't always work out well for me. Sometimes you end up with odd cut tiles right at the entrance to the kitchen. That's because the kitchen floor isn't necessarily an even multiple of the tile size you're using. The floor might be $20\frac{1}{8}$ tiles wide, instead of an even 20. The larger the tiles are, the more likely this is. What are you going to do with that one-eighth of a tile? It's not going to look good. You want to tuck it someplace out of the way, where it won't be too obvious. The entrance to the kitchen is a highly visible point. Don't put odd pieces of tile there if you can help it. I usually start my tile layouts at the entrance to the kitchen, or at whatever other place is most visible. I work toward the edge that will be covered by cabinetry. That way, if there are odd pieces that don't look right, they'll be under the kick space of the cabinets where they won't show.

Resilient Floorcoverings

Vinyl tiles and sheet goods are very common in kitchens. Unlike bathrooms, people expect to see vinyl in kitchens. Some people even prefer it. It's a low-maintenance surface that's easy to clean, and easy to replace when it wears out or goes out of style. There are hundreds of designs of vinyl tile and sheet vinyl to choose from.

Here again, it's important to match the floorcovering to the style of the kitchen, especially if you're doing an old-fashioned kitchen style. You don't want to put a modern pattern in a 1940s-style kitchen. It would spoil the effect. A 1940s floorcovering should be cute and fussy, with little old-fashioned designs. The '50s and '60s styles are more modern, with bright colors and geometric designs.

It's interesting to note that in the '50s, people really liked linoleum. They used it all over the house, including the bedrooms and sometimes even in the living room. You may come across some if you're working on a house that was remodeled during the 1950s. It's often underneath carpeting that was installed later. If you find linoleum under carpet, it's usually still there because it was too hard to get it off. Sometimes, however, linoleum was put down over an underlayment of plywood. Then you can take it all up without too much trouble. Another thing I've found occasionally is sheet vinyl that was just laid down and not glued at all. In that case, you can just roll it up and throw it away. The floor underneath may be in perfect condition. If the linoleum was glued down to an original wood floor, the floor isn't completely ruined, but it is seriously damaged. It'll have to completely sanded down and refinished.

If you're planning to extend the '50s look to other rooms in the house, using '50s-style vinyl tiles is a good way to do it. This kind of floorcovering, used in rooms other than the kitchen, was only fashionable in the '50s. These same rooms would have had wooden floors in the '40s, and carpeted floors in the '60s and later. Linoleum floors are so unique to this period that they instantly give a room the '50s look, even without other decor items.

Keep in mind, however, that sheet vinyl and vinyl tile are *not* luxury floorcoverings, even in the kitchen. They're fine for a moderate-priced home, but they'll detract from a kitchen that's supposed to be completed in top-of-the-line materials. If you're working on upscale housing, it's better to use ceramic tile.

Adding Kitchen Space

Victorian kitchens often had other rooms adjacent to them, such as a walk-in pantry or a "summer kitchen." These extra rooms can be very valuable to you in the course of remodeling. Today, an extra-large kitchen with areas set aside for special uses, such as a meal-planning area, is considered luxurious. If you remodel a modern house, this extra space has to be added on from the ground up. That's expensive. The extra rooms around the Victorian kitchen are perfect for expanding kitchen space. They can be converted into special use areas at minimal cost. You can have a very expensive effect for a fraction of what it would cost to build on.

The Summer Kitchen

A summer kitchen was an attached porch with a wood-burning stove. It had a lot of porch-type windows which could be opened to vent the heat from the stove. If there's any porch off the kitchen, you can treat it like a summer kitchen.

Today, kitchens with "sunspace" — areas with lots of windows and light — are very popular. These spaces are expensive to add on. If a house has a summer kitchen, you're in luck. It's perfect to convert into a sunspace. It even has the windows already!

Unfortunately, if the windows are porch-type windows, you'll probably have to rip them out. They don't seal well. You need all-weather windows to make the space usable in all seasons. At least the openings are there, so half the work is done.

The door is another problem. There's probably an exterior door from the porch to the kitchen. For a sunspace conversion, remove the doorway and replace it with a larger opening. Ideally, you'll take out the entire wall and open the space up to the kitchen. Keep in mind, however, that this is a load-bearing exterior wall. The load will have to be transferred to a beam, and the beam attached to something suitably strong. The details of how to do this are discussed in Chapter 12.

The typical summer kitchen was finished as a porch, with some kind of exterior siding that's not suitable for a kitchen interior. You'll need to drywall the room. You may be able to hang the drywall right over the siding. If the porch was in good condition, you might not need to do much to the room beyond replacing the windows, drywalling and decorating.

In most cases, the space you'll get from converting the summer kitchen won't be part of the kitchen work area. It's too far from the work triangle. Don't put kitchen cabinets and countertops in this room. They'll look funny, and never be used. Instead, use this added area as a kitchen office, family room, or breakfast nook. A sunny breakfast area is an especially appealing addition to any kitchen.

Be sure to decorate the added space to match the kitchen. Use the same floorcovering, wall treatment, and so on. If you decorate it differently, it will look like separate room. People will wonder what it's supposed to be. By decorating it to match the kitchen, you clearly define it as an extension of the kitchen.

🐦 The Pantry

Food storage pantries aren't as important as they used to be. In Victorian times, you couldn't just go out to the store and buy food when you needed it. Dry goods, such as flour, sugar and salt, were purchased in large quantities and stored in the pantry along with jars of fresh fruits and vegetables canned for year-round consumption. Everything that was bought or canned had to be put someplace until it was used. Today, there's no reason to keep a six-month supply of food piled up in the kitchen. Most people use the pantry for general storage now. It's a great place for keeping cleaning supplies, as well as all those handy kitchen appliances that you don't use every day.

If the kitchen is small, however, the pantry may be a lot more valuable as kitchen space than storage space. Even a small pantry can supply the room needed to modernize an old, undersized kitchen.

There are quite a few ways you can make use of pantry space. It depends on the size of the pantry and where it's located. If the pantry is large and centrally-located, you might be able to just remove the partition wall and open it up to the rest of the kitchen. The pantry area will then become part of a larger kitchen.

Too often, however, the pantry is a little room tucked into a corner that you can't easily integrate into a larger kitchen. Even if you remove the partition, you'll still have a little alcove off in the corner. This won't add to the available work space. It's too far from the work triangle. But this space makes an excellent kitchen office. An alcove, set apart from the rest of the kitchen, creates a quiet area for paying bills, writing letters, making phone calls, or watching TV while dinner cooks.

If the pantry's large enough, you may be able to convert it to a breakfast nook or eating area — if you can add light. If the pantry is located on an outside wall, you may be able to add windows and brighten it up. However, there isn't much you can do if it's an interior room. If that's the case, you should probably use if for something else. It might make a good bathroom conversion that opens to another room, as we discussed in the last chapter.

Any remodeler can build a brand-new kitchen in a brand-new space or redo a kitchen from a totally gutted space. The trick to maximum value remodeling is to work in the existing space, using many of the existing features and materials, and build something that looks like a brand-new kitchen. It won't work in every situation, but it's always worth considering. If you can pull it off, the savings to the homeowner, and the profit to you, will be enormous.

Chapter 22

Adding Living Space

Not all Victorian houses were large. Many were just little cottages. Today these smaller houses are most likely in need of additional living space, and adding that space can greatly increase their value.

Once again, the standard of the neighborhood is the key. In terms of space, the homeowners will get the best return on their remodeling investment if the house size is brought up to the same level as the others in the neighborhood. Of course, this standard works best if this particular house is the only small house remaining in a neighborhood of larger homes. If you add enough space to bring it up to the same size as those around it, its value will rise to be roughly equivalent to the others. The nicer the neighborhood, the more value you can add. In upscale neighborhoods the price differential can be huge. That's because wealthy people don't like to live in small houses. They won't buy a little house for themselves, even if it's a great deal. However, if that small house is expanded to be as spacious and desirable as the others around it, they'll snap it up. That's a perfect example of maximum value remodeling.

One thing to keep in mind here is that it doesn't pay to expand a house *beyond* the size of the other houses around it. Certainly, if the homeowners have a large family and need the space, you should expand the house to match their needs. But they'll only get the added value out of the remodeling through the added comfort it provides. They won't recover the cost when and if they decide to sell.

Converting Unused Space

One job that's always profitable is adding a third bedroom to a two-bedroom house. A two-bedroom house is too small to be desirable in any neighborhood. If the homeowners want you to add a bedroom, look for unused space that you can convert. I prefer to concentrate on converting existing space, rather than building additions, because converting space accomplishes the same thing for a lot less money. It produces the maximum value that I always strive for. Adding another room to a small house by converting unused space can be very profitable. It can easily raise the property value by 200 to 300 percent of the cost of the job.

An addition, on the other hand, is a lot more expensive. It can still be profitable,

Figure 22-1
A Victorian double porch

especially if the house is so small that it's almost unusable. In that case, the only alternative to building an addition might be to demolish the house and start over. An addition, even an expensive one, is usually

Figure 22-2
Enclosed room above front porch

cheaper than building a whole new house. However, an addition won't provide you the huge profit percentages that I like to aim for. It may return 100 to 150 percent of its cost, but you're unlikely to see the 200 to 300 percent return that you can get from converting space. Let's consider some of the spaces you may be able to convert on a Victorian house.

The Attic

Unfortunately, the attic area of a Victorian house is rarely an ideal location to convert into living space. The typical steep roofline creates an attic space that's usually too high and narrow to use. Often the angle is so steep that even the walls of the upstairs bedrooms may be angled to accommodate the roofline. This gives you an attic that has very little floor area with the 7 feet of vertical clearance required by code.

Generally, there's no way to make the attic into a room unless you want to tear off the roof, build new side walls, and then add a new roof. That would be like adding another floor to the house. It's a big, expensive job. It may be better than nothing, but it's definitely not my first choice. I'd look elsewhere for space.

Porch Conversions

While Victorian attics don't lend themselves well to conversion, the porches do. Luckily, Victorian houses were designed with lots of porches. You may have a variety of spaces to work with.

Many Victorian houses have two-story front porches. That is, they have a front entrance porch, with another porch above it. Figure 22-1 shows a typical example. Can you convert one without the other? Sure! Victorian designers did this all the time. They commonly put rooms over porches, and porches over rooms. Figure 22-2 is an original Victorian home with an enclosed room over the front porch.

You're usually better off converting the upstairs porch. Victorian houses are supposed to have entrance porches, so if you turn the existing porch into a room, you'll have to build another entry in front of the old one. This arrangement can be awkward. You'll also have the problem of blending the new, enclosed porch space with the original entrance hall or parlor. This can turn into a very odd space that's difficult to coordinate into the interior design. You may have to redesign the entire area. For the most part, I prefer to use another porch area for additional space whenever possible, and leave the front entrance as it is.

There are a lot of different upstairs porch designs, but my favorite to work with are upstairs sleeping porches. They make ideal bedroom conversions. They were actually designed as cool places to sleep on hot summer nights. (Remember, not even the richest Victorians had air conditioning!) Figure 22-3 is a sleeping porch above an enclosed back porch. Sleeping porches can be converted into rooms without too much trouble or expense. Figure 22-4 shows a dust porch. These are not usually big enough for room conversions, but they can often be used to make an adjoining room larger.

❧ Converting a Porch

Most Victorian second-floor porches already have roofs. All you need to do is put up sidewalls, and you've got a room. But first, check carefully for signs of rot damage on the porch. Since the porch was open to the weather for years, water may have accumulated in the corners and caused damage. Even if the room is enclosed, like a sleeping porch, it may have been open at one time. Rot damage that occurred 100 years ago may still be there, having never been repaired. Replace all rot-damaged wood. Remember, the new room will add a lot of weight to the structure. Defects that may not be a problem now may become a problem once the extra weight is added.

Also, make sure that the understructure is capable of holding the weight you're adding. Check the foundation. Every foundation is built with a certain load-bearing capacity in mind, and you might be exceeding that load. Luckily, many Victorian houses were massively overbuilt. You may find that the house has a stone foundation 2 feet thick, with huge oak beams resting on it for sup-

Figure 22-3
Enclosed rear porch with sleeping porch above

Figure 22-4
Open upstairs porch

port. If these are all in good condition, the new addition will pose no problems. Some Victorian structures are so strong that you could add six stories to the house before you overloaded them.

But if you have any doubts about the structure, strengthen it before you do any further work. It's a lot harder to jack the structure back up once it's been pushed down and serious damage has occurred. Use the techniques we discussed in Chapter 12, under structural repairs. Adding a few more posts, beams, and joists never hurt any building, and it's an especially good idea on an old one. By distributing the load over more support members, you lessen the load each individual member has to carry. That makes failures much less likely.

Even if the structure is strong enough, there's one more problem when you're working with porches. You're likely to run into floors that are sloped for rain runoff. That won't do for a bedroom. You'll have to make the floor level.

If the floor is solid, you can level it out with sleepers. You'll need to cut 2 x 4s or 2 x 6s (depending on the amount of slope) in an angle that's the reverse of the slope of the floor. Nail these over the existing flooring, locating them over the joists. Then lay a new layer of ¾-inch plywood subfloor over the sleepers. If the floor seems at all shaky, you may want to skip the sleepers and install new floor joists instead. They'll give you a level surface for the subfloor, and a lot more strength as well.

Interior Access Problems

A big problem with second-floor porch conversions is that they don't always have a separate entrance from a hallway. Rather, you have to go through a bedroom to reach them. This creates a flow problem. Bedrooms really need to have their own entrances. Pass-through bedrooms are considered inferior, and generally can't be called "bedrooms" in real estate listings. They're usually called sitting rooms.

There are a couple of ways to deal with this problem. First of all, is it important that

the extra room be a bedroom? Even as a pass-through, it would make a perfectly fine home office, library, or nursery. It could also have the effect of turning the bedroom it's connected to into a bedroom suite, with a sitting room.

The second solution would be to use the space for a bathroom. This is particularly helpful if the porch is attached to the master bedroom. A master bedroom with its own bath is a nice feature. If the house is short of space, converting a porch may be the only way to add a second bath. A drawback to this location is that the plumbing may present a problem. It might be necessary to do some complicated plumbing runs in order to supply water and drains to the room. Of course, this area may not be any worse than any other possible bathroom location in the house. Plumbing is always a problem in Victorian houses, no matter where the bathrooms are located. If you do decide to install a bathroom in a porch conversion, be sure to make the floor extra strong. Bathrooms weigh a lot more than bedrooms.

If you were originally thinking of locating a bathroom somewhere else upstairs, you can use that space for something else if you use the porch for the bathroom. Perhaps that area would make a better bedroom than the porch would have, especially if it has its own entrance off the hallway. Sometimes you have to do a lot of rearranging before you come up with a layout that works well in a Victorian home.

Another alternative use for the porch space is to simply remove the wall between the addition and the attached bedroom, and make one large, luxurious room. As I mentioned earlier, this is probably the best use for a dust porch anyway.

And finally, if you're planning to make major alterations in the room layouts, you may be able to redirect the hallway to provide the new room with a hall access. This might seem like a lot of work, but all you're really doing is moving partitions around. If it solves the problem, it's well worth it. It's a lot less expensive than the alternative, which is building an addition from the ground up.

Drywalling the New Spaces

Since you'll probably drywall the converted space, rather than plastering it, you should design the room with that in mind. Victorians often used a lot of odd angles and sloping ceilings where the roof line intersected the corners of the room. It wasn't any harder to plaster these than to plaster anything else. However, it's a lot harder to drywall these angles. Drywall is designed for 90-degree angles. Anything else is very difficult. Even corner trowels are made for 90-degree corners.

If you have to work on a 135-degree corner, everything slows down. It takes me longer to finish a couple of 135-degree joints properly than it does to finish a whole room. Standard drywall tools don't work well on them. The joints come out wavy, and you have to go over them again and again. If possible, try to plan out the room to avoid creating odd angles. If you absolutely must have odd angles, allow a lot of extra time in your estimate for drywalling them.

Heating the Additions

We discussed bringing heat to added or converted rooms in both Chapters 4 and 14. My best advice is to think about how you're going to supply heat to the room while the room is still in the early planning stages. That can save you a lot of extra effort. For instance, if you need to bring in other services, such as electricity or plumbing for a bathroom, you might be able to just box in a corner somewhere and bring plumbing, heat, and electrical service to the areas where they're needed. This would solve three problems at once. Look for corner spaces in the rooms below that wouldn't be ruined with the addition of a boxed-in area.

If you're planning to add space onto an existing room, the heat that's already going to that room may be enough to heat the larger area. If not, you may be able to add a booster fan in the duct of a gas forced-air system that will heat the new room adequately. If there's a hot water heating system, you can easily add on another loop of baseboard heaters to serve the new area.

If all else fails, you can use electric baseboard heaters. These are best used in areas with a mild climate since they're expensive to operate. However, even in cold areas, it won't cost too much to boost the heat in one room.

Windows

When installing windows in converted spaces, be sure to use styles that match the existing windows. Try to locate them in similar positions, as well. That is, if all the other bedrooms have one window in the middle of the wall, the new room should, too.

Old sleeping porches have a lot of windows. They may have windows on three walls, extending half the height of the wall. It's tempting to leave all these windows, especially if they're in good shape. I don't advise it. The porch was meant to be cool in summer, and not used in winter. The windows are too drafty for year-round use and they'll make the room almost unheatable.

It's best to block off some of the window openings. The new room should have the same number of windows as the other bedrooms, in similar locations and in a matching style. Otherwise, anyone familiar with older homes will know that the room is a converted sleeping porch. They'll assume that it's drafty and unpleasant in cold weather, even if it isn't. In terms of resale, that will reduce the value of the addition. Since you want your jobs to add maximum value, you should make the room as desirable as possible and not leave anything that might be considered a defect.

The only time you might consider keeping the windows is if you're using the porch for a sitting area or office off the master suite. In that case, you would have to replace the windows with all-weather Thermopane windows. They'll keep the room at a usable temperature year-round, and you'll have a bright, airy room addition with windows on three sides. It will be a nice place to sit in or work in, but it won't be very private. Bedrooms should provide both privacy and warmth.

≥ Costs

The cost of converting a porch to a bedroom varies, depending on what you have to work with. It can be surprisingly low. If the porch is in good condition, you may only need to level the floor, replace the windows, drywall, and install electric heat. Most of the materials for a job like this are quite cheap. The only expensive items are the windows. Even then, all the materials may cost under $1,000. If everything goes smoothly, you can complete the job in about 50 hours. If your labor costs are $20 per hour, the entire project will cost about $2,000. That's pretty cheap for an additional bedroom. Actually, it would be cheap at three times the price!

≥ Over-Wing Additions

Some two-story Victorian houses have downstairs wings projecting out from the structure that don't have rooms above them. If these wings have second-floor porches above them, you can convert the porches into rooms. If they don't have a porch above, you may still be able to add on a room. Just be aware that it will be more work than converting a porch. You have to take off the roof, strengthen the ceiling sufficiently to allow it to serve as a floor, put up sidewalls, and then add a new roof. All this work has to be done before rain comes in and ruins the room below. Also, if the room below has a wet plaster ceiling, the vibrations from the work above will very likely crack and ruin it. If you add a room like this, remember to add the price of a new ceiling to your estimate.

Blending the Exteriors of Converted Spaces

One of the biggest problems when converting a space is making the exterior match the rest of the house. Unfortunately, many spaces that are ideal for conversion from the inside will cause problems from the outside. Front porches are a good example. The front of a house is the most important area, in terms of design. It's very important that any converted space in the front match the rest of the house, and look good. If it adds space, but looks lousy, it will take away from the value of the house, rather than adding to it. I've seen a lot of upstairs front porches that have been converted into bedrooms. Many of them look really bad. They're obvious additions, and look like something that was just tacked on without any concern for the style of the house — or any style at all, for that matter.

If you're converting a porch on the side or in the rear of the house, the style isn't quite as important. On many houses, these areas are out of view or not easily seen from the street. This is especially true in older neighborhoods, where the houses are very close together. In a situation like this, you're lucky. You can do almost anything you want, design-wise, because nobody can see it.

In many ways, it can actually be easier to work on Victorian homes than on later styles. Because Victorian houses often have all sorts of little projections built onto them as part of the original design, you can blend an addition in and make it look like it's always been there. For a front porch conversion, your first thought might be to simply enclose the porch, using materials similar to those used on the rest of the house. You *can* do that, but you'll end up with a boxy shape that isn't in keeping with the tall, thin shape of the original porch. The alteration would be very obvious.

Instead, why not make the sidewalls extra tall, and turn it into a little tower? Towers were often used as design elements on Victorian houses, and it would be perfectly normal to have one on the front of the house. If you trimmed it out to match the rest of the house, you'd be improving the original design rather than detracting from it. If you wanted to be fancy, you could make it octagonal and turn it into a turret. In either case, the change to the house would be in keeping with its original design. The house is tall and thin, and the addition would be tall and thin as well.

Of course, the addition doesn't necessarily have to be a tower. It could be a gable, or a dormer, or a bay, or any other Victorian design element. Use the original parts of the house for guidance. Any Victorian design element that's in keeping with the rest of the house will look fine. What's important is that it *is* a Victorian design element, and not just a box on the front of the house.

Victorian Basements

The basements of Victorian homes are rarely suitable for converting to living space. The ceilings are low and the room dark and dank. They were designed to store potatoes in, not live in.

In order to get adequate headroom in a basement like this, you'll have to dig out the floor. This is a difficult job. You're not going to be able to get a backhoe down the basement stairs — all of the digging will have to be done by hand. You'll also need to leave at least 1 foot of undisturbed space around the basement walls so you don't undermine the footings. And even with all this work, you may not end up with much living space. Most of these old basements aren't very large to begin with.

Victorian basements frequently have dampness problems, especially in locations where there's a lot of rain or high humidity. The moisture control techniques we discussed in Chapter 12 will be adequate for a basement used as storage space, but may not be good enough for prime living space. Basements without floor drains or foundation drains will never be perfectly dry.

What does all this boil down to? It will usually cost more to convert the basement to living space than to build an outside addition. If the house is located in an area where no additions are permitted, converting the basement may be the only option. However, as with the attic, you're generally better off looking for space someplace else.

Major Additions

What if you can't find any space to convert and decide to add another floor, or an addition on the side or back of the house? Keep in mind that it will substantially alter the look of the house. Integrating an addition into the existing design can be difficult. I've seen jobs where another floor was added, but no attempt was made to work it into the design. The additions were obvious add-ons that stuck out like a sore thumb. Jobs like this look terrible, and don't add much to the value of the house. The improved livability doesn't balance out with the destruction of the home's style.

If you must add another floor, or if you're working with a house where a floor has already been added, try to make it blend with the rest of the house. One thing that you have on your side is the fact that the house was originally tall and thin. Adding another floor will make it taller, but the basic shape will be maintained. If you use the same steep roofline on the addition, you can preserve most of the original look.

An addition should be sided with the same material as the rest of the house. It should also have the same kind of trim, decorations, and windows. I've seen modern additions on old houses that have tiny, aluminum-frame casement windows right above large, double-hung Victorian windows. These look terrible when you see them together on the same wall. Not only does this type of work scream "addition," it also screams "low-quality workmanship." If you find aluminum casement windows anywhere on a Victorian house, get rid of them!

Always use windows that match the originals as closely as possible. Having windows made to order is one way to get the correct style. They'll cost some money, but you'll get the best possible effect. If you're working with upscale housing, getting a good match is worth the effort and expense. One source I use for made-to-order windows is Marvin Windows & Doors. Call them at 1-800-346-5128 for a free catalog.

If the homeowner's budget is tight, try to find an inexpensive stock window that matches the original windows as closely as possible. You may not be able to find one that matches exactly, but you should be able to find one that's at least the same size and shape. If you trim it out with decorations like those on the existing windows, the difference won't be obvious.

It's important that the trim on any added or converted space in a Victorian house match the rest of the house. But, it doesn't have to be an exact match. If you look at pictures of original Victorian homes, you'll see that they often used different decorative designs in different places on the house. However, the designs were complementary; they looked good together, even though they weren't the same. The Victorians liked it that way. They liked having some variety to make the decorations more interesting. You can use this to your advantage. The trim on the added space can be a similar design, or a different but complementary design. As long as it has something in common with the original design, in pattern or shape, it will look like it was intended to be that way. Remember, the original designers of these houses were creative, sometimes even fanciful. You can be, too. As long as your creativity is in keeping with the basic principles of Victorian design that we have discussed, it will look fine.

Photographs

One way to visualize the changes you want to make before you begin is to take a photograph of the house and make some photocopies of it. Enlarge the copies to show more detail. You can then draw precise elevations by tracing the copy, and work from the tracings. Or, you can just draw your proposed changes right on the copy. In either case, you'll be able to get a much better idea of what your ideas will look like.

Copies are also good for experimenting with colors. Try coloring in the black-and-white copies with some of the colors you're considering for the house. It will give you a good idea of how they'll actually look. When you come up with what you think is the right design and color combinations for the house, show it to the homeowners, and discuss the changes and colors with them. You'll get a lot better results doing this than just trying to imagine it completed.

Chapter 23

Victorian Outbuildings

*M*ost Victorian houses were originally built with a number of outbuildings. Many of these, like the outhouse, are long gone. Others, such as barns and carriage houses, may still be standing and in use today.

Carriage Houses

Old outbuildings can be very interesting. The carriage house of a stately Victorian mansion may be larger than many homes are today. The buildings often contained a second floor living area for the coachman. Sometimes the living quarters were quite spacious — large enough that they can be rented out as apartments today. Carriage houses can also be converted into living space for the primary home, used as guest quarters, or possibly even sold off as a completely separate home. In most cases, the local zoning and building codes will determine how the carriage house can be used. Selling it or renting it may not be allowed. However, living space is always valuable. As part of the property, it can be used as a studio, home office, guest house, or even a garage.

The Garage

You'll often find old garages behind Victorian houses. Of course, Victorian houses didn't originally have garages — there weren't any cars when most of these houses were built. The garages you'll find were most likely added during the 1920s, like the one in Figure 23-1. They're usually too small for today's two- or three-car families, but some of them are still in good condition. If an old garage isn't in good condition, it's probably not worth putting a lot of money into. If it isn't an original building and it has no historic significance, there isn't much point in keeping it. It's better to tear it down and add a new, more convenient garage that matches the style of the house.

Many times, original buildings such as the stable or the carriage house were converted into garages. If they've been well maintained, they're worth restoring. Be sure to keep any authentic decor items from an old garage if you must tear it down. I found an antique Victorian lightning rod on an old garage that I did some work on (Figure 23-2). These are the kinds of things that add authenticity to a building. Always save them,

Figure 23-1
1920s garage

even if you can't save the building. If you can save the structure, then you can put the items back in their original position when your repairs are completed. If you have to build a new garage, the antique fixtures will help blend it to the style of the house. In any case, if you don't have a use for them now, either save them for another job or sell them to an antique dealer. They are valuable.

Figure 23-2
Antique Victorian lightning rod

❧ Adding a New Garage

If you have to build a new garage, you'll want to build a Victorian garage. Of course, there's no such thing as a Victorian garage, but that never stopped us before. Just build the kind of garage Victorians would have built, if they had built garages!

You'll simply need to copy the style elements of the house. Foremost is the roof line. Modern garages have low roofs, either hip or gable. This is their distinguishing characteristic. If you put a high, gabled roof on the garage, with the same pitch as the house, it will instantly take on an antique look. Use the same type of exterior siding and shingles that are on the house, then finish it up with an "old-fashioned" garage door. Be sure and add some Victorian trim, the same style as on the house. Gable decorations look especially nice. You'll end up with a garage that complements the house, instead of one that detracts from it, as a modern garage would. It will be the nicest garage in the neighborhood.

Barns

It isn't unusual to find a Victorian house with a barn, even in the middle of a city. Many cities grew so quickly that they gobbled up farms, farmhouses and barns. As a result, there are barns still standing in downtown Detroit, just a mile or so from the skyscrapers of the business district. It's rather startling to come across a barn there; it seems totally out of place.

Barns are even more common in the suburbs, since many suburbs were farmland only a few years ago. Many are unique and historic features of the homes they belong to. This is especially true of the old picturesque red barns like the one in Figure 23-3. Nobody builds them anymore. Farmers use metal pole buildings for storage today. They're much cheaper to build and maintain, so gradually all the old wooden barns are being allowed to fall down.

As this process continues, the remaining barns will become more and more rare, and therefore more and more valuable. If a home has a barn, it's a shame to let it fall into disrepair. A well-maintained barn will add charm and value to a property and give it an authentic "antique" feel. It can easily add tens of thousands of dollars to the value of a home. Today it would cost about $100,000 to build a classic barn, using the same quality of materials that used to be standard, such as oak beams and flooring. Tearing a barn like that down is like throwing money away.

Unfortunately, maintaining a barn is also expensive. That's why so many of them are allowed to fall down. The work isn't complicated — usually just roofing and painting. However, the buildings are so huge that even simple work can run up a tremendous bill. A barn roof can take hundreds of squares of shingles, and barn walls can easily take 50 to 100 gallons of paint. If you add labor costs, you could be looking at a total bill of $10,000 to $20,000. And that's for a barn that's in pretty good shape! A homeowner may be reluctant to spend this kind of money on a barn. After all, it isn't living space. It's just a huge, empty building. What good is a barn unless you're a farmer?

Actually, barns have a lot of uses, even in the city. A barn offers an enormous amount of useful storage. It's perfect for anything that needs to be kept out of the weather, but doesn't need to be kept heated. It's a great place to store recreational vehicles out of season. It's big enough to hold a large sailboat, camper, an antique car collection, and any other large items that people like to keep. If the homeowners don't have any of these things, perhaps they might want to rent the space out to someone who does. Rent for garage storage space starts at about $50 per month for a car-sized space. A good-sized barn may have as many as 40 car-sized spaces. That's a potential income of $2,000 per month! Suddenly, the barn isn't quite so useless anymore, is it?

Homeowners may be a lot more willing to put money into a barn if it can make some money for them in return. In fact, if they do rent the barn out, the maintenance cost then becomes a tax write-off. It's a business expense, rather than a personal expense. The

Figure 23-3
Classic red barn

tax savings alone can be very worthwhile. It's yet another reason for fixing up and keeping a barn.

❧ Working on Barns

If you're used to working on houses, working on a barn can be a real experience. The buildings are enormous. Everything is industrial-sized. Even simple repairs become huge jobs because everything is just so big!

Barns were originally built to store hay. Hay was piled up from the floor to the ceiling. That's why they're so tall. Because these huge piles of hay were heavy, the floors needed to be very strong. The floors were generally made from large beams or tree trunks which were covered over with heavy oak planks. A floor like this, in good condition, can hold cars, boats, RVs, and other extremely heavy items. Barns often have several floors. They may have a main floor for hay storage, a hay loft above the main floor, and a basement below. And all of these levels offer useful storage.

A wood barn will most likely need a new roof and paint. It's fairly simple work, no different from any other roofing and painting. The most important thing about doing this kind of work is to estimate the sizes correctly.

Figure 23-4
Old hay barns are very large structures

Figure 23-5
Rotted floor in barn

Remember, the structure itself is considerably larger than the houses you're used to working on. Looking at the roofer on top of the barn in Figure 23-4, you can get an idea of just how big these buildings are. It's a long way down to the ground!

Don't just eyeball a barn and come up with an estimate. The size will fool you. Measure carefully, and multiply everything out. Sometimes the square footage is amazing. A standard-size barn has 6,400 square feet of floor space, and 5,600 square feet of walls. Also keep in mind that all that weathered barn wood will suck up a lot of paint. You'll get about half the coverage you normally would from a gallon. Be sure to allow for the size and the increased paint usage in your estimate.

I've found that exterior solid-color stain works well on barns. The wood has often been poorly cared for, going years without any paint. The wood grain may be raised and porous. You'll need a good coating that will sink in and protect wood like this. That's why I prefer exterior stain. It seems to protect better than ordinary paints. I've used Olympic stain with good results; Navajo Red is their classic barn red.

Common Damage

Most of the other damage on a barn consists of wood rot and termite damage, resulting from long-term roof leaks. If the roof is really bad, the wood rot can be extensive. I've worked on barns where almost the entire floor was rotted out. I had to pick my way carefully over the remaining solid spots, or I'd have fallen into the basement. You can see that type of damage in Figure 23-5. The floor of this barn was supported by beams made from tree trunks (Figure 23-6), but over time, some of the beams rotted completely

Figure 23-6
Floor beams made from tree trunks

through. Repairs on floors like this consist mostly of replacing the bad wood. Here again, though, the size of the job makes it difficult. You may have to replace huge oak beams and thousands of square feet of flooring.

Post and Beam Construction — One thing that makes an old barn difficult to work on is the post and beam construction. This type of construction was used in very old houses as well, mostly houses built before 1840. You may not run into any houses built like this unless you're working in the East. They're most common in old towns along the coast, especially in the original thirteen states. If you do happen to come across a house built with old post and beam construction, you'll find yourself doing the same kind of work that you'll need to do on these old barn projects.

Post and beam construction wasn't designed to be handled by a two-man crew. The main supports for a barn were made from huge oak beams, sometimes up to 40 feet long. You may find some that were hand-hewn, and held together with pegs, like the one in Figure 23-7. Figure 23-8 shows another hand-hewn oak beam with a forged iron latch hanging on it. The latch was made by hand by a blacksmith probably more than 100 years ago. Barns were originally built using lots of men and lots of horses. Since you don't have the horses, and most likely don't have lots of men on your crew, you'll need heavy equipment instead. You can replace the smaller beams, such as the ones that hold up the floor, easily enough. They're not so big that two men can't handle them without special equipment. But if the barn has major structural damage — if it's leaning, or one or more of the main beams are rotted out — you may want to call in a contractor who specializes in this type of heavy work, and who has the proper equipment for lifting this kind of weight.

Once I had the idea that I could replace rotted-out beams with similar beams. I had some nice 10-foot-long sections of 12-inch diameter maple tree trunks that I thought would work well. I had to give up that idea real quick. The beams weighed 400 pounds each! They were just too hard to work with.

Figure 23-7
Hand-hewn beams held together with pegs

Figure 23-8
Hand-forged iron latch

Instead, I used three treated pine 2 x 12s nailed together. They were almost as strong, and a whole lot easier to handle.

If any of the large main support beams of the barn need to be replaced, you'll probably have to replace them with steel I-beams. You can't get 40-foot-long oak beams anymore. And even if you could, they'd be ridiculously expensive. You can buy steel I-beams in just about any length you want. If you get them second-hand, from a scrap steel yard, they can be surprisingly inexpensive. However, they're also heavy and hard to work with. You'll need heavy equipment to handle them as well. They won't look as nice as the oak, but at least they'll hold the barn up.

The Floor — The original flooring in barns is often one or two layers of heavy oak planks. Some of the planks may be up to 2 inches thick. They are tremendously strong. Many of them will still have a great deal of weight-bearing capacity, even if they're slightly damaged by rot or termites. Don't tear them out unless you really need to. Sometimes the top layer of flooring may be damaged, but the bottom layer may still be intact. If that's the case, just tear out the rotted boards. The underlayer can remain to add strength to the new flooring.

It would be nice to replace the rotted flooring with the same kind of oak planks that were originally used, but that isn't practical. You can't even buy planks like those anymore. If you could, they'd be too expensive to use in a barn. Instead, you can use two to three layers of ¾-inch plywood. The multiple layers will provide the strength you need. Plywood may not look as good, but it's strong. I hate to give up historical authenticity, but there comes a point where the cost just can't be justified. That is, unless you're dealing with someone who prizes authenticity above cost, at any price. (You hear about these people, but I never seem to run into them.)

Be sure to replace any rot-damaged floor beams as well. If someone's going to be parking cars or RVs on it, the floor needs to be really strong. If in doubt, add some posts in the basement for extra support. You don't want cars falling through the floor.

Check the foundation carefully. Most barns have stone foundations and the stones may be coming loose. Repair them the same way as you would a house foundation (see Chapter 12).

The Doors — Old barn doors may be in poor condition. Before you spend a lot of time repairing them, stop and think. Are these doors necessary anymore? Some barns had a lot of doors, each with a special purpose. For instance, there was usually a set of big doors in the front, and another the same size in the back. The doors were designed so that a fully-loaded horse-drawn wagon could be pulled in one side and out the other without having to turn around. It's very difficult to turn horse-drawn wagons around in an enclosed space. Now however, the owners probably don't have any horse-drawn wagons to worry about, so they may not need all the doors. If some of the doors are no longer needed, rather than fixing them so that they open and close properly, you can just nail them down and turn them into wall sections. That will save a lot of work.

Modifications to the Barn

If the barn is going to be used as a storage building, workshop, or warehouse, you may need to make some improvements. The most obvious is wiring. Since most barns were just used to store hay, they didn't need much in the way of lighting or electrical outlets. However, a storage building or workshop does. You'll need to install adequate lighting to light up whatever part of the structure will be used on a regular basis. The last barn I worked on required forty-four 100-watt light bulbs to provide decent lighting. I distributed these evenly throughout the barn, using inexpensive ceramic fixtures. You may wonder why I didn't put in fluorescent fixtures. That's because the barn was located in a cold climate, and not heated. Fluorescent fixtures don't work well in the cold. Below 20 degrees, they won't fire up properly. They just flicker dimly. Incandescent bulbs, on the other hand, work in any temperature. If a barn is to be used all year long in a cold climate, you'll need to use incandescent lighting.

Electrical outlets are also very helpful to have. If anyone wants to work in the barn, repairing boats or RVs, for example, they'll need electric power. You should have at least six or eight outlets distributed throughout the barn. It's best to have these on three or four different circuits. That will allow several power tools and lights to run at one time without blowing any fuses.

You may also want to add a few windows to the barn. There are usually two small windows way up at the top of the side walls, but that's it. That's not really enough for such a large building. Adding a few more windows will bring in a lot more daylight. The windows don't need to be elaborate, a single pane of glass is fine.

Figure 23-9
Old outbuilding was used as a chicken coop

Figure 23-10
Interior framed with full-size oak 2 x 4s

If the barn has a hayloft, there are probably no stairs to access the loft level. People normally climbed up a ladder to reach the loft. However, a ladder may not be adequate if the loft is to be used for storage. It's very hard to carry bulky items up a ladder. A simple staircase will greatly increase the usefulness of the loft area.

Other Outbuildings

Victorians used a lot of other outbuildings in their daily lives. You may find old woodsheds, stables, chicken coops or smokehouses. If the buildings are sturdy, they may still be of some use. They might be usable as storage space, a workshop, studio or even an office, if they are large enough. A small building can be made into a great playhouse for children. Don't tear them down unless they're unsalvageable, an eyesore, or absolutely no use.

Figure 23-9 shows an old chicken coop that I recently converted into a guest cottage. This is a job that I did for myself. As you can see, the original building appeared to be in pretty poor condition. However, it looked a lot worse than it actually was. It needed a new roof and siding, but the basic structure was rock-solid.

The chicken coop had been built with oak 2 x 4s, a full 2 inches by 4 inches thick. You can see them in Figure 23-10. That should give you an idea of the building's age; oak wasn't used for 2 x 4s after 1920. The 2 x 4s were so tough I could barely cut through them. Even my Sawzall wouldn't cut them very well. I finally had to cut the window and door openings with a chain saw! You don't usually think of a chain saw as a carpentry tool (unless you build log homes). However, sometimes it's the only thing that will cut through old oak beams and 2 x 4s. You might want to have one available if you're going to

Figure 23-11
Ceiling joists and electric wiring added first

Figure 23-12
*Large window provides a nice
view and needed light*

Figure 23-13
Windows, subfloor and drywall completed

be working on a project like this. It's also the perfect tool for cutting up scrap for disposal. Just keep in mind that it isn't a good idea to use a gas-powered chain saw in an enclosed space. I tried it once. Within seconds the fumes became unbearable. If you need to use a chain saw inside, use an electric one. They don't have fumes.

Figure 23-11 shows the ceiling joists and wiring for the cottage conversion being put in. The building had no ceiling joists, because it had no ceiling. I cut a large window in the end of the building to take in the beautiful view to the south and lighten up the interior (Figure 23-12). Next came the subfloor, new windows and drywall shown in Figure 23-13. Figure 23-14 shows the bath framed-in and drywalled. I used ½-inch drywall throughout, and finished and painted it just like a house. I added plumbing for a kitchenette, as well as the bath. The wiring included a 220-volt line for an electric stove in the kitchenette.

On the outside, I used rough-sawn exterior siding to give the cottage a rustic look.

Figure 23-14
New bathroom addition for cottage

Figure 23-15
Exterior view during siding installation

Figure 23-15 shows the siding going up and the new roofing completed. The building was beginning to take shape, both inside and out. Figure 23-16 shows the exterior view of the cottage entry, with the siding completed and the new door installed. What a difference!

The entire project cost about $3,000 in materials, and took about 160 manhours. Most of the labor was interior drywall and trim. The drywall turned out to be a little more difficult than I first anticipated, because the interior walls weren't completely even. After all, it was built to be a chicken coop, not a house. I'm sure the original builders never dreamed that the interior would someday be finished, especially with drywall!

Of course, this project was somewhat fanciful; kind of a labor of love. This isn't the kind of job you would do very often. I certainly don't expect to make a living doing chicken-coop-to-guest-cottage conversions! However, it does give you an idea of the possibilities you can find in old outbuildings.

Figure 23-16
Exterior view of cottage

Remember, if you decide to tear one of these buildings down, examine the wood carefully. The old oak pieces may be valuable enough to recycle. Even if you only get a few dollars for them, it's better than paying someone else to haul them away as rubbish.

Chapter 24

Landscaping Victorian Houses

You need to consider landscaping and yard design when you add any new construction, such as a deck or gazebo, to an established yard. How will your project fit in with the overall design? I know, you're going to say "That's landscaping — it's not my job!" That's true, to a point. You don't want to forget, however, that other people looking at the yard won't know where your work ended and a landscaper failed to begin. Also, if the whole picture doesn't look good, the homeowners won't be happy with it, even if they don't exactly know why. Maybe it looks bad because a couple of ugly, scraggly bushes are blocking the view of the beautiful new gazebo, or because all the grass is dead. Your job is to tell the homeowner what's needed to make the whole project look picture perfect. If you don't, all your good work won't make your customer happy or generate referrals, whether it's your fault or not.

Like it or not, you need to consider the property as a whole, and that includes landscaping. It has a major effect on how people view your work. You can see how this works when you look at new homes being built. They always look a lot better after the landscaping is in. The landscaping gives the project a finished look and makes everything look better. It shouldn't matter, but it does. It's the icing on the cake.

Simple Landscaping Ideas

Landscaping, of course, is a career in itself. You don't have time to learn about all the different kinds of shrubs and plants, and the care each one needs. If the yard needs extensive landscaping, you should bring in a professional landscaper. However, if the homeowner doesn't want, or can't afford, a complete landscaping job, there are some simple things you can easily do yourself.

Bad landscaping will detract from your exterior work. You don't need to be a plant expert to know how to deal with it: tear it out. Take out diseased or dying shrubs, trees, or plants. An empty space looks better than a half-dead bush. In some cases, you'll find bushes that are healthy, but ugly. The cause is often an uneven amount of sunlight. The leaves that don't get enough light fall off, leaving a very scraggly-looking shrub. Before you tear it out, try drastic pruning. Cut it down to about 6 inches off the ground. With most bushes, the vitality of the plant is in the roots. It'll quickly grow back. If you're lucky, it'll grow back into a symmetrical, attractive plant. If not, nothing is lost. It wasn't a nice plant anyway.

Just cleaning up a yard can help a lot. You'll need to do some cleaning up after you finish work, anyway. It only takes a few minutes more to clean up some of the landscaping as well. It's especially important to clean up areas that are near your work. Overhanging branches, dead leaves, vines, and all sorts of other unsightly growth can combine to make your work look less appealing. I know that cleaning the yard isn't part of your job, but it's a good idea to take care of anything that reflects on the work you've done. After all, you want satisfied customers. You want them to like your work, to hire you again, and to recommend you to their friends. If a few minutes of yard cleanup will enhance your work, it's well worthwhile.

Nice grass always helps a yard look good. However, before you invest in a big load of sod, make sure someone will be available to water it every day. Who's going to do it? Are you going to be there every day? The homeowners may say they'll water, but will they do it? If they don't, the sod will die, and it'll be your fault. They won't say, "Oh, we forgot to water the sod and it died. Don't worry about it." More likely what you'll hear is, "You put the sod in wrong. Replace it!" If no one's living in the house while you're working, it's best not to start any project that you won't be able to finish yourself. If you're not going to be around to water the sod, don't get involved with it at all.

If the landscaping is okay but just looks blah, it never hurts to add a few flowers. Annual flowers, like marigolds and petunias, are cheap. You can buy a whole flat of them for $10. It takes about an hour to plant a flat of flowers and that may be the finishing touch that makes the project look great. That's especially true if the house has planters. A planter without plants is just a box of dirt, and it looks very unattractive. With flowers in it, it fulfills its purpose. A few well-placed flowers will also bring the

deck, walkways, gazebo, or planters into focus. They will brighten up any of these projects at a very small cost.

Victorian Detail and Landscaping

The Victorian love of detail and order extended to the landscaping as well. The front of the Victorian home should be landscaped with an appealing selection of shrubs and flowering plants. Victorians were very fond of shrubbery that could be trimmed into interesting shapes and designs. If there are tall shrubs, you can trim them into neat rectangles, or columns; smaller shrubs can be made into round balls or squares. The Victorians also loved to use hedges to enclose spaces or delineate property lines. Often, hedges were used instead of fencing to provide privacy between neighboring houses. A neatly-trimmed privet hedge is a lot more attractive than chain link.

Most homes you'll work on will already have some established landscaping. You can just make sure it has a well-maintained appearance, and add decorative color touches. How much you do depends a great deal on the size of the property and what you have to work with. The front of the home and walkway leading to the house should be as attractive as possible. Remember, it introduces the home to strangers and visitors alike.

If a house has some unattractive features that can't be remedied, you may be able to just hide them with some carefully placed landscaping. A big bush, a trellis with a climbing plant, or an ornamental fence can disguise a lot of features. These may not offer the ideal solution to the problem, but they still might provide a workable improvement, and one that doesn't cost much.

Whatever you add to the landscaping should connect visually to the existing landscaping scheme and to the style of the house. You want it to look like it's part of an integrated design, not like it's been stuck there to hide something. Use groups of bushes, flowering plants or walkways to connect old and new design elements.

The back garden can be as elaborate as you and the homeowners want to make it. A classic Victorian garden is very similar in design to a Victorian house: full of interesting detail and color. The Victorians liked complicated gardens, with a variety of shrubs, flowers and trees, and fussy accessories such as statuary, fountains, benches, arbors and gazebos. They especially liked walkways and pathways that led to private little sitting areas or special gardens.

Even people who weren't wealthy enjoyed complicated gardens. This type of landscaping made the most of the available space, and added interest to the smallest area. When you're in a Victorian garden, you can't really tell how big it is because you never see it all at once. With a well-placed hedge or cluster of bushes you can create private walkways or corners that are separate from the main section of the garden. Every time you go around a corner, you find something new. It gives the illusion that there's a lot more to the garden than there really is.

You can also build a number of simple structures to add interest and decoration to a Victorian garden. Some of these can turn yards that are liabilities into assets. If a home has a small uninteresting backyard, you can build an arbor or a deck, add a walkway and line it with some flowering plants, build a decorative fence, put a birdbath or statue in a corner, or do all these things. The possibilities are limited only by your imagination and the homeowner's budget. Any of these ideas would fit nicely in a Victorian garden. In this chapter we'll cover these items and more, so you'll have several suggestions to offer the next time a homeowner says to you, "What can I possibly do with this tiny yard?"

Decks

Wooden decks, like skylights, are features that Victorians rarely built. However, just because they didn't, doesn't mean you can't.

The main reason Victorians didn't build decks is because they didn't have treated wood. Most ordinary species of wood, if untreated, will decay very quickly when exposed to sun and rain. The Victorians built covered porches instead; the roof protected the rest of the structure from the weather. Because the Victorians built a lot of porches, we can assume that they were very fond of them, and that they would have been just as fond of wooden decks had they had the appropriate building materials for them.

Victorians did build open porches with masonry decks. Masonry was the only material available to the Victorians that could withstand years of exposure to the weather. These porches are nice, but very expensive to build, so you only find them on the most expensive Victorian homes.

If you want to build a Victorian deck, build it the way the Victorians would have. By now, you can probably guess what features it would have. There would have been lots of decorative woodworking, the same as the decorations on the rest of the house. You want the deck to look like it was completed at the same time as the rest of the construction. The deck should have turned posts, railings with fancy balusters, and fretwork in the corners and any place there's room to add it. All the post tops should have some kind of decoration on them, such as balls or acorns, and everything should be neatly trimmed out, including the skirts around the deck.

It's important that the deck be painted, not left natural or that green treated-wood color. That won't do. The Victorians would have hated it. Of course, treated wood isn't supposed to need paint, but it does need some kind of coating to keep it from checkering and cracking from exposure. A coat of paint isn't much more trouble than a coat of wood preservative, and it will look far more authentic. You can use a roller to paint the floor. The fretwork and balusters are the only parts that will take a lot of time to paint. Be sure that the treated wood is completely dry before you paint it. And don't use wood that has recently been treated. It may ooze chemicals for weeks and ruin your paint job. Treated wood needs to dry thoroughly before it's safe to paint. Also, I recommend using a stain-killing primer to prevent any bleed-through from chemicals or pine resins.

Painting gives you the opportunity to tie the color of the deck into the rest of the house. To connect the house visually, paint the deck and trim in the same color combinations as the house. The final effect will be very Victorian. Historians will know that the deck isn't historically accurate, but no one else will.

Victorian Gazebos

One outdoor feature that's authentically Victorian is a gazebo. Victorians loved their gardens, and a gazebo was considered the perfect embellishment. They also liked to have garden houses, arbors, and just about anything else they could construct in a garden.

Victorian-style gazebos are quite popular right now. You can find plans for them at most lumberyards or you can order plans from places like Vintage Wood Works. There are plans available for any price range, from simple and cheap to big and elaborate. The one you choose will depend on the homeowner's taste, budget, and garden space.

Gazebos are a bargain, in terms of space per dollar. Of course, it isn't living space; it's semi-enclosed exterior space. But it can seem like living space — especially in the summer. This extra space can be very important for people who have a small house. Small houses can feel claustrophobic on hot summer days. A gazebo provides a place to go and be apart from the other people living in the house. It's a separate building; and psychologically, it's almost like having another little house. A gazebo isn't as useful as adding another room, especially for the winter months, but it can make a house seem larger. In terms of property value, it will add value to a home that might otherwise seem undesirably small.

In its simplest form, a gazebo isn't much more than a free-standing deck with a roof over it. That being the case, you can build it using deck-construction techniques. It's best to support it on 4 x 4s that are set on concrete piers. If you set the 4 x 4s directly into the ground, they'll eventually rot, even if they're treated. They'll last a couple of decades, but then the gazebo won't be a truly permanent structure.

You can also build gazebos on concrete footings or pads, almost like a garage. I prefer not to do this. Concrete is expensive. And doing that much concrete work will really tear up a yard. If there isn't anything in the yard, that may not matter. But if there are any nice trees, extensive concrete work may kill them. That's something to keep in mind when you're building garages, patios, driveways, or any other large concrete areas in, or adjacent to, the yard. The excavation work required for the concrete footings may cut through the trees' major root systems, and the pressure of the heavy equipment or the permanent placement of the concrete may compress the earth and kill the roots. If you're using any heavy equipment, try to keep it as far away from the trees as possible.

Trees take a long time to grow to maturity and can't be easily replaced. A large, attractive tree is a very valuable asset. Each mature tree can add at least $1,000 to the value of a property. You don't want to kill them. I always try to use the least-damaging construction methods I can when I'm working around trees. That's why I prefer building with concrete piers. Piers only require a few small holes and no heavy equipment. They do very little root damage.

Arbors

If a homeowner can't afford a gazebo, how about an arbor? A simple arbor is just like a big trellis. They're usually made of lattice or slats, designed to hold up roses, grape vines, or anything else that needs a support to grow on. If you plant grapevines on one, the grapes hang down inside for you to pick. You can make an arbor any size and shape you want. A big arbor can be almost as nice as a small gazebo.

Figure 24-1
*Arbor posts are set 8 feet
apart to form a square*

Figure 24-2
Fill in sides and top with lattice

Generally, arbors are a lot smaller and cheaper to construct than gazebos. You can build a simple arbor by setting four treated 4 x 4s into the ground, 4 feet apart, to form a square. Placing 4 x 4s directly into the ground wouldn't be advisable for a gazebo or deck, but an arbor is a less permanent structure. It's simple and inexpensive to build, and considered a decorative addition, more like a fence than a building. It will last 10 or 20 years, or even longer, but no one will expect it to last forever.

Figure 24-1 shows a large arbor being constructed. This one was designed to be almost like a gazebo. I set the posts for this arbor 8 feet apart, forming an 8-foot square. Then I connected the tops and bottoms of the 4 x 4s with treated 2 x 4s as shown in Figure 24-2. For a simple arbor, you would just fill in the sides and the top with treated lattice, attaching it to the 4 x 4s and 2 x 4s. The front and back would be left open so people could walk through it. Pretty easy, isn't it? As you can see, I made the one in Figure 24-3 a little more complicated. I closed in all the sides, made an arched doorway in the front and double-arched window openings, like the ones in Figure 24-4, on the other three sides. The materials for this arbor cost under $400, and it only took about 12

hours to build. Anybody can afford something like this. Once grapes or roses grow over it, it will be very attractive.

This type of design allows you to offer a nice, but simple, backyard structure to people who otherwise wouldn't be able to afford one. If the budget is a little bigger, you can expand it a little more. You can make the square larger, or turn it into a rectangle or octagon. Just add more 4 x 4s at 4-foot intervals. If the arbor is wide enough, you can

Figure 24-3
Completed arbor/gazebo

373

Figure 24-3
Arbor with arched window openings

build benches and attach them to the 4 x 4s on the sides, creating a nice semi-protected sitting area. You can also add a simple floor made of patio blocks, and have an arbor that's almost as nice as many gazebos, but much less expensive to build.

Walkways

Garden structures should be connected to the main part of the house, and to each other, by walkways. Otherwise, people will wear footpaths in the grass that will turn to mud when it rains. That looks terrible. Besides, the Victorians loved pathways, and finishing them nicely will add an authentic touch. Garden structures, connected by pathways, make a small yard look like a little private park. It creates a luxurious, intimate atmosphere, like you might find on the grounds of a mansion. There are a number of materials you can use to build walkways. The most luxurious is brick.

૨૭ Brick

Keep in mind that common brick, the kind normally used for brick walls, isn't really suitable for walks or patios. They're too soft to withstand heavy foot traffic. You can use them for trim or areas that have very light foot traffic, but they'll break down under constant pressure. Even the pressure of patio furniture legs will destroy them.

Brick pavers are much harder. They're designed for heavy traffic walkways and patios. You can even use them for driveways. They're available in a variety of attractive colors and shapes. The only real problem with using brick is the cost. Brick is expensive — about $2 per square foot for material, and about $4 per square foot for labor. Laying brick for walkways isn't a particularly difficult job, but it does need to be done carefully.

To construct a brick walkway, you'll need to dig out an area as wide as the desired walk, and about 8 inches deep. Cover the bottom of this area with a thick layer of sand to provide a level bed for the bricks to lay on. A sand bed doesn't hold moisture, so it cuts down on the problems caused by bricks moving during freezing and thawing spells. Level the sand so that when the bricks are laid, they will be level with the sod. This way, a lawnmower can pass over them without catching the edges of the bricks and shattering them. Lay the brick on the sand bed in whatever pattern you like to work with. You don't need to mortar them into place, you just need to make sure they fit tightly together.

Sand isn't the only type of bed you can use when you build a brick walkway. You can also set the bricks in concrete, with all the bricks mortared together. However, I find that setting them in sand is an easier and less expensive method to use, and provides a perfectly acceptable result.

Another way to make the job easier is to use a roto-tiller to dig out the channel for the walkway. Roto-tillers cut a nice straight even groove through sod or soil. I've tried digging pathways out with a spade, but a spade makes a very ragged uneven channel that's hard to work with. A roto-tiller shreds the sod and breaks up the soil. Then you can easily scoop out the loose dirt with a flat shovel. What's left is a perfectly straight, flat channel, ready

374

to lay sand in. You can get the width perfect almost to the inch, so that very little backfilling is necessary.

ᘒ Patio Blocks

It's also possible to make an attractive walkway out of patio blocks. The advantage of using patio blocks is that they're quite cheap, usually selling for around $1.00 each. Sometimes I find them for a lot less, even less than half that price. They don't look as good as brick, and they're rather fragile, but they still make a nice walkway. They're stronger than common brick for walking on, but won't hold up well under the stress of patio furniture.

Constructing a patio block walkway is about like making a brick walk. I use a rototiller to cut a channel, and then put down a layer of sand for the blocks. The only difference is in the depth of the channel. It doesn't need to be as deep, because the patio blocks aren't as thick. A 4-inch-deep channel is usually good enough.

ᘒ Chips and Gravel

You can also make pathways out of loose material, like marble chips, gravel, or wood chips, but I haven't had a great deal of success with them. Wood chips are often used for pathways in parks and seem to look nice, but they're a maintenance problem. They rot, and you have to constantly add more to make up for the ones that have rotted away. Marble chips and gravel tend to migrate and disappear into children's pockets or into the surrounding grass. A lawnmower can then turn them into dangerous projectiles, or at best, into frequent lawnmower repair bills. Constructing a border of landscape timbers can help keep most of them in place, but they still tend to disappear, most likely as they sink into the ground under the pressure of people walking on them. They have to be replenished every couple of years with a fresh layer. Otherwise, they'll eventually be replaced by a layer of mud.

Weeds are another problem with loose materials. There's very little you can do to stop the weeds from growing up through them. Putting plastic down underneath helps for a while, but eventually the pressure of people walking on the path forces the stones or chips through the plastic, making a whole bunch of little holes. The holes are just about the right size for weeds to grow through, and once the weeds get going, it's very hard to control them. They grow back as fast as you pull them out, or so it seems. About the only way to get rid of them is to poison them with herbicides. I prefer not to use a lot of herbicides; they're bad for the garden, and they're not too good for humans either.

Another problem with loose materials is that they're hard to remove if you decide you don't want them any longer. Long after you have taken them out, you'll still be finding pieces in the grass. They'll be turning up for years. I don't want to deal with these problems, so I don't use chips or gravel any more. Bricks or patio blocks look nicer, work better, and last longer. They're worth the extra work and expense.

Ornamental Fencing

Fencing can be a very effective design element. An attractive fence will dress up the exterior entrance to a house or make the back garden more appealing. Victorian mansions were often surrounded by wrought-iron fences. These are quite expensive to put up now, so you'd probably only want to go to that kind of expense on a really nice property. Wooden picket fences are also authentically Victorian, and are much more affordable than wrought iron.

You can buy preassembled 8-foot fence sections at almost any home-improvement store. They run between $20 and $40 dollars per section, depending on the height, wood type and fence design. The fancier designs will naturally cost more. At that price, however, it isn't worth my time to build a fence from scratch. The materials would almost cost as much as these finished sections cost!

Figure 24-5
Unique fencing and entrance decorate home

All you need to do is install the posts and sections and them paint them an attractive color to complement the house. Preassembled fencing sections save a lot of time and effort.

You can also use fencing to set off a fancy entranceway. The picket fencing on either side of the ornamental arbor in Figure 24-5 helps create a unique entranceway. Combining something like this with an attractive walkway will make a memorable first impression for any house.

Figure 24-6
Neat fence defines entrance and traffic flow into yard

Defining Space with Fencing

Fences are also helpful in terms of delineating space, and establishing visible property lines. They're especially appropriate on lots where it's hard to tell where one property ends and another begins. Defining the property lines with an ornamental fence not only adds beauty, but can eliminate confusion and sometimes prevent difficulties between neighbors.

A fence is also valuable for establishing traffic flow. A neat little fence like the one in Figure 24-6 lets people know that they're welcome to enter the property to visit, but not to use the front yard as a pathway or shortcut to another house. Having people cut through or across a front lawn can be a real nuisance when a house is on a corner lot. People tend to cut off the corner and eventually wear a pathway across the grass. Even a small fence will prevent this from happening and save the homeowners a lot of frustration.

Privacy Fencing

Privacy fencing can also be an effective design element, especially if a house has an unattractive view. Many older homes now back up to shopping centers or light industrial areas. Privacy fencing can block them off from these unsightly areas. It's also a useful means of creating a pleasant atmosphere in a small backyard. Often small yards lack privacy, and there are a lot of people who never enjoy their gardens because of this. When the neighbors are just too close, and the homeowners need some separation, privacy fencing can turn wasted space into a pleasant secluded retreat.

Avoid using chain link fencing where it can be seen. A chain link fence is fine for a dog kennel, but it really doesn't belong with a nice home. If the homeowners need to keep their dog in, suggest another type of fencing where it will be visible, and only use chain link in back areas where it will be seen just by the owners. If it adjoins a neighbor, plant vines or shrubs next to it that will eventually grow up and cover it.

Exterior Lighting

Now that you've added all these beautiful exterior features, why not light them up so that everyone can see them? Walkway lights and deck lights are inexpensive and quite popular today. They can beautify any yard, even one that doesn't have many outstanding features.

Most walkway lights and deck lights are low-voltage. They come with power transformer-timers. These plug into regular 120-volt outlets, but feed out 12 volts to power the lights. The advantage of this is that 12 volts of power can't hurt anybody. If a dog chews through a 12-volt power line, he'll get a shock but it won't really hurt him.

Because they are safer, the code requirements for installing a 12-volt line are much less demanding than those for 120-volt line. A 12-volt wire doesn't have to be buried 2 feet underground, or encased in conduit. You can just tuck it under the sod.

If you've installed an attractive walkway, highlight it with lights. Consider where you want to place the lights carefully, however. If they're not well placed, they can make mowing the lawn difficult. Try to keep them away from areas that need to be mowed. Tuck them into flower beds, by the fence at the entry, or next to the porch instead.

You can use these lights to highlight any special features on the house as well. They're available in a mini-floodlight form, as well as the more common tier lamps. Mix and match the lamp types to light up the walkway and highlight features all with one set of lights.

The timer-transformers are weatherproof for outside use, but I prefer to keep them inside, anyway. I plug them in either on a porch or in the basement, drilling a small hole in the wall for the 12-volt cable. Very few older houses have exterior electrical outlets. And if they do, I'd rather not use one up for the walk lights. It's better to save these outlets for other, less permanent uses. I think it's safer and better to run these lines into the basement. The timer-transformer has a short power cord that plugs into the 120-volt outlet. If the homeowner's dog chews on the 120-volt cord, it'll be electrocuted. I'd just as soon keep the cord in the basement, out of the way.

❧ Deck Lights

Many people enjoy using their decks in the evening, but lighting the decks can present a problem. Floodlights cast a harsh glaring light and tend to attract a lot of bugs. That spoils the effectiveness of the lighting; most people will go inside rather than deal with these problems.

Low-voltage deck lights aren't very bright, but then, most of the time people don't really need or want bright lighting. Unless they're working outside on the deck at night, they just want a pleasant light that they can see by. Install deck lights about 3 feet up off the deck to provide the maximum effect. If you tuck them under the railings, the lights themselves will be invisible. All that will be visible is a soft glow, which should provide just the right amount of illumination.

Deck lights have the same kind of timer-transformer and 12-volt lines as the walk lights. You can install them the same way. Keep the wires tucked up out of sight. The lighting will look better, and there will be less chance that the wires will get damaged.

All of these low-voltage light systems are timer controlled. It's a good idea to set them to come on at dusk and go off late at night. It isn't necessary to leave them on all night. No one is going to see them when it's very late. I usually set them to turn off at about 2 a.m. Leaving them on all night won't use much electricity, but it will make the light bulbs burn out sooner.

❧ Victorian Lampposts

Reproductions of Victorian-style lampposts are now available at almost any garden store. Originally made of iron, the new reproductions are made of a durable grade of plastic, making them a lot cheaper and easier to handle. Some of them are beautiful and quite authentic. A few years ago they were considered specialty items, but now you can even find them at most builder's supply stores, starting at around $99.

Victorian lampposts will dress up any yard or garden, but of course they look especially nice with Victorian homes. They also provide a substantial amount of lighting, making a yard more usable at night, as well as providing better security. The soft lighting provided by the lampposts is far more pleasant than the sodium lights many people use for security.

There are a couple of manufacturers that offer catalogues that will help give you an idea of what's available. Call Classic Lamp Posts at 1-800-654-5852 for a copy of their catalog. They have quite a selection to choose from. Another good source for lampposts is Mel-Nor. You can call them at 1-800-828-0302 for a free brochure, or write to:

Mel-Nor
303 Gulf Bank
Houston, TX 77037

Elaborate lampposts also make good "distracters." They're large, unusual, and eye-catching. If a house has some unattractive exterior feature that you can't get rid of, consider putting a fancy lamppost in front of it. The feature will still be there, but it won't attract as much attention because everyone will be distracted by the lamppost.

The only problem with lampposts is that the installation is a lot of work. Since they're 120-volt fixtures, you have to put them on their own circuit with a ground-fault circuit interrupter. The wiring will need to be UF-type cable, protected by conduit, and buried 18 inches underground. Digging the trench can be a big job. If the trench is very long, you might want to rent a trenching machine. However, if there are other services buried in the same area, such as gas pipe, the trench may have to be dug by hand anyway to prevent damage to the pipeline.

Chapter 25

Craftsman and Prairie Homes

During the 20th century, the pace of life has increased tremendously with each decade. Even early in the century, people began to feel stressed by the details and demands that filled their lives. They felt the need to simplify everything around them, including their homes. Their need to make life less constricting led to the development and popularity of the Craftsman style of architecture. The small dark high-ceiling rooms of the Victorian gave way to a design that included fewer, but larger, rooms with lower ceilings, larger windows and less elaborate trim. The Craftsman style is simple and open, with a flowing floor plan designed to accommodate smaller family groups in a less formal atmosphere.

Between 1915 and 1930, millions of Craftsman houses were built all across America. In spite of that fact, very few people recognize the style. Most people just call Craftsman homes "bungalows" or "old style houses." In reality, the Craftsman home is a very distinct and carefully designed architectural style.

The Craftsman Home

Craftsman-style homes are far more similar to modern homes than the Victorian. You can identify them by their low-pitched gabled roofs with wide eaves, and porches that often extend across the entire front of the house. The porches are supported by pillars, which are frequently quite massive at the base and topped with one or more wooden columns. The roof of the house always overhangs the walls, with exposed rafters in the overhangs, and beams or braces under the roof on the gable side.

The home in Figure 25-1 is a beautiful example of Craftsman design. Its broad, massive structure is counterbalanced by an abundance of windows which provide for a light and bright interior. Figure 25-2 shows a less elaborate home, with the wide fieldstone porch and triangular eave braces that were also common features of the Craftsman. Many of the less-pronounced characteristics of these homes may have been covered over or removed by now, but you can still identify a Craftsman home by its basic design. Figure 25-3 is a small, simple single-story home, but it is still quite obviously a Craftsman design.

The father of the Craftsman style was Gustav Stickley, also known for Stickley furniture. The style was an outgrowth of the American Arts & Crafts movement, which took place shortly after the turn of the century. This movement was a reaction to the elaborate Victorian style, and included all kinds of arts and crafts. It was especially

Figure 25-1
A beautiful example of the Craftsman style

Figure 25-2
A more typical Craftsman home

strong in pottery, furniture, and home design. Gustav Stickley designed homes and everything that went in them. His architectural designs became very popular throughout the country, and other designers began to build similar homes.

The style featured simpler, more solid lines, utilizing finely-crafted, but sturdy, materials. Craftsman homes typically have beautiful oak woodwork, trim, and built-in cabinetry with leaded glass, all in rather straight lines or simple geometric shapes. The tile work and leaded glass were also the product of the artists and crafts people of the period.

The furniture from this period, often called Mission Oak, is designed in the same fashion. Its solid and sturdy styling is enjoying a revival today. Original pieces have become collector's items and are selling for hundreds of thousands of dollars. If you bought a Craftsman-style house today and filled it with Mission Oak furniture, leaded glass cabinetry and Pewabic pottery, you'd see that everything matched, even though you bought it in different places and at different times. That's because these were all created during the same period, as part of the Arts & Crafts style.

Figure 25-3
Small Craftsman home

Prairie-Style Homes

At about the same time, Frank Lloyd Wright was becoming well-known as an architect. His "Prairie" house, built in Chicago in 1903, caused an instant sensation in the architectural world. It had a lot of the same features as the Craftsman style, but it was a little less elaborate. Its basic shape was wide and low, with a broad overhanging roof and massive masonry pillars holding up the porch. The design was entirely different from the tall, elaborate Victorian. As you can see in Figure 25-4, the Prairie style is very similar to the Craftsman. It also uses simple geometric shapes and lots of oak and leaded glass.

Just like the Craftsman, millions of these homes were built all across America between 1910 and 1930. As they were copied by different builders, various alterations were made. The result is that most houses built in the Craftsman and Prairie styles don't look just like the original Stickley and Wright designs, although the overall spirit is the same. The modified Prairie style in Figure 25-5 is an example of this evolution. This narrow city lot did not allow room for a wide, low home, so the builder adjusted the design to make it narrower and taller. However, you can see the Prairie-style features in the sloping roof, wide overhangs, sturdy look and masonry pillars.

Other factors also played a part in evolving the designs of these homes. When Frank Lloyd Wright built the original Prairie house, money was no object. Unfortunately, the builders that followed him didn't always have the luxury of unlimited funds. Figure 25-6 shows a later Prairie-style house built on a very tight budget. The builder tried to include as many of the style features as he could. But let's face it, there's not a lot you can do when you've only got one or two thousand dollars to work with. Even adjusting for inflation, that wasn't a lot of money in 1925. This little house probably sold new for about $2,000. A lot of cost-cutting went into the design to bring it down to that affordable price.

Figure 25-4
Prairie-style home

The Merging of the Styles

Over time, many features of the Craftsman and Prairie styles became intermingled. Eventually it became hard to tell which was which. Figure 25-7 is an example of this. Is this a Craftsman-style house, or a Prairie style? You've probably seen hundreds of houses like this; they're all over the U.S. This house has endured all the modifications that you typically find on houses of this age: the porch has been screened-in, the original wooden porch steps have been replaced with

Figure 25-5
*A modified Prairie-style,
somewhat neglected*

Figure 25-6
Small Prairie-style home

Figure 25-7
*Basic shape identifies this old home
as a Craftsman-style house*

concrete, and the house has been re-sided with vinyl siding. All of these things make it hard to identify the style. However, the shape is basically Craftsman. This house probably had a lot of Craftsman detailing at one time, like triangular braces and exposed rafters. The details have either been removed or covered over now. For our purposes, it doesn't really matter which style it is. The Craftsman and Prairie styles have enough in common in their designs, especially in the interior, that anything I say about one will apply to the other.

The popularity of these styles corresponded to a tremendous period of expansion in American cities. From 1910 to 1930, thousands of people converged on the cities to find jobs in new industries. Block after block of Prairie- and Craftsman-style houses were built in the newly-emerging neighborhoods during this time. If you work in an area like this, it's well worth your while to get to know these styles. You'll be able to put that knowledge to good use over and over again.

Like the Victorian, the Craftsman and Prairie styles are also enjoying a resurgence of popularity now. People are restoring the older homes, and many builders are putting up brand new homes in the Craftsman style. The style has come to symbolize good, solid quality in the minds of many people. This isn't surprising. As a rule, they were well-built homes, solidly crafted out of quality materials. As a matter of fact, the originals are usually a lot better-built than the modern copies. These fine old homes are well worth preserving and keeping for a few more generations.

Chapter 26

Craftsman Interiors

*I*f you compare the floor plan of a Craftsman house to a Victorian, you'll see that a major change in lifestyle occurred between the times these two styles were built. Victorian lifestyles were different from ours, and their houses were designed to suit their lives. Craftsman homes, on the other hand, were built for people who lived very much the way we do now.

Craftsman houses all had central heat, rather than wood-burning stoves, so they didn't need the features the Victorians had for moving heat. Gas stoves were widely used for cooking, not wood-burners, so there was no need for woodsheds and summer kitchens. Food was stored in iceboxes, so they didn't need large root cellars, though many homes were still built with basements. The cleaning problems remained, however, since vacuum cleaners weren't generally available until the mid-1920s. You'll find that many Craftsman homes have dust porches upstairs, and hardwood floors throughout, rather than wall-to-wall carpeting.

The very formal manners of the Victorian era had also gone out of style. The Craftsman- and Prairie-style homes didn't need to have both a formal and informal parlor. Instead, they had one large living room like a modern home. They were also designed with fewer, but larger, bedrooms than the Victorian houses, as the size of families grew smaller. Overall, a Craftsman house seems quite modern. They even have driveways and garages. Most of the time it only takes a few alterations to bring a Craftsman or Prairie home up to modern standards.

Oak Woodwork: The Signature of the Craftsman Style

Oak is a basic material in Craftsman and Prairie homes. Oak was still plentiful during the time these homes were built, but it was beginning to rise in value. It had become too expensive to use for studs and joists (you'll never find oak studs in a house built after 1920). Since it was considered valuable, designers decided to showcase it by using massive oak trim throughout the house. The door frames, window frames, mantels and stairways were all built of heavy oak. Beautiful built-in cabinetry and flooring were built from matching oak.

Figure 26-1
*Craftsman interiors included many
beautiful oak-trimmed windows*

Figure 26-2
*Windows are often arranged
in groups of three*

Craftsman designers liked earth tones, and natural materials. They used tiles set in geometric patterns in the kitchens and bath. The nicer homes have leaded glass set into built-in cabinetry as well as an abundance of windows. The result is a house that's solid, but airy. Figure 26-1 shows the living room of a Craftsman home. Notice the number of windows and all the oak trim. The flooring, door and window trim are all dark-finished oak. In spite of the dark wood trim, the room is very light and bright because of all the windows.

The designers also liked groupings of three, and often placed windows in groups like this. Figure 26-2 shows a common three-window grouping in a Craftsman living room. You can see that a large portion of the wall space in both these homes is taken up by windows. These three-window groupings, and other repeated geometric patterns, are common in Prairie homes as well.

🐦 Painted Woodwork

In the 1930s, the natural look went out of style. Many of these houses were redecorated in a style almost the reverse of Craftsman. All the beautiful woodwork was painted white, and the windows were cov-

ered over with heavy drapes. I bought a Prairie-style house a few years ago that was still decorated like this. When my wife first saw it, she said "I don't like this house. It's dark and depressing." When the former owners moved out, they took their heavy drapes with them. What a difference that made! The house was no longer dark. In fact, it was particularly light and airy, with lots of big, bright windows. Taking down the drapes completely changed the character of the house.

As we discussed in the section on Victorian homes, removing paint from woodwork is a real problem. It's a bigger problem on a Craftsman-style home, where large amounts of natural oak are a major part of the design. A Victorian house with painted woodwork is still clearly Victorian. However, a Craftsman house with all the beautiful woodwork painted over really loses its character. The design doesn't make sense with one of the major elements hidden. Because of this, stripping the woodwork is more important in a Craftsman house than in a Victorian. It's a little less difficult than a Victorian, because the woodwork is a simpler design. It's easier to strip straight, flat pieces than it is curly designs, but it's still a big, time-consuming job.

Selecting the Pieces to Refinish

It would be nice if you could take the time to strip all the woodwork in the house, but that would be very expensive. You can get much the same effect at a lot less cost by just stripping a few important pieces. I recommend doing the mantel and fireplace surround, the stairway, the trim around the opening between the living and dining rooms, and the built-in cabinetry in the dining room. These are large, centrally-located items, right in your line of vision. While they contain only a small percentage of the total square feet of wood in the house, they get a large percentage of the attention.

As you can see in Figure 26-3 and Figure 26-4, stripping a few special pieces still provides much of the original effect. It draws your attention to the massive oak woodwork. Maybe there isn't as much as in the original design, but there's a lot by today's standards.

Keep in mind that every room looks different once it's furnished. A lot of the woodwork that's visible when the room is empty will be hidden by furniture and window treatments when the room is occupied. It's less important to refinish the parts that will be covered. The most important parts,

the mantel, stairway, and so on, will not be covered, no matter what furniture or window treatments are used. Give them top priority in stripping.

If there's more money available, strip more of the woodwork, in order of its visibility. Are there any built-in bookcases like the one in Figure 26-5? Those tend to attract attention, and should be stripped, if possible. Any especially beautiful or noticeable windows? Strip those. The most noticeable doors and door frames should also be stripped. On the other hand, anything out of the line of sight, like base molding, doesn't absolutely need to be stripped. If the floors are carpeted, the base molding won't be noticed once the furniture is in place.

As far as the windows are concerned, a lot depends on what window treatments the homeowners have in mind. Do they want to install a window treatment like blinds, which leave the window frame uncovered? If so, it would be good to strip the window frames as well, since they'll be highly visible. On the other hand, if the homeowners are going to hang drapes that cover the window frames, why should they spend a lot of money to have them stripped?

Figure 26-3
Stripped and refinished, staircase is an outstanding feature of this house

Figure 26-4
Refinish highly visible trim

Figure 26-5
*Refinished built-in oak bookcase becomes
centerpiece of room*

What if the woodwork isn't painted, but it's dark and dingy? Before you strip it, try cleaning it. Some of this darkening may be nothing more than many years of dirt and grime. Use a strong detergent cleaning solution, like *Fantastic* or *409*, to see if you can clean and lighten the wood. A careful cleaning job could yield a whole house full of beautiful oak woodwork.

Window Replacements

Craftsman homes often have very distinctive windows, with the upper sash divided into three or four vertical panes. The lower sash is usually one large pane. (You can see examples of this type of window in Figure 26-1.) If you need to replace one or more of these windows on a Craftsman home, you may have a problem. At the moment, I don't know any place you can buy ready-made windows in this style. You can have them made to order, but that's expensive.

Another option is to replace the windows with double-hung sash windows that have just one large pane of glass in each sash. They will work nicely, although they won't look quite as good as the original windows. If you want to try to restore the original look, you can use thin strips of molding to copy the original muntins. If you install the molding pieces in exactly the same positions as the muntins on the original windows, it'll be hard to tell that they aren't real. As a matter of fact, if the muntins on the original windows are still intact, you might be able to take them off the old windows and use them on the new windows. Your new Craftsman-copy windows won't be authentic, but that's still better than the new windows they make today with fake muntins. From the street, which is where most people will see them, they'll look perfect.

The style of the windows is more important on the front of the house than the back or sides, which aren't as easily visible. It wouldn't look too bad if they weren't authentically styled. I wouldn't bother making fake muntins for the back and side windows unless they're clearly visible from the street, if the house is on a corner lot, for instance.

Walls and Trim

One advantage to working in Craftsman homes, as opposed to Victorian, is that you don't have to worry about elaborate plasterwork. Craftsman houses don't have elaborate wall detail; they usually don't even use arches. Everything is done in straight lines, with lots of oak trim. The trim is the major focus of attention in the Craftsman house, not the plasterwork. This makes drywall work a lot easier. You can use straight simple drywall installation techniques throughout, without interfering with the style. Of course, the original walls will be wet plaster over furring strips, as they are in all the old houses we've talked about. You need to handle them with care (refer back to the section on wall repair in Chapter 15). However, you don't need to make any special allowances for the style.

❧ Floors

Craftsman- and Prairie-style houses usually have oak flooring throughout, stained to match the oak trim. This can be a problem if the floor needs refinishing, but not the trim. It's difficult to get a good match, as we discussed in Chapter 16. However, if the woodwork needs stripping, you can strip everything down and refinish it all the same way. It may not be exactly the same as it was, but as long as there aren't any pieces with the original finish left in the room, no one will be able to compare.

As I said earlier in the book, there are subcontractors who do nothing but refinish floors. If the floor absolutely has to match existing woodwork, you might want to seek out one of these contractors. Otherwise, be prepared to spend a long time fussing with it before you get it right.

The Craftsman Bathroom

An original Craftsman bathroom may present you with many of the same problems as a Victorian bath. You'll find the cast-iron footed tubs and sinks with separate hot and cold water faucets. However, by Craftsman times, the more elaborate fixtures and decorations common in Victorian houses had gone out of style. Original Craftsman bathrooms are just as inconvenient as Victorian bathrooms, but plainer. If you find a bathroom like this, it isn't a great sacrifice to tear it out and start over. You won't have to feel bad about destroying any objects of beauty. In an original Craftsman bathroom, there aren't any.

❧ Later Styles

The bathroom in the home may not be original. It could be of any age, from 1915 to the present. Some of the later bathrooms were very attractive. Depending on their age, many are functionally equal to modern bathrooms. If that's the case, they may be well worth saving, at least in part.

From a style point of view, this situation is very similar to the kitchens we discussed in the section on Victorian interiors. Each decade had its own distinctive style, although sometimes it can be difficult to see what that style was. Later modifications may have turned the bathroom into a hodgepodge of styles that don't fit any time period. Nevertheless, you may still be able to restore the original style. Of course, not everybody wants or likes old styles, especially in the bathroom. However, if the homeowners are interested in an old-fashioned design, you could offer them a stylish, nicely-coordinated bathroom for a very small amount of money.

The 1930s Bathrooms

Bathroom design didn't change much from Victorian times through the 1920s. The first major design change took place during the 1930s. Around this same time, built-in tub/shower combinations began to replace the common cast iron, rolled-edge tub. This innovation completely altered the design of the bathroom, and limited what you can do as far as rearranging and changing the style of a bathroom. It's a lot harder to create an authentic antique look with a modern tub/shower unit already built in.

A 1930s bathroom in good condition is almost the same as a modern one. Besides the tub/shower assemblies, they also had tiled floors, tiled tub surrounds, and often the walls were tiled up to a height of 3 or 4 feet. This is strikingly different from the wood wainscoting you'll find in bathrooms built in the 1920s. By today's standards, some '30s tile work is rather plain, especially if it's just white. However, combinations of black and white were commonly used, as well as black and green. Black and green are the only colors you'll find. They didn't have the wide selections of pastel colors that you find today.

The fixtures of this period featured the "streamlined" look, with rounded, swept-back edges. The modern look of chrome first made its appearance in the 1930s as well, and you'll find chrome medicine cabinets, light fixtures, towel holders and sink legs. Sinks with single, central water faucets first began to be used at this time, however separate hot-

and-cold water faucets were still the more common type.

So you see, its possible to find a 1930s bathroom that's pretty much up to modern standards. Except for the separate hot-and-cold water faucets, the bathroom may need very little updating. If the homeowners can live with the bathroom as it is, your best bet, from a "home value versus remodeling cost" point of view, would be to just leave the bathroom alone. The homeowners would get better value for their remodeling dollar by having another project done — adding a second bathroom, for example. It isn't cost-effective to remodel a bathroom that doesn't really need it.

If the homeowners can't stand the old-fashioned sink, you can replace it with a new one of similar design that uses a modern faucet. A pedestal-style sink is a modern design that will still fit nicely into a '30s bathroom decor. Since they're popular now, you can find several that are similar to 1930s styles. You can get a good one for about $200 — less if you want to shop around. You can add a top-quality faucet for another $100, and pay a plumber about $50 to put it all in. The result will be a bathroom that's totally up to modern standards of convenience for only about $350. That's certainly a lot cheaper than remodeling an entire bathroom!

Another reason for preserving the 1930s look is that 1930s designs are popular once again. Many new bathrooms are being built with the same colors, designs, and tile work, so a bathroom may be modern and stylish, even though it's now 60 years old. It would be a shame to rip out a perfectly good bathroom unless there's a very good reason.

The Tub — Old bathtubs are often chipped or worn in spots. You can either have them reglazed, or replace them. Reglazing can be quite expensive, but it's generally less expensive than replacing the tub. Unlike the footed tubs in older bathrooms, a 1930s tub doesn't need to be replaced to modernize the bathroom and improve livability. A replacement tub will probably be very similar to the existing tub, unless you're planning to dramatically expand the bathroom.

One thing to consider when deciding whether or not to replace a tub is the condition of the tile. If you pull out the old tub, you'll damage the tile. It will then need to be repaired or replaced. If you're planning on keeping the tile, the expense of repairing it after replacing the tub needs to be added onto the job. That may make the job too expensive to justify replacing the tub. But if you need to replace the tile anyway, it's not an extra expense. It's just part of the overall job.

If you're going replace the tub, you might suggest installing a more luxurious model, like a whirlpool, or an extra-deep or extra-wide tub. These more modern tubs will give the elegant look of a deluxe bathroom. After all, replacing a tub with one that's exactly the same isn't much of an improvement for all the work involved. When you're doing an expensive job, with high labor costs, the results should be worth the cost and the effort. For a little more money you can install a very nice tub and make the job much more beneficial in terms of overall home value.

The Tile — Much of the tile work from the 1930s is still stylish and attractive. However, not every job from that period is worth saving. Some of them were really ugly, even in 1930.

Before you just tear out the tile, take a careful look at it. Why is it ugly? What's wrong with it? For example, many 1930s bathrooms were simply too plain. They were tiled in plain white throughout, giving them an institutional look. It may be possible to improve on this without tearing out all the tile. Try removing one row of tile, and replacing it with an accent stripe of colored tiles, like I did in the bathroom in Figure 26-6. Or, remove a few individual tiles and replace them with colored tiles to create a checkerboard stripe around the bathroom. Both of these designs were popular in the 1930s, and they're back in style today.

For a different effect, remove a few tiles in strategic locations and replace them with decorative tile inserts. These are tiles with pictures on them, often simple designs or flowers. If your client wants something more elaborate, you can get large scenes made up of many tiles set together. Tile inserts are available in a wide variety of designs to match any style.

These ideas won't solve the design problems in every bathroom, but they're worth considering. If one of them works, you can make a great improvement in the looks of a bathroom for just a few dollars. You can order a brochure full of ideas on how to use decorative insert tiles from:

Summitville Tile
Summitville, Ohio 43962
Phone (216) 223-1511

Brightening the Bathroom

Don't forget paint and wallpaper. Very often, new decorating can make the ugliest bathroom look a thousand times better. Simple redecorating can often create the effect of a complete remodel, at a tiny fraction of the cost. For instance, if you have white tile against white walls, the room will look like the bathroom in a bus station. On the other hand, if you paint the walls a strong color, the white tile will stand out against it in contrast. When you add a row of colored tiles or a few color inserts, a matching wallpaper border, and some complementary-colored accessories, the bathroom will be bright, attractive and best of all, new. You may even want to include matching window and shower curtains so that the homeowners will have a complete, finished look. The cost of these extra items is minimal, and it's worth the little extra effort to please the customer and make sure everything comes out right.

Jobs like this can have tremendous profit potential. You'll often come across a situation where the customer says, "I hate this bathroom, but I can't afford to pay $10,000 to have it remodeled. I don't have anywhere near that much money." If a complete remodel is the only option offered, chances are the job just won't happen. On the other hand, if you could totally change the existing look and brighten up the bathroom for, perhaps, $1,000, the homeowner would jump at it. Changing a few of the tiles, painting, adding

Figure 26-6
Add an accent stripe of colored tile to a plain bathroom

wallpaper, replacing trim and accessories, and finishing with new curtains and a few decorator items won't cost that much, but the bathroom will have an entirely new look. The homeowners will feel like they have a whole new bathroom for only $1,000.

From your point of view, you can make more profit on this $1,000 job than your competitor would have made on the $10,000 complete remodel. Your material costs can be as low as $100 to $200, and you may be able to complete the job in as little as one day. That's about $100 an hour! Of course, this approach won't work on every bathroom, but it's always worth considering.

Bathrooms Built after 1940

Any bathroom built after 1940 is essentially modern. Many are quite attractive, although unless they've been remodeled recently, they won't have the latest luxury features, such as spas or whirlpool baths.

I generally don't tear out bathrooms from the 1940s or later unless they're in really bad shape. I don't find that it's cost effective. Redecorating is usually all these bathrooms need.

The exception would be a bathroom renovation in a high-priced home. Once again, the house needs to be up to the standards of the neighborhood. If the other homes have spa-type baths, with all the latest features, then the house you're working on should too. A spartan 1940s bathroom simply will not do in this case, except as a second or third bath. All luxury homes need to have at least one luxury bathroom, but all the bathrooms don't have to be extravagant. Keep the older bathrooms for the extra baths, and if the homeowners like the idea, decorate them in the period to which they belong. A "fabulous '50s" bathroom, with '50s memorabilia, can be fun. Everyone will get a kick out of it.

The Craftsman Kitchen

You won't usually find a spacious, empty Victorian-type kitchen in a Craftsman house. It's more likely to have a 1930s- to 1950s-style kitchen. If it's in good condition, you might want to consider redecorating it in the original style as we discussed in Chapter 21, when dealing with updated Victorian kitchens.

❧ Adding Space

It's often more difficult to remodel a Craftsman kitchen, or any later kitchen, than it is to remodel a Victorian. That's because there's less space to work with. Kitchens were built smaller after 1920, and they rarely had pantries or summer kitchens that you could cut into for extra space. Many times, however, they did have large back porches that you can use to expand the kitchen area.

Sometimes you can steal space from the dining room. Craftsman homes always had formal dining rooms; they were considered very important. Even small houses had them. The kitchen, on the other hand, was still considered a service area. People were willing to sacrifice space in the kitchen in order to get a better dining room.

Today, the reverse is true. People prefer a big, luxurious kitchen, even at the expense of a formal dining room. Most lower-priced new homes don't even have formal dining rooms anymore, and it doesn't seem to bother anyone. So, if you really need the space, and the homeowners don't object, you can use all of the dining room to expand and modernize the kitchen. Your best bet is to remove the wall between the kitchen and dining room, and create one large room. That will give you the space to do anything the homeowners want (and can afford).

Having a room that's expendable is one reason a Craftsman home is easier to remodel than later designs. The formal dining room gives you some extra space to work with. If you're remodeling a later model home, with no dining room, you're stuck. Often, your only alternative for adding space to the kitchen is to build an addition from the ground up, and that's a lot more expensive. Given that choice, people often have to get by with the space they have.

❧ Dealing with Small Kitchens

It's difficult to build a luxurious kitchen in a small space. You can add more windows to make the room look larger, but that may just take away from the amount of wall space available for cabinets. A skylight will also make a room seem larger, but you can't add a skylight if there's a room above. However, there is something you can do: use especially nice, or even luxurious, materials. About the only advantage to a small room is that expensive materials won't run up a big bill, because you won't need very much. Since the labor is the same whether you use cheap materials or expensive ones, you might as well go with the best quality. The difference in the total cost of the job will be small, but the result will be a big difference in the look and convenience of the kitchen. I think it's a good idea to take this approach. If a kitchen can't be big, at least it can be the best that the homeowners can afford.

Besides using nice materials, you can maximize the usefulness of the cabinets in a small kitchen by adding turntables and roll-out racks. You can find them moderately priced at retailers such as Home Depot or Handy Andy, and they only take a few minutes to install. Racks like these are a nice touch in any kitchen, but they're especially valuable in a small kitchen. If you don't have room to install additional cabinets, you should make the most of the space in the ones that are there.

Figure 26-7
Attic storage in a Craftsman house

Converting Space for Living

Craftsman and Prairie homes were built in all sizes. Some were large and luxurious and others were just small cottages. There are millions of the smaller cottage-size homes all over the United States. Most of them are two bedroom, one bath homes that can greatly benefit from a little extra living space. How can this space can be obtained at minimum cost? Let's consider the possibilities.

❧ Attic Conversions

Craftsman and Prairie attics tend to be tall and broad, like the rest of the home. It sometimes takes very little work to make them into rooms. That's a big advantage over Victorian attics. Figure 26-7 shows an attic storage space in a Craftsman home. This area could easily be converted into a livable room. All it needs is a window and maybe a skylight, heating ducts, electrical wiring and lighting fixtures, and some interior finishing work. It already has a stairway access, which many times is the most difficult part of the addition.

Most building codes require that at least 50 percent of a bedroom ceiling be at least 7 feet high. You'll probably need to add a dormer somewhere in the attic to meet this height standard. In the Craftsman and Prairie styles, dormers were often used as part of the design. The house is likely to have a small, decorative dormer in the middle front of the attic. Unfortunately, the original dormers, like the one in Figure 26-8, are usually too small to be of any use. They're really just decorations. They are valuable as a model for your new dormer, though. You can use the same design, only many times bigger. The new dormer can be made the size of a room. However, the shape of the dormer is more important than the size. It should copy the style of the original dormer so that it will fit in with the style of the house.

The large new dormer will have an over-sized look about it. That's okay, because that look is quite stylish now. Modern Craftsman-type designs are a little different from the originals. They incorporate a number of "postmodern" design elements, including the

Figure 26-8
Small decorative dormer on a Prairie-style home

use of oversized features, such as very large dormers. These design elements come out of the postmodern school of architecture, popular in the 1980s. The addition will look like it was professionally designed in the style of a modern Craftsman home. No one, except someone very familiar with the style, will realize that the dormer was added to scavenge up a little more living space.

On the rear of the house, the design of the dormer is less important. This is especially true if the houses are close together. It may be almost impossible to see the rear roof from the ground. In that case, you can use whatever dormer type provides the most interior space. (A shed dormer is usually the most spacious.) It won't matter if it doesn't match the style of the house, since no one will ever see it.

Height Problems

In some cases, the ridge board of the attic may be less than 7 feet high. That creates a problem. You can, of course, tear off the entire roof, add sidewalls, and build a new roof on the new walls. We discussed this briefly in the section on attic conversions in Victorian houses (Chapter 22). But raising the roof line is an expensive alternative and creates a whole batch of new design problems. If you do this, you'll have a house with two complete stories, instead of one. The exterior design will then need to be reworked to accommodate the changes.

A better alternative might be to build a rear dormer that extends above the ridgeboard, creating a two-level roof. This design is often used in modern housing. The space between the two roofs is usually filled with clerestory windows which brighten the interior of the new room, almost like having a skylight. It also makes it look like you wanted the space between the roofs for that very purpose, rather than appearing like an unfortunate add-on. While this is not an authentic Craftsman design, it's close enough. If you trim up the front of the house with Craftsman detail, you can preserve the major style elements of the house and play down the elements that aren't authentic.

Venting and Insulating

It's very important to maintain adequate roof venting in a converted attic. Don't let the ceiling insulation block the flow of air under the roof decking. Otherwise, the roof will overheat, and the shingles will fail. This may seem obvious, but I've seen this mistake made time and again. In Michigan, where I live, a roof with no venting will fail in two to three years. Further south, they fail even faster.

If you use fiberglass insulation, you'll need to install baffles under the decking to make sure the insulation doesn't bunch up against the underside of the roof. I prefer to avoid this problem by using Styrofoam board insulation instead of fiberglass. Styrofoam board lays flat, and stays put. It costs more than fiberglass, but it's ideal for problem areas like this.

Adding Skylights

Skylights aren't an authentic Craftsman feature, but they look nice anyway. I'm sure Craftsman builders would have used skylights if modern skylight technology and quality had been available. The natural lighting that skylights provide is very much in keeping with the Craftsman "look."

If you want to add a skylight, you can use just about any normal, modern installation design and it will look good in a Craftsman house. They're very helpful in brightening up small dark bedrooms, especially those with sloping ceilings, like you'll probably have in an attic conversion. When the roof line intersects a small room, and cuts down on the ceiling height, it can make the room seem claustrophobic. Adding a skylight on the sloping part of the roof can be a tremendous improvement.

Sloping ceilings can also make a small bathroom seem even smaller. Again, a skylight will help make the bathroom appear larger. Keep this in mind if you have a bathroom that's functional, but unpleasant to be in. Installing a skylight isn't a cheap job, but it's a lot less expensive than tearing out a whole bathroom and replacing it.

ᴣᴗ Porch Conversions

Craftsman homes weren't designed with as many porches as Victorians. They often have only one downstairs, a broad front porch that extends across the entire width of the house. A front porch doesn't convert well into living space, and closing it in will spoil the look of the house. Besides, the porch space is right next to the living room and is only useful for increasing the size of that area. What most of these houses need is another bedroom, not a larger living room.

I've seen homes where the front porch was enclosed, and partitioned off to make a bedroom. The remodeled porch always looks lousy, and the resulting bedroom is awkward and undesirable. It isn't ever a good idea to do this kind of remodeling. I never do them, but I frequently tear them out!

Back Porches

Some Craftsman houses have a broad back porch as well as a front porch. This design is more common on larger houses than on the cottages. Back porches are ideal for expanding kitchens or turning into family rooms or kitchen offices, but they don't make very good bedrooms. They aren't positioned well for that use. Homeowners don't really want a bedroom that opens up onto the kitchen, convenient though it may be for the midnight snacker.

In some cases, the back porch extends across the back of an existing bedroom. If you enclose the porch and open a door to the existing bedroom, you'll have a "pass-through" bedroom. This also makes a substandard bedroom arrangement. However, it can be used for an office, a library, or a nursery, as we discussed when we considered pass-through rooms in Victorian houses (Chapter 19). You could also expand the existing bedroom out onto the porch area and create one large bedroom. That won't solve the problem of not having enough bedrooms, but it does add living space. If you're working on a two-bedroom house and this is the only

option for adding space, it's better to have one of the bedrooms be as large as possible.

Enclosing the back porch can create problems in the kitchen. If some of the kitchen windows open onto the porch and you have to block them off, the kitchen may become dark and uninviting. You'll need to either add more windows on another wall, or use a skylight to bring in needed light. If you're planning to remodel the kitchen anyway, these changes might not be a problem. If you weren't planning to redo the kitchen, this is an added expense that you'll need to consider.

Other Porches

You may find that the house has an upstairs dust porch or sleeping porch. These are perfect for converting into extra rooms. They can be remodeled the same way as the equivalent porches on Victorian houses. We discussed these in Chapter 22.

ᴣᴗ Garage Conversions

I discussed converting garages into living space in detail in *Profits in Buying & Renovating Homes*. I won't cover the same ground in this book because older homes generally don't have attached garages. Victorian homes, as I mentioned earlier, didn't originally have garages at all. Craftsman houses had garages, but they were built on the back of the property, usually quite far from the house. There's no way that they could be useful as converted living space.

Of course, it's possible that an attached garage has been added to the house. On rare occasions, I've seen them on Victorians. The ones I've seen were pretty awful, suitable only for demolition. I've never seen an attached garage on a Craftsman-style house, and believe me, I've looked at plenty of Craftsman homes. I think you don't see them because Craftsman houses tend to be built close together, and there's no room to add a full garage on the side. It would run over onto the neighbor's property.

Chapter 27

Craftsman Exteriors

With any house design, it's important that modifications to both the inside and the outside be in keeping with the original style. If your modifications will show from the outside, they need to be integrated into the exterior design.

This is somewhat more difficult with Craftsman houses than with Victorians. Victorians were fond of odd shapes and projections that stuck out from the house. It was part of the design. Craftsman and Prairie homes, however, were supposed to have a simple basic shape. You can't tack on a lot of odd additions without ruining the design. Anything you add must be in keeping with the original spirit of the house.

Maintaining Design Elements

Symmetry and balance were primary design elements of the Craftsman exterior. If the house was designed originally as a single story and you add a second story, you've thrown the balance off. You have to alter other elements of the house in order to restore that balance.

In many cases, you can restore this balance by restyling the front porch. This may seem an odd approach, but it works. The front porch is one of the most important design elements on a Craftsman house. It works together with the shape of the house to create a visual harmony which is an integral part of the Craftsman design statement. If you alter the shape of the house, you need to alter the shape of the porch to coincide with the new design.

You'll be able to see the connection clearly if you look around a neighborhood of Craftsman homes. You'll notice that most of the one-story houses have one kind of porch, while the two-story houses have another. The porches on one-story houses are smaller and shorter, while those on the two-story houses tend to be taller and have heavier columns.

One important point to keep in mind is that the overall shape of a Craftsman house is basically a square. Prairie houses are also squarish and tend to be low and wide. This is totally different from Victorian houses, which are generally tall and thin. If you add height to a Craftsman house, you've made it taller and thinner. To balance this, you need to add something sideways to make it appear visually wider and restore the original shape.

Figure 27-1
Porte-cochere

Widening the porch may provide the effect you need. It doesn't actually make the house wider, but it will make it look wider. Another way to restore the original design balance is to add another structure to the side of the house, like a porte-cochere.

❧ Adding a Porte-Cochere

The common term for a porte-cochere is carport. I like the name porte-cochere better, because I feel like I can charge more for adding a porte-cochere than a carport. It sounds like a more elaborate job.

Porte-cocheres were commonly used in both Victorian and Craftsman designs. All they are is a roof on columns that extends over the driveway. They function the same as a carport; providing a covered area to park and can get out of the car in bad weather. They're really quite convenient. Figure 27-1 shows a porte-cochere which is only connected to the house by means of a covered porch. More often, they're connected directly to the house. They aren't a substitute for a garage however; they're supposed to be used in addition to a garage. The porte-cochere offers a temporary parking place, but the garage is where you keep a car overnight.

A proper porte-cochere should include the same design elements as the house. It should have the same kind of roof: a low-pitched, hipped, Craftsman-style roof. The pitch should be the same as the pitch on the

house, and the shingles should also be the same. The columns supporting the porte-cochere should match the columns on the porch. If you construct it in this way, the porte-cochere will look like part of the original design.

This project has a number of advantages. First, it doesn't cost much to build. It's just a roof, with one side attached to the house and the other held up by columns. It's less expensive than expanding the porch, because you don't have to worry about a floor or foundation. Its floor is the existing driveway.

Second, a porte-cochere can be a visually attractive addition. It will make the house look much larger, even though it doesn't actually add living space. If you're dealing with a small house in a neighborhood of larger homes, adding on a structure like this can prevent the house from looking like the "runt" of the neighborhood. It will make it look like a larger, more solid home. It's by far the cheapest way to add visual size to a house.

Third, porte-cocheres are a luxury feature, normally found only on Victorian or Craftsman mansions. They were, however, occasionally used on modest homes. A porte-cochere looks fine on a cottage as well as a mansion.

You may be able to create work for yourself by suggesting the addition of a porte-cochere. It isn't the type of thing that homeowners usually think of on their own. If they don't like the exterior look of their house, a porte-cochere might be just the answer they're looking for. It makes a big change in the appearance of the house, without costing too much. You won't have to worry about competitive bids from other contractors. No other contractor will even know what a porte-cochere is!

Problems

The biggest problem you may run into if you decide to add a porte-cochere is the local zoning ordinance. The porte-cochere needs to go over the driveway, and many driveways are pretty close to the property line. Most ordinances prohibit construction within so many feet of the property line, or another structure. You're more likely to see porte-cocheres on older homes because the zoning ordinances weren't in effect when the home was built. An existing porte-cochere on an older house was "grandfathered" in when the ordinance became effective.

The exact number of feet of clearance you'll need between a structure and the property line varies from city to city. Check the zoning ordinances before you suggest a project like this. Unfortunately, most Craftsman style houses are in neighborhoods where the houses were built quite close together. I've come across this problem many times. Several houses I've worked on would have been perfect for candidates for this kind of addition, but they weren't on wide enough lots, so I couldn't get a permit. If you're working on a house that has a little extra footage on the side, a porte-cochere could be worth considering.

Exterior Detail and Style Elements

Craftsman houses often have details that aren't used much anymore. Some of these include brackets under the eaves, porch roofs that are open with exposed rafters, and unusual pillars and columns. Figure 27-2 is a good example of these design elements, including the eave brackets and the massive brick pillars topped with multiple columns. Notice how the arched openings in the brick on the porch duplicate the arch in the porch roof, providing symmetry and balance in the design.

You don't often find all of the exterior detail on these homes still intact. Much of the time, some or all of it has been removed in an attempt to modernize the exterior of the house. The resulting combination of old and new, as in Figure 27-3, can create a very striking, unique look. You have the quaint Craftsman porch with its multiple columns and the modern look of a front picture window. The overall effect, though not authentic, is still appealing.

Figure 27-2
Brackets under the eaves and unusual pillar and column design are typical

It's good to keep details like these in mind; they can be useful problem solvers. You can dress up some neglected place on the house, or add a striking feature to something that's too plain. Adding special detail also works as a good "distracter." That is, if there's a part of the house that's unattractive, and you can't fix it for some reason, you can distract attention from it by adding some striking feature nearby. People will look at this new feature, and will fail to notice the flaw. It won't make the problem area go away, but it compensates for it somewhat by making other areas more pleasing.

Figure 27-3
Unique porch columns make this little house interesting

Figure 27-4
Lattice arbor makes a nice entranceway

When you are adding detail, never mix and match different architectural styles in your decorations. Don't use Victorian turnings or fretwork on a Craftsman house. Craftsman designers hated fancy fretwork. The whole point of Craftsman design was to get away from Victorian detailing. Of course the same would apply to using Craftsman columns and geometric shapes on a Victorian; it simply doesn't work. Using the wrong details with any style will destroy the character of a house. It will turn it into a confusing composite that won't make any sense.

ﺔ‌ Exterior Entrances

Craftsman houses sometimes have little decorative roofed entrance porches over a single doorway or as an entry to another, larger porch. These are about the size of a canopy, but they're made of wood and permanently installed. Craftsman designers liked these little roofed entries a lot, and you can find them over side and back doors as well as front porches. This style is very popular with the newer, postmodern designers and you will see them more often in newer designs than with the original Craftsman homes. Postmodern designers use these entranceways as distinctive style elements to dress up the front of the house.

Several styles are popular for these entranceways. One is just a roof held up by four columns that extends out from the house. Another more elaborate style includes lattice privacy screening. They often include other Craftsman elements or details which add distinction to the style of the house.

The house in Figure 27-3 is a good example of how these fancy entranceways can change the look of a house. You can see that this is basically a small, plain house. The covered entranceway changes it from a boring little box into a striking house, and gives it the visual impact of a much larger home. Adding a simple structure like this to a house can make an amazing difference.

An alternative to changing the face of the house is adding a decorative arbor at the entranceway, like the one shown in Figure 27-4. It's just a framework covered with lattice and thin wood strips, but it adds charm and appeal to the front of the home.

Keep these ideas in mind when a homeowner says to you (as they often do), "I don't like the front of this house, but I don't know what to do about it. And, even if I could do something, I haven't got very much money." A decorative entranceway can totally change the way a house looks, without costing the owner an arm and a leg.

ﺔ‌ Privacy Screening

Another popular treatment that can be added to an entranceway is lattice screening, especially with decorative window openings cut into it. You can use it to decorate porches and provide privacy. As privacy screening, lattice is very useful. People don't sit out and socialize on their porches as much as they did in the early part of the century when most Craftsman homes were built. Often large, beautiful porches go unused today because people feel they are too exposed. They are self-conscious about sitting out where everyone can see them. Privacy screening can solve this problem. It changes the way a porch feels. Rather than appearing to be sitting out in an open space, the screening makes the porch feel like a room. Of course, it isn't entirely enclosed, but it disrupts other people's view of the house.

Lattice screening allows a substantial amount of light and air to circulate on the porch, as do the window openings. The windows also preserve the view. It gives the homeowners as much privacy as they would have in a sunroom or screened-in porch. They can see out, but it's difficult for others to see in. For many people, this extra privacy can make the difference between a useful, fun area for entertaining and relaxing, and a useless space that's only there as a decoration.

Figure 27-5 shows a porch with lattice privacy screening that I'm in the process of finishing. This example is quite an open design, with Craftsman style railings and just short sections of lattice screening on each side of the porch. There are window openings cut into each lattice panel with decorative pots of blooming flowers. This is actually more of a postmodern touch than an authentic Craftsman design. However, the spirit is the same. It includes the geometric shapes that Craftsman designers liked, so it blends right in with this Craftsman home.

❧ Decks

Decks didn't exist during the Craftsman era, for the same reason they didn't exist in Victorian times: treated wood wasn't available. However, there's no reason you can't build a deck on a Craftsman house, as long as you follow Craftsman design principles.

What makes a deck a Craftsman style, or any other particular style for that matter? Generally, it's the detailing. After all, there isn't really that much to a deck. It's basically just a floor, with a railing around it. The style of the deck is determined by the shape of that floor, and by the type of the railing.

A Craftsman-styled deck should be a geometric shape. Don't use modern, free-form shapes. The deck should be a square or a rectangle, or a square and a rectangle together, or any other regular geometric shape. The railing should be geometric as well. Balusters should be square or flat. Don't use turnings. The balusters should either be straight, or in

Figure 27-5
Decorative privacy screening on porch

Figure 27-6
Craftsman-style porch railing

a geometric design. Figure 27-6 shows an interesting Craftsman-style railing. The balusters are geometrically offset. You'll find these geometric patterns included in all aspects of Craftsman design, including Mission Oak furniture. You can, by the way, use Mission Oak furniture as a good source of ideas for Craftsman styles. Any detail you see on the furniture can be reproduced as detailing for a Craftsman house. It'll match perfectly.

When you build railings, you must make them strong because people are likely to lean against them. Your code will also require a certain minimum strength. The top of the railing in Figure 27-6 is 8 inches wide. I made

Figure 27-7
Decorative screening with window cut-out

it extra wide, so that it would be more useful than just an ordinary handrail. It's wide enough to put drinks on, or to hold potted plants and planter boxes. I also added lattice screening to this deck. In this case, the lattice is used more for decoration and to screen off objects in the background than for privacy. You can see in Figure 27-7 that the window cutout shows off the landscape, while the lattice blocks the view of the barn.

I made the screening for this deck out of heavy-duty lattice, and used treated 1 x 4s (ripped down to 3 inches) for the straight side pieces of the window frames and treated 1 x 8s for the curved top pieces. I drew arcs onto the 1 x 8s using a pencil attached to a piece of string, then cut the curved pieces out with a jigsaw. The finished pieces were 3 inches wide. The original 1 x 8s were wide enough to accommodate the entire curved piece for each window opening.

I made two of each top and side piece for each section, sandwiched the lattice between them, and nailed them together. Then I toe-nailed the completed unit to the top railing. The interior edge of each unit is trimmed with a thin strip ripped off a treated 2 x 4. The strip was thin enough that I was able to bend it around the curve of the top piece, and nail it in place.

In all, I made three units, a total of 20 feet wide. From the porch deck to the top

they stand 12 feet tall, including the height of the rails. This height provides a total visual barrier. Also, the design had to be fairly tall for the window cutouts to make sense. The assembly (including the rails for that section) took about 24 hours to build, and cost $250 for materials. The additional railings and stairs for this deck cost $150 and took 16 hours to build. The railings were fairly time-consuming because of the fancy baluster treatment (shown in Figure 27-6). Another special treatment that I added to this deck was extra-wide stairs. Wide stairs are really nice on porches and decks. People can sit on them and talk. It's like having an extension to the deck, and they only cost a little bit more to build.

One important point to remember is that Craftsman exteriors were always painted. Therefore, the deck, railings and lattice should be painted or stained as well to match the porch or house.

৯ Gazebos

As we discussed in Chapter 24, gazebos can add interest to any backyard setting. They can stand alone or be attached to a deck or walkway, if desired. You can make a whole complex of backyard structures, if the homeowners have the space. In a large yard, it's sometimes nice to construct a gazebo towards the back of the property. You can build a walkway leading to it so that people can wander through the yard and end up at the gazebo, as though they're in their own private park.

There are many books of gazebo plans available. However, you need to pick the right plan to match the house. A Craftsman house should have a Craftsman-style gazebo. These aren't as common as Victorian gazebos, because gazebos were more of a Victorian idea and interest faded in the early 20th century. The designs you see everywhere, full of fretwork and turnings, are all Victorian, not Craftsman styles. They should not be used with a Craftsman house.

Gazebos built during the Craftsman times had the regular geometric shapes that

Craftsman designers loved. They were square or rectangular, not octagonal like Victorian gazebos. They had either a solid roof or a sunscreen roof supported by pillars or columns; round columns were more common. A gazebo with a solid roof would be hipped, to match the house. The space between the columns had railings that were either straight or geometric in design.

If you build a gazebo close to the house, it's best to match it to the styling of the porch. It should have the same kind of roof, railings, columns, and other details. That way, all the exterior features will look coordinated. If the gazebo is a good distance from the house, it's less important that it be perfectly coordinated. If it isn't visible from the house at all, you can do anything you want in terms of design, but it's still best if it has the same general spirit as the house. A Craftsman gazebo will always look best with a Craftsman house.

❧ Landscaping Features

Don't forget about other exterior landscaping features, such as walkways and planters. We discussed these items in regard to Victorian homes in Chapter 24, and many of the same basic ideas also apply to Craftsman homes. For instance, if there are any buildings or structures in the yard that will be used frequently, connect them with walkways. Otherwise a path will be worn into the grass by people walking back and forth, and eventually it will turn into mud. Making this type of improvement is just common sense and would apply to any home.

Planters, garden seats, privacy fencing and privacy screening can all be used to make any backyard a more pleasant, useful space. Remember, the smaller the yard, the more important these features are. They can turn a useless little square of dirt into a pleasant garden.

Garages

Unlike Victorian homes, Craftsman homes usually had garages. However, the garage may or may not be usable. We discussed the repairs needed by old garages in Chapter 2, and the other garage problems in Chapter 23, in the section on Victorian outbuildings.

The major problem with old garages today is that they're just too small. They were built to house one car and nothing else. That's no longer the only use for a garage. Even if the homeowners only have one car, it would still be too small, and you'll probably have to build a new one. However, the old garage can be useful as a shed or storage area for lawnmowers, bicycles and patio furniture. In that case, a little paint and simple decoration can make it a lot more attractive.

If a one-car garage is in poor condition and doesn't have a proper foundation, there isn't much point in trying to save it. You're better off tearing it down and building a new one rather than trying to repair it, even for storage. Tearing one of these down is really easy — sometimes all it takes is a good push and they fall right over. However, remember to check the local zoning ordinances before you do anything. As we discussed earlier, you don't want to tear the garage down, and then find out you won't be allowed to build another.

If you replace the garage, you'll want to replace it with an original Craftsman style. Of course, you won't want to use old-style wooden pull doors on a new garage. Instead, look for a modern, roll-up door with a pattern of windows similar to that of the original Craftsman style. It'll look almost the same, but be far more convenient to use. The roof line and siding on the new garage should match the house. If the house has a hipped roof, the garage should, too. Use the same colors of siding and shingles as well. Trim it up with the Craftsman detailing we discussed earlier in this chapter, such as triangular corner brackets on the eaves. Any special detailing on the house should be duplicated on the garage. If you do a careful job, the garage will look like it has been there as long as the house.

Conclusion

This brings us to the end of our discussion of maximum value remodeling for the older home. Older homes have a lot of unique problems, but they also offer a lot of unique opportunities. The trick is to see an older home's unusual features as assets, not liabilities; as something to be cherished and enhanced, not ripped out. If you can do this, you'll be able to work with the spirit and style of an older home, not against it. By getting into the "flow" of the design, you can turn a house that looked like an old hunk of junk into a thing of beauty — without it costing anyone too much money.

I've presented a lot of unique and cost-effective ideas in this book — ideas you won't find anyplace else. These ideas can give you a big edge in the competitive remodeling business. Because some of the work I've discussed isn't commonly done by remodelers, you'll find that there aren't many other contractors who'll be able to bid against you. Your creative, cost-effective proposal will stand out from all the others. You'll be able to get jobs because you work better, not cheaper; smarter, not harder.

I've found from my own experience that the ideas presented in this book are real money-makers. The best part is that they make money for both you and the homeowner. Of course, all my suggestions won't apply to all situations. However, there's enough good, common-sense advice contained in this book, that everybody should find something that they can use. Even if you only find one type of repair or improvement that you can apply to your work, you'll find that it'll save you a hundred times the price you paid for this book.

On the facing page, you'll find a sample of the checklist I use to estimate repair costs. It contains all the common defects you're likely to find in an average older house, as well as other information that you'll be glad to have later, such as whether the attic or crawl space has adequate work area. Feel free to photocopy it for your own use. Make as many copies of the bathroom, bedroom, porch, hall and staircase checklists as you need for the house you're estimating. Take the list with you when you make inspections and check off the items as you come across them. If you don't like this checklist, modify it to suit your work or make up one of your own. You need to have some kind of prepared list because it's very easy to be distracted and leave out something important. With a checklist to go by, you don't need to write as much — just check off boxes.

❧ Success in Remodeling

The key to getting jobs in this business is making your customers happy. But that isn't enough. You also have to make yourself happy. You can't do that by competing on price alone. You may be able to make the customer happy by working cheap, but you'll go broke. *You've got to make money too* if you're going to be a success in this business. By zeroing in on maximum value jobs, you can make top dollar for your labor, and still please your customers. You'll be making big profits and providing your customers top value for their money. It's a "win-win" situation. Everybody wins, nobody loses, and that's a proven prescription for success.

Good Luck!